An Introduction to 3D Computer Graphic and Animation in OpenGL a.

Fore June

An Introduction to 3D Computer Graphics, Stereoscopic Image, and Animation in OpenGL and C/C++

Copyright @ 2011 by Fore June

CreateSpace, a DBA of On-Demand Publishing, LLC.

ISBN-13: 978-1466488359

ISBN-10: 1466488352

First Edition:	November, 2011
Second Edition:	August, 2012
Third Edition:	December, 2014
Fourth Edition:	December, 2015

Contents

x

About the Author

Fore June is an independent Internet Service Provider (ISP) who provides various kinds of Internet services to the public and information technology consulting to a couple of small companies. Fore has written a few books and holds an M.S.E.E. degree in Electrical Engineering and Computer Science.

xii

Preface

I worked for a toy company in the Far East for a couple of years about ten years ago. After I returned to the US, I resumed my job as an independent Internet Service Provider (ISP), enjoying every bit of the freedom and peaceful life such a job can provide. One day, when I sat down and reviewed my work, I suddenly found that ten years had past and I was shocked by the rapid advance of the computing technologies in this period. Mobile devices have become ubiquitous and their computing capacities are amazingly huge. Ten years ago, ARM processor was a popular but small player in the microprocessor market. Then suddenly people are talking about the rivalry between ARM and Intel, the world's largest microprocessor designer and manufacturer. Open-source movement is no longer a quixotic thought but has become a reality and has made profound impact in this world. The open-source mobile OS Android came from nowhere a couple of years ago to become the major mobile system. If we measure the purchasing power of a person in terms of computing power that the person can buy, almost everyone in this nation has become a multimillionaire overnight.

Just like my work on video compression, which is summarized in my other book, my work on graphics resulted from developing embedded stereoscopic videos for toys. This book is resulted from the work of those days when I worked for a toy company. Some of the images used in the book were downloaded from the Internet over the years, and I have lost track the exact URLs of the sources. I would like to take this chance to thank all the authors of the images.

The source code of this book can be obtained from the web site

http://www.forejune.com/stereo/
or
http://www.forejune.co/stereo/

by entering the password 'mr_liu'.

Fore June
Nov. 2011

Chapter 1   Introduction

1.1   The Value of Knowledge

Most of us might have heard about the value of knowledge but many of us may overlook the underlying significance of acquiring knowledge in the modern world, not recognizing fully its real value. Though the jobless rate in this nation hovers around 9%, there is a serious shortage of good engineers and scientists. Many large newspapers such as New York Times and Wall Street Journal reported in 2011 that Silicon Valley saw strong hiring demand in the year. In July, 2011, more than 6,500 new jobs were advertised online for IT related openings in the Silicon Valley, up 9% from the same period a year ago. Some claimed that recruiting in Silicon Valley was more competitive and intense and furious than college football recruiting of high school athletes.

In March, 2011, New York Times reported: "As the rest of the country fights stubbornly high unemployment, the shortage of qualified engineers has grown acute in the last six months, tech executives and recruiters say, as the flow of personal or venture capital investing has picked up. In Silicon Valley, along the southern portion of the San Francisco Bay in California, and other tech hubs such as New York, Seattle and Austin, start-ups are sprouting by the dozen, competing with well-established companies for the best engineers, programmers and designers. At the same time, all the companies are seeking ever more specialized skills. Tech recruiters have also expanded their searches. They still scout college campuses, particularly Stanfords computer science department, where this year it was common for seniors to receive half a dozen offers by the end of first quarter. But since college degrees are not mandatory, recruiters are also going to computer coding competitions and parties, in search of talent that is reminiscent of the dot-com mania."

This book is written in the spirit of helping readers acquire a knowledge that will be valuable to their own development. Even though the book presents the materials at an introductory level, some readers may still find some of the materials difficult, depending on their background and willingness of paying efforts in learning. But our knowledge is valuable only if we need to pay effort to gain it. The more effort we pay to acquire knowledge, the wealthier and happier we will be. Topics that are easy to us are also easy to our competitors. In the coming decades, the competition between nations will be a competition of acquiring knowledge. The economic regions that censor information and block the flow of knowledge would eventually fall behind.

Renowned management specialist Peter Drucker (1909 - 2005) had long advocated the emergence of knowledge society and the importance of knowledge workers. The social transformations from an industrial society to a knowledge society would be the most significant event of the century and its lasting legacy. Science and technology have been advancing so rapidly that manufacturing becomes irrelevant in the modern society. A DVD containing certain data that we pay twenty dollars to purchase may just cost a few cents to manufacture. Though it is very rare for the productivity between two labour workers differs by a factor more than two, the productivity of a good knowledge worker can be easily a factor of 100 or higher than that of an average knowledge worker. Nathan Myhrvoid, former Chief Technology Officer at Microsoft Corporation, and a co-founder of Intellectual Ventures, once said the following:

> *The top software developers are more productive than*
> *average software developers not by a factor of 10X or*
> *100X or even 1000X but by 10,000X.*

Putting this in another perspective, we see that under an ideal situation (discarding exploition by 'leaders'), if an average engineer earns \$100K a year, a top engineer could earn $10000 \times \$100K = \$1$ billion a year.

To become proficient in a certain field, one must learn with his or her heart, overcoming difficulties, barriers and frustrations. After enduring the hard work, one would enjoy the pleasure of understanding difficult materials and acquiring valuable knowledge. Fauja Singh, the 100-year-old marathoner runner who became the world's oldest person to complete a full-length marathon in October 2011 after crossing the line at the Scotiabank Toronto Waterfront event in eight hours and 25 minutes, said: "Anything worth doing is going to be difficult."

While the position of a labour worker can be easily substituted by another one with little training, it is very difficult to replace a specialist of a field in the knowledge economy, for the new worker must also go through the same learning barriers and hard work to acquire the knowledge.

1.2   The Open Source Movement

In the past few decades, the open source movement may be the most important development in the software industry and in knowledge acquirement. Open source software is made available to anybody to use as its source code can be read by everyone. Open source software promotes learning and understanding, and expedite software development, making software more robust.

Nowadays, open source applications are abundant and they have been propelling the technolgy world moving forward rapidly. This book along with its programs and utilities are 100% written using open source software.

Very often, it takes an abundant amount of computing power to create the stunning visual effects behind blockbuster movies such as King Kong, the Lord of the Rings trilogy and the $230 million movie *Avatar* produced by James Cameron. The stereoscopic 3D movie *Avatar* of 2009 was exceptionally successful and has set off a phenomenal trend in making 3D films. The movie has also become the top grossing movie of all time, eclipsing James Cameron's former top grossing movie, *Titanic*. Probably the main reason of its huge success is the use of open source technologies to create the fantastic stereoscopic 3D effects. It is interesting to note that Cameron wrote the script for the film more than 15 years ago, but the open source technology was not mature enough to portray his vision of the film, which might be the major cause of the long delay of its production.

While the audience are moved and amazed by the realistic 3D effects, few realise that open source software is the driving force behind the creation of those 3D graphics and animation rendering. Linux has played a silent but an important role in the creation of the movie. Weta Digital, co-founded by Peter Jackson, is a digital visual effects company that gave life to the flora and fauna of Pandora in the movie. It uses Linux and other Linux-based software to achieve all those cutting edge graphics. Weta Digital renders the imaginary landscapes of Middle Earth and Pandora at a campus of studios, production facilities, soundstages and data center consisting of a 40,000 CPU farm. Figure 1-1 below shows some of the high-density server and networking gear inside the Weta Digital data center used to render the animation of the movie *Avatar*. The image was downloaded from the site *http://www.datacenterknowledge.com/archives/2009/12/22/the-data-crunching-powerhouse-behind-avatar/*.

According to an article posted at *http://www.datacenterknowledge.com/* in 2009, the Weta Digital data center got a major hardware refresh and redesign in 2008 and used more than 4,000 HP BL2x220c blades, 10 Gigabit Ethernet networking gear from Foundry and storage from BluArc and NetApp. The system ranked about 195 in the Top 500 list of the most powerful supercomputers. There were more than 90 cameras (configured in a grid) that hang around the perimeter of a sound stage. Later on, a computer replaced the studio walls, the floor and the ceiling with digitally rendered three-dimensional environments and structures.

Figure 1-1   Weta Digital Data Center

Fast-forward to 2011, the year in which open source movement scored a couple of stunning triumps. In February of the year, the whole world was watching with great interest and excitement the human-versus-machine competition on the quiz show *Jeopardy*. On the human side were Brad Butter, the biggest all-time money winner on *Jeopardy*, and Ken Jennings, the record holder for the longest championship streak. On the machine side was an artificial intelligence computer system named *Watson*, which was capable of answering questions posed in natural language, and was developed in IBM's DeepQA project by a research team led by principal investigator David Ferrucci. Watson was named after IBM's first president, Thomas J. Watson. In a two-game, combined-point match, broadcast in three *Jeopardy* episodes, Watson beat both Brad Rutter and Ken Jennings without any connection to the Internet during the game. The audience was much amazed by the intelligence of Watson. However, much of the audience might not know that Watson was actually powered by open source software. IBM did not build Watson from scratch but had leveraged existing open source projects to provide many of the building blocks for the Watson project. Watson's software was written in both Java and C++ and uses Apache Hadoop framework for distributed computing, Apache UIMA (Unstructured Information Management Architecture) framework, IBMs DeepQA software and SUSE Linux Enterprise Server 11 operating system. Watson can run on a few operating systems but to compete on *Jeopardy*, Watson was running SUSE Linux Enterprise Server OS. Just like the human players, Watson had no access to Google or any other outside sources of information during the competition. It played with its own "knowledge".

Another big triump of open source software in 2011 is that Android has become the most popular mobile phone operating system, capturing nearly 50% of smart phone market. Google first unveiled Android as a Linux-based open-source mobile operating system in late 2007 and it was embraced immediately by many big carriers such as Sprint, T-Mobile, Verizon and AT&T. Since its debut, Android has been gaining market rapidly. Android is an open-source software stack for mobile devices, and the Android project is led by Google. The Android Open Source Project (AOSP) includes individuals working in a variety of roles. Google is responsible for Android product management and the engineering process for the core framework and platform; however, the project considers contributions from any source, not just Google. The Android team created Android in response to their own experiences of launching mobile apps. They wanted to make sure that there was no central point of failure, so that no industry player can restrict or control the innovations of any other. That's why Android was created, and its source code was made open. For details, please refer to the Android official web site at *http://www.android.com/*. It is convenient to develop graphics applications in the Android platform using OpenGL.

1.3   Computer Graphics Applications

The development of computer graphics has made computers easier to interact with, to understand and to interpret different types of data. Developments in computer graphics have made profound impact on many types of media and have revolutionized the film, video game and publishing industries. Beyond these, applications of computer graphics are ubiquitous. The following lists some of the common and important applications.

1. **Computer Graphics and Image Processing**
   The fields of computer graphics and image processing are interwined with each other more and more each year. In general, *computer graphics* applications create pictures and images, synthesizing them using a certain model in a computer. On the other hand, *image processing* is concerned with the analysis and manipulation of images by computer. It improves or alters images that were created elsewhere. Figure 1-2 below shows the segmentation of an image using image processing techniques.

   Original Image   Segmented Image
   Figure 1-2 Image Segmentation

2. **Art, Entertainment, and Publishing**
   Computer graphics have revolutionized movie production, animation, creating special film effects, browsing World Wide Web, producing slides, book publication and magazine design.

3. **Video Games**
   Latest computer graphics technologies are always rapidly incorporated into video game development. Popular video games such as Warcraft, and Halo 3 are created with the state-of-the-art computer graphics technologies.

4. **Monitoring a Process**
   Computer graphics can be used for monitoring, controlling, testing, and acquiring data from an industrial process control system .

5. **Computer-aided Design (CAD)**
   Computer-aided Design makes use of interactive computer graphics to provide the user with input-tools to streamline design processes, drafting, documentation, and manufacturing processes. It is widely used in architectural design, and electrical circuit design.

6. **Displaying Simulations**
   Computer graphics can display simulations generated by software such as the *flight simulator*, which displays objects as if they physically exist, when in reality they are only models

inside the computer. Virtual reality (VR) has been a research field as well as a graphics application that empolys computer-simulated environments to simulate physical presence in places in the real world, as well as in imaginary worlds. Most virtual reality environments involve mainly visual experiences; graphics scenes are usually displayed either on a head-mounted computer screen or through special stereoscopic displays. Some simulations may include additional sensory information, such as information from sound coming through speakers or headphones. Some advanced, haptic systems may include tactile information or remote communication environments, which are common in medical and gaming applications. Figure 1-3 below shows a US Navy personnel using a VR parachute training simulator to acquire the skill of using actual parachute. The image was taken from the site

http://en.wikipedia.org/wiki/Virtual_reality.

Figure 1-3 US Navy personnel Using a VR Parachute Trainer

7. **Scientific Analysis and Visualization**
Graphical presentations of scientific data can help us understand the underlying significance of the data and gain new insights into the investigating process.

8. **Digital Shape Sampling and Processing (DSSP)**
DSSP uses scanning hardware and processing software to digitally capture physical object shapes and forms. It automatically creates accurate 3D models with associated structural properties for design, engineering, inspection and custom manufacturing. What digital signal processing (DSP) is to audio, DSSP is to 3D geometry. Computer graphics is to used to display and model the scanned data. (See for example, *http://www.geomagic.com/en*) Figure 1-4 shows a spaceship engine fan that is rebuilt using DSSP software; in the figure, (a) shows the spaceship that uses the engine fan, (b) shows a blade of the fan; the upper image shows the actual object and the lower one is the object created by graphics reconstruction, (c) shows the rebuilt fan. The images were downloaded from the site *http://www.geomagic.com*.

9. **Video Compression**
For some video applications where the images do not change abruptly from frame to frame such as news announcement or company meetings, graphics techniques can be used to compress the videos. A graphics model is constructed to represent the largely static features of the scene and a few parameters are transmitted to produce a dynamic scene. Video compression standard MPEG-4 Visual specifies support for animated face and body models. For example, a face model described by Facial Definition Parameters (FDPs) is used to animate a human face using the transmitted Facial Animation Parameters (FAPs) . In a similar way,

Body Definition Parameters (BDP) are used to describe a human body and Body Animation Parameters (BAP) are used to animate a human body.

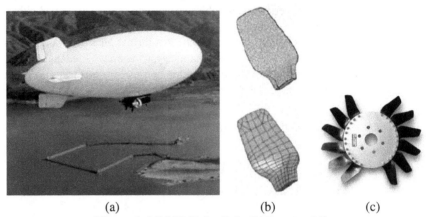

(a)   (b)   (c)

Figure 1-4 DSSP Helps Rebuild Damaged Fan

1.4   This Book

This book, *An Introduction to 3D Computer Granphics, Stereoscopic Image, and Animation in OpenGL and C/C++*, is written based on the author's experience of developing stereoscopic video programs to be embedded in some toys. However, to develop the programs one has to learn the basics of graphics programming. So this book is more about basic graphics programming than advanced stereoscopic video development. The materials are discussed at an introductory level and the code is presented in C/C++. The implementations of more advanced topics are not included. The programs presented are mainly for illustrating the principles of graphics and how to implement them; very often error checking and handling are not included. For the purpose of making the materials easy to understand, sometimes the parameters are hard-coded. Nevertheless, the programs can be used as a starting point for further development.

We have to admit that the programs were written over a period of time and thus the notations may not be very consistent. Also, we have not optimized the code for memory usage or computing time. All the code presented in this book can be found at the site,

http://www.forejune.com/stereo/

and you can download the programs using the password "mr_liu". The programs have been compiled and tested in Linux platforms. The C/C++ programs of this book reside in subdirectories with numbering reflecting the related chapters. For example, the programs discussed in Chapter 8 will be in directory **8/**. If the programs of another chapter need to use the programs developed in Chapter 8, we just need to link their object files in **8/**. We also put most of the sample data files in the directory **data/**.

In our description, when we use the term *into*, we usually refer to a many-to-one mapping such as the mapping of a 3D object to a 2D image. When we say *onto*, we refer to a one-to-one mapping; such a mapping is reversible. In describing a program, we usually express variables in italics.

We hope you enjoy reading this book.

Chapter 2   OpenGL Basics

2.1   What Is OpenGL?

OpenGL, which stands for **Open Graphics Library**, is the computer industry's standard graphics application program interface (API) described in the C programming language. The interface defines over 700 distinct "commands" which are actually C-type functions. Out of the 700 functions, about 650 are in the core OpenGL and 50 in the OpenGL Utility Library. The functions allow users to create interactive two dimensional and three dimensional graphics applications. OpenGL is designed as a streamlined, hardware-independent interface to be implemented on many different hardware platforms. We use the words "commands" and "functions" interchangeably in describing OpenGL functions.

Prior to OpenGL, any company developing a graphical application typically had to rewrite the graphics part of it for each operating system platform and had to customize for the specific graphics hardware platform. Nowadays, an application can use OpenGL to create the same graphics look-and-feel in any platform that supports OpenGL.

Each OpenGL command (functon) directs a drawing action or causes special effects. The outputs of an OpenGL command do not depend on the windowing characteristics of any operating system; OpenGL provides special functions for each operating system to enable OpenGL to work in that system's windowing environment. OpenGL comes with a large number of built-in graphics processing functions, including hidden surface removal, alpha blending, antialiasing, texture mapping, pixel operations, viewing and modeling transformations, and creating atmospheric effects. It employs a pipeline architecture to process a graphics scene at each stage of the pipeline and passes the result to the next stage for further execution.

Silicon Graphics, a company which makes advanced graphics workstations, first started the development of OpenGL. Other companies on the industry-wide Architecture Review Board (ARB) including DEC, Intel, IBM, Microsoft, and Sun Microsystems contribute to its later development. Note that OpenGL is not a development "toolkit". However, such toolkits are available. For example, Silicon Graphics's Open Inventor is an object-oriented programming 3D graphics toolkit for development.

OpenGL is an open-source API; one does not need to pay any royalty to any party when using it. The libraries for various platforms are also free for download. For example, Mesa is an open-source implementation of the OpenGL specification. A variety of device drivers allows Mesa to be used in many different environments ranging from software emulation to complete hardware acceleration for modern graphics processing units (GPUs). One can download the Mesa package from the site *http://www.mesa3d.org/* The site *http://www.opengl.org/* provides documentation, tutorials and examples on OpenGL.

To maintain the hardware-independent characteristics, core OpenGL does not provide commands for performing windowing tasks or obtaining user inputs. One may use the OpenGL Utility Library or other means to perform these tasks. Also, OpenGL does **not** provide high-level commands for three-dimensional modelling, which are commonly used in specifying relatively complicated shapes such as automobiles, parts of the body, airplanes, or molecules. To create complicated objects using OpenGL, one must build up a desired model from a small set of geometric primitive such as points, lines, and polygons. On the other hand, OpenGL Utility Library provides some commands to create some common graphics object models such as spheres, teapots, and cubes.

2.2 OpenGL Programming

2.2.1 Basics of OpenGL Code

The OpenGL functions are contained in two libraries usually called **gl**, and **glu** (or GL and GLU). The first library, gl, is the core OpenGL library; it contains all the required OpenGL functions. The second library is the OpenGL Utility Library (GLU), which contains functions that are written using the core OpenGL functions to provide many helpful functions for modeling. Most OpenGL releases also include the **OpenGL Utility Toolkit** (GLUT), which contains window management functions. Both GLU and GLUT include a number of built-in graphical elements that we can use. To use the functions, we have to include the following header statements in our programs:

```
#include<GL/gl.h>
#include<GL/glu.h>
#include<GL/glut.h>
```

Names of functions in the GL library begin with **gl** (e.g. $glColor3f()$). On the other hand, names of functions in the GLU library begin with **glu** (e.g. $gluLookAt()$), and those in GLUT begin with **glut** (e.g. $glutMainLoop()$).

The goal of most OpenGL applications is to create images from models using computers, a process known as **rendering**. We construct models, or objects from geometric primitives such as points, lines, and polygons, which are defined by one or more vertices. The final rendered image consists of pixels drawn on the screen. **Pixel** is the abbreviation of **picture element**, which is the smallest visible element the display hardware can put on the screen. We may organize pixels into bitplanes. A bitplane is a 2D array that holds one bit of information for every pixel of the screen. Therefore, if each pixel holds 24 bits of information, the screen consists of 24 bitplanes. We may then organize bitplanes into a framebuffer, which holds all the information that the graphics display needs to control the color and intensity of all the pixels on the screen. We can imagine that a framebuffer is a 2D array with each location holding the information of a pixel. Bitplanes are artificial and are not necessary when developing graphics programs. However, the concept of framebuffer is fundamental. We can always consider that framebuffer is a memory buffer with each location corresponding to a pixel on the screen; when we change the value at a specified location of the framebuffer, the appearance of the corresponding pixel on the screen will be changed.

OpenGL function calls are enclosed between the functions **glBegin**() and **glEnd**(). For example, the following code draws three points:

```
glBegin( GL_POINTS );
   glVertex2i( 100, 40 );
   glVertex2i( 120, 50 );
   glVertex2i( 140, 80 );
glEnd();
```

Each OpenGL command starts with the prefix **gl** followed by a capital letter just like the command **glVertex2i**(). Also, OpenGL-defined constants begin with **GL_**, consisting of all capital letters. Words in the defined constants are separated by underscores (e.g. GL_POINTS and GL_LINES).

In the above example, the function **glVertex2i**() can be decomposed into several parts as shown in the following table:

gl	Vertex	2	i
gl library	basic command	number of arguments	type of argument

glVertex2i(..)

In this example, the number of arguments is 2, indicating the two dimensional x-y coordinates of the vertex, and the data type of argument is i (integer). If the suffix **i** in the command is replaced by **f**, it would indicate that the argument type is floating-point numbers. Having different formats allows an OpenGL program to accept a user's data in a preferred specified data format.

Some OpenGL commands accept as many as 8 different data types for their arguments. Table 2-1 shows the suffix letters used to specify these data types for ISO C implementations of OpenGL, along with the corresponding OpenGL type definitions. Variations of OpenGL implementations exist and some implementations might not follow this scheme exactly. For example, an implementation of OpenGL in C++ or Ada may differ from this scheme. Therefore, using OpenGL defined types such as **GLbyte** and **GLshort** instead of C-specific types **char** and **short** to write OpenGL programs may ease the difficulties of porting the programs from one platform to another. However, as this book is an introduction to graphics, for simplicity and ease of readability, we often use the C-language types in our programs.

Table 2-1 OpenGL Command Suffixes and Argument Data Types

Suffix	Data Type	OpenGL Type Definition	Corresponding C-Language Type
b	8-bit integer	GLbyte	signed char
s	16-bit integer	GLshort	short
i	32-bit integer	GLint, GLsizei	int or long
f	32-bit floating-point	GLfloat, GLclampf	float
d	64-bit floating-point	GLdouble, GLclampd	double
ub	8-bit unsigned integer	GLubyte, GLboolean	unsigned char
us	16-bit unsigned integer	GLushort	unsigned short
ui	32-bit unsigned integer	GLuint, GLenum, GLbitfield	unsigned int or unsigned long

As a consequence of Table 2-1, the two commands

```
glVertex2i(6, 4);
glVertex2f(6.0, 4.0);
```

are equivalent, except that the first function specifies the vertex's coordinates as 32-bit integers, and the second specifies them as single-precision floating-point numbers. The number of arguments of **glVertex*()** and many OpenGL commands can be 2, 3, or 4; in our notation here, the asterisk * stands for all variations of the command that we can use to specify a vertex.

Some OpenGL functions can take a final letter **v**, which stands for "vector" to indicate that the command takes a pointer (i.e. a vector or an array) rather than a series of individual arguments. (A vector here does **not** mean an Euclidean vector. It simply means an array.) The absence of the suffix "v" indicates a scalar format. Many commands have both vector and scalar versions, but some commands accept only scalar formats and others require that at least some of the arguments be specified in vector formats. For example, the following glColor*() commands are equivalent:

```
glColor3f( 1.0, 0.0, 0.0 );

GLfloat color_array[] = {1.0, 0.0, 0.0};
glColor3fv( color_array );
```

2.2.2   The Event Loop

OpenGL programs often run in an event loop. After initialization, the program falls into an infinite loop, waiting for events to happen. The application program has to specify how it handles various events, such as displaying, mouse movement, key pressing and window reshaping. The events are placed in an **event queue** and are processed sequentially. The application only needs to use a set of **callback functions** to specify how the program should react to specific events. Typically, an OpenGL program has a display callback function, which is invoked whenever the OpenGL program discovers that the window needs to be redrawn, including the first time when the window is created and opened. Consequently, if we put our rendering commands in the display callback function, it is guaranteed that they will be executed at least once.

After registering the callback functions, the program typically executes **glutMainLoop**() to get into an infinite loop to wait for events to happen. The following code is a typical piece of code that registers callback functions and puts the program in an infinite loop:

```
glutMouseFunc( myMouse );
glutMotionFunc( myMovedMouse );
glutKeyboardFunc( myKeyboard );
glutDisplayFunc( display );
glutReshapeFunc( reshape );
glutMainLoop();                    //go into perpetual loop
```

The above code has used the following callback functions to invoke various events:

1. **glutMouseFunc**(void (*func)(int button, int state, int x, int y)) associates a mouse button with a routine, which will be called when the mouse button is pressed or released.
2. **glutMotionFunc**(void (*func)(int x, int y)) associates a mouse motion to a routine, which will be called when the mouse is moved while a mouse button is also pressed.
3. **glutKeyboardFunc**(void (*func)(unsigned char key, int x, int y) links a keyboard key with a routine, which will be called when the key is pressed or released.
4. **glutDisplayFunc**(void (*func)(int w, int h)) links window display to a routine, which will be invoked each time the window needs to be redrawn.
5. **glutReshapeFunc**(void (*func)(int w, int h)) links window reshaping to a routine, which will be called when the window is resized.

Besides these functions, another popularly used callback function is **glutIdleFunc**(void (*func)(void)), which is particularly useful in animation graphics. This callback specifies a function that's to be executed when no other events are pending (i.e. when the event loop would otherwise be idle). This routine takes the pointer to a function as its only argument.

2.2.3   OpenGL as a State Machine

We can consider a running OpenGL program as a state machine consisting of state variables such as object color, line width, and object position. We may briefly classify state variables into three kinds:

1. *On-Off state variables* can be set to GL_FALSE (off) or GL_TRUE (on). We can use the functions glEnable() and glDisable() to set or reset these variables. For example, if GL_LINE_SMOOTH is enabled, lines are drawn with antialiasing, which makes lines look smooth, otherwise lines are drawn with aliasing.
2. *Mode state variables* require a function specific to the state variable in order to change its state. For example, glShadeModel (GL_SMOOTH) enables smooth shading, and glShade-Model (GL_FLAT) tells the program to draw with flat shading, which is the default.
3. *Value state variables* require commands specific to the state variables in order to change them. For example, the command "glColor3f(0.0, 1.0, 0.0)" changes the color state to green.

OpenGL also provides functions that can query the current state of the state machine. At any instance, we can use these functions to query the system for any variable's current value. Typically, we use one of these four commands to make the query: **glGetBooleanv**(), **glGetDoublev**(),

glGetFloatv(), or **glGetIntegerv**(). For example, the following code returns the current color state (RGBA values) to the array *color_state* and prints out the values:

```
glColor3f( 0.6, 0.4, 0.2 );
float color_state[4];
glGetFloatv( GL_CURRENT_COLOR, color_state );
char *colors[4] = { "Red", "Green", "Blue", "Alpha"};
for ( int i = 0; i < 4; i++ )
      printf("%s=%4.1f, ", colors[i], color_state[i]);
```

The code gives the following outputs:

```
Red= 0.6, Green= 0.4, Blue= 0.2, Alpha= 1.0
```

The following is another state-query example which prints out the current version of OpenGL used in the program:

```
const char *version;
version = (const char *) glGetString(GL_VERSION);
printf("\nOpenGL Version: %s\n", version );
```

This code may typically print out the following:

```
OpenGL Version: 2.1 Mesa 7.0.3
```

Besides querying, we can also save the current state in a stack. We can save a collection of state variables on an attribute stack using the command **glPushAttrib**(), and retrieve the attributes later by **glPopAttrib**().

2.2.4 Demo Programs

In this section we present a couple of very simple but complete programs. Each of them can be compiled independently to an executable file. The first program, **draw.cpp** presented in Listing 2-1 shows you how to write an OpenGL program to draw some primitive objects such as points, lines, and rectangles.

Program Listing 2-1: Draw Demo

```
--------------------------------------------------------------------
//draw.cpp : demo program for drawing 3 dots,lines,ploylines,rectangles
#include <GL/glut.h>
#include <stdio.h>

//initialization
void init( void ) {
  glClearColor( 1.0, 1.0, 1.0, 0.0 );     //get white background color
  glColor3f( 0.0f, 0.0f, 0.0f );          //set drawing color to black
  glPointSize( 4.0 );                     //a dot is 4x4 pixels
  glMatrixMode( GL_PROJECTION );          //matrix for projection
  glLoadIdentity();                       //load identity matrix
  gluOrtho2D( 0.0, 300.0, 0.0, 300.0 );   //2D 300x300 world window
}

void display( void ) {
  glClear( GL_COLOR_BUFFER_BIT );         //clear screen
  glBegin( GL_POINTS );                   //draw points
```

```
    glVertex2i( 100, 50 );                    //draw a point at (100, 50)
    glVertex2i( 100, 150 );                   //draw a point
    glVertex2i( 200, 200 ); //draw a point
  glEnd();

  //Two points specify a line.
  glBegin( GL_LINES );                        //draw lines
    glVertex2i( 20, 20 );                     //horizontal line
    glVertex2i( 250, 20 );
    glVertex2i( 20, 10 );                     //vertical line
    glVertex2i( 20, 250 );
  glEnd();
  //draw line connecting all points
  glBegin( GL_LINE_STRIP );                   //draw polyline
    glVertex2i( 100, 100 );   glVertex2i( 200, 50 );
    glVertex2i( 250, 100 );   glVertex2i( 100, 50 );
  glEnd();
  glColor3f( 0.6, 0.6, 0.6 );                 //bright grey color
  glRecti( 200, 200, 250, 280 );              //draw rectangle

  glFlush();                                  //send all output to screen
}

/*  Main Loop
 *  Open window with initial window size, title bar,
 *  RGB display mode.
 */
int main(int argc, char** argv) {
  glutInit(&argc, argv);                      //initialize toolkit
  glutInitDisplayMode (GLUT_SINGLE | GLUT_RGB ); //set display mode
  glutInitWindowSize(300, 300);               //set window size on screen
  glutInitWindowPosition( 100, 150 );         //set window position on screen
  glutCreateWindow(argv[0]);                  //open screen widow
  init();                                     //customized initialization
  glutDisplayFunc (display);                  //points to display function
  glutMainLoop();                             //go into perpetual loop
  return 0;
}
```

Figure 2-1 below shows the display output of the program and the following is a sample **Makefile** to compile the program.

```
#sample Makefile for using OpenGL
PROG = draw
TOP = /usr/include/GL
CFLAGS  = -w -s -O2 -ansi -DSHM
LIBS    = -lglut -lGLU -lGL -lGLEW
INCLS   = -I/usr/X11R/include  -I$(TOP)
LIBDIR  = -L/usr/X11/lib -L/usr/X11R6/lib

#source codes
SRCS   = $(PROG).cpp

#substitute .cpp by .o to obtain object filenames
```

```
OBJS   = $(SRCS:.cpp=.o)

#$< evaluates to the target's dependencies,
#$@ evaluates to the target

$(PROG): $(OBJS)
    g++ -o $@ $(OBJS)  $(LIBDIR) $(LIBS) $(XLIBS)


$(OBJS):
    g++ -c  $*.cpp $(INCLS)


clean:
    rm $(OBJS); rm $(PROG)
```

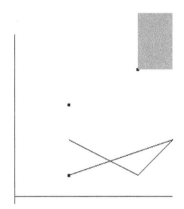

Figure 2-1   Display Output of Program **draw.cpp**.

2.3   OpenGL Drawing Primitives

OpenGL supports several basic primitive types, including points, lines, quadrilaterals, and general polygons. We can specify a primitive using a sequence of vertices. OpenGL does not have any primitive for drawing curves or circles. However, we can always approximate any curve using a sequence of small line segments. Figure 2-2 below shows some of the OpenGL primitives and Table 2-2 describes the meanings of the OpenGL primitives. Usually there are several ways to draw the same primitive. The way we choose depends on our vertex data, which specify the coordinates of the vertex and are parameters of the **glVertex***() command. We can also use special commands to provide additional vertex-specific data such as a color, a normal vector, texture coordinates, or a combination of these for each vertex. For example, the following piece of code specifies the normal of the vertices.

```
int v[3][3]={{100, 200,0},{200, 100,0},{200, 200, 0}};
int n[3] =  {0, 0, 1};

glBegin ( GL_TRIANGLES );
  glNormal3iv ( n );
  glVertex3iv( v[0] );
  glVertex3iv( v[1] );
  glVertex3iv( v[2] );
glEnd();
```

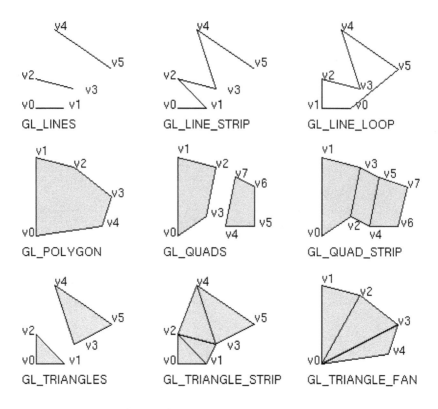

Figure 2-2 OpenGL Drawing Primitives

Providing the data of a normal vector to a plane is important in generating realistic scenes when light sources exist; OpenGL uses the normal vector to calculate the color at each pixel when filling the polygon.

Table 2-2 OpenGL Primitives Names and Meanings

Value	Meaning
GL_POINTS	individual points
GL_LINES	independent line segments, each joining two vertices
GL_LINE_STRIP	connected line segments
GL_LINE_LOOP	connected line segments that form a loop
GL_TRIANGLES	triangles, each specified by 3 vertices
GL_TRIANGLE_STRIP	linked strip of triangles, a vertex may be shared by 2 or more triangles
GL_TRIANGLE_FAN	linked fan of triangles, all having a common vertex
GL_QUADS	four-sided polygons, each joining four vertices
GL_QUAD_STRIP	connected strip of quadrilaterals, shared vertices
GL_POLYGON	simple bounded convex polygon

2.4 Displaying Points, Lines and Polygons

By default, a point is drawn as a single pixel on the screen; a line is drawn solid and one pixel wide, and a polygon is drawn with solidly-filled in color. We can change these default display modes using OpenGL functions as described below.

2.4.1   Point and Line Details

Points

We can change point attributes using the function **void glPointSize**(GLfloat *size*), which works as follows.

1. It sets the width of a rendered point in pixels with *size* > 0.0; the default *size* is 1.0.
2. The default is that antialiasing is disabled. In this case fractional widths are rounded to integer widths. For example, if *size* = 2, the dot is 2 × 2 pixels and looks like a small square.
3. We can enable antialiasing using the function **glEnable(GL_POINT_SMOOTH)**. In this case, a circular group of pixels is drawn and a point looks like a filled circle.

Line Stipple

We can draw lines with different widths using the function **glLineWidth**(GLFloat *width*), where *width* sets the line width in pixels for the rendered line and its value must be larger than 0.0. The default line width value is 1.0. The actual rendering of lines is affected by the antialiasing mode, in the same way as for points.

We can also draw lines that are stippled in various ways such as dotted, dashed, dotted-dash and so on. To make stippled lines, we use the function **glLineStipple**() to define the stipple pattern, and enable line stippling with glEnable():

void **glLineStipple** (GLint *factor*, GLushort *pattern*) sets the current stippling pattern for lines *pattern* is a 16-bit number that sets the pattern with 1 implying drawing and 0 implying no drawing *factor* ranges 1 to 256 specifying the repeating pattern

For example, the hexadecimal number 0x3F07 can be expressed in binary as

$$0011111100000111$$

If we repeat the binary pattern twice, the binary number becomes

$$00001111111111110000000000111111$$

Therefore, the command *glLineStipple(2, 0x3F07)* would draw a line with 6 pixels on, 10 off, 12 on, and 4 off.

2.4.2   Polygon Details

A **polygon** is a plane figure specified by a set of three or more vertices (coordinate positions). A **simple** (standard) polygon is a polygon whose edges do not cross each other. Each polygon in a scene is contained within a plane of infinite extent, which can be described by an equation like the following,

$$Ax + By + Cz + D = 0 \qquad (2.1)$$

where A, B, C and D are constants and (x, y, z) is any point on the plane. The plane divides the three dimensional space into three regions; a point can be behind the plane, on the plane, or in front of the plane. For an arbitrary given point (x, y, z), if

$$Ax + By + Cz + D < 0$$

the point (x, y, z) is **behind** the plane. If

$$Ax + By + Cz + D > 0$$

the point (x, y, z) is **before** the plane.

Polygons are typically drawn by coloring all the pixels enclosed within the boundary of the polygon, but we can also draw only the outlines of them or simply draw only the points at the vertices of the polygons. A filled polygon might be solidly filled or stippled with a certain pattern.

Back and Front Faces

A polygon has two sides, **front face** and **back face**. The back face of a polygon is the side that faces into the object interior and the front face is the outward side that is visible to the viewer.

We can render the back face, the front face or both faces of a polygon and can obtain a cutaway view of an object by appropriately rendering the faces of the polygons of an object. By default, both front and back faces are drawn in the same way. We may use the function **glPolygonMode**() to change this, or to draw only outlines or vertices:

void **glPolygonMode**(GLenum *face*, GLenum *mode*):

- Controls the drawing mode of drawing a polygon.
- Parameter *face* can be GL_FRONT, or GL_BACK, or GL_FRONT_AND_BACK to indicate whether we draw only the front faces, only the back faces or both front faces and back faces of the polygons.
- Parameter *mode* can be GL_POINT, GL_LINE, or GL_FILL to indicate whether we draw a polygon as points, or draw its outline or draw it as a filled polygon. By default, both the front and back faces are drawn filled.

For example, we can draw a polygon with its front face filled and its back face outlined by making the following two calls to this function:

```
glPolygonMode(GL_FRONT, GL_FILL);
glPolygonMode(GL_BACK, GL_LINE);
```

By convention, when we specify the vertices of a polygon in counterclockwise order, the side that appears on the screen is called **front-facing**. However, we can also make clockwise order as front-facing by the following command:

```
glFrontFace( GL_CW );  //clockwise as front-facing
```

We can change the facing to counterclockwise by

```
glFrontFace( GL_CCW ); //counterclockwise as front-facing
```

The orientation vertices is also known as **winding**.

Culling

Culling is the discarding (ignoring) of invisible polygons during rendering. This feature is helpful in drawing an object that is composed of polygons. For example, we can cull the back faces of an object enclosed by opaque polygons. The feature can be enabled by the command **glEnable**(GL_CULL_FACE). We can also specify whether we want to cull the back face, front face or both back and front faces by the commands,

```
glCullFace ( GL_FRONT );
glCullFace ( GL_BACK );
glCullFace ( GL_FRONT_AND_BACK );
```

As an example, consider the following piece of code. Assuming that everything has been initialized properly, *what do you expect to see on the screen when the code is executed?*

```
glEnable( GL_CULL_FACE );
glCullFace ( GL_BACK );        //discard back faces
glColor3f( 1.0, 0.0, 0.0 ); //red
glFrontFace ( GL_CCW );        //counterclockwise as front facing
glPolygonMode( GL_FRONT, GL_FILL );
glBegin( GL_POLYGON );         //draw solid polygon
  glVertex2i( 0, 0 );
  glVertex2i( 0, 100 );
  glVertex2i( 100, 100 );
  glVertex2i( 100, 0 );
glEnd();
```

The answer to the above question is that you should see nothing. This is because the code discards the back face of any polygon and uses counterclockwise as front facing; the polygon it specifies is a square whose vertices are specified in counterclockwise order $((0,0),(0,100),(100,100),(100,0))$ and therefore is a back face and will be discarded while rendering.

The area of an n-sided polygon with vertices $(x_0, y_0), (x_i, y_i), ..., (x_{n-1}, y_{n-1})$ can be calculated according to the following formula.

$$A = \frac{1}{2} \sum_{i=0}^{n-1} x_i y_{i+1} - x_{i+1} y_i \tag{2.2}$$

where $i+1$ is taken mod n. If we set counterclockwise ordering as front-facing (i.e. GL_CCW), then the side of a polygon with $A > 0$ is a front face, otherwise it is a back face. On the other hand, if we use clockwise ordering as front-facing (i.e. GL_CW), then the side of a polygon with $A < 0$ is a front face, otherwise it is a back face.

Figure 2-3 below shows three polygons, (a), (b), and (c) that are drawn using the following three modes respectively:

(a) glPolygonMode(GL_FRONT, GL_FILL);
(b) glPolygonMode(GL_FRONT, GL_LINE);
(c) glPolygonMode(GL_FRONT, GL_POINT);

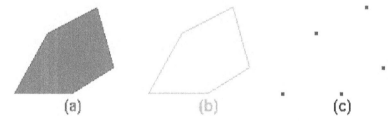

Figure 2-3 Polygons Drawn with Various Modes

2.5 Two Dimensional Graphics

OpenGL was designed primarily for making 3D graphics, but it can be used for 2D drawing as well. In 3D graphics, we need three coordinates, x, y, and z to specify a vertex. In 2D graphics, we just need the two coordinates x and y. The third coordinate, z, usually representing depth is ignored. The depth values (z values) are stored separately in a memory buffer called depth-buffer or z-buffer. The depth values are used to determine which objects are in front of others by depth-test. As we do not need the z coordinate in 2D graphics, it is better for us to turn off the depth-test. This can be done by the command

```
glDisable(GL_DEPTH_TEST);
```

Under this situation, we just need two parameters to specify a vertex. For example,

```
glVertex2f ( 10.0, 30.0 );
glVertex2i ( 100, 200 );
```

are valid commands that specify vertex locations.

The following class **Point2** defines some basic functions of handling a point in 2D graphics.

Listing 2-1: *Point2* Class

```
--------------------------------------------------------------------------
   class Point2
   {
     public:
       float x, y;
       Point2();                          //constructor 1
       Point2(float x0, float y0);        //constructor 2
       void set(float x0, float y0); //set x, y values
       void draw(void);                   //draw the point
   };
--------------------------------------------------------------------------
```

Implementation of the *Point2* class is straightforward. For example, its **set**() and **draw**() functions can be implemented as follows.

```
   void Point2::set(float x0, float y0)
   {
     x = x0;   y = y0;
   }

   void Point2::draw(void)
   {
     glBegin(GL_POINTS);     //draw this point
       glVertex2f( (GLfloat)x,  (GLfloat) y );
     glEnd();
   }
```

World Window

We can use the command **glutInitWindowSize**() to specify the initial window size. For example, the command

```
   glutInitWindowSize (500, 500);
```

sets the initial window size to 500×500 pixels. This window is called the **screen window** and its size is measured in pixels. In the real world, we do not describe the size or coordinates of an object in pixels. For example, the value of the sine function $y = sin(x)$ varies between -1 and 1 and the function is periodic, repeating itself after 2π. Therefore, if we want to display the curve of a sine function, we may want to set the range of x values from 0 to 2π and the range of y values from -1 to 1; the window size for displaying the sine curve is $2\pi \times 2$. This window is referred to as **world window**. We can use the command **gluOrtho2D**(), which defines a 2D orthographic projection matrix, to setup a world window.

For example, the command

```
gluOrtho2D(-3.1416, 3.1416, -1.0, 1.0 );
```

setup the world window for displaying the sine curve from $-\pi$ to $+\pi$.

Even though OpenGL is designed for 3D modeling, at the end each scene is projected on a 2D screen. We shall discuss the projection mechanism in details in next chapter. For 2D drawing, we can use a 2D projection scheme. Using the sine-curve as an example, the following code shows the setup of the projection.

```
const double Xleft=-3,14, Xright=3.14, Ybottom=-1.0, Ytop=1.0;
glMatrixMode (GL_PROJECTION)
glLoadIdentity ();
glOrtho2D(Xleft, Xright, Ybottom, Ytop);
glMatrixMode (GL_MODELVIEW)
```

The following sample code setup the world window and draws the sine curve from $-\pi$ to $+\pi$. The output of the code is shown in Figure 2-4 below.

```
------------------------------------------------------------------------
//Output of Code is shown in Figure 2-4
const double pi = 3.1416;

void init(void)
{
  glClearColor (1.0, 1.0, 1.0, 0.0);
  gluOrtho2D (-pi-0.2, pi+0.2, -1.1, 1.1);
}

void display(void)
{
  glClear (GL_COLOR_BUFFER_BIT);
  glColor3f ( 0.0, 0.0, 0.0 );    //black color
  glLineWidth ( 2 );
  double x, y, incx;
  int N = 100;
  incx = 2 * pi / N;
  //draw the sine curve
  glBegin( GL_LINE_STRIP );
    x = -pi;
    for ( int i = 0; i <= N; i++ ) {
      y = sin ( x );
      glVertex2f ( x, y );
      x += incx;
    }
  glEnd();
  //draw the rectangle
  glBegin( GL_LINE_LOOP );
    glVertex2f(-pi, -1.0);
    glVertex2f( pi, -1.0);
    glVertex2f( pi,  1.0);
    glVertex2f(-pi,  1.0);
  glEnd();
  glFlush ();
}
------------------------------------------------------------------------
```

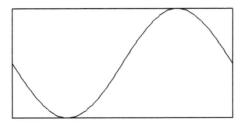

Figure 2-4 Sine Curve in World Window

Viewport

A **viewport** is a rectangular space defined in the screen window. Objects inside the world window are displayed in the viewport. We can display a viewport in anywhere of the screen window. The OpenGL command to set a viewport is **glViewport**():

> void glViewport(GLint *x*, GLint *y*, GLint *width*, GLint *height*);

where (*x*, *y*) specifies the coordinates of the lower-left corner of the viewport, and *width* and *height* are the width and height of the viewport in pixels respectively.

The following sample code displays a sine curve in four different viewports; the output is shown in Figure 2-5.

```
-------------------------------------------------------------------
    int main(int argc, char** argv)
    {
      ....
      glutInitWindowSize (480, 240);
      init();
      glutDisplayFunc(display);
      ....
    }

    const double pi = 3.1416;
    void init(void)
    {
       glClearColor (1.0, 1.0, 1.0, 0.0);
       gluOrtho2D (-pi-0.2, pi+0.2, -1.1, 1.1);
    }

    void drawSine()
    {
       double x, y, incx;
       int N = 100;
       incx = 2 * pi / N;
       //draw the sine curve
       glBegin ( GL_LINE_STRIP );
         x = -pi;
         for ( int i = 0; i <= N; i++ ) {
           y = sin ( x );
           glVertex2f ( x, y );
           x += incx;
         }
       glEnd();
```

```
    //draw the rectangle
    glBegin( GL_LINE_LOOP );
      glVertex2f(-pi, -1.0);
      glVertex2f( pi, -1.0);
      glVertex2f( pi,  1.0);
      glVertex2f(-pi,  1.0);
    glEnd();
  }

  void display(void)
  {
    glClear (GL_COLOR_BUFFER_BIT);
    glColor3f ( 0.0, 0.0, 0.0 );      //black color
    glLineWidth ( 2 );
    glViewport (0, 0, 240, 120 );     //lower left
    drawSine();
    glViewport (240, 0, 240, 120);    //lower right
    drawSine();
    glViewport (0, 120, 240, 120);    //upper left
    drawSine();
    glViewport (240, 120, 240, 120);  //upper right
    drawSine();
    glFlush ();
  }
```

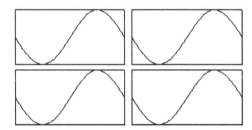

Figure 2-5 Sine Curve Drawn in Four Viewports

One interesting application of 2D graphics is to create turtle graphics, which is a valuable tool for kids to learn graphics, arts, or creating patterns and logos.

2.5.1 Turtle Graphics

Turtle graphics is a style of computer graphics using a relative cursor (the "turtle") to draw on a 2D plane. It is based on preserved state (position and orientation) and a small number of operations against that state (forward, turn, pen-up and pen-down). Usually the drawing state is referred to as the turtle and programs specify the turtle how to draw. Turtle graphics is easy for kids to pick up and is a key feature of the Logo programming language.

We may imagine that the drawing pen of a plotter is a turtle, and we have control of this little "creature" that exists in a mathematical plane or on a computer display screen. The turtle can respond to a few simple commands: FORWARD moves the turtle in the direction it is facing some number of units. TURN rotates it counterclockwise in its place some number of degrees. The turtle may simply move forward or draws a line while it moves, the exact operation depending on the pen-up and pen-down commands.

If the current position of the "turtle" is given, and we specify the direction (the angle θ with respect to the horizontal axis) and the distance d that we want the turtle to move, then the destination position can be calculated. For example, if the current position of the turtle is (x_0, y_0) and the distance is d as shown in Figure 2-6, we can calculate the destination position according to the following formulas.

$$x = x_0 + d \times \cos \theta$$
$$y = y_0 + d \times \sin \theta$$
(2.3)

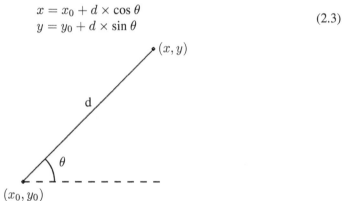

Figure 2-6 Calculating New Position

The following class (*Turtle*) defines some useful functions of turtle graphics. The **forward**() function is the main function in the class as it instructs the "turtle" to move with "pen" down or up (i.e. *isVisisble* is nonzero or zero).

Listing 2-2:   *Turtle* Class

```
class Turtle
{
public:
  Point2 cp;        //current turtle position
  float  angle;     //direction of turtle in degrees
  Turtle();         //constructor
  //move turtle to specified position
  void moveTo(float x, float y);
  void moveTo(Point2 p);
  //move certain displacement
  void moveRel(float dx, float dy);
  //draw line to specified point
  void lineTo(float x, float y);
  void lineTo(Point2 p);
  //turn to direction specified by angle
  void turnTo( float angle );
  //turn to direction pointing from turtle position to p
  void turnTo( Point2 p );
  //turn the specified amount of angle
  void turn( float angle );
  //Move forward by dist. If isVisible != 0, a line is drawn
  //  while moving forward, otherwise no line is drawn.
  void forward ( float dist, int isVisible );
};
```

Implementation of the *Turtle* class is also straightforward. For example, we can implement the **turnTo**() and **forward**() functions as follows.

```
//turns to the specific direction
void Turtle::turnTo( float a )
{
  angle = a;    //set current direction
}

//pointing towards p
void Turtle::turnTo( Point2 p )
{
  if ( p.x == cp.x && p.y == cp.y )
    angle = 0;
  else {
    if ( cp.x == p.x ) {
      if ( p.y < cp.y )
        angle = -90;
      else
        angle = 90;
    }else {
        float a=atan((p.y - cp.y) /(p.x - cp.x));//find angle
        angle = 180 * a / 3.1415926;    //convert to degree
    }
  }
}

//move line forward by amount dist;if isVisible nonzero,line is drawn
void Turtle::forward ( float dist, int isVisible )
{
  //radians per degree = 3.14159265389/180
  const float radPerDeg = 0.017453393;
  float x = cp.x + dist * cos ( radPerDeg * angle );
  float y = cp.y + dist * sin ( radPerDeg * angle );
  //special treatment for 0 and 90 degrees for better results
  if ( ( (int) angle % 180 )  == 0 )
    y = cp.y;
  else if ( (int) angle % 90 == 0 )
    x = cp.x;

  if ( isVisible )
    lineTo( x, y );
  else
    moveTo ( x, y );
}
```

Complete programs of all the code discussed in this book can be downloaded from the site

http://www.forejune.com/stereo/.

The following sample code makes use of turtle graphics to draw a box and then uses the box-drawing routine to draw a window; the output of the code is shown is Figure 2-7.

```
Turtle turtle;

void box()
{
  for ( int i = 0; i < 4; i++ ) {
    turtle.forward( 80, 1);
    turtle.turn( 90 );
  }
}

void display(void)
{
    int i;
```

```
glClear (GL_COLOR_BUFFER_BIT);
glLineWidth( 2 );
Point2 p1 (100, 200);
turtle.moveTo ( p1 );
box();      //draw box
//draw window
Point2 p2 ( 300, 280 );   //window center
turtle.moveTo ( p2 );
for ( int i = 0; i < 4; i++ ){
  box();
  turtle.turn ( 90 );
}
glFlush();
}
```

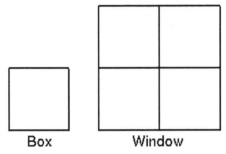

Figure 2-7 Drawing Boxes by Turtle Graphics

Chapter 3   Modeling and Viewing Transformations

3.1   Viewing

Any graphical object that we create in 3D space will be transformed and projected on a two-dimensional screen. OpenGL makes use of three computer operations, namely, transformations, clipping, and viewport mapping to convert an object's three-dimensional coordinates to pixel positions on the screen. All the operations are carried out by matrix operations.

A **transformation** is represented by a matrix multiplication, including modeling, viewing, and projection operations. Rotation, translation, reflection, scaling, orthographic projection, and perspective projection are examples of transformation operations. A **modelview transformation** is a transformation, which consists of modeling and positioning of the view point (camera or eye position). This includes rotation, translation, and scaling. A **projection transformation** is a transformation that involves the projection of 3D scene on a 2D plane.

Since the scene is rendered on a rectangular window, lines or objects (or parts of objects) that lie outside the window will not be rendered. In practice, we are only interested to see objects within a certain space that we define. The defined space is referred to as **viewing volume**. **Clipping** is the process of removing the parts of the objects that lie outside the viewing volume. All the points in space are transformed accordingly in a viewing transformation. Therefore, points that lie outside a viewing volume will be still outside after such a transformation. Consequently, the operation is more efficient if we remove those points before the transformation. We can carry out clipping either in three-dimensional space, or in projected 2D space.

We discussed in Chapter 2 that a viewport is a rectangular region on a display device that objects are drawn or rendered and is described in pixels. On the other hand, objects are drawn in world coordinates and the units or scales can be anything in the real world. To display the objects properly in the viewports, a correspondence must be established between the transformed world coordinates of the objects and the screen pixels of the viewport; this process is referred to as **viewport mapping**.

Figure 3-1 summarizes these operations. The figure shows that graphics rendering is like a manufacturing assembly line with each stage adding something to the previous one. This rendering architecture is referred to as **pipeline** architecture, which is supported by OpenGL.

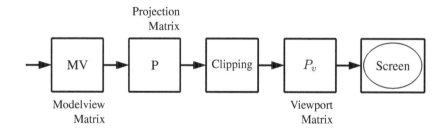

Figure 3-1   Graphics Pipeline

In traditional OpenGL programming, a fixed-function pipeline architecture is used. That is, the operations of the functions in each stage of Figure 3-1 are fixed. There is a trend to replace this fixed-function architecture with a programmable one. The OpenGL Shading Language (glsl) is introduced for this purpose. OpenGL for Embedded Systems (OpenGL ES), a subset of the OpenGL API designed for embedded systems and maintained by the nonprofit technology consortium, the Khronos Group, Inc., has eliminated most of the fixed-function rendering pipeline in favor of a programmable one in version 2.0 released in March 2007.

3.2 Points and Vectors

We discuss in this section points and geometric vectors intuitively. Later in this chapter, we will have a more formal, rigid and mathematical discussion of this topic. We know that both points and geometric vectors can be represented by (x, y, z). Given a 3-tuple (x, y, z), we really cannot tell whether it represents a point or a vector. At the surface, points and vectors appear to be the same but in reality, they are very different. A **point** denotes a position or a location; it does not have any direction or magnitude. On the other hand, a **vector** specifies a direction rather than a location; it has a magnitude and directional components. It makes sense to add two vectors but it does **not** make any sense to add two points. In some situations, a vector may be considered as a special point located at infinity. A common way to distinguish between a point and a vector denoted by (x, y, z) is to introduce an additional component, usually expressed as 'w', with '$w = 1$' denoting a point and '$w = 0$' denoting a vector. Therefore, in two-dimensional space, $(x, y, 1)$ represents a point and $(x, y, 0)$ represents a vector. If we consider three-dimensional situations, $(x, y, z, 1)$ represents a point and $(x, y, z, 0)$ represents a vector. With this representation, the operations on points and vectors are consistent with our intuition or understanding of points and vectors. For example, a point $(x_1, y_1, z_1, 1)$ plus a vector $(x_2, y_2, z_2, 0)$ is a point $(x_1 + x_2, y_1 + y_2, z_1 + z_2, 1)$, and a point $(x_1, y_1, z_1, 1)$ minus a point $(x_2, y_2, z_2, 1)$ is a vector $(x_1 - x_2, y_1 - y_2, z_1 - z_2, 0)$. A point $(x_1, y_1, z_1, 1)$ plus another point $(x_2, y_2, z_2, 1)$ gives $(x_1 + x_2, y_1 + y_2, z_1 + z_2, 2)$, which is an invalid representation and therefore, adding two points is an illegal operation. The operations may be summarized in the following table:

Table 3-1

Operation		Result
Vector	+	Vector	Vector
Vector	-	Vector	Vector
Vector	+	Point	Point
Vector	-	Point	Illegal
Point	+	Point	Illegal
Point	-	Point	Vector
Point	+	Vector	Point
Point	-	Vector	Point

Though it is illegal to add two points, we may form linear combinations of points:

$$P = c_0 P_0 + c_1 P_1 + \ldots + c_{n-1} P_{n-1} \tag{3.1}$$

where $P_i = (x_i, y_i, z_i, 1)$ is a point and c_i's are constant coefficients. The combination is legitimate if the summing coefficients are summed up to 1, and the combination gives a valid new point. i.e.,

$$c_0 + c_1 + \ldots + c_{n-1} = 1 \tag{3.2}$$

Linear combination of points satisfying (3.2) is in general referred to as affine combination of points. (The word "affine" has the Latin root "affinis" meaning "connected with"; "finis" means border or end, and "af" means sharing a common boundary.) This is the principle behind point interpolation and extrapolation. To construct a valid interpolation or extrapolation of points, the combination must be affine.

3.3   Vector, Affine, and Projective Spaces

Graphical scenes and objects are defined by points and vectors. Therefore, when we manipulate a graphical object, we basically process points and vectors. We have introduced the concepts of points and vectors in the previous section. It is important for us to have a deeper understanding of vectors and points in order to process our objects properly.

3.3.1   Vector Space

A **vector space** V is a set of objects called vectors that is closed under finite vector addition and scalar multiplication. That is, addition of two vectors yields another vector in the set, and multiplication of a vector by a scalar also produces a vector in the set. For a vector space to be valid, the following axioms must be satisfied for every vector $\mathbf{u}, \mathbf{v}, \mathbf{w}$ in V and every scalar a and b.

1. $(\mathbf{u} + \mathbf{v}) \in V$ (V is closed under addition)

2. $\mathbf{u} + \mathbf{v} = \mathbf{v} + \mathbf{u}$ (commutative property)

3. $(\mathbf{u} + \mathbf{v}) + \mathbf{w} = \mathbf{u} + (\mathbf{v} + \mathbf{w})$ (associative property)

4. There exists a vector in V, called the zero vector and denoted $\mathbf{0}$ such that $\mathbf{u} + \mathbf{0} = \mathbf{u}$ (additive identity)

5. For every vector $\mathbf{u}$ in V, there exists a vector $-\mathbf{u}$ also in V such that $\mathbf{u} + (-\mathbf{u}) = 0$ (additive inverse)

6. $a\mathbf{u} \in V$ (V is closed under scalar multiplication)

7. $a(\mathbf{u} + \mathbf{v}) = a\mathbf{u} + a\mathbf{v}$

8. $(a + b)\mathbf{u} = a\mathbf{u} + b\mathbf{u}$

9. $a(b\mathbf{u}) = (ab)\mathbf{u}$

10. $1\mathbf{u} = \mathbf{u}$

We specify both a magnitude and a direction for a geometric vector quantity. On the other hand, we specify a scalar quantity with just a number. Any number of vector quantities of the same type (i.e., same units) can be combined by basic vector operations. Figure 3-2 shows the vector addition and scalar multiplication properties.

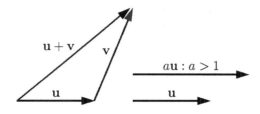

Figure 3-2   Vectors

Actually, there are many sets that satisfy the above properties. For example, polynomials of degree n form an n-dimensional vector space. Here, we are only concerned with geometric vectors which obviously satisfy the definition.

3.3.2 Affine Space

We define an n-dimensional **affine space** as a set of points, which associates with an n-dimensional vector space, and two operations, subtraction of two points in the set and addition of a point in the set to a vector in the associated vector space. In an affine space, we can subtract one point from another to get a vector, or add a vector to a point to get another point, but we cannot add points together directly. Also, there is no particular point which serves as the 'origin' of all the points. The solution set of an inhomogeneous linear equation is either empty or an affine space. Figure 3-3 shows the subtraction and addition operations; in the figure, P and Q are points and $\mathbf{u}$ is a vector.

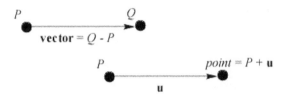

Figure 3-3   Affine Space Operations

3.3.3 Projective Space and Projective Equivalence

From an n-dimensional affine space, we can define an $(n+1)$-dimensional projective space, which embeds the points of the n-dimensional affine space. We denote the extra coordinate dimension as w and say that the affine points lie in the $w = 1$ plane of the projective space.

Figure 3-4 illustrates the $n = 2$ case. The xy plane is the affine 2D plane which is the $w = 1$ plane of a 3D projective space. (The image is copied from *http://www.ccs.neu.edu.*)

All projective space points on the line from the projective space origin through an affine point on the $w = 1$ plane are said to be projectively equivalent to the affine space point. Therefore, in a 4D projective space, the following points are projectively equivalent,

$$\begin{pmatrix} 1 \\ 2 \\ 3 \\ 1 \end{pmatrix}, \quad \begin{pmatrix} 2 \\ 4 \\ 6 \\ 2 \end{pmatrix}, \quad \begin{pmatrix} 0.5 \\ 1.0 \\ 1.5 \\ 0.5 \end{pmatrix}, \quad \begin{pmatrix} -1 \\ -2 \\ -3 \\ -1 \end{pmatrix}$$

and are "projected" into the same affine space point,

$$\begin{pmatrix} 1 \\ 2 \\ 3 \end{pmatrix}$$

In Figure 3-4, all points on a line that is not parallel to the xy plane are projectively equivalent to the point symbolized by the dot on the affine (i.e. $w = 1$) plane. Basically, for any nonzero α, all the 4D projective space points in the form

$$\begin{pmatrix} \alpha x \\ \alpha y \\ \alpha z \\ \alpha \end{pmatrix}$$

are projectively equivalent to the 3D affine point

$$\begin{pmatrix} x \\ y \\ z \end{pmatrix}$$

We may use the symbol $\sim$ to denote the "projectively equivalent" relation:

$$\begin{pmatrix} \alpha x \\ \alpha y \\ \alpha z \\ \alpha \end{pmatrix} \sim \begin{pmatrix} x \\ y \\ z \end{pmatrix} \tag{3.3}$$

Therefore, to find the affine point that is equivalent to a given projective space point, we can simply divide the first three coordinates by the fourth one. *Then what would happen if the fourth component is zero? What is the significance of the projective space point*

$$\begin{pmatrix} x \\ y \\ z \\ 0 \end{pmatrix} ?$$

It is obvious that a line from the projective space origin through this point is parallel to the $w = 1$ plane implying that it does not intersect the $w = 1$ plane, or we can imagine that they meet at infinity. It turns out that we can interpret this point as the 3D vector

$$\begin{pmatrix} x \\ y \\ z \end{pmatrix}$$

as we have discussed in the previous section. We can interpret vectors as special points at infinity of the $w = 1$ plane of a projective space.

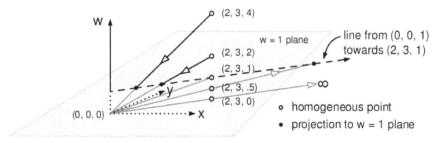

Figure 3-4   Projective Space

The idea of a projective space relates to perspective projection. It is the way that an eye or a camera projects a 3D scene into a 2D image. All points lying on a projection line (i.e., a "line-of-sight"), intersecting with the focal point of the camera, are projected onto a common image point. We can conveniently represent perspective projections in projective space. This means that we can represent them using the same formalism as ordinary transformations such as rotations, translations, and scales. This greatly eases the task of integrating perspective transformations with other transformations, which would not otherwise be true if we restrict ourselves to affine space and their associated operations.

We can study projective spaces as an independent field in mathematics, but we can also apply them to various fields, in particular geometry. We can represent geometric objects, such as points, lines, or planes, as elements in projective spaces using **homogeneous coordinates** discussed below. Consequently, we can describe various relations among these objects in a simpler way as compared to the case without using homogeneous coordinates. Moreover, we can make more consistent statements in geometry without making exceptions. For example, in standard geometry two lines always intersect at a point except when the lines are parallel. However, when we represent lines and points in a projective space, such an intersection point exists even for parallel lines, and we can compute it in the same way as other intersection points.

3.4 Homogeneous coordinates

Homogeneous coordinates are a system of coordinates used in projective geometry in a way that Cartesian coordinates are used in Euclidean geometry. In 3D graphics, a point P in homogeneous coordinates is a point in the corresponding projective space and is represented by four coordinates in the form

$$P = \begin{pmatrix} x \\ y \\ z \\ w \end{pmatrix}$$

We may sometimes simply express it as $P = (x, y, z, w)$. We have learned that a point (x, y, z) in an affine space is mapped to many points in a projective space in the form $(\alpha x, \alpha y, \alpha z)$ with nonzero α. Conversely, a projective space embeds an affine space at the $w = 1$ plane. Therefore, a 3D affine point is given by

$$P = \begin{pmatrix} x \\ y \\ z \\ 1 \end{pmatrix} \tag{3.4}$$

and a 3D vector $\mathbf{v}$ is represented by

$$\mathbf{v} = \begin{pmatrix} x \\ y \\ z \\ 0 \end{pmatrix} \tag{3.5}$$

For a "point" to be a valid affine point, the fourth component needs to have a value of 1 and for it to be a valid vector, the fourth component's value is 0.

Because of the restriction on the value of the fourth component of 3D points and vectors, we can always form linear combinations of 3D vectors, but we can form legitimate linear combinations of 3D points only if it satisfies the condition that the sum of the combination coefficients is equal to 0 or 1. That is,

$$\sum_{i=0}^{n-1} c_i P_i = \begin{cases} \text{point} & \text{if} \quad \sum_{i=0}^{n-1} c_i = 1 \\[2ex] \textbf{vector} & \text{if} \quad \sum_{i=0}^{n-1} c_i = 0 \\[2ex] \text{invalid} & \text{otherwise} \end{cases} \tag{3.6}$$

The advantage of using homogeneous coordinates is that we can use finite coordinates to represent all the coordinates of points, including points at infinity. Formulas involving homogeneous coordinates are often simpler and more symmetric than their Cartesian counterparts. Homogeneous coordinates are particularly convenient when we use them to represent points and vectors in 3D graphics as all the affine transformations, and projective transformations can be represented by matrices that have the same form. In general, such a transformation is represented by a 4×4 matrix M that has the following form:

$$M = \begin{pmatrix} m_{00} & m_{01} & m_{02} & m_{03} \\ m_{10} & m_{11} & m_{12} & m_{13} \\ m_{20} & m_{21} & m_{22} & m_{23} \\ 0 & 0 & 0 & 1 \end{pmatrix} \tag{3.7}$$

In projective space, an affine point is embedded in the $w = 1$ plane, and we describe an affine transformation in that projective space. The property that the bottom row of the transformation matrix M is $(0, 0, 0, 1)$ guarantees that transformed points are in the same affine space. That is, the fourth coordinate of the transformed point will be always 1. This can be easily verified by carrying out the matrix multiplication directly:

$$P' = MP = \begin{pmatrix} m_{00} & m_{01} & m_{02} & m_{03} \\ m_{10} & m_{11} & m_{12} & m_{13} \\ m_{20} & m_{21} & m_{22} & m_{23} \\ 0 & 0 & 0 & 1 \end{pmatrix} \begin{pmatrix} x \\ y \\ z \\ 1 \end{pmatrix} = \begin{pmatrix} x' \\ y' \\ z' \\ 1 \end{pmatrix} \tag{3.8}$$

The 4×4 matrix M of (3.7) can be used to represent both affine transformations and projection transformations. This is the main reason that virtually all graphics APIs, including OpenGL, employ 4×4 matrices to represent all transformations and why most graphics hardware includes support for 4×4 matrix multiplication.

OpenGL uses 4-tuples to represent homogeneous coordinates for 3D space points extensively. For example, the function call **glVectex4f**(x, y, z, w) specifies a point (x, y, z, w) in homogeneous coordinates. If we specify a point with only three (nonhomogeneous) coordinates, such as a function call to **glVectex3f**(x, y, z), OpenGL translates it to $(x, y, z, 1)$.

3.5   General Transformations

In general, an invertible $n \times n$ matrix M represents a transformation from one coordinate system to another. The columns of M give the images to which the principal axes of the original system are mapped in the new coordinate system. For example, when the 4×4 matrix M of (3.7) operates on the vectors $(1, 0, 0, 0)$, $(0, 1, 0, 0)$, and $(0, 0, 1, 0)$, we have

$$\begin{pmatrix} m_{00} & m_{01} & m_{02} & m_{03} \\ m_{10} & m_{11} & m_{12} & m_{13} \\ m_{20} & m_{21} & m_{22} & m_{23} \\ 0 & 0 & 0 & 1 \end{pmatrix} \begin{pmatrix} 1 \\ 0 \\ 0 \\ 0 \end{pmatrix} = \begin{pmatrix} m_{00} \\ m_{10} \\ m_{20} \\ 0 \end{pmatrix} \tag{3.9a}$$

$$\begin{pmatrix} m_{00} & m_{01} & m_{02} & m_{03} \\ m_{10} & m_{11} & m_{12} & m_{13} \\ m_{20} & m_{21} & m_{22} & m_{23} \\ 0 & 0 & 0 & 1 \end{pmatrix} \begin{pmatrix} 0 \\ 1 \\ 0 \\ 0 \end{pmatrix} = \begin{pmatrix} m_{01} \\ m_{11} \\ m_{21} \\ 0 \end{pmatrix} \tag{3.9b}$$

$$\begin{pmatrix} m_{00} & m_{01} & m_{02} & m_{03} \\ m_{10} & m_{11} & m_{12} & m_{13} \\ m_{20} & m_{21} & m_{22} & m_{23} \\ 0 & 0 & 0 & 1 \end{pmatrix} \begin{pmatrix} 0 \\ 0 \\ 1 \\ 0 \end{pmatrix} = \begin{pmatrix} m_{02} \\ m_{12} \\ m_{22} \\ 0 \end{pmatrix} \tag{3.9c}$$

Conversely, the columns of M^{-1} give the images to which the principal axes of the new coordinate system are mapped in the original coordinate system. Therefore, given any arbitrary independent vectors **u**, **v**, and **w**, we can construct a transformation matrix which maps these vectors to the vectors $(1, 0, 0, 0)$, $(0, 1, 0, 0)$, and $(0, 0, 1, 0)$. From (3.9), if **u**, **v**, and **w** form the columns of the inverse of the transformation matrix, we have

$$\begin{pmatrix} u_x & v_x & w_x & 0 \\ u_y & v_y & w_y & 0 \\ u_z & v_z & w_z & 0 \\ 0 & 0 & 0 & 1 \end{pmatrix}^{-1} \begin{pmatrix} u_x \\ u_y \\ u_z \\ 0 \end{pmatrix} = \begin{pmatrix} 1 \\ 0 \\ 0 \\ 0 \end{pmatrix} \tag{3.10a}$$

$$\begin{pmatrix} u_x & v_x & w_x & 0 \\ u_y & v_y & w_y & 0 \\ u_z & v_z & w_z & 0 \\ 0 & 0 & 0 & 1 \end{pmatrix}^{-1} \begin{pmatrix} v_x \\ v_y \\ v_z \\ 0 \end{pmatrix} = \begin{pmatrix} 0 \\ 1 \\ 0 \\ 0 \end{pmatrix} \qquad (3.10b)$$

$$\begin{pmatrix} u_x & v_x & w_x & 0 \\ u_y & v_y & w_y & 0 \\ u_z & v_z & w_z & 0 \\ 0 & 0 & 0 & 1 \end{pmatrix}^{-1} \begin{pmatrix} w_x \\ w_y \\ w_z \\ 0 \end{pmatrix} = \begin{pmatrix} 0 \\ 0 \\ 1 \\ 0 \end{pmatrix} \qquad (3.10c)$$

In representing transformations using matrices, we need to keep in mind a few matrix multiplication properties. Suppose A, B, and C are matrices that we can carry out multiplications. The following are some basic but important properties of matrix operations.

Noncommutative multiplication: $AB \neq BA$
Associative: $(AB)C = A(BC)$
Transpose Property: $(AB)^T = B^T A^T$
Inverse Property: $(AB)^{-1} = B^{-1} A^{-1}$

We can concatenate multiple transformations and represent the resultant transformation by a single matrix. For example,

$$M\mathbf{V} = M_1 M_2 M_3 \mathbf{V} \qquad (3.11)$$

So the composite matrix is

$$M = M_1 M_2 M_3 \qquad (3.12)$$

3.5.1 Orthogonal Matrix

We define an invertible $n \times n$ matrix M to be **orthogonal** if and only if its inverse is equal to its transpose (i.e. $M^{-1} = M^T$). Orthogonal matrices have a few interesting properties that we want to study. First, with this definition, we can prove the following theorem.

Theorem 3.1
If the vectors $\mathbf{v_0}, \mathbf{v_1}, ..., \mathbf{v_{n-1}}$ form an orthonormal set, then the $n \times n$ matrix M constructed by setting the j-th column equal to v_j for all $0 \leq j < n$ is orthogonal.

Proof
Since v_j's are orthonormal, $(M^T M)_{ij} = \mathbf{v_i} \cdot \mathbf{v_j} = \delta_{ij}$ where δ_{ij} is the Kronecker delta symbol which is defined as

$$\delta_{ij} = \begin{cases} 0 & \text{if } i \neq j \\ 1 & \text{if } i = j \end{cases}$$

So $M^T M = I$. Therefore, $M^T = M^{-1}$ and according to our definition, M is orthogonal.

Another property of orthogonal matrix relates to length and angle preservation. We say that a matrix M **preserves length** if for any vector $\mathbf{V}$ we have

$$|M\mathbf{V}| = |\mathbf{V}| \qquad (3.13)$$

A matrix M that preserves lengths also **preserves angles** if for any two vectors $\mathbf{U}$ and $\mathbf{V}$, we have

$$(M\mathbf{U}) \cdot (M\mathbf{V}) = \mathbf{U} \cdot \mathbf{V} \qquad (3.14)$$

Now we prove the following theorem.

Theorem 3.2
If an $n \times n$ matrix M is orthogonal, then M preserves lengths and angles.

Proof
Let M be orthogonal and $\mathbf{U}, \mathbf{V}$ are two vectors. We use the conventional notation that a vector $\mathbf{U}$ is a column matrix and its transpose $\mathbf{U}^T$ is a row matrix. The dot product of any two vectors is equal to the product of the corresponding row matrix and column matrix. For example, the dot product of two vectors $\mathbf{u}$ and $\mathbf{v}$ is given by:

$$\mathbf{u} \cdot \mathbf{v} = \mathbf{u}^T \mathbf{v} = (u_x, u_y, u_z, 0) \begin{pmatrix} v_x \\ v_y \\ v_z \\ 0 \end{pmatrix} = u_x v_x + u_y v_y + u_z v_z$$

Therefore,

$$\begin{aligned} (M\mathbf{U}) \cdot (M\mathbf{V}) &= (M\mathbf{U})^T (M\mathbf{V}) \\ &= (\mathbf{U}^T M^T)(M\mathbf{V}) \\ &= \mathbf{U}^T M^T M \mathbf{V} \\ &= \mathbf{U}^T \mathbf{V} \\ &= \mathbf{U} \cdot \mathbf{V} \end{aligned}$$

where we have made use of the transpose property of matrix (i.e. $(AB)^T = B^T A^T$), and the orthogonal property of M (i.e. $M^T M = M^{-1} M = I$). Therefore,

$$(M\mathbf{U}) \cdot (M\mathbf{V}) = \mathbf{U} \cdot \mathbf{V} \tag{3.15}$$

implying that the matrix M preserves angles.

Moreover, when $\mathbf{U} = \mathbf{V}$, (3.15) is reduced to

$$|M\mathbf{U}|^2 = |\mathbf{U}|^2 \tag{3.16}$$

which implies that $|M\mathbf{U}| = |\mathbf{U}|$ and thus the length is preserved.

For example, the following scaling matrix represents a reflection about the yz plane (i.e. $x \rightarrow -x$).

$$S = \begin{pmatrix} -1 & 0 & 0 & 0 \\ 0 & 1 & 0 & 0 \\ 0 & 0 & 1 & 0 \\ 0 & 0 & 0 & 1 \end{pmatrix} \tag{3.16}$$

It is obvious that in (3.16), $S^T = S^{-1} = S$ and thus the reflection matrix S is orthogonal, preserving both lengths and angles, which is consistent with our knowledge about reflection. In general, orthogonal matrices preserve the overall structure of a coordination system as they preserve lengths and angles. Orthogonal matrices can thus represent only combinations of rotations and reflections.

3.6   3D Affine Transformations

In geometry, an **affine transformation** (or affine map) is a linear transformation (rotation, scaling or shear) followed by a translation. Under such a transformation, a point P in 3D graphics is transformed to another point Q by the equation,

$$Q = AP + \mathbf{v} \tag{3.17}$$

where A is a matrix and $\mathbf{v}$ is the translational vector. Several linear transformations can be combined into a single one, so that the general formula of (3.17) is still applicable. In the one-dimensional case, A and $\mathbf{v}$ are called **slope** and **intercept** respectively. Geometrically, one can show that an affine transformation in Euclidean space satisfies the following properties:

1. It preserves the collinearity relation between points. That is, the points which lie on a line continue to be on the same line after the transformation.

2. It preserves the ratios of distances along a line implying that for distinct collinear points p_1, p_2, p_3, the ratio $\dfrac{|p_2 - p_1|}{|p_3 - p_2|}$ remains the same after transformation.

If we use homogeneous coordinates that we have discussed in section 3.4, the translational vector can be "absorbed" in the transformation matrix M; in this case, (3.17) can be expressed as:

$$Q = MP \qquad\qquad (3.18)$$

Equations (3.18) and (3.8) above represent affine transformations in homogeneous coordinate systems. In 3D graphics, affine transformation includes translation, scaling, and rotation. The affine transformation matrix M is always in the form given in (3.7). In the special case that $m_{ij} = \delta_{ij}$ (i.e. $m_{ii} = 1$, and $m_{ij} = 0$ for $i \neq j$), M is reduced to the identity matrix I:

$$I = \begin{pmatrix} 1 & 0 & 0 & 0 \\ 0 & 1 & 0 & 0 \\ 0 & 0 & 1 & 0 \\ 0 & 0 & 0 & 1 \end{pmatrix}$$

In OpenGL, we can set the transformation matrix to the identity matrix using the command **glLoadIdentity**(). OpenGL provides a few functions to change or examine the values of the transformation matrix M:

1. void **glLoadIdentity**(void);
   Sets the transformation matrix to the 4×4 identity matrix

2. void **glLoadMatrix**{fd}(const TYPE *m);
   Sets the sixteen values of the transformation matrix to those specified by m.

3. void **glMultMatrix**{fd}(const TYPE *A);
   Multiplies the transformation matrix by the sixteen values pointed to by A. The 16 values pointed by A are not changed. i.e. $M \leftarrow MA$

4. void **glPushMatrix**(void);
   Pushes the transformation matrix onto stack. The current stack is determined by **glMatrixMode**().

5. void **glPopMatrix**(void);
   Pops matrix at top of stack and sets the transformation matrix to the 16 values of the popped matrix. The current stack is determined by **glMatrixMode**().

We can use the function **glGetFloatv**() or **glGetDoublev**() to retrieve and examine the values of the transformation matrix. Note that OpenGL operates in a column-major data format. That is, it first reads the first column of the transformation matrix M into memory, followed by the second column and so on. In the same way, when it loads data from a memory array to the transformation matrix, the first four elements in the memory are loaded into the first column of M, and the next four elements into the second column and so on. Therefore, if we use the above commands to read the transformation matrix into a 2D 4×4 array (e.g. double a[4][4];), we will end up storing the transpose of the transformation matrix in the array.

3.6.1   Translation

If we let **t** to be the translational vector, the functional form for **translation** can be expressed as

$$
\begin{aligned}
x' &= x + \mathbf{t}_x \\
y' &= y + \mathbf{t}_y \\
z' &= z + \mathbf{t}_z
\end{aligned}
\tag{3.19}
$$

When represented in the matrix form of (3.18) or (3.8), this becomes:

$$
\begin{pmatrix} x' \\ y' \\ z' \\ 1 \end{pmatrix}
=
\begin{pmatrix}
1 & 0 & 0 & \mathbf{t}_x \\
0 & 1 & 0 & \mathbf{t}_y \\
0 & 0 & 1 & \mathbf{t}_z \\
0 & 0 & 0 & 1
\end{pmatrix}
\begin{pmatrix} x \\ y \\ z \\ 1 \end{pmatrix}
\tag{3.20}
$$

We can use the OpenGL command **glTranslate**{fd}() to perform a translation operation:

> void **glTranslate**{fd}(TYPE *tx*, TYPE *ty*, TYPE *tz*);
> Multiplies the current transformation matrix by a matrix that translates an object by the given *tx*, *ty*, and *tz* values.

This command sets $M = MT$, where T is the translation matrix:

$$
T =
\begin{pmatrix}
1 & 0 & 0 & \mathbf{t}_x \\
0 & 1 & 0 & \mathbf{t}_y \\
0 & 0 & 1 & \mathbf{t}_z \\
0 & 0 & 0 & 1
\end{pmatrix}
\tag{3.21}
$$

3.6.2   Scaling

Scaling is the process of resizing a graphical object. The functional form for scaling is given by

$$
\begin{aligned}
x' &= s_x x \\
y' &= s_y y \\
z' &= s_z z
\end{aligned}
\tag{3.22}
$$

Equation (3.22) scales the x, y, and z coordinates independently. In matrix form, this becomes

$$
\begin{pmatrix} x' \\ y' \\ z' \\ 1 \end{pmatrix}
=
\begin{pmatrix}
s_x & 0 & 0 & 0 \\
0 & s_y & 0 & 0 \\
0 & 0 & s_z & 0 \\
0 & 0 & 0 & 1
\end{pmatrix}
\begin{pmatrix} x \\ y \\ z \\ 1 \end{pmatrix}
\tag{3.23}
$$

In this case, the transform matrix is the scaling matrix S:

$$
S =
\begin{pmatrix}
s_x & 0 & 0 & 0 \\
0 & s_y & 0 & 0 \\
0 & 0 & s_z & 0 \\
0 & 0 & 0 & 1
\end{pmatrix}
\tag{3.24}
$$

OpenGL provides the functions "**glScale**{fd}(TYPE *sx*, TYPE *sy*, TYPE *sz*)" to do scaling transformation. That is, it sets $M = MS$.

OpenGL does not have any special commands for reflections or shearing transformations. A **reflection** transforms points across some plane to generate mirror-image points. Reflections across the coordinate planes are special cases of scaling transformations. For example, a reflection across the yz-plane can be done by setting s_x of S shown in (3.24) to -1, and s_y, and s_z to 1; such a reflection transformation matrix is

$$S = \begin{pmatrix} -1 & 0 & 0 & 0 \\ 0 & 1 & 0 & 0 \\ 0 & 0 & 1 & 0 \\ 0 & 0 & 0 & 1 \end{pmatrix} \tag{3.25}$$

This corresponds to executing the command,

    glScalef(-1.0, 1.0, 1.0);

The code below shows an example of scaling and reflection; the output of the code is shown in Figure 3-5. The teapot in the upper half of the figure is the original wired teapot. The one in the second half is a reflection of the upper one about the zx-plane (.i.e. $y \to -y$); it has also been scaled in the x-direction by a factor of 1.5. Note that we have used **glLoadIdentity**() to isolate the effects of modeling transformations. This function initializes the transformation matrix values to δ_{ij} to prevent successive transformations from having a cumulative effect. Even though using **glLoadIdentity**() repeatedly has the desired effect, it may be inefficient, because we may have to re-specify viewing or modeling transformations repeatedly.

```
glMatrixMode (GL_MODELVIEW);
glLoadIdentity();
glTranslatef ( 0, 0.8, 0 );      //move teapot upward
glutWireTeapot( 1.0 );

glLoadIdentity();
glColor3f (0.0, 1.0, 0.0);       //green color
glTranslatef ( 0, -0.8, 0 );     //move reflected teapot downward
glScalef ( 1.5, -1.0, 1.0 );     //scale and reflect
glutWireTeapot( 1.0 );
```

A **shearing** transformation is a more complicated kind of transformation. There is no direct OpenGL command that does a shearing transformation but we can always produce the effect by combining scaling, rotation and translation transformations. However, it may be easier to perform a desired transformation by setting the transformation matrix M to predefined values using the commands **glLoadMatrixf**() or **glMultMatrix**() discussed above.

Figure 3-5   Scaling and Reflection

3.6.3 Rotations

Rotations about the coordinate axes are the simplest kinds of rotations and they form the basis of an arbitrary rotation. Rotations about an arbitrary axis can be done by appropriately combining translations and coordinate-axis rotations. We refer to coordinate-axis rotations as **elementary rotations**.

Conventionally, a counterclockwise rotation about an axis is given by a positive rotation angle; the direction is determined by the right-hand thumb rule. That is, if our right-hand fingers are wrapping in the counterclockwise direction our thumb points in the positive direction of the axis as shown in Figure 3-6.

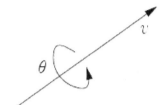

Figure 3-6 Counterclockwise rotation

Borrowing aviation terminology, rotations about z-axis, y-axis, and x-axis in counterclockwise direction are referred to as **yaw, pitch**, and **roll** respectively. Sometimes people also refer to these rotations as z-roll, y-roll, and x-roll. Figure 3-7 shows these rotations.

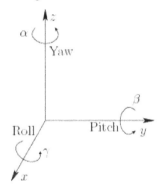

Figure 3-7 Yaw, Pitch, and Roll

z-axis rotation (yaw or z-roll)

The functional form for a rotation about the z-axis for an angle θ is given by

$$x' = x \cos \theta - y \sin \theta$$
$$y' = x \sin \theta + y \cos \theta \qquad (3.26)$$
$$z' = z$$

In homogeneous coordinate matrix form, this becomes

$$\begin{pmatrix} x' \\ y' \\ z' \\ 1 \end{pmatrix} = \begin{pmatrix} \cos \theta & -\sin \theta & 0 & 0 \\ \sin \theta & \cos \theta & 0 & 0 \\ 0 & 0 & 1 & 0 \\ 0 & 0 & 0 & 1 \end{pmatrix} \begin{pmatrix} x \\ y \\ z \\ 1 \end{pmatrix} \qquad (3.27)$$

A positive rotation about the z-axis rotates the x-axis towards the y-axis. This rotation is usually denoted by $R_z(\theta)$, which is the rotation matrix

$$R_z(\theta) = \begin{pmatrix} \cos \theta & -\sin \theta & 0 & 0 \\ \sin \theta & \cos \theta & 0 & 0 \\ 0 & 0 & 1 & 0 \\ 0 & 0 & 0 & 1 \end{pmatrix} \qquad (3.28)$$

Figure 3-8 shows an example of such a rotation. In the figure, a teapot is rotated by 135° about the z-axis.

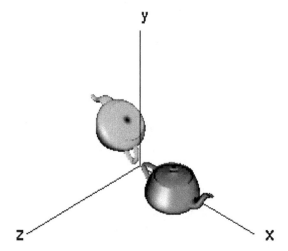

Figure 3-8 Rotation about z-axis for 135°

y-axis rotation (pitch or y-roll)

A rotation about the y-axis for an angle θ can be specified by the equations

$$
\begin{aligned}
x' &= x \cos \theta + z \sin \theta \\
y' &= y \\
z' &= -x \sin \theta + z \cos \theta
\end{aligned}
\tag{3.29}
$$

A positive rotation about the y-axis rotates the z-axis towards the x-axis. This rotation is usually denoted by $R_y(\theta)$, which is the rotation matrix

$$
R_y(\theta) = \begin{pmatrix}
\cos \theta & 0 & \sin \theta & 0 \\
0 & 1 & 0 & 0 \\
-\sin \theta & 0 & \cos \theta & 0 \\
0 & 0 & 0 & 1
\end{pmatrix}
\tag{3.30}
$$

x-axis rotation (roll or x-roll)

A rotation about the x-axis for an angle θ can be specified by the equations

$$
\begin{aligned}
x' &= x \\
y' &= y \cos \theta - z \sin \theta \\
z' &= y \sin \theta + z \cos \theta
\end{aligned}
\tag{3.31}
$$

A positive rotation about the x-axis rotates the y-axis towards the z-axis. This rotation is usually denoted by $R_x(\theta)$, which is the rotation matrix

$$
R_x(\theta) = \begin{pmatrix}
1 & 0 & 0 & 0 \\
0 & \cos \theta & -\sin \theta & 0 \\
0 & \sin \theta & \cos \theta & 0 \\
0 & 0 & 0 & 1
\end{pmatrix}
\tag{3.32}
$$

Composite Rotations

We can place a 3D object in any orientation using yaw, pitch, and roll rotations. We can form a single rotation matrix R by multiplying the yaw, pitch, and roll rotation matrices as follows.

$$R(\alpha, \beta, \gamma) = R_z(\alpha)R_y(\beta)R_x(\gamma) =$$

$$\begin{pmatrix} \cos\alpha\cos\beta & \cos\alpha\sin\beta\sin\gamma - \sin\alpha\cos\gamma & \cos\alpha\sin\beta\cos\gamma + \sin\alpha\sin\gamma & 0 \\ \sin\alpha\cos\beta & \sin\alpha\sin\beta\sin\gamma + \cos\alpha\cos\gamma & \sin\alpha\sin\beta\cos\gamma - \cos\alpha\sin\gamma & 0 \\ -\sin\beta & \cos\beta\sin\gamma & \cos\beta\cos\gamma & 0 \\ 0 & 0 & 0 & 1 \end{pmatrix} \quad (3.33)$$

Note that matrix operations on points start from the right side first. In (3.33), we perform the rotation $R_x(\gamma)$ first, $R_y(\beta)$ second, and $R_z(\alpha)$ last. That is, we obtain the final point, say P_3, from an initial point P_0 that undergoes matrix multiplications in the following order:

$$\begin{aligned} P_3 &= R(\alpha, \beta, \gamma)P_0 \\ &= R_z(\alpha)R_y(\beta)R_x(\gamma)P_0 \\ &= R_z(\alpha)R_y(\beta)P_1 \\ &= R_z(\alpha)P_2 \\ &= P_3 \end{aligned} \quad (3.34)$$

This means that $R(\alpha, \beta, \gamma)$ performs the roll first, then the pitch, and finally the yaw. If the order of these operations is changed, a different rotation matrix would result as matrix multiplications are not commutative. Note also that 3D rotations depend on three parameters, α, β, and γ, whereas 2D rotations depend only on a single parameter, θ. The angles α, β, and γ, are often called **Euler angles**.

Euler's Rotation Theorem

We have discussed rotations about coordinate axes and their rotation matrices. In practice, very often we need to rotate an object about an axis that points in an arbitrary direction. It turns out that every rotation can be represented in this way as stated by Euler's rotation theorem.

Euler's rotation theorem
Any rotation (or sequence of rotations) about a point is equivalent to a single rotation about some axis through that point.

We skip the derivation steps and proof of the theorem here. We just present the matrix that represents an arbitrary rotation about a vector pointing in a specific direction. Suppose $\mathbf{u}$ is a unit vector. That is, $\mathbf{u} = (u_x, u_y, u_z)$, and $|\mathbf{u}| = 1$. One can show that a rotation $R_\mathbf{u}(\theta)$, through an angle θ around axis $\mathbf{u}$ is given by

$$R_\mathbf{u}(\theta) = \begin{pmatrix} (1-c)u_x^2 + c & (1-c)u_xu_y - su_z & (1-c)u_xu_z + su_y & 0 \\ (1-c)u_xu_y + su_z & (1-c)u_y^2 + c & (1-c)u_yu_z - su_x & 0 \\ (1-c)u_xu_z - su_y & (1-c)u_yu_z + su_x & (1-c)u_z^2 + c & 0 \\ 0 & 0 & 0 & 1 \end{pmatrix} \quad (3.35)$$

where $c = \cos\theta$ and $s = \sin\theta$. OpenGL provides a command to perform such an operation:

glRotatef(float $theta$, float u_x, float u_y, float u_z);

This command rotates an object for an angle $theta$ around an axis through the origin in the direction of the vector $\mathbf{u}$. That is, it sets the transformation matrix $M = MR_\mathbf{u}(\theta)$. The vector $\mathbf{u}$ must not be **0**. If the vector provided in the argument is not a unit vector, OpenGL will normalize it to a unit vector. The rotation angle *theta* is measured in degrees, and the direction of rotation follows the right-hand rule discussed above. The functions, glRotatef(*theta*, 1, 0, 0); glRotatef(*theta*, 0, 1, 0); and glRotatef(*theta*, 0, 0, 1); reduce to the elementary rotations, x-roll, y-roll, and z-roll respectively.

If we need to rotate an object about an axis that does not pass through the origin of the coordinate system, all we need to do is to translate the origin of the coordinate system to a point on the rotating axis and perform the rotation around the axis. After rotation, we translate the system back.

Euler's rotation theorem also implies that the composition of two rotations is also a rotation. Consequently, the set of rotations has a structure known as a *rotation group*.

3.7   Composite Transformations

3.7.1   Modelview Transformation

As we have mentioned before, affine transformations can be combined to give a resultant affine transformation. This is done by multiplying matrices in the form of (3.7). We often use affine transformations to do modelling transformation but we can also use them for viewing transformation. OpenGL combines the modelling and viewing steps into one stage called **modelview transformation** (Figure 3-1). It is important to note that matrix multiplication is not commutative. That is, for two matrices of (3.7), M_1 and M_2, we have

$$M_2 M_1 \neq M_1 M_2 \qquad (3.36)$$

Therefore, the process of *translate-then-rotate* is different from the process of *rotate-then-translate*. The operation *translate-then-rotate* is given by

$$M = RT \qquad (3.37)$$

Figure 3-8 above shows the situation of translating a teapot from the origin to another position along the x-axis and then rotating it by 135° around the z-axis. On the other hand, *rotate-then-translate* is

$$M = TR \qquad (3.38)$$

Figure 3-9 below shows the corresponding *rotate-then-translate* situation.

Note again that matrix operations on a point start from the right. For example,

$$MP_0 = R(TP_0) = RP_1 = P_2$$

The following code shows an example of composite transformation:

```
glLoadIdentity();      //M = I
glTranslatef(..);      //M = I.T = T
glRotate(..);          //M = M.R = T.R
glScale(..);           //M = M.S = T.R.S
draw_a_point( P );     //Q = M.P = T.R.S.P
```

The equivalent order of operation on P is : scale, rotate, translate. Therefore, the code for *translate-then-rotate* that generates the image of Figure 3-8 is:

```
glLoadIdentity();            //M = I
glRotatef (135, 0, 0, 1 );   //M = MR = IR = R
glTranslatef ( 1.0, 0.0, 0 ); //M = MT = RT
glutSolidTeapot( 0.6 );       //P' = MP = (RT)P = R(TP)
```

As usual, the statements of the code are executed sequentially, from top to bottom. In the graphics pipeline, a vertex is always multiplied by the current modelview transformation matrix M before rendering (Figure 3-1). Thus, as shown in the comments of the code, any point P is transformed to $P' = MP = RTP = R(TP)$, showing that the translation effect takes place first, though in reality the vertex is transformed by multiplying its coordinates by the transformation matrix M.

Similarly, the code for *rotate-then-translate* (Figure 3-9) is:

```
glLoadIdentity();              //M = I
glTranslatef ( 1.0, 0.0, 0 ); //M = MT = IT = T
glRotatef (135, 0, 0, 1 );     //M = MR = TR
glutSolidTeapot( 0.6 );        //P' = MP = (TR)P = T(RP)
```

Beginners need to pay special attention in writing this kind of transformation code as its statements appear to be in "reverse order".

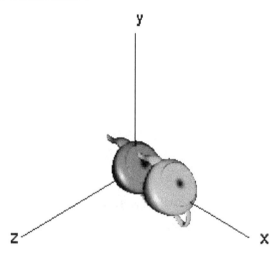

Figure 3-9 Rotation around z-axis for 135° then Translate along x-axis

3.7.2 Affine Transformations Properties

Here are some useful and pleasing properties of affine transformations.

1. **Affine transformations preserve affine combination of points**.
   Suppose C is an affine combination of two points A and B:

$$C = aA + bC$$

   where $a + b = 1$. Under an affine transformation with matrix M,

$$MC = M(aA + bC) = a(MA) + b(MC)$$

   So the affine transformation of a combination of points is equal to the combination of the affine transformation of each of the points.

2. **Lines and planes are preserved.**
   A straight line passing through points A, B is given by

$$L(t) = (1 - t)A + tB$$

where $-\infty < t < \infty$. Under an affine transformation M, the image of $L(t)$ is the same affine combination of the images of A and B:

$$L'(t) = ML(t) = (1-t)MA + tMB$$

Therefore, a line is still a line after the transformation.

A plane can be written as an affine combination of 3 points, A, B, and C:

$$P(s,t) = sA + tB + (1-s-t)C$$

When each point is transformed, this becomes:

$$MP(s,t) = sMA + tMB + (1-s-t)MC$$

Therefore, a plane maps to a plane under the transformation.

3. **Parallelism of Lines and Planes is Preserved.**
   Consider two lines with the same direction $\mathbf{b}$:

$$L_1(t) = A + \mathbf{b}t$$

$$L_2(t) = B + \mathbf{b}t$$

Under an affine transformation M, they become

$$L_1'(t) = MA + (M\mathbf{b})t$$

$$L_2'(t) = MB + (M\mathbf{b})t$$

Both of the transformed lines have the same direction $(M\mathbf{b})$.

Two planes with same directional normal can be described by

$$P_1(s,t) = A + \mathbf{a}s + \mathbf{b}t$$

$$P_2(s,t) = B + \mathbf{a}s + \mathbf{b}t$$

Under affine transformation M, the planes become

$$P_1'(t) = MA + (M\mathbf{a})s + (M\mathbf{b})t$$

$$P_2'(t) = MB + (M\mathbf{a})s + (M\mathbf{b})t$$

Again, both of the transformed planes have the same directional normal, characterized by $M\mathbf{a}$ and $M\mathbf{b}$.

3.8   Viewing Transformations

In OpenGL, viewing and modeling transformations are inextricably related. They are considered in the same stage of the graphics pipeline as shown in Figure 3-1. The modeling and viewing transformation matrices are combined into a single **modelview** matrix.

In general, a viewing transformation changes the position and orientation of the viewpoint. A viewing transformation on a graphics scene is generally composed of translations and rotations. It is like moving the camera to some position and rotating it to a desired direction when taking a photo. To achieve a certain scene composition in the final image, we can either move the camera to capture the image view or move all the objects in the opposite direction into the field of view of the camera. Therefore, a modeling transformation that rotates an object counterclockwise achieves the same effect as one that rotates the camera clockwise for the same number of degrees. Because of the matrix characteristics that matrix operations on a point starts from the right side, we must first call the viewing transformation functions before performing any modeling transformations, so that the modeling transformations take effect on the objects first. The following code shows an example of the structure with V denoting a viewing transformation matrix and D denoting a modeling matrix (as usual, M is the current transformation matrix):

```
glLoadIdentity();         //M = I
ViewingTransform();       //M = MV = V
ModelTransform();         //M = MD = VD
glutSolidTeapot( 0.6 );   //P' = MP = (VD)P = V(DP)
```

In an OpenGL program, if we do not do anything to set the viewpoint (camera location), the default location and orientation of the viewpoint are used. The default viewpoint is at the origin, looking down the negative z-axis. We may also use one of the following two methods to set the viewpoint.

1. We may use the modeling transformation functions such as **glTranslatef**() and **glRotatef**() to move the objects relative to the default viewpoint. Actually, we are **not** setting the viewpoint directly. We simply transform the objects relative to a fixed point.

2. We can use the Utility Library routine **gluLookAt**() to define a line of sight and a camera position. This routine makes use of a series of rotations and translations to set the viewpoint.

Of course, we can always create our own utility routine that encapsulates rotations and translations to set the camera position and orientation. For some applications, it might be more convenient to use custom routines to specify the viewing transformation. For example, we might want to render a scene at various viewpoint positions of a roller-coaster; in this case it is more convenient to specify a transformation in terms of the coordinates of a **Frenet frame**, which defines a local coordinate system at any point of a given curve.

3.8.1   The gluLookAt() Utility Routine

The utility function **gluLookAt**() lets us set the viewpoint position and a line of sight. The function takes three sets of arguments; one set specifies the location of the viewpoint; the second set defines a reference point towards which the camera is aimed, and the third set specifies the upward direction of the camera, usually referred to as the **up-vector**. We can choose the viewpoint to yield the desired view of the scene. Typically, the reference point is somewhere in the middle of the scene. (For example, if we build a scene around the origin, it is desirable to set the reference point to be the origin.) The setting of the up-vector is not as obvious; we shall explain this below. The following is the prototype and details of **gluLookAt**().

void **gluLookAt**(GLdouble *eyex*, GLdouble *eyey*, GLdouble *eyez*,
   GLdouble *centerx*, GLdouble *centery*, GLdouble *centerz*,
   GLdouble *upx*, GLdouble *upy*, GLdouble *upz*);
   The function defines a viewing matrix V and multiplies it to the right of the current matrix (i.e. $M = MV$). The desired viewpoint is specified by (*eyex, eyey*, and *eyez*).
   The (*centerx, centery*, and *centerz*) arguments specify a point along the desired line of sight (i.e. the camera is aiming at the point (*centerx, centery*, and *centerz*)).
   The (*upx, upy*, and *upz*) arguments specify the up-vector, indicating which direction is up (that is, the direction from the bottom to the top of the viewing volume).

For example, the command "**gluLookAt** (0.0, 0.0, 5.0, 0.0, 0.0, 0.0, 0.0, 1.0, 0.0);" does the following:

1. Sets the camera location (viewpoint) at (0.0, 0.0, 5.0).

2. Points the camera towards the point (0.0, 0.0, 0.0).
3. Specifies the orientation of camera by the up-vector (0.0, 1.0, 0.0). (So in this example, y-axis is the up-down axis.)

Now lets take a more detailed look at what exactly **gluLookAt()** does. We have discussed the concept of world coordinates. All the object positions and most of the parameters of OpenGL functions, including those of **gluLookAt()** are specified in world coordinates. However, we can always attach a coordinate system to an object and move it along with the associated object; this system is called the **object coordinate system**. At the end, we want to specify the object positions relative to the eye (or camera). When the coordinates are specified relative to the eye, the coordinate system is called **eye coordinate system**. For convenience of discussion, lets assume that e is a point where the eye is located, C is the point that the camera (or eye) is aiming at, and $\mathbf{U}$ is the normalized up-vector (i.e. $|\mathbf{U}| = 1$). (If the up-vector provided is not normalized, gluLookAt() will normalize it.) So we have

$$e = \begin{pmatrix} e_x \\ e_y \\ e_z \\ 1 \end{pmatrix}, \quad C = \begin{pmatrix} C_x \\ C_y \\ C_z \\ 1 \end{pmatrix}, \quad \mathbf{U} = \begin{pmatrix} U_x \\ U_y \\ U_z \\ 0 \end{pmatrix}$$

The corresponding gluLookAt() function to use these parameters is

$$\text{gluLookAt}(e_x, e_y, e_z, C_x, C_y, C_z, U_x, U_y, U_z);$$

When the function is called, it computes a forward-vector $\mathbf{F}$ given by

$$\mathbf{F} = C - e = \begin{pmatrix} C_x - e_x \\ C_y - e_y \\ C_z - e_z \\ 0 \end{pmatrix}$$

(Recall that the difference between two points is a vector.) It then normalizes $\mathbf{F}$ to

$$\mathbf{f} = \frac{\mathbf{F}}{|\mathbf{F}|}$$

We can then define a unit backward-vector $\mathbf{b} = -\mathbf{f}$ and compute a unit side-vector $\mathbf{s}$ given by

$$\mathbf{s} = \mathbf{U} \times \mathbf{b}$$

and another unit up-vector $\mathbf{u}$ given by

$$\mathbf{u} = \mathbf{b} \times \mathbf{s}$$

The vectors $\mathbf{s}, \mathbf{u}$, and $\mathbf{b}$ are orthogonal unit vectors; they form the axes of a new orthonormal coordinate system. We can construct a viewing transformation matrix V as follows

$$V = \begin{pmatrix} s_x & u_x & b_x & 0 \\ s_y & u_y & b_y & 0 \\ s_z & u_z & b_z & 0 \\ 0 & 0 & 0 & 1 \end{pmatrix} \tag{3.39}$$

The function call "gluLookAt($e_x, e_y, e_z, C_x, C_y, C_z, U_x, U_y, U_z$);" is equivalent to

$$\begin{aligned} &\text{glMultMatrixf}(V^T); \\ &\text{glTranslatef}(-e_x, -e_y, -e_z); \end{aligned} \tag{3.40}$$

We need to use the transpose of V, which is V^T in (3.40) because as we mentioned earlier, OpenGL array operations are column-major. So the first row of V^T, which is $(s_x, s_y, s_z, 0)$, will become the first column of the corresponding OpenGL matrix.

What (3.40) means is that we move the origin of the coordinate system to the eye location and use the orthogonal unit vectors, **s**, **u**, and **b** as the coordinate axes. (See also discussions in Section 3.5.) That is, we align the view volume with the line-of-sight of the camera. The effect of this command is to change the coordinates of the scene vertices into the **camera's coordinate system** (which is also called eye coordinate system).

The following few code segments show some examples of the usage of **gluLookAt**(); the outputs are shown on the right side of the code segments. Each code segment uses the following parameters and **drawLine**() routine that draws a line to draw the coordinate axes:

```
float origin[3] = {0, 0, 0};
float axes[3][3] = {{2.0, 0, 0}, {0, 2.0, 0}, {0, 0, 2.0}};
void drawLine( float v0[], float v1[] ) {
   glBegin( GL_LINE );
      glVertex3fv( v0 );
      glVertex3fv( v1 );
   glEnd();
}
```

Example 3-1

Line of sight = negative z-axis, **up** = (0, 1, 0)
The z-axis in this example is pointing out of the page.

```
void display(void)
{
   .....
   glMatrixMode (GL_MODELVIEW);
   glLoadIdentity();
   gluLookAt ( 0.0, 0.0, 5.0, 0.0, 0.0, 0.0, 0.0, 1.0, 0.0);
   for ( int i = 0; i ¡ 3; i++ )
      drawLine ( origin, axes[i] );
   glutSolidTeapot( 0.6 );
}
```

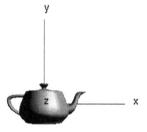

Figure 3-10

Example 3-2

Line of sight = negative z-axis, **up** = (1, 0, 0)
The z-axis in this example is pointing out of the page.

```
void display(void)
{
   .....
   glMatrixMode (GL_MODELVIEW);
   glLoadIdentity();
   gluLookAt ( 0.0, 0.0, 5.0, 0.0, 0.0, 0.0, 1.0, 0.0, 0.0);
   for ( int i = 0; i ¡ 3; i++ )
      drawLine ( origin, axes[i] );
   glutSolidTeapot( 0.6 );
}
```

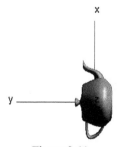

Figure 3-11

Example 3-3

Line of sight = (5, 5, 5) - (0, 0, 0), **up** = (1, 1, 0)
x, y, z axes are pointing out of the plane.

```
void display(void)
{
    .....
    glMatrixMode (GL_MODELVIEW);
    glLoadIdentity();
    gluLookAt ( 5.0, 5.0, 5.0, 0.0, 0.0, 0.0, 1.0, 1.0, 0.0);
    for ( int i = 0; i ¡ 3; i++ )
        drawLine ( origin, axes[i] );
    glutSolidTeapot( 0.6 );
}
```

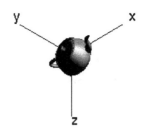

Figure 3-12

3.8.2 More Explanations on **up** Vector

We discussed above that we use three sets of coordinates in defining **gluLooAt()**:

```
gluLooAt ( ex, ey, ez, ax, ay, az, upx, upy, upz );
```

The first three parameters specify the observation point (eye or camera position):

$$e = (e_x, e_y, e_z)$$

The next three parameters specify the point that the camera (or eye) is aiming at:

$$a = (a_x, a_y, a_z)$$

The last three parameters define the up-direction of the system:

$$\mathbf{up} = (up_x, up_y, up_z)$$

It is easy to understand the points e and a. These two points define a look-at direction, the direction along which the observer is looking at:

$$\mathbf{LOOK} = a - e$$

But what exactly does the **up** vector mean?

We can imagine that we are holding a regular camera at e, aiming at a scene along **LOOK**. Normally, we know the up direction of our camera, which should be perpendicular to **LOOK**. Once **LOOK** is fixed, we cannot tilt our camera because if we tilt it, we would change **LOOK**, which is defined independently by e and a. So the up direction of the camera is not the same as the **up** vector specified in **gluLookAt**. However, we can rotate our camera about the axis along **LOOK** and define **up** as the up-direction of the camera. For instance, consider that the camera is on the z-axis, say, at $(0, 0, 5)$, looking along the negative z-axis, at the origin $(0, 0, 0)$. If we set **up** $= (0, 1, 0)$, the up-direction is the y-axis and we hold the camera in the usual orientation; if we set **up** $= (1, 0, 0)$, the up-direction is the $x - axis$, which means we have to rotate our camera right $90°$ to take the photo. These are easy to understand and have been explained above.

What if we set **up** $= (1, 0, 1)$? We cannot tilt our camera so that its up-direction matches this **up**, otherwise it will look at scenes at different directions! However, we can imagine (yes, just imagine) that we can tilt the camera's film, onto which the scene is projected. When the film is tilted, we will still obtain the same projected scene, assuming that we have a larger film to cover the original projected scene. The up-direction of the film is what the **up** vector of **gluLookAt** wants to specify. Actually, in a graphics system, we want to define a vector **v**, which along with the **LOOK** vector specify the orientation of the final projection plane. However, it is more difficult for users to specify **v** directly. So OpenGL let users specify the **up** vector instead. Their relation is given by:

$$\mathbf{v} = \mathbf{LOOK} \times \mathbf{up}$$

Therefore, many different **up** vectors could give us the same vector **v** as shown in Figure 3-13 below.

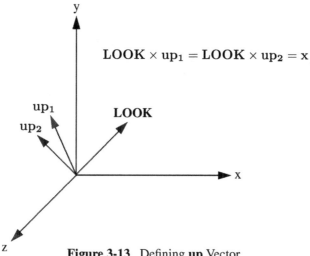

$$\mathbf{LOOK} \times \mathbf{up_1} = \mathbf{LOOK} \times \mathbf{up_2} = \mathbf{x}$$

Figure 3-13   Defining **up** Vector

For example, if

$$\mathbf{LOOK} = \begin{pmatrix} 0 \\ 0 \\ -1 \end{pmatrix}$$

which is a direction looking along the negative z-axis. For any up-vector **u** lying in the y-z plane,

$$\mathbf{u} = \begin{pmatrix} 0 \\ 1 \\ z_t \end{pmatrix}$$

where z_t can be of any value, we have

$$\mathbf{v} = \mathbf{LOOK} \times \mathbf{u} = \begin{pmatrix} 1 \\ 0 \\ 0 \end{pmatrix}$$

Therefore, regardless of the value of z_t, **v** always points in the x-direction. So all the commands,

```
gluLooAt ( 0, 0, 5, 0, 0, 0, 0, 1, 0 );
gluLooAt ( 0, 0, 5, 0, 0, 0, 0, 1, 5 );
gluLooAt ( 0, 0, 5, 0, 0, 0, 0, 1, 10 );
gluLooAt ( 0, 0, 5, 0, 0, 0, 0, 0.1, 2 );
```

will give us the same projection results. That is, no matter how much we tilt the film, we still get the same projection. The only exception is that the film cannot lie on the x-z plane, when the **up** vector is parallel to the **LOOK** vector. Therefore, the command

```
gluLooAt ( 0, 0, 5, 0, 0, 0, 0, 0, 1 );
```

would not give us any projected scene. In practice, it is not good to set the **up** vector to be nearly parallel to **LOOK**.

3.9 Coding Examples

3.9.1 Robot Arm

Suppose we want to rotate an object about a 'z' axis through $(-1, 0, 0)$. We can achieve this by moving everything by 1 in the x-direction, performing the rotation, and moving things back by 1. This may be a simple example of applying modeling transformation. However, if we are not careful, we may end up applying the wrong order of transformations which will lead to undesirable results. Consider the following two code segments. *Which one is the correct code to rotate an object about a 'z' axis through* $(-1, 0, 0)$?

Code 1:

```
glTranslatef ( 1.0, 0.0, 0.0 );
glRotatef( degrees, 0.0, 0.0, 1.0 );
glTranslatef ( -1.0, 0.0, 0.0 );
draw_object();
```

Code 2:

```
glTranslatef ( -1.0, 0.0, 0.0 );
glRotatef( degrees, 0.0, 0.0, 1.0 );
glTranslatef ( 1.0, 0.0, 0.0 );
draw_object();
```

Before reading on, try to answer the above question and convince yourself that your answer is correct.

The problem requires us to rotate objects about a 'z' axis passing through $(-1, 0, 0)$. Therefore, we need to shift the origin of the coordinate system to $(-1, 0, 0)$. This is equivalent to shifting the objects by $(+1, 0, 0)$. Remember that all the OpenGL transformation commands such as glTranslatef() and glRotatef() operate on objects, not the coordinate system and that the latest command before drawing a vertex is the first one to operate on the vertex. Thus **Code 2** is the correct answer.

To build a robot arm, we can call the function **glutWireCube**() to create cubes and then scale them to be used as the segments of the robot arm. However, we need to first call the appropriate modeling transformations to align each segment. When we use **glutWireCube**() to create a cube, it is created around the origin of the coordinate system. In other words, the origin is at the center of the cube. As a rotating axis always passes through the origin $(0, 0, 0)$, if we want to rotate an object about another axis (e.g. an axis passing through a cube edge), we first move the cube so that one of its edges passes through the origin, which will be the pivot point for rotation. We can do this using glTranslatef(); after rotation, we move the objects back with glTranslatef() again. The following code builds the first arm segment (upper arm):

```
glTranslatef (-1.0, 0.0, 0.0);
glRotatef ( angle1, 0.0, 0.0, 1.0);
glTranslatef (1.0, 0.0, 0.0);
glPushMatrix();
glScalef (2.0, 0.4, 0.5);
```

```
glutWireCube (1.0);
glPopMatrix();
```

In the code, the command **glPushMatrix**() before glScalef() and the command **glPopMatrix**() are to guarantee that the scaling function only operates on the cube but does not have any effect on any other objects. We build the second segment (lower arm) by moving the local system (the cube) to the next pivot point:

```
glTranslatef (1.0, 0.0, 0.0);
glRotatef (angle2, 0.0, 0.0, 1.0);
glTranslatef (1.0, 0.0, 0.0);
glPushMatrix();
glScalef (2.0, 0.4, 0.4);
glutWireCube (1.0);
glPopMatrix();
```

Note here that we move the cube by +1 unit by "glTranslate(1.0, 0.0, 0.0);" so that we rotate it around an axis passing through it left-side edge. After the rotation, we move the object a further +1 unit (the top "glTranslatef (1.0, 0.0, 0.0);" statement) so that the left-side edge of this rotated cube is at the right-side edge of the previous cube (upper arm) as shown in Figure 3-14. The dots in the figure show the pivot points. The following is the code that creates the robot arm of Figure 3-14.

```
/*
  glutWireCube ( 1.0 )
  produces a cube: -0.5 to 0.5
  R = rotation, T = translation, S = scaling,  T(2)=T(1).T(1)
*/
void display(void)
{  ......
  glPushMatrix();                    //Save M0
  glTranslatef (-1.0, 0.0, 0.0);     //M1 = T(-1)
  drawDot ( 0, 0, 0 );               //Draw dot at (0,0,0)
  glRotatef(angle1, 0.0, 0.0, 1.0);  //M2=T(-1).R1
  glTranslatef (1.0, 0.0, 0.0);      //M3 = T(-1).R1.T(+1)
  glPushMatrix();                    //Save M3
  glScalef (2.0, 0.4, 0.5);          //M4 = T(-1).R1.T(+1).S
  glutWireCube (1.0);                //P' = T(-1).R1.T(+1).S.P

  glPopMatrix();                     //Restore M3 = T(-1).R1.T(+1)
  glTranslatef (1.0, 0.0, 0.0);      //M5 = T(-1).R1.T(+1).T(+1)
  drawDot ( 0, 0, 0 );               //P' = T(-1).R1.T(+1).T(+1).P
  glRotatef(angle2, 0.0, 0.0, 1.0);  //M6 = T(-1).R1.T(+2).R2
  glTranslatef (1.0, 0.0, 0.0);      //M7 = T(-1).R1.T(2).R2.T(+1)
  glPushMatrix();                    //Save M7
  glScalef (2.0, 0.4, 0.4);          //M8 = T(-1).R1.T(2).R2.T(+1).S
  glutWireCube (1.0);                //P' = T(-1).R1.T(2).R2.T(+1).S.P
  glPopMatrix();                     //Restore M7
  glPopMatrix();                     //Restore M0
}
```

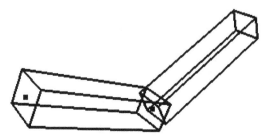

Figure 3-14 Robot Arm

3.9.2 Solar System

This simple example shows how to use affine transformations to model a solar system. In our example, we have three planets revolving around the sun about the y-axis; the most distant planet has a moon revolving around it about the z-axis of the local coordinate system of the planet; a satellite revolves around the moon about the y-axis of the local coordinate system of the moon. The following code segment shows how this is done.

```
void satellite()
{
   glColor3f ( 0.1, 1, 0.1 );
   glPushMatrix();
   glRotatef ( angleSat, 0, 1, 0 );
   glTranslatef ( 0.5, 0.0, 0 );
   glutSolidSphere( 0.1, 32, 24 );
   glPopMatrix();
}

void moon()
{
   glColor3f ( 1, 1, 0 );  //yellow
   glPushMatrix();
   glRotatef ( angleMoon, 0, 0, 1 );
   glTranslatef ( 1, 0.0, 0 );
   glutSolidSphere( 0.2, 32, 24 );
   satellite();  //satellite revolving around moon
   glPopMatrix();
}

// r is radius of planet, d is distance from the sun
void planet( float r, float d, int n )
{
   float angle = anglePlanet / d;
   glPushMatrix();
   glColor3f (0.6, 0.4, 0.5);
   glRotatef ( angle, 0, 1, 0 );
   glTranslatef ( d, 0.0, 0 );
   glutSolidSphere( r, 32, 24 );
   if ( n == 2 )
      moon();      //moon revolving around outermost planet
   glPopMatrix();
}

void display(void)
{
   glColor3f (1.0, 0.0, 0.0);     // red color
   glutSolidSphere( 1.5, 32, 24 );// the sun

   planet( 0.5, 2, 0 );  //planets revolving around sun
   planet( 0.8, 4, 1 );
   planet( 0.4, 6, 2 );
}
```

We can add animation to the scene by making use of the function **glutIdleFunc**(), which will be discussed in Chapter 11. A snapshot of such an animated solar system is shown in Figure 3-15 below. We can also add lighting, which will be discussed in Chapter 7, to the scene to make the model look more realistic.

Figure 3-15   Solar System

Chapter 4   Projection Transformations

4.1   Projections

We create a 3D graphics scene using certain models. At the end, all the 3D objects will be projected on a 2D screen. In this chapter, we examine the principles of projection and how to define the desired projection matrix to transform the vertices in our scene.

In the projection process, we define a **viewing volume**, which is bounded by a **near plane**, a **far plane**, and four side-planes as shown in Figure 4-1. All the scenes inside the viewing volume are projected into the near plane, which is also called the **view plane**. All the objects or portions of objects that lie outside the viewing volume are clipped and will not appear in the final projected image. The position of the eye (viewpoint) is called the **center of projection** (point O of Figure 4-1).

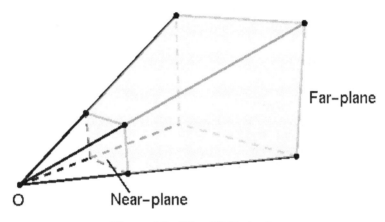

Figure 4-1   3D to 2D Projection

In most cases, people use one of the two techniques, **perspective projection** or **orthographic projection** to make 3D-to-2D projection in graphics.   In perspective projection, the farther an object is from the viewpoint, the smaller it appears in the projected image. In contrast, orthographic projection projects objects in the same way whether they are near or far away from the viewpoint. Figure 4-2 shows a cube that is rendered with (a) orthographic projection, and (b) perspective projection.

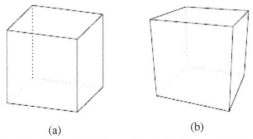

(a)   (b)

Figure 4-2   Cubes Rendered with (a) Orthographic Projection, and (b) Perspective Projection

Figure 4-3 shows a scene that is rendered with (a) orthographic projection, and (b) perspective projection. Note in the scene that in orthographic projection, the diamond-shaped texture pattern appears the same whether it is near or far away from the viewpoint; however, in perspective projection, the far-away pattern appears smaller.

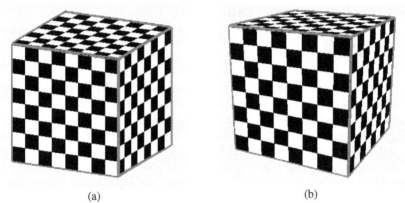

(a)   (b)

Figure 4-3 Scenes Rendered with (a) Orthographic Projection, and (b) Perspective Projection

4.2   Perspective Projections

4.2.1   Vanishing Points

A perspective projection is characterized by the fact that a distant object appears smaller as compared to a near object with the same size. Typically, such a projection is associated with one, two or three vanishing points. A **vanishing point** is a point in a perspective drawing or an image obtained from perspective projection to which parallel lines appear to converge.

A **one-point perspective** image consists of one vanishing point. Any objects that are made up of lines either directly parallel with the viewer's line of sight or directly perpendicular to it. Figure 4-4(a) below shows a cube that is rendered as a one-point perspective image. Figure 4-5 shows two one-point perspective photos.

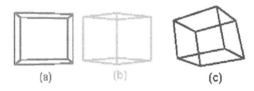

(a)   (b)   (c)

Figure 4-4 Cubes Rendered with (a)One-point, (b)Two-point, and (c) Three-point Perspectives

Figure 4-5 One-point Perspective Photos

A **two-point perspective** image consists of two vanishing points. One point represents one set of parallel lines, and the other point represents the other set. For example, when we look at a house from a corner, one wall would recede towards one vanishing point, and the other wall would recede towards the opposite vanishing point. Figure 4-4(b) shows a cube rendered with the two-point perspective technique. Figure 4-6 shows two-point perspective drawings.

A **three-point perspective** image consists of three vanishing points meaning that we have three sets of parallel lines that converge to three different points. For example, when we look up at a tall building from a corner, the third vanishing point is high in space. Figure 4-4(c) shows a cube rendered with three-point perspective. Figure 4-7 shows a three-point perspective image.

Figure 4-6   Two-point Perspective Drawing

Figure 4-7   Three-point Perspective Image

4.2.2   Perspective Projection Transformations

Perspective projection is accomplished through the use of a frustum-shaped viewing volume as shown in Figure 4-8 below. In the figure, **O** is the center of projection (viewpoint or camera position). The view-frustum is the volume bounded by a near plane, a far plane and the field of view (fov). Objects that fall within the viewing volume are projected towards the center of projection where the camera or viewpoint is at. Objects or portions of objects outside the frustum are clipped.

In Figure 4-8, the eye or the camera is at the origin O, looking towards the negative z direction; the near-plane is at $z = -n$ and the far-plane is at $z = -f$; more detailly,

$$
\begin{aligned}
n &= \text{near distance} & f &= \text{far distance} \\
l &= \text{left} & r &= \text{right} \\
b &= \text{bottom} & t &= \text{top} \\
O &= (0,0,0)
\end{aligned}
\qquad (4.1)
$$

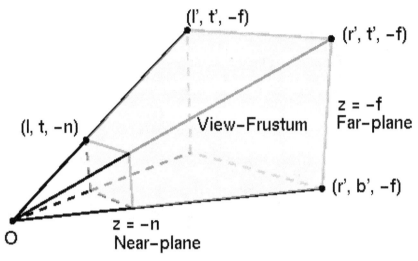

Figure 4-8 Frustum-shaped Viewing Volume

Any point (x, y, z) inside the frustum is projected into a point (x', y', z') on the screen at $z = -n$ (near-plane). Obviously, z' is always equal to $-n$. The values of x' and y' can be easily calculated using similar triangles shown in Figure 4-9. For example, $\frac{x}{x'} = \frac{z}{z'} = \frac{z}{-n}$. Thus, $x' = \frac{-nx}{z}$. Equation (4.2) shows the calculated values.

$$\begin{pmatrix} x' \\ y' \\ z' \end{pmatrix} = \begin{pmatrix} \frac{-nx}{z} \\ \frac{-ny}{z} \\ -n \end{pmatrix} \tag{4.2}$$

Any point lying outside the frustum is **not** projected. Therefore, $l \le x' \le r$ and $b \le y' \le t$. That is,

$$l \le \frac{nx}{-z} \le r$$
$$b \le \frac{ny}{-z} \le t \tag{4.3}$$

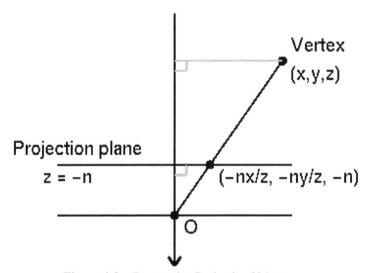

Figure 4-9 Perspective Projection Values

Obviously, the mapping given by Equation (4.2) is a **many-to-one** mapping. Many different (x, y, z) points in the frustum may be projected into the same (x', y', z') at the near-plane. We want to find a transformation matrix that will map (x, y, z) to (x', y', z') of (4.2) in a form similar to that of an affine transformation (translation, rotation, and scaling) that we discussed in Chapter 3. However, each mapping in Equation (4.2) involves a **division** by the z coordinate! We know that matrix multiplications of affine transformations only have additions and multiplications! *How can we combine this perspective transformation with the affine transformations?*

The trick is to make use of the characteristics of homogeneous coordinates that we have discussed in the previous chapter. Recall that in the homogeneous coordinate representation, the point (x, y, z, w) represents the **same** point as does $(\alpha x, \alpha y, \alpha z, \alpha w)$ with $\alpha \neq 0$. Thus $(x, y, z, 1)$ and $(\frac{x}{w}, \frac{y}{w}, \frac{z}{w}, \frac{1}{w})$ are equivalent provided $w \neq 0$. For example, the point $(1, 2, 3)$ has the representations $(1, 2, 3, 1), (2, 4, 6, 2), (0.03, 0.06, 0.09, 0.03), (-1, -2, -3, -1)$, and so on in homogeneous coordinate system. Therefore, to convert from homogeneous coordinates to ordinary coordinates, we need to

1. divide all components by the fourth component, and
2. discard the fourth component.

For example, $(3, 6, 2, 3) \rightarrow (1, 2, \frac{2}{3}, 1) \rightarrow (1, 2, \frac{2}{3})$. On the other hand, to convert from ordinary coordinates to homogeneous coordinates, we simply append a 1 as the fourth component. For example, $(2, 3, 4) \rightarrow (2, 3, 4, 1)$.

So, both representations

$$\begin{pmatrix} \frac{-nx}{z} \\ \frac{-ny}{z} \\ -n \\ 1 \end{pmatrix} \quad \text{and} \quad \begin{pmatrix} x \\ y \\ z \\ \frac{-z}{n} \end{pmatrix}$$

represent the **same** 3D point

$$\begin{pmatrix} \frac{-nx}{z} \\ \frac{-ny}{z} \\ -n \end{pmatrix}$$

Therefore, finding the matrix that maps

$$\begin{pmatrix} x \\ y \\ z \\ 1 \end{pmatrix} \longrightarrow \begin{pmatrix} \frac{-nx}{z} \\ \frac{-ny}{z} \\ -n \\ 1 \end{pmatrix}$$

is the same as finding the matrix that maps

$$\begin{pmatrix} x \\ y \\ z \\ 1 \end{pmatrix} \longrightarrow \begin{pmatrix} x \\ y \\ z \\ \frac{-z}{n} \end{pmatrix}$$

Such a matrix is given by

$$
\begin{pmatrix}
1 & 0 & 0 & 0 \\
0 & 1 & 0 & 0 \\
0 & 0 & 1 & 0 \\
0 & 0 & \frac{-1}{n} & 0
\end{pmatrix}
\begin{pmatrix}
x \\
y \\
z \\
1
\end{pmatrix}
=
\begin{pmatrix}
x \\
y \\
z \\
\frac{-z}{n}
\end{pmatrix}
\tag{4.4}
$$

Therefore, the perspective matrix A_0 that projects a point in the frustum into a point in the near-plane is given by

$$
A_0 =
\begin{pmatrix}
1 & 0 & 0 & 0 \\
0 & 1 & 0 & 0 \\
0 & 0 & 1 & 0 \\
0 & 0 & \frac{-1}{n} & 0
\end{pmatrix}
\tag{4.5}
$$

Matrix A_0 no longer involves any division by the z coordinate. It seems that we can now seamlessly combine this matrix with the matrix of an affine transformation. However, there is a catch here. The matrix given in (4.5) is **singular**, meaning that its inverse does not exist. That is, it is noninvertible. This is because we have many points in the 3D view-frustum projected into the same point at the 2D view-plane. The solution to this problem is to treat the z coordinate separately. We actually don't care about the z coordinate after the transformation; all we care about are the x and y coordinates where the point is rendered on the screen. We therefore modify the transformation matrix A_0 to A that operates on a point P as follows:

$$
P' = AP =
\begin{pmatrix}
1 & 0 & 0 & 0 \\
0 & 1 & 0 & 0 \\
0 & 0 & 1 & \frac{-1}{n} \\
0 & 0 & \frac{-1}{n} & 0
\end{pmatrix}
\begin{pmatrix}
x \\
y \\
z \\
1
\end{pmatrix}
=
\begin{pmatrix}
x \\
y \\
z - \frac{1}{n} \\
\frac{-z}{n}
\end{pmatrix}
\tag{4.6}
$$

Of course, we know that in homogeneous coordinate system, we can always divide each coordinate of the projected point given on the right side of (4.6) by the fourth coordinate, which is $\frac{-z}{n}$. Thus, the projected point is equal to the following:

$$
P' =
\begin{pmatrix}
x \\
y \\
z - \frac{1}{n} \\
\frac{-z}{n}
\end{pmatrix}
=
\begin{pmatrix}
\frac{-nx}{z} \\
\frac{-ny}{z} \\
-n + \frac{1}{z} \\
1
\end{pmatrix}
\tag{4.7}
$$

Converting back to ordinary 3D space, the point (x, y, z) now maps to $(\frac{-nx}{z}, \frac{-ny}{z}, -n + \frac{1}{z})$, which will be projected onto the screen at $(\frac{-nx}{z}, \frac{-ny}{z}, 0)$; the third component has been peeled off for depth testing.

The transformation matrix A is nonsingular. Its inverse is given by

$$
A^{-1} =
\begin{pmatrix}
1 & 0 & 0 & 0 \\
0 & 1 & 0 & 0 \\
0 & 0 & 1 & \frac{-1}{n} \\
0 & 0 & \frac{-1}{n} & 0
\end{pmatrix}^{-1}
=
\begin{pmatrix}
1 & 0 & 0 & 0 \\
0 & 1 & 0 & 0 \\
0 & 0 & 0 & -n \\
0 & 0 & -n & -n^2
\end{pmatrix}
\tag{4.8}
$$

We have derived the perspective transformation matrix A given by (4.6) and its inverse A^{-1} given by (4.8). However, in the derivation process we have assumed that the camera (viewpoint) is at the origin looking at the negative z direction; the projection plane is perpendicular to the z-axis and is at a distance n from the origin. Any point (x, y, z) inside the viewing frustum is projected into (x', y') at the view-plane. One may refer to this coordinate system as the **eye coordinate**

system because the origin is at the eye position (viewpoint). Some authors may write (x, y, z) as (x_e, y_e, z_e) with the subscript e signifying "eye"; they may express the projected point (x', y', z') as (x_p, y_p, z_p) with the subscript p signifying "projection". For simplicity, we shall stick to our notations (x, y, z) and (x', y', z') to denote these quantities. *What if the camera is not at the origin and it is not aiming at the negative z direction?* In this case, we have to first transform the camera to the origin and align its orientation to be the same as that shown in Figure 4-8. This is what the function **gluLookAt**() does. In other words, in the OpenGL pipeline, after the modelview transformation, coordinates are expressed in the eye coordinate system. Note that at this point, the coordinate values are still expressed in the world coordinate system (**WCS**). For example, we may limit the range of the x coordinates from $-\pi$ to $+\pi$. The parameters l, r, b, and r are all specified in world coordinates. The next step is to transform the world coordinates to device coordinates. For example, a screen may be specified as 800×640 pixels and we need to define the position of a point in terms of pixels. To ensure that graphics output is independent of the display device, OpenGL will first map the projected values to normalized device coordinates (NDC) that we are going to discuss in the next section.

4.2.3 Normalized Device Coordinates

After we have projected the desired scenes into the world window bounded by l, r, b, t, we need to determine where to display the scene on the screen or a display device. That is, we need to specify our viewport and we specify it in device coordinates such as pixel column and pixel row. However, if we want to run our programs on several hardware platforms or graphic devices, we will run into the difficulties of obtaining identical scenes in various platforms or devices. There are two common conventions for device coordinate systems (DCS):

1. The origin is at the lower left corner, with x to the right and y upward.
2. The origin is at the top left corner, with x to the right and y downward.

Also, many different resolutions for graphics display devices exist. For example,

1. Workstations commonly have 1280×1024 frame buffers.
2. A PostScript page has 612×792 points, but it has 2550×3300 pixels at 300 dpi resolution.

Moreover, different devices may have different aspect ratios.

If we map directly from a world coordinate system to a device coordinate system, then changing our device requires rewriting the program to change many of the display parameters in order to obtain the same look-and-feel display as before. This is certainly a tedious task. A better approach is to use **normalized device coordinates** (NDC) as an intermediate coordinate system that gets mapped to the device layer as shown in Figure 4-10. In the figure, the world window bounded by l, r, b, t is mapped to the unit square bounded by $-1, 1, -1, 1$ in the NDC space. Normalized device coordinates (NDC) are also referred to as **normalized coordinates** because this representation makes a graphics package independent of the coordinate range for any specific output device. The coordinate systems for display devices are generally called **device coordinates**, or **screen coordinates** for the case of a video monitor. Often, the normalized coordinates are specified in left-handed coordinate system; that is, when we use our left hand to roll our fingers from the x axis to the y axis, our thumb points to the z-axis. In this representation, increasing positive distances from the xy plane (the screen or view-plane) can be interpreted as farther from the viewing position.

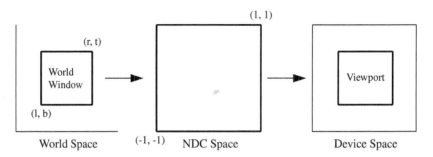

Figure 4-10 NDC as Intermediate Platform

OpenGL also uses this approach, mapping world coordinates to normalized device coordinates before transforming them to device coordinates. The truncated pyramid frustum shown in Figure 4-8 above is mapped to a cube with length 2 in normalized coordinates. The x-coordinate is from $[l, r]$ to $[-1, 1]$, the y-coordinate from $[b, t]$ to $[-1, 1]$ and the z-coordinate from $[-n, -f]$ to $[-1, 1]$. These are shown in Figure 4-11 and Figure 4-12. Figure 4-11 shows the view-frustum of perspective projection in the eye coordinate system as discussed in the above section; Figure 4-12 shows that the view-frustum is mapped to a $2 \times 2 \times 2$ cube in normalized device coordinate.

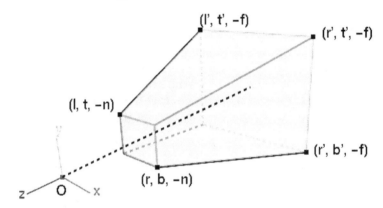

Figure 4-11 View-frustum of Perspective Projection in Eye Coordinates

Note that the eye coordinates are specified in right-handed coordinate system, but normalized coordinates are defined using left-handed coordinate system. As shown in Figure 4-11, the camera at the origin is looking along the $-z$ axis in eye space, but as shown in Figure 4-12, it is looking along $+z$ axis in normalized coordinate.

Now we want to find the transformation that projects a point (x, y, z) into $(x', y'z')$ of (4.2) at the near-plane (i.e. $z' = -n$) and then maps the projected point $(x', y', -n)$ to a point (x^n, y^n, z^n) in the NDC space. We assume a linear relationship in mapping the range $[l, r]$ to $[-1, 1]$ and $[b, t]$ to $[-1, 1]$. Thus

$$x^n = \frac{1 - (-1)}{r - l}x' + c = \frac{2x'}{r - l} + c \tag{4.9}$$

where c is a constant which can be found by boundary conditions. When $x' = r$, we have $x^n = 1$. Substituting this into (4.9), we obtain

$$1 = \frac{2r}{r - l} + c \tag{4.10}$$

From (4.10), we can then solve for c:

$$c = 1 - \frac{2r}{r - l} = -\frac{r + l}{r - l} \tag{4.11}$$

Substituting c into (4.9), we obtain the following:

$$x^n = \frac{2x'}{r-l} - \frac{r+l}{r-l} \tag{4.12}$$

From (4.2), we know that $x' = \frac{-nx}{z}$. Substituting this into (4.12), we obtain

$$x^n = \frac{2nx}{r-l}\left(\frac{1}{-z}\right) - \frac{r+l}{r-l} \tag{4.13}$$

We can similarly obtain the equation for y^n:

$$y^n = \frac{2ny}{t-b}\left(\frac{1}{-z}\right) - \frac{t+b}{t-b} \tag{4.14}$$

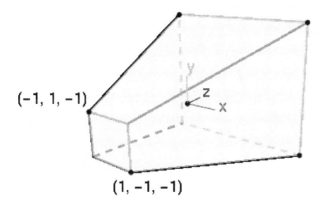

(-1, 1, -1)

(1, -1, -1)

Figure 4-12 View-frustum of Perspective Projection in Normalized Coordinates

Mapping the z-coordinate of a point in the view-frustum to the range $[-1, 1]$ is more complicated. We wish to find a function that maps $-n \rightarrow -1$ and $-f \rightarrow 1$. (Note again that such a mapping reflects the z-axis, resulting in a left-handed coordinate system.) As we have mentioned in the above section, z-coordinates are used for depth information and we have to interpolate their reciprocals in the transformation. Therefore, we construct this mapping as a function of $\frac{1}{z}$, consequently allowing projected depth values to be interpolated linearly. Our mapping function thus has the form

$$z^n = \frac{c}{z} + d \tag{4.15}$$

where c and d are constants to be determined by boundary conditions. Since $z^n = -1$, when $z = -n$, and $z^n = 1$, when $z = -f$, we have

$$\begin{aligned} -1 &= -\frac{c}{n} + d \\ 1 &= -\frac{c}{f} + d \end{aligned} \tag{4.16}$$

Solving for c and d, we obtain

$$\begin{aligned} c &= \frac{2nf}{f-n} \\ d &= \frac{f+n}{f-n} \end{aligned} \tag{4.17}$$

Substituting this back to (4.15), we obtain the mapping function for the z-coordinate:

$$z^n = \frac{2nf}{f-n}\left(\frac{1}{-z}\right) + \frac{f+n}{f-n} \tag{4.18}$$

We can rewrite (4.13), (4.14), and (4.18) by multiplying $-z$ to both sides of the equations:

$$-zx^n = \frac{2nx}{r-l} + \frac{r+l}{r-l}z$$

$$-zy^n = \frac{2ny}{t-b} + \frac{t+b}{t-b}z \tag{4.19}$$

$$-zz^n = -\frac{2nf}{f-n} - \frac{f+n}{f-n}z = -\frac{f+n}{f-n}z - \frac{2nf}{f-n}$$

We know that a 3D point (x^n, y^n, z^n) when represented in homogeneous coordinates is equivalent to the point $P^n = (-zx^n, -zy^n, -zz^n, -z) = (x^n, y^n, z^n, 1)$. The equations of (4.19) are linear functions of the coordinates x, y, and z. We can therefore represent them using a 4×4 matrix N to calculate the point P^n as follows:

$$P^n = \begin{pmatrix} x^n \\ y^n \\ z^n \\ 1 \end{pmatrix} = \begin{pmatrix} -zx^n \\ -zy^n \\ -zz^n \\ -z \end{pmatrix} = \begin{pmatrix} \frac{2n}{r-l} & 0 & \frac{r+l}{r-l} & 0 \\ 0 & \frac{2ny}{t-b} & \frac{t+b}{t-b} & 0 \\ 0 & 0 & -\frac{f+n}{f-n} & -\frac{2nf}{f-n} \\ 0 & 0 & -1 & 0 \end{pmatrix} \begin{pmatrix} x \\ y \\ z \\ 1 \end{pmatrix} \equiv NP \tag{4.20}$$

Therefore, the transformation matrix that transforms a point inside the frustum in the eye coordinate system (i.e. the eye is at the origin looking down the $-z$ axis) to a point in the normalized coordinate system is given by

$$N = \begin{pmatrix} \frac{2n}{r-l} & 0 & \frac{r+l}{r-l} & 0 \\ 0 & \frac{2n}{t-b} & \frac{t+b}{t-b} & 0 \\ 0 & 0 & -\frac{f+n}{f-n} & -\frac{2nf}{f-n} \\ 0 & 0 & -1 & 0 \end{pmatrix} \tag{4.21}$$

Matrix N of (4.21) is nonsingular. Its inverse is given by

$$N^{-1} = \begin{pmatrix} \frac{r-l}{2n} & 0 & \frac{r+l}{2n} & 0 \\ 0 & \frac{t-b}{2n} & \frac{t+b}{2n} & 0 \\ 0 & 0 & 0 & -1 \\ 0 & 0 & -\frac{f-n}{2fn} & -\frac{f+n}{2fn} \end{pmatrix} \tag{4.22}$$

The transformation matrix N given by (4.21) is the OpenGL perspective projection matrix generated by the function **glFrustum**(l, r, b, t, n, f) to do the projection. Points in the eye-coordinate system are transformed by the matrix N into homogeneous clip space in such a way that the w-coordinate holds the negation of the original z-coordinate (i.e. $-z$). We can use this value for depth-test.

The projection matrix N of (4.21) is for a general frustum. If the viewing volume is symmetric, (i.e. $r = -l$, and $t = -b$), then it can be simplified to N_s as follows:

$$N_s = \begin{pmatrix} \frac{n}{r} & 0 & 0 & 0 \\ 0 & \frac{n}{t} & 0 & 0 \\ 0 & 0 & -\frac{f+n}{f-n} & -\frac{2nf}{f-n} \\ 0 & 0 & -1 & 0 \end{pmatrix} \tag{4.23}$$

We can also construct a view frustum that is not bounded by depth by allowing the far-plane distance f to go to infinity. The resulted projection matrix N_{inf} is given by

$$N_{inf} = \lim_{f \to \infty} N = \begin{pmatrix} \frac{2n}{r-l} & 0 & \frac{r+l}{r-l} & 0 \\ 0 & \frac{2n}{t-b} & \frac{t+b}{t-b} & 0 \\ 0 & 0 & -1 & -2n \\ 0 & 0 & -1 & 0 \end{pmatrix} \tag{4.24}$$

The matrix of (4.24) is a valid projection matrix that renders objects at any depth greater than or equal to n. Moreover, a vertex $(x, y, z, 0)$ with w-coordinate value 0 can be rendered correctly; such a vertex lies infinitely far from the viewpoint in the direction of (x, y, z). This is consistent with our earlier discussion that a vector is a special point lying at infinity.

glFrustum and gluPerspective

In OpenGL, there are two popular ways to define a view-volume of perspective projection. One way is to use the function **glFrustum**():

void **glFrustum**(double l, double r, double b, double t, double n, double f);
Creates a matrix for a perspective-view frustum and multiplies the current matrix by it. The frustum's viewing volume is defined by the parameters $(l, b, -n)$ and $(r, t, -n)$; they specify the (x, y, z) coordinates of the lower-left and upper-right corners of the near clipping plane; n and f give the distances from the viewpoint to the near and far clipping planes. They should always be positive.

This command specifies a view-frustum like that shown in Figure 4-8 above and creates the transformation matrix given by (4.21).

Another way to define a viewing volume is to use the function **gluPerspective**(). As shown in Figure 4-13. We need to provide the following information to this function:

1. Specify the angle of the field of view (fov) in the y-direction. **Field of view** or vision (fov) is the extent of the observable world that the viewer can see; it determines how much of the world is taken into the picture. A larger field of view implies a smaller object projection size.
2. Specify the aspect ratio of width to height (w/h) of the projection plane.
3. Specify the distance n from the viewpoint to the near-plane (projection plane) and the distance f from the viewpoint to the far-plane.

In Figure 4-13, the viewpoint is the origin O, which is the point where the camera is located. The angle a is the angle of the field of view in the y-direction. w is the width of the near-plane and h is its height. The function **gluPerspective**() provides an alternative way to define the view-volume and works as follows.

void **gluPerspective**(GLdouble $fovy$, GLdouble $aspect$, GLdouble $near$, GLdouble far);
Creates a matrix for a symmetric perspective-view frustum and multiplies the current matrix by it. $fovy$ is the angle of the field of view in the $y - z$ plane; its value must be in the range $[0.0, 180.0]$. $aspect$ is the aspect ratio of the frustum, its width divided by its height. $near$ and far values are the distances between the viewpoint and the clipping planes, along the negative z-axis. They should be always positive.

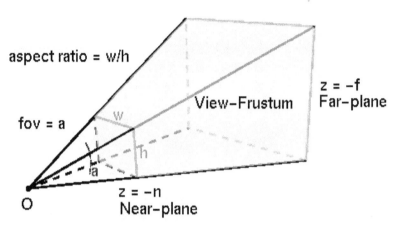

Figure 4-13   Setup for gluPerspective()

Example 4-1

Suppose $t = r = 1$, $b = l = -1$, $n = 2$, and $f = 10$, corresponding to the command " glFrustum (-1.0, 1.0, -1.0, 1.0, 2.0, 10.0);". Then the NDC perspective projection matrix N can be calculated from (4.23) and is equal to:

$$N = \begin{pmatrix} \frac{2}{1} & 0 & 0 & 0 \\ 0 & \frac{2}{1} & 0 & 0 \\ 0 & 0 & -\frac{10+2}{10-2} & -\frac{2\times2\times10}{10-2} \\ 0 & 0 & -1 & 0 \end{pmatrix} = \begin{pmatrix} 2 & 0 & 0 & 0 \\ 0 & 2 & 0 & 0 \\ 0 & 0 & -1.5 & -5 \\ 0 & 0 & -1 & 0 \end{pmatrix} \quad (4.25)$$

If the viewpoint is located at $(0, 0, 5)$ and the **up** vector is pointing at the y direction corresponding to the command "gluLookAt (0.0, 0.0, 5.0, 0.0, 0.0, 0.0, 0.0, 1.0, 0.0);", the composite projection P matrix can be found by multiplying N by the appropriate affine transformation matrix:

$$P = \begin{pmatrix} 2 & 0 & 0 & 0 \\ 0 & 2 & 0 & 0 \\ 0 & 0 & -1.5 & -5 \\ 0 & 0 & -1 & 0 \end{pmatrix} \begin{pmatrix} 1 & 0 & 0 & 0 \\ 0 & 1 & 0 & 0 \\ 0 & 0 & 1 & -5 \\ 0 & 0 & 0 & 1 \end{pmatrix} = \begin{pmatrix} 2 & 0 & 0 & 0 \\ 0 & 2 & 0 & 0 \\ 0 & 0 & -1.5 & 2.5 \\ 0 & 0 & -1 & 5 \end{pmatrix} \quad (4.26)$$

We can verify this using the following piece of OpenGL code.

```
//Use template so that we can print double, float or int
template<class T>
void print_mat ( T m[][4] )        //print 4 x 4 matrix
{
  cout.precision ( 2 );
  cout << fixed;                   //fixed-point format
```

```
  for ( int i = 0; i < 4; ++i ) {
    cout << "\t";
    for ( int j = 0; j < 4; ++j )
      cout <<  m[j][i] << "\t";   //OpenGL is column-major
    cout << endl;
  }
  cout << endl;
}

void display(void)
{
    float p[4][4];                    //4 x 4 matrix

    glMatrixMode (GL_PROJECTION); //Current matrix is projection
    glLoadIdentity ();                //set matrix to identity
    glFrustum (-1.0,1.0,-1.0,1.0,2.0,10.0); //set view-volume
    glGetFloatv(GL_PROJECTION_MATRIX,&p[0][0]);
    cout << "NDC Perspective Projection Matrix:" << endl;
    print_mat ( p );                  //print matrix
    gluLookAt (0.0, 0.0, 5.0, 0.0, 0.0, 0.0, 0.0, 1.0, 0.0);
    glGetFloatv(GL_PROJECTION_MATRIX,&p[0][0]);
    cout << "Perspective Projection Matrix:" << endl;
    print_mat ( p );
}
```

In the code, the word **template** in front of the function **print_mat**() is a C++ keyword. It allows the function to handle various data types such as float, double or int; the data type used is determined by the calling function and in our example, data type float is used. The following is the output of the above code which is consistent with our calculations of (4.25) and (4.26).

```
NDC Perspective Projection Matrix:
        2.00    0.00    0.00    -0.00
        0.00    2.00    0.00    -0.00
        0.00    0.00    -1.50   -5.00
        0.00    0.00    -1.00   -0.00

Perspective Projection Matrix:
        2.00    0.00    0.00    0.00
        0.00    2.00    0.00    0.00
        0.00    0.00    -1.50   2.50
        0.00    0.00    -1.00   5.00
```

Example 4-2

In designing our graphics scene, we need to estimate the field of view if we use **gluPerspective**() to define the view-frustum. Suppose the field of view is θ and the largest object size is about S, which is at a distance d from the viewpoint. Then we can estimate the field of view as follows.

$$tan\frac{\theta}{2} = \frac{S/2}{d} \tag{4.27}$$

This implies that

$$\theta = 2tan^{-1}\frac{S}{2d} \tag{4.28}$$

The following piece of code segment shows how to calculate this angle in degree, which can be used for the $fovy$ parameter of **gluPerspective**().

```
const double PI = 3.14159265389;

double fov(double size, double distance)
```

```
{
    double angle_rad, angle_deg;

    angle_rad = 2.0 * atan2 (size/2.0, distance);
    angle_deg = ( 180.0 * angle_rad ) / PI;
    return ( angle_deg );
}
```

4.3 Orthographic Projection

Orthographic projection, also known as **orthogonal projection**, is a form of parallel projection, where all the projection lines are orthogonal (perpendicular) to the projection plane. Most often we use orthographic projection to produce the front, side, and top views of an object as shown in Figure 4-14. Front, side, and rear orthographic projections of an object are referred to as *elevations*. A top orthographic projection is called a *plane view*.

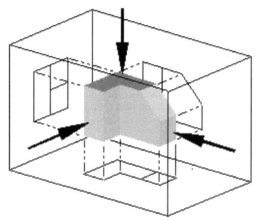

Figure 4-14 Front, Side and Top Views of an Object

With an orthographic projection, the viewing volume is a rectangular parallelepiped (box) as shown in Figure 4-15.

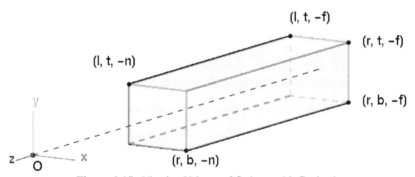

Figure 4-15 Viewing Volume of Orthographic Projection

Unlike perspective projection, the size of the planes bounding the volume does not change from one end to the other. Therefore, the distance of the viewpoint from the viewing volume does not affect how large an object appears. This type of projection is commonly used for engineering and architectural drawings because lengths and angles are accurately depicted and can be measured from the drawings.

The OpenGL function **glOrtho**() creates an orthographic parallel viewing volume. As with **glFrustum**(), we specify the corners of the near clipping plane and the distance to the far clipping plane (Figure 4-15):

> void **glOrtho**(double l, double r, double b, double t, double n, double f);
> Creates a matrix for orthographic projection and multiplies the current matrix by it. $(l, b, -n)$ and $(r, t, -n)$ are points on the near clipping plane that are mapped to the lower-left and upper-right corners of the viewport window, respectively. $(l, b, -f)$ and $(r, t, -f)$ are points on the far clipping plane that are mapped to the same respective corners of the viewport. Both n and f can be positive or negative.

Constructing the GL_PROJECTION matrix for orthographic projection is a lot simpler than for perspective projection. In this case, we map all x, y and z coordinates in eye space linearly to NDC. We just need to scale a rectangular volume to a cube, then move it to the origin. As in the case of perspective projection, we want to find the transformation that projects a point (x, y, z) into $(x', y'z')$ at the near-plane (i.e. $z' = -n$) and then maps the projected point $(x', y', -n)$ to a point (x^n, y^n, z^n) in the NDC space. Since there is no perspective distortion, we can interpolate depth values in an orthographic projection linearly. Thus, our mapping to normalized coordinates can be performed linearly in all three axes. For x and y coordinates, we have a linear relationship in mapping the range $[l, r]$ to $[-1, 1]$ and $[b, t]$ to $[-1, 1]$, which are given by

$$x^n = \frac{2x}{r - l} - \frac{r + l}{r - l} \tag{4.29}$$

and

$$y^n = \frac{2y}{t - b} - \frac{t + b}{t - b} \tag{4.30}$$

Similarly, by negating z so that $-n \to -1$ and $-f \to 1$, we can show that the function that maps the z coordinate from the range $[-f, -n]$ to the range $[-1, 1]$ is given by

$$z^n = \frac{-2z}{f - n} - \frac{f + n}{f - n} \tag{4.31}$$

Again, we can express this in matrix from. Suppose the orthograhic matrix O transforms a point $P = (x, y, z, 1)$ into normalized coordinates $P^n = (x^n, y^n, z^n, 1)$, then

$$P^n = OP \tag{4.32}$$

where

$$O = \begin{pmatrix} \frac{2}{r - l} & 0 & 0 & -\frac{r + l}{r - l} \\ 0 & \frac{2}{t - b} & 0 & -\frac{t + b}{t - b} \\ 0 & 0 & \frac{-2}{f - n} & -\frac{f + n}{f - n} \\ 0 & 0 & 0 & 1 \end{pmatrix} \tag{4.33}$$

The inverse of O is given by

$$O^{-1} = \begin{pmatrix} \frac{r - l}{2} & 0 & 0 & \frac{r + l}{2} \\ 0 & \frac{t - b}{2} & 0 & \frac{t + b}{2} \\ 0 & 0 & \frac{f - n}{-2} & -\frac{f + n}{2} \\ 0 & 0 & 0 & 1 \end{pmatrix} \tag{4.34}$$

The orthographic projection matrix O can be further simplified to O_s if the viewing volume is symmetric with $r = -l$, and $t = -b$.

$$O_s = \begin{pmatrix} \frac{1}{r} & 0 & 0 & 0 \\ 0 & \frac{1}{t} & 0 & 0 \\ 0 & 0 & \frac{-2}{f-n} & -\frac{f+n}{f-n} \\ 0 & 0 & 0 & 1 \end{pmatrix} \tag{4.35}$$

The matrix O of (4.33) is the orthographic projection matrix generated by the OpenGL function **glOrtho**(l, r, b, t, n, f). Note that the w coordinate of the point remains 1 after the transformation, and therefore no perspective projection has taken place.

Example 4-3

Suppose $t = r = 1$, $b = l = -1$, $n = 2$, and $f = 10$, corresponding to the command " glOrtho(-1.0, 1.0, -1.0, 1.0, 2.0, 10.0);". Then the NDC orthographic projection matrix O can be calculated from (4.33) and is equal to:

$$O = \begin{pmatrix} 1 & 0 & 0 & 0 \\ 0 & 1 & 0 & 0 \\ 0 & 0 & -0.25 & -1.5 \\ 0 & 0 & 0 & 1 \end{pmatrix} \tag{4.36}$$

If the viewpoint is located at $(0, 0, 5)$ and the **up** vector is pointing at the y direction corresponding to the command "gluLookAt (0.0, 0.0, 5.0, 0.0, 0.0, 0.0, 0.0, 1.0, 0.0);", the composite projection P matrix can be found by multiplying N by the appropriate affine transformation matrix:

$$P = \begin{pmatrix} 1 & 0 & 0 & 0 \\ 0 & 1 & 0 & 0 \\ 0 & 0 & -0.25 & -1.5 \\ 0 & 0 & 0 & 1 \end{pmatrix} \begin{pmatrix} 1 & 0 & 0 & 0 \\ 0 & 1 & 0 & 0 \\ 0 & 0 & 1 & -5 \\ 0 & 0 & 0 & 1 \end{pmatrix} = \begin{pmatrix} 1 & 0 & 0 & 0 \\ 0 & 1 & 0 & 0 \\ 0 & 0 & -0.25 & -0.25 \\ 0 & 0 & 0 & 1 \end{pmatrix} \tag{4.37}$$

We can verify this with the following OpenGL code. The function **print_mat**() has been presented in Example 4-1.

```
void display(void)
{
    float p[4][4];

    glMatrixMode (GL_PROJECTION);   //Current matrix is for projection
    glLoadIdentity ();              // clear the matrix
    glOrtho (-1.0, 1.0, -1.0, 1.0, 2.0, 10.0);
    glGetFloatv(GL_PROJECTION_MATRIX,&p[0][0]);
    cout << "NDC Orthographic Projection Matrix:" << endl;
    print_mat ( p );
    gluLookAt (0.0, 0.0, 5.0, 0.0, 0.0, 0.0, 0.0, 1.0, 0.0);
    glGetFloatv(GL_PROJECTION_MATRIX,&p[0][0]);
    cout << "Orthographic Projection Matrix:" << endl;
    print_mat ( p );
}
```

The following is the output of the code, which is consistent with our calculations in (4.36) and (4.37).

```
NDC Orthographic Projection Matrix:
        1.00    0.00    -0.00    0.00
        0.00    1.00    -0.00    0.00
        0.00    0.00    -0.25   -1.50
        0.00    0.00     0.00    1.00

Orthographic Projection Matrix:
        1.00    0.00     0.00    0.00
        0.00    1.00     0.00    0.00
        0.00    0.00    -0.25   -0.25
        0.00    0.00     0.00    1.00
```

In general, the 3D to 2D projection is a many-to-one mapping and is not reversible. However, if we specifiy a z value, we can map a projected 2D point (x', y') back to a 3D point (x, y, z). OpenGL provides the function **gluUnproject**() to achieve this purpose.

4.4   Rasterization

After the transformation to NDC, the graphics data will go through a process called **rasterization** or **scan conversion**, which converts the graphics objects to pixel data. The piece of code that performs the conversion is referred to as **rasterizer**. The output of a rasterizer is a set of **fragments** for each graphics primitive. Pixel values for displayed are saved in a framebuffer. We can think of a fragment as a set of data consisting of information such as color and depth value to form a potential pixel; the information will be used to update the corresponding pixel in the frame buffer. Fragments usually contain depth information that can be used to determine whether a particular fragment lies behind or in front of other previously rasterized fragments for a given pixel; typically, we discard the fragment if it lies behind otherwise we overwrite the one in the framebuffer with the new one.

The rasterizer takes vertices in normalized coordinates as inputs and outputs fragments in **window coordinates** or **screen coordinates**, units of the display device. The projection of the clipping volume must be in the assigned viewport. Suppose the viewport is bounded by x_{vmin} and x_{vmax} in the x direction, and by y_{vmin} and y_{vmax} in the y direction. Then the transformation of the normalized coordinates (x^n, y^n) to the screen coordinates (x^s, y^s) can be easily calculated. The x^s coordinate is given by

$$x^s = x_{vmin} + \frac{x^n - (-1)}{1 - (-1)}(x_{vmax} - x_{vmin})$$

which can be simplified to

$$x^s = x_{vmin} + \frac{x^n + 1}{2}(x_{vmax} - x_{vmin}) \tag{4.38}$$

Similarly,

$$y^s = y_{vmin} + \frac{y^n + 1}{2}(y_{vmax} - y_{vmin}) \tag{4.39}$$

Note that the z coordinates are scaled nonlinearly in perspective projection. However, their original depth order is preserved and thus we can use them for depth test or hidden surface removal.

Chapter 5   Color

5.1   Color Spaces

To describe an image, we need a way to represent the color information. To describe a gray-level image, we only need one number to indicate the brightness or luminance of each spatial sample. We need more numbers if we want to describe a color image. In reality, our perception of light depends on the light frequency and other properties. When we view a source of light, our eyes respond to three main sensations. The first one is the **color**, which is the main frequencies of the light. The second one is the **intensity** (or brightness), which represents the total energy of the light; we can quantify brightness as the luminance of the light. The third one is the **purity** (or saturation) of the light, which describes how close a light appears to be a pure spectral color, such as red, green or blue. Pale colors have low purity and they appear to be almost white, which consists of a mixture of the red, green and blue colors. We use the term **chromaticity** to collectively refer to the two characteristics of light, color purity and dominant frequency (hue).

Very often, we employ a **color model** to precisely describe the color components or intensities. In general, a color model is any method for explaining the properties or behavior of color within some particular context. No single model can explain all aspects of color, so people make use of different models to help describe different color characteristics. Here, we consider a **color model** as an abstract mathematical model that describes how colors are presented as tuples of numbers, typically as three or four values or color components; the resulting set of colors that define how the components are to be interpreted is called a **color space**. The commonly used **RGB** color model naturally fits the representation of colors by computers. However, it is not a good model for studying the characteristics of an image.

5.2   RGB Color Model

X-ray, light, infrared radiation, microwave and radio waves are all electromagnetic (EM) waves with different frequencies. Light waves lie in the visible spectrum with a narrow wavelength band from about 350 to 780 nm. The retina of a human eye can detect only EM waves lying within this visible spectrum but not anything outside. The eye contains two kinds of light-sensitive receptor cells, **cones** and **rods** that can detect light.

The **cones** are sensitive to colors and there are three types of cones, each responding to one of the three primary colors, red, green and blue. Scientists found that our perception of color is a result of our cones' relative response to the red, green and blue colors. We can form any color by mixing these three colors with certain intensity values. The human eye can distinguish about 200 intensities of each of the red, green and blue colors. Therefore, it is natural that we represent each of these colors by a byte, which can hold 256 values. In other words, 24 bits are enough to represent the 'true' color. More bits will not increase the quality of an image as human eyes cannot resolve the extra colors. Each eye has 6 to 7 million cones located near the center of the eye, allowing us to see the tiny details of an object.

On the other hand, the **rods** cannot distinguish colors but are sensitive to dim light. Each eye has 75 million to 150 millions rods located near its corner, allowing us to detect peripheral objects in an environment of near darkness.

We can characterize a visible color by a function $C(\lambda)$ where λ is the wavelength of the color in the visible spectrum. The value for a given wavelength λ gives the relative intensity of that wavelength in the color. This description is accurate when we measure the color with certain physical instrument. However, the human visual system (HVS) does not perceive color in this way. Our brains do not receive the entire distribution $C(\lambda)$ of the visible spectrum but rather three values – the **tristimulus values** – that are the responses of the three types (red, green and blue) of cones to a color. This human characteristics leads to the formulation of the trichromatic theory: *If two colors produce the same tristimulus values, they are visually indistinguishable.* A consequence of of this theory is that it is possible to match all of the colors in the visible spectrum by appropriately mixing three primary colors. In other words, any color can be created by combining red, green, and blue in varying proportions. This leads to the development of the **RGB color model**.

The RGB (short for red, green, blue) color model decomposes a color into three components, Red (R), Green (G), and Blue (B); we can represent any color by three components R, G, B just like the case that a spatial vector is specified by three components x, y, z. If the color components R, G and B are confined to values between 0 and 1, all definable colors lie in a unit cube as shown in Figure 5-1. This color space is most natural for representing computer images, in which a color specification such as (0.1, 0.8, 0.23) can be directly translated into three positive integer values, each of which is represented by one byte.

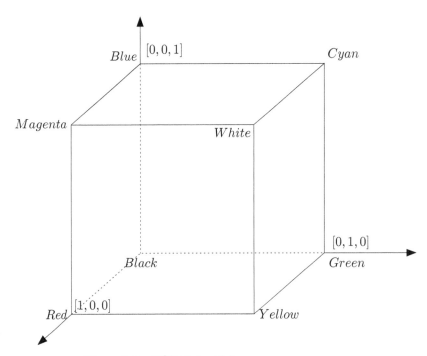

Figure 5-1 RGB Color Cube

In this model, we express a color C in the vector form,

$$C = \begin{pmatrix} R \\ G \\ B \end{pmatrix} \qquad 0 \le R, G, B \le 1 \tag{5.1}$$

In some other notations, the authors may consider $R, G,$ and B as three unit vectors like the three spatial unit vectors $\mathbf{i}, \mathbf{j},$ and $\mathbf{k}$. Just as a spatial vector $\mathbf{V}$ can be expressed as $\mathbf{V} = x\mathbf{i} + y\mathbf{j} + z\mathbf{k}$, any color is expressed as $C = (rR + gG + bB)$, and the red, green, blue intensities are specified by the values of $r, g,$ and b respectively. In our notation here, $R, G,$ and B may represent the intensity values of the color components. The next few sections discuss in more detail the color representation of various standards.

Suppose we have two colors C_1 and C_2 given by

$$C_1 = \begin{pmatrix} R_1 \\ G_1 \\ B_1 \end{pmatrix}, \qquad C_2 = \begin{pmatrix} R_2 \\ G_2 \\ B_2 \end{pmatrix}$$

Does it make sense to add these two colors to produce a new color C? For instance, consider

$$C = C_1 + C_2 = \begin{pmatrix} R_1 + R_2 \\ G_1 + G_2 \\ B_1 + B_2 \end{pmatrix}$$

You may immediately notice that the sum of two components may give a value larger than 1 which lies outside the color cube and thus does not represent any color. Just like adding two points in space is illegitimate, we cannot arbitrarily combine two colors. A linear combination of colors makes sense only if the sum of the coefficients is equal to 1. Therefore, we can have

$$C = \alpha_1 C_1 + \alpha_2 C_2 \tag{5.2}$$

when

$$0 \leq \alpha_1, \alpha_2 \quad and \quad \alpha_1 + \alpha_2 = 1$$

In this way, we can guarantee that the resulted components will always lie within the color cube as each value will never exceed one. For example,

$$R = \alpha_1 R_1 + \alpha_2 R_2 \leq \alpha_1 \times 1 + \alpha_2 \times 1 = 1$$

which implies

$$R \leq 1$$

The linear combination of colors described by Equation (5.2) is called *color blending*.

5.3 Color Systems

In the RGB model described above, a given color is a point in a color cube as shown in Figure 5-1, and can be expressed as

$$C = \begin{pmatrix} R \\ G \\ B \end{pmatrix} \qquad 0 \leq R, G, B \leq 1$$

However, RGB systems do not produce identical perceptions and they vary significantly from one to another. For example, suppose we have a yellow color described by the triplet (0.9, 0.8, 0.0). If we feed these values to a CRT and a film image recorder, we shall see different colors, even though in both cases the red is 90 percent of the maximum, the green is 80 percent of the maximum, and there is no blue. The reason is that the CRT phosphors and the film dyes have different color distribution responses. Consequently, the range of displayable colors (or the color **gamut**) is different in each case.

Different organizations have different interests and emphasis on color models. For example, the graphics community is interested in device-independent graphics; it will be a burden for them to develop graphics APIs that address the real differences among display properties. Fortunately, this bas been addressed in colorimetery literature, and standards exist for many common color systems. For example, the National Television System Committee (NTSC) defines an RGB system which forms the basis for many CRT systems. We can view the differences in color systems as the differences between various coordinate system for representing the tristimulus values. For example, if

$$C_1 = \begin{pmatrix} R_1 \\ G_1 \\ B_1 \end{pmatrix}, \quad \text{and} \quad C_2 = \begin{pmatrix} R_2 \\ G_2 \\ B_2 \end{pmatrix} \tag{5.3}$$

are the representations of the same color in two different systems, we can find a 3×3 color conversion matrix M such that

$$C_2 = MC_1 \tag{5.4}$$

Regardless of the way we find this matrix, it allows us to produce similar displays on different color systems.

However, this is not a good approach because the color gamuts of two systems may not be the same; even after the conversion of the color components from one system to another, the color may not be producible on the second system. Also, the printing and graphic arts industries use a four color subtractive system (CMYK) that includes black (K) as the fourth primary. Moreover, the linear color theory is only an approximation to human perception of colors. The distance between two points in the color cube does not necessarily measure how far apart the colors are perceptually. For example, humans are particularly sensitive to color shifts in blue.

The International Commission on Illumination, referred to as the CIE (Commission Internationale de l'Eclarage) defined in 1931 three standard primaries, which are actually imaginary colors. CIE defined the three standard primaries mathematically with positive color-matching functions shown in Figure 5-2. If the spectral power distribution (SPD) for a colored object is weighted by the curves of Figure 5-2, the CIE chromaticity coordinates can be calculated. This provides an international standard definition of all colors. The CIE primaries also eliminate negative-value color-matching and other problems related to the selection of a set of real primaries.

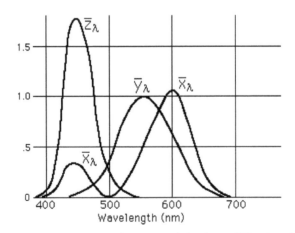

Figure 5-2 Matching functions of the three CIE primaries

5.3.1 The XYZ Color Model

The set of CIE primaries defines a color model that is in general referred to as the **XYZ color model,** where parameters X, Y, and Z represent the tristimulus values, the amount of each CIE primary required to produce a given color. The tristimulus values do not correspond to real colors, but they do have the property that any real color can be represented as a positive combination of them. Therefore, an RGB model describes a color in the same way as the XYZ model does. Actually, most color standards are based on this theoretical XYZ model. In this model, the Y primary is the luminance of the color and all colors can be represented by positive tristimulus values.

Due to the nature of the distribution of cones in the eye, the tristimulus values depend on the observer's field of view. To eliminate this variable, the CIE defined the standard (colorimetric) observer, which is characterized by three color matching functions. The color matching functions are the numerical description of the chromatic response of the observer. The three color-matching functions are referred to as $\overline{X}(\lambda), \overline{Y}(\lambda)$, and $\overline{Z}(\lambda)$, which can be thought of as the spectral sensitivity curves of three linear light detectors that yield the CIE XYZ tristimulus values X, Y, and Z. The tabulated numerical values of these functions are known collectively as the CIE standard observer.

The tristimulus values for a color with a spectral power distribution $I(\lambda)$ are given in terms of the standard observer by:

$$X = \int_0^\infty \overline{X}_\lambda I(\lambda) d\lambda$$

$$Y = \int_0^\infty \overline{Y}_\lambda I(\lambda) d\lambda \tag{5.5}$$

$$Z = \int_0^\infty \overline{Z}_\lambda I(\lambda) d\lambda$$

where λ is the wavelength of the equivalent monochromatic light.

A color can be specified by the tristimulus values, X, Y, and Z:

$$C = \begin{pmatrix} X \\ Y \\ Z \end{pmatrix} \tag{5.6}$$

We may also represent a color in the XYZ color space as an additive combination of the primaries using unit vectors $\mathbf{X}, \mathbf{Y}$, and $\mathbf{Z}$. Therefore, we can express Equation (5.6) as

$$C = X\mathbf{X} + Y\mathbf{Y} + Z\mathbf{Z} \tag{5.7}$$

We can use 3×3 matrices to convert from XYZ color representation to representations in other standard systems. Also, it is convenient to normalize the X, Y, and Z values against the sum $X + Y + Z$, which is the total light energy. The normalized values are usually referred to as the **chromaticity coordinates**:

$$x = \frac{X}{X+Y+Z}, \quad y = \frac{Y}{X+Y+Z}, \quad z = \frac{Z}{X+Y+Z} \tag{5.8}$$

As $x + y + z = 1$, any color can be represented with just the x and y coordinates if the total energy is known. The parameters x and y depend only on hue and purity of the color and are called **chromaticity values**. Instead of using the total energy, people typically use the luminance Y and the chromaticity values x, and y to specify a color. The other two CIE values can be calculated as

$$X = \frac{x}{y}Y, \quad Z = \frac{z}{y}Y \tag{5.9}$$

where $z = 1 - x - y$. Using chromaticity coordinates (x, y), we can represent all colors on a two-dimensional diagram known as chromaticity diagram.

Color Gamuts

The gamut is the set of possible colors within a color system. No one system can reproduce all possible colors in the visible spectrum. It is not possible for a designer to create every color in the spectrum with either additive or subtractive colors. Both systems can reproduce a subset of all visible color, and while those subsets generally overlap, there are colors which can be reproduced with additive color and not with subtractive color and vice versa.

5.3.2 YUV Color Model

While the RGB color model is well-suited for displaying color images on a computer screen, it is not an effective model for image processing or video compression. This is because the human visual system (HVS) is more sensitive to luminance (brightness) than to colors. Therefore, it is more effective to represent a color image by separating the luminance from the color information and representing luma with a higher resolution than color.

The YUV color model, defined in the TV standards, is an efficient way of representing color images by separating brightness from color values. Historically, YUV color space was developed to provide compatibility between color and black /white analog television systems; it is not defined precisely in the technical and scientific literature. In this model, Y is the luminance (luma) component, which is the same as the Y component in the CIE XYZ color space, and U and V are the color differences known as chrominance or chroma, which is defined as the difference between a color and a reference white at the same luminance. The conversion from RGB to YUV is given by the following formulas:

$$
\begin{aligned}
Y &= k_r R + k_g G + k_b B \\
U &= B - Y \\
V &= R - Y
\end{aligned}
\tag{5.10}
$$

with

$$
\begin{aligned}
&0 \leq k_r, k_b, k_g \\
&k_r + k_b + k_g = 1
\end{aligned}
\tag{5.11}
$$

Note that equations (5.10) and (5.11) imply that $0 \leq Y \leq 1$ if the R, G, B components lie within the unit color cube. However, U and V can be negative. Typically,

$$
k_r = 0.299, k_g = 0.587, k_b = 0.114
\tag{5.12}
$$

which are values used in some TV standards.

The complete description of an image is specified by Y (the luminance component) and the two color differences (chrominance) U and V. If the image is black-and-white, $U = V = 0$. Note that we do not need another difference ($G - Y$) for the green component because that would be redundant. We can consider (5.10) as three equations with three unknowns, R, G, and B. We can always solve for the three unknowns and recover R, G, and B. A fourth equation is not necessary.

It seems that there is no advantage of using YUV over RGB to represent an image as both system requires three components to specify an image sample. However, as we mentioned earlier, human eyes are less sensitive to color than to luminance. Therefore, we can represent the U and V components with a lower resolution than Y and the reduction of the amount of data to represent chrominance components will not have an obvious effect on visual quality. Representing chroma with less number of bits than luma is a simple but effective way of compressing an image.

The conversion from RGB space to YUV space can be also expressed in matrix form:

$$\begin{pmatrix} Y \\ U \\ V \end{pmatrix} = \begin{pmatrix} 0.299 & 0.587 & 0.114 \\ -0.299 & -0.587 & 0.886 \\ 0.701 & -0.587 & -0.114 \end{pmatrix} \begin{pmatrix} R \\ G \\ B \end{pmatrix} \tag{5.13}$$

The conversion from YUV space to RGB space using matrix is accomplished with the inverse transformation of (5.13):

$$\begin{pmatrix} R \\ G \\ B \end{pmatrix} = \begin{pmatrix} 1 & 1 & 0 \\ 1 & 0 & 1 \\ 1 & -0.509 & -0.194 \end{pmatrix} \begin{pmatrix} Y \\ U \\ V \end{pmatrix} \tag{5.14}$$

5.3.3   YCbCr Color Model

The YCbCr color model defined in the standards of ITU (International Telecommunication Union) is closely related to YUV but with the chrominace components scaled and shifted to ensure that they lie within the range 0 and 1. It is sometimes abbreviated to YCC. It is also used in the JPEG and MPEG standards. In this model, an image sample is specified by a luminance (Y) component and two chrominance components (Cb, and Cr). The following equations convert an RGB image to one in YCbCr space.

$$Y = k_r R + k_g G + k_b B$$

$$C_b = \frac{B - Y}{2(1 - k_b)} + 0.5$$

$$C_r = \frac{(R - Y)}{2(1 - k_r)} + 0.5 \tag{5.15}$$

$$k_r + k_b + k_g = 1$$

An image may be captured in the RGB format and then converted to YCbCr to reduce storage or transmission requirements. Before displaying the image, it is usually necessary to convert the image back to RGB. The conversion from YCbCr to RGB can be done by solving for R, G, B in the equations of (5.15). The equations for converting from YCbCr to RGB are shown below:

$$R = Y + (2C_r - 1)(1 - k_r)$$

$$B = Y + (2C_b - 1)(1 - k_b)$$

$$G = \frac{Y - k_r R - k_b B}{k_g} \tag{5.16}$$

$$= Y - \frac{k_r(2C_r - 1)(1 - k_r) + k_b(2C_b - 1)(1 - k_b)}{k_g}$$

If we use the ITU standard values $k_b = 0.114, k_r = 0.299, k_g = 1 - k_b - k_r = 0.587$ for (5.15) and (5.16), we will obtain the following commonly used conversion equations.

$$Y = 0.299R + 0.587G + 0.114B$$
$$C_b = 0.564(B - Y) + 0.5$$
$$C_r = 0.713(R - Y) + 0.5$$

$$(5.17)$$

$$R = Y + 1.402C_r - 0.701$$
$$G = Y - 0.714C_r - 0.344C_b + 0.529$$
$$B = Y + 1.772C_b - 0.886$$

In equations (5.15), it is obvious that $0 \leq Y \leq 1$ as $0 \leq R, G, B \leq 1$. It turns out that the chrominance components C_b and C_r defined in (5.15) also always lie within the range [0, 1]. We prove this for the case of C_b. From (5.15), we have

$$
\begin{aligned}
C_b &= \frac{B - Y}{2(1 - k_b)} + \frac{1}{2} \\
&= \frac{B - k_r R - k_g G - k_b B + 1 - k_b}{2(1 - k_b)} \\
&= \frac{B}{2} + \frac{-k_r R - k_g G + 1 - k_b}{2(1 - k_b)} \\
&\geq \frac{B}{2} + \frac{-k_r \times 1 - k_g \times 1 + 1 - k_b}{2(1 - k_b)} \\
&= \frac{B}{2} \\
&\geq 0
\end{aligned}
$$

Thus

$$C_b \geq 0 \qquad (5.18)$$

Also,

$$
\begin{aligned}
C_b &= \frac{B - Y}{2(1 - k_b)} + \frac{1}{2} \\
&= \frac{B - k_r R - k_g G - k_b B}{2(1 - k_b)} + \frac{1}{2} \\
&\leq \frac{B - k_b B}{2(1 - k_b)} + \frac{1}{2} \\
&= \frac{B}{2} + \frac{1}{2} \\
&\leq \frac{1}{2} + \frac{1}{2} \\
&= 1
\end{aligned}
$$

Thus

$$C_b \leq 1 \qquad (5.19)$$

Combining (5.18) and (5.19), we have

$$0 \leq C_b \leq 1 \qquad (5.20)$$

Similarly

$$0 \leq C_r \leq 1 \tag{5.21}$$

In summary, we have the following situation.

$$\text{If} \quad 0 \leq R, G, B \leq 1$$

$$\tag{5.22}$$

$$\text{then} \quad 0 \leq Y, C_b, C_r \leq 1$$

Note that the converse is not true. That is, if $0 \leq Y, C_b, C_r \leq 1$, it does **not** imply $0 \leq R, G, B \leq 1$. A knowledge of this helps us in the implementations of the conversion from RGB to YCbCr and vice versa. We mentioned earlier that the eye can only resolve about 200 different intensity levels of each of the RGB components. Therefore, we can quantize all the RGB components in the interval [0,1] to 256 values, from 0 to 255, which can be represented by one byte of storage without any loss of visual quality. In other words, one byte (or an 8-bit unsigned integer) is enough to represent all the values of each RGB component. When we convert from RGB to YCbCr, it only requires one 8-bit unsigned integer to represent each YCbCr component. This implicitly implies that all conversions can be done efficiently in integer arithmetic.

5.4   RGBA Color Model

A computer monitor displays different amounts of red (R), green (G), and blue (B) light at each pixel position. The R, G, and B values form a certain color. These values are usually packed together and the packed value is referred to as the **RGB** value. Very often, an RGB value is packed with another value called **alpha** value to form the **RGBA** value. The alpha (α) value is used for color blending and denotes the degree of transparency of the associated pixel or object. If alpha is 1, the object is opaque and blocks objects behind it; if alpha is 0, the object is totally transparent and cannot be seen; if its value is between 0 and 1, the object is translucent. When initializing an OpenGL program, we can select the RGB mode with the command

> **glutInitDisplayMode** (GLUT_RGB);

or the RGBA mode using

> **glutInitDisplayMode** (GLUT_RGBA);

In OpenGL, the alpha value has meaning only if we enable color blending which is enabled by the command

> **glEnable**(GL_BLEND);

The default is that all objects are opaque. We can specify an RGB value or an RGBA value using

> glColor3f(r, g, b);

or

> glColor4f(r, g, b, a);

All the values r, g, b, a lie within the range $[0, 1]$. That is, $0 \leq r, g, b, a \leq 1$. We may also use array specifications such as

> float a[3] = { 1, 1, 0 };
> glColor3fv(a);

or

    float a4[4] = { 1, 1, 0, 1 };
    glColor4fv(a4);

We can assign an OpenGL color specification to individual vertices within the **glBegin/glEnd** pairs.

OpenGL represents color information in floating-point format internally. We can specify color values in integer format, but they will be converted automatically to floating-point values. For example, we can specify a color with an unsigned byte using the command,

    glColor4ub(0, 255, 0, 1);

which is equivalent to

    glColor4f(0.0, 1.0, 0.0, 1.0);

As we have discussed before, our eye can only resolve about 200 values for each of the primary colors. Therefore, most applications do not need to use other integer formats such as **unsigned int** (ui) which is a 32-bit integer format to specify a color component.

5.5 Color Blending

When we render only opaque polygons, the z-buffer for hidden surface removal is enough to render objects properly. However, when an OpenGL program runs in RGBA mode and **blending** is enabled, the alpha (A) value controls how RGB values are written into the frame buffer; fragments from different objects are combined to form the color of the same pixel, and we say that we **blend** or **composite** these objects together. (A fragment is all the data in a location of the frame buffer necessary to generate a pixel.) In the blending process, we combine the color value of the fragment being processed (source color) with that of the pixel already stored in the frame buffer (destination color). The combined color is put back to the same pixel location of the frame buffer. The new destination color is the combination of the old destination color and the source color. This process is shown in Figure 5-3. Blending occurs after our scene has been rasterized and converted to fragments.

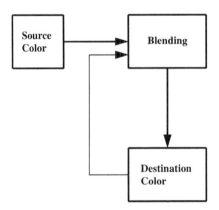

Figure 5-3 Color Blending

The alpha component (A) of an RGBA quantity is a measure of the *opacity* of a surface, which is the percentage of light that is blocked by the surface. An opacity of 1 (A = 1) indicates that the surface is totally opaque and blocks all light incident on it. An opacity of 0 (A = 0) corresponds to a totally transparent surface where all incident light passes through it. The *transparency* or *translucency* of a surface is 1 - A. Therefore, an alpha value is meaningful only if it lies within the range $[0, 1]$.

In the rasterization process, polygons are usually rendered one at a time into the frame buffer. Without blending, each new fragment overwrites any existing color values in the frame buffer (color buffer), which holds the color for display. With blending, we need to apply opacity as part of fragment processing. Usually the polygon color that we are working on is considered as the **source color** and the color in the color buffer is the **destination color**. We combine the two colors using source and destination factors. Suppose we represent the source (polygon) colors, destination colors, source factors, and destination factors using 4-tuples (RGBA), C_s, C_d, S and D respectively :

$$C_s = \begin{pmatrix} R_s \\ G_s \\ B_s \\ A_s \end{pmatrix}, \quad C_d = \begin{pmatrix} R_d \\ G_d \\ B_d \\ A_d \end{pmatrix}, \quad S = \begin{pmatrix} S_r \\ S_g \\ S_b \\ S_a \end{pmatrix}, \quad D = \begin{pmatrix} D_r \\ D_g \\ D_b \\ D_a \end{pmatrix} \tag{5.23}$$

Then the blended color (new destination color) C_d' is given by

$$C_d' = \begin{pmatrix} R_s S_r + R_d D_r \\ G_s S_g + G_d D_g \\ B_s S_b + B_d D_b \\ A_s S_a + A_d D_a \end{pmatrix} \tag{5.24}$$

Each component is clamped to $[0, 1]$.

The next question is how to generate the blending factors. OpenGL provides the function **glBlendFunc()** to do so. Before using this function, we need to enable blending using the command

glEnable(GL_BLEND);

(We can disable blending using "glDisable(GL_BLEND);".) After blending has been enabled, we can set up the source and destination factors by the command

glBlendFunc(*sourceFactor*, *destinationFactor*);

where *sourceFactor* and *destinatiionFactor* are type **GLenum**. OpenGL defines a number of blending factors, including the values 1 (GL_ONE) and 0 (GL_ZERO), the source alpha S_a and $1-S_a$ (GL_SRC_ALPHA and GL_ONE_MINUS_SRC_ALPHA), and the destination alpha D_a and $1 - D_a$ (GL_DST_ALPHA and GL_ONE_MINUS_DST_ALPHA). Table 5-1 shows the source and destination factors that the function **glBlendFunc()** can take as parameters.

We can also specify a (R_c, G_c, B_c, A_c) using the **glBlendColor()** function. For example, suppose we select GL_SRC_ALPHA for the source blending factor and GL_ONE_MINUS_SRC_ALPHA for the destination blending factor, then the new destination color is given by

$$C_d' = \begin{pmatrix} R_d' \\ G_d' \\ B_d' \\ A_d' \end{pmatrix} = \begin{pmatrix} R_s S_a + R_d(1 - S_a) \\ G_s S_a + G_d(1 - S_a) \\ B_s S_a + B_d(1 - S_a) \\ A_s S_a + A_d(1 - S_a) \end{pmatrix} \tag{5.25}$$

Actually, this is one of the most commonly used options in computing the composite color.

Note that unlike most OpenGL functions that users do not need to worry about the order in which polygons are rasterized, the effect of color blending depends on the order of rendering polygons. The destination and source factors could be interchanged if the order of rendering two polygons is interchanged.

Table 5-1 Blending Factors

GL Constant	Computed Blend Factor
GL_ZERO	$(0, 0, 0, 0)$
GL_ONE	$(1, 1, 1, 1)$
GL_DST_COLOR	(R_d, G_d, B_d, A_d)
GL_SRC_COLOR	(R_s, G_s, B_s, A_s)
GL_ONE_MINUS_DST_COLOR	$(1, 1, 1, 1)\text{-}(R_d, G_d, B_d, A_d)$
GL_ONE_MINUS_SRC_COLOR	$(1, 1, 1, 1)\text{-}(R_s, G_s, B_s, A_s)$
GL_SRC_ALPHA	(A_s, A_s, A_s, A_s)
GL_ONE_MINUS_SRC_ALPHA	$(1, 1, 1, 1)\text{-}(A_s, A_s, A_s, A_s)$
GL_DST_ALPHA	(A_d, A_d, A_d, A_d)
GL_ONE_MINUS_DST_ALPHA	$(1, 1, 1, 1)\text{-}(A_d, A_d, A_d, A_d)$
GL_SRC_ALPHA_SATURATE	$(f, f, f, 1)$; f=min$(A_s, 1\text{-}A_d)$
GL_CONSTANT_COLOR	(R_c, G_c, B_c, A_c)
GL_CONSTANT_ALPHA	(A_c, A_c, A_c, A_c)

Example 5-1

This example draws two overlapping colored triangles, one red and one green, each with an alpha value of 0.8. The background is white. Blending is enabled and the parameters for source and destination blending factors for the function **glBlendFunc()** are set to GL_SRC_ALPHA and GL_ONE_MINUS_SRC_ALPHA respectively. When the program starts up, a red triangle is drawn on the left and then a green triangle is drawn on the right with part of it overlapping with the red triangle as shown in case (a) of Figure 5-4. Case (b) of Figure 5-4 shows a similar drawing except that the green triangle is drawn on the left first.

For case (a), when the red triangle is first drawn, its color $C_r = (1, 0, 0, 0.8)$, which is the source, is blended with the background white color $C_w = (1, 1, 1, 1)$, which is the original destination color to give the new destination color C_d. In this case, the source blending factor is 0.8 (source alpha), and the destination blending factor is 0.2 (one minus source alpha). Thus

$$C_d = \begin{pmatrix} 1 \times 0.8 + 1 \times 0.2 \\ 0 \times 0.8 + 1 \times 0.2 \\ 0 \times 0.8 + 1 \times 0.2 \\ 0.8 \times 0.8 + 1 \times 0.2 \end{pmatrix} = \begin{pmatrix} 1 \\ 0.2 \\ 0.2 \\ 0.84 \end{pmatrix} \tag{5.26}$$

When the green triangle is drawn on the right side, besides the white background, we have three different regions, the nonoverlapping 'red' region on the left, the 'red-green' overlapping region at the center and the nonoverlapping 'green' region as shown in Figure 5-4(a). The color of the nonoverlapping 'red' region is given by (5.26). Similarly, the color of the nonoverlapping 'green' region is $(0.2, 1, 0.2, 0.84)$. To calculate the color of the overlapping region, we use $C_g = (0, 1, 0, 0.8)$ as the source color and $C_d = (1, 0.2, 0.2, 0.84)$ as the destination color; the new destination color is given by

$$C_d^{(a)} = \begin{pmatrix} 0 \times 0.8 + 1 \times 0.2 \\ 1 \times 0.8 + 0.2 \times 0.2 \\ 0 \times 0.8 + 0.2 \times 0.2 \\ 0.8 \times 0.8 + 0.84 \times 0.2 \end{pmatrix} = \begin{pmatrix} 0.2 \\ 0.84 \\ 0.04 \\ 0.808 \end{pmatrix} \tag{5.27}$$

We see that green is the dominant component, followed by red in the overlapping region.

In case (b), the green triangle is drawn first. The color for the overlapping region can be similarly calcualted:

$$C_d^{(b)} = \begin{pmatrix} 0.84 \\ 0.2 \\ 0.04 \\ 0.808 \end{pmatrix}$$

(5.28)

In this case, red is the dominant color followed by green.

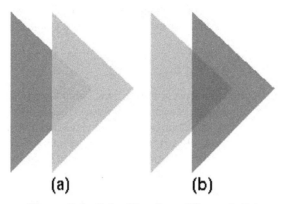

(a)   **(b)**

Figure 5-4   Color Blending of Example 5-1

The following is the code for this example.

```
static void init(void)
{
  glEnable (GL_BLEND);
  glBlendFunc (GL_SRC_ALPHA, GL_ONE_MINUS_SRC_ALPHA);
  glShadeModel (GL_FLAT);
  glClearColor (1.0, 1.0, 1.0, 1.0);
}

static void triangle( float color[4] )
{
  glColor4fv( color );
  glBegin (GL_TRIANGLES);
    glVertex3f(-2, -1.9, 0.0);
    glVertex3f( -1, -0.9, 0.0);
    glVertex3f( -2,   0, 0.0);
  glEnd();
}

void display(void)
{
  glClear(GL_COLOR_BUFFER_BIT);
  glOrtho (-2.2, 2.2, -2.2, 2.2, -2.0, 10.0);

  //draw red triangle first, then green
  float red[4] = { 1, 0, 0, 0.8};
  triangle( red );
  glTranslatef( 0.5, 0, 0 );
  float green[4] = { 0, 1, 0, 0.8};
  triangle( green );

  //draw green triangle first, then red
  glTranslatef( 1.2, 0, 0 );
  triangle ( green );
  glTranslatef( 0.5, 0, 0 );
  triangle ( red );
```

```
    glFlush();
}
```

Note that when we enable blending, we usually do not enable hidden surface removal. This is because objects behind any object already rendered would not be rasterized and thus its color would not combine with the frame buffer color. If a scene consists of both opaque and transparent objects, any object behind and opaque one should not be rendered, but translucent objects in front of opaque objects should be composited. A simple solution to this problem is to enable hidden-surface removal as usual and make the z buffer read-only for any object that is translucent. This can be done using the command

glDepthMask(GL_FALSE);

When the z buffer is read-only, a translucent object lying behind any opaque object already rendered is discarded. On the other hand, a translucent object lying in front of a rendered opaque object will be blended; however, as the z buffer is read-only, the depth value in the buffer will not be changed. When we render opaque objects, we set the depth mask to true (so that the z buffer is writable) and render them as usual. In summary, when drawing translucent objects, we enable depth buffering but make the depth buffer read-only and draw the objects in the following order:

1. First draw all opaque objects, with depth buffer in normal operation.
2. Preserve the depth values by making depth buffer read-only.
3. Draw the translucent objects only if they are in front of the opaque ones, and blend them with the opaque ones.

Finally, one should note that in some systems, the hardware frame buffer may not fully support blending and the blending result may not be exactly the same as what we expect.

Chapter 6   Depth Test and OpenGL Buffers

6.1   Buffers

We briefly mentioned in previous chapters two types of standard buffers, *depth buffers* and *color buffers*, which are most commonly used. Depth buffers are also referred to as z buffers. In graphics, we can generally consider a buffer as a block of memory arranged in the form of a two-dimensional array with size $m \times n$ with each location corresponding to a pixel position of the screen. Each memory location may save a k-bit datum. For example, in RGBA mode, very often an RGBA value is 32-bit as 8-bit is required to save the value for each of the red, green, blue and alpha components. Therefore, an RGBA color buffer location stores a 32-bit value (i.e. $k = 32$). Similarly, for RGB display, k is 24. For the z buffer, its k is determined by the depth precision the graphics system supports; very often, it is 32 bits which is the size of a floating point number or an integer in most C/C++ programs. We refer to any of the k $n \times m$ one-bit 'planes' in a buffer as a **bitplane**. The k bit datum at a particular buffer location describes a pixel shown on the screen.

In general, OpenGL supports a number of different types of buffers including,

1. Color buffers: front-left, front-right, back-left, back-right, and any number of auxiliary color buffers
2. Depth buffer
3. Accumulation buffer
4. Stencil buffer

The buffers are collectively known as **frame buffer** in OpenGL. When we work with the frame buffer, we usually work with one of the above buffers at a time. Therefore, when we use the term *buffer*, we refer to one particular buffer listed above, which is a constituent of the frame buffer. Exactly what kind of buffers and what value of k is used in a system is determined by the particular OpenGL implementation used. We may use the function **glGetIntegerv**() to query the OpenGL system about the storage information of each buffer location. For example, the following code queries the number of bits used to specify a depth value; the number is returned in the variable *depth*:

```
int depth;
glGetIntegerv ( GL_DEPTH_BITS, &depth );
```

The general syntax of this command is

    void glGetIntegerv(GLenum *pname*, GLint *p*);

where *pname* specifies the parameter value (see Table 6-1) to be returned and *p* points to the memory location that the value or values will be returned. Other commands that perform the same task but operate on different data types include

glGetBooleanv(), **glGetDoublev**(), and **glGetFloatv**().

Table 6-1 lists the parameters that can be used with **glGetIntegerv**() to query the bits-per-pixel information of an OpenGL system. If we know the internal format of how data are stored in any of the buffers, we can often write applications that run more efficiently. Moreover, this knowledge helps us encode the image data into some standard image formats such as PNG, GIF and JPEG formats.

Table 6-1   Parameters for **glGetIntegerv**() to Query Per-Pixel Buffer Storage

Parameter	Meaning
GL_RED_BITS, GL_GREEN_BITS, GL_BLUE_BITS, GL_ALPHA_BITS	Number of bits per R, G, B, or A component in the color buffers
GL_INDEX_BITS	Number of bits per index in color buffers
GL_DEPTH_BITS	Number of bits per pixel in depth buffer
GL_STENCIL_BITS	Number of bits per pixel in stencil buffer
GL_ACCUM_RED_BITS, GL_ACCUM_GREEN_BITS, GL_ACCUM_BLUE_BITS, GL_ACCUM_ALPHA_BITS	Number of bits per R, G, B, or A component in the accumulation buffer

Color Buffers

The color buffers are the ones to which we store the color data for each pixel. They contain color-index, RGB or RGBA color data. If an OpenGL implementation supports double-buffering, the color buffers consist of front and back buffers. On the other hand, a single-buffered system only has the front buffer. If the system also supports stereoscopic viewing, the color buffers will have left and right buffers for the left and right stereo images. If stereo is not supported, only the left buffer is used. Every OpenGL implementation must provide a front-left color buffer.

Some implementations may also support nondisplayable auxiliary color buffers. OpenGL does not specify any particular uses for these buffers, so we can define and use them in our own way.

We can use the parameters GL_STEREO or GL_DOUBLEBUFFER for **glGetBooleanv**() to find out whether our system supports stereo or double-buffering, and use parameter GL_AUX_BUFFERS to find out how many auxiliary buffers are present.

Depth Buffer

The depth buffer is also called z buffer. It stores a depth value (z coordinate) for each pixel. It is used to remove any hidden-surface in the scene. We usually measure depth in terms of distance to the viewpoint, so pixels with larger depth-buffer values are overwritten by pixels with smaller values.

Accumulation Buffer

The accumulation buffer is simply an extra image buffer that is used to accumulate composite images. It is typically used for accumulating a series of images into a final, composite image to create some special graphics effects such as antialiasing, depth-of-field, and motion blur. We shall use this buffer to create stereoscopic images by accumulating images for the left and right eyes. The accumulation buffer stores RGBA color data just like the color buffers do in RGBA mode. Actually, we do not draw directly into the accumulation buffer; accumulation operations are always performed in rectangular blocks, usually transferring data to or from a color buffer.

Stencil Buffer

The data in a stencil buffer do not represent colors or depths but have application-specific meanings. Unlike the data of a color buffer, the stencil buffer data are not directly visible. By calling the stencil function and the stencil operations, we can change the bits in the stencil planes.

We can also use the stencil function along with a stencil test to control whether we want to discard a fragment. Also we can make use of the stencil operation to determine how we update the stencil planes.

A common use for the stencil buffer is to restrict drawing to certain portions of the screen. For example, if we want to draw an image as it would appear through a window of a train, we can store an image of the window's shape in the stencil buffer, and then draw the entire scene. The stencil buffer prevents anything that are not visible through the window from being drawn. Therefore, if our application is a simulation of a running train, we can draw all the items inside the train only once, and as the train moves, we only need to update the outside scene. Another example of application is the use of stencil buffer to define a shadow volume in the process of creating shadows; we only shadow objects within the shadow volume.

Clearing Buffers

It is always computing-expensive to clear the screen or a constituent of the frame buffer. To clear a 512×512 RGBA color buffer requires clearing a memory of more than one million bytes. It may take more time to clear a buffer than computing the drawing of the scene in a simple graphics application. Very often, a machine has special hardware to handle the buffer-clearing process.

OpenGL provides a number of functions to specify values to clear the buffers:

    void glClearColor(float red, float $green$, float $blue$, float $alpha$);
    void glClearIndex(float $index$);
    void glClearDepth(double $depth$);
    void glClearStencil(int s);
    void glClearAccum(float red, float $green$, float $blue$, float $alpha$);

The above functions are for clearing the color buffer in RGBA mode, the color buffer in color-index mode, the depth buffer, the stencil buffer, and the accumulation buffer respectively with the values specified by the parameters passed to their arguments. The color values are clamped to be between 0.0 and 1.0. The default clearing values for the functions are 0 except the depth-clearing value, which is defaulted to 1.0. The actual clearing occurs when the command **glClear**() is executed with the specified buffer. For example, the commands,

    glClearColor(1.0, 1.0, 1.0, 0);
    glClear(GL_COLOR_BUFFER_BIT);

will fill the color buffer with white color values.

6.2 Depth Test

When rendering a graphics scene, we do not want to display a fragment which is from an object behind another opaque object. The elimination of parts of solid objects that are obscured by others is called **hidden-surface removal**. Back face culling is also a form of hidden-surface removal. From another point of view, hidden-surface removal is to discover what part of a surface is visible to the viewer and thus the process is also referred to as **visible-surface determination**. There are two approaches to do this. One approach is to use visible-surface algorithms to find the surfaces that are visible. The other approach is to use hidden-surface-removal algorithms to remove those surfaces that should not be visible to the viewer, and there are two types of such algorithms:

1. **Object-space algorithms** attempt to order the surfaces of the objects in the scene according to their distances from the viewer so that drawing surfaces in a particular order provides the correct image. These algorithms may not work well with pipeline architectures. The **painter's algorithm** is an example of such algorithms. It works as follows:

(a) First draw the objects that are farthest from the viewpoint.
(b) Continue to draw objects from far to near and draw the closest objects last.
(c) Objects drawn later overwrite those drawn earlier at the same location of the projection plane just like the way we paint. Consequently, the nearer objects will obscure the farther objects as we draw from far to near.

Painter's algorithm is very simple and there are variants of it. The problem of this algorithm is that objects must be drawn in a particular order based upon their distances from the viewpoint. If the viewing position is changed, the drawing order must be changed.

2. **Image-space algorithms** work as part of the projection process. Such an algorithm finds the relationship among object points in each projection step. This works well with pipeline architectures.

The **z-buffer algorithm** is the most commonly used algorithm of this type. OpenGL also uses the z-buffer algorithm to remove hidden surfaces. The feature is enabled by the command:

glEnable (GL_DEPTH_TEST);

6.2.1   The z-Buffer Algorithm

Because of its ease of implementation and fitting naturally with pipeline architectures, the z-**buffer algorithm** is the most widely used hidden-surface removal algorithm. The algorithm uses a depth or z buffer to keep track of the distance from the projection plane to each point of the object. For each pixel position, the frame buffer only retains the point of the surface that has the smallest z coordinate. Very often, the depth or z values are normalized to values in the range $[0, 1]$. During the rendering process, the depth-buffer value (normalized z coordinate) $d[i][j]$ contains the depth of the closest object rendered so far at that pixel. As the rendering process proceeds pixel by pixel across a scanline and fills the face of the current polygon, the algorithm tests whether the depth of current point of the face is less than the depth $d[i][j]$ stored in the depth-buffer at the corresponding location. If so, the color of the point of the closer surface replaces the color $c[i][j]$ of the color buffer, and this smaller depth replaces the old value in $d[i][j]$, otherwise no replacement takes place. Polygons and other graphics primitives such as lines and points can be drawn in any order. The following is the algorithm in detail:

1. Clear the color buffer to the background color.
2. Initialize the values at all locations of the depth buffer to 1.
3. For each fragment of each surface, compare depth values to those already stored in the depth buffer:
   (a) Calculate the distance from the projection plane for each xy position on the surface.
   (b) Normalize the distance to $[0, 1]$, which is the depth value of the fragment.
   (c) If the distance is less than the value currently stored in the depth buffer,
       i. set the corresponding position in the color buffer to the color of the fragment,
       ii. set the value in the depth buffer to the distance to that object,
       otherwise
           leave the color and depth buffers unchanged.

Note that specialized hardware depth buffers are much faster than software buffers, and the number of bitplanes associated with the depth buffer determines the depth precision or resolution.

6.2.2   OpenGL z-Buffering

OpenGL uses z-buffering for hidden-surface removal. As we have mentioned above, the z buffer is also referred to as depth buffer. Since using a depth buffer means we need a lot of extra memory, we have to inform OpenGL our request of the extra memory. This can be done in the initialization steps using a command like the following:

glutInitDisplayMode (GLUT_DOUBLE | GLUT_RGB | GLUT_DEPTH);

Before using the depth buffer, we must enable it and clear it. Very often, we clear the depth buffer whenever we clear the color buffer. This is done by the command,

glClear (GL_COLOR_BUFFER_BIT | GL_DEPTH_BUFFER_BIT);

Depth test is enabled by

glEnable (GL_DEPTH_TEST);

and disabled by

glDisable (GL_DEPTH_TEST);

We use the function **glDepthFunc**() to set the comparison function for the depth test. This function specifies the function used to compare each incoming pixel depth value with the depth value present in the depth buffer. The comparison is performed only if depth testing is enabled. Its syntax is as follows:

void glDepthFunc (GLenum $func$);

where $func$ specifies the comparison function, which may be

GL_NEVER, GL_ALWAYS, GL_LESS, GL_LEQUAL, GL_EQUAL, GL_GEQUAL,
GL_GREATER, or GL_NOTEQUAL

For example, when $func$ is GL_GEQUAL, the depth test passes if the incoming pixel depth value is greater than or equal to the stored depth value. The default of $func$ is GL_LESS. Initially, depth testing is turned off (disabled). If depth testing is disabled or if no depth buffer exists, the program works as if the depth test always passes. Table 6-2 lists all the valid values of $func$ and their meanings.

Table 6-2   Valid Parameters for **glDepthFunc**()

func	Depth Test
GL_NEVER	Never passes.
GL_LESS	Passes if the incoming depth value is less than the stored depth value.
GL_EQUAL	Passes if the incoming depth value is equal to the stored depth value.
GL_LEQUAL	Passes if the incoming depth value is less than or equal to the stored depth value.
GL_GREATER	Passes if the incoming depth value is greater than the stored depth value.
GL_NOTEQUAL	Passes if the incoming depth value is not equal to the stored depth value.
GL_GEQUAL	Passes if the incoming depth value is greater than or equal to the stored depth value.
GL_ALWAYS	Always passes.

We can turn on depth buffering by

glEnable(GL_DEPTH_TEST);

and turn it off by

glDisable(GL_DEPTH_TEST);

Each time prior to drawing the scene, we clear the depth buffer when we clear the color buffer in the display callback:

glClear (GL_COLOR_BUFFER_BIT | GL_DEPTH_BUFFER_BIT | ...);

We usually use a single **glClear** command to clear all buffers.

If necessary, we may change the depth range so that z values may lie in a range other than $[0, 1]$. This is done using

void **glDepthRange**(GLclampd $near$, GLclampd far);

where $near$ and far specify the minimum and maximum values that can be stored in the depth buffer. By default, $near$ and far are 0.0 and 1.0 respectively. The data type **GLclampd** specifies a floating-point (double) value clamped to $[0, 1]$.

We can also enable or disable writing to the depth buffer using the following command:

void **glDepthMask**(GLboolean $flag$);

where $flag$ specifies whether the depth buffer is enabled for writing:

- GL_TRUE enables writing
- GL_FALSE disables writing

Writing is enabled by default. When writing is disabled, the depth buffer is read-only; its value will not be changed after a depth test.

We can similarly use the function **glColorMask**() to enable or disable the writing of a color component to the color buffer:

void glColorMask(GLboolean $rflag$, GLboolean $gflag$, GLboolean $bflag$,
GLboolean $aflag$);

The parameters $rflag, gflag, bflag$, and $aflag$ are flags specifing whether red, green, blue, and alpha color components can or cannot be written into the color buffer. For example, if $bflag$ is GL_FALSE, no change is made to the blue component of any pixel in any of the color buffers, regardless of the drawing operation we have used. Note that we cannot control changes to individual bits of components. Rather, changes are either enabled or disabled for entire color components. The initial values of all the flags are GL_TRUE, indicating that we can write the color components to the buffer. Making use of this function, we can easily create a red-blue stereoscopic pair of images; when creating the red image, we enable only the writing of the red component and when creating the blue image, we enable only the writing of the blue component. We shall have more detailed discussions and examples on this in later chapters.

6.3 Writing to Buffers

We have learned the principles and usage of the buffers in OpenGL. In an application, we may want to read and write into the buffers directly and we would like to do these efficiently. OpenGL provides a few functions to transfer data to and from these buffers in large chunks.

In general, we call a frame buffer with one bit per pixel a **bitmap**, and a frame buffer with multiple bits per pixel a **pixmap**. We also use these terms to describe other rectangular arrays;

we may refer to any pattern of binary values as a bitmap, and multicolor pattern as a pixmap. Specifications for a pixel array may consist of a pointer to the color matrix, the size of the matrix, and the position and size of the screen area involved in the data reading or writing. Figure 6-1 shows an example of data transfer of an $m \times n$ block of pixels from a **source buffer** to another buffer, the **destination buffer**. Sometimes the source buffer and the destination buffer can be the same constituent of the frame buffer.

In Figure 6-1, the operation writes an $m \times n$ source block whose lower-left corner is at (x_0, y_0) to the destination buffer starting at a location (u_0, v_0). The transfer of the entire block is usually performed by a single function call in the following form:

writeBlock (*source*, x_0, y_0, *destination*, u_0, v_0, m, n);

where *source* and *destination* points to the memory locations of the source and destination blocks respectively.

In OpenGL, the commands that perform block data transfer include **glReadPixels()**, **glDrawPixels()**, **glCopyPixels()**, and **glBitmap()**. Some commands require the functions **glRasterPos*()** to help specify the frame buffer location that the data are read from or written to. We discuss these functions below.

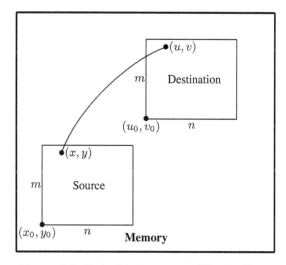

Figure 6-1   Transfer of an $m \times n$ Block of Data

6.3.1   OpenGL Pixel-Array Function

OpenGL provides a bitmap function and a pixmap function to define a shape or pattern specified by a rectangular array. Also, OpenGL provides several other functions for saving, copying, and manipulating arrays of pixel values.

Bitmap Function

The OpenGL functions **glRasterPos*()** and **glBitmap()** specify the position and draw a single bitmap on the screen. The commands **glPasterPos*()** specify the current raster position which is the origin where the next bitmap is to be drawn. The suffix codes and parameters are the same as those for the **glVertex** functions. Therefore, a current raster position is specified in world coordinates, and it is transformed to screen coordinates by the modelview and projective transformations. The color for the bitmap is the color that is in effect when the **glRasterPos** command is invoked.

Any subsequent color changes do not affect the bitmap. Once we have set the desired raster position, we can use the **glBitmap**() function to draw the scene specified by the data passed to the function:

$$\text{void glBitmap}\quad(\text{GLsizei } width, \text{ GLsizei } height, \text{ GLfloat } x0, \text{ GLfloat } y0,$$
$$\text{GLfloat } xi, \text{ GLfloat } yi, \text{ const GLubyte } *bitmap);$$

where $bitmap$ is a pointer to the bitmap image to be drawn. The origin of the bitmap image is at the current raster position. If the current raster position is invalid, nothing is drawn or changed. We use the arguments $width$ and $height$ to specify the width and height, in pixels, of the bitmap image. i We use the parameters $x0$ and $y0$ to define the origin of the bitmap image relative to the current raster position; a positive $x0$ shifts the origin right and a positive $y0$ shifts it upwards relative to the raster position. Negative values shift it down and left. Parameters xi and yi specify the x and y increments that are added to the raster position after the bitmap has been rasterized. This means that xi and yi are measured in pixels rather than world coordinates. After the bitmap image has been drawn, the current raster position is advanced by xi and yi in the x and y directions respectively. Figure 6-2 below shows an example illustrating these parameters, with $width = 10$, $height = 12$, $(x0, y0) = (0, 0)$, and $(xi, yi) = (11, 0)$; each square represents a pixel.

Figure 6-3 shows an example of a bitmap which is the image pattern of an upward arrow. In this example, the width is 9 pixels and the height is 10 pixels. The image is saved in a rectangular bit array where each row of it is stored in multiples of 8 bits (16 here) and the binary data are arranged as a set of 8-bit unsigned characters. When this image pattern is applied to the pixels in the frame buffer, all bit values beyond the 9-th column are ignored. Suppose we are going to draw this bitmap and that the current raster color is green. Wherever there is a 1 in the bitmap, the corresponding pixel is replaced by a green pixel. If there is a 0 in the bitmap, the contents of the pixel are unaffected. Therefore, an upward arrow will be drawn using this bitmap. Actually, the most common use of bitmaps is for drawing characters on the screen.

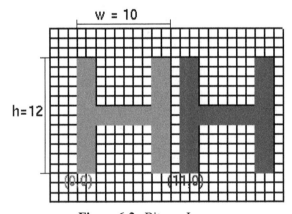

Figure 6-2 Bitmap Image

```
9 │0│0│0│0│1│0│0│0│0│0│0│0│ │ │ │ │   0x08  0x00
  │0│0│0│1│1│1│0│0│0│0│0│0│ │ │ │ │   0x1c  0x00
  │0│0│1│1│1│1│1│0│0│0│0│0│ │ │ │ │   0x3e  0x00
  │0│1│1│1│1│1│1│1│0│0│0│0│ │ │ │ │   0x7f  0x00
  │1│1│1│1│1│1│1│1│1│0│0│0│ │ │ │ │   0xff  0x80
  │0│0│0│1│1│1│0│0│0│0│0│0│ │ │ │ │   0x1c  0x00
  │0│0│0│1│1│1│0│0│0│0│0│0│ │ │ │ │   0x1c  0x00
  │0│0│0│1│1│1│0│0│0│0│0│0│ │ │ │ │   0x1c  0x00
  │0│0│0│1│1│1│0│0│0│0│0│0│ │ │ │ │   0x1c  0x00
0 │0│0│0│1│1│1│0│0│0│0│0│0│ │ │ │ │   0x1c  0x00
   0               8    11        15
```

Figure 6-3 10×9 Bit Pattern Saved in 10×16 Block

We can display the arrow image of Figure 6-3 by applying the bit pattern to a frame buffer location with the following code:

```
void display(void)
{
   glMatrixMode(GL_PROJECTION);
   glLoadIdentity();
   glOrtho (-1.0, 1.0, -1.0, 1.0, -10.0, 10.0);
   glClearColor (1.0, 1.0, 1.0, 0.0);
   glClear (GL_COLOR_BUFFER_BIT );
   glColor4f(0, 0, 0, 0);
   GLubyte arrow[20] = {0x1c, 0x00, 0x1c, 0x00, 0x1c, 0x00,
                        0x1c, 0x00, 0x1c, 0x00, 0xff, 0x80,
                        0x7f, 0x00, 0x3e, 0x00, 0x1c, 0x00,
                        0x08, 0x00};
   //set pixel storage mode, byte-alignment
   glPixelStorei(GL_UNPACK_ALIGNMENT,1);
   glRasterPos2f( 0.1, 0.2 );
   glBitmap ( 9, 10, 0, 0, 20, 30, arrow );
   glBitmap ( 9, 10, 0, 0, 20, 30, arrow );
   glBitmap ( 9, 10, 0, 0, 20, 30, arrow );
}
```

In the above code, we specify the array values for $arrow$ row by row, starting at the bottom of the rectangular-grid pattern as shown in Figure 6-3. We set the storage mode of the bitmap using the the function **glPixelStorei**(). The parameter GL_UNPACK_ALIGNMENT specifies the alignment requirements for the start of each pixel row in memory. The allowable values are 1 (byte-alignment), 2 (rows aligned to even-numbered bytes), 4 (word-alignment), and 8 (rows start on double-word boundaries). We have used the value 1 in the code. Thus, the data values are to be aligned on byte-boundaries. We use the function **glRasterPos2f**() to set the current raster position to $(0.1, 0.2)$, which are in world coordinates. The parameters to the function **glBitmap**() indicate that the bit pattern is given in the array $arrow$, and that this array has 9 columns (width) and 10 rows (height). The location of this pattern in the block is $(0, 0)$, which is the lower left corner of the grid. We illustrate a raster position increment with values $(20, 30)$ which are the offset between two successive arrows drawn; after each call to the function **glBitmap**(), the raster position is incremented by this amount in **pixels**. Therefore, the code displays three arrows, each with displacement $(20, 30)$ relative to the preceding one. Figure 6-4 shows the output of the code.

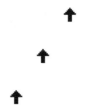

Figure 6-4 Output Of Bitmap Example Code

Pixmap Function

A **pixmap** is a general **image** which is similar to a bitmap, but instead of containing only a single bit for each pixel in a rectangular region of the screen, a pixmap can contain much more information such as a complete (R, G, B, A) color of each pixel. The image sources of a pixmap include the following,

1. a photo image that is taken by a digital camera,
2. a photograph that is digitized with a scanner,
3. an image that was first generated on the screen by a graphics program using the graphics hardware. and then read back, pixel by pixel, and
4. a software program that generates the image in memory pixel by pixel.

OpenGL provides three functions for manipulating image data:

1. **glReadPixels** () – Reads a rectangular array of pixels from the frame buffer and stores the data in processor memory.
2. **glDrawPixels**() – Writes a rectangular array of pixels from data kept in processor memory into the frame buffer at the current raster position specified by glRasterPos*().
3. **glCopyPixels**() – Copies a rectangular array of pixels from one part of the frame buffer to another. This function behaves similarly to a call to **glReadPixels**() followed by a call to **glDrawPixels**(), except that the data are never written into processor memory.

Figure 6-5 shows the OpenGL pixel data flow and the tasks of these functions.

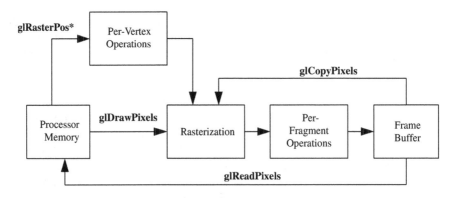

Figure 6-5 Pixel Data Flow

6.3.2   Pixel Data Block Transfer

The three pixmap functions discussed above provide an efficient way to transfer data between the processor memory and the frame buffer in large blocks. The following shows more details of these functions.

> void **glReadPixels**(GLint $x0$, GLint $y0$, GLsizei $width$, GLsizei $height$,
>   GLenum $format$, GLenum $type$, GLvoid *$pixels$);
> Reads pixel data from the framebuffer rectangle whose lower-left corner is at $(x0, y0)$ in screen coordinates (pixels) and whose dimensions are $width$ and $height$ and stores it in the array pointed to by $pixels$. Parameter $format$ indicates the kind of pixel data elements that are read (an index value or an R, G, B, or A component value, as listed in Table 6-1 below), and $type$ indicates the data type of each element shown below.

> void **glDrawPixels**(GLsizei $width$, GLsizei $height$, GLenum $format$,
>   GLenum $type$, const GLvoid *$pixels$);
> Draws a rectangle of pixel data with dimensions $width$ and $height$. The pixel rectangle is drawn with its lower-left corner at the current raster position. Parameters $format$ and $type$ have the same meaning as with **glReadPixels**(). The array pointed to by $pixels$ contains the pixel data to be drawn.

> void **glCopyPixels**(GLint $x0$, GLint $y0$, GLsizei $width$, GLsizei $height$,
>   GLenum $buffer$);
> Copies pixel data from the frame buffer rectangular region whose lower-left corner is at $(x0, y0)$ and whose dimensions are $width$ and $height$. The data are copied to a new position whose lower-left corner is given by the current raster position. Parameter $buffer$ is either GL_COLOR, GL_STENCIL, or GL_DEPTH, specifying the frame buffer that is used. **glCopyPixels**() behaves similarly to a **glReadPixels**() followed by a **glDrawPixels**(), with the following translation for the $buffer$ to $format$ parameter:

- If $buffer$ is GL_DEPTH or GL_STENCIL, then GL_DEPTH_COMPONENT or GL_STENCIL_INDEX is used respectively.
- If GL_COLOR is specified, then GL_RGBA or GL_COLOR_INDEX is used, depending on whether the system is in RGBA or color-index mode.

Table 6-1   Pixel Formats for **glReadPixels**() or **glDrawPixels**()

Format Constant	Pixel Format
GL_COLOR_INDEX	A single color index
GL_RGB	Red, green, blue color components
GL_RGBA	Red, green, blue, alpha color components
GL_RED	A single red color component
GL_GREEN	A single green color component
GL_BLUE	A single blue color component
GL_ALPHA	A single alpha color component
GL_LUMINANCE	A single luminance component
GL_LUMINANCE_ALPHA	A luminance component followed by an alpha
GL_STENCIL_INDEX	A single stencil index
GL_DEPTH_COMPONENT	A single depth component

Example 6-1

This example presents a code section shown below that displays a 16×16 checker board of alternate black and white squares on the screen. Each black or white square is 16×16 pixels. It uses **glDrawPixels()** to draw a pixel rectangle in the lower-left corner of a window. The function **getBoard()** creates a 256×256 RGBA array representing the black-and-white checker board image. The function call **glRasterPos2i**(0,0) positions the lower-left corner of the image at the origin of the world coordinate system. The output of this code is shown in Figure 6-6.

```
const int width = 256, height = 256;
unsigned char board[width][height][4];

//create checker board image
void getBoard(void)
{
  int  c;

  for ( int i = 0; i < width; i++ ) {
    for ( int j = 0; j < height; j++ ) { //start from lower-left corner
      c = ((((i&16)==0)^((j&16))==0))*255; //0 or 255-->black or white
      board[i][j][0] =  c; //red component
      board[i][j][1] =  c; //green component
      board[i][j][2] =  c; //blue  component
    }
  }
}

//initialization
void init(void)
{
  glClearColor (0.8, 0.8, 1.0, 1.0);
  glShadeModel (GL_FLAT);
  getBoard();    //create checker image array
  //Sets pixel-storage mode: byte-aligned
  glPixelStorei(GL_UNPACK_ALIGNMENT, 1);
}

void display(void)
{
  glClear(GL_COLOR_BUFFER_BIT);
  glRasterPos2i(0, 0);
  glDrawPixels(width, height, GL_RGBA, GL_UNSIGNED_BYTE, board);
  glFlush();
}
```

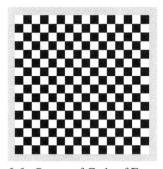

Figure 6-6 Output of Code of Example 6-1

6.4   Displaying and Saving Images

OpenGL does not provide functions to handle images in standard formats such as PNG, JPEG, TIFF, GIF, and PPM. This is because there exists too many proprietary image and video file formats, each with clear strengths and weaknesses. The file formats are generally not a user-defined option and many of the features are specified by the vendors. Because of the lack of OpenGL support, we have to write our own routines to read image data from files to the frame buffer or to take images formed in the frame buffer and save them in a standard format. We are certainly interested in exploring all the file formats. Often, we may use some open-source libraries to process the images. As an illustration of the basic ideas of OpenGL pixel functions, here we develop our own simple routines that read and write data in the PPM format, which is the simplest of all image formats. We shall also discuss a couple of simple standard formats and some related tools that can convert from one format to the other.

6.4.1   Portable Pixel Map (PPM)

The Portable Pixel Map (PPM) file format is a lowest and simplest common denominator color image format. A PPM file contains very little information about the image besides basic colors and the data are not compressed. Therefore, it is easy to write programs to process the file, which is the purpose of this format. A PPM file consists of a sequence of one or more PPM images. There are no data, delimiters, or padding before, after, or between images. The PPM format closely relates to two other bitmap formats, the PBM format, which stands for Portable Bitmap (a monochrome bitmap), and PGM format, which stands for Portable Gray Map (a gray scale bitmap). All these formats are not compressed and consequently the files stored in these formats are usually quite large. In addition, the PNM format means any of the three bitmap formats. You may use the unix manual command **man** to learn the details of the PPM format:

$**man ppm**

The three bitmap formats can be stored in two possible representations:

1. an ASCII text representation (which is extremely verbose), and
2. a binary representation (which is comparatively smaller).

Each PPM image consists of the following (taken from unix ppm manual):

1. A "magic number" for identifying the file type. A ppm image's magic number is the two characters "P6".
2. Whitespace (blanks, TABs, CRs, LFs).
3. A width, formatted as ASCII characters in decimal.
4. Whitespace.
5. A height, again in ASCII decimal.
6. Whitespace.
7. The maximum color value (*Maxval*), again in ASCII decimal. Must be less than 65536 and more than zero.
8. Newline or other single whitespace character.
9. A raster of *Height* rows, in order from top to bottom. Each row consists of *Width* pixels, in order from left to right. Each pixel is a triplet of red, green, and blue samples, in that order. Each sample is represented in pure binary by either 1 or 2 bytes. If the *Maxval* is less than 256, it is 1 byte. Otherwise, it is 2 bytes. The most significant byte is first. A row of an image is horizontal. A column is vertical. The pixels in the image are square and contiguous.

10. In the raster, the sample values are "nonlinear". They are proportional to the intensity of the ITU-R Recommendation BT.709 red, green, and blue.

In summary, a PPM file has a header and a body, which may be created using a text editor. The header is very small with the following properties:

1. The first line contains the magic identifier "P3" or "P6".
2. The second line contains the *width* and *height* of the image in ascii code.
3. The last part of the header is the maximum color intensity integer value.
4. Comments are preceded by the symbol #.

Here are some header examples:

Header example 1

```
P6 1024 788 255
```

Header example 2

```
P6
1024 788
# A comment
255
```

Header example 3

```
P3
1024   # the image width
788    # the image height
       # A comment
1023
```

The following is an example of a PPM file in P3 format.

```
P3
# feep.ppm
4 4
15
0   0   0     0   0   0     0   0   0    15   0  15
0   0   0     0  15   7     0   0   0     0   0   0
0   0   0     0   0   0     0  15   7     0   0   0
15   0  15     0   0   0     0   0   0     0   0   0
```

You can simply use a text editor to create it; for example, copy-and-paste the content into a file named "feep.ppm", which then becomes a PPM file and can be viewed by a browser or the unix utility **xview**. When you execute the unix command,

$ xview feep.ppm

you should see a tiny image appear on the upper left corner of your screen along with the following messages displayed in the console,

```
feep.ppm is a 4x4 PPM image with 16 levels
  Building XImage...done
```

6.4.2   The **Convert** Utility

Once we obtain an image in PPM format, we can easily convert it to other popular formats such as PNG, JPG, or GIF using the **convert** utility, which is a member of the ImageMagick suite of tools. Conversely, if you obtain an image from other sources in another format, you may also use **convert** to convert it to the PPM format. Besides making conversion between image formats, the utility can also resize an image, blur, crop, despeckle, dither, draw on, flip, join, re-sample, and do much more. It can even create an image from text. We use the unix manual command to see the details of its usage:

   $ **man convert**

We can also run 'convert -help' to get a summary of its command options. The following are some simple examples of its usage.

```
$convert feep.ppm  feep.png
$convert house.jpg house.ppm
$convert house.jpg -resize 60% house.png
$convert -size 128x32 xc:transparent -font \
    Bookman-DemiItalic -pointsize 28 -channel RGBA \
    -gaussian 0x4 -fill lightgreen -stroke green \
    -draw "text 0,20 'Freedom'" freedom.png
```

The last command creates a PNG (Portable Network Graphics) file named "freedom.png" from the text "Freedom". Figure 6-7 shows the image thus created.

Figure 6-7   Image Created by **convert**

If you want to convert a PDF file to PPM, you may use the utility **pdftoppm**. You may run **"pdftoppm –help"** to find out the details of its usage.

6.4.3   Read and Write PPM Files

To process any PPM and related graphics file, you may use the the **netpbm** library, which can be downloaded from the Internet at

   http://netpbm.sourceforge.net

However, for the purpose of this book, we just need something very simple to read or write a PPM file. In this section, we present a simple C program that shows how to read or write a PPM file.

The C/C++ program shown in **Listing 6-1** briefly demonstrates the reading and writing of PPM files; the file names and some parameters are hard-coded; the class **CImage** with public members *red, green*, and *blue* is used to save the color data of one pixel. In a C++ program, a public **class** is the same as a C **struct**.

   Program Listing 6-1   Read and Write PPM Files

```
-----------------------------------------------------------------
/* ppmdemo.cpp
 * Demostrate read and write of PPM files.
 */
//A public class is the same as a 'struct'
class CImage {
public:
  unsigned char red;
  unsigned char green;
```

```
    unsigned char blue;
};

// Create PPM header from image width and height. "P6" format used.
// PPM header returned in integer array ppmh[].
void make_ppm_header ( int ppmh[], int width, int height )
{
  //standard header data, 'P' = 0x50, '6' = 0x36, '\n' = 0x0A
  int ca[] = {0x50, 0x36, 0x0A,                    //"P6"
      //image width=260, height = 288
      0x33, 0x36, 0x30, 0x20, 0x32, 0x38,
              //color levels / pixel = 256
              0x38, 0x0A, 0x32, 0x35, 0x35, 0x0A };

  //only have to change width and height
  char temp[10], k;

  sprintf(temp, "%3d", width );              //width in ascii code
  k = 0;
  for ( int i = 3; i <= 5; ++i )             //replace width
    ca[i] = temp[k++];

  sprintf(temp, "%3d", height );             //height in ascii code
  k = 0;
  for ( int i = 7; i <=9; ++i )              //replace height
    ca[i] = temp[k++];

  for ( int i = 0; i < 15; ++i )             //form header
    ppmh[i] = ca[i];
}

void save_ppmdata (FILE *fp, CImage *ip, int width, int height)
{
  int size = width * height;
  for ( int i = 0; i < size; ++i ){
    putc ( ip[i].red, fp );
    putc ( ip[i].green, fp );
    putc ( ip[i].blue, fp );
  }
}

void ppm_read_comments ( FILE *fp )
{
  int c;
  while ( (c = getc ( fp ) )  == '#' ) {
    while ( getc( fp ) != '\n' )
        ;
  }
  ungetc ( c, fp );
}
.....
------------------------------------------------------------------------
```

6.4.4   Saving Graphics with glReadPixels

With the PPM functions developed in the above section, we can save an OpenGL graphics scene to a PPM file. We first use the function **glReadPixels**() to read the specified scene on the screen into a buffer and then save the data in the buffer in a PPM file. Then we can use the **convert** utility to convert the PPM file to a file in any standard image format such as PNG, JPEG, TIFF, or GIF. The following code section shows an example that saves the graphics scene in the file "teapot.ppm"; the code for error-checking and lighting is omitted here. The scene saved is shown in Figure 6-8.

```
void save_ppmRGB ( FILE *fp, unsigned char *p, int width, int height )
{
  //save data up-side-down
  int k;
  for ( int i = 0; i < height; i++ ) {
    k = (height - 1 - i) * width * 3;
    for ( int j = 0; j < width; j++ ) {
      putc( p[k++], fp );
      putc( p[k++], fp );
      putc( p[k++], fp );
    }
  }
}

void ppm_save_image ( char *n1, int x0, int y0, int width, int height )
{
  unsigned char *imgBuffer;
  imgBuffer = ( unsigned char *) malloc( 3 * width * height );
  //read the screen data to buffer pointed by
  glPixelStorei(GL_PACK_ALIGNMENT, 1);
  glReadPixels(x0,y0, width,height, GL_RGB, GL_UNSIGNED_BYTE, imgBuffer);

  int ppmh[20], c;                    //PPM header
  make_ppm_header ( ppmh, width, height );
  FILE *fpo = fopen ( n1, "wb" );
  for ( int i = 0; i < 15; ++i )    //save PPM header
    putc ( ppmh[i], fpo );
  save_ppmRGB ( fpo, imgBuffer, width, height );
  fclose ( fpo );
  delete imgBuffer;
}

void display(void)
{
  glClear(GL_COLOR_BUFFER_BIT | GL_DEPTH_BUFFER_BIT);
  glMatrixMode (GL_PROJECTION);
  glLoadIdentity ();                   // clear the matrix
  glFrustum (-1.0, 1.0, -1.0, 1.0, 1.5, 20.0);
  glMatrixMode (GL_MODELVIEW);
  glLoadIdentity();
  gluLookAt ( 0.0, 0.0, 5.0, 0.0, 0.0, 0.0, 0.0, 1.0, 0.0);
  glColor3f (1.0, 0.0, 0.0);       //red color
  glutSolidTeapot( 0.6 );          //draw a teapot
  glColor3f (0.0, 1.0, 0.0);       //green color
  glTranslatef(-0.5, -0.5, -1.0);
  glutSolidSphere( 0.6, 40, 40 );//draw a sphere
  glFlush ();
  int x0 = 140, y0 = 160, width = 200, height = 150;
  ppm_save_image ( "teapot.ppm", x0, y0, width, height );
}
```

Note that in the function **save_ppmRGB**(), we save the image data in the buffer *imgBuffer* in an "up-side-down" manner. This is because **glReadPixels** considers the lower-left corner of the screen window as $(0, 0)$ but the PPM image format considers the upper-left corner as $(0, 0)$.

We can view the image from the program with the UNIX command "**xview teapot.ppm**" which displays the image as shown in Figure 6-8 along with the following message:

```
$ xview teapot.ppm
teapot.ppm is a 200x150 Raw PPM image with 256 levels
  Building XImage...done
```

Figure 6-8   PPM Image Created by Above Code

The command "convert teapot.ppm teapot.png" converts the PPM data to PNG format.

6.4.5   Displaying PPM Images with glDrawPixels

If we want to display a PPM image in an OpenGL application, we can use the function **glRead-Pixels**() to do so. The following code section demontrates how this is done; it calls the function **read_ppm_image**() to read in the data of the ppm file "../data/soolee.ppm" into a buffer. The function then uses **glDrawPixels**() to display the image at the specified location $(x0, y0)$ which is $(0, 0)$ in the example. The code also uses the function **glutSolidSphere**() to create a sphere that simulates an exaggerated table tennis ball and superimpose it on the PPM image. The error-checking statements are omitted in the program. (Readers can download complete programs which may contain error-checking statements from this book's web site.) The output of the code is shown in Figure 6-9.

```
void read_ppm_image( char *n1, float x0, float y0 )
{
  FILE *fpi = fopen( n1, "rb");
  int width, height, c, colorlevels;;
  unsigned char *imgBuffer;
  char temp[100];

  ppm_read_comments ( fpi );
  fscanf ( fpi, "%2s", temp );
  temp[3] = 0;
  if ( strncmp ( temp, "P6", 2 ) )
    throw ppm_error();
  ppm_read_comments ( fpi );
  fscanf ( fpi, "%d", &width );
  ppm_read_comments ( fpi );
  fscanf ( fpi, "%d", &height );
  ppm_read_comments ( fpi );
  fscanf ( fpi, "%d", &colorlevels );
  ppm_read_comments ( fpi );
  while ( ( c = getc ( fpi )) == '\n' );//get rid of extra line returns
  ungetc ( c , fpi);

  imgBuffer = ( unsigned char *) malloc( 3 * width * height );
  //read image up-side down
  int k;
  for ( int i = 0; i < height; i++ ) {
    k = (height - 1 - i) * width * 3;
    for ( int j = 0; j < width; j++ ) {
```

```
        imgBuffer[k++] = (unsigned char) getc( fpi );
        imgBuffer[k++] = (unsigned char) getc( fpi );
        imgBuffer[k++] = (unsigned char) getc( fpi );
    }
  }

  //read data pointed by imgBuffer to frame buffer for display
  glPixelStorei(GL_UNPACK_ALIGNMENT, 1);
  glRasterPos2f ( x0, y0 );
  glDrawPixels(width, height, GL_RGB, GL_UNSIGNED_BYTE, imgBuffer);

  fclose ( fpi );
  delete imgBuffer;
}

void display(void)
{
   glClear(GL_COLOR_BUFFER_BIT | GL_DEPTH_BUFFER_BIT);
   glMatrixMode (GL_PROJECTION);
   glLoadIdentity ();                    // clear the matrix
   glOrtho (-1.0, 1.0, -1.0, 1.0, -10.0, 10.0);
   glMatrixMode (GL_MODELVIEW);
   glLoadIdentity();
   float x0 = -1.0, y0 = -1.0;
   read_ppm_image ("../data/soolee.ppm", x0, y0);
   glColor3f (1.0, 0.8, 0.0);
   glutSolidSphere( 0.2, 40, 40 );//draw a ball
   glFlush ();
}
```

Figure 6-9   Display PPM Image Using glDrawPixels

6.4.6   Portable Network Graphics (PNG)

We have seen that PPM image format is very simple and easy to process. It is an excellent format for illustration and testing certain graphics programming concepts. However, the data are stored without any compression and the header contains only very little information about the image data. If we want to read and write image data from and to a file more efficiently, it is better to use one of the more sophisticated open standards. We feel that the best open format that we should use is the **portable network graphics** (PNG), which is an open, extensible image format with lossless compression and the following features:

1. It is designed in 1995 specifically in response to the patent problems with the LZW algorithm used in GIF.
2. It is 'completely' patent-free.
3. It supports alpha channels and allows up to 254 levels of partial transparency.
4. It supports gamma correction.
5. One can find more detailed information of PNG at the site *http://www.libpng.org/*.

Instead of writing our own routines to process PNG files, we shall use a simple open-source library to accomplish the task. The library that we shall use is the **imageio library utility** developed by Adrien Treuille of CMU. It is particularly simple to compile and use. One can download the library source code from the site

   http://www.cs.cmu.edu/~treuille/resc/imageio/

or from this book's web site. This simple library allows users read and write png and tiff files. The package consists of the program "imageio.cpp" and the header file "imageio.h". Assuming that the OpenGL directories are accessible, we can compile the program with the command,

   g++ -c imageio.cpp

which generates the object file "imageio.o". To use the functions of the programs, we include the header file "imageio.h" in our application program:

   #include "imageio.h"

Then we link the object file with our application program using a command like the following:

   g++ -o *program program.o* imageio.o -ltiff -lpng

Display PNG Image

We can use **loadImageRGBA**() of **imageio** to read a PNG image into memory:

   unsigned char *loadImageRGBA(unsigned char *fileName*, int *width*, int *height*);

This function returns a pointer pointing to the uncompressed image data loaded from the file specified by *filename*. Parameters *width* and *height* will contain the image width and height respectively. The byte order of images created with this library is compatible with that used by OpenGL. We can use **glDrawPixels** to write the data to screen. The following piece of code is an example of using this function to render an image on the screen:

```
int width, height;
char *filename = "soolee.png";
unsigned char *ibuff = loadImageRGBA( filename, &width, &height);
glPixelStorei(GL_UNPACK_ALIGNMENT, 1);
glRasterPos2f ( 1.0, 2.0 ); //position to display image
glDrawPixels ( width, height, GL_RGBA, GL_UNSIGNED_BYTE, ibuff );
```

Save Graphics Scene in PNG

We can save memory data into a PNG file using the function **saveImageRGBA**() of **imageio**:

bool saveImageRGBA(char *fileName, unsigned char *buffer, int width, int height);

This function returns true if the image data stored in *buffer* is successfully saved in the file specified by *filename*, otherwise it returns false. The parameters *width* and *height* specify the width and height of the image. The following code section is an example that saves a graphics scene into a PNG file:

```
void png_save_image( char *n1, int x0, int y0, int width, int height)
{
  unsigned char *imgBuffer;
  imgBuffer = ( unsigned char *) malloc( 4 * width * height );
  if ( imgBuffer == NULL ) {
    printf("\nError in allocating memory!\n");
    return;
  }
  glPixelStorei(GL_PACK_ALIGNMENT, 1);
  glReadPixels(x0,y0, width,height, GL_RGBA,GL_UNSIGNED_BYTE,imgBuffer);
  saveImageRGBA(n1, imgBuffer, width, height);
  delete imgBuffer;
}
```

Chapter 7   Lighting and Texture

7.1   Importance of Lighting and Local Illumination

Lighting and shading are important features in graphics for making a scene appear more realistic and more understandable. Lighting provides crucial visual cues about the curvature and orientation of surfaces. It also helps viewers perceive a graphics scene having three-dimensionality. Figure 7-1 shows a lit and an unlit sphere drawn in the same way. We can see that the lit sphere gives us a 3D perception but the unlit sphere simply looks like a 2D disk.

Lit Sphere   Unlit Sphere

Figure 7-1   A Lit Sphere and an Unlit Sphere

Shading refers to the process of making colors and brightness vary smoothly across a surface. Gouraud shading and Phong shading are the two most popular shading methods that make use of interpolation to create a smooth appearance to surfaces. We shall discuss a local model of illumination and shading called **Phong lighting model**, which is the simplest and by far the most popular lighting and shading model. This model gives good shading and illumination and we can implement it efficiently in hardware or software. This is also the model that OpenGL has used. Here, we mainly discuss the lighting features and do not address the shading details.

The Phong lighting model (also called Phong illumination or Phong reflection model) is considered as a local model of lighting because it only considers the effects of a light source shining directly on a surface and then being reflected directly to the viewpoint; second bounces are ignored. In general, a local lighting model only considers the light property and direction, the viewer's position, and the object material properties. It considers only the first bounce of the light ray but ignores any secondary reflections, which are light rays that are reflected for more than once by surfaces before reaching the viewpoint. Nor does a basic local model consider shadows created by light. Actually, the Phong model is not based on real physics but on empirical graphical experience. The model consists of the following features:

1. All light sources are modeled as point light sources.
2. Light is composed of red (R), green (G), and blue (B) colors.
3. Light reflection intensities can be calculated independently using the principle of superposition for each light source and for each of the 3 color components (R, G, B). Therefore, we describe a source through a three-component intensity or illumination vector

$$\mathbf{I} = \begin{pmatrix} R \\ G \\ B \end{pmatrix} \tag{7.1}$$

Each of the components of $\mathbf{I}$ in (7.1) is the intensity of the independent red, green, and blue components.

107

4. There are three distinct kinds of light or illumination that contribute to the computation of the final illumination of an object:

- **Ambient Light**: light that arrives equally from all directions. We use this to model the kind of light that has been scattered so much by its environment that we cannot tell its original source direction. Therefore, ambient light shines uniformly on a surface regardless of its orientation. The position of an ambient light source is meaningless.
- **Diffuse Light**: light from a point source that will be reflected diffusely. We use this to model the kind of light that is reflected evenly in all directions away from the surface. (Of course, in reality this depends on the surface, not the light itself. As we mentioned earlier, this model is not based on real physics but on graphical experience.)
- **Specular Light**: light from a point source that will be reflected specularly. We use this to model the kind of light that is reflected in a mirror-like fashion, the way that a light ray reflected from a shinny surface.

5. The model also assigns each surface material properties, which can be one of the four kinds:

- Materials with **ambient reflection properties** reflect ambient light.
- Materials with **diffuse reflection properties** reflect diffuse light.
- Materials with **specular reflection properties** reflect specular light.
- Materials with **emissive properties** emits light. The emissivity of a surface controls how much light the surface emits in the absence of any incident light. Note that light emitted from a surface does not act as light source that illuminates other surfaces. It only affects the color of the object seen by the observer.

Note that if an object only possesses ambient reflection properties, it only reflects ambient light even if light sources of other types (diffuse and specular) exist in the environment. In general, we assign the four material properties to an object and the final illumination at a point observed by the viewer is the sum of ambient, diffuse, and specular reflections plus the light emitted by the object.

7.2 Phong Reflection Model

Figure 7-2 shows the fundamental vectors of the Phong lighting model. As shown in the figure, a point on the surface is illuminated by a point light source and viewed from some viewpoint (eye position). To calculate the illumination at the point, we need to know the vectors, $\mathbf{n}$, $\mathbf{v}$, and $\mathbf{l}$, where

$$
\begin{aligned}
\mathbf{n} &= \text{unit normal vector to the surface} \\
\mathbf{v} &= \text{unit vector of viewpoint (eye) direction} \\
\mathbf{l} &= \text{unit vector of point light source direction}
\end{aligned}
\tag{7.2}
$$

These are unit vectors. That is, $|\mathbf{n}| = |\mathbf{v}| = |\mathbf{l}| = 1$. These three vectors along with the attributes of the light source and the properties of the surface material are used by the Phong model to determine the amount (intensity) of light reaching the eye.

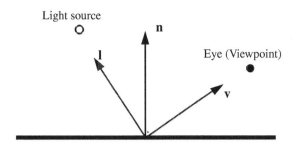

Figure 7-2 Phong Lighting Vectors

7.2.1 Specular Reflection

In the specular reflection model, the amount of light that can be received by an observer depends on her position of observation (viewpoint). If the surface is perfectly smooth, mirror-like reflections occur and the eye can see the reflected light only if it is positioned at a point along perfect-reflection direction. But for non-perfect surface we still can see specular highlight when the eye moves a little bit away from the perfect reflection (mirror) direction. The larger the deviation of the view angle from the mirror direction, the less light we can see. Phong model makes use of this observation to derive a formula to calculate the specular reflection. Figure 7-3 shows the setup for calculating the specular reflection. In addition to the unit vectors $\mathbf{n}$, $\mathbf{v}$, and $\mathbf{l}$ above, we have the following quantities:

$$
\begin{aligned}
\theta &= \text{angle of incidence} = \text{perfect reflection angle} \\
\mathbf{r} &= \text{unit vector of direction of perfect reflection, coplanar with } \mathbf{l} \text{ and } \mathbf{n} \\
\phi &= \text{deviation of view angle from perfect reflection direction} \\
|\mathbf{r}| &= |\mathbf{n}| = |\mathbf{v}| = |\mathbf{l}| = 1 \\
\mathbf{l}\cdot\mathbf{n} &= \mathbf{r}\cdot\mathbf{n} = \cos\theta \\
I_s^{in} &= \text{incidence specular light intensity} \\
I_s &= \text{reflected specular light intensity}
\end{aligned}
\tag{7.3}
$$

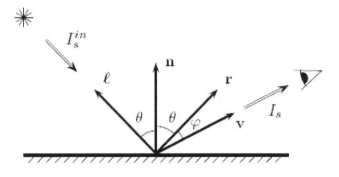

Figure 7-3 Setup for Calculating Specular Reflection

The reflection direction is determined by the incident direction and the normal to the surface. The colplanar condition implies that we can express $\mathbf{r}$ as a linear combination of $\mathbf{l}$ and $\mathbf{n}$:

$$
\mathbf{r} = a\mathbf{l} + b\mathbf{n}
\tag{7.4}
$$

where a and b are constants which can be determined by taking the dot product of $\mathbf{n}$ and Equation (7.4). This gives

$$\mathbf{n} \cdot \mathbf{r} = a\mathbf{n} \cdot \mathbf{l} + b\mathbf{n} \cdot \mathbf{n}$$
$$\Rightarrow \quad \cos \theta = a\cos \theta + b \tag{7.5}$$

Squaring (7.4), we obtain

$$\mathbf{r} \cdot \mathbf{r} = a^2 + 2ab\mathbf{l} \cdot \mathbf{n} + b^2$$
$$\Rightarrow \quad 1 = a^2 + 2ab\cos \theta + b^2 \tag{7.6}$$

Solving (7.5) and (7.6), we obtain

$$a = -1$$
$$b = 2\cos \theta = 2\mathbf{l} \cdot \mathbf{n} \tag{7.7}$$

Therefore, the reflection direction is given by

$$\boxed{\mathbf{r} = 2(\mathbf{l} \cdot \mathbf{n})\mathbf{n} - \mathbf{l}} \tag{7.8}$$

The Phong model calculates the specular reflection using an empirical formula which can be expressed in the following form:

$$\begin{aligned} I_s &= c_s I_s^{in} (\mathbf{r} \cdot \mathbf{v})^f \\ &= c_s I_s^{in} (\cos \phi)^f \end{aligned} \tag{7.9}$$

where c_s is a constant called the *specular reflectivity coefficient* and the exponent f is a value that can be adjusted empirically on an ad hoc basis to achieve desired lighting effect. The exponent f is ≥ 0, and values in the range 50 to 100 are typically used for shinny surfaces. The larger the exponent factor f, the narrower the beam of specularly reflected light becomes. When $f \to \infty$, (7.9) is reduced to mirror-like perfect reflection. Figure 7-4 shows a general specular reflection.

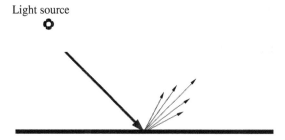

Figure 7-4   Specular Reflection

Note that the light intensity I is composed of any of the three components, red, green, and blue and each component operates independently. We can think of the quantity I_s in Equation (7.9) as an element of the set $\{R_s, G_s, B_s\}$. That is, $I_s \in \{R_s, G_s, B_s\}$.

Therefore, (7.9) actually represents three equations, one for each color component. For example,

$$R_s = c_s^R R_s^{in} (\cos \phi)^f \tag{7.10}$$

where R_s denotes the brightness of the reflected red color component, R_s^{in} is the incident brightness of the red component, and c_s^R is the specular reflectivity coefficient for the red color component.

In general, the reflectivity coefficient c_s depends on the surface and the wavelength of the of the light. We may need to use a different c_s for each of the red, green, and blue components. The material property of an object is defined by the reflectivity coefficients. A perfectly red ball would have $c_s^R = 1, c_s^G = 0$, and $c_s^B = 0$, which yields $R_s = R_s^{in}, G_s = 0, B_s = 0$. It reflects all the incoming red light and absorbs all the green and blue light that strikes it.

Figure 7-5 shows two spheres with specular properties exposed to specular light from the same direction. The two spheres have different exponent factors f. The one with a lot larger f has much more concentrated reflection.

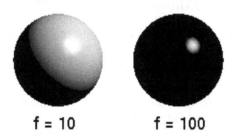

Figure 7-5   Lit Spheres with Same Specular Material Properties but Different Exponents f

7.2.2   Diffuse Reflection

In the model of diffuse reflection, a surface receives illumination from a light source and reflects equally in all direction. The eye position does not matter and has no effect on the amount of light it receives from reflection. However, the amount of reflection depends on the incident angle θ of the light.

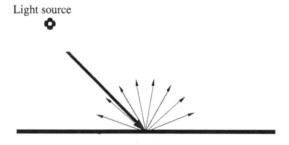

Figure 7-6   Diffuse Reflection

The intensity of reflected light is calculated based on Lamberts law, which says that if a light beam is incident on a small surface at an angle θ to the surface normal, the radiant energy that the small surface receives is equal to the product of the incoming light intensity and $\cos \theta$. Therefore, the reflected diffuse light intensity is given by

$$I_d = c_d I_d^{in} \cos \theta \tag{7.11}$$

where $\cos \theta = 1 \cdot \mathbf{n}$, I_d^{in} is the incident diffuse light intensity and c_d is a constant called the *diffuse reflectivity coefficient*. Maximum reflection occurs when $\theta = 0$, meaning that the incoming light is incident normally on the surface. The illuminated sphere on the left side of Figure 7-7 below is an example of diffuse reflection; the sphere is illuminated by diffuse light only. Again we can assume that $I_d \in \{R_d, G_d, B_d\}$, and $c_d \in \{c_d^R, c_d^G, c_d^B\}$.

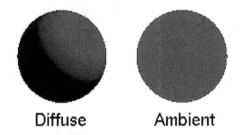

Diffuse   **Ambient**

Figure 7-7 Diffuse and Ambient Reflections

7.2.3 Ambient Reflection and Emissivity

Ambient light is the illumination of an object caused by multiple reflections from other surfaces. The Phong model assumes ambient light is uniform in the environment. It is a very rough approximation of global illumination. In the model, the amount of ambient light incident on each object is a constant for all surfaces in the scene and the amount of ambient light reflected by an object is independent of the object's position or orientation. Surface properties are used to determine how much ambient light is reflected. The intensity of the reflected light is given by

$$I_a = c_a I_a^{in} \tag{7.12}$$

where I_a^{in} is the incident ambient light intensity and c_a is a constant called the *ambient reflectivity coefficient*; $I_a \in \{R_a, B_a, G_a\}$ and $c_a \in \{c_a^R, c_a^G, c_a^B\}$.

In addition, a surface can also be given an emissive intensity constant $\mathbf{I}_e$, which is equal to the light emitted by the surface.

The illuminated sphere on the right side of Figure 7-7 is an example of ambient reflection; the sphere is illuminated by ambient light only.

7.2.4 Phong Reflection

Putting all these together, we obtain the Phong model which states that the total intensity I of the reflected light of a particular wavelength is the sum of all of the above reflected intensities. That is,

$$\begin{aligned} I &= I_a + I_d + I_s + I_e \\ &= c_a I_a^{in} + c_d I_d^{in}(\mathbf{l} \cdot \mathbf{n}) + c_s I_s^{in}(\mathbf{r} \cdot \mathbf{v})^f + I_e \end{aligned} \tag{7.13}$$

To write a single equation that incorporates all three wavelengths (red, green, blue) at once, we use boldface variables to denote a 3-tuple as we do for denoting a vector and use the symbol $\odot$ to denote component-wise multiplication on 3-tuples. That is,

$$\mathbf{I_s} = \begin{pmatrix} R_s \\ G_s \\ B_s \end{pmatrix} \qquad\qquad \mathbf{c_s} = \begin{pmatrix} c_s^R \\ c_s^G \\ c_s^B \end{pmatrix}$$

and

$$\mathbf{c_s} \odot \mathbf{I_s} = \begin{pmatrix} c_s^R \\ c_s^G \\ c_s^B \end{pmatrix} \odot \begin{pmatrix} R_s \\ G_s \\ B_s \end{pmatrix} = \begin{pmatrix} c_s^R R_s \\ c_s^G G_s \\ c_s^B B_s \end{pmatrix} \tag{7.14}$$

and so on. We can rewrite (7.13) as

$$
\begin{aligned}
\mathbf{I} \ &= \mathbf{I}_a + \mathbf{I}_d + \mathbf{I}_s + \mathbf{I}_e \\
&= \mathbf{c}_a \odot \mathbf{I}_a^{in} + \mathbf{c}_d \odot \mathbf{I}_d^{in}(\mathbf{l} \cdot \mathbf{n}) + \mathbf{c}_s \odot \mathbf{I}_s^{in}(\mathbf{r} \cdot \mathbf{v})^f + \mathbf{I}_e
\end{aligned}
\tag{7.15}
$$

Equation (7.15) is for one light source. If there are multiple light sources in the scene, we simply sum the contributions from all the light sources. Suppose there are L light sources and the incident light direction at a point on a surface of light number i is l_i and the perfect reflection direction is $\mathbf{r}_i$. The i-th light also has an intensity $\mathbf{I}^{in,i}$ that represents the intensity of the light reaching the observed point on the surface. This intensity may be moderated by the surface from the light and other factors such as spotlight effects. Moreover, if $\mathbf{n} \cdot \mathbf{l}_i \leq 0$, the light is not shining from above the surface; in this case, we set $\mathbf{I}^{in,i}$ to 0. The overall illumination at the point is given by

$$
\mathbf{I} \ = \mathbf{c}_a \odot \mathbf{I}_a^{in} + \mathbf{c}_d \odot \sum_{i=1}^{L} \mathbf{I}_d^{in,i}(\mathbf{l}_i \cdot \mathbf{n}) + \mathbf{c}_s \odot \sum_{i=1}^{L} \mathbf{I}_s^{in,i}(\mathbf{r}_i \cdot \mathbf{v})^f + \mathbf{I}_e
\tag{7.16}
$$

Figure 7-8 shows a sphere rendered with Phong illumination. Two light sources have been used.

Figure 7-8   Phong Illumination

7.3   OpenGL Lighting

OpenGL implements the full Phong lighting model and supports all material properties, including the ambient, diffuse, and specular reflectivity coefficients and emissivity. We may assign ambient, diffuse and specular intensities and some special effects such as spotlighting and distance attenuation independently to each light source.

The reflectivity coefficient of a surface determines the reflectance of the surface; its ambient reflectance is combined with the ambient component of each incoming light source, the diffuse reflectance with the light's diffuse component, and similarly for the specular reflectance and component.

By default, Phong lighting is disabled in OpenGL and a vertex color is set by a **glColor***() command. However, after we have enabled lighting, the **glColor***() commands will have no effect on the scene. We can use the following command to enable Phong lighting:

glEnable (GL_LIGHTING);

In general, we can create up to eight point light sources in a graphics scene of OpenGL using commands of **glLight***(). The light sources are named GL_LIGHT0, GL_LIGHT1, GL_LIGHT2, and so on. Each light source must be enabled explicitly using **glEnable**(). For example, we can "turn on" or enable light sources 0 and 1 (GL_LIGHT0 and GL_LIGHT1) by the commands,

```
glEnable( GL_LIGHT0 );
glEnable( GL_LIGHT1 );
```

To turn light source 1 off but leave light 0 on, we can disable only light source 1 using the command

```
glDisable( GL_LIGHT1 );
```

OpenGL provides the options of rendering one side or both sides of a polygon. A polygon consists of a front face and a back face. In general, the face that faces the exterior of an object is the front face and the one that faces the interior is the back face. By default, OpenGL does not light the back faces. To tell OpenGL to light the back faces too, we can use the command

```
glLightModeli ( GL_LIGHT_MODEL_TWO_SIDE, GL_TRUE );
```

where i can be $0, 1, ..., , 7$, denoting the i-th light. The functions **glLightModel*()** set the lighting model parameters. The first parameter specifies a single-valued lighting model parameter, which can be

```
GL_LIGHT_MODEL_LOCAL_VIEWER
GL_LIGHT_MODEL_COLOR_CONTROL
GL_LIGHT_MODEL_TWO_SIDE
```

The second parameter passes the appropriate value to the function for the specified lighting model. In summary, to set up lighting properly in OpenGL, we need to perform the following tasks:

1. Set light properties.
2. Enable or disable lighting.
3. Set surface material properties.
4. Provide correct surface normals.
5. Set light model properties.

7.3.1 Light Properties

Light sources have a number of properties, such as color, position, and direction. We can use the functions **glLight*()** to specify all properties of lights. The functions take three arguments to identify the light source, the property, and the desired value for that property:

```
void glLight{if} ( GLenum light_source, GLenum pname, TYPE param );
void glLight{ifv} ( GLenum light_source, GLenum pname, TYPE *param );
```

The functions create the light specified by *light_source*, which can be GL_LIGHT0, GL_LIGHT1, ... , or GL_LIGHT7. The characteristic of the light being set is specified by *pname*, which is a named parameter as shown in Table 7-1. The parameter *param* indicates the values to which the *pname* characteristic is assigned; it can be a pointer to a group of values if the vector version is used, or the value itself if the nonvector version is used. We can use the nonvector version to set only single-valued light characteristics.

Example:

```
float light[] = { 0.5, 0.5, 0.8 };
float light_position[] = { 1.0, 1.0, 1.0, 0.0 };
glLightfv(GL_LIGHT0, GL_DIFFUSE, light );
glLightfv(GL_LIGHT0, GL_POSITION, light_position);
```

Table 7-1   Default Values for *pname* Parameter of **glLight***()

pname	Default Value	Meaning
GL_AMBIENT	(0.0, 0.0, 0.0, 1.0)	ambient RGBA intensity of light
GL_DIFFUSE	(1.0, 1.0, 1.0, 1.0)	diffuse RGBA intensity of light
GL_SPECULAR	(1.0, 1.0, 1.0, 1.0)	specular RGBA intensity of light
GL_POSITION	(0.0, 0.0, 1.0, 0.0)	(x, y, z, w) position of light
GL_SPOT_DIRECTION	(0.0, 0.0, -1.0)	(x, y, z) direction of spotlight
GL_SPOT_EXPONENT	0.0	spotlight exponent
GL_SPOT_CUTOFF	180.0	spotlight cutoff angle
GL_CONSTANT_ATTENUATION	1.0	constant attenuation factor
GL_LINEAR_ATTENUATION	0.0	linear attenuation factor
GL_QUADRATIC_ATTENUATION	0.0	quadratic attenuation factor

The default values listed for GL_DIFFUSE and GL_SPECULAR in Table 7-1 apply only to GL_LIGHT0. For other lights, the default values are (0.0, 0.0, 0.0, 1.0) for both GL_DIFFUSE and GL_SPECULAR.

7.3.2 Types of Light

OpenGL supports two types of lights:

1. point light source at a fixed location, and
2. directional light (location of source at infinite distance).

To specify which type of light we are going to use, we assign a nonzero or a zero value to the fourth component (w) of the light position in homogeneous coordinates. If $w = 0$, we specify a directional light (an infinite-distance light source). If $w \neq 0$, we specify a finite point source located at $(x/w, y/w, z/w)$.

   The following code section is an example indicating that light source 0 is a finite point source located at $(2, 1, 0.5)$ and light source 1 is a directional light which shines along the direction $(-4, -2, -1)$ (i.e. from the point $(4, 2, 1)$ to the origin $(0, 0, 0)$).

```
float x = 4, y = 2, z = 1, w = 2;
float light_position0[4] = { x, y, z, w };
glLightfv(GL_LIGHT0, GL_POSITION, light_position0);
w = 0;
float light_position1[4] = { x, y, z, w };
glLightfv(GL_LIGHT1, GL_POSITION, light_position1);
```

7.3.3 Surface Material Properties

We use OpenGL functions **glMaterial***() to set the surface material properties. We can use the functions to specify the ambient, diffuse and specular reflectivity coefficients and the emissive intensity. Note again that an ambient surface interacts with ambient light, a diffuse surface interacts with diffuse light, and so on. For example, to set the diffuse reflectivity coefficients, we may use a code similar to the following:

```
float r = 0.8, g = 0.6, b = 0.5, a = 1.0;
float color[4] = {r, g, b, a};
glMaterialfv( GL_FRONT, GL_DIFFUSE, color );
```

In this example, the function **glMaterialfv**() has three parameters. The first parameter GL_FRONT indicates that we are handling the front faces of polygons. If we want to set the back faces or both front and back faces, we can use the parameters GL_BACK and GL_FRONT_AND_BACK respectively. The second parameter GL_DIFFUSE indicates that we are setting diffuse reflectivity coefficients. Other valid parameters for this argument include GL_AMBIENT, GL_SPECULAR, GL_EMISSION, and GL_AMBIENT_AND_DIFFUSE. The third parameter, *color*, is an array containing the reflectivity coefficients for the red, green, blue and alpha components.

The color components specified for materials have different meaning from that of lights. For a light, the numbers correspond to a percentage of full intensity for each color. If the R, G, and B values for a light's color are all 1.0, the light is the brightest possible white. If their values are all the same but less than 1, the light is still white but appears gray. If $R = G = 0$ and $B = 1$, the light is blue.

For materials, the numbers are reflectivity coefficients, corresponding to the reflected proportions of those colors. Therefore, if $R = 1$, and $G = B = 0$ for a material, that material reflects only 100% of all incoming red light, but absorbs all green, and blue light. For example, if an OpenGL light has components $(1, 0.9, 0.8)$, and a material has components $(0.6, 0.5, 0.4)$, then the light that arrives at the eye is $(1 \times 0.6, 0.9 \times 0.5, 0.8 \times 0.4) = (0.6, 0.45, 0.36)$.

If we have two lights L_1 and L_2 with components,

$$L_1 = \begin{pmatrix} R_1 \\ G_1 \\ B_1 \end{pmatrix} \qquad L_2 = \begin{pmatrix} R_2 \\ G_2 \\ B_2 \end{pmatrix}$$

shining at the same point. OpenGL adds the components, giving

$$L = L_1 + L_2 = \begin{pmatrix} R_1 + R_2 \\ G_1 + G_2 \\ B_1 + B_2 \end{pmatrix} \tag{7.17}$$

If any of the sums is larger than 1, OpenGL clamps it to 1.

7.3.4 Surface Normals

We need to provide correct normals for OpenGL to produce 'correct' lighting. Equations (7.13) and (7.8) show that the diffuse and specular reflections depend on the normal at the point where light is incident on the surface. In general, we associate a normal to each vertex of the polygons that make up the surface similar to the following code where (xn, yn, zn) specifies the normal at the point (x, y, z):

```
glBegin ( ... );
  glNormal3f ( xn, yn, zn );
  glVertex3f ( x, y, z );
  ---
glEnd()
```

The normals we provide need to have a unit length. We can use "**glEnable** (GL_NORMALIZE);" to have OpenGL normalize all the normals. When we use the "glut" utilities to create a graphics object such as **glutSolidSphere**(), the normals at various points of the object have been calculated by the called functions.

7.3.5 Attenuation and Spotlighting

We can create some special lighting effects using the distance **attenuation** and **spotlighting** features supported by OpenGL. We know that for real-world point-source lights, the intensity of light decreases as distance from the light increases. Since a directional light is infinitely far away, it does not make sense to attenuate its intensity over distance, so attenuation is disabled for a directional light. However, we can attenuate a positional light. OpenGL provides functions to attenuate a light source by multiplying the contribution of that source by an attenuation factor ρ:

$$\rho = \frac{1}{k_c + k_l d + k_q d^2} \tag{7.18}$$

where k_c, k_l, and k_q are the *constant attenuation factor*, the *linear attenuation factor*, and the *quadratic attenuation factor* respectively; d is the distance from the light source to the incident point of a surface. An incident intensity value is multiplied by the distance attenuation factor before being used in the Phong lighting calculations. By default, $k_c = 1.0, k_l = k_q = 0.0$. We can assign different values to these parameters using the function **glLightf**(). For example, the code

```
glLightf(GL_LIGHT0, GL_CONSTANT_ATTENUATION, 2.0);
glLightf(GL_LIGHT0, GL_LINEAR_ATTENUATION, 1.0);
glLightf(GL_LIGHT0, GL_QUADRATIC_ATTENUATION, 0.5);
```

will set $k_c = 2.0, k_l = 1.0, k_q = 0.5$ for light 0; if $d = 2$, the attenuation factor will be

$$\rho = \frac{1}{2.0 + 1.0 \times 2 + 0.5 \times 2^2} = \frac{1}{2.0 + 2.0 + 2.0} = 0.17$$

We can make use of the spotlight effect to make a positional light act as a narrow beam of light like that shown in Figure 7-9. A spot light source usually has the following characteristics:

1. It is a point light source that emits light only within a specified volume of a cone.
2. The cone is parameterized by direction and cutoff angle (see Figure 7-9).
3. Light is parameterized by position and intensity.
4. An exponent parameter is used to control the intensity distribution within the cone and how fast the light intensity attenuates from the central axis of the spotlight.
5. Intensity falls off with the square of the distance from the source.

In OpenGL, properties of a spot light are specified by setting light parameters

GL_SPOT_DIRECTION
GL_SPOT_EXPONENT
GL_SPOT_CUTOFF

The following is a sample code of setting these parameters:

```
float direction[3] = {x, y, z};
glLightfv( GL_LIGHT1, GL_SPOT_DIRECTION, direction );
const float theta = 60;
glLightf( GL_LIGHT1, GL_SPOT_CUTOFF, theta );
const float e = 2.0;
glLightf( GL_LIGHT1, GL_SPOT_EXPONENT, e );
```

Light Source

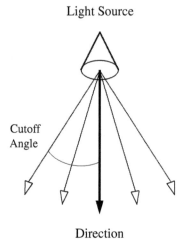

Cutoff
Angle

Direction

Figure 7-9   Spot Light

Example 7-1

This example presents the code that shows the basic steps of lighting objects in a scene. The following is the code of this example that displays a sphere illuminated by two light sources, as shown earlier in Figure 7-8.

```
void init(void) {
   //Material properties: reflectivity coefficients
   GLfloat mat_specular[] = { 0.6, .8, 1, 1.0 };
   GLfloat mat_ambient[] = { 0.1, 0.1, 0.1, 1.0 };
   GLfloat mat_diffuse[] = { 0.6, 0.4, 0.2, 1.0 };
   GLfloat mat_shininess0[] = { 20.0};
   GLfloat mat_shininess1[] = { 100.0};
   //Light properties
   GLfloat light_position0[] = {1.0, 1.0, 1.0, 0.0};//directional light
   GLfloat light0[] = { 1, 1, 1 };   //light source 0
   GLfloat light1[] = {1, 1, 1 };    //light source 1
   GLfloat light_position1[] = {1.0, 1.0, 0.0, 0.0};//directional light

   glClearColor (1.0, 1.0, 1.0, 0.0);
   glShadeModel (GL_SMOOTH);
   glMaterialfv(GL_FRONT, GL_SPECULAR, mat_specular);
   glMaterialfv(GL_FRONT, GL_SHININESS, mat_shininess0);
   glMaterialfv(GL_FRONT, GL_DIFFUSE, mat_diffuse);
   glMaterialfv(GL_FRONT, GL_AMBIENT, mat_ambient);

   glLightfv(GL_LIGHT0, GL_POSITION, light_position0);
   glLightfv(GL_LIGHT0, GL_DIFFUSE, light0 );
   glLightfv(GL_LIGHT0, GL_AMBIENT, light0 );
   glLightfv(GL_LIGHT0, GL_SPECULAR, light0 );

   glMaterialfv(GL_FRONT, GL_SHININESS, mat_shininess1);
   glLightfv(GL_LIGHT1, GL_DIFFUSE, light1 );
   glLightfv(GL_LIGHT1, GL_AMBIENT, light1 );
   glLightfv(GL_LIGHT1, GL_POSITION, light_position1);
   glLightfv(GL_LIGHT1, GL_SPECULAR, light1 );

   glEnable(GL_LIGHTING);
   glEnable(GL_LIGHT0);
   glEnable(GL_LIGHT1);
   glEnable(GL_DEPTH_TEST);
```

```
   }

void display(void) {
   glClear (GL_COLOR_BUFFER_BIT | GL_DEPTH_BUFFER_BIT);
   glutSolidSphere (0.5, 64, 64);
   glFlush ();
}
```

7.4 Texture Mapping

Texture mapping is the mapping of a separately defined graphics image, a picture, or a pattern to a surface. The technique helps us to combine pixels with geometric objects to generate complex images without building large geometric models. For example, we can apply texture mapping to 'glue' an image of a brick wall to a polygon and to draw the entire wall as a single polygon. Texture mapping ensures that all the right things happen as the polygon is transformed and rendered. A texture map can hold any kind of information that affects the appearance of a surface. The map is simply a table consisting of data that will be mapped to various pixel locations. We can think of texture mapping as a table lookup process that retrieves the information affecting a particular point on the surface as it is rendered. Figure 7-10 shows an example of texture mapping; a two-dimensional world map is mapped onto the surface of a sphere.

Texture mapping does not require intensive computing. Consequently, people like to use texture maps in real-time rendering such as video games and animations to produce special visual effects. We can apply texture maps at various situations in constructing a graphics scene:

1. A texture map can hold colors to be applied to a surface in *replace* or *decal* mode. In this case, the colors of the texture map simply overwrite the original colors of the object. Lighting should not be turned on as the texture data will overwrite the data generated by any lighting effects.
2. After applying a lighting model to a scene, a texture map can hold color attributes such as color intensities and transparency to change the the surface appearance of the objects in the scene. The texture map attributes are blended with, or modulate, the surface colors generated from the lighting model.
3. A texture map can hold the parameters of a lighting model such as reflectivity coefficients and normals. We can use the texture map values to modify the surface properties that are input to the lighting model.

Figure 7-10 A World Map is Mapped onto the Surface of a Sphere

Actually, texture mapping is just one of the general techniques that apply discrete data for surface rendering. We can classify these techniques into three major types:

1. **Texture mapping** uses a pattern (or texture) to determine the color of a fragment. It can be 1, 2, 3, or 4 dimensional. Figure 7-10 above shows an example of this mapping.
2. **Bump mapping** distorts the normal vectors during a shading process to make the surface appear to have small variations in shape like the bumps on a real orange. Figure 7-11 below shows an orange without bump mapping and another one with bump mapping which makes the orange look a lot more realistic.

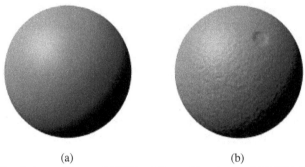

(a)   (b)

Figure 7-11   Rendering an Orange (a) Without Bump Mapping, and (b) With Bump Mapping

3. **Environment mapping** (also called reflection mapping) stores the image of the environment surrounding of the rendered object as a texture image and then maps the image to the object surface. Figure 7-12 shows an example of environment mapping.

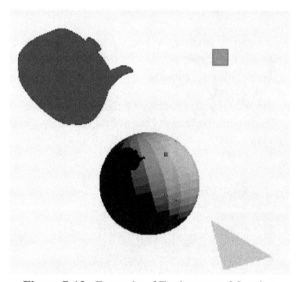

Figure 7-12   Example of Environment Mapping

7.4.1   Two Dimensional Texture Mapping

Just like calling a picture element a pixel, we call a texture element a **texel**. We denote the texture coordinates of a texel as (s, t) and describe the texture pattern by $T(s, t)$. $T(s, t)$ here represents the attributes of the texture at the texel coordinates (s, t). A texture map associates a texel with each point on a geometric object that is itself mapped to screen coordinates for display. If homogeneous coordinates (x, y, z, w) are used to specify a point of an object, then a texture map is described by

$$
\begin{aligned}
x &= x(s, t) \\
y &= y(s, t) \\
z &= z(s, t) \\
w &= w(s, t)
\end{aligned}
\tag{7.19}
$$

Conversely, given a point (x, y, z, w) of the object, the texel coordinates are obtained by the inverse functions:

$$
\begin{aligned}
s &= s(x, y, z, w) \\
t &= t(x, y, z, w)
\end{aligned}
\tag{7.20}
$$

For parametric (u, v) surfaces, we need an additional function to map from (u, v) to (x, y, z, w). We also need the mapping from (u, v) to (s, t) and its inverse.

A parametric surface is described by two parameters, u, and v. That is, the position of a point P on the surface is a function of u and v:

$$
P(u, v) = \begin{pmatrix} x(u, v) \\ y(u, v) \\ z(u, v) \end{pmatrix}
\tag{7.21}
$$

A simple mapping that is commonly used is the **linear mapping**; we map a point on the texture $T(s, t)$ to a point $P(u, v)$ on the parametric surface. This mapping is given by

$$
\begin{aligned}
u &= as + bt + c \\
v &= ds + et + f
\end{aligned}
\tag{7.22}
$$

where $a, b, c, d, e,$ and f are constants. The mapping is invertible if $ae \neq bd$.

Linear mapping makes it easy to map a texture to a group of parametric surface patches. Suppose the rectangle in st space specified by (s_{min}, t_{min}) and (s_{max}, t_{max}) is mapped to the one in uv space specified by (u_{min}, v_{min}) and (u_{max}, v_{max}) as shown in Figure 7-13.

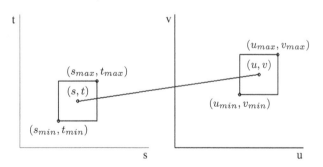

Figure 7-13 Mapping Texture to Surface Patches

The mapping is given by the following linear equations:

$$
\begin{aligned}
u &= u_{min} + \frac{s - s_{min}}{s_{max} - s_{min}}(u_{max} - u_{min}) \\
v &= v_{min} + \frac{t - t_{min}}{t_{max} - t_{min}}(v_{max} - v_{min})
\end{aligned}
\tag{7.23}
$$

Example 7-2 Mapping Texture to Surface of Revolution

The surface generated by revolving a profile (curve) around the z-axis can be expressed in the following parametric form:

$$P(u,v) = \begin{pmatrix} r(u)cos(v) \\ r(u)sin(v) \\ z(u) \end{pmatrix} \qquad (7.24)$$

where v is the angle of revolution and r is the radius of revolution at a certain height (z value) which depends on the parameter u. We can set u lie in the range $[0,1]$, and v in $[0,2\pi]$. That is,

$$\begin{aligned} 0 &\leq u \leq 1 \\ 0 &\leq v \leq 2\pi \end{aligned} \qquad (7.25)$$

Suppose the texture coordinates are normalized so that $0 \leq s \leq 1$ and $0 \leq t \leq 1$. Then the mapping between (u,v) and (s,t) is given by

$$\begin{aligned} s &= u \\ t &= \frac{v}{2\pi} \end{aligned} \qquad (7.26)$$

Example 7-3 Mapping Texture to Sphere

We can define a sphere parametrically by

$$P(\theta,\phi) = \begin{pmatrix} r\sin\theta\cos\phi \\ r\sin\theta\sin\phi \\ r\cos\theta \end{pmatrix} \qquad (7.27)$$

where

$$\begin{aligned} r &= radius \\ \theta &= u = \text{angle from } z\text{-axis } (0 \leq \theta \leq \pi) \\ \phi &= v = \text{angle from } x\text{-axis } (0 \leq \phi \leq 2\pi) \end{aligned} \qquad (7.28)$$

The texture mapping is

$$\begin{aligned} s &= \frac{\phi}{2\pi} \\ t &= \frac{\theta}{\pi} \end{aligned} \qquad (7.29)$$

Given a point (x,y,z), we can obtain (s,t) from

$$\begin{aligned} t &= \frac{1}{\pi}cos^{-1}\frac{z}{r} \\ s &= \frac{1}{2\pi}cos^{-1}\frac{x}{rsin(t\pi)} \end{aligned} \qquad (7.30)$$

The following code section shows this texture mapping. The function takes the coordinates x, y, and z, as well as the radius r as inputs; it then calculates the corresponding texture coordinates s and t and returns their values.

```
const double PI = 3.141592654;
const double TWOPI = 6.283185308;
```

```
void
sphereMap(double x,double y,double z,double r,double *s,double *t)
{
    *t = acos (z / r ) / PI;
    if (y >= 0)
        *s = acos ( x / ( r * sin(PI*(*t)) ) ) ) / TWOPI;
    else
        *s = ( PI + acos ( x / (r * sin(PI*(*t))) ) ) ) / TWOPI;
}
```

7.4.2   OpenGL Texture Mapping

To use texture mapping in OpenGL, we need to perform the following steps.

1. **Enable texture mapping**.
   We need to enable texturing before we can apply texture to any object. We usually think of a texture as a 2D image but it can also be 1D. Texturing is enabled or disabled by the functions **glEnable**() or **glDisable**() with symbolic constants GL_TEXTURE_1D or GL_TEXTURE_2D for one or two dimensional texturing respectively:

   ```
   glEnable ( GL_TEXTURE_1D );
   glEnable ( GL_TEXTURE_2D );
   glDisable ( GL_TEXTURE_1D );
   glDisable ( GL_TEXTURE_2D );
   ```

   If both are enabled, 2D texturing is used.

2. **Specify an image or a pattern to be used as texture**.
   Before applying the texture to an object, we need to specify the image or pattern that will be used as texture. In the process, we use the function **glGenTextures**() to generate texture names. We then use **glBindTexture**() to bind a named texture to a texturing target. The function **glBindTexture**() lets us create or use a named texture. When a texture is bound to a target, the previously bound target is automatically released. We can switch between different textures we want using this function. This essentially chooses what texture we are working with.
   The following example code illustrates this step.

   ```
   GLuint handles[2];
   glGenTextures(2, handles);

   glBindTexture(GL_TEXTURE_2D, handles[0]);
   //Initialize texture parameters; load a texture with glTexImage2D

   glBindTexture(GL_TEXTURE_2D, handles[1]);
   //Initialize texture parameters and load another texture
   ```

3. **Indicate how the texture is to be applied to each pixel**.
   The data describing a texture may consist of one, two, three, or four elements per texel, representing anything from a modulation constant to an (R, G, B, A) quadruple. We can choose any of four possible functions for computing the final RGBA value from the fragment color and the texture-image data:

   (a) **decal** mode – the texture color is the final color; the texture is painted on top of the fragment.
   (b) **replace** mode – it is a variant of the decal mode.

   (c) **modulate** mode – use texture to modulate or scale the fragment's color; this technique
       is useful for combining the effects of lighting with texturing.
   (d) **constant** mode – a constant color is blended with that of the fragment, based on the
       texture value.

4. **Draw the scene, supplying both texture and geometric coordinates**.
   We need to specify both texture coordinates and geometric coordinates of the object so that
   we can "glue" the texture image onto the object surface in the way we want. For example, in
   2-D texture mapping, the texture coordinates are in the range [0.0, 1.0]. The object coordinates can be anything. We may associate a texture coordinate with a geometric coordinates
   using the commands **glTexCoord2f**() and **glVertex3f**(). For example, the commands

   glTexCoord2f(0.0, 0.0);
   glVertex3f(-2.0, -2.0, 0.0);

   associate the texture coordinates $(0, 0)$ with the geometric coordinates $(-2.0, -2.0, 0.0)$.

5. **Delete the texture from memory when it is no longer used**.
   After we have finished texturing, we have to delete the texture from memory using the
   function **glDeleteTextures**() so that the allocated memory will be freed for other uses. For
   example, the command

   glDeleteTextures(2, *handles*);

   frees two textures specified by the array *handles*.

7.4.3 Texture Programming Examples

In this section, we present some simple programming examples to illustrate the usage of texture in
OpenGL.

Example 7-4 Mapping Texture to Quads

   In this example, the 2D texture image is generated by the program; it is the same checker
board image used in Example 6-1 of Chapter 6. The program applies this texture to two quads
independently, which are rendered using perspective projection as shown in Figure 7-14. The
following is the code that gives this output display.

```
//checker_tex.cpp
const int width = 256, height = 256;
unsigned char board[width][height][4];
GLuint handle;

void getBoard(void)
{
  int c;

  for ( int i = 0; i < width; i++ ) {
    for ( int j = 0; j < height; j++ ){//start from lower-left corner
      c = ((((i&16)==0)^((j&16))==0))*255;//0 or 255-->black or white
      board[i][j][0] =  c; //red component
      board[i][j][1] =  c; //green component
      board[i][j][2] =  c; //blue  component
      board[i][j][3] =  255; //alpha
    }
  }
}
```

```
void init(void)
{
  glClearColor (0.8, 0.8, 1.0, 1.0);
  glShadeModel(GL_FLAT);
  glEnable(GL_DEPTH_TEST);
  getBoard();

  glPixelStorei(GL_UNPACK_ALIGNMENT, 1);

  glGenTextures(1, &handle);
  glBindTexture(GL_TEXTURE_2D, handle);

  glTexParameteri(GL_TEXTURE_2D, GL_TEXTURE_WRAP_S, GL_REPEAT);
  glTexParameteri(GL_TEXTURE_2D, GL_TEXTURE_WRAP_T, GL_REPEAT);
  glTexParameteri(GL_TEXTURE_2D, GL_TEXTURE_MAG_FILTER, GL_NEAREST);
  glTexParameteri(GL_TEXTURE_2D, GL_TEXTURE_MIN_FILTER, GL_NEAREST);
  glTexImage2D(GL_TEXTURE_2D, 0, GL_RGBA, width, height,
               0, GL_RGBA, GL_UNSIGNED_BYTE, board);
}

void display(void)
{
  glClear(GL_COLOR_BUFFER_BIT | GL_DEPTH_BUFFER_BIT);
  glMatrixMode (GL_PROJECTION);
  glLoadIdentity ();
  glFrustum (-2.5, 2.5, -2.5, 2.5, 5, 20.0);
  glMatrixMode (GL_MODELVIEW);
  glLoadIdentity();
  gluLookAt ( 0.0, 0.0, 5.5, 0.0, 0.0, 0.0, 0.0, 1.0, 0.0);

  glEnable(GL_TEXTURE_2D);
  glTexEnvf(GL_TEXTURE_ENV, GL_TEXTURE_ENV_MODE, GL_DECAL);
  glBindTexture(GL_TEXTURE_2D, handle);
  glBegin(GL_QUADS);    //draw two quads
    glTexCoord2f(0.0, 0.0); glVertex3f(-2.0, -2.0, 0.0);
    glTexCoord2f(1.0, 0.0); glVertex3f( 0.0, -2.0, 0.0);
    glTexCoord2f(1.0, 1.0); glVertex3f(0.0, 0.0, 0.0);
    glTexCoord2f(0.0, 1.0); glVertex3f(-2.0, 0.0, 0.0);

    glTexCoord2f(0.0, 0.0); glVertex3f(0.5, -2.0, 0.0);
    glTexCoord2f(1.0, 0.0); glVertex3f( 2.5, -1.5, 0.0);
    glTexCoord2f(1.0, 1.0); glVertex3f( 2.5, 0.5, 0.0);
    glTexCoord2f(0.0, 1.0); glVertex3f( 0.5, 0.0, 0.0);
  glEnd();
  glFlush();
}
```

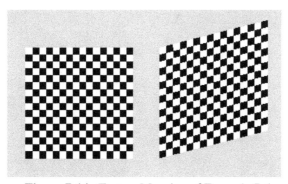

Figure 7-14 Texture Mapping of Example 7-4

In this example, we use the routine **getBoard**() to create the texture image, and perform all the texture-mapping initialization in the routine **init**(). The functions **glGenTextures**() and **glBind-Texture**() name and create a texture object for a texture image. The texture map is specified by **glTexImage2D**(), whose input parameters include the size of the image, type of the image, location of the image, and other properties of it. The four calls to **glTexParameter***() specify how the texture is to be wrapped and how the colors are to be filtered if there is no exact match between pixels in the texture and pixels on the screen. In the routine **display**(), texturing is turned on by **glEnable** (GL_TEXTURE_2D), and **glTexEnvf**() sets the drawing mode to GL_DECAL so that the textured polygons are drawn using the colors from the texture map. We then draw two quads with the texture by specifying the texture coordinates along with vertex coordinates. The function **glTexCoord2f**() sets the current texture coordinates that will associate with vertices specified by subsequent **glvertex***() commands until **glTexCoord2f**() is called again.

Example 7-5 Mapping Texture to a Sphere

Figure 7-10 above shows that a world map is mapped onto the surface of a sphere. The following code section is the code that does this mapping, which maps a 2D image onto a sphere. It is a more detailed implementation of Example 7-3 that explains the principles and presents the code for mapping of texture to a sphere. The texture image used in the mapping is given by the file "../data/earth.png". The loading of this image and the initialization of the texture features are all done in the routine **init**(); to load the image, **init**() calls **makeTexImage**() that in turn calls **loadImageRGBA**() of the imagio library that we have discussed in Chapter 6.

The function **createSphere**() creates a sphere composed of quads. Alternatively, one may use triangles to build a sphere (i.e. use GL_TRIANGLE_STRIP for the argument of glBegin() instead of using GL_QUAD_STRIP for it). This function also does the mapping between the texture coordinates and the geometric coordinates as explained in Example 7-3. We also cull the back faces of the polygons using the command **glCullFace** (GL_BACK) so that only the exterior surface of the sphere is rendered.

```
int texImageWidth;
int texImageHeight;
static GLuint handles[6]; //texture names
char maps[][20] = {"../data/earth.png"};

class Point3 {
public:
  double x;
  double y;
  double z;
  Point3()
  {
    x = y = z = 0.0;
  }

  Point3 ( double x0, double y0, double z0 )
  {
    x = x0; y = y0;    z = z0;
  }
};

//load texture image
GLubyte *makeTexImage( char *loadfile )
{
    int i, j, c, width, height;
    GLubyte *texImage;
```

```
    /*
      Only works for .png or .tif images. NULL is returned for errors.
      loadImageRGBA() is from imageio library discussed in Chapter 6.
    */
    texImage = loadImageRGBA( (char *) loadfile, &width, &height);
    texImageWidth = width;
    texImageHeight = height;

    return texImage;
}

void init(void)
{
    glClearColor (1, 1, 1, 0.0);
    glShadeModel(GL_FLAT);

    glEnable(GL_DEPTH_TEST);

    glPixelStorei(GL_UNPACK_ALIGNMENT, 1);
    //handles is global
    glGenTextures(1, handles);

    for ( int i = 0; i < 1; ++i ) {
     GLubyte *texImage = makeTexImage( maps[i] );
     if ( !texImage ) {
       printf("\nError reading %s \n", maps[i] );
       continue;
     }
     glBindTexture(GL_TEXTURE_2D, handles[i]); //now we work on handles
     glTexParameteri(GL_TEXTURE_2D, GL_TEXTURE_WRAP_S, GL_REPEAT);
     glTexParameteri(GL_TEXTURE_2D, GL_TEXTURE_WRAP_T, GL_REPEAT);
     glTexParameteri(GL_TEXTURE_2D, GL_TEXTURE_MAG_FILTER, GL_NEAREST);
     glTexParameteri(GL_TEXTURE_2D, GL_TEXTURE_MIN_FILTER, GL_NEAREST);
     glTexImage2D(GL_TEXTURE_2D, 0, GL_RGBA, texImageWidth,
                  texImageHeight, 0, GL_RGBA, GL_UNSIGNED_BYTE, texImage);

     delete texImage;      //free memory holding texture image
   }
}

const double PI = 3.141592654;
const double TWOPI = 6.283185308;
/*
 *    Create a sphere centered at c, with radius r, and precision n
 *    Draw a point for zero radius spheres
 */
void createSphere(Point3 c,double r,int n)
{
    int i,j;
    double phi1, phi2, theta, u, v;
    Point3 p, q;

    if ( r < 0 || n < 0 )
       return;
    if (n < 4 || r <= 0) {
       glBegin(GL_POINTS);
       glVertex3f(c.x,c.y,c.z);
       glEnd();
       return;
    }

    for ( j=0; j < n; j++ ) {
       phi1 = j * TWOPI / n;
```

```
      phi2 = (j + 1) * TWOPI / n; //next phi

      glBegin(GL_QUAD_STRIP);
      for ( i=0; i <= n; i++ ) {
        theta = i * PI / n;

        q.x = sin ( theta ) * cos ( phi2 );
        q.y = sin ( theta ) * sin ( phi2 );
        q.z = cos ( theta );
        p.x = c.x + r * q.x;
        p.y = c.y + r * q.y;
        p.z = c.z + r * q.z;

        glNormal3f ( q.x, q.y, q.z );
        u = (double)(j+1) / n; // column
        v = 1 - (double) i / n; // row
        glTexCoord2f( u, v );
        glVertex3f( p.x, p.y, p.z );

        q.x = sin ( theta ) * cos ( phi1 );
        q.y = sin ( theta ) * sin ( phi1 );
        q.z = cos ( theta );
        p.x = c.x + r * q.x;
        p.y = c.y + r * q.y;
        p.z = c.z + r * q.z;

        glNormal3f ( q.x, q.y, q.z );
        u = (double) j / n; // column
        v = 1 - (double) i / n; // row
        glTexCoord2f( j / (double) n, 1 - i / (double) n );
        glVertex3f ( p.x, p.y, p.z );
      }
      glEnd();
    }
}

void display(void)
{
    glClear(GL_COLOR_BUFFER_BIT | GL_DEPTH_BUFFER_BIT);
    glEnable(GL_TEXTURE_2D);
    glTexEnvf(GL_TEXTURE_ENV, GL_TEXTURE_ENV_MODE, GL_DECAL);
    glEnable( GL_CULL_FACE );
    glCullFace ( GL_BACK );

    glPointSize ( 6 );
    Point3 c;

    createSphere( c, 3.0 , 40 );

    glFlush();
    glDisable(GL_TEXTURE_2D);
}
```

Example 7-6 Mapping Texture to a Cube

In this example, a cube is drawn with texture images. It is similar to Example 7-4, where we "glue" images to quads except that now our images data are loaded from files and the images are "glued" to the six faces of a cube. Again we use **loadImageRGBA**() of **imageio** library to load the images from the files. The following is the code that does the mapping and Figure 7-15 shows the graphics output of the code.

```
int texImageWidth;
```

```
int texImageHeight;
static GLuint handles[6];    //texture names

//images for texture maps for 6 faces of cube
char maps[][40] = {"../data/front.png", "../data/back.png",
                   "../data/right.png", "../data/left.png",
                   "../data/up.png", "../data/down.png" };

//load texture image
GLubyte *makeTexImage( char *loadfile )
{
    int i, j, c, width, height;
    GLubyte *texImage;

    texImage = loadImageRGBA( (char *) loadfile, &width, &height);
    texImageWidth = width;
    texImageHeight = height;

    return texImage;
}

void init(void)
{
    glClearColor (1, 1, 1, 0.0);
    glShadeModel(GL_FLAT);
    glEnable(GL_DEPTH_TEST);
    glPixelStorei(GL_UNPACK_ALIGNMENT, 1);

    //handles is global
    glGenTextures(6, handles);
    for ( int i = 0; i < 6; ++i ) {
      GLubyte *texImage = makeTexImage( maps[i] );
      if ( !texImage ) {
        printf("\nError reading %s \n", maps[i] );
        continue;
      }
      glBindTexture(GL_TEXTURE_2D, handles[i]);//now we work on handles
      glTexParameteri(GL_TEXTURE_2D, GL_TEXTURE_WRAP_S, GL_REPEAT);
      glTexParameteri(GL_TEXTURE_2D, GL_TEXTURE_WRAP_T, GL_REPEAT);
      glTexParameteri(GL_TEXTURE_2D, GL_TEXTURE_MAG_FILTER,GL_NEAREST);
      glTexParameteri(GL_TEXTURE_2D, GL_TEXTURE_MIN_FILTER,GL_NEAREST);
      glTexImage2D(GL_TEXTURE_2D, 0, GL_RGBA, texImageWidth,
              texImageHeight, 0, GL_RGBA, GL_UNSIGNED_BYTE,texImage);

      delete texImage;       //free memory holding texture image
    }
}

void display(void)
{
    glClear(GL_COLOR_BUFFER_BIT | GL_DEPTH_BUFFER_BIT);
    glEnable(GL_TEXTURE_2D);
    glTexEnvf(GL_TEXTURE_ENV, GL_TEXTURE_ENV_MODE, GL_DECAL);
    float x0 = -1.0, y0 = -1, x1 = 1, y1 = 1, z0 = 1;
    float face[6][4][3] = {
      {{x0, y0, z0}, {x1, y0, z0}, {x1, y1, z0}, {x0, y1,z0}},  //front
      {{x0, y1, -z0}, {x1, y1, -z0},{x1, y0, -z0},{x0, y0,-z0}},//back
      {{x1, y0, z0}, {x1, y0, -z0}, {x1, y1, -z0}, {x1, y1,z0}},//right
      {{x0, y0, z0}, {x0, y1, z0}, {x0, y1, -z0}, {x0, y0,-z0}},//left
      {{x0, y1, z0}, {x1, y1, z0}, {x1, y1, -z0}, {x0, y1,-z0}},//top
      {{x0, y0, z0}, {x0, y0, -z0}, {x1, y0, -z0}, {x1,y0,z0}}  //bottom
    };
    glEnable( GL_CULL_FACE );
```

```
glCullFace ( GL_BACK );

glPushMatrix();
glRotatef( anglex, 1.0, 0.0, 0.0);      //rotate the cube along x-axis
glRotatef( angley, 0.0, 1.0, 0.0);      //rotate along y-axis
glRotatef( anglez, 0.0, 0.0, 1.0);      //rotate along z-axis

for ( int i = 0; i < 6; ++i ) {         //draw cube with texture images
  glBindTexture(GL_TEXTURE_2D, handles[i]);
  glBegin(GL_QUADS);
    glTexCoord2f(0.0, 0.0); glVertex3fv ( face[i][0] );
    glTexCoord2f(1.0, 0.0); glVertex3fv ( face[i][1] );
    glTexCoord2f(1.0, 1.0); glVertex3fv ( face[i][2] );
    glTexCoord2f(0.0, 1.0); glVertex3fv ( face[i][3] );
  glEnd();
}
glPopMatrix();
glFlush();
glDisable(GL_TEXTURE_2D);
}
```

Figure 7-15 Cube Mapping of Example 7-6

Chapter 8   Depth Perception

8.1   Stereoscopic Depth Perception

When we observe the three dimensional world with our eyes, the three dimensional environment is reduced to two-dimensional images on the two retinae of our eyes as shown in the figure below.

Figure 8-1 3D to 2D Projection on Retina
(Image from *http://www.mind.ilstu.edu/curriculum/vision_science_intro/vision_science_intro.php*)

We usually call the "lost" dimension *depth*, which is crucial for almost all of our interaction with our environment. Our brain tries to estimate the depth from the retinal images as good as it can with the help of different cues and mechanisms. *Depth perception* is the visual ability to perceive the world in three dimensions (3D) and the distance of an object. *Depth sensation* is the ability to move accurately, or to respond safely, based on the distances of objects in an environment. In nature, depth sensation is crucial for the survival of many animal species.

The main reason for humans to have depth perception is that we have two eyes located in our forehead and the two eyes are separated by a distance of about 2.5 inches. Because the left eye and right eye are at different positions, the 2D images of the 3D environment projected onto their retinae are not the same. The slight difference in the two projected images can be utilized to extract depth information. We usually refer to the discrepancies perceived by the two eyes as **binocular disparities**. Our brain converts binocular disparity to depth information based on our experience.

It turns out that eagles have a similar distance between the eyes as humans do as shown in the figure below. Therefore, eagles also can sense depth well. Actually, eagles have better vision than humans at the day time because their eyes have better cone cells.

Figure 8-2 Eagle Eyes and Human Eyes

Some readers may wonder whether some small animals with two eyes close to each other may have difficulties to extract depth information from the binocular disparities as the two projected images will be very close to each other. Indeed, animals such as insects and small birds whose eye separations are very small cannot resolve depth from binocular disparities; they have to rely on other methods such as object motions to infer the distance of an object. It turns out that even if we see with one eye, we still can extract a lot of depth information based on our perspective experience of the world. Actually, the problem of finding depth from 2D retinal images is an under-determined problem. However, in most situations we can perceive depths of objects in 2D images with ease.

What information contained in a 2D image makes us perceive depth? This approach of correlating information in the retinal image with depth in the scene is called *cue approach*. This approach tries to relate the elements of information contained in a 2D scene to the depth of the objects in the scene. According to cue theories, we make a connection between these cues and the actual depth by our accumulated knowledge from prior experience. The association becomes automatic after repeated experience of observing this 3D world. These include some heuristics, which may confuse us in pathological cases. We can roughly divide depth cues in a few different categories:

1. **Oculomotor**: Cues based on our ability to sense the tension in the eye muscles.
2. **Monocular**: Cues that work with one eye.
3. **Motion-based**: Cues that depend on motion of objects.
4. **Binocular**: Cues that depend on two frontal eyes.

8.2 Oculomotor Cues

Convergence and accommodation of our eyes can induce 3D information. *Accommodation* is the process by which our eye changes shape to maintain a clear image (focus) on an object as its distance changes. When looking at nearby objects, our eyes move inwards. This is called *convergence*. When looking at far away objects, our eyes move outward. Our eyes are relaxed and are non-convergent as shown in the right image of the figure below.

Figure 8-3 Converged Eyes and Non-converged Eyes

When the eyes move inward, there is a tightening of the muscles that hold the lens to get the eye to focus close by (left of Figure 8-3). When the eye moves outward, muscles relax (right of Figure 8-3). These two situations give us different sensations of our eye muscles which give us an estimate about the depth of the object. We can experience this by moving an object at our arms length closer and closer to the eye to feel the tightening of the muscles and then move it back again to feel the muscles relax. Actually, we can relax our eye muscles and thus improving our eyesight by alternating our staring at nearby and far away objects over a short period of time. So playing table tennis or badminton are good for our eyes.

There is a direct relationship between the effort of accommodation and the effort of convergence. We measure the effort of accommodation in *diopters*, and the effort of convergence in *degrees*. A diopter, or dioptre, is a unit of measurement of the optical power of a lens or a curved mirror. It is equal to the reciprocal of the focal length measured in metres. Therefore, its unit is the reciprocal of length. For example, a 3-diopter lens brings parallel rays of light to focus at $\frac{1}{3}$ meter from the lens.

There are three main types of eye refraction: emmetropia (normal-sightedness), myopia (near-sightedness), and hyperopia (farsightedness). Emmetropia is the normal condition of perfect vision, where parallel light rays are focused on the retina without the need for accommodation. When an emmetropic person is looking at a distant object, accommodation and convergence are at in a resting state; the axes of the eyes are parallel, and there is no effort of convergence (the angle of intersection is zero degrees). When the emmetropic (normal sighted) person is looking at a nearby object, some effort of accommodation and convergence is necessary. When an emmetropic person is looking at the distance of one meter, the effort of accommodation is 1.00 diopter, and if the eye separation is $65mm$, the angle of convergence θ is:

$$\theta = tan^{-1}\frac{65}{1000} = 3.7^o$$

Similarly, at a distance of 0.5 meters, if the effort of accommodation is 2.00 diopters, the angle of convergence is about 7.4 degrees. At a distance of 0.33 meters, if the effort of accommodation is 3.00 diopters, the convergence is about 11 degrees. Figure 8-4 shows the convergence of a nearby object and the convergence of a far object.

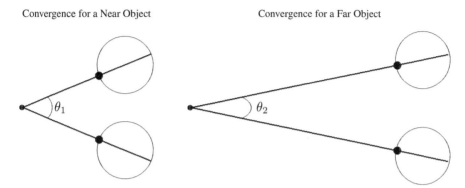

Figure 8-4   Angles of Convergence ($\theta_1 > \theta_2$)

8.3 Monoscopic Depth Cues

We can extract a lot of 3D information from a single 2D view. As we have discussed above, the 3D world is projected into a 2D image on the retina of an eye. People with one blind eye can only detect 2D images. However, you might know of some people with one blind eye who still can sense this three dimensional world. They might behave like a normal person and you might not be even aware of their handicap. They can move to a chair and sit properly on it; they do not bump into a wall and drop glasses over the table edges. They achieve these by extracting 3D information from a single 2D image they receive. The depth cues that are obtained from the 2D image of only one eye are called *monocular cues* or *pictorial cues*, which usually do not provide absolute information about depth, but relative depth with respect to other objects in the environment. Monocular cues include the following different types.

8.3.1   Occlusion

When an object is hidden fully or partially, this hidden (occluded) object is considered to be farther away, behind the object (occluding object) which is covering it. For example, if a house hides half a man, we know that the house is in front of him. *Occlusion* is also referred to as *interposition*. Figure 8-5 shows that the square is behind the circle as the circle hides part of the square.

Figure 8-5 Occlusion

Figure 8-6 also shows how depth cues can be obtained from occlusion. Sometimes, the depth information they present may be ambiguous as shown in Figure 8-6(b). Actually, many common optical illusions are based on these ambiguities. Despite the potential for ambiguity, combining many depth cues produces a powerful sense of three dimensionality. Figure 8-6(c) shows that the shadow cues resolve contradicting depth cues deduced from occlusion and relative object heights.

(a)   (b)   (c)

Figure 8-6   (a) Occlusion Cues

(b) Contradicting Occlusion and Relative Height Cues

(c) Shadows Resolving Contradiction

8.3.2 Relative Height

Relative height, also called *height in field*, is another cue to infer depth. We judge an object's distance by considering its height in our visual field relative to other objects. The usual assumption is that where the base of a shape is higher than that of a similar shape, then the one with the higher base is farther away. This cue relates objects to the horizon. As objects move away from us, objects get closer to the horizon. Therefore, we perceive objects nearer to the horizon as more distant than objects that are farther away from the horizon. This effect is shown in Figure 8-1 above and Figure 8-7 below. This means that below the horizon, objects higher in the visual field appear farther away than those that are lower. However, above the horizon, the effect is reversed; objects lower in the visual field appear farther away than those that are higher. These effects are shown in Figure 8-8. The clouds higher up in the image appear to be closer as they are above the horizon.

Figure 8-8 Clouds Higher Up in Sky Appear Closer

Figure 8-7 Distance to Horizon Induces Depth

8.3.3   Aerial Perspective, Atmosphere Blur, Saturation, and Color Shift

If the air is smoggy, particles suspended in the air make distant objects look blur like the images shown in Figure 8-9 below. Moreover, relative colours of objects give us some cues to their distances. Diffusion of water particles in the air will generate a bluish color shift and pollution-based diffusion will generate grey to brown color shifts.

Figure 8-9 Smoggy Atmosphere

Due to the scattering of blue light in the atmosphere, distant objects such as distant mountains appear more blue. Contrast of objects also provide clues to their distance. When the scattering of light blurs the outlines of objects, the object is perceived as distant. Mountains and objects are perceived to be closer when they appear clear. These effects are shown in Figure 8-10. Figure 8-11 shows a Chinese landscape painting using *atmospheric perspective* to show recession in space. Figure 8-12 shows aerial perspective as viewed towards a sunset; scattering has resulted in a shift of colour towards red.

Figure 8-10 Aerial Perspective

Figure 8-11 Atmospheric Perspective
in Painting

Figure 8-12 Color Shifting

8.3.4 Shadows and Highlights

We can extract depth information of an object from highlights and shadows. Because our visual system assumes light comes from above, a totally different perception is obtained if an image is viewed upside down. Figure 8-13 shows two rows of shadowed circular shapes which appear to be bumps on the left three columns; the illustration of the right three columns is obtained by viewing the left three columns upside down. The bumps become holes!

Figure 8-6 above shows an example where the occlusion and the relative height cues contradict each other. Shadows play an important role in this case to resolve the contradiction. The presence of the shadow removes the contradiction by telling us that the vase is in front of the glass but at a higher position.

Figure 8-13   Right-Half is Upside-Down View of Left-Half

8.3.5 Linear Perspective

Lines in the 3D environment that are perpendicular to the retinal image plane and are parallel will not be projected into parallel lines in the 2D image. Rather, the lines tend to merge with increasing distance and seem to converge to a point at infinity, which is referred to as a **vanishing point**. Consequently, when common objects with parallel-line features such as roads, railway lines, and electric wires subtend a smaller and smaller angle in a 2D image, we interpret them as being farther away. This linear perspective helps us obtain depth cues. Figure 8-14 shows an example of this effect; the road seems to converge to a single point at infinity.

The simplest version of such illusions deriving from linear perspective is called the *Ponzo illusion*, which is an optical illusion first demonstrated by the Italian psychologist Mario Ponzo in 1913. Ponzo suggested that the human mind judges an object's size based on its background. He showed this by drawing two identical lines across a pair of converging lines, similar to those shown in Figure 8-15; in the figure, even though both horizontal lines are of the same size, we perceive the upper line as longer. This is because we interpret the converging sides according to linear perspective as parallel lines receding into the distance. In this context, we interpret the upper line as if it were farther away. So it appears longer to us as a farther object would have to be longer than a nearer one for both to produce retinal images of the same size.

Some researchers believe that the Moon illusion is an example of the Ponzo illusion. The Moon illusion is a phenomenon where the Moon appears larger near the horizon than it does when it is higher up in the sky; in this situation, the trees and houses play the role of Ponzo's converging lines, and foreground objects which trick our brain into thinking the moon is bigger than it really is. There are many other explanations of the Moon illusion. Some believe its due to the variations of the angular size when the moon is at different positions and some believe its due to the atmospheric effects. Ponzo illusion may just account for part of the magnitude in Moon illusion.

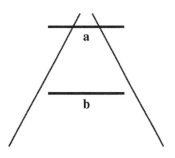

Figure 8-15 Ponzo Illusion

Figure 8-14 Linear Perspective

8.3.6   Relative Size and Familiar Size

Retinal image size allows us to judge distance based on our past and present experience and familiarity with similar objects. For example, if a building and a lady look the same size, we can assume that the building is farther away because from our real-life experience, a building is much larger than a lady. If two objects are equal in size, one that is farther away will have a smaller field of view than the closer one. We can combine this information with our previous knowledge of the object's size to determine the absolute depth of the object. For example, we are generally familiar with the size of an average automobile. We combine this prior knowledge with information about the angle it subtends on the retina to determine the distance of an automobile in a scene. This effect is shown in Figure 8-16; as a car drives away, the retinal image of it becomes smaller and smaller. We interpret a retinal image of a small car as a distant car.

Figure 8-16 Familiar and Relative Size Cues

8.3.7   Texture Gradient

If we view a texture surface from a slanting direction, rather than directly from above, we will see a *texture gradient* meaning that the texture pattern does not appear uniform but appears smaller at distant positions. Though texture gradient relates in a sense to relative size, it is a depth cue in its own right. Many surfaces in the real world, such as walls and roads and a field of flowers in bloom, have a texture. The texture becomes denser, smoother and less detailed as the surface gets farther away from us and recedes into the background. This information helps us to judge depth.

Figure 8-17 shows an example of texture gradient. It is a photo image of a dried river bank. The diamond-shaped dried mud blocks are the key patterns. The mud blocks get progressively smaller as the river bank recedes in depth; eventually the blocks are not clearly distinguishable from each other. In the distant surface, only the general roughness of the river bank is noticeable and then this roughness becomes less noticeable at farther distance.

Figure 8-17   Texture Gradient

8.3.8   Familiar Shapes

We store the information of the shape of an object that we have encountered in our brain. When we see the object again, we will retrieve the shape information of the object from our memory. The object shape can give depth cues of the object. Figure 8-18 shows two objects of similar texture. However, we will perceive the left object as a convex soccer ball, until it skews and we identify it a a ball-textured concave plate shown on the right.

Shapes alone may not give strong depth perception. However, when we combine the knowledge of the shape of an object with other depth sense, we obtain strong depth cues. Studies have suggested that under many circumstances, the brain combines cues using weighted linear combination, where individual cues are first processed largely independent of each other to yield an estimate of an environmental property. The brain combines estimates from different depth cues by weighing each source of information proportional to its statistical reliability.

8.4   Motion-based Depth Cues

By analyzing the movements of objects, our brain can reveal the objects' speeds and directions, as well as their placement in the 3D environment. We can estimate how far away a moving object is by watching how fast it seems to move. For example, an airplane in sky looks stationary but appears to move very fast on the runway. If information about the direction and velocity of movement is known, motion *parallax*, which is the relative position of an object's retinal image at various times can provide absolute depth information. Some small animals such as birds rely on motion parallax to determine depth.

On the other hand, our head movements change our viewpoints of the environment frequently. These point-of-view (PoV) movements also cause motion parallax by which images of nearby objects cross the retinal image plane faster than those of distant objects. We observe this phenomenon when we sit inside a train and look outside through a window like the situation shown in Figure 8-19; we see that nearby objects speedily pass by in a blur, but distant objects move slightly. We can use the speed of these passing objects to estimate the distance of the objects.

Figure 8-18   Depth Cues from Shapes

Figure 8-19   Motion Parallax
(From *http://www.morguefile.com/ archive/display/1696*)

The sequence of images in Figure 8-20 below shows another example of motion parallax induced by PoV movement. As the viewpoint moves side to side, the displacements of nearby objects in Figure 8-20 are much larger than those of distant objects. When the sequence of images are shown as consecutive frames in a movie or a video game, the distant objects will appear to move more slowly than the objects close to the camera. Moreover, our eye movement also leads to deletion and accretion of objects as shown in the figure. As we move, parts of objects get revealed or occluded. We obtain depth information of the objects from the rate of these deletion and accretion.

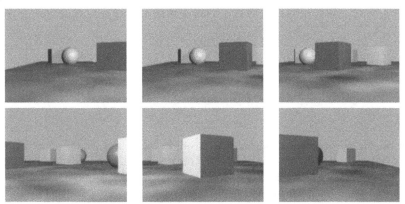

Figure 8-20   Motion Parallax Example
(Images from *http://en.wikipedia.org/wiki/Parallax*)

8.5   Binocular Cues

Animals that have frontal eyes can use information derived from the different projection of objects into each retina to deduce depth. The two eyes of a human are about 7 cm apart and hence they view the same scene with slightly different angles. Consequently, the projected 2D retinal images on the two eyes are different from each other. Though there is a significant overlap of view from the two eyes, their views are not identical as their locations are different. This difference in view is called *binocular disparity* and the brain converts it to depth information. The information provided by the disparity is called *stereopsis*.

The distance to an object can be derived with a high degree of accuracy using a process called *triangulation*, in which we determine the location of a point by measuring angles to it from known points at either end of a fixed baseline. In other words, given a baseline and two angles measured from the baseline, we can fix the whole triangle. Figure 18-21 shows how this is done. Suppose e is the known distance between the two points A and B. (For example, e can be the eye separation.) Then the distance d of the third point C from the baseline AB can be determined by trigonometric identities.

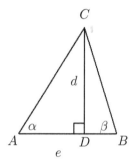

Figure 18-21 Triangulation

That is,

$$
\begin{aligned}
e &= AD + DB \\
&= \frac{d}{\tan \alpha} + \frac{d}{\tan \beta} \\
&= d[\frac{\cos \alpha}{\sin \alpha} + \frac{\cos \beta}{\sin \beta}] \\
&= d[\frac{\cos \alpha \sin \beta + \cos \beta \sin \alpha}{\sin \alpha \sin \beta}] \\
&= d[\frac{sin(\alpha + \beta)}{\sin \alpha \sin \beta}]
\end{aligned}
$$

Therefore, the distance d to the baseline is given by

$$
d = \frac{e \times \sin \alpha \sin \beta}{sin(\alpha + \beta)}
\tag{8.1}
$$

We may be able to triangulate the distance to an object with a high degree of accuracy. Equation (8.1) shows that one can derive the distance of an object from the eye separation and the viewing angles of the eyes. However, it does not show the relation between the object distance and the disparity of the retina images. In reality, if an object is far away, the disparity of the images projected on both retinas is small. If the object is near, the disparity is large. It is *stereopsis* that tricks us into thinking of perceiving depth when viewing a 3-D movie or a stereoscopic photo.

One popular approach to generate stereo displays in cinema is to use different polarized light to project the images from two different viewpoints on the same screen. The viewers are provided with polarized glasses. The left glass allows one direction of polarization and the right glass allows the other. Though a viewer is watching the same screen, the two eyes receive two different images. The right image is blocked by the left glass and the left image is blocked by the right glass. This creates a compelling sense of depth. A simpler approach is to use colored glasses; the left glass allows one color such as red to pass through and the right glass allows another color such as blue to go through; the viewers are presented with two images of the same scene from two viewpoints, one created using red color and the other using blue color leading to a depth sensation. Similar technologies are used in head-mounted displays where a head gear with two micro-screens, one in front of each eye, is mounted on the head of the viewer. A sense of depth is created by projecting two images of the same scene generated from two different viewpoints on two different screens.

8.5.1 Horopter

Horopter, derived from the Greek words *horos* (boundary) and *opter* (observer), is a 3D curve used for modeling the human visual system. It consists of the points for which the light falls on corresponding areas in the two retinas. This is the same as the set of points of intersection of a *cylinder* and a *hyperbolic paraboloid*. A horopter can be regarded as a one-turn helix curve around a cylinder like the one shown in Figure 8-22. In the special case that he horopter is in the horizontal plane through the eyes that contain the centers of the retinas, it is referred to as the *Vieth-Muller circle* . In this case, the horopter takes the form of a circle, plus the line along the cylinder, and it is referred to as the *vertical horopter*. The center region of the retina, where the light falls on when we look straight to an object, is called the *fovea*. The eye structure is shown in Figure 8-23; light enters the pupil and is focused and inverted by the cornea and lens; it is then projected onto the retina at the back of the eye where seven layers of alternating cells process and convert the light signal into a neural signal.

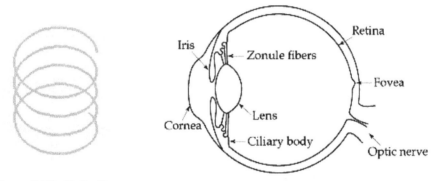

Figure 8-22   Helix Curve

Figure 8-23   Eye and Retina

The Vieth-Muller circle is the theoretical horopter, which can be computed based on the geometry of the eyes and the viewing distance. The more general horopter of an individual is found empirically, where the horopter is the locus of points in space that appear binocularly fused to the observer; all the points lying on the horopter are imaged at corresponding points in the two eyes. *Corresponding retinal points* are the locations in each retina connected to the same place in the visual cortex; they give rise to the same visual direction. We can determine these points by locating the matching points on the retina when one retina could be slid on top of another. Anywhere else in space appears as a double image to the observer. The actual horopter measured in a laboratory is referred to as *empirical horopter*. These are shown in Figure 8-24. In the figure, the fixation point is the point in the visual field that is fixated by the two eyes in normal vision and for each eye is the point that directly stimulates the fovea of the retina. The nodal point is the point in the eye where light entering or leaving the eye and is undeviated. This allows similar triangles to be used to determine the retinal image size of an object in space. The horopter varies across individuals and with fixation distance and gaze angle.

The images of points closer than the horopter do not lie on corresponding points across the retina. Moving an object slightly off the horopter creates a small amount of *retinal disparity* that gives rise to stereoscopic depth perception as shown in Figure 8-25.

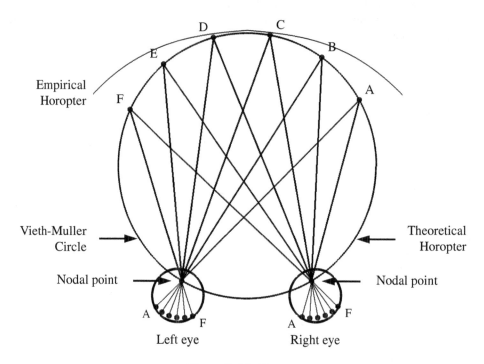

Figure 8-24 Horopter

There are physiological evidence that we are sensitive to retinal disparity. Researchers have identified cells in the visual cortex that respond selectively to different ranges of disparities. Though humans can convert retinal disparities to depth information with utter ease, it is not easy to devise computer vision algorithms to do so.

Note that only animals with frontal eyes such as cats, dogs, and humans make use of disparity to perceive depth. Some animals such as rabbits, buffaloes and birds which have lateral eyes located on both sides of the head cannot use disparity to sense depth. However, those animals have a wider view of the world than animals with frontal eyes. In such animals, the eyes often move independently to increase the field of view. Even without moving their eyes, some birds have a 360-degree field of view. They have much better ways of using motion cues to sense depth. In the process of evolution, predators like eagles grow frontal eyes as depth perception is very important for them to hunt successfully. On the other hand, animals lower in the food chain, herbivores such as rabbits and deers usually grow lateral eye so that they can have a larger field of view to see a larger part of the environment to detect predators more effectively.

8.5.2 Vision Fusion

As we have two eyes, we should receive two images of an object. Yet we do not see an object double because our brain fuses the two images into one. *Fusion* is the neural process that brings the retinal images in the two eyes to form one single image. It is the fusion process that enables us to have binocular vision, which gives accurate depth perception.

Fusion takes place when the images are from the same object. When the objects are different but their field of view overlaps, suppression, superimposition or binocular (retinal) rivalry may occur to avoid confusion. *Suppression* is the neural process of eliminating one image to prevent confusion. *Superimposition* occurs when one image is presented on top of the other image.

When two very different images are shown to the same retinal regions of the two eyes, our perception settles on one for a few moments, then the other, then the first, and so on, for as long as we care to look. This alternation of perception between the images of the two eyes is referred to as *binocular rivalry* or *retinal rivalry* . This usually occurs when lines with different orientation, size or brightness are presented to the two eyes.

You can experiment the fusion process with the images shown in Figure 8-26 by placing a pen between yourself and the figure. Keep your eyesight on the tip of the pen and move it slowly from the screen towards you. You should see the two images fused together.

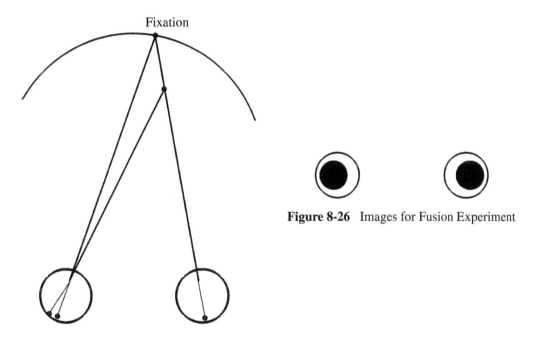

Fixation

Figure 8-26 Images for Fusion Experiment

Figure 8-25 Retinal Disparity

Chapter 9   Principles of 3D Stereoscopic Graphics

9.1   Anaglyph

We discussed in the previous chapter that retinal disparity enables us to perceive depth. Therefore, if we could present to our left eye a 2D image of an object slightly different from that presented to the right eye, we can deceive our brain to sense depth and think that we are seeing a real 3D object. There are many different ways of creating and viewing stereoscopic 3D images. They all rely on independently presenting different images to the left and right eye. Besides the method of using polarized glasses mentioned in the previous chapter to view stereoscopic images, one can also use LCD shutter glasses to view frame-sequential stereo, where the left and right eye images are presented alternatively and are synchronized with the LCD shutter. Figure 9-1 shows an example of this kind of glasses. LCD shutter glasses are expensive, ranging from around $60 to $800 per pair. A system of two pairs of glasses and an emitter range from $1000 to $2000.

Figure 9-1 LCD Shutter Glasses

A simple and inexpensive way to experience stereoscopic 3D effects is to use **anaglyphs**. An anaglyph is a stereoscopic picture where the left and right eye images are superimposed, but in different colors. A color filter over each eye only transmits the image component suitable for that eye. For example, the lenses of a pair of anaglyph glasses consists of chromatically opposite colors such as "red and cyan" or "red and blue". An anaglyph image is made up of two color layers, superimposed, but offset with respect to each other to produce a depth effect. In general the main subject is at the center, while the foreground and background are shifted laterally in opposite directions. The picture contains two differently filtered colored images, one for each eye. When we view superimposed image through a pair of color-coded anaglyph glasses, we will see a 3D object or scene that looks realistic. Anaglyph glasses are usually cheap. Paper anaglyph filter may cost less than 50 cents and better glasses cost about $3. Figure 9-2a shows a low-cost paper anaglyph filters and Figure 9-2b shows a red-green anaglyph glasses.

Many stereoscopic photographers do not like anaglyphs because of the poor color, ghosting and retinal rivalry they produce. However, most Internet 3D stereoscopic images are presented in anaglyph format as using anaglyphs is the cheapest way to create and project stereoscopic 3D images using digital cameras and a single digital projector. NASA publishes anaglyphs extensively. Some children's books also often use anaglyphs to show 3D images. Figure 9-3 shows an example of anaglyph where the left eye image is in red and the right eye image is in cyan; they are superimposed to form one single image.

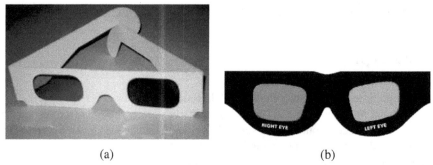

(a)   (b)

Figure 9-2 Anaglyph Glasses

Figure 9-3 An Anaglyph (red on left, cyan on right)

Despite its popularity, there are a few disadvantages of using anaglyphs to present 3D scenes, which include the following.

1. **Ghosting**. The viewers may see a faintly-colored ghost image if some color from the left image gets into the right eye or that from the right gets into the left. Increasing the parallax (stereo depth) separates the two images further and makes the 3D effect more pronounced but it also makes the ghosting effect worse. Ideally, a computer color display would show red, green and blue without any overlap between the colors. However, researchers have shown from spectral analysis that practical screens have "cross-talk" between the colors. For example, a green pixel component may also emit some red light. If each RGB component does not emit its own colour exclusively, it is not possible for a pair of anaglyph glasses to filter the colors precisely; those monitors will produce ghosting effects. In general LCD screens have less color cross-talk than CRT monitors.

2. **Retinal rivalry**. We explained in the previous chapter that retinal rivalry may occur if image attributes such as brightness or size of the two images are different. Very often, the brightness of the two images of an anaglyph is not the same in each eye, leading to retinal

rivalry which gives an unpleasant viewing effect. Some anaglyph glasses have one filter darker than the other, which will routinely cause retinal rivalry.

9.2   Creating Anaglyphs with GIMP

We can create an anaglyph using the open-source graphics package *GIMP*, the *GNU Image Manipulation Program*, which is a freely distributed piece of software for such tasks as *photo retouching*, *image composition* and *image authoring*. It works on many operating systems, and in many languages. You can download it from its official web site at *http://www.gimp.org/*. The following steps show you how to make an anaglyph using GIMP.

1. Take two photos of an object using a digital camera located at two different positions. The distance between two locations of the camera should be about 70 mm. Note that our cameras are mimicking our eyes, which always focus on something; at the two camera positions, the camera should not view straight ahead separately. Rather, we should point the camera to focus at the same focal point from the two camera locations.

2. Transfer the two images to your computer.

3. Start GIMP and open the right image. Note that objects in the right image are more to the left when overlaid with the left eye image.

4. From the color selector, choose color "red" (ff0000). (**Dialogs** > **Colors** > Enter "ff0000" in the text box)

5. Create a layer above the right image and fill it with this color (**Layer** > **New Layer**> Select 'Foreground Color').

6. Duplicate this layer (**Layer** > **Duplicate Layer**) and click on **Colors** > **Invert**. This will change the color of the duplicated red layer to a cyan color (direct opposite). The resulted RGB color will have $R = 000, G = 255$, and $B = 255$.

7. Select the red layer. Click on **File** > **Open as Layers** and open the left image. (You can use Ctrl-Tab to cycle through all layers in an image if your window manager doesn't trap those keys. You can always access the layers through **Dialog** > **Layer**.)

8. The above step will put the left image just above the red layer and you should now have 4 layers in the following order, from bottom to top: the right image, the red layer, the left image and the cyan layer as shown in the figure below.

9. You can check the alignment of the image pair by turning off the red and cyan layers and adjusting the opacity of the left image to 50%. Make sure that both images are on the same vertical plane and shift up/down appropriately. When finished checking the alignment, change the opacity of the left image back to 100%. (A layer can be turned off by clicking the eye icon at the left of the Layers dialog box; you can turn it on again by clicking the position again.)

10. Select the cyan layer and change the transfer mode to *screen* by clicking on **Dialogs** > **Layers** > **Mode: Screen**.

11. Turn off the lower layer (the right image) and the red layer by clicking on the small eye icon, which is at the left side of the **Layers** menu.

12. Merge the cyan and left image layers together by clicking on **Image** > **Merge Visible Layers** > **Merge**. You should now see a faint image of your photo. Turn off this new cyan layer by clicking on the eye icon of the Layer dialog box.

13. Turn the red and right image layers back on and change the red layer transfer mode to *screen*. Then merge them in the same way you merged the cyan and left image layers in above. Again you will see a faint red image similar to the cyan image you saw before.

14. Turn on the new merged cyan/left image layer and select it. Change the transfer mode to multiply. You should now see the superimposed 3D image. Put on your anaglyph glasses (red on left, cyan on right) and you should see the realistic 3D effect. The anaglyph shown in Figure 9-3 was created in this way.

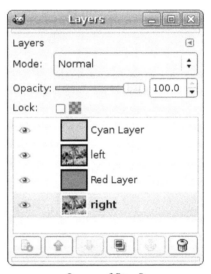

Layers of Step 8

9.3 Horizontal Parallax

As we have discussed in the previous chapter, when we view an object along two different lines of sight, we will see the object appear at difference positions; the displacement of the object (i.e. the difference of the apparent positions of the object) is referred to as **parallax**. Sometimes people define parallax as the angle subtended by the two lines of sight. Therefore, we may measure parallax by the angle or semi-angle of inclination between the two lines of sight. Nearby objects have a larger parallax than distant objects when observed from different positions. As a result we can use parallax to determine depth.

In astronomy, parallax is the apparent difference in position or angle of a body such as the sun or a star, as seen from some point on the earth's surface. Astronomers use the principle of parallax to measure distances to celestial objects, including the distances to the Moon, the Sun, and to stars beyond the Solar System. For example, the Hipparcos satellite took measurements for over 100,000 nearby stars, which provide a basis to pinpoint other distant stars. In this case, *parallax* is the angle or semi-angle of inclination between two lines of sight to the star.

When we look at a stereoscopic picture, our brain extracts and computes the size of the dispar- ities to access the distance of the objects. Figure 9-4 shows the projections of a single model point on a plane for two different eye positions. Our left and right eyes see two different projections of the model point; the projection for the left eye is on the left and the projection for the right eye is on the right. The two projected points are called **homologous points**.

In general, two projected points (one for the left eye and one for the right eye) are **homolo- gous** if they are projected from a common model point. The horizontal distance between the two homologous points is called the **horizontal parallax**. We may also define horizontal parallax as the angle subtended by the horizontal distance between the two homologous points. Similarly, the vertical distance between two homologous points is called the **vertical parallax**. Since our eyes are horizontal, when we talk about parallax, we refer to horizontal parallax unless otherwise stated.

In Figure 9-4, since the projections are on the same side as the respective eyes, we call the parallax a positive parallax. Note that the maximum positive parallax occurs when the object (model point) is at infinity; at this point the horizontal parallax is equal to the interocular (i.o.) distance, which is the separation between the two eyes.

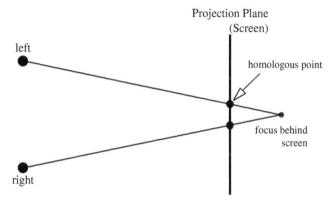

Figure 9-4 **Positive Parallax** with two **homologous points** on the plane

Figure 9-5 shows the case of **negative parallax**, where the projection for the left eye is on the right and the projection for the right eye is on the left. In this case, the model point is in front of the projection plane. Obviously, when the model point is half way between the projection plane and the center of the eyes, the interocular distance is equal to the negative horizontal parallax. The negative horizontal parallax increases to infinity as the model point moves closer to the viewer, and it goes to zero as the model point moves towards the projection plane.

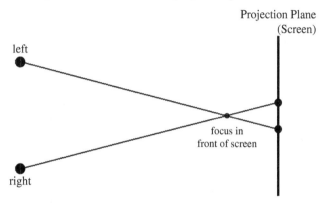

Figure 9-5 **Negative Parallax**

Figure 9-6 shows the case of zero parallax , where objects are at the projection plane. In this case, the projections for the left eye and the right eye converge to the same location at which the model point is located.

In summary, objects associated with positive parallax are seen to be behind the projection plane; those with negative parallax are seen to be in front of the plane and those with zero parallax are at the plane.

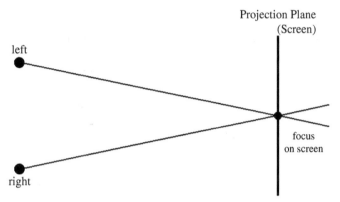

Figure 9-6 Zero Parallax

To create good stereo pairs, it is crucial to achieve appropriate horizontal parallax. On the other hand, we should avoid or at least strictly limit vertical parallax. In general, we will have difficulties in fusing and holding images together in the presence of vertical parallax. One way vertical parallax will be introduced is that we use different projection planes for the left eye and the right eye. For example, the toe-in method that some people use to generate stereo pairs is simple and quick. However, it also introduces vertical parallax that could make viewers uncomfortable when viewing the stereo images with glasses. We will discuss this method in more detail in the next chapter.

We can use shear transformation to implement positive and negative horizontal parallax. Actually, shear transformations mechanisms are included in the left and right eye projection matrices.

We can measure parallax in inches or degrees. The parallax distance between homologous points would be in inches and the parallax angle θ describing the angle made by the homologous points and the viewer would be in degrees. So if we describe parallax in inches, we refer to the distance and if we describe parallax in degrees, we refer to the angle. The parallax distance p in inches and the angle θ in degrees is related by the formula,

$$p = 2d \times tan\frac{\theta}{2} \tag{9.1}$$

where d is the distance from the viewer to the projection plane (stereo plane). Lastly, if the stereo images are projected on a computer screen, we may describe parallax in terms of pixels.

In practice, *when we create stereo images on a computer screen, what parallax value should we use?* There are a few rules we may follow to generate good stereo pairs. Ideally, maximum positive parallax should be equal to the typical human eye separation. In this way we will not force our eyes into divergence, which is what will happen if the positive parallax is greater than our eye separation. If the positive parallax is equal to our eye separation, the object we view will appear to be at infinity as we can tell from Figure 9-4. Maximum negative parallax should be also equal to the eye separation, which occurs when the object being viewed is half way between the screen and our eyes. Actually, negative parallax is more flexible because we can cope with larger changes in negative parallax than with positive. However, measurements of parallax depend on the screen size and viewing distance as shown in Equation (9.1) above. This implies that stereo images that work well on a small screen may not work well when viewed on a large screen. The following calculation gives a guideline for estimating the maximum positive parallax p_{max} in pixels for a given screen size:

$$p_{max} = \frac{i.o.}{w} \times N \qquad (9.2)$$

where $i.o.$ is the human interocular distance (eye separation), which is about 2.5 inches, w is the screen width in inches, and N is the number of horizontal pixels. For example, a small 24-inch wide HD monitor would have a maximum positive parallax of

$$p_{max} = \frac{2.5}{24} \times 1920 = 200 \; (pixels)$$

In other words, the interocular distance covers a range of 200 pixels. If the screen is 30 feet wide but with the same number of horizontal pixels, then the maximum parallax is

$$p_{max} = \frac{2.5}{360} \times 1920 = 13.3 \; (pixels)$$

9.4   Calculating Stereo Pairs

9.4.1   Perspective Projection

We discussed in Chapter 4 the concept of perspective projection, and in particular perspective projection transformations in Section 4.2.2. This projection is important in creating stereoscopic images. Figure 9-7 below shows a viewing frustum; any object inside the frustum will be projected into the near-plane.

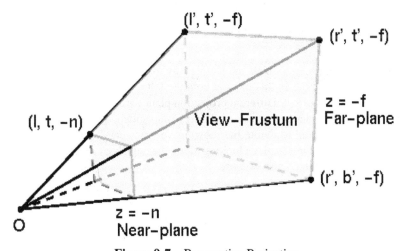

Figure 9-7   Perspective Projection

In Figure 9-7, the eye (viewing point) is at the origin O, looking towards the negative z direction; the near-plane is at $z = -n$ and the far-plane is at $z = -f$; more detailly,

$$
\begin{array}{llll}
n = & \text{near distance} & f = & \text{far distance} \\
l = & \text{left} & r = & \text{right} \\
b = & \text{bottom} & t = & \text{top} \\
O = & (0,0,0) & &
\end{array} \qquad (9.3)
$$

Any point (x, y, z) inside the frustum is projected into a point (x', y', z') on the screen at $z = -n$. Obviously z' is always equal to $-n$. The values of x' and y' can be easily calculated using similar triangles as shown in Figure 9-8. The calculated values are shown in Equation (9.4) below.

$$\begin{pmatrix} x' \\ y' \\ z' \end{pmatrix} = \begin{pmatrix} \frac{-nx}{z} \\ \frac{-ny}{z} \\ -n \end{pmatrix} \qquad (9.4)$$

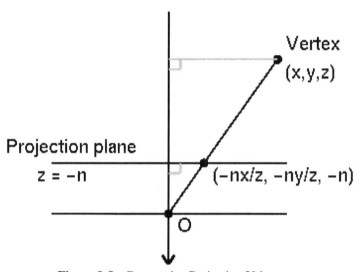

Figure 9-8 Perspective Projection Values

9.4.2 Rotation or Toe-in Method

The rotation or Toe-in method is a quick and simple way to create graphics stereo pairs. However, this is also an incorrect method. In this method both the left and right eyes point towards a single focal point as shown in Figure 9-9. Different projection planes are used for the two eyes. If the eye separation is known, the center between the two eyes is specified, and the focal point is defined, then other parameters required to define the viewing volumes can be calculated. For instance, consider that the eyes are in the x-y plane looking along the negative z direction and the mid-point of the two eyes is at the origin O, and suppose

$$\begin{aligned} O &= \quad (0,0,0) \\ f &= \quad \text{focal length} \\ e &= \quad \text{eye separation} \end{aligned} \qquad (9.5)$$

Then we can calculate the eye positions and their distances to the projection plane. For example,

Left eye position $\qquad\qquad E_l = (-\frac{e}{2}, 0, 0)$

Distance from left eye to projection plane $\quad d = \sqrt{f^2 + (e/2)^2}$ $\qquad (9.6)$

We can obtain similar equations for the right eye. Once the eye position and its distance to the projection plane (which is the near plane in this case) are known, we can specify the viewing volume and calculate its projected values according to Equation (9.4). OpenGL users usually use the function **gluPerspective** to do the projection.

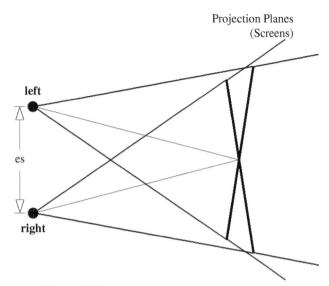

Figure 9-9   Toe-in Method (es = eye separation)

Though the Toe-in method is simple and gives workable stereo pairs, it is not a friendly way to generate stereo pairs. It causes vertical parallax and distorts the stereo plane. The vertical parallax is most noticeable when objects are placed at the outer field of view.

9.4.3   Two-Center Projection (Off-axis Projection)

The two-center or off-axis projection is sometimes known as **parallel axis asymmetric frustum perspective projection**. In this case, the view vector for each eye position remains parallel as shown in Figure 9-10. Instead of projecting objects into two different planes, this method projects the objects into a unique single plane and will not cause vertical parallax. Usually, OpenGL users use the **glFrustum** function to describe the perspective projections of this method.

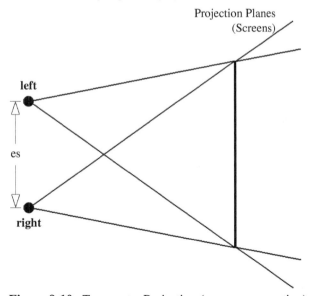

Figure 9-10   Two-center Projection (es = eye separation)

As discussed in Chapter 4, for any given point $P(x_0, y_0, z_0)$ inside the viewing frustum, it is not difficult to find where it will be projected into the projection plane. For instance, consider the setup of the eye positions shown in Figure 9-11 with index l denoting left and r denoting right. Suppose the camera is looking along the negative direction, eye separation (i.o. distance) is e, the middle of the two eye positions is at $(0,0,0)$ and the projection is at $z = -d$ as shown in the figure. We can use parametric equations to determine a point $P = (x, y, z)$ on the line joining the points $P_0 = (x_0, y_0, z_0)$ given that the left eye position is $E_l = (e/2, 0, 0)$:

$$P = P_0 + t(E_l - P_0) \qquad\qquad 0 \le t \le 1 \qquad\qquad (9.7)$$

Equation (9.7) actually consists of three equations:

$$\begin{aligned} x &= x_0 + t(e/2 - x_0) \\ y &= y_0 + t(0 - y_0) \\ z &= z_0 + t(0 - z_0) \end{aligned} \qquad\qquad (9.8)$$

At the projection plane, $z = -d$. So we can solve for t:

$$-d = z_0 + t(0 - z_0) \qquad\qquad (9.9)$$

which implies

$$t = \frac{z_0 + d}{z_0} \qquad\qquad (9.10)$$

Knowing t, we obtain the x, y coordinates at the viewing (projection) plane, where $x = x_l, y = y_l$:

$$\begin{aligned} x_l &= -\frac{d \times x_0}{z_0} + \frac{e \times d}{2z_0} + \frac{e}{2} \\ y_l &= -\frac{d \times y_0}{z_0} \end{aligned} \qquad\qquad (9.11)$$

Similarly, we can solve for the right eye position:

$$\begin{aligned} x_r &= -\frac{d \times x_0}{z_0} + \frac{e \times d}{2z_0} - \frac{e}{2} \\ y_r &= -\frac{d \times y_0}{z_0} \end{aligned} \qquad\qquad (9.12)$$

Equations (9.11) and (9.12) demonstrate how the projected points on the view plane can be calculated for the two different eye positions, left and right. However, in reality we do not need to carry out the calculations in our applications. In OpenGL, we can simply implement this shift by translation in the modelview matrix. We can recalculate the e term for each frame in an animation based on a set of parallax angles. An additional shift (yielding both positive and negative parallax) is created by altering the projection matrix so that the perspective view volume is asymmetrical.

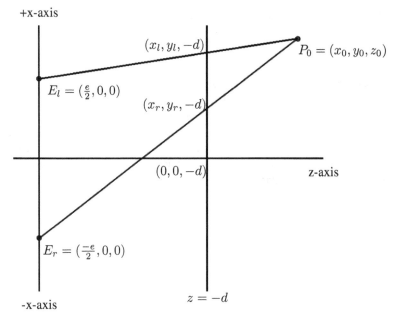

Figure 9-11   Two-center Projection Calculations

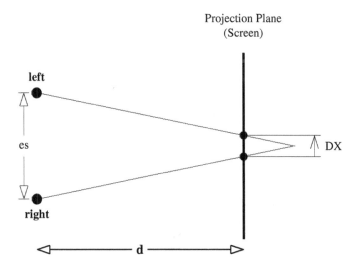

Figure 9-12   Stereo Effect Measurement

9.4.4   Stereo Effect

As we mentioned before, objects that lie in front of the projection plane will appear to be in front of the computer screen and objects that lie behind the projection plane will appear to be "into" the screen. It is generally easier to view stereo pairs of objects that recede into the screen (positive parallax). To achieve this, we would place the focal point closer to the camera than the objects of interest. A common measure of the **stereo effect** is the parallax angle, which is defined as

$$\theta = 2tan^{-1}\frac{DX}{2d} \tag{9.12}$$

where DX is the horizontal separation of a projected point on the screen for the two eye positions and d is the distance of the eyes from the projection plane as shown in Figure 9-12 above. For easy fusing by the majority of people, we should make the absolute value of θ be less than 1.5 degrees for all points in the scene. Note that θ is positive for points behind the scene and negative for points in front of the screen. It is a fairly common practice to restrict the negative value of θ to some value closer to zero since negative parallax is more difficult to fuse especially when model objects overlap with the boundary of the projection plane.

Chapter 10   Creating Stereoscopic Images with OpenGL

10.1   Multirendering using Accumulation Buffer

The accumulation buffer in OpenGL is one of the few buffers that help users processing graphics data more conveniently. It has the same spatial resolution as the frame buffer but the accumulation buffer has greater depth resolution. It is a higher precision buffer that can be used to accumulate intermediate rendering results. We can alter the viewing and projection matrices to provide multiple samples. These multiple samples result in multiple images, which are typically added into the accumulation buffer. Very often, the resulting accumulated images are scaled to produce an average filtered image. The following are the properties of the OpenGL accumulation buffer.

1. We may think of the accumulation buffer as a special color buffer that stores color values in floating point numbers and accumulates values.
2. Images are not rendered into it directly. Rather, images rendered into one of the color buffers are added to the contents of the accumulation buffer after rendering. Special graphics effects such as antialiasing, motion blur, and depth-of-field can be created by accumulating images generated with different transformation matrices.
3. It helps us to do image processing in a convenient way.

The function that operates on the accumulation buffer is **glAccum**(), which works as follows.

void **glAccum** (GLenum *op*, GLfloat *mult*);

   op   Specifies the accumulation buffer operation. Valid symbolic constants include GL_ACCUM, GL_LOAD, GL_ADD, GL_MULT, and GL_RETURN.

 mult   Specifies a floating-point value used in the accumulation buffer operation. The first parameter *op* determines how this value is used.

The operations specified by the parameter *op* are as follows:

GL_ACCUM
The operation obtains integer values of R, G, B, and A from the buffer currently selected for reading. Each component value is divided by $2^n - 1$, where n is the number of bits allocated to each color component in the currently selected buffer. This results in a floating-point number in the range $[0, 1]$; this number is multiplied by the parameter *mult* and added to the corresponding pixel component in the accumulation buffer, thereby updating the accumulation buffer.

GL_LOAD
The operation is similar to GL_ACCUM, except that it does not use the current value in the accumulation buffer to calculate the new value. Here, the integer values of R, G, B, and A from the currently selected buffer are divided by $2^n - 1$, multiplied by *mult*, and then stored in the corresponding accumulation buffer location, overwriting the current value.

GL_ADD
The operation adds *mult* to each of the R, G, B, and A components in the accumulation buffer.

GL_MULT

The operations multiplies each of the R, G, B, and A components in the accumulation buffer by *mult* and returns the scaled component to its corresponding accumulation buffer location.

GL_RETURN

The operation transfers accumulation buffer values to the color buffer or buffers currently selected for writing. It multiplies each R, G, B, and A component by *mult*, then multiplies the product by $2^n - 1$, clamps the result to the range $[0, 2^n - 1]$, and stores the result in the corresponding display buffer location. The only fragment operations that are applied to this transfer are pixel ownership, scissor, dithering, and color writemasks.

We can 'clear' the accumulation buffer with specified color components using the functions **glClearAccum**() and **glClear**() (with accumulation buffer enabled). The function **glClearAccum** (float R, float G, float B, float A) set the R, G, B, and A values when the accumulation buffer is cleared.

The following code section shows an example of using this function to display four images at the same time:

```
glutInitDisplayMode (GLUT_DOUBLE | GLUT_RGB | GLUT_ACCUM );
......

glClear(GL_ACCUM_BUFFER_BIT);
for ( int i = 0; i < 4; i++ ) {
   glClear(GL_COLOR_BUFFER_BIT|GL_DEPTH_BUFFER_BIT);//clear screen
   draw_image( i );              //construct i-th image
   glAccum(GL_ACCUM, 0.25);     //scale each image by 0.25
}
glClear( GL_COLOR_BUFFER_BIT );//clear screen
glAccum(GL_RETURN, 1.0);         //render the accumulated image
```

Example 10-1   Blending Colors of 3 Triangles

In this example, we make use of the accumulation buffer to blend the colors of three partially overlapped triangles. The function **glRotatef**() is used to slightly offset each triangle so that they only partially overlap with each other. The following is the complete listing of the program.

```
/*
  accumtest.cpp :
  Partially overlap three triangles with blending colors
  using accumulation buffer.
*/
#include <GL/glut.h>
void init( void ) {
  glClearColor( 1.0, 1.0, 1.0, 0.0 ); //get white background color
  glMatrixMode( GL_PROJECTION );
  glLoadIdentity();
  gluOrtho2D( 0.0, 400.0, 0.0, 400.0 );
}

void draw_triangle() {
  glBegin( GL_TRIANGLES );
    glVertex2i( 100, 100 );
    glVertex2i( 100, 300 );   glVertex2i( 300, 300 );
  glEnd();
}

void setColor( int i ) {
```

```
      switch ( i ){
      case 0:
        glColor3f( 1, 0, 0 );   break;
      case 1:
        glColor3f( 0, 1, 0 );   break;
      case 2:
        glColor3f( 0, 0, 1 );   break;
      default:
        glColor3f( 0, 0, 0 );   break;
      }
    }

    void display( void ) {
      glClear(GL_ACCUM_BUFFER_BIT);
      for ( int i = 0; i < 3; i++ ) {
        glClear(GL_COLOR_BUFFER_BIT);//clear screen
        glPushMatrix();
        //slightly displace each triangle
        glRotatef ( i*5.0, 0, 0, 1 );
        setColor ( i );    draw_triangle();
        glPopMatrix();
        glAccum(GL_ACCUM, 0.33);     //accumulate color data
      }
      glClear(GL_COLOR_BUFFER_BIT);  //clear screen
      glAccum(GL_RETURN, 1.0);//render data saved in accumulation buffer
      glFlush();                     //send all output to screen
    }

    int main(int argc, char** argv) {
      .....
      //set display mode with accumulation buffer operations
      glutInitDisplayMode (GLUT_RGB | GLUT_ACCUM);
      .....
    }
```

The main accumulating task is done in the call-back function **display**(), where the command **glAccum**(GL_ACCUM, 0.33) accumulates the data in the accumulation buffer. Inside the for-loop, whenever the function **draw_triangle**() is called, data are written into the color buffer and at the same time the normalized color data are multiplied by 0.33 and added to the original data in the accumulation buffer. This is essentially a color-blending process. When the program exits the for-loop, the color buffer is cleared by the command **glClear**(GL_COLOR_BUFFER_BIT). The next statement **glAccum**(GL_RETURN, 1.0) sends the data to the color buffer without further modification as the scaling factor is 1.0 (second parameter of glAccum) and thus render them on the screen. Figure 10-1 below shows the output of this code.

Figure 10-1   Color Blending using Accumulation Buffer

10.2   OpenGL Stereo

The above section describes the general method of using the accumulation buffer to superimpose different images and render them simultaneously. This is the general technique of creating stereo pairs. We create one image for the left eye and one for the right eye and accumulate both images in the buffer for superimposition. Nowadays, some system may offer special hardware to facilitate the process. In general, there are four types of OpenGL-based stereo viewing systems:

1. **Hardware with OpenGL stereo support.** This makes creating stereo pairs a lot easier. We may initialize the GLUT library for stereo operation with a code section like the following:

```
if (stereo)
  glutInitDisplayMode(GLUT_DOUBLE|GLUT_RGB|GLUT_DEPTH|GLUT_STEREO);
else
  glutInitDisplayMode(GLUT_DOUBLE | GLUT_RGB | GLUT_DEPTH);
```

   In stereo mode, this defines two buffers, namely GL_BACK_LEFT and GL_BACK_RIGHT. We need to select the appropriate buffer for operations. For example, the following code clears the two buffers:

```
glDrawBuffer(GL_BACK_LEFT);
glClear(GL_COLOR_BUFFER_BIT | GL_DEPTH_BUFFER_BIT);
if (stereo) {
  glDrawBuffer(GL_BACK_RIGHT);
  glClear(GL_COLOR_BUFFER_BIT | GL_DEPTH_BUFFER_BIT);
}
```

2. **Hardware without OpenGL stereo support**. This is used by software that does not know about stereo. These are the low-cost stereo devices targeting consumers, mostly 3D games. They work by using library wrappers that intercept the 3D information sent to OpenGL by the application and convert it to left and right views before displaying the data needed to work with the hardware. These drivers mostly do not work for applications that know about stereo; this may cause a lot of confusion for people trying to use them with true stereo programs.

3. **Hardware without OpenGL support**. This is used by software that knows how to directly produce stereo for a given system without any special hardware support. This may involve using a low-cost stereo device like one of those mentioned in 2. This may suffer from the problem of platform-dependent coding.

4. **Simulated OpenGL stereo support**. This is for software that knows about stereo. This approach allows one to use real stereo applications (as in case 1) on low cost hardware (as in case 2) without the application having to do all the work when porting the application from one platform to another one.

10.3   3D Stereo Rendering Using OpenGL

10.3.1   Using glColorMask

In this section, we discuss the general technique to render 3D stereo images without any special hardware support. The following are the general steps of using OpenGL to create 3D stereo images.

1. Use the function **glColorMask**() to handle colors of different situations of the scene. This function has the following prototype.

void glColorMask(GLboolean *red*, GLboolean *green*, GLboolean *blue*, GLboolean *alpha*);

The function specifies whether *red*, *green*, *blue*, and *alpha* can be written into the frame buffer. The default values are all GL_TRUE meaning that all R, G, B, and A components can be written into the buffer. For instance, if we want to filter out the blue component, we simply set the *blue* variable to GL_FALSE.

2. Create the scene with all the surfaces colored with pure white.

3. Render the scene twice with different colors, once for each eye.
   Suppose we use red color for the left eye, and blue color for the right eye. Then we can do the following to create the two colored scenes.

   a) Call
      glColorMask (GL_TRUE, GL_FALSE, GL_FALSE, GL_FALSE);
      before rendering the left-eye scene so that the scene is drawn with red color only.
   b) Call
      glColorMask (GL_FALSE, GL_FALSE, GL_TRUE, GL_FALSE);
      before rendering the right-eye scene so that the scene is drawn with blue color only.

4. Render the scene twice and use the accumulation buffer to superimpose the two images. (If the OpenGL hardware supports stereo buffers, then the above steps can be implemented directly without using the accumulation buffer.)

10.3.2   Using Accumulation Buffer

If the hardware of our system does not support stereo buffers, we may use the accumulation buffer to merge the two images created for the left and right eyes. Alternatively, we may use the color blending techniques that we have discussed in Chapter 5 to combine the images. However, the accumulation buffer technique is more flexible and provides more image processing functions. The following are the typical steps of using this method:

1. Initialize the accumulation buffer in glut:

   glutInitDisplayMode (GLUT_DOUBLE | GLUT_ACCUM | GLUT_RGB | GLUT_DEPTH);

2. Set the clear-colour for the accumulation buffer:

   glClearAccum (0.0, 0.0, 0.0, 0.0);

3. Clear the accumulation buffer when necessary:

   glClear (GL_ACCUM_BUFFER_BIT);

4. Copy the current drawing buffer to the accumulation buffer. We usually do this after the left eye image has been drawn:

   glAccum (GL_LOAD, 1.0);

5. Add the current drawing buffer, which now contains the right eye image, to the accumulation buffer:

   glAccum (GL_ACCUM, 1.0);

6. Copy the accumulation buffer content to the current drawing buffer:

   glAccum (GL_RETURN, 1.0);

10.3.3   Toe-in Projection Method

We have discussed in the previous chapter the principles of the toe-in method in creating stereo image pairs. Figure 9-9 of the chapter shows the setup of this method, in which both the left and right eyes point towards a single focal point. Here we discuss the implementation of this method. We shall use the function **gluPerspective**() to do the projection of the two images as both the left and right eyes will have the same values of *viewing angle* (field of view), *aspect ratio, near distance*, and *far distance*.

As we did in Chapter 7, we use a *Point3* class for handling positions, and use a *Vector3* class for handling vectors in 3D space. Their declarations are straight forward and similar; each class defines the public data members **x, y, z** to describe the coordinates of a point or the components of a vector, (x, y, z). Details of these classes are defined and discussed in Chapter 12. Here, for clarity, we just use a simplified version of each of those classes.

Since we have two eye positions to deal with, we define a *Camera* class that can handle different viewpoints and different orientations:

```cpp
class Camera {
public:
    Point3 p;            // View position
    Point3 focus;        // Point at which camera focuses
    Vec3   v;            // View direction vector
    Vec3   up;           // View up direction
    double f;            // Focal Length along v
    double fov;          // Camera aperture (field of view)
    double es;           // Eye separation
    int    w;            // Viewplane width
    int    h;            // Viewplane height

    //constructors
    Camera ()
    {
        // default parameters
        f = 10.0;
        es = f / 30;
        fov = 60;
        w = 400;
        h = 300;
        p = Point3 ( 0, 0, 10 );  //viewpoint
        focus = Point3( 0, 0, 0); //focus
        v = Vec3 ( 0, 0, 1 );     //view direction
        up = Vec3 ( 0, 1, 0 );    //up vector
    }

    void setCamera(double f0, double es0, double fov0, int w0, int h0)
    {
        f   = f0;
        es  = es0;
        fov = fov0;
        w   = w0;
        h   = h0;
    }

    void lookAt ()
    {
        gluLookAt(p.x,p.y,p.z, focus.x,focus.y,focus.z, up.x,up.y,up.z);
    }

    void lookAt(const Point3 &eye,const Point3 &focus,const Vec3 &up0)
    {
        p = eye;
```

```
        up = up0;
        gluLookAt(p.x,p.y,p.z, focus.x,focus.y,focus.z, up.x,up.y,up.z);
    }
};
```

In the *Camera* class, we define two **lookAt**() functions which work in the same way as the OpenGL **glutLookAt**() function. The first one, which does not take any input parameters, uses the data members to set up the camera orientation. The second one, which takes three input parameters, uses the input parameters and calls **glutLookAt**() to do the setup.

Listing 10-1 below lists the code segment that creates a stereo pair of a wireframe cube and solid teapot using this toe-in method. In the example, the function **drawScene**() does the job of creating the graphics scene; it is independent of the way we render it. The camera is first setup in the **init**() routine using the parameters common to both the left and right eye positions. The two images are rendered in the callback function **display**(). The camera first moves to the left eye position, takes a 'shot' with a red 'filter', scales and saves the data in the accumulation buffer. It then moves to the right eye position and takes a 'shot' using a blue 'filter'. The positions are calculated according to Equation (9.6). That is, the left-eye location E_l, and the right-eye location E_r are given by

$$\text{Left eye position} \quad E_l = (-\tfrac{e}{2}, 0, 0)$$

$$\text{Right eye position} \quad E_r = (+\tfrac{e}{2}, 0, 0)$$

(10.1)

where e is the eye separation and we assume that the mid-point between the eyes is at $(0,0,0)$. However, in the program we assume the mid-point is at $(0,0,d)$ implying that the origin $(0,0,0)$ is at the center of the projection planes and the mid-point is at a distance d from the center.

The two images are superimposed in the accumulation buffer and rendered with the command "**glAccum**(GL_RETURN,1.0);" at the end. We have used a black background implying that the color components are all zero. Therefore, when we "accumulate" the scene, the background will not contribute any value in the process. Also, the color is filtered by a color-filter, the background will not have any effect as zero component remains to be zero. Figure 10-2 shows the output of this program.

Program Listing 10-1: Toein Projection Implementation (toein.cpp)

```
/*
    Create the scene
*/
void drawScene(void)
{
    glPushMatrix();
    glRotatef ( 20, 1, 0, 0 );
    glRotatef ( 45, 0, 1, 0 );
    glLineWidth ( 3 );
    glutWireCube( 4 );
    glPopMatrix();
    glPushMatrix();
    glTranslatef ( 1, 0, 4 );
    glRotatef ( 25, 0, 1, 0 );
    glutSolidTeapot ( 1 );
    glPopMatrix();
}

Camera camera;

void init(void)
{
```

```
        glEnable(GL_DEPTH_TEST);
        glPolygonMode(GL_FRONT_AND_BACK,GL_FILL);
        glFrontFace(GL_CW);
        glClearColor ( 0, 0, 0, 0.0 );      //black background
        glClearAccum ( 0.0, 0.0, 0.0, 0.0 );

        glMatrixMode(GL_PROJECTION);
        glLoadIdentity();
        //setup camera
        double focalLength = 15;
        double eyeSeparation = focalLength / 30.0;
        double fov = 60;
        camera.setCamera ( focalLength, eyeSeparation, fov, 400, 300 );
        Point3 focus ( 0, 0, 0 );
        Vector3 up ( 0, 1, 0 );
        camera.focus = focus;
        camera.up = up;
        double aspectRatio = (double) camera.w / camera.h;
        gluPerspective( camera.fov, aspectRatio, 0.1, 10000.0 );
}

void display(void)
{
    // Set the buffer for writing and reading
    glDrawBuffer(GL_BACK);
    glReadBuffer(GL_BACK);

    // Clear things
    glClear ( GL_COLOR_BUFFER_BIT | GL_DEPTH_BUFFER_BIT );
    glClear ( GL_ACCUM_BUFFER_BIT );
    // Left eye  projection
    glMatrixMode(GL_MODELVIEW);
    glDrawBuffer(GL_BACK_RIGHT);
    glLoadIdentity();
    // setup camera for left eye
    double d = 10;
    Point3 viewPoint ( -camera.es / 2, 0, d );
    camera.p = viewPoint;              //change camera viewpoint
    camera.lookAt();

    // Left eye filter
    glColorMask(GL_TRUE,GL_FALSE,GL_FALSE,GL_TRUE);

    drawScene();
    // Write over the accumulation buffer
    glAccum( GL_LOAD, 1.0 );
    glDrawBuffer(GL_BACK);
    glClear(GL_COLOR_BUFFER_BIT | GL_DEPTH_BUFFER_BIT);

    //right side projection
    glMatrixMode(GL_MODELVIEW);
    glDrawBuffer(GL_BACK_LEFT);
    glLoadIdentity();
    viewPoint.x = camera.es / 2;
    camera.p = viewPoint;              //change camera viewpoint
    camera.lookAt();
    // Right eye filter
    glColorMask(GL_FALSE,GL_FALSE,GL_TRUE,GL_TRUE);
    drawScene();
    glFlush();
    // Addin the new image and copy the result back
    glAccum(GL_ACCUM, 1.0);
```

```
    // Allow all colors
    glColorMask(GL_TRUE,GL_TRUE,GL_TRUE,GL_TRUE);

    glAccum(GL_RETURN,1.0);
    glutSwapBuffers();
}
```

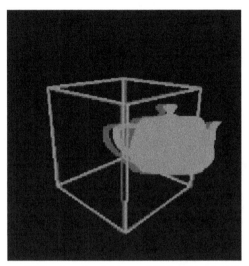

Figure 10-2   Anaglyph Created Using Toe-in Method

10.3.4   Two-center Projection Method

The two-center or the off-axis projection, where the view vector for each eye position remains parallel as shown in Figure 9-10, is the correct method of creating proper anaglyph pairs. We have discussed in Section 9.4.3 the general technique to calculate the projected points on the view plane. However, in our implementation, we do not calculate the projected points directly. We make use of the OpenGL projection functions to do the calculations for us. Since the view vector for each eye remains parallel, we use the OpenGL function **glFrustum**() to describe the perspective projection. Our task is to make the proper setup to use **glFrustum**().

Consider Figure 10-3 that shows the two-center projection (see also Figure 9-13 of Chapter 9). Suppose we let $\overline{AB} = d_{left}$ and $\overline{BD} = d_{right}$. We can make use of similar triangles to find the parameters to call **glFrustum**() for each of the eyes.

In this method, both the left and right eyes use the same projection plane. However, the projected images will be mapped to different near-planes which will define two different frustum as shown in Figure 10-3. In this way, the fields of view for both eyes are the same. Let us first consider the case of the left eye. Referring to the figure, we let

$$L = left = -\overline{AB} = -d_{left} \qquad R = right = \overline{BD} = d_{right}$$
$$B = bottom \qquad\qquad T = top$$
$$N = neardistance \qquad F = fardistance$$
$$f = \text{focal length of camera} \qquad \theta = \text{field of view} \qquad\qquad (10.2)$$
$$e = \text{eye separation} \qquad\qquad \rho = \text{aspect ratio} = \frac{width(W)}{height(H)}$$

where W and H are the width and height of the near-plane, and L, R, B, T denote the left, right, bottom and top boundary coordinates of the near-plane respectively. As we usually do, we also assume that the near-plane lies in the x-y plane with y-axis pointing upward. These imply that

$$T = N \tan \frac{\theta}{2}$$
$$B = -T \tag{10.3}$$
$$H = T - B = 2T$$

Applying similar triangle properties, we can calculate the half-width a of the projection plane of Figure 10-3. First we notice that

$$\frac{2a}{f} = \frac{W}{N} \tag{10.4}$$

Therefore,

$$\frac{a}{f} = \frac{W}{2N} = \frac{\rho \times 2T}{2N} = \rho \times \frac{T}{N} = \rho \times \tan \frac{\theta}{2} \tag{10.5}$$

From (10.5), we obtain

$$a = f \times \rho \times \tan \frac{\theta}{2} \tag{10.6}$$

Once a is known, we can determine the distances b and c of Figure 10-3 by:

$$b = a - \frac{e}{2}$$
$$c = a + \frac{e}{2} \tag{10.7}$$

From similar triangles, we have

$$\frac{d_{left}}{b} = \frac{N}{f} = \frac{d_{right}}{c} \tag{10.8}$$

Also,

$$L = -d_{left} = -b \times \frac{N}{f}$$
$$R = d_{right} = c \times \frac{N}{f} \tag{10.9}$$

Combining (10.7), (10.8), and (10.9), we obtain

$$L = -b \times \frac{N}{f} = -a \times \frac{N}{f} + \frac{e}{2} \times \frac{N}{f} = -\rho \times \frac{H}{2} + \frac{e}{2} \times \frac{N}{f}$$
$$R = c \times \frac{N}{f} = a \times \frac{N}{f} + \frac{e}{2} \times \frac{N}{f} = \rho \times \frac{H}{2} + \frac{e}{2} \times \frac{N}{f} \tag{10.10}$$

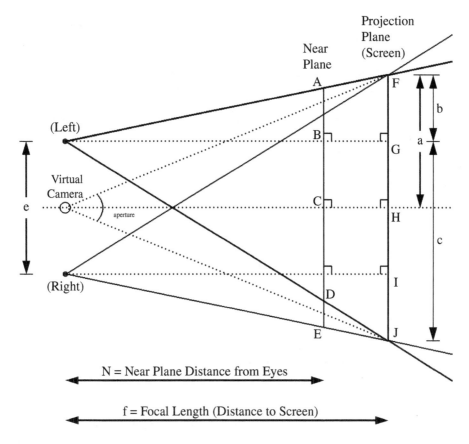

Figure 10-3 Off-axis Projection Calculations

The variables $L, R, T,$ and B are used as the input parameters for the **glFrustum**() function of the left eye. Using the same code notations that we have used in the toein method implementation, we can implement this using a code section like the following.

```
/*
  L = left, R = right, T = top, B = bottom, N = near, F = far,
  f = focal length, e = eye separation, theta2 = (field of view)/2
  a = half-width of projection plane, ratio = aspect ratio
*/
double L, R, T, B, N, F, e, f, theta2, a, b, c, ratio;
glMatrixMode(GL_PROJECTION);
glLoadIdentity();
...              //set N and F to near and far distances
f = camera.f;         // focal length
e = camera.es;        // eye separation
theta2 = (3.1415926/180) * camera.fov / 2;  //theta / 2 in radians
ratio  = (double) camera.w / camera.h;
a = f * ratio * tan ( theta2 );
b = a - e / 2.0;
c = a + e / 2.0;
T = N * tan ( theta2 );
B = -T;
L = -b * N / f;
R =  c * N / f;
glFrustum( L, R, B, T, N, F );

//viewpoint = (-e/2, 0, f), focus = (-e/2, 0, 0), up=(0, 1, 0)
gluLookAt ( -camera.es/2, 0, f, -camera.es/2, 0, 0, 0, 1, 0 );
```

The above formulas and code are for the left eye. We have assumed that the origin $(0,0,0)$ is at the center of the projection plane; the eye is looking along the $-z$ direction and is at a distance f from the projection plane.

We can similarly obtain the equations and code for the right eye. If the center of the eye separation has x-y coordinates $(0,0)$, then there are some symmetries between the two eyes and the right eye parameters can be obtained directly from those of the left eye. Firstly, we note that the top and bottom boundaries of the near-plane are the same for both eyes. Secondly, we note that the value of the left boundary for the right eye is equal to the negative value of the right boundary for the left eye and the value of the right boundary for the left eye is equal to the negative value of the left boundary for the right eye. Suppose we use the subscript l to denote the left eye and the subscript r to denote the right eye. Then we have

$$T_r = T_l = N\tan\frac{\theta}{2}$$
$$B_r = -T_r$$
$$L_r = -R_l = -c \times \frac{N}{f} = -\rho \times \frac{H}{2} - \frac{e}{2} \times \frac{N}{f}$$
$$R_r = L_l = b \times \frac{N}{f} = \rho \times \frac{H}{2} - \frac{e}{2} \times \frac{N}{f}$$

(10.11)

Listing 10-2 below lists the code segment that creates a stereo pair using this two-center method. The setup of the camera and the functions **init**() and **drawScene**() are very similar to those of the toe-in method of Listing 10-1 that we have explained above. In this example, we use the function **glColorMask**() to filter the colors for the left and right eyes. The output of this program is shown in Figure 10-4 below.

Program Listing 10-2:   Two-center Projection Implementation (twocenter.cpp)

```
void init(void)
{
    glEnable(GL_DEPTH_TEST);
    glClearColor(0.0,0.0,0.0,0.0);    //black background
    glClearAccum(0.0,0.0,0.0,0.0);    // The default
}

void display(void)
{
    /*
      L=left,R=right,T=top,B=bottom,N = near,F = far,f=focal length
      e = eye separation, a = half-width of projection plane,
      ratio = aspect ratio, theta2 = (field of view)/2
    */
    double theta2, near,far;
    double L, R, T, B, N, F, f, e, a, b, c, ratio;

    // Clip to avoid extreme stereo
    near = camera.f / 5;
    far = 1000.0;
    f = camera.f;

    // Set the buffer for writing and reading
    glDrawBuffer(GL_BACK);
    glReadBuffer(GL_BACK);

    // Clear things
    glClear(GL_COLOR_BUFFER_BIT | GL_DEPTH_BUFFER_BIT);
    glClear(GL_ACCUM_BUFFER_BIT);
```

```
// Left eye filter
glColorMask(GL_TRUE,GL_FALSE,GL_FALSE,GL_TRUE);

// Create the projection
glMatrixMode(GL_PROJECTION);
glLoadIdentity();
theta2 = ( 3.1415926 / 180 ) * camera.fov / 2;  //theta / 2 in radians
ratio  = camera.w / (double)camera.h;
a = f * ratio * tan ( theta2 );
b = a - camera.es / 2.0;
c = a + camera.es / 2.0;
N = near;
F = far;
T = N * tan ( theta2 );
B = -T;
L = -b * N / f;
R =  c * N / f;
glFrustum( L, R, B, T, N, F );

// Create the model for left eye
glMatrixMode(GL_MODELVIEW);
glLoadIdentity();
camera.p = Point3( -camera.es/2, 0, f );   //change camera viewpoint
camera.focus = Point3 ( -camera.es/2, 0, 0 );
camera.lookAt();
drawScene();
glFlush();
glColorMask(GL_TRUE,GL_TRUE,GL_TRUE,GL_TRUE);

// Write over the accumulation buffer
glAccum(GL_LOAD,1.0);

glDrawBuffer(GL_BACK);
glClear(GL_COLOR_BUFFER_BIT | GL_DEPTH_BUFFER_BIT);

//now handle the right eye
glMatrixMode(GL_PROJECTION);
glLoadIdentity();

// Obtain right-eye parameters from left-eye, no change in T and B
double temp;
temp = R;
R = -L;
L = -temp;
glFrustum( L, R, B, T, N, F );

// Right eye filter
glColorMask(GL_FALSE,GL_FALSE,GL_TRUE,GL_TRUE);

glMatrixMode(GL_MODELVIEW);
glLoadIdentity();
camera.p = Point3( camera.es/2, 0, f );   //change camera viewpoint
camera.focus = Point3 ( camera.es/2, 0, 0 );
camera.lookAt();
drawScene();
glFlush();
glColorMask(GL_TRUE,GL_TRUE,GL_TRUE,GL_TRUE);

// Add  the new image and copy the result back
glAccum(GL_ACCUM,1.0);
glAccum(GL_RETURN,1.0);
```

```
glutSwapBuffers();
}
```

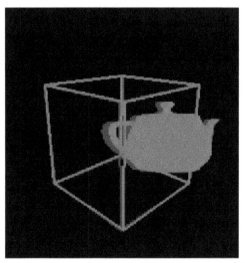

Figure 10-4 Anaglyph Created Using Two-center Method

In the implementation, we have again used a black background. It is not appropriate to use a white background to create a stereo pair. This is because when we use the OpenGL commands to accumulate the colors, all values in the color buffer, including the background values will be added and this could lead to undesired values. More importantly, stereo pairs do not work well with a white background. With a black background, when a region with blue color passes through the red filter of our left eye, it becomes black and 'disappears', and our left eye will not see the region. On the other hand, if a white background is used, the blue region simply becomes a black region and our left eye still can see a black region on a white background. This means that the left eye will see something that is in not supposed to be seen in the real 3D world. As a consequence, this will largely compromise the stereoscopic effect.

In some special cases that we do need a non-black background, we can first start with a black background and use the accumulation buffer to accumulate the objects we need to render. In the process, we use the stencil buffer to keep track of the pixels that the objects have mapped to. The stencil buffer creates a mask for the objects. At the end, we put in the special background we want but will mask off the pixels the objects have occupied. We will present the implementation of this technique in Chapter 14, where we discuss the creation of stereo pairs using extrusion and surface of revolution.

Chapter 11   Animation

11.1   Introduction

Animation is an optical illusion of motion due to the phenomenon of persistence of vision. The following figure shows a sequence of images of a ball at various heights. When the images are shown in sequence repetitively at a rate of about 20 frames (images) in one second, we shall see the ball bouncing on the ground.

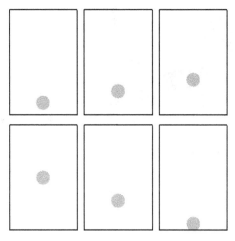

Figure 11-1   Sequence of Images Used in Animation

People had applied traditional animation techniques in traditional movies long before the use of computerized animation in applications. In early animation techniques, started in the 1880s, sequential drawings are employed to produce movement. The technique requires drawing a series of pictures, each picture showing an instantaneous snapshot of objects in motion. Figure 11-2 shows an animation picture of "Fantasmagorie" created by Emile Cohl in 1908. Production of animated short films (Cartoon) became an industry in the 1910s.

Figure 11-2   Fantasmagorie by Emile Cohl, 1908

Cel animation is a traditional animation technique, where individual frames are photographs of drawings, which are first drawn on paper. Drawings are traced or photocopied onto transparent acetate sheets called **cels**, and then photographed by a rostrum camera.

Stop motion animation is another popular technique used in traditional animation. People take photographs of real physical objects one frame at a time and play them back to create an illusion of motion. This technique consists of several kinds which are listed below:

1. **Clay animation (claymation)** uses clay to create figures. Figure 11-3 shows a claymation scene from a TV show.

Figure 11-3   A Claymation Scene from a TV Show

2. **Cutout animation** uses 2-D pieces of materials such as paper, cloth, card or even photographs to do animation. Nowadays computer software is frequently used to create cutout-style animation with scanned images or vector graphics taking the role of physically cut materials.

3. **Graphic animation** uses non-drawn flat visual graphic material such as photographs, newspaper clippings, and magazines, which are sometimes manipulated frame-by-frame, to create object movement.

4. **Model animation** uses models that interact with live-action world to create the illusion of a real-world fantasy sequence. The technique was used in the the films *The Lost World* (1925), *King Kong* (1933), and *The Son of Kong* (1933).

5. **Object animation** uses regular objects such as LEGOs, dolls, and toys to do animation.

6. **Pixilation** uses live humans to create surreal effects such as disappearances and reappearances, allowing people to appear to slide across the ground.

7. **Puppet animation (pupperty)** manipulates puppets to creation object motion.

11.2   Computer Animation

Nowadays, we use computer and in particular computer graphics to do much of the work of animation. We can consider computer animation as a digital successor to the stop motion techniques discussed above. Modern computer animation usually uses 3D computer graphics, although 2D computer graphics are still used for stylistic, low bandwidth, and faster real-time renderings. To create the illusion of movement, we display an image on the computer screen and repeatedly replace it by a new image that is similar to the previous image, usually at a rate of 24 or 30 frames/second. This technique is identical to how the illusion of movement is achieved with television and motion pictures.

For 3D animations, we usually build graphical objects using a virtual skeleton of rigid links connected by joints. The joints of a skeleton can be given characteristics that controls their motion. The movement of the rest of the object is synchronized with that of the skeleton. One such technique is called **skinning**, which allows the "skin", or surface, of a creature to move in sync with the skeleton movement. For 2D figure animations, we may use separate objects with or without a virtual skeleton. Other features of the figure such as limbs, eyes, mouth, and clothes are moved by the animator on key frames. The differences in appearance between key frames are interpolated by the computer using the tweening or morphing technique. At the end, the animation is rendered.

In fact, several aspects of computer animation are direct extensions of traditional animation techniques. The following are some prominent features of computer animation.

1. **keyframing**. Keyframing is a simple form of animating an object by specifying the states of objects at keyframes and filling in intermediate frames by interpolation. The technique is based on the notion that an object has a beginning state or condition and will be changing over time, in position, form, color, luminosity, or any other property, to some different final stare. Keyframing takes the stance that we only need to show the "key" frames, or conditions, that describe the transformation of this object, and that all other intermediate positions can be interpolated. In traditional animations of movies, the keyframes (keys) are drawn by senior animators. Other artists, *inbetweeners* and *inkers*, draw intermediate frames. This is important for creating a sequence of frames that are coherent and for division of labour. In computerized keyframing, people make use of spline curves to interpolate points.

2. **Motion Capture**. Motion capture uses real world object movements to guide animated motion. Special sensors, called *trackers* can be used to record the motion of a human. In motion capture sessions, movements of one or more actors are sampled many times per second. These animation data are mapped to a 3D model so that the model performs the same actions as the actor.

3. **Compositing**. Compositing is the process of overlaying visual elements from separate sources to form a single image, often to create the illusion that all those elements are parts of the same scene. It makes use of the alpha channel of the images to achieve the effect. Using compositing we can combine images of real characters and objects with computer graphics to create special scenes and effects.

4. **Procedural Methods**. Procedural method is the process of generating contents algorithmically rather than manually; the computer program follows the steps of an algorithm to generate motions. They can be used to easily generate a family of similar motions. The algorithms can be based on actual physical laws to simulate real physical motions. For example, *flexible dynamics* simulates behaviors of flexible objects, such as clothes and paper. We usually build a model using triangles, with point masses at the triangles' vertices. We join the triangles at edges with hinges, which open and close in resistance to springs that hold the two hinge halves together. Parameters in the model include point masses, positions, velocities, accelerations, spring constants, and wind force. Procedural methods are particularly useful in modeling particle systems, which model fuzzy objects such as fire, water and smoke.

5. **Computer Animation Software**. Popular computer animation software include the following:

   - 3D Studio MAX (Autodesk)
   - Softimage (Microsoft)
   - Alias/Wavefront (SGI)
   - Lightwave 3D (Newtek)
   - Prisms 3D Animation Software (Side Effects Software)
   - HOUDINI (Side Effects Software)

- Apple's toolkit for game developers
- Digimation
- Blender (Open Source)
- Maya

In particular, Blender is a free open-source 3D content creation suite, available for all major operating systems under the GNU General Public License. It is a very powerful tool that can create sophisticated 3D graphical objects and models for animation. For details, one can refer to its official site *http://www.blender.org/*.

11.3   Computer Animation Systems

Most computer animation systems use a model representation of the image, similar to a stick figure to control the movements of the animation. Each segment of the model is controlled by an animation variable. However, these systems are only appropriate in animating rigid bodies. Today, computer animation can model systems beyond rigid bodies. These include the following kinds of systems.

1. **Rigid Bodies**. We may treat a rigid body as a system of particles, where the distance between any two particles is fixed. Therefore, its shape never changes. A rigid body may be controlled directly with positions and orientation or indirectly with velocity and angular velocity.

2. **Flexible Objects**. Flexible objects are squishy or bendable objects such as cloth, rope, and paper. A simple and intuitive technique to simulate or animate flexible objects is the mass-spring model, where differential equations are employed to calculate the force that acts on each mass-point and we can animate the mass-point by numerical integration of the force.

3. **Camera Viewpoint**. The camera is our eye. In computer animation, every scene is rendered from the camera's point of view. We need to move the camera to follow the viewer's viewpoint without having excessive jerkiness, oscillation or other jitter.

4. **Articulated Rigid Bodies** (**multibodies**). An articulated rigid body is an assembly of hierarchically linked rigid bodies; joints may be rotational or translational (e.g. robot arms, skeletons of humans). There are two categories of articulated rigid bodies, kinematics and dynamics, which can be further classified as follows:

   - **Forward Kinematics** determines the positions of the links in the structure when the joint settings are known.
   - **Inverse Kinematics** determines the joint settings (angles) to achieve a desired position. This is much more difficult than Forward Kinematics.
   - **Forward Dynamics** is the same as physical simulation. That is, given the initial physical parameters such as positions, orientations, and velocities, the process computes the movement of the articulated object as a function of time.
   - **Inverse Dynamics** determines what forces must be applied to achieve certain motion.

5. **Particle Systems**. Particle systems are for modeling fuzzy objects such as water, cloud, fire, and smoke. The objects are non-rigid, dynamic, and do not have well-defined shapes. They differ from normal image representation in 3 ways:

   - In a particle system, we do **not** represent an object by a set of patches or a polygon mesh but as clouds of primitive particles that define its volume.

- They are not static. New particles are created and destroyed.
- Object form may not be specific. Stochastic processes are used to change an object's shape and appearance. However, particle systems can also be used to create well-shaped objects such as a human head or body.

Figure 11-4 below is an image created using particle system techniques. The image is taken from the film *Star Trek II: Wrath of Khan*, which was one of the first films to extensively use electronic images and computer graphics to expedite the production of shots, to show the effect of *Genesis*, which was a powerful terraforming device. The film contained a one minute computer-generated imagery (CGI) sequence depicting a simulation of the birth of a planet (the *Genesis effect*). The Genesis effect made the first onscreen use of a particle rendering system to achieve its fiery effects.

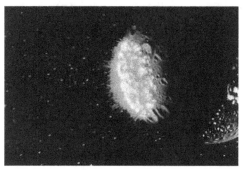

Figure 11-4 Genesis Effect of Star Trek II

11.4 Interpolation

Interpolation is the foundation of all animations. In animation, interpolation refers to inbetweening, or filling in frames between the key frames. It typically calculates the in-between frames through use of piecewise polynomial interpolation to draw images semi-automatically. The simplest case is interpolating the position of a point. An animator has a list of values associated with a given parameter at specific frames (called key frames or keys). The parameter to be interpolated may be one of the following:

- a coordinate of the position of an object,
- a joint angle of an appendage of a robot,
- the transparency attribute of an object, or
- any other parameter used in the display and manipulation of computer graphic elements.

The simplest kind of interpolation is the linear interpolation, where the points are related by a linear equation. Suppose two polylines Q and R are formed by n points:

$$Q = \{Q_0, Q_1, .., Q_i, ...Q_{n-1}\}$$
$$R = \{R_0, R_1, .., R_i, ...R_{n-1}\} \tag{11.1}$$

We construct polyline P with points $\{P_0, P_1, .., P_i, ...P_{n-1}\}$ by 'interpolating' Q and R. That is,

$$P_i(t) = (1-t)Q_i + tR_i \tag{11.2}$$

Note that (11.2) is an affine combination of points as the sum of the coefficients $(1-t)$ and t is always equal to 1, and thus the result is always a valid point. We also have the special situation:

$$\text{When } t = 0, P_i = Q_i(i.e.P = Q)$$
$$\text{When } t = 1, P_i = R_i(i.e.P = R) \tag{11.3}$$

So when t changes from 0, to 0.1, 0.2, ..., to 1, P begins with the shape Q and gradually morphs to R. Figure 11-5 below shows an example of tweening; figures (a) and (d) are the key frames at $t = 0$ and $t = 1$ respectively; (b) and (c) are obtained by interpolation.

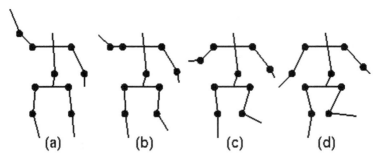

(a)   (b)   (c)   (d)

Figure 11-5 Interpolation

By rewriting (11.2) as

$$P_i(t) = Q_i + (R_i - Q_i) \times t \tag{11.4}$$

we can implement the linear interpolation with a code like the following:

```
class Point2{
public:
   float x;
   float y;
};

Point2 tween( const Point2 &Q, const Point2 &R, float t )
{
    Point2 P;
    P.x = Q.x + ( R.x - Q.x ) * t;
    P.y = Q.y + ( R.y - Q.y ) * t;
    return P;
}
```

The following listing is the program of the above example of tweening that generates the figures of Figure 11-5. In the program, the functions **make*()** creates three figures from the key frames (i.e. at $t = 0$, and $t = 1$); the three figures together simulates the skeleton of a human body. The function **tween()** does the interpolation of points at t with ($0 \le t \le 1$. The function **drawTween()** calls the **tween()** function to do the interpolation and draws the figures. The value of t and the position of a figure can be changed by pressing the key 'a', which animates and moves the skeleton across the screen. Pressing the key 'r' reverses the direction of motion.

Program Listing 11-1:   Animation by Interpolation (tween.cpp)

```
/*
 * tween.cpp
 * Demo of in-between principle and animation.
 */
#include <GL/gl.h>
#include <GL/glut.h>

class Point2{
public:
   float x;
   float y;
   Point2()
   { x = y = 0; }
```

```
   ......
};

Point2 tween( const Point2 &Q, const Point2 &R, float t )
{
  Point2 P;
  P.x = Q.x + ( R.x - Q.x ) * t;
  P.y = Q.y + ( R.y - Q.y ) * t;
  return P;
}

void drawTween( const Point2 A[], const Point2 B[], int n,
                float t, const Point2 &c )
{
  glColor3f (0, 0, 0 );
  glEnable ( GL_POINT_SMOOTH );
  glPointSize ( 8 );

  // draw the tween at time t between polylines A and B
  Point2 P0 = tween(A[0], B[0],t);
  Point2 P1 = Point2( P0.x + c.x, P0.y + c.y );
  for(int i = 1; i < n; i++)
  {
    Point2 P, P2;
    if ( i == n )
       P = tween( A[0], B[0],t );
    else
       P = tween( A[i], B[i],t );
    P2 = Point2( P.x + c.x, P.y + c.y );
    if ( i < n - 1 ) {
      glBegin( GL_POINTS );
        glVertex2f ( P2.x, P2.y );
      glEnd();
    }
    glBegin( GL_LINES );
      glVertex2f ( P1.x, P1.y );
      glVertex2f ( P2.x, P2.y );
    glEnd();
    P1 = P2;
  }
}

//create two figures for demo use
void makeHand( Point2 A[], Point2 B[] )
{
  A[0].x = 1.2; A[0].y = 9.8;  A[1].x = 2; A[1].y = 8;
  A[2].x = 3; A[2].y = 7;  A[3].x = 6; A[3].y = 7;
  A[4].x = 7; A[4].y = 5; A[5].x = 7; A[5].y = 4;

  B[0].x = 1; B[0].y = 4;  B[1].x = 2; B[1].y = 5;
  B[2].x = 3; B[2].y = 7;  B[3].x = 6; B[3].y = 7;
  B[4].x = 7.5; B[4].y = 5.5; B[5].x = 8; B[5].y = 5;
}

void makeBody( Point2 A[], Point2 B[] )
{
  A[0].x = 4.5; A[0].y = 8;  A[1].x = 4.7; A[1].y = 5;
  A[2].x = 4.5; A[2].y = 4;

  B[0].x = 4.5; B[0].y = 8;  B[1].x = 5; B[1].y = 5;
  B[2].x = 4.5; B[2].y = 4;
}
```

```
void makeLeg( Point2 A[], Point2 B[] )
{
  A[0].x = 3.5; A[0].y = 0.2;  A[1].x = 3; A[1].y = 2;
  A[2].x = 3.2; A[2].y = 4;   A[3].x = 5.8; A[3].y = 4;
  A[4].x = 6; A[4].y = 2; A[5].x = 6.2; A[5].y = 0.2;

  B[0].x = 3.2; B[0].y = 0.2;  B[1].x = 3.5; B[1].y = 2;
  B[2].x = 3; B[2].y = 4;   B[3].x = 5.8; B[3].y = 4;
  B[4].x = 4.8; B[4].y = 2; B[5].x = 7; B[5].y = 1.8;
}

Point2 A[10], B[10];
Point2 A1[10], B1[10];
Point2 A2[10], B2[10];
Point2 center( 0, 0 );
float t = 0, deltat = 0.1;
float deltax = 2, deltay = 0;

void init ( void )
{
  gluOrtho2D ( 0.0, 30.0, 0.0, 30.0 );
  makeHand( A, B ); //create figure A and B
  makeBody( A1, B1 ); //create figure A1 and B1
  makeLeg( A2, B2 ); //create figure A2 and B2

  glLineWidth ( 2 );
  glClearColor( 1.0, 1.0, 1.0, 0.0 );
}
void display(void)
{
  glClear(GL_COLOR_BUFFER_BIT);

  drawTween( A, B, 6, t, center );
  drawTween( A1, B1, 3, t, center );
  drawTween( A2, B2, 6, t, center );

  glFlush();
  glutSwapBuffers();
}

void animate()
{
  t += deltat;
  //move center for clarity of display
  center.x += deltax; center.y += deltay;
  if ( t > 1 ){
    t = 1.0;
    deltat = -deltat;  //reverse direction
    deltax = -deltax;
    deltay = -deltay;
  } else if ( t < 0 ) {
    t = 0;
    deltat = -deltat;  //reverse direction
    deltax = -deltax;
    deltay = -deltay;
  }
  glutPostRedisplay ();
}

int main( int argc, char *argv[] )
{
  // Set things (glut) up
   glutInit(&argc,argv);
```

```
    glutInitDisplayMode(GLUT_DOUBLE | GLUT_RGB );

    // Create the window and handlers
    glutCreateWindow("Tweening Demo");
    glutReshapeWindow( 500, 500 );
    glutInitWindowPosition(100, 100);
    glutDisplayFunc(display);
    glutKeyboardFunc(keyboard);
    init();
    //perpetual loop
    glutMainLoop();
    return(0);
}
```

Equation (11.2) is for linear interpolation and it is used by the above example. We can easily generalize the idea to do quadratic or cubic interpolation. For instance, we note that

$$1 = 1^2 = ((1-t)+t)^2 = (1-t)^2 + 2t(1-t) + t^2 \qquad (11.5)$$

As the sum of $(1-t)^2$, $2t(1-t)$, and t^2 is always equal to 1, we can use them as the coefficients for combining three points so that the result is a valid point. This gives us quadratic interpolation. In this case, we construct polyline $P = \{P_0, P_1, .., P_i, ...P_{n-1}\}$ from the interpolation of three polylines, say, Q, R, and S. The equation corresponding to (11.2) for quadratic interpolation is given by

$$P_i(t) = (1-t)^2 Q_i + 2t(1-t)R_i + t^2 S_i \qquad (11.6)$$

Note that when $t = 0$, $P = Q$, and when $t = 1$, $P = S$. So P starts from Q and morphs to S at the end. Similarly, we can do cubic interpolation by noting that

$$1 = 1^3 = ((1-t)+t)^3 = (1-t)^3 + 3(1-t)^2 t + 3(1-t)t^2 + t^3 \qquad (11.7)$$

Now, we need four polylines, say, Q, R, S, and W to do the interpolation:

$$P_i(t) = (1-t)^3 Q_i + 3(1-t)^2 t R_i + 3(1-t)t^2 S_i + t^3 W_i \qquad (11.8)$$

For more sophisticated graphics, people often use Bezier curves or B-splines to interpolate points.

11.5   Animation in OpenGL

People often use the OpenGL callback functions **glutIdleFunc**() and/or **glutVisibilityFunc**() to do animation.

The function **glutIdleFunc**() sets the global idle callback with prototype,

  void glutIdleFunc (void (*func)());

It sets the global idle callback to be *func* so that an OpenGL program can perform tasks in the background or continuous animation when window system events are not being received. The callback routine *func* does not take any parameters. We should minimize the amount of computation and rendering done in an idle callback to avoid disturbing the program's interactive response. In general, we should not process more than one frame of rendering in an idle callback. If we want to disable the generation of the idle callback, we can simply pass NULL to **glutIdleFunc**(). To use this function in the program, we can add a statement like the following in the **main**() routine of the program:

```
glutIdleFunc ( idle );
```

The following is a typical callback idle function to animate a window:

```
void idle(void)
{
    time += 0.02;
    glutSetWindow ( window );
    glutPostRedisplay();
}
```

Note in this example that the idle callback function does not do any actual drawing. It only advances the time scene state global variable. The actual drawing is done by the window's display callback function, which is called by the call to **glutPostRedisplay**().

If we use the idle callback for animation, we should make sure that we stop rendering when the window is not visible. This can be easily done by setting up with a visibility callback like the following:

```
void visible ( int vis )
{
    if ( vis == GLUT_VISIBLE )
        glutIdleFunc ( idle );
    else
        glutIdleFunc ( NULL );   //disable idle callback
}
```

Also, for animation applications, it is better **not** to set up the idle callback before calling **glutMain-Loop**(), but to use the visibility callback to install idle callback when the window first becomes visible on the screen.

For simplicity, we make slight modifications to the program **tween.cpp** of Listing 11-1 to illustrate the use of **glutIdleFunc**() to animate the tweening figures. To specify the frame rate, the rate at which we want to display a new figure, we need a function that gives us the the time lapse between the execution of statements of a program. We use the a function provided by the Simple Directmedia Layer (SDL) Library (*http://www.libsdl.org/*) to accomplish this. The SDL function **SDL_GetTicks**() is used to give an estimate of the time delay between two frames as shown in the following piece of code where a frame rate of 20 frames per second (fps) is assumed:

```
static unsigned int prev_time = SDL_GetTicks();
static unsigned int current_time=SDL_GetTicks();

current_time = SDL_GetTicks();       //ms since library starts
int diff = current_time - prev_time;
if ( diff < 50 ){       //20 fps = 50 ms / frame
   int delay = 100 - ( current_time - prev_time );
   SDL_Delay ( delay );
}
```

The function **SDL_GetTicks**() returns the number of milliseconds since the SDL library has been initialized. This value wraps around if the program runs for more than 49.7 days. The SDL function **SDL_Delay**() waits a specified number of milliseconds before returning. The delay granularity is at least 10 ms. To use these functions, we have to include the header statement,

```
#include <SDL/SDL.h>
```

and links the SDL library with the linking option "-lSDL". (Alternatively, one may use the standard C function **gettimeofday**() function to obtain the current time by including the header "#include <sys/time.h>".)

Listing 11-2 presents the program that does the tweening animation. It is a modification of **tween.cpp** of Listing 11-1, which moves the skeleton when the user presses the key 'a'. Here, the skeleton moves across the screen automatically. The parts that are identical to **tween.cpp** are not listed.

Program Listing 11-2:   Animation using glutIdleFunc (tween1.cpp)

```
#include <SDL/SDL.h>

void idle ()
{
   static unsigned int prev_time = SDL_GetTicks(),
   current_time = SDL_GetTicks();

   current_time = SDL_GetTicks();  //ms since library starts
   int diff = current_time - prev_time;
   if ( diff < 100 ){    //10 fps ~ 100 ms / frame
      int delay = 100 - ( current_time - prev_time );
      SDL_Delay ( delay );
   }
   prev_time = current_time;
   animate();
}

int main( int argc, char *argv[] )
{
   glutInit(&argc,argv);
   glutInitDisplayMode(GLUT_DOUBLE | GLUT_RGB );

   glutCreateWindow("Tweening Demo");
   glutReshapeWindow( 500, 500 );
   glutInitWindowPosition(100, 100);
   glutDisplayFunc(display);
   glutIdleFunc ( idle );    //for animation

   glutKeyboardFunc(keyboard);
   init();
   glutMainLoop();
   return 0;
}
```

Another way to do animation in OpenGL is to use the function **glutVisibilityFunc**(), which sets the visibility callback for the current window. It has the following prototype,

   void glutVisibilityFunc (void (*func)(int state));

where the parameter func is the new visibility callback function. The visibility callback for a window is called when the visibility of a window changes. The state callback parameter is either GLUT_NOT_VISIBLE or GLUT_VISIBLE depending on the current visibility of the window. GLUT_VISIBLE does not distinguish a window being totally versus partially visible. GLUT_NOT_VISIBLE indicates that no part of the window is visible, i.e., until the window's visibility changes, all further rendering to the window is discarded. Note that GLUT considers a window visible if any pixel of the window is visible or any pixel of any descendant window is visible on the screen. Passing NULL to **glutVisibilityFunc**() disables the generation of the visibility callback.

Very often, this function works along with the function **glutTimerFunc**() to set the frame rate of animation. The function **glutTimerFunc**() has the following prototype,

```
      void glutTimerFunc ( unsigned int  msecs,
                           void (*func)(int value), value);
```

where parameters

msecs specifies the number of milliseconds to pass before calling the callback,
func specifies the timer callback function, and
value specifies the integer value to pass to the timer callback function.

This function registers the timer callback *func* to be triggered in at least *msecs* milliseconds. The *value* parameter to the timer callback will be the value of the *value* parameter to **glutTimerFunc**(). Multiple timer callbacks at same or differing times may be registered simultaneously.

We again slightly modify **tween.cpp** of Listing 11-1 above to make use of these two functions to animate the tweening figures. Listing 11-3 below presents the modified code; functions identical to those of Listing 11-1 are omitted. In this program (**tween2.cpp**), the function **timerHandle**() calls **animate**() to change the skeleton to a new form and move it to a new positon; it then calls **glutPostRedisplay**() to render the new scene. At the end, it calls **glutTimerFunc**() to call itself after 100 ms. Note that in this example, the *value* parameter is not used. The visibility callback function **visHandle**() initiates the call to **timerHandle**() when the window becomes visible.

Program Listing 11-3: Animation using glutTimerFunc (tween2.cpp)

```
void timerHandle ( int value )
{
   animate();
   glutPostRedisplay();
   glutTimerFunc ( 100, timerHandle, 0 );
}

void visHandle( int visible )
{
   if (visible == GLUT_VISIBLE)
      timerHandle ( 0 );   //start animation when visible
}

int main( int argc, char *argv[] )
{
   glutInit(&argc,argv);
   glutInitDisplayMode(GLUT_DOUBLE | GLUT_RGB );

   glutCreateWindow("Tweening Demo");
   glutReshapeWindow( 500, 500 );
   glutInitWindowPosition(100, 100);
   glutDisplayFunc(display);
   glutVisibilityFunc( visHandle );

   glutKeyboardFunc(keyboard);
   init();
   glutMainLoop();
   return(0);
}
```

Chapter 12   Normal Vectors and Polygon Mesh

A polygon mesh (or mesh) is a collection of polygons which share edges and vertices. We can construct any 3D graphical object using polygon meshes. In general, we can use different representations of polygon meshes for different applications and goals. However, triangles are the most commonly used polygons to form polygon meshes because a triangle is the simplest polygon, having three sides and three angles, and is always coplanar. Any other simple polygon can be decomposed into triangles. The process of decomposing a polygon into a set of triangles is referred to as **triangulation**.

Depending on the number of polygons used, a mesh can represent an object with various degrees of resolution, from a very coarse representation to a very fine-detailed description. A mesh can be used for graphics rendering or for object recognition. There are many ways to represent a mesh. A simple way is to use the *wire-frame* representation where the model consists of only the vertices and edges of the object model. Figure 3-5 of Chapter 3 shows the wire-frame representation of a teapot and its mirror image. In general the wire-frame model assumes that the polygons are planar, consisting of straight edges. A popular generalization of the wire-frame representation is the *face-edge-vertex* representation where we specify an object by the faces, edges and vertices. The information can be saved in different lists as discussed below. To specify the face of a surface, besides the vertices, we also need to calculate the normal to it.

A normal to a plane is a vector perpendicular to the plane. If a surface is curved, we have to specify a normal at each vertex and a normal is a vector perpendicular to the tangential plane at the vertex of the surface. Normals of a surface are important in calculating the correct amount of light that it can receive from a light source. In this chapter we discuss how to construct simple objects using polygon meshes and how to import these objects from an external application to an OpenGL program and export them from an OpenGL program to another application.

12.1   3D Vectors

A 3D vector is the difference between two points in 3D space, possessing a magnitude (or length) and a direction. It is usually represented by bold face. If P_1 and P_2 are two points, then $\mathbf{A} = P_2 - P_1$ is a vector directing from P_1 to P_2. The three standard unit vectors in Euclidean Space along the x, y, and z directions are denoted by $\mathbf{i}$, $\mathbf{j}$, and $\mathbf{k}$, and represented as

$$\mathbf{i} = \begin{pmatrix} 1 \\ 0 \\ 0 \end{pmatrix}, \qquad \mathbf{j} = \begin{pmatrix} 0 \\ 1 \\ 0 \end{pmatrix}, \qquad \mathbf{k} = \begin{pmatrix} 0 \\ 0 \\ 1 \end{pmatrix} \qquad (12.1)$$

A vector $\mathbf{A}$ can be expressed as $\mathbf{A} = A_x\mathbf{i} + A_y\mathbf{j} + A_z\mathbf{k}$, or as

$$\mathbf{A} = \begin{pmatrix} A_x \\ A_y \\ A_z \end{pmatrix} \qquad (12.2)$$

The magnitude of $\mathbf{A}$ is $|\mathbf{A}| = \sqrt{A_x^2 + A_y^2 + A_z^2}$.

The dot product of two vectors $\mathbf{A}$ and $\mathbf{B}$ is a scalar and is given by

$$\mathbf{A} \cdot \mathbf{B} = |\mathbf{A}||\mathbf{B}|cos\,\theta \qquad (12.3)$$

where θ is the angle between **A** and **B** as shown in the following figure.

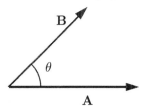

Figure 12-1 $\mathbf{A} \cdot \mathbf{B} = |\mathbf{A}||\mathbf{B}|cos\theta$

The cross product of two vectors **A** and **B** is another vector **C**, which is perpendicular to both **A** and **B** and is denoted by

$$\mathbf{C} = \mathbf{A} \times \mathbf{B} \tag{12.4}$$

The magnitude of the cross product is given by

$$|\mathbf{C}| = |\mathbf{A}||\mathbf{B}|sin\,\theta \tag{12.5}$$

where θ is the angle between the two vectors as shown in Figure 12-2.

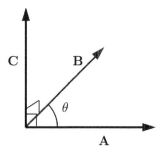

Figure 12-2 $\mathbf{C} = \mathbf{A} \times \mathbf{B}$

The direction of the cross-product **C** is determined by the right-hand rule; when we roll our fingers from **A** to **B** with our right hand, our thumb points in the direction of **C**. The cross product can be also calculated by the following formula.

$$\mathbf{C} = \mathbf{A} \times \mathbf{B} = (A_y B_z - A_z B_y)\mathbf{i} + (A_z B_x - A_x B_z)\mathbf{j} + (A_x B_y - A_y B_x)\mathbf{k} \tag{12.6}$$

The components of the cross product can be obtained in the way we calculate the determinant of a 3×3 matrix as shown in the following figure; the x, y, and z components of the product are obtained by collecting the **i**, **j**, and **k** terms respectively.

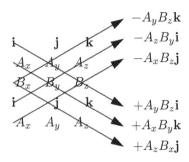

Figure 12-3 Calculating Cross Product of Two Vectors

The following are some basic properties of 3D vectors. Suppose a and b are scalars, and **A**, **B**, and **C** are 3D vectors. We let $A = |\mathbf{A}|$. Then

1. $\mathbf{A} \times \mathbf{B} = -(\mathbf{B} \times \mathbf{A})$

2. $(a\mathbf{A}) \times \mathbf{B} = a(\mathbf{A} \times \mathbf{B})$

3. $\mathbf{A} \times (\mathbf{B} + \mathbf{C}) = \mathbf{A} \times \mathbf{B} + \mathbf{A} \times \mathbf{C}$

4. $\mathbf{A} \times \mathbf{A} = 0 = \begin{pmatrix} 0 \\ 0 \\ 0 \end{pmatrix}$

5. $(\mathbf{A} \times \mathbf{B}) \cdot \mathbf{C} = (\mathbf{C} \times \mathbf{A}) \cdot \mathbf{B} = (\mathbf{B} \times \mathbf{C}) \cdot \mathbf{A}$

6. $\mathbf{A} \times (\mathbf{B} \times \mathbf{A}) = \mathbf{A} \times \mathbf{B} \times \mathbf{A} = A^2\mathbf{B} - (\mathbf{A} \cdot \mathbf{B})\mathbf{A}$

7. $a(\mathbf{A} + \mathbf{B}) = a\mathbf{A} + a\mathbf{B}$

8. $(\mathbf{A} + \mathbf{B}) + \mathbf{C} = \mathbf{A} + (\mathbf{B} + \mathbf{C})$

Implementations

We have discussed the difference between points and vectors in Chapter 3. Since both a point and a vector are specified by three coordinates, it is convenient to define a class called *XYZ* that has the common properties of points and vectors; we define a *Vector3* class (for 3D vectors) and a *Point3* class (for 3D points) that will inherit the properties of *XYZ* as shown in Figure 12-4. The empty-head arrow in the figure denotes the inheritance relation; it points toward the parent class *XYZ*; the child classes are at the tail.

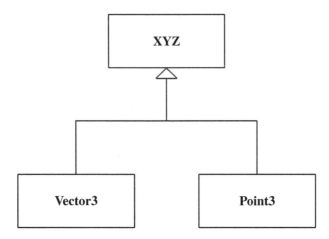

Figure 12-4. Relations between vector and point classes

We shall overload several operators for the two child classes. (In C++, *overload an operator* means *redefine a built-in operator*. An overloaded operator can be implemented as a global function or as a member function of a class.) The overloaded operators for **Vector3** and **Point3** include the following:

    −   vector or point subtraction

    +   vector addition or vector-point addition

    ∧   vector cross product operation

    ∗   vector dot product operation

   *   multiplication of a scalar and a vector

Listing 12-1 below shows the declaration of the class *XYZ*.

```
class XYZ {
  public:
    double x;
    double y;
    double z;
    XYZ ();
    XYZ ( double x0, double y0, double z0 );
    void set ( double x0, double y0, double z0 );
    XYZ getXYZ();
    void getXYZ( double a[]  );
    void print();
};
```

Listing 12-1 Class XYZ

The functions **getXYZ**() return the information of the triple (x, y, z) of an *XYZ* object. They are implemented as follows:

```
XYZ XYZ::getXYZ()
{
  XYZ a( x, y, z );

  return a;
}

void XYZ::getXYZ( double a[] )
{
  a[0] = x;   a[1] = y;   a[2] = z;
}
```

Listing 12-2 shows the declaration of the class *Point3*, which inherits all the data and function members (except constructors) of *XYZ*.

```
class Vector3;            //forward declaration

class Point3: public XYZ
{
  public:
    Point3();
    Point3( double x0, double y0, double z0 );
    Point3( const Point3 &p);
    Vector3 operator-(const Point3 &p); //point-point-> vector
    Point3  operator+(const Vector3 &v);//point+vector-> point
};
```

Listing 12-2 Class *Point3*

Implementation of the overloaded operators '-' and '+' are straightforward. For example, the subtraction operator '-' which calculates the difference between two points and returns the difference as a vector can be implemented as follows:

```
Vector3 Point3::operator - ( const Point3 &p )
{
  Vector3 v1;
```

```
    v1.x = x - p.x;
    v1.y = y - p.y;
    v1.z = z - p.z;

    return v1;
}
```

In this implementation, the argument of the operator function is a *Point3* object. The '&' before *p* in the argument means that we are using pass-by-reference to pass the object to the function; this is a more efficient way of passing an object to a function than using "pass-by-value", in which the passing object is copied and pushed onto the stack, and the called function has to pop it from the stack, which could be time-consuming when the object is large. Pass-by-reference simply passes the address of the object. To inform the user that our purpose of using "pass-by-reference" is for efficiency but not because we want to alter the content of the object, we put the keyword **const** in front of the data type. In general, "pass-by-reference" is more efficient but "pass-by-value" is more robust as it cleanly separates the calling and called functions.

Listing 12-3 below shows the declaration of the class *Vector3* and the overloaded operator '*'.

```
class Point3;              //forward declaration

class Vector3: public XYZ
{
  public:
    Vector3();
    Vector3( double x0, double y0, double z0 );
    Vector3( const Vector3 &v );
    Vector3 operator + (const Vector3 &v);//vec + vec->vector
    Vector3 operator - (const Vector3 &v);//vec - vec->vector
    Vector3 operator ^ (const Vector3 &v);//cross product
    double  operator * (const Vector3 &v);//dot product
    Point3  operator + (const Point3 &p); //vec+point->point
    double magnitude();
    void  normalize();                    //make it a unit vector
};

Vector3 operator * ( double a, const Vector3 &v );
Vector3 operator * ( const Vector3 &v, double a );
```

Listing 12-3   Class *Vector3*

Listing 12-4 shows the implementations of this class and the overloaded operators.

Program Listing 12-4:   *Vector3* class implementation

```
Vector3::Vector3():XYZ()
{ }

Vector3::Vector3( double x0, double y0, double z0 ): XYZ( x0, y0, z0 )
{ }

Vector3::Vector3( const Vector3 &v )
{
  x = v.x;
  y = v.y;
  z = v.z;
}
```

```
Vector3 Vector3::operator + ( const Vector3 &v )
{
  Vector3 v1;
  v1.x = x + v.x;
  v1.y = y + v.y;
  v1.z = z + v.z;

  return v1;
}

Vector3 Vector3::operator - ( const Vector3 &v )
{
  Vector3 v1;
  v1.x = x - v.x;
  v1.y = y - v.y;
  v1.z = z - v.z;

  return v1;
}

//cross product
Vector3 Vector3::operator ^ ( const Vector3 &v )
{
  Vector3 v1;
  v1.x = y * v.z - z * v.y;
  v1.y = z * v.x - x * v.z;
  v1.z = x * v.y - y * v.x;

  return v1;
}

//dot product
double Vector3::operator * ( const Vector3 &v )
{
  double d;
  d = x * v.x + y * v.y + z * v.z;

  return d;
}

//vector + point --> point
Point3 Vector3::operator + ( const Point3 &p )
{
  Point3 p1;

  p1.x = x + p.x;
  p1.y = y + p.y;
  p1.z = z + p.z;

  return p1;
}

double Vector3::magnitude()
{
  return sqrt(x * x + y * y + z * z );
}

void Vector3::normalize()
{
  double d = x*x + y*y + z*z;

  if ( d > 0 ) {
```

```
    d = sqrt ( d );
    x /= d;
    y /= d;
    z /= d;
  }
}
//----------------- external functions --------------
//scalar times vector
Vector3 operator * ( double a, const Vector3 &v )
{
  Vector3 v1;
  v1.x = a * v.x;
  v1.y = a * v.y;
  v1.z = a * v.z;

  return v1;
}

Vector3 operator * ( const Vector3 &v, double a )
{
  return a * v;
}
```

Listing 12-5 below is a sample program that demonstrates the usage of the *Vector3* and *Point3* classes operators.

Program Listing 12-5:   Example of Using *Vector3* and Point3 classes

```
//vpdemo.cpp
int main()
{
  Vector3 v1 ( 1.0, 2.0, 4.0 );   //a vector
  XYZ a; //an XYZ object
  a = v1.getXYZ (); //get XYZ object of v1
  cout << "v1 = ";
  v1.print(); //prints  (x, y, z) values
  Vector3 v2 ( 2.0, 4.0,  6.0 );
  cout << "v2 = ";
  v2.print(); //prints (x, y, z) values of v2
  Vector3 v3 ( v2 ); //construct v2 from v2
  v3.normalize(); //normalize v3
  cout << "v3 = ";
  v3.print(); //now v3 is a unit vector
  cout << "magnitude of v3 is ";
  cout << v3.magnitude() << endl; //magnitude should be 1

  Vector3 v4 = v2 + v1; //addition of two vectors
  cout << "v2 + v1 = ";
  v4.print();
  Vector3 v5 = v2 - v1; //subtraction of two vectors
  cout << "v2 - v1 = ";
  v5.print();
  Vector3 v6 = v1 ^ v2;
  cout << "v1 X v2 = ";
  v6.print();
  double d = v1 * v2;
  cout << "Dot product of v1 and v2 is " << d << endl;
  Vector3 v7 = 3 * v1;
  cout << " 3 * v1 = ";
  v7.print();
```

```
Point3 p1 ( 0.0, 1.0, 2.0 );
cout << "Point p1 = ";
p1.print();
Point3 p2 = v1 + p1;
cout << "v1 + p1 is the point ";
p2.print();

return 0;
}
```

When executed, the program of Listing 12-5 generates the following outputs.

```
v1 = (1, 2, 4)
v2 = (2, 4, 6)
v3 = (0.267261, 0.534522, 0.801784)
magnitude of v3 is 1
v2 + v1 = (3, 6, 10)
v2 - v1 = (1, 2, 2)
v1 X v2 = (-4, 2, 0)
Dot product of v1 and v2 is 34
3 * v1 = (3, 6, 12)
Point p1 = (0, 1, 2)
v1 + p1 is the point (1, 3, 6)
```

12.2 Normal to a Surface

12.2.1 Normal Vector

A **normal vector** (or normal for short) to a surface at a point is a vector pointing in a direction which is perpendicular to the surface at that point. For a plane (flat surface), one perpendicular direction is the same for every point on the surface. A normal to a surface at a point is the same as a normal to the tangent plane to that surface at that point. We know that any three points P_1, P_2, P_3 determine a unique plane. To find a normal to the plane, we build two vectors

$$\mathbf{A} = P_2 - P_1$$
$$\mathbf{B} = P_3 - P_1 \tag{12.7}$$

In forming the vectors, the points P_1, P_2, P_3 should appear counter-clockwise when we look at the plane (i.e. front face) formed by the three points. The normal to the plane is given by

$$\mathbf{N} = \mathbf{A} \times \mathbf{B} \tag{12.8}$$

The corresponding unit normal is given by

$$\mathbf{n} = \frac{\mathbf{N}}{N} \tag{12.9}$$

where $N = |\mathbf{N}|$ is the magnitude of normal $\mathbf{N}$, and $|\mathbf{n}| = 1$.

12.2.2 Equation of a Plane

Suppose $P = (x, y, z)$ is an arbitrary point in the plane formed by the three points P_1, P_2, P_3 discussed above. Then $\mathbf{V} = P - P_1$ is a vector directing from P_1 to P. That is,

$$\mathbf{V} = \begin{pmatrix} x \\ y \\ z \end{pmatrix} - \begin{pmatrix} x_1 \\ y_1 \\ y_1 \end{pmatrix} \tag{12.10}$$

Since $\mathbf{V}$ is on the plane, it is perpendicular to the normal. Therefore, $\mathbf{V} \cdot \mathbf{N} = 0$. As a result,

$$xN_x + yN_y + zN_z - (x_1N_x + y_1N_y + z_1N_z) = \mathbf{V} \cdot \mathbf{N} = 0 \tag{12.11}$$

Equation (12.11) can be expressed in the form,

$$ax + by + cz - d = 0 \tag{12.12}$$

where $(a, b, c) = (N_x, N_y, N_z)$, and $d = (x_1N_x + y_1N_y + z_1N_z)$; it is the general equation of a plane. Conversely, if we are given the equation of a plane represented by

$$Ax + By + Cz + D = 0 \tag{12.13}$$

we immediately know its normal, which is

$$\mathbf{N} = \begin{pmatrix} A \\ B \\ C \end{pmatrix} \tag{12.14}$$

Also, suppose $O = (0, 0, 0)$ is the origin of the coordinate system of the 3D space. Then

$$\mathbf{v_1} = P_1 - O = \begin{pmatrix} x_1 \\ y_1 \\ z_1 \end{pmatrix} \tag{12.15}$$

is the vector directing from the origin to the point P_1, and $\mathbf{v_1} \cdot \mathbf{n}$ is the perpendicular distance from the origin to the plane containing the point P_1. This is equal to the value of d of equation (12.12) divided by N (i.e. $\frac{d}{N}$); this is shown in Figure 12-5 below.

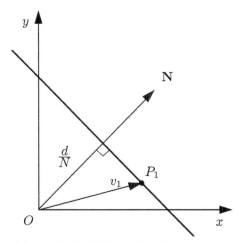

Figure 12-5 Distance to a Plane

If we want to find the distance d_0 from a point $P_0 = (x_0, y_0, z_0)$ to the plane rather than from the origin, we can first calculate v_1 by

$$\mathbf{v_1} = P_1 - P_0 = \begin{pmatrix} x_1 \\ y_1 \\ z_1 \end{pmatrix} - \begin{pmatrix} x_0 \\ y_0 \\ z_0 \end{pmatrix} \tag{12.17}$$

Then the distance is gvien by

$$
\begin{aligned}
d_0 &= \mathbf{v_1} \cdot n \\
&= x_1 n_x + y_1 n_y + z_1 n_z - (x_0 n_x + y_0 n_y + z_0 n_z) \\
&= \frac{d - (ax_0 + by_0 + cz_0)}{|\mathbf{N}|} \\
&= -\frac{ax_0 + by_0 + cz_0 - d}{\sqrt{a^2 + b^2 + c^2}}
\end{aligned}
\tag{12.18}
$$

Example

Find the unit normal to the plane described by the equaiton $x + 2y + z - 6 = 0$ and the distance from the point $(1, 0, 1)$ to the plane.

Solution

1. A normal to the plane is given by

$$\mathbf{N} = \begin{pmatrix} 1 \\ 2 \\ 1 \end{pmatrix}$$

2. The unit normal to the plane is

$$\mathbf{n} = \frac{\mathbf{N}}{N} = \frac{\mathbf{N}}{\sqrt{1^2 + 2^2 + 1^2}} = \frac{1}{\sqrt{6}} \begin{pmatrix} 1 \\ 2 \\ 1 \end{pmatrix}$$

3. The distance from $(1, 0, 1)$ to the plane is given by

$$d_0 = -\frac{1 \times 1 + 2 \times 0 + 1 \times 1 - 6}{\sqrt{6}} = \frac{2\sqrt{2}}{\sqrt{3}}$$

Example

Find the unit normal to the plane containing the three points, $(1, 2, 0)$, $(1, 1, 1)$, and $(2, 0, -1)$.

Solution

Let $P_1 = (1, 2, 0)$, $P_2 = (1, 1, 1)$, and $P_3 = (2, 0, -1)$. When looking at the plane formed by the three points, P_1, P_2, P_3 appear anti-clockwise. Therefore, we form the vectors

$$\mathbf{A} = P_2 - P_1 = \begin{pmatrix} 0 \\ -1 \\ 1 \end{pmatrix}$$

$$\mathbf{B} = P_3 - P_1 = \begin{pmatrix} 1 \\ -2 \\ -1 \end{pmatrix}$$

A normal to the plane is given by

$$\mathbf{N} = \mathbf{A} \times \mathbf{B} = \begin{pmatrix} 3 \\ 1 \\ 1 \end{pmatrix}$$

The unit normal is

$$\mathbf{n} = \frac{\mathbf{N}}{N} = \frac{1}{3.32} \begin{pmatrix} 3 \\ 1 \\ 1 \end{pmatrix} = \begin{pmatrix} 0.90 \\ 0.30 \\ 0.30 \end{pmatrix}$$

12.3   Polygon Mesh Modeling

As we mentioned above, a polygon mesh is a collection of polygons and we can construct any graphics object using a polygon mesh. In order for a mesh to be lit with appropriate light, we need to know the normal to each polygon of the mesh. There are many ways to model and render a polygon mesh. One simple way is to specify the mesh using a vertex list, a normal list, and a face list. Lets consider the following example, which is taken from the popular graphics textbook, "Computer Graphics Using OpenGL" by Hill and Kelly, to illustrate this method. In this example, a barn is represented by seven polygons as shown in Figure 12-6. The mesh consists of 10 vertices numbered from 0 to 9 and 7 polygons; the arrows denote the 7 normals of the 7 polygons.

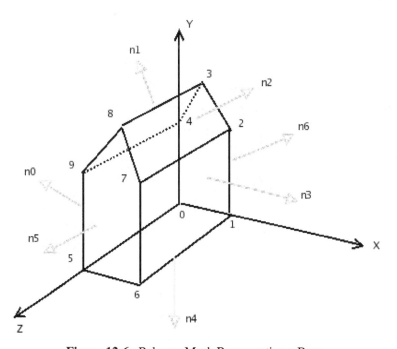

Figure 12-6   Polygon Mesh Representing a Barn

Tables 12-1 to 12-3 show the list of normals, the list of polygons and the associated vertices of each polygon, and the list of vertices of the mesh respectively.

Table 12-1 Normal List

Normal	n_x	n_y	n_z
0	-1	0	0
1	-0.707	0.707	0
2	-0.707	0.707	0
3	1	0	0
4	0	-1	0
5	0	0	1
6	0	0	-1

Table 12-2 Polygon List

Polygon	Vertices	Normals
0 (left)	0,5,9,4	0,0,0,0
1 (roof left)	3, 4, 9, 8	1,1,1,1
2 (roof right)	2, 3, 8, 7	2,2,2,2
3 (right)	1, 2, 7, 6	3,3,3,3
4 (bottom)	0, 1, 6, 5	4,4,4,4
5 (front)	5, 6, 7, 8, 9	5,5,5,5,5
6 (back)	0, 4, 3, 2, 1	6,6,6,6,6

Table 12-3 Vertex List

Vertex	Coordinates (x, y, z)
0	$(0, 0, 0)$
1	$(1, 0, 0)$
2	$(1, 1, 0)$
3	$(0.5, 1.5, 0)$
4	$(0, 1, 0)$
5	$(0, 0, 1)$
6	$(1, 0, 1)$
7	$(1, 1, 1)$
8	$(0.5, 1.5, 1)$
9	$(0, 1, 1)$

Implementation

To simplify the implementation of the mesh model, we make use of the C++ standard template library (STL) class **vector** to implement the vertex, normal, and polygon lists. Of course, the C++ STL **vector** class has a total different meaning from the **vector3** class we have presented above. The STL **vector** class is essentially a dynamic array that can work with different data types. To use this class, we have to include the following header line in our program:

```
#include <vector>
```

To specify a face (a polygon), we just need to specify the vertices of the polygon and the corresponding normals; actually, we just need to specify the indices of the coordinates of the vertices and normals as shown in Table 12-2. So we define the *Polygon* class to represent a face, which consists of a vector to hold the vertex indices and a vector to hold the normal indices:

```
class Polygon {
public:
    int n;                  //n sides
    vector <int> vertices;  //vertex indices of vertexList;
    vector <int> normals;   //indices of normals at vertices
};
```

For those who are not familiar with C++ STL syntax, the statement **vector <int> vertices** means we declare the variable *vertices* as a **vector** of data type **int**.

Now we can define the class *Mesh* to represent the polygon mesh, which has a vertex list, a normal list and a face (polygon) list. Each of these lists is declared as a **vector**. The vertex list is a vector of *Point3*; the normal list is a vector of *Vector3*, and the face list is a vector of *Polygon* as shown Listing 12-6 below:

Program Listing 12-6:   *Mesh* class

```
#include <vector>
#include <fstream>
#include <GL/glut.h>
#include "Point3.h"
#include "Vector3.h"

using namespace std;

class Polygon {
public:
  int n;                  //n sides
  vector <int> vertices; //vertex indices of vertexList
  vector <int> normals;  //indices of normals at vertices
};

class Mesh {
public:
  int nVertices;          //number of vertices
  int nNormals;           //number of normals
  int nFaces;             //number of polygons
  vector<Point3> vertexList;
  vector<Vector3> normalList;
  vector <Polygon> faceList; //each face is a polygon
  Mesh();
  bool readData( char fileName[] );
  void renderMesh();      //render the mesh
};
```

Table 12-4   Data of Barn Example

10 7 7	number of vertices, normals, faces
0 0 0 1 0 0 1 1 0 0.5 1.5 0 0 1 0	vertice coordinates (x, y, z)
0 0 1 1 0 1 1 1 1 0.5 1.5 1 0 1 1	
-1 0 0 -0.707 0.707 0 0.707 0.707 0	normal coordinates (x, y, z)
1 0 0 0 -1 0 0 0 1 0 0 -1	
4 0 5 9 4 0 0 0 0	a face with 4 vertices and normals
4 3 4 9 8 1 1 1 1	a face with 4 vertices and normals
4 2 3 8 7 2 2 2 2	a face with 4 vertices and normals
4 1 2 7 6 3 3 3 3	a face with 4 vertices and normals
4 0 1 6 5 4 4 4 4	a face with 4 vertices and normals
5 5 6 7 8 9 5 5 5 5 5	a face with 5 vertices and normals
5 0 4 3 2 1 6 6 6 6 6	a face with 5 vertices and normals

Listing 12-7 below shows the implementation of the two member functions, **readData**() and **renderMesh**() of the class *Mesh*. The function **readData**() reads the data from a file. It first reads the number of vertices, the number of normals and the number of faces (polygons) of the mesh. Secondly, it reads all the 3D coordinates of the vertices; the coordinates of each vertex are read as a *Point3* object, which is pushed onto the back of the vertex list, *vertexList*, by the STL vector function **push_back**(). (More precisely, the **push_back**() function creates a copy of the object and it inserts the copy into the list.) It then reads the coordinates of the normals, each of which is read as a *Vector3* object and is pushed onto the back of the normal list, *normalList*. At the end, the number of vertices, the indices of the vertices and normals of each face are read as a *Polygon* object and pushed onto the back of the face list, *faceList*. The data of the file should be organized in the order that the function reads them. Table 12-4 above shows the data and its organization of the data file of the Barn example of Figure 12-6 and Tables 12-1 to 12-3.

Program Listing 12-7:   Implementation of *Mesh* Functions

```
Mesh::Mesh()
{
  nVertices = nNormals = nFaces = 0;
}

//Read mesh data from file
bool Mesh::readData ( char fName[] )
{
  fstream ins;                              //file input stream
  ins.open ( fName, ios::in );
  if( ins.fail() ) return false;        // error - can't open file
  if( ins.eof() )  return false;        // error - empty file
  // read in number of vertices, normals, and faces
  ins >> nVertices >> nNormals >> nFaces;
  for (int i = 0; i < nVertices; i++){ //read vertices
    Point3 p;
    ins >> p.x >> p.y >> p.z;
    vertexList.push_back ( p );  //insert into list at the tail
  }
  for (int i = 0; i < nNormals; i++){  //read normals
    Vector3 v;
    ins >> v.x >> v.y >> v.z;
    normalList.push_back ( v );  //insert into list at tail
  }
  for ( int i = 0; i < nFaces; i++ ) {
    Polygon p;
    ins >> p.n;
    for ( int j = 0; j < p.n; j++ ) {
      int vertexIndex;
      ins >> vertexIndex;         //read vertice index
      p.vertices.push_back ( vertexIndex );
    }
    for ( int j = 0; j < p.n; j++ ) {
      int normalIndex;
      ins >> normalIndex;         //read normal index
      p.normals.push_back ( normalIndex );
    }
    faceList.push_back ( p );
  }
  return true;
}

//render the mesh
void Mesh::renderMesh()
{
  //Draw each polygon of the mesh
  glEnable ( GL_CULL_FACE );
```

```
    glCullFace ( GL_BACK );  //do not render back faces

  //draw one polygon at a time
  for ( int i = 0; i < nFaces; i++ ) {
    glBegin ( GL_POLYGON );
      //specifying vertices of the polygon
      for (int j = 0; j<faceList[i].n; j++){ //traverse the list
        int vi = faceList[i].vertices[j];    //vertex index
        int ni = faceList[i].normals[j];      //normal index
        glNormal3f ( normalList[ni].x, normalList[ni].y,
                                         normalList[ni].z );
        glVertex3f ( vertexList[vi].x, vertexList[vi].y,
                                         vertexList[vi].z );
      } //for j
    glEnd();
  }  //for i
}
```

The function **renderMesh**() renders the polygon mesh. We use the function **glCullFace**() to cull the back faces of the mesh. That is, we won't display any face that is facing inside the mesh (back face). Since each polygon of the face is saved in the face list, to render the mesh, all we need to do is to traverse this list and render one polygon at a time as shown in the code above. Listing 12-8 shows a code section that makes use the *Mesh* functions to render a barn; the file name of the data is hard-coded to be *data.txt*. The rendered barn is shown in Figure 12-7.

Program Listing 12-8:   Sample Code for Rendering Barn of Figure 12-6

```
void display(void)
{
  glMatrixMode( GL_PROJECTION );
  glLoadIdentity();
  glOrtho(-2.0, 2.0, -2.0, 2.0, 0.1, 100 );
  glMatrixMode(GL_MODELVIEW); // position and aim the camera
  glLoadIdentity();
  gluLookAt(8.0, 8.0, 8.0, 0.0, 0.0, 0.0, 0.0, 1.0, 0.0);
  glClear(GL_COLOR_BUFFER_BIT | GL_DEPTH_BUFFER_BIT);
  glColor3f( 0, 0, 0 );
  barn.renderMesh();
  glFlush();
}

int main( int argc, char *argv[] )
{
  if ( !barn.readData ( "data.txt" ) ) { //hard-coded filename
    cout << "Error opening file" << endl;
    return 1;
  }
  glutInit( &argc, argv );
  .....
}
```

Figure 12-7   Rendered Barn of Figure 12-6

12.4   COLLADA

12.4.1   3D Graphics Formats

We mentioned that we can represent any 3D graphical object by a polygon mesh. Very often a graphical object is created by an artist using a graphics application package such as Blender or Maya; the object is represented by a mesh, which will be saved in a file along with other attributes of the object such as lighting, field of view, camera position and texture. A programmer can parse the file, transform and render the object using OpenGL. In order that the programmer can parse the object effectively, the data of object created by the artist need to be saved in an agreed upon format. There are quite a lot of popular graphics file format in the market. The following table lists a few most commonly used formats and their host organizations.

Table 12-5   Graphics Formats

format	affiliation
3DS	3D Studio
BLEN	BLENDER
DAE	COLLADA
DXF	AutoCAD
LWO	Lightwave
OBJ	Wavefront Technologies
SKP	Google sketchup
WRL	VRML

   Each of the formats listed in Table 12-5 has its special characteristics, goals, virtues and short-comings. Among all of these formats, we are most interested in COLLADA which is the only format we shall use and discuss in this chapter (*http://collada.org*). COLLADA, short for COL-LAborative Design Activity, is an open-source 3D graphics format managed by the Khronos Group (*http://www.khronos.org/*), which is a nonprofit industry consortium whose main tasks are to create open standards and royalty-free APIs to enhance the authoring and acceleration of parallel computing, graphics and dynamic media on a wide variety of platforms and devices. COLLADA is royalty-free and is an XML-based schema. XML, short for Extensible Markup Language, is a metalanguage using extra "markup" (information enclosed between angle brackets) for defining a set of rules to encode documents in a format that can be understood by humans and machines easily. It is produced and maintained by the World Wide Web Consortium (W3C).

COLLADA defines an XML database schema that helps 3-D authoring applications to freely exchange digital assets without loss of information, and enables multiple software packages to be combined into powerful tool chains. Many large technology companies or organizations support the work of COLLADA. These include Sony Computer Entertainment, NVIDIA, ATI, Softimage, Autodesk, Google, and Intel. Moreover, some major game engines such as OGRE, C4 Engine, AgentFX, Multiverse, PhyreEngine, and CryEngine also support COLLADA.

12.4.2 COLLADA Features

One main feature of COLLADA is that it is an open-source standard. Its schema and specifications are freely available from The Khronos Group. The standard allows graphics software packages interchange data in an effective way. One can import art assets created with other software packages or to export them to other packages. An **art asset** or sometimes referred to as media asset in computer graphics is an individual piece of digital media used in the creation of a larger graphics scene. Art assets include synthetic and photographic bitmaps, 3D models of meshes, shaders, motion captured or artificial animation data, and video samples. The term "art" here refers to a piece of work created from a piece of software; its data are not necessarily represent anything artistic. COLLADA supports a wide variety of graphics and related features, which include the following:

1. Mesh geometry
2. Transform hierarchy (rotation, translation, shear, scale, matrix)
3. Effects
4. Shaders (Cg, GLSL, GLES)
5. Materials
6. Textures
7. Lights
8. Cameras
9. Skinning
10. Animation
11. Physics (rigid bodies, constraints, rag dolls, collision, volumes)
12. Instantiation
13. Techniques
14. Multirepresentations
15. Assets
16. User data
17. Kinematics
18. Boundary representations (B-reps)
19. Geographic coverage
20. Custom image initialization
21. Math formulas

Since a COLLADA file is a text file consisting of data with XML tags, all COLLADA documents can be edited by an ordinary text editor such as **vi**, **notepad** and **emacs**. After we have edited a COLLADA document, we should always validate it manually to ensure that the document is correctly formatted. A COLLADA file ends with extension ".dae" and there are a couple of ways to validate a COLLADA document.

Validating COLLADA Document

We can use the XML tool, **xmllint** of the **libxml** package, which we will discuss below, to validate a COLLADA document against the COLLADA schema. Suppose we have a COLLADA file called "cube.dae". We check whether this file is correctly formatted using a command like the following:

```
$xmllint --noout --schema  \
 http://www.khronos.org/files/collada_schema_1_4 cube.dae
```

It may be more convenient if we first download the schema and save it as a local file; this can be done by the command,

```
$wget http://www.khronos.org/files/collada_schema_1_4
```

and then rename the downloaded file to "colladaSchema.xsd":

```
$mv collada_schema_1_4 colladaSchema.xsd
```

Then we can validate the document using the command

```
$xmllint --noout --schema colladaSchema.xsd cube.dae
```

The option "–noout" is used to prevent superfluous output. If the file is valid, the following message is displayed:

```
cube.dae validates
```

If the document is invalid, we may see a message similar the following:

```
cube.dae:9: element source_data: Schemas validity error : Element
'{http://www.collada.org/2005/11/COLLADASchema}source_data':
'file://' is not a valid value of the atomic type 'xs:anyURI'.
cube.dae:196: element instance_rigid_body: Schemas validity error :
Element
'{http://www.collada.org/2005/11/COLLADASchema}instance_rigid_body':
Missing  child element(s). Expected is
({http://www.collada.org/2005/11/COLLADASchema}technique_common ).
cube.dae:194: element physics_scene: Schemas validity error : Element
'{http://www.collada.org/2005/11/COLLADASchema}physics_scene':
Missing child element(s). Expected is one of (
{http://www.collada.org/2005/11/COLLADASchema}instance_physics_model,
{http://www.collada.org/2005/11/COLLADASchema}technique_common ).
cube.dae fails to validate
```

12.4.3 COLLADA Format

In the subsequent discussions of COLLADA, we will refer to a COLLADA file called "cube.dae" to explain the basic format of COLLADA. The file "cube.dae" is exported from the free open-source 3D content creation suite, **Blender** (*http://www.blender.org/*), version 2.61. This file is part of the resource distribution at this book's web site at

http://www.forejune.com/stereo/.

Actually, you can easily obtain a similar file from Blender which always starts with a default cube object similar to the one we have used. We will discuss briefly the Blender suite later in this chapter.

Like viewing any COLLADA file, we can view "cube.dae" with a text editor such as **vi** and **emacs**, or we can view it using a browser such as Firefox that supports XML. If we view it with a browser, we should see the structure of the file which looks like the following:

```
-<COLLADA version="1.4.1">
  -<asset>
    -<contributor>
       <author>Blender User</author>
       <authoring_tool>Blender 2.61.0 r42614</authoring_tool>
    </contributor>
    <created>2012-01-04T10:45:03</created>
    <modified>2012-01-04T10:45:03</modified>
    <unit name="meter" meter="1"/>
    <up_axis>Z_UP</up_axis>
  </asset>
 -<library_cameras>
  -<camera id="Camera-camera" name="Camera">
    -<optics>
      -<technique_common>
        -<perspective>
           <xfov sid="xfov">49.13434</xfov>
           <aspect_ratio>1.777778</aspect_ratio>
           <znear sid="znear">0.1</znear>
           <zfar sid="zfar">100</zfar>
        </perspective>
      </technique_common>
    </optics>
  </camera>
 </library_cameras>
...........
 -<scene>
    <instance_visual_scene url="#Scene"/>
 </scene>
</COLLADA>
```

The '-' sign in front of a tag indicates the beginning of a structure (node). We can click on the '-' sign to collapse the structure, which also changes the '-' sign to '+'. For example, when we click on the '-' sign in front of the <COLLADA> tag, the whole document will collapse to a single line like the following:

```
+<COLLADA version="1.4.1"> </COLLADA>
```

Clicking on the '+' sign will expand the document.

XML organizes data in a tree structure and refers to each structure enclosed by a beginning tag and ending tag as a node. For example, the <mesh> node starts with <mesh> and ends with </mesh>. The <COLLADA> node is the root of a COLLADA document. COLLADA defines a lot of nodes to describe various graphics object attributes. As an introduction, we only consider a few simple nodes. We list some of the COLLADA nodes below.

Reading Geometry Data

   1. **<library_geometries>**:

This node is a library that contains geometry type nodes that define geometries in the scene.

2. **\<mesh\>**:

   This node contains the geometry data of the mesh. It usually contains a few \<source\> child nodes that define the data of vertices, normals and texture.

3. **\<source\>**:

   This node contains child nodes such as \<float_array\> and \<technique_common\> that define the geometry data.

4. **\<float_array\>**:

   This node contains floating point numbers for defining various attributes, which are described by a sibling node of type \<technique_common\>.

5. **\<technique_common\>**:

   This node's \<accessor\> child node specifies the data usage for the arrays defined in \<float_array\> or \<Name_array\>. (\<Name_array\> is similar to \<float_array\> except that it specifies strings instead of floating point numbers.)

In the file "cube.dae", you will find one \<library_geometries\> node, which has one \<geometry\> child node. The \<geometry\> node has one \<mesh\> child node that defines the polygon mesh of the cube object. The following is a \<source\> node example taken from "cube.dae", which defines the data of the vertices of a cube. As you can imagine, a cube has 8 vertices, and each vertex has 3 coordinate values. So there are totally 24 data values.

```
<source id="Cube-mesh-positions">
  <float_array id="Cube-mesh-positions-array" count="24">1 1 -1 1 -1 -1
        -1 -0.98 -1 -0.97 1 -1 1 0.95 1 0.94 -1.01 1 -1 -0.97 1 -1 1 1
  </float_array>
  <technique_common>
    <accessor source="#Cube-mesh-positions-array" count="8" stride="3">
      <param name="X" type="float"/>
      <param name="Y" type="float"/>
      <param name="Z" type="float"/>
    </accessor>
  </technique_common>
</source>
```

In this example, the \<float_array\> node defines 24 floats (i.e. count="24"). The \<accessor\> node tells us how to interpret the data; it has three \<param\> child nodes describing the (x, y, z) coordinates of a vertex. The attribute stride="3" means the next vertex is 3 floats away from the current one; the count="8" attribute indicates that there are 8 vertices. In summary, the \<source\> node describes that there are 8 vertices, each with 3 components, which are saved in \<float_array\> as 24 float values; the components are called "X", "Y" and "Z". (If the \<source\> contains texture coordinates, then the components would be called "S", "T" and "P".) Actually, such a node could also describe the (x, y, z) coordinates of a normal vector. To distinguish whether we are processing a vertice or a normal vector, we have to read another child node of \<mesh\> called \<vertices\> to find the vertices source; this node contains a child node named \<input\> with a semantic attribute of "POSITION" value.

```
<vertices id="Cube-mesh-vertices">
  <input semantic="POSITION" source="#Cube-mesh-positions"/>
</vertices>
```

If you navigate through the file "cube.dae", you will find 2 \<source\> nodes (they are children of \<mesh\>). One of them defines the vertices as discussed above. You might have guessed that the other \<source\> node defines the normal coordinates. Indeed, your guess is right; the normal \<source\> structure is very similar to that of the vertex \<source\>. The following is the corresponding normal segment taken from the file "cube.dae":

```
<source id="Cube-mesh-normals">
  <float_array id="Cube-mesh-normals-array" count="18">0 0 -1  0 0 1
```

```
    1 -2.83e-7 0   -2.83e-7 -1 0   -1 2.23e-7 -1.34e-7 2.38e-7 1 2.08e-7
  </float_array>
  <technique_common>
    <accessor source="#Cube-mesh-normals-array" count="6" stride="3">
        <param name="X" type="float"/>
        <param name="Y" type="float"/>
        <param name="Z" type="float"/>
    </accessor>
  </technique_common>
</source>
```

As you can see, a cube has 6 faces and thus we have 6 normals, one for each face. Therefore, the accessor source count is "6". Since each normal is specified by 3 numbers, we need a total of $6 \times 3 = 18$ data values. So the float_array count is "18".

In the file "cube.dae", another child of <source> is the <polylist> node. You might have guessed that this node describes the list of polygons of the mesh. Again, your guess is right. This node defines the polygon (face) list of the mesh just as we discuss in Section 12.3. The following shows the xml code of this node taken from the file "cube.dae".

```
<polylist material="Material1" count="6">
  <input semantic="VERTEX" source="#Cube-mesh-vertices" offset="0"/>
  <input semantic="NORMAL" source="#Cube-mesh-normals" offset="1"/>
  <vcount>4 4 4 4 4 4 </vcount>
  <p>0 0   1 0   2 0   3 0    4 1   7 1   6 1   5 1
      0 2   4 2   5 2   1 2    1 3   5 3   6 3   2 3
      2 4   6 4   7 4   3 4    4 5   0 5   3 5   7 5</p>
</polylist>
```

In the node <polylist>, we see that count="6" indicating that the list has 6 polygons. Inside the <polylist> node, the child node **vcount** indicates "vertex count", the number of vertices a polygon (face) has. Obviously, each face of a cube has 4 vertices. That is why we see six 4's for the six faces in the <vcount> node. The <p> node consists of the indices of the vertex and the normal coordinates of each of the six faces. The two <input> nodes tell us which is which. For each polygon, the first index is for the vertex tuple (offsets="0") and the second index is for the normal tuple. So the first polygon is specified by

```
    0 0   1 0   2 0   3 0
```

meaning that the polygon consists of vertices 0, 1, 2, and 3, and the normal at each of the vertex is normal 0.

From these data, we can reconstruct tables similar to those of Table 12-1 to 12-3, specifying a normal list, a polygon list and a vertex list. The following are the tables thus constructed.

Table 12-6   Vertex List

Vertex	Coordinates (x, y, z)
0	$(1, 1, -1)$
1	$(1, -1, -1)$
2	$(-1, -0.98, -1)$
3	$(-0.97, 1, -1)$
4	$(1, 0.95, 1)$
5	$(0.94, -1.01, 1)$
6	$(-1, -0.97, 1)$
7	$(-1, 1, 1)$

Table 12-7   Normal List

Normal	(n_x, n_y, n_z)
0	$(0, 0, -1)$
1	$(0, 0, 1)$
2	$(1, -2.83 \times 10^{-7}, 0)$
3	$(-2.83 \times 10^{-7}, -1, 0)$
4	$(-1, -2.23 \times 10^{-7}, -1.34 \times 10^{-7})$
5	$(2.38 \times 10^{-7}, 1, 2.08 \times 10^{-7})$

Table 12-8 Polygon List

Polygon	vcount	Vertices	Normals
0	4	0, 1, 2, 3	0,0,0,0
1	4	4, 7 , 6, 5	1,1,1,1
2	4	0, 4, 5, 1	2,2,2,2
3	4	1, 5, 6, 2	3,3,3,3
4	4	2, 6, 7, 3	4,4,4,4
5	4	4, 5, 3, 7	5,5,5,5

For example, face (polygon) 2 has 4 vertices, which are vertex 0, 4, 5, and 1 and the coordinates of these vertices are shown in Table 12-6 as

$$(1, 1, -1), (1, 0.95, 1), (0.94, -1.01, 1), (1, -1, -1)$$

The normal to this face is normal 2 with components shown in Table 12-7 as

$$(1, -2.83 \times 10^{-7}, 0)$$

12.4.4 Parsing COLLADA Files

After understanding the basic features of a COLLADA file, the next thing we want to do is to extract the mesh data and process or render them using our OpenGL programs. The collada.org provides a package called **COLLADA Document Object Model (DOM)** for loading, saving, and parsing COLLADA files. The package is a C++ library which provides rich features to process COLLADA data. However, this package is huge and require special libraries such as the *Boost Filesystem* library to build; it is fairly difficult to compile. For beginners who are interested to work in the open-source environment, we want something simpler to accomplish our tasks of studying, understanding, and developing graphics applications with COLLADA files. Since a COLLADA file is basically an xml file, to parse it, all we need is a simple xml parser. There are quite a few C/C++ open-source xml parsers. The one we have chosen to study and use is the *libxml* library maintained by Daniel Veillard (*http://xmlsoft.org/*). Actually, the one we are going to use is *libxml2*, which is a newer version of the library. Interestingly, the DOM package is also built on top of libxml.

12.5 The libxml Library

12.5.1 Introduction

The *libxml2* library, a newer version of *libxml*, is an XML parser and toolkit developed for the Gnome project. It is written in C and is free software available under the MIT License. It is known to be fast and very portable, working effectively on a variety of systems, including Linux, Unix, Windows, CygWin, MacOS, MacOS X, RISC Os, OS/2, VMS, QNX, MVS, and VxWorks.

According to its offical website at *http://xmlsoft.org/*, *libxml2* implements a number of existing standards related to markup languages:

1. the XML standard: http://www.w3.org/TR/REC-xml
2. Namespaces in XML: http://www.w3.org/TR/REC-xml-names/
3. XML Base: http://www.w3.org/TR/xmlbase/
4. RFC 2396 : Uniform Resource Identifiers http://www.ietf.org/rfc/rfc2396.txt

5. XML Path Language (XPath) 1.0: http://www.w3.org/TR/xpath
6. HTML4 parser: http://www.w3.org/TR/html401/
7. XML Pointer Language (XPointer) Version 1.0: http://www.w3.org/TR/xptr
8. XML Inclusions (XInclude) Version 1.0: http://www.w3.org/TR/xinclude/
9. ISO-8859-x encodings, as well as rfc2044 [UTF-8] and rfc2781 [UTF-16] Unicode encodings, and more if using iconv support
10. part of SGML Open Technical Resolution TR9401:1997
11. XML Catalogs Working Draft 06 August 2001:
    http://www.oasis-open.org/committees/entity/spec-2001-08-06.html
12. Canonical XML Version 1.0: http://www.w3.org/TR/xml-c14n and the Exclusive XML Canonicalization CR draft http://www.w3.org/TR/xml-exc-c14n
13. Relax NG, ISO/IEC 19757-2:2003, http://www.oasis-open.org/committees/relax-ng/spec-20011203.html
14. W3C XML Schemas Part 2: Datatypes REC 02 May 2001
15. W3C xml:id Working Draft 7 April 2004

The *libxml* web site provides coding examples and details of the API's of the library. There are 3 main API modules; the *Parser API* provides interfaces, constants and types related to the XML parser; the *Tree API* allows users to access and process the tree structures of an XML or HTML document; and the Reader API provides functions to read, write, and validate XML files, and allows users to extract the data and attributes recursively.

Moreover, the web site also provides some information about XML, detailed enough to understand and use *libxml*.

12.5.2   Reading and Parsing an XML File

We can find practical coding examples of libxml2 at

> *http://xmlsoft.org/examples*

We will first discuss how to read and parse an XML file. We present a program called "readxml.cpp" to illustrate the concept; most of the code we are presenting is from the above site's program "reader1.c", which uses the function **xmlReaderForFile**() to parse an XML file and print out the information about the nodes found in the process. To use the function, we have to include the header statement,

> #include <libxml/xmlreader.h>

For simplicity, we hard-code the file name for testing to be "cube.dae"; this is the COLLADA file we have used in the above section. In this program, the **main**() function will open the file "cube.dae" for parsing:

```
int main()
{
  // Initializes library and check whether correct version is used.
  LIBXML_TEST_VERSION

  const char filename[] = "cube.dae";
  xmlTextReaderPtr reader = xmlReaderForFile( filename, NULL, 0 );
  if ( reader == NULL ) {
      fprintf(stderr, "Unable to open %s\n", filename);
      return 1;
  }

  int ret = xmlTextReaderRead(reader);
  while (ret == 1) {
```

```
      processNode(reader);
      ret = xmlTextReaderRead(reader);
  }
  xmlFreeTextReader(reader);
  if (ret != 0) {
    fprintf(stderr, "%s : failed to parse\n", filename);
  }

  //Cleanup function for the XML library.
  xmlCleanupParser();

  return 0;
}
```

The function **xmlReaderForFile**() is used to open the file; this function can parse an XML file from the filesystem or the network (the first input parameter can be an URL); it returns a pointer *reader*, pointing to the new **xmlTextReader** or NULL if an error has occurred. This returned *reader* will be used as a handle for further processing of the document.

Next, the function **xmlTextReaderRead**() is used to move the position of the current node pointer to the next node in the stream, exposing its properties; it returns 1 if the node was read successfully, and 0 if there are no more nodes to read, or -1 in case of error. Therefore, we setup a while loop so that as long as the returned value is 1 (node read successfully), we call the function **processNode**() discussed below to process the information contained in the node. When finished reading the file, the function **xmlFreeTextReader**() is called to deallocate all the resources associated with the reader. At the end, the function **xmlCleanupParser**() is called to clean up the memory allocated by the library; this function name is somewhat misleading as it does not clean up parser state. It is a cleanup function for the XML library. It tries to reclaim all related global memory allocated for the library processing but it does not deallocate any memory associated with the document.

One can write the function **processNode**( ) to process the information of the current node in any way the application requires. In our example, we just print out the attributes and the value of the node. We used the following libxml2 functions to obtain the information:

1. **xmlTextReaderConstValue**() reads the text value of the current node; the function returns the string of the value or NULL if the value is not available. The result will be deallocated on the next read operation.
2. **xmlTextReaderDepth**() reads the depth of the node in the tree; it returns the depth or -1 in case of error.
3. **xmlTextReaderNodeType**() gets the node type of the current node; it returns the xmlNode-Type of the current node or -1 in case of error. The node type is defined at the link,

    http://www.gnu.org/software/dotgnu/pnetlib-doc/System/Xml/XmlNodeType.html

4. **xmlTextReaderIsEmptyElement**() checks whether the current node is empty; it returns 1 if empty, 0 if not and -1 in case of error.
5. **xmlTextReaderHasValue**() is used to check whether the node can have a text value; it returns 1 if true, 0 if false, and -1 in case or error.

When we compile the program, we need to link it with the libxml2 library. We may use a command similar to the following to generate the executable:

```
  g++  -o readxml readxml.cpp  -lxml2 -L/{\it libxml2\_dir}/libxml2/lib \
      -I/{\it libxml2\_dir}/libxml2/include/libxml2
```

When "readxml" is executed, it will read the COLLADA file "cube.dae" and prints out the information of each node, which looks like the following output:

```
 1:  0 1 COLLADA 0 0
 2:  1 14 #text 0 1     value=

 3:  1 1 asset 0 0
 4:  2 14 #text 0 1     value=

 5:  2 1 contributor 0 0
 6:  3 14 #text 0 1     value=

 7:  3 1 author 0 0
 8:  4 3 #text 0 1     value= Blender User
 9:  3 15 author 0 0
10:  3 14 #text 0 1     value=

11:  3 1 authoring_tool 0 0
12:  4 3 #text 0 1     value= Blender 2.61.0 r42614
13:  3 15 authoring_tool 0 0
14:  3 14 #text 0 1     value=

15:  2 15 contributor 0 0
16:  2 14 #text 0 1     value=

17:  2 1 created 0 0
18:  3 3 #text 0 1     value= 2012-01-04T10:45:03
19:  2 15 created 0 0
20:  2 14 #text 0 1     value=
.....
39:  4 1 technique_common 0 0
40:  5 14 #text 0 1     value=

41:  5 1 perspective 0 0
42:  6 14 #text 0 1     value=

43:  6 1 xfov 0 0
44:  7 3 #text 0 1     value= 49.13434
45:  6 15 xfov 0 0
46:  6 14 #text 0 1     value=

47:  6 1 aspect_ratio 0 0
48:  7 3 #text 0 1     value= 1.777778
49:  6 15 aspect_ratio 0 0
50:  6 14 #text 0 1     value=

51:  6 1 znear 0 0
52:  7 3 #text 0 1     value= 0.1
53:  6 15 znear 0 0
54:  6 14 #text 0 1     value=
.....
609: 1 15 library_visual_scenes 0 0
610: 1 14 #text 0 1     value=

611: 1 1 scene 0 0
612: 2 14 #text 0 1     value=

613: 2 1 instance_visual_scene 1 0
614: 2 14 #text 0 1     value=
615: 1 15 scene 0 0
616: 1 14 #text 0 1     value=
617: 0 15 COLLADA 0 0
```

12.5.3   Parsing a File To a Tree

The example here, "treexml.cpp" is based on the program "tree1.c" example the libxml2 web site. The program parses an xml file to a tree. It first uses **xmlDocGetRootElement**() to get the root element. Then it scans the document and prints all the element names in document order. In the program, we have to include the following header statements:

    #include <libxml/parser.h>
    #include <libxml/tree.h>
    #include <libxml/xmlreader.h>

For simplicity, we again hard-code "cube.dae" as our file name. The **main**() of the program uses **xmlReadFile**(), which belongs to the parser API of libxml2, to open "cube.dae"; this function parses an XML file from the filesystem or the network; it returns a pointer pointing to the document tree and NULL on failure. The **main**() function then uses **xmlDocGetRootElement**() to obtain the pointer pointing to the root of the document tree and calls **print_element_names**() recursively to print out all the element names of the nodes in the tree:

```
int main()
{
  xmlDoc *doc = NULL;
  xmlNode *root = NULL;
  const char filename[] = "cube.dae";

  // Initialize library and check whether correct version is used.
  LIBXML_TEST_VERSION
  // parse the file and get the DOM
  doc = xmlReadFile( filename, NULL, 0);

  if ( doc == NULL ) {
    printf( "error: could not parse file %s\n", filename );
    return 1;
  }

  // Get the root element node
  root = xmlDocGetRootElement( doc );

  //starts printing from the root at level -1
  print_element_names( root, -1 );

  xmlFreeDoc(doc);
  xmlCleanupParser();

  return 0;
}
```

The function **print_element_names**() takes in two input arguments; the first is a pointer pointing to an **xmlDoc** node, a root of a subtree of the document tree. The second argument is the relative level of the node. each time the pointer moves a level deeper, the value of level is incremented by one; a '+' is printed for the advance of a level along with the node element name:

```
void print_element_names(xmlNode *root, int level )
{
  xmlNode *cur_node = NULL;
  ++level;   //one level deeper in next call

  for (cur_node = root; cur_node; cur_node = cur_node->next) {
    if (cur_node->type == XML_ELEMENT_NODE) {
      for ( int i = 0; i < level; i++ )
        printf(" +");  //signifies level of node
      printf(" %s\n", cur_node->name);
    }
    print_element_names( cur_node->children, level );
```

```
        }
    }
```

Again, this program can be easily compiled and linked with a command like "g++ -o treexml treexml.cpp -lxml2". When we run the executable "treexml", outputs similar to the following will be generated:

```
COLLADA
+ asset
+ + contributor
+ + + author
+ + + authoring_tool
+ + created
+ + modified
+ + unit
+ + up_axis
+ library_cameras
+ + camera
+ + + optics
+ + + + technique_common
+ + + + + perspective
+ + + + + + xfov
+ + + + + + aspect_ratio
+ + + + + + znear
+ + + + + + zfar
+ library_lights
+ + light
+ + + technique_common
+ + + + point
+ + + + color
+ + + + constant_attenuation
+ + + + linear_attenuation
+ + + + quadratic_attenuation
+ + + extra
+ + + technique
. . . . . . . . . . . .
+ library_visual_scenes
+ + visual_scene
+ + + node
+ + + + translate
+ + + + rotate
+ + + + rotate
+ + + + rotate
+ + + + scale
+ + + + instance_geometry
+ + + + + bind_material
+ + + + + + technique_common
+ + + + + + + instance_material
+ + + node
+ + + + translate
+ + + + rotate
+ + + + rotate
+ + + + rotate
+ + + + scale
+ + + + instance_camera
+ scene
+ + instance_visual_scene
```

12.5.4   Searching For a Node

A COLLADA file is an XML file organizing information in a tree structure. The previous section shows how to parse such a file into a tree. Given the tree, we can search for a particular node and extract the information from the node or the subtree rooted at the searched node. Here, we discuss how to search for a node and a few ways to extract the information of the node. Again, we use the COLLADA file "cube.dae" generated by Blender in our example.

Given the root of a subtree of the document, we can search a target node specified by a key string. We first search the root, its siblings and all the children of them and then we search recursively the subtrees of each child until the target is found. This can be accomplished by the following function **searchNode**(), which returns a pointer to the node associated with the target key or NULL if the target is not found:

```
xmlNode *searchNode ( xmlNode *a_node, char target[] )
{
  xmlNode *nodeFound = NULL;

  for ( xmlNode *cur = a_node; cur; cur= cur->next) {
    if (cur->type == XML_ELEMENT_NODE) {
      if ( !xmlStrcmp ( cur->name, (const xmlChar* )target ) ) {
        printf("Found %s \n", cur->name );
        nodeFound = cur;
        break;
      }
    }
    //search recursively until node is found.
    if ( nodeFound == NULL && cur != NULL )
      nodeFound = searchNode ( cur->children, target );
  }

  return nodeFound;
}
```

In practice, there could be more than one node that has the same target key. If we need all the targeted nodes, we can save the node in a vector rather than breaking out of the **for** loop of **searchNode**() after one node has been found. The following main code first searches for nodes associated with key strings "source" and print out the subtrees rooted at the "source" nodes. It then searches for "float_array" from the first "source" subtree. If the node is found, it calls **parseNode**() to print out the data of the node. The function **parseNode**() makes use of **xmlNodeListGetString**() to get the content of the node; this function builds the string equivalent to the text contained in the node list made of TEXTs and ENTITY_REFs; it returns a pointer to the string copy, which must be freed by the caller with **xmlFree**():

```
void parseNode ( xmlDocPtr doc, xmlNodePtr cur )
{
  xmlChar *key;
  cur = cur->xmlChildrenNode;
  while (cur != NULL) {
    key = xmlNodeListGetString(doc, cur, 1);
    printf(" %s\n", key);
    xmlFree(key);
    cur = cur->next;
  }
  return;
}

int main(int argc, char **argv)
{
  xmlDoc *doc = NULL;
  xmlNode *root_element = NULL;
  const char filename[] = "cube.dae";

  // Initialize library and check whether correct version is used.
  LIBXML_TEST_VERSION

  // parse the file and get the DOM
```

```
    doc = xmlReadFile( filename, NULL, 0);

    if ( doc == NULL ) {
        printf( "error: could not parse file %s\n", filename );
    }
    // Get the root element node
    root_element = xmlDocGetRootElement( doc );

    xmlNode *nodeFound;

    nodeFound = searchNode ( root_element, "source" );
    //print subtrees rooted at "source"
    print_element_names(nodeFound, -1);
    //find "float_array" within first "source" subtree
    if ( nodeFound != NULL ){
        nodeFound = searchNode ( nodeFound, "float_array" );
    }
    //print out data of node found
    if ( nodeFound != NULL )
      parseNode ( doc, nodeFound );
    printf("----------------------------------------------------------\n");
    ......
}
```

When this code is executed, it will generate an output similar to the following:

```
Found source
 source
 + float_array
 + technique_common
 + + accessor
 + + + param
 + + + param
 + + + param
 source
 + float_array
 + technique_common
 + + accessor
 + + + param
 + + + param
 + + + param
 vertices
 + input
 polylist
 + input
 + input
 + vcount
 + p
Found float_array
 1 1 -1 1 -1 -1 -1 -0.9999998 -1 -0.9999997 1 -1 1 0.9999995 1
 0.9999994 -1.000001 1 -1 -0.9999997 1 -1 1 1
----------------------------------------------------------
```

If you use **xmlNodeListGetString**() to find and print the "content" of a node, very often you may find that an empty line is printed. According to the documentation of libxml2, the empty lines of the elements that do not have text content but have child elements in them are actually part of the document, even if they are supposedly only for formatting; libxml2 could not determine whether a text node with blank content is for formatting or data for the user. The application programmer has to know whether the text node is part of the application data or not and has to do the appropriate filtering. On the other hand, libxml2 provides a function called **xmlElemDump**() that allows a user to dump the subtree rooted at the specified node to a file; actually, we can use the function to dump to a pipe and use some popular text processing utilites such as **sed** and **awk** to further parse it, or we can direct it to a buffer using the C function **setvbuf** for further processing in our program. The following code segment of **main**() shows how this is done. (For simplicity, we have omitted some error-checking code.)

```
int main(int argc, char **argv) {
  xmlDoc *doc = NULL;
  doc = xmlReadFile( filename, NULL, 0);
  ......
  printf("----------------------------------------------------------\n");
  nodeFound = searchNode ( root_element, "library_geometries" );
  nodeFound = searchNode ( nodeFound, "vertices" );
  if ( nodeFound == NULL ) {
    printf("\nvertices Node not found!\n");
    return 1;
  }
  //send information to screen
  xmlElemDump ( stdout, doc, nodeFound );
  printf("\nparsing the node:\n");
  //open a pipe, which will execute the awk command when writing
  FILE *fp = popen ( "awk 'BEGIN {} {for(i=NF;i > 0;i--)
                                     printf(\"%s\\n\",$i); } END {} '", "w" );
  //print the parsed text to screen
  xmlElemDump ( fp, doc, nodeFound );
  pclose ( fp );  //close the pipe
  printf("----------------------------------------------------------\n");
  //search a new node
  nodeFound = searchNode ( nodeFound, "polylist" );
  if ( nodeFound == NULL ) return 1;
  //open a temporary file
  FILE *f = fopen ("temp.$$$", "w" );
  const int bufsize = 20000;
  char buf[bufsize];            //create a buffer
  bzero ( buf, bufsize );  //set buffer to zeros
  //send the output stream to buf before writing to "temp.$$$"
  setvbuf ( f, buf, _IOFBF, bufsize );

  //dump the element of node to the buffer
  xmlElemDump ( f, doc, nodeFound );
  printf("%s\n", buf ); //print content of node

  /*free the document */
  xmlFreeDoc(doc);
  xmlCleanupParser();
  return 0;
}
```

In the code, we first search for the "library_geometries" node and then search this subtree to find the "vertices" node. Then we use the statement "xmlElemDump (stdout, doc, nodeFound);" to dump the subtree rooted at "vertices" to screen. To demonstrate how to parse the information, we open a pipe using **popen**(), which has the prototype,

FILE *popen(const char *command, const char *type);

where *command* is the command to be issued and *type* is a string indicating the operation mode with "r" indicating reading data from the pipe obtained from output of *command*, and "w" indicating writing data to the pipe which sends them to the command. In our example the *command* is to use awk to parse the text.

   The last part of the code demonstrates the dumping of a subtree to a buffer. We first search for the "polylist" node. After we have found the node, we open a temporary file named "temp.$$$" for writing information. We declare a buffer named *buf* and use the **setvbuf**() to buffer the file output so that the node information will be dumped to *buf* when the function **xmlElemDump**() is called. Then we print out the text stored in *buf*.

   When this code is executed, outputs similar to the following will be generated:

```
Found library_geometries
```

```
Found vertices
<vertices id="Cube-mesh-vertices">
        <input semantic="POSITION" source="#Cube-mesh-positions"/>
        </vertices>
parsing the node:
id="Cube-mesh-vertices">
<vertices
source="#Cube-mesh-positions"/>
semantic="POSITION"
<input
</vertices>
---------------------------------------------------------------
Found polylist
<polylist material="Material1" count="6">
        <input semantic="VERTEX" source="#Cube-mesh-vertices" offset="0"/>
        <input semantic="NORMAL" source="#Cube-mesh-normals" offset="1"/>
        <vcount>4 4 4 4 4 4 </vcount>
        <p>0 0 1 0 2 0 3 0 4 1 7 1 6 1 5 1 0 2 4 2 5 2 1 2 1 3 5 3 6 3 2
                 3 2 4 6 4 7 4 3 4 4 5 0 5 3 5 7 5</p>
        </polylist>
```

12.6   Blender

Blender is an open-source 3D content creation suite, free and available for all major operating systems including Linux, Windows and Mac OS/X under the GNU General Public License (*http://www.blender.org/*). One can do and create a lot of amazing graphics using Blender. To name a few, we can use Blender to model a human head basemesh that can easily be used as a starting point for sculpting, to create a modern wind turbine with lighting, to model an entire building exterior from photo references, to use simple shapes and alpha masked leaves to create a tree with realistic look, or to create an animated movie. There are a lot of tutorials on the Web about using Blender. For example, besides the official site (www.blender.org), the site of **BlenderArt Magazine** (*http://blenderart.org/*) also offers a few good tutorials. Our COLLADA file "cube.dae" used in the examples of the previous sections is created using Blender. Figure 12-8 shows a screen capture of the Blender interface when creating the cube.

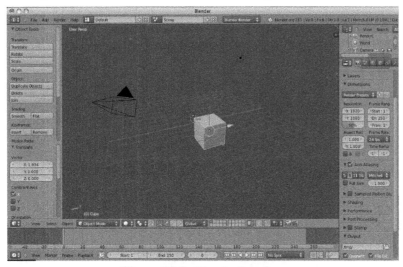

Figure 12-8   Blender Interface

With the help of Blender, we can largely extend our capabilities of creating graphics using OpenGL and C/C++. Very often, our application may need a graphics object that is difficult to create from sketch using OpenGL; in this case, we can use Blender to create the object and save it as a COLLADA file. Our C/C++ OpenGL program can parse the COLLADA file using libxml2 discussed above, and further fine-tune or process it with OpenGL commands. Or sometimes we can use Blender to import a graphics object from the Internet saved in another 3D file format, and use Blender to export the file to the COLLADA format, which can then be parsed and rendered by our application. (The site at *http://www.hongkiat.com/blog/60-excellent-free-3d-model-websites/* lists 60 excellent free 3D model Websites, which have free 3D models in various formats available for download.) The import and export procedures are straightforward. Using a 3DS file as an example, to import the 3DS object, we can issue the following sequence of "commands" (clicking menu or entering file name) in the Blender IDE:

File > **Import** > **3D Studio (3ds)** > *Select 3DS file* > **Import 3DS**

The imported object will appear in the Blender IDE.

To export a graphics object from the Blender IDE to a COLLADA file, we can issue the following sequence of "commands":

File > **Export** > **COLLADA (.dae)** > *Enter File name* > **Export COLLADA**

After obtaining the exported COLLADA file, we can parse it and incorporate it in our OpenGL application.

In conclusion, the availability of open-source software packages has created unlimited opportunities for every body. It brings democracy to the world, enriches our life, and makes big positive impact to the planet. As long as one pays effort to acquire the knowledge of the modern world, he or she will find that the world is abundant and beautiful.

Chapter 13   Curves and Surfaces

Curves and surfaces are important in graphics design. We can create an interesting graphics object by simply revolving a simple curve around an axis. Skies and terrains, important features of a video game, can be created using surfaces. Historically, ship builders used mathematical models of surfaces to model ships. In the 1960s, automobile and aircraft industries began to apply curve and surface math models to design vehicles. Such techniques are rapidly borrowed by other areas of computer graphics applications such as video games and animated movies. We discuss in this chapter the application of some of these models in computer graphics. The terminology of some terms used in this field is quite confusing. Different authors may use different terms to refer to the same subject or they may define the same thing in different ways. We simply follow the terminology that a majority of people use in the Internet.

13.1   Representation of Curves and Surfaces

There are 3 common ways to represent curves and surfaces, namely, explicit, implicit and parametric representations. Each representation has some advantages and disadvantages. In computer graphics, the parametric representation is more commonnly used as it can generate a curve or a surface by varying one or two parameters.

13.1.1   Explicit Representation

In the explicit representation, the coordinates of a point on a curve is represented as a funtcion of the other coordinate. In general, if $P = (x, y)$ is a point on a 2D curve, the y coordinate is expressed as a function of the x coordinate:

$$\textbf{2D Curve:} \quad y = f(x) \tag{13.1}$$

Similarly, the y and z coordinates of a point $P = (x, y, z)$ on a 3D curve is expressed as functions of the x coordinate:

$$\textbf{3D Curve:} \quad \begin{aligned} y &= f(x) \\ z &= g(x) \end{aligned} \tag{13.2}$$

For example, a 2D line and a 2D circle are given by:

$$\begin{aligned} \text{2D line:} &\quad y = mx + b \\ \text{2D circle segment:} &\quad y = \sqrt{r^2 - x^2} \qquad 0 \leq |x| < r \end{aligned} \tag{13.3}$$

An explicit 3D surface is represented as a function of two variables:

$$\textbf{3D Surface:} \quad z = f(x, y) \tag{13.4}$$

For example, the upper hemisphere surface of a sphere centered at the origin is given by:

$$\text{3D hemisphere surface:} \quad z = \sqrt{r^2 - x^2 - y^2} \qquad x^2 + y^2 \leq r \tag{13.5}$$

In this representation, it is simple to compute the points and plot them and it is also easy to check whether a point lies on the curve. However, the representation has a few disadvantages.

Firstly, it is not possible to get multiple values for a single x. In many situations, we need to break curves like circles and ellipses into segments. For example, a complete circle centered at the origin is composed of two segments:

$$y = \sqrt{r^2 - x^2} \qquad\qquad y = -\sqrt{r^2 - x^2} \qquad\qquad (13.6)$$

Secondly, the form has problem representing curves with infinite slope (i.e. vertical tangent). In particular, if $f(x)$ is a polynomial, it is impossible to represent such a curve with infinite slope. Thirdly, it is not invariant under an affine transformation; its form may be changed under such a transformation. A curve or a surface may not have an explicit representation. This representation is rarely used in computer graphics.

13.1.2 Implicit Representation

In the implicit representation, the (x, y) coordinates of a point on a 2D curve satisfy an equation of the form

$$\textbf{2D Curve:} \quad F(x, y) = 0 \qquad\qquad (13.7)$$

For example, a 2D line and a 2D circle can be represented as:

$$\begin{aligned} \text{2D line:} &\quad ax + by + c = 0 \\ \text{2D circle:} &\quad x^2 + y^2 - r^2 = 0 \end{aligned} \qquad\qquad (13.8)$$

An implicit surface in 3D space has the form

$$\textbf{3D Surface:} \quad F(x, y, z) = 0 \qquad\qquad (13.9)$$

For example, a plane and a spherical surface can be expressed as:

$$\begin{aligned} \text{A plane:} &\quad ax + by + cz + d = 0 \\ \text{A spherical surface:} &\quad x^2 + y^2 + z^2 - r^2 = 0 \end{aligned} \qquad\qquad (13.10)$$

Actually, we can represent a curve as the intersection of two surfaces:

$$\begin{aligned} F(x, y, z) &= 0 \\ G(x, y, z) &= 0 \end{aligned} \qquad\qquad (13.11)$$

If we can solve a variable, say z of the implicit equation of (13.9) as a function of the other two variables, then we obtain an explicit representation of the surface, $z = f(x, y)$. This is always possible at least locally when $\frac{\partial F}{\partial z} \neq 0$.

Sometimes the function F is referred to as an inside-outside function because we can easily determine whether a point is inside or outside the curve or the surface. In 3D space, we have

1. $F(x, y, z) = 0$ for all (x, y, z) on the surface,
2. $F(x, y, z) > 0$ for all (x, y, z) outside the surface, and
3. $F(x, y, z) < 0$ for all (x, y, z) insdie the surface.

In implicit form, we can represent curves with infinite slope, as well as closed and multivalued curves such as a circle or an ellipse. On the other hand, when we join curve segments together, it is difficult to determine whether their tangent directions agree at the joint points. Like explicit representation, an implicit function is not invariant under an affine transformation. Also, some implicit curves are difficult to trace.

If the function $F(x, y, z)$ of (13.9) is a polynomial of the x, y, z, then the function represents algebraic surfaces. Of particular importance are the quadratic surface or quadrics where each term in $F(x, y, z)$ can have degree up to 2 (e.g. $x, xy,$ or z^2 but not xy^2):

$$ax^2 + by^2 + cz^2 + dxy + eyz + hxz + kx + ly + mz + n = 0 \qquad (13.12)$$

The web site at *http://wims.unice.fr/gallery/* has an interesting gallery of animated algebraic surfaces. Ellipsoid, elliptic cone and elliptic cylinder with special cases of sphere, circular cone and circular cylinder respectively are examples of quadrics:

$$
\begin{aligned}
\text{Ellipsoid:} && \frac{x^2}{a^2} + \frac{y^2}{b^2} + \frac{z^2}{c^2} - 1 &= 0 \\
\text{Elliptic Cylinder:} && \frac{x^2}{a^2} + \frac{y^2}{b^2} - 1 &= 0 \\
\text{Elliptic Cone:} && \frac{x^2}{a^2} + \frac{y^2}{b^2} - z^2 &= 0
\end{aligned}
\qquad (13.13)
$$

Quadrics are useful in modeling objects. Some researchers claim that 85% of manufactured objects can be modeled using quadrics. An implicit curve or surface in general is hard to render as we have to solve a set of non-linear equations but an algebraic surface usually can be rendered more efficiently than an arbitrary surface.

13.1.3   Parametric Representation

In this representation, we express each coordinate of a point on a curve in terms of an independent variable, u, the parameter. A point in 3D space is expressed as

$$P(u) = \begin{pmatrix} x(u) \\ y(u) \\ z(u) \end{pmatrix} \qquad u \in [u_1, u_2]. \qquad (13.14)$$

The form is the same for two and three dimensions. A useful interpretation of the parametric form is to visualize the locus of points $P(u)$ being drawn as the parameter u varies. Sometimes we may even interpret u as a time variable t. The spatial variables $x(u), y(u),$ and $z(u)$ are usually polynomial or rational functions in u and $u \in [u_1, u_2]$, where u_1, and u_2 are real numbers.

For example, a 3D helix curve with radius a and rises $2\pi b$ units per turn can be described by the parametric equations,

$$
\begin{aligned}
x(u) &= a \cos (u) \\
y(u) &= a \sin (u) \\
z(u) &= bu
\end{aligned}
\qquad (13.15)
$$

In this example, $u \in [0, 2\pi]$. Figure 13-1 below shows a helix curve.

Figure 13-1   Parametric Helix Curve

To describe a 3D surface, we need two parameters, u and v. We express the coordinates of a point $P = (x, y, z)$ of a surface patch as a function of parameters u and v in a closed rectangle:

$$
\begin{aligned}
x &= x(u, v) \\
y &= y(u, v) \\
z &= z(u, v)
\end{aligned}
\tag{13.16}
$$

with $u_1 \leq u \leq u_2$, and $v_1 \leq v \leq v_2$. For example, we can express a torus with major radius R and minor radius r parametrically as

$$
\begin{aligned}
x &= cos(u)(R + rcos(v)) \\
y &= sin(u)(R + rcos(v)) \\
z &= rsin(v)
\end{aligned}
\tag{13.17}
$$

for $u, v \in [0, 2\pi]$. Figure 13-2 below shows a torus with $R = 2$ and $r = 0.6$; the diagram on the right side of the figure shows the relations between parameters (u, v) and the (x, y, z) coordinates.

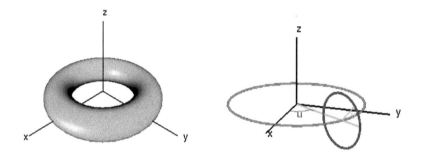

Figure 13-2 Torus with $R = 2, r = 0.6$.

13.1.4 Geometric Continuity

The smoothness of a parametric curve relates to its continuity. We say that a parametric curve $f(u)$ has C^k continuity if its k-th derivative,

$$
\frac{d^k f(u)}{du^k}
$$

exists and is continuous throughout the curve. For example, a curve that describes the trajectory of the motion of an object with a parameter of time, must have C^1 continuity for the object to have finite acceleration.

The continuity of the piecewise curve determines how the curve segments join at the joints. We can describe the various order of parametric continuity as follows:

- C^{-1}: Curves consist of discontinuities. They may not be joined.
- C^0: Curves are joined.
- C^1: First derivatives are continuous.
- C^2: First and second derivatives are continuous.
- C^k: First through k-th derivatives are continuous.

In real applications, we may have to join a number of small curves to form a long curve to represent the profile of an object. The point where two curve segments meet within a piecewise curve is referred to as a *breakpoint*. If the curve segments have the same k-*th* derivative at the breakpoint, then the curve has C^k continuity. While computer graphics has relied heavily on mathematical descriptions of point sets based on parametric functions, we need a different notion, *geometric continuity* to describe the smoothness of curves and surfaces.

We have learned that two C^k functions join smoothly at a boundary to form a joint C^k function if, at all common points, their i-*th* derivatives agree for $i = 0, 1, ..., k$. However, it is neither necessary nor sufficient to characterize the smoothness of curves or surfaces by the continuities of the derivatives of the component functions. As an example, consider the piecewise curve formed by three curve segments as shown in Figure 13-3 below:

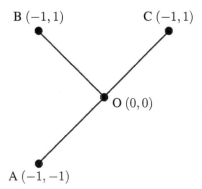

Figure 13-3 Geometric Continuity

We can parameterize the curve segments OB and OC with two parabolic arcs with equal derivatives at the point O:

$$P_{BO}(u) = (1-u)^2 B + 2(1-u)uO + u^2 O \qquad u \in [0,1]$$
$$P_{OC}(u) = (1-u)^2 O + 2(1-u)uO + u^2 C \qquad u \in [0,1]$$

$\hspace{10cm}$ (13.18)

We see that the curve is C^1 continuous at the breakpoint O with $P_{BO}(1) = P_{OC}(0) = O$ and $\left.\dfrac{dP_{BO}(u)}{du}\right|_{u=1} = \left.\dfrac{dP_{OC}(u)}{du}\right|_{u=0} = O$ However, the two segments are not joining smoothly at the joint point O, showing that matching derivatives do not always imply smoothness. On the other hand, smoothness does not necessarily imply matching derivatives. We can similarly parameterize AO and OC with two parabolic arcs with unequal derivatives at the joint point O, even though the shape is geometrically continuous.

To study the smoothness of curves and surfaces, people define k-th order geometric continuity, G^k, as agreement of derivatives after suitable reparametrization. The geometric continuity can be considered as a relaxation of parametrization but not as a relaxation of smoothness. For $k \leq 2$, it has the following properties:

- G^0: Curves are joined. There may be a sharp turn at where they meet.
- G^1: First derivatives are continuous. Two curve segments have identical tangents at the breakpoint; they join smoothly.
- G^2: First and second derivatives are continuous. Two curve segments have identical curvature at the breakpoint. (Curvature is the rate of change of the tangents.)

In general, G^k continuity exists if we can reparameterize the curves to have C^k continuity. A reparametrization of a curve only affects the parameters but the reparametrized curve is geometrically identical to the original.

13.2 Interpolation

13.2.1 Polynomial Parametric Curves

In parametric representation, a popular approach is to represent a curve or a surface as a polynomial of the parameters. A polynomial parametric curve of degree n (= $order - 1$ in OpenGL), is of the form

$$p(u) = \sum_{k=0}^{n} u^k c_k \tag{13.19}$$

where each c_k has independent x, y, z components. That is,

$$p(u) = \begin{pmatrix} x(u) \\ y(u) \\ z(u) \end{pmatrix}, \quad c_k = \begin{pmatrix} c_{kx} \\ c_{ky} \\ c_{kz} \end{pmatrix} \tag{13.20}$$

A parametric polynomial surface is similarly defined by two parameters, u and v in the form

$$p(u) = \begin{pmatrix} x(u,v) \\ y(u,v) \\ z(u,v) \end{pmatrix} = \sum_{i=0}^{n} \sum_{j=0}^{m} c_{ij} u^i v^j \tag{13.21}$$

In particular, the commonly used parametric cubic polynomial curves have the form

$$p(u) = \sum_{k=0}^{3} c_k u^k = c_0 + c_1 u + c_2 u^2 + c_3 u^3 \tag{13.22}$$

We can express this in matrix form

$$p(u) = \begin{pmatrix} x(u) \\ y(u) \\ z(u) \end{pmatrix} = \begin{pmatrix} c_{0x} & c_{1x} & c_{2x} & c_{3x} \\ c_{0y} & c_{1y} & c_{2y} & c_{3y} \\ c_{0z} & c_{1z} & c_{2z} & c_{3z} \end{pmatrix} \begin{pmatrix} 1 \\ u \\ u^2 \\ u^3 \end{pmatrix} \tag{13.23a}$$

Or equivalently,

$$p(u) = \begin{pmatrix} x(u) & y(u) & z(u) \end{pmatrix} = \begin{pmatrix} 1 & u & u^2 & u^3 \end{pmatrix} \begin{pmatrix} c_{0x} & c_{0y} & c_{0z} \\ c_{1x} & c_{1y} & c_{1z} \\ c_{2x} & c_{2y} & c_{2z} \\ c_{3x} & c_{3y} & c_{3z} \end{pmatrix} \tag{13.23b}$$

13.2.2 Interpolation Polynomial

An interpolation polynomial is of the form

$$f(x) = \sum_{k=0}^{n} a_k x^k = a_n x^n + a_{n-1} x^{n-1} + \ldots + a_1 x_1 + a_0 \tag{13.24}$$

If $f(x)$ interpolates the data points (x_i, y_i), then

$$f(x_i) = y_i \quad \text{for all } i \in 0, 1, \ldots, n$$

That is, the polynomial curve passes through the data points. We can find the coefficients a_i using a Vandermonde matrix, which is a matrix with the terms of a geometric progression in each row.

Cubic parametric interpolating polynomial is a commonly used parametric curve that interpolates four control points ($n = 4$). By adjusting the four control points, we obtain different curves. Suppose the four control points are P_0, P_1, P_2, and P_3, where

$$P_k = \begin{pmatrix} x_k & y_k & z_k \end{pmatrix} \tag{13.25}$$

In this case, the curve is described by

$$p(u) = c_0 + c_1 u + c_2 u^2 + c_3 u^3 \qquad 0 \le u \le 1 \tag{13.26}$$

To solve for (u), we have to find the coefficients c_i so that the polynomial $p(u)$ passes through (interpolates) the four control points. An easy way to find $p(u)$ is to specify the four control points, P_0, P_1, P_2, and P_3 at $u = 0, 1/3, 2/3$, and 1 respectively. That is,

$$
\begin{aligned}
P_0 &= p(0) = c_0 \\
P_1 &= p(\tfrac{1}{3}) = c_0 + c_1(\tfrac{1}{3}) + c_2(\tfrac{1}{3})^2 + c_3(\tfrac{1}{3})^3 \\[4pt]
P_2 &= p(\tfrac{2}{3}) = c_0 + c_1(\tfrac{2}{3}) + c_2(\tfrac{2}{3})^2 + c_3(\tfrac{2}{3})^3 \\
P_3 &= p(1) = c_0 + c_1 + c_2 + c_3
\end{aligned}
\tag{13.27}
$$

We can express this in matrix form:

$$P = AC \tag{13.28}$$

where

$$
\begin{pmatrix} P_0 \\ P_1 \\ P_2 \\ P_3 \end{pmatrix} =
\begin{pmatrix}
x_0 & y_0 & z_0 \\
x_1 & y_1 & z_1 \\
x_2 & y_2 & z_2 \\
x_3 & y_3 & z_3
\end{pmatrix}
\tag{13.29}
$$

$$
A = \begin{pmatrix}
1 & 0 & 0 & 0 \\
1 & \tfrac{1}{3} & (\tfrac{1}{3})^2 & (\tfrac{1}{3})^3 \\
1 & \tfrac{2}{3} & (\tfrac{2}{3})^2 & (\tfrac{2}{3})^3 \\
1 & 1 & 1 & 1
\end{pmatrix}
\qquad
C = \begin{pmatrix} c_0 \\ c_1 \\ c_2 \\ c_3 \end{pmatrix} =
\begin{pmatrix}
c_{0x} & c_{0y} & c_{0z} \\
c_{1x} & c_{1y} & c_{1z} \\
c_{2x} & c_{2y} & c_{2z} \\
c_{3x} & c_{3y} & c_{3z}
\end{pmatrix}
\tag{13.31}
$$

The inverse of matrix A can be calculated and is

$$
A^{-1} = \begin{pmatrix}
1 & 0 & 0 & 0 \\
-5.5 & 9 & -4.5 & 1 \\
9 & -22.5 & 18 & -4.5 \\
-4.5 & 13.5 & -13.5 & 4.5
\end{pmatrix}
\tag{13.32}
$$

As P in (13.28) consists of control points which are known, we can solve for the coefficients C by

$$C = A^{-1}P \tag{13.33}$$

The curve $p(u)$ of (13.26) can be expressed as

$$p(u) = UC \tag{13.34}$$

where

$$U = \begin{pmatrix} 1 & u & u^2 & u^3 \end{pmatrix} \tag{13.35}$$

Example

Find the cubic polynomial curve $p(u)$, $u \in [0, 1]$ that interpolates the points $(0, 0, 0), (1, 2, 2), (2, 3, 4), (4, 5, 3)$. What is $p(0.8)$?

Solutions:

We let the curve $p(u)$ pass through the points at $u = 0, 1/3, 2/3, 1$. Then

$$
C = A^{-1}P = \begin{pmatrix} 1 & 0 & 0 & 0 \\ -5.5 & 9 & -4.5 & 1 \\ 9 & -22.5 & 18 & -4.5 \\ -4.5 & 13.5 & -13.5 & 4.5 \end{pmatrix} \begin{pmatrix} 0 & 0 & 0 \\ 1 & 2 & 2 \\ 2 & 3 & 4 \\ 4 & 5 & 3 \end{pmatrix} = \begin{pmatrix} 0 & 0 & 0 \\ 4 & 9.5 & 3 \\ -4.5 & -13.5 & 13.5 \\ 4.5 & 9 & -13.5 \end{pmatrix}
$$

Thus

$$
p(u) = UC = \begin{pmatrix} 1 & u & u^2 & u^3 \end{pmatrix} \begin{pmatrix} 0 & 0 & 0 \\ 4 & 9.5 & 3 \\ -4.5 & -13.5 & 13.5 \\ 4.5 & 9 & -13.5 \end{pmatrix} \qquad (13.36)
$$

When $u = 0.8$, we have

$$
p(0.8) = \begin{pmatrix} 1 & 0.8 & 0.64 & 0.512 \end{pmatrix} \begin{pmatrix} 0 & 0 & 0 \\ 4 & 9.5 & 3 \\ -4.5 & -13.5 & 13.5 \\ 4.5 & 9 & -13.5 \end{pmatrix}
$$

$$
= \begin{pmatrix} 2.624 & 3.568 & 4.128 \end{pmatrix}
$$

The cubic polynomial curve of this example is shown in Figure 13-4 below.

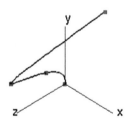

Figure 13-4 Cubic Polynomial Interpolation

13.2.3 Lagrange's Method

Langrange interpolation is a simplest form of numerical solution for polynomial interpolation. Though it is simple, the method is susceptible to Runge's phenomenon, which is a problem of oscillation at the edges of an interval caused by polynomial interpolation with high degree polynomials. Also, when an interpolation point is changed, the method requires recalculating the entire interpolant.

The Lagrange interpolating polynomial is the polynomial $y(x)$ of degree $\leq (n - 1)$ passing through the set of n points $\{(x_1, y_1), (x_2, y_2), ..., (x_n, y_n)\}$ with $y(x_i) = y_i$, and no two x_i are the same. It is given by

$$y(x) = \sum_{i=1}^{n} y_i \frac{\prod\limits_{\substack{j \neq i}}^{n} (x - x_j)}{\prod\limits_{\substack{j \neq i}}^{n} (x_i - x_j)} \tag{13.37}$$

The following function **polyint**() shows an implementation of this method. The class *Point3*, which has been discussed in Chapter 12, is a class that defines a 3D point.

```
//Langrange polynomial interpretation for N points
double polyint ( Point3  points[], double x, int N )
{
  double y;

  double num = 1.0;      //numerator
  double den = 1.0;      //denominator
  double sum = 0.0;

  for ( int i = 0; i < N; ++i ) {
    num = den = 1.0;
    for ( int j = 0; j < N; ++j ) {
      if ( j == i ) continue;
      num = num * ( x - points[j].x );              //x - xj
    }
    for ( int j = 0; j < N; ++j ) {
      if ( j == i ) continue;
      den = den * ( points[i].x - points[j].x );    //xi - xj
    }
    sum += num / den * points[i].y;
  }
  y = sum;

  return y;
}
```

13.2.4 Neville's Algorithm and Barycentric Formula

The Lagrange interpolation is simple and its implementation is straightforward but it is quite inefficient when the degree of the polynomial becomes large as it involves $O(n^2)$ multiplications. Neville's algorithm improves Lagrange method by calculating values recursively, which can be easily extended to calculate derivative values. The Barycentric formula extends the idea further, which only requires $O(n)$ multiplications in the evaluation of $y(x)$. In this method, we let

$$\begin{aligned}
l(x) &= (x - x_0)(x - x_1) \cdots (x - x_n) \\
w_i &= \frac{1}{\prod\limits_{\substack{j \neq i}}^{n} (x_i - x_j)}, \quad i = 0, \cdots, n \\
l_i(x) &= l(x) \frac{w_i}{(x - x_i)}
\end{aligned} \tag{13.38}$$

where w_i are referred to as barycentric weights. Then equation (13.37) can be rewritten as

$$y(x) = \sum_{i=0}^{n} l_i y_i = l(x) \sum_{i=0}^{n} \frac{w_i}{(x - x_i)} y_i \tag{13.39}$$

The formula requires $O(n^2)$ operations for calculating some quantities and the numbers w_i, but once the quantities are obtained, it only requires $O(n)$ operations to evaluate $y(x)$. The following code segment shows an implementation of this method.

```
const int N = ..;
double w[N];

void calculate_weights( Point3 points[] )
{
  for ( int i = 0; i < N; i++ ) {
    w[i] = 1.0;
    for ( int j = 0; j < N; j++ ) {
      if ( j == i ) continue;
        w[i] /= points[i].x - points[j].x;
    }
  }
}


//Barycentric polynomial interpretation for N points
double barycentric ( Point3  points[], double x )
{
  double sum = 0.0, lx = 1.0, y;

  for ( int i = 0; i < N; i++ ) {
    if ( x == points[i].x )
      return points[i].y;
    lx *= x - points[i].x;
  }

  for ( int i = 0; i < N; i++ )
    sum += w[i] * points[i].y / ( x - points[i].x );

  y = lx * sum;
  return y;
}
```

Another simple method of interpolation based on polynomials is the Hermite interpolation which extends the basic polynomial interpolation to consider both the data points and the derivatives (slopes) at the the data points. Hermite interpolation is simple and efficient but it may not be very effective as sometimes a small change of the interpolating curve requires a large variation of the magnitude of the tangent vector.

In a curve interpolation, we generate a curve that passes through all of the control points. Under the constraint of restricting the curve to pass through a set of data points, we have too little local control of the curve. In many applications, we do not require the curve passing through all of the control points. All we need is that the curve passes through the first and the last control points; other points are used to shape the curve. This gives us a lot more control in shaping the curve by varying the control points. We can imagine that the shape of such as curve is obtained by fixing the two ends of an elastic magnetic string on a table. We then fix some small magnets at various positions of the table. The magnets attract the elastic string towards them and thus generate a curved shape. The magnets act like control points in a curve design algorithm. A curve generated by a set of control points but does not necessarily pass through all of them is called an *approximating curve*. In the following sections, we discuss some common algorithms used by designers to produce such a curve.

13.3 Bezier Curves and Surfaces

13.3.1 Bezier Curve

A commonly used family of approximating curves is the spline curves or splines for short. A spline curve is a smooth curve specified succinctly by a few control points. This term originates from traditional drafting design, where a spline is a thin strip, which is held in place by weights to create a curve for tracing. In a similar way we generate a curve using a set of control points.

Bezier curves and B-spline curves are two main classes of splines. Bezier curve is named after the French Pierre Bezier, who developed the method for the body design of the Renault car in the 1970s. Given a set of of $n+1$ points $P_0, P_1, ..., P_n$, the Bezier parametric curve is of the form

$$p(u) = \sum_{k=0}^{n} P_k B_{k,n}(u) \qquad u \in [0,1] \tag{13.40}$$

where $B_{k,n}(u)$ is a Bernstein polynomial given by

$$B_{k,n}(u) = \frac{n!}{k!(n-k)!} u^k (1-u)^{n-k} \qquad u \in [0,1] \tag{13.41}$$

Note that

$$\sum_{k=0}^{n} B_{k,n}(u) = \sum_{k=0}^{n} \binom{n}{k} u^k (1-u)^{n-k} = (u + (1-u))^n = 1^n = 1 \tag{13.42}$$

Thus Equation (13.40) is an affine combination of points and gives a valid point. The curve always passes through the first control point ($p(0) = P_0$) and the last control point ($p(1) = P_n$). Because $B_{k,n}(u) \geq 0$ for $u \in [0,1]$, the curve always lies within the convex hull of the control points. Also, the curve is tangent to $P_1 - P_0$ and $P_n - P_{n-1}$ at the end points.

In general, $B_{k,n}$ is called a blending function as it 'blends' the control points to form the Bezier curve; its degree is always one less than the number of control points. We can generate closed curves by making the last control point P_n the same as the first one P_0.

A rational Bezier curve adds adjustable weights to provide better approximation to arbitrary shapes; it is defined by

$$p(u) = \frac{\displaystyle\sum_{k=0}^{n} B_{k,m}(u) w_k P_k}{\displaystyle\sum_{k=0}^{n} B_{k,m}(u) w_k} \qquad u \in [0,1] \tag{13.43}$$

where $B_{k,m}$ is a Bernstein polynomial with degree m, P_k are the control points, and the weight w_k of P_k is the last ordinate (w) of the homogeneous point P_k^w.

13.3.2 Cubic Bezier Curve

The most commonly used Bezier curves are the degree three Bezier Curves, also known as cubic Bezier curves, which are defined by four control points.Two of these are the end points of the curve, while the other two effectively define the gradients at the end points, pulling the curve towards them.

From equations (13.40) and (13.41), a degree 3 (four control points) Bezier curve is given by

$$p(u) = B_0(u)P_0 + B_1(u)P_1 + B_2(u)P_2 + B_3(u)P_3 \qquad u \in [0,1] \qquad (13.44)$$

where

$$B_k(u) = B_{k,3}(u) = \binom{3}{k} u^k (1-u)^{3-k} = \frac{3!}{k!(3-k)!} u^k (1-u)^{3-k} \qquad (13.45)$$

are the blending functions for the curve. In explicit form,

$$
\begin{aligned}
B_0 &= (1-u)^3 & B_1 &= 3u(1-u)^2 \\
B_2 &= 3u^2(1-u) & B_3 &= u^3
\end{aligned}
\qquad (13.46)
$$

The figure below presents some examples of degree three Bezier curves, showing how the control points shape the curves.

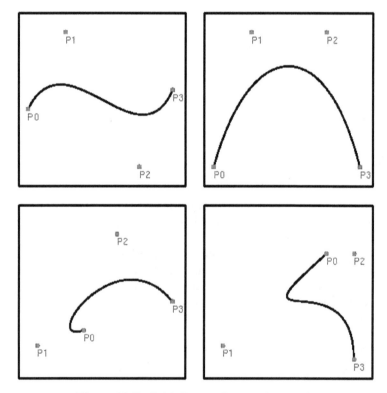

Figure 13-5 Cubic Bezier Curves (Degree 3)

Figure 13-6 below shows a plot of the blending functions for $u \in [0, 1]$; at any value of u, $B_0 + B_1 + B_2 + B_3 = 1$.

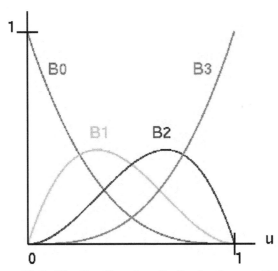

Figure 13-6 Blending Functions for Bezier Curves of Degree 3

If we expand (13.46) and substitute the expanded terms into (13.44), we can express $p(u)$ explicitly as

$$p(u) = (1 - 3u + 3u^2 - u^3)P_0 + (3u - 6u^2 + 3u^3)P_1 + (3u^2 - 3u^3)P_2 + u^3 P_3 \qquad (13.47)$$

or in matrix form

$$p(u) = \begin{pmatrix} 1 & u & u^2 & u^3 \end{pmatrix} \begin{pmatrix} 1 & 0 & 0 & 0 \\ -3 & 3 & 0 & 0 \\ 3 & -6 & 3 & 0 \\ -1 & 3 & -3 & 1 \end{pmatrix} \begin{pmatrix} P_0 \\ P_1 \\ P_2 \\ P_3 \end{pmatrix} \qquad (13.48)$$

The derivative of $p(u)$ is given by

$$p'(u) = \frac{dp(u)}{du} = \begin{pmatrix} 0 & 1 & 2u & 3u^2 \end{pmatrix} \begin{pmatrix} 1 & 0 & 0 & 0 \\ -3 & 3 & 0 & 0 \\ 3 & -6 & 3 & 0 \\ -1 & 3 & -3 & 1 \end{pmatrix} \begin{pmatrix} P_0 \\ P_1 \\ P_2 \\ P_3 \end{pmatrix} \qquad (13.49)$$

Therefore,

$$p'(0) = 3(P_1 - P_0) \qquad p'(1) = 3(P_3 - P_2) \qquad (13.50)$$

This means that the curve $p(u)$ starts at $u = 0$, traveling in the direction of the vector from P_0 to P_1 and at the end, it travels in the direction of P_2 to P_3.

The following code segment shows an implementation of cubic Bezier curves.

```
-----------------------------------------------------------------
//blending functions with degree 3; 0 <= k <=3, 0 <= u <= 1
float blend3 ( float u, int k ) {
   float b = 1;
   switch ( k ) {
     case 0:
         for ( int i = 0; i < 3; i++ )
           b *= ( 1 - u );
```

```
            break;
        case 1:
            b = 3 * u * ( 1 - u ) * ( 1 - u );
            break;
        case 2:
            b = 3 * u * u * ( 1 - u );
            break;
        case 3:
            b = u * u * u;
            break;
    }
    return b;
}

//blending functions with degree n (n+1 control points), 0 <= u <= 1
float blend ( float u, int n, int k ) {
    float b = 1;
    if ( n <= 0 || n < k ) return b;

    int j = n - k;
    float u1 = 1 - u;
    for ( int i = 1; i <=n; i++ ) {
        b *= i;
        if ( k >= 1 ) {
            b *= u / k;    k--;
        }
        if ( j >= 1 ) {
            b *= u1 / j;   j--;
        }
    }
    return b;
}

//render the  curve
void display(void) {
    float x, y, z;
    int i, j, k;

    Point3 data[4], *p[4];
    float B[4], u;
    .............  //data[] contains four control points
    glBegin(GL_LINE_STRIP);
        for (i = 0; i <= 80; i++) {
            u = (float) i / 80.0;
            for ( k = 0; k < 4; k++ ) {
                //B[k] = blend3 ( u, k );
                B[k] = blend ( u, 3, k );  //degree 3 blending functions
                p[k] = (Point3 *) &data[k];
            }
            x = y = z = 0;
            for ( k = 0; k < 4; k++ ){
                x += B[k] * p[k]->x;
                y += B[k] * p[k]->y;
                z += B[k] * p[k]->z;
            }
```

```
            glVertex3f ( x, y, z );
       }
    glEnd();
    glFlush();
}
```

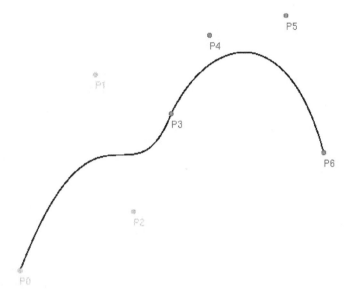

Figure 13-7 Joining Cubic Bezier Curves to Form Piecewise Curve

Although a cubic Bezier curve is simple and easy to compute, it is not possible to use it to closely approximate a curve that has many turns as a cubic Bezier curve only uses four control points. A common practice is to break a long curve into a number of segments, each defined by a separate cubic Bezier curve and joined to another one to form a piecewise curve. Figure 13-7 above shows an example of joining multiple cubic curves to approximate a curve fit to an arbitrary number of data points.

13.3.3 Bezier Surface

By blending functions of two orthogonal Bezier curves, we can form a Bezier surface, which can be also defined as a parametric surface. We can specify an order $(n + 1)(m + 1)$ Bezier surface using two parameters, u and v with $(n + 1)(m + 1)$ control points P_{ij}:

$$p(u,v) = \sum_{i=0}^{n} \sum_{j=0}^{m} B_{i,n}(u) B_{j,m}(v) P_{ij} \qquad u, v \in [0,1] \qquad (13.51)$$

where $B_{k,n}$ are the Bernstein polynomials given by (13.41).

The corresponding properties of Bezier curve apply to Bezier surface. For example, the surface is contained within the convex hull of the control points, and in general does not pass through all the control points except for the corners of the control point grid. We can form closed surfaces by setting the last control point to be the same point as the first. If the tangents of the first two control points are also equal to that of the last two control points then the closed surface will have first order continuity.

Using Bezier surfaces to construct patch meshes is better than constructing meshes using poly-gons such as triangles because Bezier surfaces are easier to manipulate and are much more compact. Moreover, they have more superior continuity properties. Some common parametric surfaces such as spheres and cylinders can be well approximated by relatively small numbers of cubic ($n = m = 3$) Bezier patches.

However, Bezier patch meshes are difficult to render directly because it is difficult to calculate their intersections with lines. It is also difficult to combine them directly with perspective projection algorithms. Therefore, Bezier patch meshes are in general decomposed into meshes of flat triangles in the 3D graphics processing pipeline.

13.4 B-Splines

13.4.1 B-Spline Properties

In many computer applications such as computer aided design (CAD), we may need to construct curves which are long and have complicated shapes. One approach would be to use high-degree Bezier curves. However, a high-degree Bezier curve is expensive to compute and does not have good local control; each of the $n + 1$ control points of a degree n Bezier curve affects the whole curve. When we change the position of one control point, the whole curve will be changed. Another approach is to construct the long curve by joining piecewise cubic Bezier curves with some constraints at the joints. In most cases, the constraint is that the curves are joined smoothly, which in turn requires at least C^1-continuity but desirably C^2-continuity. Piecewise Bezier curves interpolate the control points at the joints (which are end points for the segments) and have local control, but they need not be C^2-continuous. It turns out that piecewise cubic Bezier curves cannot be C^2-continuous and have local control at the same time. This is because C^2-continuous property implies second derivatives at the joined points are continuous; this requires that the two "interior" control points p_1^k, and p_2^k of segment k depend on $p_3^k(= p_0^{k+1})$, which in turn depend on the "interior" control points of the next segment, i.e. there is no local control.

A B-spline, which can be considered as a generalization of the Bezier curve, addresses these problems by using a different approach to represent a complicated curve. A B-spline curve maintains local control but does not interpolate the "interior" control points. We can define a B-spline curve in the following way.

We first define a **knot vector** U (not a geometric 3D vector) as a nondecreasing sequence,

$$U = \{u_0, u_1, ..., u_T\} \tag{13.52}$$

and define n control points $p_0, p_1, ..., p_{n-1}$. We define the order as

$$m = T - n + 1 \qquad m \geq 1 \tag{13.53}$$

Degree d is defined as order minus one (i.e. $d = m - 1 = T - n$). Because $m \geq 1$, we have $T \geq n$. Also, $T = n + m - 1$. We call the entities $u_m, ..., u_T$ *internal knots*, and define the *basis* functions $N_{k,i}$ recursively as

$$N_{k,1}(u) = \begin{cases} 1 & \text{if } u_k < u \leq u_{k+1} \\ 0 & \text{otherwise} \end{cases} \tag{13.54}$$

$$N_{k,m}(u) = \left(\frac{u - u_k}{u_{k+m-1} - u_k} \right) N_{k,m-1}(u) + \left(\frac{u_{k+m} - u}{u_{k+m} - u_{k+1}} \right) N_{k+1,m-1}(u) \tag{13.55}$$

A Non-Uniform Rational B-spline (NURB) is defined by the curve

$$p(u) = \sum_{k=0}^{n-1} p_k N_{k,m}(u) \tag{13.56}$$

Note again that the basis functions sum up to 1 at any u and thus it is legitimate to use them to form a combination of points.

In (13.56), if the first m knots are 0 and the last m knots are equal to 1, then it defines a nonperiodic B-spline . If the internal knots are equally spaced, it is a uniform B-spline . If the B-spline has no internal nodes, it is reduced to a Bezier curve.

B-splines have a number of advantages in graphics design. The following list some of them:

1. A single B-spline can specify a long complicated curve.
2. B-splines can approximate curves with sharp bends and even "corners".
3. We can translate piecewise Bezier curves into B-splines.
4. B-splines act more flexibly and intuitively with a large number of control points.
5. We can have local control of B-splines. That is, changing the placement of a point only affects a small segment of the curve.
6. Compared to Bezier curves, B-splines are a lot more sensitive to the placement of control points.
7. A piecewise Bezier curve requires more control points than a corresponding B-spline curve.

13.4.2 Knot Vector and Basis Functions

As discussed above, an order m (degree $m - 1$) B-spline curve with n control points is a continuous function defined by (13.56). In defining the curve, we must specify a knot vector $U = \{u_0, u_1, ..., u_{n+m-1}\}$. Each basis function $N_{k,j}(u)$ depends only on the $j + 1$ knot values from u_k to u_{k+j}. $N_{k,j}(u) = 0$ for $u \leq u_k$ or $u > u_{k+j}$. So p_k only influences the curve segment for $u_k < u \leq u_{k+j}$. Actually, $p(u)$ is a polynomial of order j (degree $j - 1$) on each interval $u_k < u \leq u_{k+1}$. Across the knots $p(u)$ is C^{j-2}-continuous and $p(u)$ is defined for $u_{min} < u \leq u_{max}$ where $u_{min} = u_j$ and $u_{max} = u_{n+2}$.

Knot vectors are generally classified into three categories: *uniform, open uniform*, and *non-uniform*.

If the knots u_k are equally spaced, the knot vector is a **uniform** knot vector. For example,

$$\{1, 2, 3, 4, 5, 6, 7, 8, 9, 10\}$$
$$\{0.0, 0.2, 0.4, 0.6, 0.8, 1.0\}$$
$$\{-1.5, -1.0, -0.5, 0.0, 0.5, 1.0, 1.5, 2.0\}$$

are uniform knot vectors.

Open Uniform knot vectors are uniform knot vectors which have j-equal knot values at each end. That is, knot values are equally spaced but the end values are repeated j times:

$$
\begin{aligned}
u_k &= u_0, & 0 \leq k < j \\
u_{k+1} - u_k &= constant, & j - 1 \leq k < n + 1 \\
u_k &= u_{j+n}, & k \geq n + 1,
\end{aligned}
\tag{13.57}
$$

Examples:

$$\{0, 0, 0, 1, 2, 3, 4, 4, 4\} \qquad\qquad k = 3, n = 5$$
$$\{1, 1, 1, 1, 2, 3, 4, 5, 6, 6, 6\} \qquad\qquad k = 4, n = 7$$
$$\{0.1, 0.1, 0.1, 0.1, 0.1, 0.3, 0.5, 0.7, 0.7, 0.7, 0.7, 0.7\} \quad k = 5, n = 7$$

Non-uniform knot vectors are general cases, where the only constraint is the standard $u_k \leq u_{k+1}$.

The shape of an $N_{k,j}$ basis function is determined entirely by the relative spacing between the knots. Scaling ($u'_k = \alpha u_k, \forall k$) or translating ($u'_k = u_k + \Delta u, \forall k$) the knot vector has no effect on the shape of the basis function $N_{k,j}$.

13.4.3 Cubic Uniform B-Splines

From discussions above, we see that when the knots are equidistant, the basis functions are just shifted copies of each other and we say that the B-spline is uniform. If the number of knots is the same as the degree, the B-spline degenerates into a Bezier curve.

Uniform B-splines of degree three, also known as cubic uniform B-splines, are one of the simplest and most useful classes of B-splines. A cubic B-Spline with $n + 1$ control points with open uniform knots is given by:

$$p(u) = \sum_{k=0}^{n} p_k N_k(u) \qquad 3 \leq u \leq n+1 \tag{13.58}$$

where p_k's are the control points, and $N_k(u) = N_{k,4}(u)$ are the blending (or basis) functions of degree 3 (order 4). For degree 3, $N_k(u) = 0$ if $u \leq k$ or $u \geq k + 4$. (i.e. For any given u value, only 4 basis functions are nonzero; see Figure 13.9 below.) Therefore, (13.58) can be expressed as

$$p(u) = \sum_{k=j-3}^{j} p_k N_k(u) \qquad u \in [j, j+1], \quad 3 \leq j \leq n \tag{13.59}$$

This equation implies that when a single control point p_k is moved, only the portion of the curve $p(u)$ with $k < u < k + 4$ will be changed. In other words, we can have local control for such a curve. Another way of understanding (13.59) is that the curve $p(u)$ is composed of a number of curve segments and each segment is controlled by four control points. In general, the blending functions have the following properties:

1. They are translates of each other, i.e. $N_k(u) = N_0(u - k)$.
2. They are piecewise degree three polynomials.
3. They are C^2-continuous, i.e. $N_k(u)$'s have continuous second derivatives.
4. They are partitions of unity, i.e. $\sum N_k(u) = 1$, for $3 \leq u \leq n + 1$. This is necessary as $p(u)$ is a valid point.
5. $N_k \geq 0$, (thus $N_k \leq 1$) for all u.
6. They have local properties, i.e. $N_k = 0$ for $u \leq k$ and $k + 4 \leq u$.

Figure 13-8 shows how these basis functions are calculated recursively.

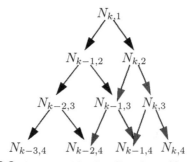

Figure 13-8 Degree 3 Blending Functions ($N_{k,1} = 1, N_i = N_{i,4}$)

Figure 13-9 shows a plot of the first five cubic blending functions with uniform knots. The knot vector is $\{0, 1, 2, 3, 4, 5, 6, 7, 8, 9, 10\}$. (If open-uniform knots are used, $N_k(u) = 0$ when $u \leq 3$.) We can see that the functions are translates of each other ($N_k(u) = N_0(u + k)$) and $N_k(u)$ is nonzero only when $k < u < k + 4$.

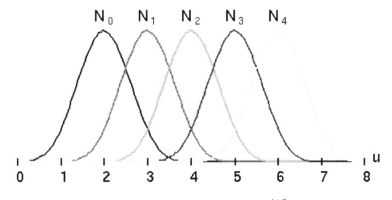

Figure 13-9 Cubic Blending Functions ($\sum_{i=j}^{j+3} N_i(u) = 1$)

13.4.4 Non Uniform Rational B-Splines (NURB)

The non uniform rational B-Spline (NURB) is the most general form of a B-Spline. An order m (or degree $m - 1$) NURB with n control points is given by (13.56). A uniform B-spline is simply a special form of NURB.

We denote the knot vector used in calculating the curve values of a NURB as $U = \{u_0, u_1, ..., u_{n+m-1}\}$. The knot vector divides the parametric space into intervals, which are usually referred to as knot spans. The number of knots in a knot vector is always equal to the number of control points plus the B-Spline order. The values in the knot vector should be in nondecreasing order. Each time the value of the parameter u gets to a new knot span, a new control point will be used and an old control point will be dropped in calculating the current $p(u)$. The steps below show a standard simple way of setting a knot vector of an order m NURB with n control points:

1. The knot vector U has totally $n + m$ knots, denoted as $U = \{u_0, ..., u_{n+m-1}\}$.
2. The values of the first m knots, $u_0, ..., u_{m-1}$ are all equal to 0.
3. The next $n - m$ knots $u_m, ..., u_{n-1}$ increments in 1, from 1 to $n - m$.
4. The final m knots, $u_n, ..., u_{n+m-1}$ are all equal to $n - m + 1$.

Examples

1. Knot vector of 8 control points ($n = 8$), order $4(m = 4)$:
$u_0 = u_1 = u_2 = u_3 = 0$
$u_4 = 1, u_5 = 2, u_6 = 3, u_7 = 4$
$u_8 = u_9 = u_{10} = u_{11} = 5$

2. Knot vector of 7 control points ($n = 8$), order $5(m = 5)$:
$u_0 = u_1 = u_2 = u_3 = u_4 = 0$
$u_5 = 1, u_6 = 2$
$u_7 = u_8 = u_9 = u_{10} = u_{11} = 3$

The following code segment shows the function **setKnotVector** that builds a knot vector using this method, the function **N_k** that calculates the blending functions, and the function **nurb** that finds a point using NURB.

```
//order m; n control points; return knots in U[]
void setKnotVector ( int m, int n, float U[] ) {
    if ( n < m  ) return;      //not enough control points
```

```
        for ( int i = 0; i < n + m; ++i ){
            if (i < m) U[i] = 0.0;
            else if (i < n) U[i] = i-m+1;   //i is at least m here
            else U[i] = n - m + 1;
        }
    }


    //order m blending functions recurvsively, U[] holds knots
    float N_k ( int k, int m, float u, float U[] ) {
      float d1, d2, sum = 0.0;
      if ( m == 1 )
      return ( U[k] < u &&  u <= U[k+1] );      //1 or 0

      //m larger than 1, so evaluate recursively
      d1 = U[k+m-1] - U[k];
      if ( d1 != 0 )
        sum = (u - U[k]) * N_k(k,m-1,u, U) / d1;
      d2 = U[k+m] - U[k+1];
      if ( d2 != 0 )
      sum += ( U[k+m] - u) * N_k(k+1, m-1, u, U ) / d2;
      return sum;
    }
    //non uniform rational B-splines, n control points, order m;
    //   p is the output point
    void nurb ( int n, int m, const Point3 control_points[],
                              float u, float U[],  Point3 &p ) {
      //sum control points,multiplied by respective basis functions
      Point3 p3;       //x, y, z components set to zero in constructor
      for ( int k = 0; k < n; ++k ){
        float Nk = N_k(k, m, u, U);   //blending (basis) function
        p3.x += Nk * control_points[k].x;
        p3.y += Nk * control_points[k].y;
        p3.z += Nk * control_points[k].z;
      }
      p = p3;                         //= is a copy command in C++
    }
```

Figure 13-10 below shows a curve obtained using the **nurb** function shown above; 8 control points and order 4 are used in the calculations.

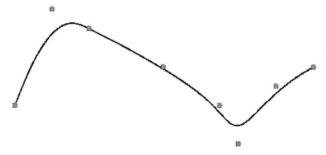

Figure 13-10   Curve Evaluated Using NURB with Order 4 and 8 Control Points

NURBS are just B-Splines with extensions made to accommodate points specified in homogeneous coordinates. They are invariant under the projective transformation. This means that if we draw two objects that are connected, they will be still connected when drawn in perspective. NURBS can also model conic sections precisely.

13.5 OpenGL Evaluators and NURBS

OpenGL provides functions to generate both Bezier (GL) and B-Spline (GLU) curves and surfaces. We can use the functions to interpolate vertices, normals, colors and textures.

13.5.1 OpenGL Evaluators for Bezier Curves and Surfaces

OpenGL supports the drawing of curves and surfaces through the use of evaluators. We use **glMap1***, which defines a one-dimensional evaluator to construct Bezier curves. This is done in the following steps, using **glMap1f** as example:

1. Specify the parameters with

```
void glMap1f(  GL_MAP1_VERTEX_3,
    float uMin,   float uMax,
    int stride,   int nPoints,
    const float *points  );
```

   This assumes 3 coordinates per vertex, and *stride* is used if we have interleaved different kinds of data in the array *points*.
2. Activate Bezier curve display by

   glEnable(GL_MAP1_VERTEX_3);

3. Display the curve by putting

   glEvalCoord1f(float *uValue*);

   in a loop insdie **glBegin/glEnd**.

For uniform spacing of u values, we can also use

   glMapGrid1f(int $nPartitions$, float $u1$, float $u2$);

to specify the number and range of u values, where $nPartitions$ is the number of partitions in the grid range interval $[u1, u2]$, $u1$ is a value used as the mapping for integer grid domain value $i = 0$, and $u2$ is a value used as the mapping for integer grid domain value $i = uPartitions$. The curve is actually drawn with

   glEvalMesh1f(enum $mode$, int $n1$, int $n2$);

where $mode$ can be GL_LINE or GL_POINT and $n1$ and $n2$ specify the part of the curve that should be drawn.

   Besides GL_MAP1_VERTEX_3, the commands **glMap1***() support other types of control points as listed in Table 13-1 below.

Table 13-1 Control Point Types for glMap1*()

Parameter	Data Types
GL_MAP1_VERTEX_3	vertex coordinates (x, y, z)
GL_MAP1_VERTEX_4	vertex coordinates (x, y, z, w)
GL_MAP1_INDEX	color index
GL_MAP1_COLOR_4	color components (R, G, B, A)
GL_MAP1_NORMAL	normal coordinates (x, y, z)
GL_MAP1_TEXTURE_COORD_1	texture coordinates s
GL_MAP1_TEXTURE_COORD_2	texture coordinates (s, t)
GL_MAP1_TEXTURE_COORD_3	texture coordinates (s, t, r)
GL_MAP1_TEXTURE_COORD_4	texture coordinates (s, t, r, q)

The following code segment shows an example of using the evaluator with 5 control points and the constructed Bezier curve is shown in Figure 13-11 below.

```
float controlPoints[Order][3] = {
    { -4.0, -1.0, 0.0}, { -2.0, 1.0, 0.0},
    { -3.0, -0.5, 0.0},
    {2.0, -1.0, 0.0}, {4.0, 1.0, 0.0}};

void init(void)
{
   glClearColor(1.0, 1.0, 1.0, 0.0);
   glShadeModel(GL_FLAT);
/*
 * GL_MAP1_VERTEX_3 -- specifies that 3-dimensional control points
 *         are provided and 3-D vertices should be produced
 * 0.0 -- low value of parmeter u
 * 1.0 -- high value of parmeter u
 * 3   -- number of floating-point values to advance in the data
 *         between two consecutive control points
 * 5   -- order of the spline (=degree+1) = number of control points
 */
   glMap1f(GL_MAP1_VERTEX_3,0.0,1.0, 3, Order, &controlPoints[0][0]);
   glEnable(GL_MAP1_VERTEX_3);
}

void display(void)
{
   int i;

   glClear( GL_COLOR_BUFFER_BIT );
   glColor3f( 0.0, 0.0, 0.0 );
   glBegin( GL_LINE_STRIP );
      for ( i = 0; i <= 30; i++ )
         glEvalCoord1f((float) i/30.0);
   glEnd();
   // The following code displays the control points as dots.
   glPointSize( 6.0 );
   glColor3f( 1.0, 0.0, 0.0 );
   glEnable ( GL_POINT_SMOOTH );
   glBegin(GL_POINTS);
     for ( i = 0; i < Order; i++ )
       glVertex3fv( &controlPoints[i][0] );
   glEnd();
   glFlush();
}
```

In the example, we use the command **glMap1f**() to define a one-dimensional evaluator that uses Equation (13.40) for Bezier curves to evaluate points. The output of the code is shown in Figure 13-11 below.

Figure 13-11   Curve Defined by glMap1f() in Above Code Segment

We can similarly construct two-dimensional Bezier surfaces or patches described by Equation (13.51); we summarize the procedures as follows, using **glMap2f**() as example:

1. Define the evaluator with

```
void glMap2f( GL_MAP2_VERTEX_3,
    float u1,     float u2,
    int ustride, int uorder,
    float v1,     float v2,
    int vstride, int vorder,
    const float *points );
```

2. Enable the evaluator by

  glEnable(GL_MAP2_VERTEX_3);

3. Display the curve by putting

  glEvalCoord2f(float *uValue*, float *vValue*);

  in a loop insdie **glBegin/glEnd**. If we do not want to use loop, we can setup and evaluate a mesh with **glMapGrid2f**() and **glEvalMesh2f**().

The following code segment presents an example of using OpenGL commands to construct a Bezier surface. The output of it is shown in Figure 13-12 below.

```
const int uOrder = 4;
const int vOrder = 4;
float controlPoints[uOrder][vOrder][3] = {
    {{-2, -1, 4.0}, {-1, -1, 3.0},
     {0, -1, -1.5}, {2, -1, 2.5}},
    {{-2, -0.5, 1.0}, {-1, -0.5, 3.0},
     {0, -0.5, 0.0}, {2, -0.5, -1.0}},
    {{-2, 0.5, 4.0}, {-1, 0.5, 1.0},
     {0, 0.5, 2.0}, {2, 0.5, 4.0}},
    {{-2, 1.5, -2.0}, {-1, 1.5, -2.0},
     {0, 1.5, 0.0}, {2, 1.5, -1.0}}
};

void init(void)
{
   glClearColor(1.0, 1.0, 1.0, 0.0);
   glMap2f(GL_MAP2_VERTEX_3, 0, 1, 3, uOrder,
        0, 1, 12, vOrder, &controlPoints[0][0][0]);
   glEnable(GL_MAP2_VERTEX_3);
   glMapGrid2f(20, 0.0, 1.0, 20, 0.0, 1.0);
   glEnable(GL_DEPTH_TEST);
```

```
    }

void display(void)
{
  int i, j;
  float u, v;

  glClear( GL_COLOR_BUFFER_BIT | GL_DEPTH_BUFFER_BIT);
  glColor3f( 0.0, 0.0, 0.0 );
  gluLookAt ( 10, 10, 10, 0, 0.0, 0.0, 0.0, 1.0, 0.0);
  glEnable ( GL_LINE_SMOOTH );
  glLineWidth( 2 );

  const int n1 = 8, n2 = 30;
  for ( i = 0; i <= n1; i++ ) {
    v = (float) i / n1;
    glBegin(GL_LINE_STRIP);
    for (j = 0; j <= n2; j++){
      u = (float) j / n2;
      glEvalCoord2f( u, v );
    }
    glEnd();
  }
  for (i = 0; i <= n1; i++) {
    u = (float) i / n1;
    glBegin(GL_LINE_STRIP);
    for (j = 0; j <= n2; j++) {
      v = (float) j / n2;
      glEvalCoord2f( u, v );
    }
    glEnd();
  }

  glFlush();
}
```

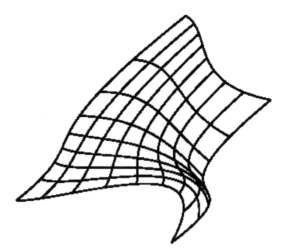

Figure 13-12 Bezier Surface Constructed using Evaluators

13.5.2 The GLU NURBS

Another way to draw Bezier curves and B-Splines is to use the NURBS interface. Internally, the NURBS interface is built on top of the evaluators discussed above. From the programmers point of view, the NURBS are simpler to use. It is also relatively easy to incorporate lighting effects and texture mapping in NURBS curves or surfaces. The following steps summarize the procedures to use NURBS:

1. We need to pass a NURBS context object into the NURBS interface each time we use the interface. Therefore, the first thing to do is to create a NURBS context object by

    GLUnurbs *nurbs = gluNewNurbsRenderer();

    This creates a pointer to a NURBS object, and we refer to this pointer when creating a NURBS curve or surface. A value of 0 is returned if there is not enough memory to allocate the object.

2. If we need to use lighting with a NURBS surface, we can enable the automatic normal-calculation feature by

    glEnable(GL_AUTO_NORMAL);

3. We may call **gluNurbsProperty**() to choose rendering values. The function has prototype,

    void gluNurbsProperty(GLUnurbs *nurbs, GLenum property, GLfloat value);

    where

    property specifies the property to be set, which can be
    GLU_SAMPLING_TOLERANCE, GLU_DISPLAY_MODE, GLU_CULLING,
    GLU_AUTO_LOAD_MATRIX, GLU_PARAMETRIC_TOLERANCE,
    GLU_SAMPLING_METHOD, GLU_U_STEP, GLU_V_STEP, or GLU_NURBS_MODE.

    value specifies the value of the indicated property, which may be a numeric value or one of
    GLU_OUTLINE_POLYGON, GLU_FILL, GLU_OUTLINE_PATCH, GLU_TRUE,
    GLU_FALSE, GLU_PATH_LENGTH, GLU_PARAMETRIC_ERROR,
    GLU_DOMAIN_DISTANCE, GLU_NURBS_RENDERER, or
    GLU_NURBS_TESSELLATOR.

4. If we need notification when encountering an error, we can call

    void gluNurbsCallback (GLUnurbs *nurb, GLenum which ,
    _GLfuncptr CallBackFunc);

5. Start rendering our curve or surface by calling

    gluBeginCurve(nurbs) or **gluBeginSurface**(nurbs)

6. Generate and render our curve or surface by calling

    gluNurbsCurve() or **gluNurbsSurface**()

    at least once with the control points, knot sequence, and order of the blending functions for the NURBS object. We might further call these functions to specify surface normals and/or texture coordinates.

7. Finish rendering the curve or surface by calling

    gluEndCurve(nurbs) or **gluEndSurface**(nurbs).

The following code segment presents an example of constructing a NURBS surface with lighting. Same control points of the evaluator example above have been used. The output of it is shown in Figure 13-13 below.

```
GLUnurbsObj *nurbs;

void nurbsError( GLenum error )
{
  const GLubyte *s = gluErrorString ( error );
  printf ( "Nurbs Error: %s\n", s );  exit (0);
}

void init(void)
{
  glClearColor(1.0, 1.0, 1.0, 0.0);
  GLfloat mat_ambient[] = { 0.5, 0.4, 0.3, 1.0 };
  GLfloat mat_diffuse[] = { 0.7, 0.8, 0.9, 1.0 };
  GLfloat mat_specular[] = { 0.9, 0.8, 0.7, 1.0 };
  GLfloat mat_shininess[] = { 50.0 };
  glMaterialfv(GL_FRONT, GL_DIFFUSE, mat_diffuse);
  glMaterialfv(GL_FRONT, GL_SPECULAR, mat_specular);
  glMaterialfv(GL_FRONT, GL_SHININESS, mat_shininess);
  glMaterialfv(GL_FRONT, GL_AMBIENT, mat_ambient);
  GLfloat light[] = { 1, 1, 1 };
  GLfloat light_position[] = { 1.0, 1.0, 1.0, 0.0 };
  glLightfv(GL_LIGHT0, GL_DIFFUSE, light );
  glLightfv(GL_LIGHT0, GL_AMBIENT, light );
  glLightfv(GL_LIGHT0, GL_SPECULAR, light );
  glLightfv(GL_LIGHT0, GL_POSITION, light_position);
  glEnable(GL_LIGHTING);     glEnable(GL_LIGHT0);
  glEnable(GL_DEPTH_TEST);
  glEnable(GL_AUTO_NORMAL);
  glEnable(GL_NORMALIZE);

  nurbs = gluNewNurbsRenderer ();
  gluNurbsProperty( nurbs, GLU_SAMPLING_TOLERANCE, 25.0);
  gluNurbsProperty( nurbs, GLU_DISPLAY_MODE, GLU_FILL);
  gluNurbsCallback( nurbs, GLU_ERROR, (GLvoid (*)()) nurbsError);
}

void display(void)
{
  glClear( GL_COLOR_BUFFER_BIT | GL_DEPTH_BUFFER_BIT);
  gluLookAt ( 10, 10, 10, 0, 0.0, 0.0, 0.0, 1.0, 0.0);
  const int uKnotCount = 8, vKnotCount = 8;
  float uKnots[uKnotCount] = {0.0, 0.0, 0.0, 0.0, 1.0, 1.0, 1.0, 1.0};
  float vKnots[vKnotCount] = {0.0, 0.0, 0.0, 0.0, 1.0, 1.0, 1.0, 1.0};
  int uStride = vOrder * 3, vStride = 3;
  gluBeginSurface ( nurbs );
    gluNurbsSurface ( nurbs,
                 uKnotCount, uKnots, vKnotCount, vKnots,
                 uStride, vStride, &controlPoints[0][0][0],
                 uOrder, vOrder, GL_MAP2_VERTEX_3);
  gluEndSurface ( nurbs );
```

```
    glFlush();
}
```

Figure 13-13   Surface Constructed by NURBS

13.6 Subdivision Surface

We discuss before that any surface can be approximated by a mesh of polygons, in particular triangles. Very often we can start from a coarse mesh and subdivide each polygon into smaller faces to obtain finer representation.

In general, we define the subdivision surfaces recursively. We start with a given polygonal mesh and apply a refinement scheme to subdivide the polygons of it, creating new vertices and new faces. We compute the positions of the new vertices using affine combinations of nearby old vertices. The refinement process produces a denser mesh than the original one, containing more polygonal faces. We can apply the same refinement process to the resulting mesh repeatedly until we obtain a smooth surface we want.

We consider a simple example to illustrate this subdivision technique; we approximate a unit sphere centered at $O = (0,0,0)$ with a mesh of triangles. We first approximate the sphere using a mesh of 20 equivalent triangles defined by 12 vertices. Each vertice is on the sphere and its coordinates are defined by three values, X, Z, and 0 where

$$X = .525731112119133606, \quad Z = .850650808352039932$$

Note that the sum of the squares of X and Z is equal to 1. That is,

$$X^2 + Z^2 = 1 \tag{13.60}$$

Therefore, any vertice $P = (x, y, z)$ of any triangle of the mesh has a unit normal at it, which can be calculated by

$$\mathbf{n} = P - O = (x, y, z) - (0, 0, 0) = (x, y, z) \tag{13.61}$$

Obvisously, the magnitude of $\mathbf{n}$ is $|\mathbf{n}| = x^2 + y^2 + z^2 = X^2 + Z^2 + 0^2 = 1$.

We define the 12 vertices and the 20 faces of the mesh using two arrays:

```
//vertex data
static double vdata[12][3] = {
    {-X, 0.0, Z}, {X, 0.0, Z}, {-X, 0.0, -Z}, {X, 0.0, -Z},
    {0.0, Z, X}, {0.0, Z, -X}, {0.0, -Z, X}, {0.0, -Z, -X},
    {Z, X, 0.0}, {-Z, X, 0.0}, {Z, -X, 0.0}, {-Z, -X, 0.0}
};
```

```
//indices for triangles
static int tindices[20][3] = {
    {0,4,1}, {0,9,4}, {9,5,4}, {4,5,8}, {4,8,1},
    {8,10,1}, {8,3,10}, {5,3,8}, {5,2,3}, {2,7,3},
    {7,10,3}, {7,6,10}, {7,11,6}, {11,0,6}, {0,1,6},
    {6,1,10}, {9,0,11}, {9,11,2}, {9,2,5}, {7,2,11} };
```

For example, the first triangle is defined by the indices {0, 4, 1} of the vertex array vdata[]; thus the coordinates of its vertices are given by vdata[0], vdata[4], and vdata[1], which have coordinate values

$$\{-X, 0.0, Z\}, \{0.0, Z, X\}, \{X, 0.0, Z\}$$

To refine the mesh, we subdivide a triangle into smaller triangles by making affine combinations of the original three vertices as shown in Figure 13-14 below. In the figure, the original triangle is defined by the three points P_1, P_2, and P_3. New triangles are formed by creating new vertices that are formed by affine combinations of the three vertices:

$$P_{12} = \tfrac{1}{2}(P_1 + P_2)$$
$$P_{23} = \tfrac{1}{2}(P_2 + P_3)$$
$$P_{31} = \tfrac{1}{2}(P_3 + P_1)$$

(13.62)

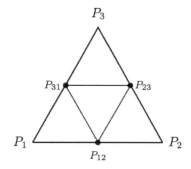

Figure 13-14   Subdividing a Triangle

Since a triangle always lies in a plane, the newly created triangles all lie in the same plane as the original one and they are beneath the the surface of the unit sphere. Obviously, these new triangles will not improve our approximation if we render them as is. To make the actual improvement, the trick is to move the new vertices P_{12}, P_{23}, and P_{31}, which are at a distance of less than 1 from the sphere center, to the surface of the sphere. This can be done by normalizing the normal to each point and moving the point to the tip of the unit normal. For example, we calculate the normal $\mathbf{N_{ij}}$ at P_{ij} by:

$$\mathbf{N_{ij}} = P_{ij} - O$$

(13.63)

We then normalize it by:

$$\mathbf{n_{ij}} = \frac{\mathbf{N_{ij}}}{|\mathbf{N_{ij}}|}$$

(13.64)

We recalculate the new position P'_{ij} of the vertex P_{ij} by:

$$P'_{ij} = \mathbf{n_{ij}} + O$$

(13.65)

Now P'_{ij} lies on the spherical surface as it is at a unit distance from the sphere center. The effect of the normalization process is to 'push out' the new vertices onto the spherical surface. (Keep in mind that the difference between two points is a vector and the sum of a vector and a point is a point. It is wrong and would be sloppy if we 'normalize' a point directly.)

As shown in Figure 13-14, we subdivide a triangle into four smaller ones and by 'pushing' the three new vertices onto the surface of the unit sphere, we have refined the mesh, which now has a total of $4 \times 20 = 80$ faces. The following code segment shows an implementation of this process and the output of it is shown in Figure 13-15 below.

```
Point3 vertices[12];

void midPoint(const Point3 &p1, const Point3 &p2, Point3  &p12)
{
  p12.x = ( p1.x + p2.x ) / 2.0;
  p12.y = ( p1.y + p2.y ) / 2.0;
  p12.z = ( p1.z + p2.z ) / 2.0;
}

void triangle(const Point3 &p1, const Point3 &p2, const Point3 &p3)
{
  glBegin(GL_TRIANGLES);
   glNormal3f( p1.x, p1.y, p1.z ); glVertex3f( p1.x, p1.y, p1.z );
   glNormal3f( p2.x, p2.y, p2.z ); glVertex3f( p2.x, p2.y, p2.z );
   glNormal3f( p3.x, p3.y, p3.z ); glVertex3f( p3.x, p3.y, p3.z );
  glEnd();
}

void subdivide(const Point3 &p1, const Point3 &p2, const Point3 &p3)
{
  Point3 p12, p23, p31;

  midPoint ( p1, p2, p12 );
  midPoint ( p2, p3, p23 );
  midPoint ( p3, p1, p31 );

  Point3 O (0, 0, 0);         //center of sphere
  Vector3 v12, v23, v31;      //3D vectors
  v12 = p12 - O;
  v23 = p23 - O;
  v31 = p31 - O;
  //normalize the vectors
  v12.normalize();
  v23.normalize();
  v31.normalize();
  //find vertices at vector tips
  p12 = v12 + O;
  p23 = v23 + O;
  p31 = v31 + O;
  triangle ( p1, p12, p31 );
  triangle ( p2, p23, p12 );
  triangle ( p3, p31, p23);
  triangle ( p12, p23, p31);
}

void init(void)
{
  glClearColor (1.0, 1.0, 1.0, 0.0);
  for ( int i = 0; i < 12; i++ )
    vertices[i] = Point3 ( vdata[i]  );
}

void display(void)
{
  glClear (GL_COLOR_BUFFER_BIT);
  glLineWidth ( 2 );
  glColor3f (0.0, 0.0, 0.0);
```

```
  glLoadIdentity ();
  gluLookAt (2.2, 2.2, 2.2, 0.0, 0.0, 0.0, 0.0, 1.0, 0.0);

  glPolygonMode( GL_FRONT_AND_BACK, GL_LINE );
  for (int i = 0; i < 20; i++) {
    int i0 = tindices[i][0];
    int i1 = tindices[i][1];
    int i2 = tindices[i][2];
    subdivide( vertices[i0], vertices[i1], vertices[i2] );
  }
  glFlush ();
}
```

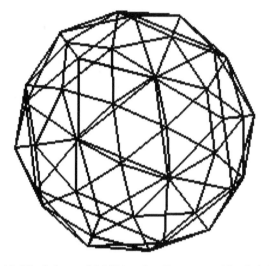

Figure 13-15 Sphere of 80 Triangles Constructed by Subdivision

We can continue to subdivide the triangles recursively until we are satisfied with the refinement of the mesh. To accomplish this recursive property, we just need to make slight modifications to the above **subdivide**() function:

```
void subdivide( const Point3 &p1, const Point3 &p2, const Point3 &p3,
                int level)
{
  Point3 p12, p23, p31;

  midPoint ( p1, p2, p12 );
  midPoint ( p2, p3, p23 );
  midPoint ( p3, p1, p31 );

  Point3 O (0, 0, 0);        //sphere center
  Vector3 v12, v23, v31;     //3D vectors
  v12 = p12 - O;
  v23 = p23 - O;
  v31 = p31 - O;
  //normalize the vectors
  v12.normalize();
  v23.normalize();
  v31.normalize();
  //find vertices at vector tips
  p12 = v12 + O;
  p23 = v23 + O;
  p31 = v31 + O;
  if ( level > 0 ) {  //subdivide recursively
    --level;
```

```
      subdivide ( p1, p12, p31, level );
      subdivide ( p2, p23, p12, level );
      subdivide ( p3, p31, p23, level );
      subdivide ( p12, p23, p31, level );
   } else {
      triangle ( p1, p12, p31 );
      triangle ( p2, p23, p12 );
      triangle ( p3, p31, p23);
      triangle ( p12, p23, p31);
   }
}
```

Figure 13-16 shows a sphere constructed with one more level of subdivision, consisting of $4 \times 80 = 320$ triangles.

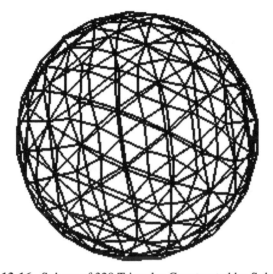

Figure 13-16   Sphere of 320 Triangles Constructed by Subdivision

Chapter 14   3D Objects from Planar Contours

In previous chapters, we have discussed how to construct a polygon mesh by specifying vertices and faces and how to use subdivision to obtain a finer mesh. Another common and simple way to create a mesh is by extrusion, which extrudes or sweeps a 2D face or a group of faces through space. By moving a uniform cross-section along a path in space, we obtain a 3D object. For example, extruding a square upward would create a cube connecting the bottom and the top faces. Thus, extrusion involves a 2D shape or a group of 2D shapes and straight line-segments in space. The cross-section of the extruded 3D object is determined by the 2D shape. In the extrusion process, we connect a starting point and the corresponding ending point of the extruded form in space by a line segment. We first duplicate the cross-section to create the top and bottom faces. Then we join the top and bottom faces together with parallel sides, which would generate outward-facing faces.

Extrusion is one of the general methods of constructing 3D surface from planar contours that represent cross sections of the objects. Besides 3D modeling, this field has applications in many scientific and engineering areas, including bio-medical applications, geology, archeology, and oceanogragphy. We may consider a contour as a continuous curve, which is the intersection of a plane and a surface.

14.1 Prisms

We first consider a simple example to illustrate the extrusion technique. We will sweep a cross-section along a straight line to obtain a prism. The cross-section we will use is composed of two triangles and a regular hexagon connected together as shown in (a) of Figure 14-1, where we assume that the cross-section lies in the xy-plane. To create a prism, we start with a **base** B consisting of the three polygons (two triangles and a hexagon) with a total of 12 vertices. We label each vertex of a polygon as $0, 1, ..., n - 1$, where n is the number of vertices in the polygon as shown in (b) of Figure 14-1. The coordinates of each vertex of the base is $(x, y, 0)$. We can sweep B in any direction $\mathbf{D}$ but for simplicity, we sweep B along the z-direction; the sweep creates an edge and another vertex for each vertex of the base as shown in (c) of Figure 14-1. The new vertices form the **cap** of the prism. The coordinates of each vertex of the cap is (x, y, H) where H is the height of the prism. To draw the prism, we simply use an array, say, $base[][3]$ to hold the coordinates of the N vertices of the base and a corresponding array, say, $cap[][3]$ to hold the vertices of the cap. If $base[][3]$ has been specified, the following code segment gives the cap:

```
for ( int i = 0; i < N; i++ ){
  cap[i][0] = base[i][0];
  cap[i][1] = base[i][1];
  cap[i][2] = H;
}
```

Polygons are formed from subsets of the base or cap vertices. We can use indices to specify a polygon of the base. For example, a polygon with n vertices can be specified by the indices $i_0, i_1, ..., i_{n-1}$ that refer to the coordinates at $base[i_0], base[i_1], ..., base[i_{n-1}]$. We can easily draw the polygons of the base and the cap. A sweeping edge joins the vertices $base[i_j]$ with $cap[i_j]$. The construction of a side face or a wall is straightforward. For the j-th wall ($j = 0, 1, ..., n - 1$), we construct a face from two vertices of the base and two vertices of the cap having indices i_j and i_{j+1}, where the operation $j + 1$ is taken $mod\ n$. (i.e., if the value of $j + 1$ is equal to n, we set it to 0.) The normal to each face can be calculated by finding the cross product of two vectors pointing in the directions of two adjacent edges. The following code segment shows the implementation of this concept for our example cross-section:

```
void drawWalls ()
{
  int i, j, k, n;
  int sides[3] = {3, 6, 3};
  for ( i = 0; i < 3; i++ ) {
    n = sides[i];
    glBegin(GL_POLYGON);
      for ( j = 0; j < n; j++ ) {
        k = indexp[i][j];
        glVertex3dv ( cap[k] );
        glVertex3dv ( base[k] );
        int next = (j + 1) % n;
        k = indexp[i][next];
        glVertex3dv ( base[k] );
        glVertex3dv ( cap[k] );
      }
    glEnd();
  }
}
```

In this code, the array *sides* contains the number of sides each polygon has. (In our example, there are three polygons in the base or the cap as shown in Figure 14-1.) The array *indexp* is a global variable that holds the indices to the vertices of the polygons; *indexp*[i][j] refers to the j-th vertex of the i-th polygon of the base or the cap.

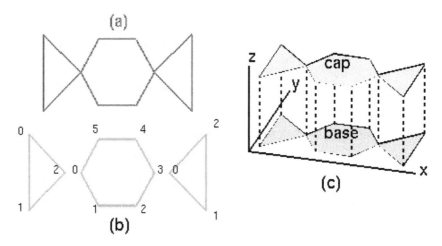

Figure 14-1 Cross-section and Walls of a Prism

Figure 14-2 below shows the prism created by the above code segment using the cross-section of Figure 14-1. Different colors have been used to render the faces of the prism. The complete code can be found in the source-code package of this book.

We should note that OpenGL can render only convex polygons reliably. If we draw the base of Figure 14-1 as one single polygon, OpenGL will fail to draw it properly as it is not a convex polygon. In this situation, we have to decompose the polygon into a set of convex polygons like what we did in our example, and extrude each one independently. Also, the windings of the base and the cap should be different. If we draw the vertices of both the base and the cap in the same order, the front face (outward face) is defined in different winding directions for the base and the cap. The front face winding direction can be changed by the command **glFrontFace**(). The following sample code will ensure that every face drawn is an outward face:

```
glFrontFace( GL_CW );      //clockwise is front facing
draw( base );       //draw base
glFrontFace( GL_CCW );   //anitclockwise is front facing
draw( cap );        //draw cap
drawWalls();
```

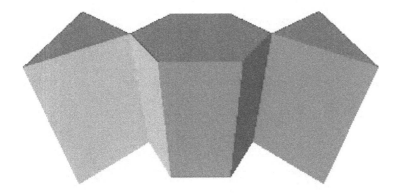

Figure 14-2 Prism by Extrusion

In the above example, the cap is just a translation of the base along the z-axis; the cap and the base have the same shape and size. We can easily generalize this by making the cap an affine transformation of the base. Suppose $b_i = (x_i, y_i, z_i)$ is the i-th vertex of the base. Then the corresponding vertex c_i of the cap is obtained by

$$c_i = M b_i \qquad (14.1)$$

where M is an affine transformation matrix and homogeneous coordinates are used.

For example, if we want the cap to have a smaller size we can choose M to have the following form:

$$M = \begin{pmatrix} 0.8 & 0 & 0 & 0 \\ 0 & 0.8 & 0 & 0 \\ 0 & 0 & 1 & H \\ 0 & 0 & 0 & 1 \end{pmatrix} \qquad (14.2)$$

The transformation given by (14.2) is a scaling in the x and y directions with scaling factor 0.8 plus a translation of H in the z-direction. Figure 14-3(a) below shows an example of this case.

If we want to 'twist' the prism, we can first rotate the base through an angle θ about the z-axis before translation; the transformation matrix will have the form,

$$M = \begin{pmatrix} \cos\theta & -\sin\theta & 0 & 0 \\ \sin\theta & \cos\theta & 0 & 0 \\ 0 & 0 & 1 & H \\ 0 & 0 & 0 & 1 \end{pmatrix} \qquad (14.3)$$

Figure 14-3(b) shows an example of such a prism. The transformation involves matrix multiplications, which will be also used in subsequent sections of this chapter and later chapters. We therefore define a few simple matrix classes to handle the special transformations. We discuss the matrix classes in the next section.

(a)   (b)

Figure 14-3 Extruded Prisms: Caps by Affine Transformation of Base

14.2 Matrix Classes

In this section, we define a few simple matrix classes that will help implement extrusion programs more effectively and systematically. For simplicity, we only consider 1×4, 4×1, and 4×4 matrices. We first define the base class *Matrix4* that has the common properties of 1×4 and 4×1 matrices. We then define the subclasses *Matrix14* for 1×4 matrix operations and *Matrix41* for 4×1 matrix operations. Their inheritance relations are shown in Figure 14-4 below. The class *Matrix44* is another independent class that can be constructed from *Matrix41* or *Matrix14*.

Both *Matrix14* and *Matrix41* have four components x, y, z, and w, which are inherited from their parent, *Matrix4*. In general, if $w = 0$, it represents a 3D vector. If $w \neq 0$, it represents a point; the position of the corresponding 3D point is specified by $(x/w, y/w, z/w)$. Conversely, if the class is constructed from a 3D vector (*Vector3*), its fourth component w is set to 0; if it is constructed from a 3D point (*Point3*), w is set to 1. In the implementation, we use the array $m[4]$ to represent x, y, z, and w with $m[0]$ representing x, $m[1]$ representing y, and so on. The following header shows the constituents of the *Matrix4* class:

```
//Matrix4.h : Base class for 1 X 4 and 4 x 1 matrix operations
class Matrix4
{
  public:
    double m[4];     //row or column elements (x, y, z, w)
    //constructors
    Matrix4();
    Matrix4 ( double x, double y, double z, double w );
    Matrix4 ( const double a[3], double w );
    Matrix4 ( const double a[4] );
    Matrix4 ( const Point3 &p );
    Matrix4 ( const Vector3 &v );
```

```
        //member functions
        void set ( double x, double y, double z, double w );
        void set ( const double a[3], double w );
        void set ( const double a[4] );
        void get3 ( double a[3] );
        void get4 ( double a[4] );
        XYZ getXYZ();
        bool isVector3();   //does it represent a 3D vector or a point?
        Point3 getPoint3();
        Matrix4 operator + ( const Matrix4 &mat );
        Matrix4 operator - ( const Matrix4 &mat );
        Matrix4 operator * ( const double a );
    };
```

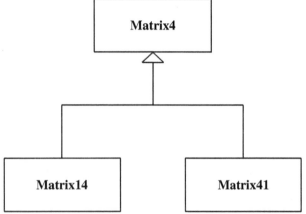

Figure 14-4. Class *Matrix4* and subclasses *Matrix14* and *Matrix41*

The following code shows the subclass *Matrix14* declaration:

```
//Matrix14.h : Class defines 1 X 4 matrix operations
#include "Matrix4.h"

class Matrix41;  //forward declaration
class Matrix44;  //forward declaration

class Matrix14: public Matrix4
{
  public:
    Matrix14();
    Matrix14 ( double x, double y, double z, double w );
    Matrix14 ( const Point3 &p );
    Matrix14 ( const Vector3 &v );
    Matrix41 transpose();
    double operator * (const Matrix41 &mat);   //(1x4)(4x1)-->(1x1)
    Matrix14 operator * (const Matrix44 &mat);//(1x4)(4x4)-->(1x4)
    void print();   //print row matrix
};
```

We have similar code for the class *Matrix41*. From the header code, we see that the operator *
represents matrix multiplications. The multiplication of a 1×4 matrix and a 4×1 matrix yields a
1×1 matrix (a scalar). Multiplying a 1×4 matrix to a 4×4 matrix gives a 1×4 matrix, and the
product of a 4×1 matrix and a 1×4 matrix is a 4×4 matrix. In general,

$$(n \times m)(m \times r) \rightarrow (n \times r)$$

In homogeneous coordinates, points and vectors are 4×1 matrices.

The other class, *Matrix44* handles 4×4 matrix operations such as affine transformations. The following code shows the *Matrix44* class declaration:

```
//Matrix44.h : Class defines 4 X 4 matrix operations

#include "Matrix4.h"
class Matrix14;   //forward declarations
class Matrix41;

class Matrix44
{
  public:
    double m[4][4];     //4 x 4 array
    Matrix44();
    Matrix44 ( const double mat44[4][4] );
    Matrix44 ( const double *a );
    Matrix44 ( const Matrix14 &r0, const Matrix14 &r1, const Matrix14 &r2,
               const Matrix14 &r3 );
    Matrix44 ( const Matrix41 &c0, const Matrix41 &c1, const Matrix41 &c2,
               const Matrix41 &c3 );
    void set ( const double *a );
    void get ( double *a );
    bool setCol ( int nCol, const double a[] );   //set one column
    bool setCol ( int nCol, double a0, double a1, double a2, double a3 );
    Matrix44 transpose();
    Matrix44 operator + ( const Matrix44 &mat );
    Matrix44 operator - ( const Matrix44 &mat );
    Matrix44 operator * ( const double d );
    Matrix41 operator * ( const Matrix41 &mat );   //(4x4)(4x1) --> (4x1)
    Matrix44 operator * ( const Matrix44 &mat );   //(4x4)(4x4) --> (4x4)
    double determinant();
    Matrix44 inverse();
};
```

There are many ways we can construct a 4×4 matrix. For example, we can construct it from a 1D array of 16 elements, or from a 2D array of 4×4 elements, or from 4 *Matrix14* objects. The member functions **transpose**(), **determinant**(), and **inverse**() calculate the transpose, determinant and inverse of the 4×4 matrix respectively.

After defining the matrix classes, we can now present the code for transforming a base to a cap through an affine transformation given by (14.2) or (14.3). The following code segment shows how we obtain the cap from a base by a rotation-translation transformation defined by (14.3).

```
const double H = 3;     //height
double theta = 3.1415926 / 6;

//define transformation matrix elements
double a[4][4] = { { cos (theta), -sin (theta), 0 , 0 },
                   { -sin (theta), cos (theta), 0, 0 },
                   { 0, 0, 1, H },
                   { 0, 0, 0, 1 } };

Matrix44 Rz ( a );   //Construct a Matrix44 object from a[4][4]

//base and cap have 3 vertices
double base[3][3] = {
   {0, 1.0, 0}, {0, 0, 0}, {1, 0.0, 0}
};
double cap[3][3];

Matrix41 Base[3]; //3 vertices, a Matrix41 object for each vertex
for ( int i = 0; i < 3; i++ ){
```

```
    Base[i].set ( base[i], 1 );    //set x, y, z, w value
    Matrix41 temp = Rz * Base[i];  //multiply matrix by a vertex
    temp.get3 ( cap[i] );          //get coordinates of transformed
                                   // vertice; save them in cap[i]
  }
```

14.3 Tubes and Snakes

14.3.1 Segmented Tubes

We have discussed that we can form a simple tube by sweeping a cross-section in space and we obtain a special shape of the tube by performing an affine transformation of the cross section. If we create various tube segments each with a particular transformation and join the segments end to end, we can obtain a long tube with a specific shape. Figure 14-5 shows a tube created in this way; we extrude a triangular base B_0 three times, in different directions with different scaling. The first cap C_0, which becomes the next base B_1 is given by $C_0 = B_1 = M_0 B_0$, where M_0 is the first transformation matrix employed to make the first segment S_0; in the notation, the matrix operates on each vertex of the base. For example, the j-th vertex of the cap is $C_{0j} = M_0 B_{0j}$. We can generalize this to the creation of segment i from base B_i with matrix M_i as

$$B_{i+1} = C_i = M_i B_0 \tag{14.4}$$

Again, it is understood that matrix M_i operates on each vertex of B_0. The various intermediate transformed bases are referred to as **waists** of the tube. In the example, the waists are given by $M_0 B_0, M_1 B_0, M_2 B_0$. Program Listing 14-1 below shows an implementation that generates the tube of Figure 14-5.

Program Listing 14-1   Implementation of Building a Segmented Tube

```
------------------------------------------------------------------
const int N0 = 3;       //number of vertices in base
double base[N0][3] = {
   {0, 0.5, 0}, {0, 0, 0}, {0.5, 0.0, 0}
};
double cap[3][N0][3];
//Three Transformation matrices
double a0[4][4] = { {0.5, 0.0, 0.0, 1.0},
                    {0.0, 0.5, 0.0, -0.2},
                    { 0, 0, 0.5, 0.5 },
                    { 0, 0, 0, 1 } };
double a1[4][4] = { {0.8, 0.0, 0.0, 2.0},
                    {0.0, 0.8, 0.0, 0.2},
                    { 0, 0, 0.8, 0.7 },
                    { 0, 0, 0, 1 } };
double a2[4][4] = { {1.5, 0.0, 0.0, 3.0},
                    {0.0, 1.5, 0.0, 1.0},
                    { 0, 0, 1.5, 1.0 },
                    { 0, 0, 0, 1 } };
Matrix44 M[3];
void init(void) {
  //setup transformation matrices
  M[0].set ( a0 );  M[1].set ( a1 );  M[2].set ( a2 );
  //calculate caps
```

```
   for ( int k = 0; k < 3; k++ ) {
     Matrix41 Base[N0];
     for ( int i = 0; i < N0; i++ ){
       Base[i].set ( base[i], 1 );
       Matrix41 temp = M[k] * Base[i];
       temp.get3 ( cap[k][i] );    //put values in cap array
     }
   }
}
void drawWalls ( double base[3][3], double cap[3][3] ) {
  int j, k, n = 0;
  for ( j = 0; j < 3; j++ ) {
    setColor ( n++ );              //use different colors
    glBegin(GL_POLYGON);
      k = j;
      glVertex3dv ( cap[k] );
      glVertex3dv ( base[k] );
      int next = (j + 1) % 3;
      k = next;
      glVertex3dv ( base[k] );
      glVertex3dv ( cap[k] );
    glEnd();
  }
}
void display(void) {
  draw( base );      //draw base
  for ( int i = 0; i < 3; i++ ) {
    draw( cap[i] );        //draw cap
    //draw walls formed between a base and a cap
    if ( i == 0 )
      drawWalls( base, cap[0] );
    else
      drawWalls( cap[i-1], cap[i] );
  }
}
```

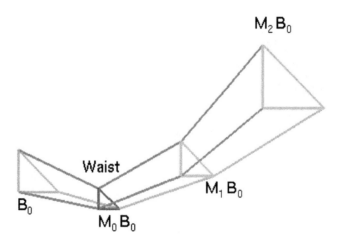

Figure 14-5 A Tube Composed of Different Segments

We can also make use of the transformation matrices to grow and shrink the cross-section of the tube to create a snake-shaped tube like the one shown in Figure 14-6.

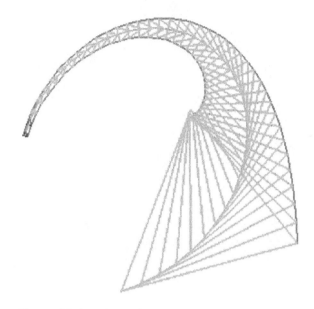

Figure 14-6   A Snake by Growing or Shrinking Caps

14.3.2 Frenet Frame

We can naturally construct a tube by wrapping a 3D shape around a curve C, which can be considered as the spine of the extrusion. In general we represent the curve parametrically by $C(u) = (x(u), y(u), z(u))$. For example, a helix curve shown in Figure 14-7 (a) can be described parametrically by by

$$
\begin{aligned}
x(u) &= cos(u) \\
y(u) &= sin(u) \\
z(u) &= bu \qquad \text{for some constant b}
\end{aligned}
\tag{14.5}
$$

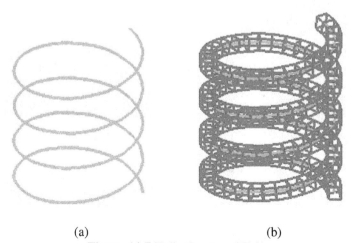

(a)   (b)

Figure 14-7 Helix Curve and Tube

Figure 14-7 (b) shows a tube obtained by sweeping a square along the helix curve of (a).

A common technique to construct a tube along a curve is to first obtain the curve values at various parametric value u_i and then build a polygon perpendicular to the curve at the point $C(u_i)$ using a Frenet frame, which is one of the most important tools used to analyze a curve. A Frenet frame is a moving frame that provides a local coordinate system at each point of the curve that adapts to the changes of the curvature of the curve. A Frenet frame along a curve C is created in the following steps:

1. We consider a point $C(u_i)$ on the curve in homogeneous coordinates:

$$C(u_i) = \begin{pmatrix} x(u_i) \\ y(u_i) \\ z(u_i) \\ 1 \end{pmatrix} \tag{14.6}$$

2. At each parametric value u_i, we calculate a normalized vector $\mathbf{T}(u_i)$, which is the unit tangent to the curve at u_i. We can find $\mathbf{T}(u)$ from the derivative $C'(u)$ of $C(u)$:

$$C'(u) = \frac{dC(u)}{du} = \begin{pmatrix} \frac{dx}{du} \\ \frac{dy}{du} \\ \frac{dz}{du} \\ 0 \end{pmatrix}, \quad \mathbf{T}(u) = \frac{C'(u)}{|C'(u)|} \tag{14.7}$$

3. We calculate the unit normal $\mathbf{N}(u)$ at u_i from the derivative of the unit tangent $\mathbf{T}(u)$ at u_i:

$$\mathbf{T}'(u) = \frac{d\mathbf{T}(u)}{du}, \quad \mathbf{N}(u) = \frac{\mathbf{T}'(u)}{|\mathbf{T}'(u)|} \tag{14.8}$$

The two unit vectors $\mathbf{T}$ and $\mathbf{N}$ are perpendicular to each other. (Any unit vector $\mathbf{a}(u)$ is always perpendicular to its derivative $\mathbf{a}'(u)$. This is because $\mathbf{a} \cdot \mathbf{a} = 1$. By differenting this equation with respect to u, we obtain $2\mathbf{a} \cdot \mathbf{a}' = 0$, implying that the two vectors are perpendicular to each other.)

4. We then find a third unit vector, binormal $\mathbf{B}$, which is perpendicular to both $\mathbf{T}$ and $\mathbf{N}$. This unit binormal vector can be found by taking the cross product of $\mathbf{T}$ and $\mathbf{N}$:

$$\mathbf{B}(u) = \mathbf{T}(u) \times \mathbf{N}(u) \tag{14.9}$$

5. The three orthonormal vectors $\mathbf{T}(u_i), \mathbf{N}(u_i)$, and $\mathbf{B}(u_i)$ constitute the Frenet frame at u_i.

6. In summary, the basis of a Frenet frame is given by

$$\begin{aligned} \mathbf{T}(u) &= \frac{C'(u)}{|C'(u)|} & \text{the unit tangent} \\ \mathbf{N}(u) &= \frac{\mathbf{T}'(u)}{|\mathbf{T}'(u)|} & \text{the unit principal normal} \\ \mathbf{B}(u) &= \mathbf{T}(u) \times \mathbf{N}(u) & \text{the unit binormal} \end{aligned} \tag{14.10}$$

If we want to reference an object in the Frenet frame at u_i, we can translate the origin $O = (0, 0, 0)$ of our world coordinate system to the spine point $C(u_i)$ and transform the basis vectors $(\mathbf{i}, \mathbf{j}, \mathbf{k})$ to the Frenet frame basis $(\mathbf{T}(u_i), \mathbf{N}(u_i), \mathbf{B}(u_i))$. The 4×4 transformation matrix M that does this is

$$M = (\mathbf{T}(u_i), \mathbf{N}(u_i), \mathbf{B}(u_i), C(u_i)) \tag{14.11}$$

This is the transformation matrix that transforms a base polygon of the tube to its position and orientation in the Frenet frame as shown in Figure 14-8 below. Note that we are **not** expressing our coordinates in the Frenet fram coordinate system. What we do is to rotate our base object in a way that the unit vectors $\mathbf{i}$, $\mathbf{j}$, and $\mathbf{k}$ are aligned with the unit vectors $\mathbf{T}$, $\mathbf{N}$, and $\mathbf{B}$ respectively.

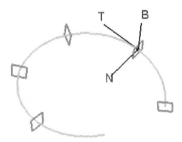

Figure 14-8 Frenet Frame

Very often people define the curvature κ and torsion τ of a curve $C(u)$ as:

$$\kappa = \kappa(u) = \left| \frac{d\mathbf{T}(u)}{du} \right|$$
$$\tau = \tau(u) = -\frac{d\mathbf{B}(u)}{du} \cdot \mathbf{N}(u) \tag{14.12}$$

Note that $\frac{d\mathbf{B}}{du}$ is parallel to $\mathbf{N}$. Therefore, $|\tau| = |\frac{d\mathbf{B}}{du}|$. With these definitions, we can derive the Frenet-Serret formulas:

$$\frac{d}{du} \begin{pmatrix} \mathbf{T} \\ \mathbf{N} \\ \mathbf{B} \end{pmatrix} = \begin{pmatrix} 0 & \kappa & 0 \\ -\kappa & 0 & \tau \\ 0 & -\tau & 0 \end{pmatrix} \begin{pmatrix} \mathbf{T} \\ \mathbf{N} \\ \mathbf{B} \end{pmatrix} \tag{14.13}$$

Example 14-1:
Consider the helix curve described by Equation (14.5). Find a Frenet frame at u_i and the transformation matrix M that transforms objects to the new coordinate system.

Solution:
In this example, the spine point on the curve at u_i is:

$$C(u_i) = \begin{pmatrix} cos(u_i) \\ sin(u_i) \\ bu_i \\ 1 \end{pmatrix} \tag{14.14}$$

A tangent vector to the curve is

$$C'(u) = \frac{dC(u)}{du} = \begin{pmatrix} -sin(u) \\ cos(u) \\ b \\ 0 \end{pmatrix}$$

Therefore the unit tangent at u_i is:

$$\mathbf{T}(u_i) = \frac{C'(u_i)}{|C'(u_i)|} = \frac{1}{\sqrt{1+b^2}} \begin{pmatrix} -sin(u_i) \\ cos(u_i) \\ b \\ 0 \end{pmatrix} \tag{14.15}$$

where we have used the trigonometry identity $sin^2\theta + cos^2\theta = 1$.

The unit normal at u_i is:

$$\mathbf{N}(u_i) = \frac{T'(u_i)}{|T'(u_i)|} = \begin{pmatrix} -cos(u_i) \\ -sin(u_i) \\ 0 \\ 0 \end{pmatrix} \tag{14.16}$$

The unit binormal at u_i is:

$$\mathbf{B}(u_i) = \mathbf{T}(u_i) \times \mathbf{N}(u_i) = \frac{1}{\sqrt{1+b^2}} \begin{pmatrix} b \times sin(u_i) \\ -b \times cos(u_i) \\ 1 \\ 0 \end{pmatrix} \tag{14.17}$$

The three unit vectors $(\mathbf{T}(u_i), \mathbf{N}(u_i), \mathbf{B}(u_i))$ form an orthonormal basis, which is a Frenet frame.

Let $c = \dfrac{1}{\sqrt{1+b^2}}$. The transformation matrix $M = (\mathbf{T}(u_i), \mathbf{N}(u_i), \mathbf{B}(u_i), C(u_i))$ is:

$$M = \begin{pmatrix} -c \times sin(u_i) & -cos(u_i) & c \times b \times sin(u_i) & cos(u_i) \\ -c \times cos(u_i) & -sin(u_i) & -c \times b \times cos(u_i) & sin(u_i) \\ c \times b & 0 & c & b \times u_i \\ 0 & 0 & 0 & 1 \end{pmatrix} \tag{14.18}$$

The implementation of transforming objects to a Frenet frame of the above example is straight forward. All we need to do is to calculate the transformation matrix of (14.18) and then multiply the vertex coordinates of any object by this matrix. The following code segment presents an example implementation.

Program Listing 14-2   Example Code for Frenet Frame Transformationdd

```
----------------------------------------------------------------
//Matrix for transforming to Frenet frame of Helix Curve
void setM( Matrix44 &M, float u, float b ) {
  float c = 1.0 / sqrt ( 1 + b*b );
  M.setCol( 0, -c * sin(u), c * cos(u), b * c, 0);      //Tangent   T(u)
  M.setCol( 1,  -cos(u), -sin(u), 0, 0 );               //Normal    N(u)
  M.setCol( 2, c * b * sin(u), -c * b * cos(u), c, 0 ); //Binormal  B(u)
  M.setCol( 3, cos(u), sin(u), b * u, 1 );              //The curve C(u)
```

```
}
//An array is not copyable; so we define this class mainly for copying
class Cdouble3 {
  public:
     double p3[3];
};

void display(void) {
  const float b = 0.1;         //constant of Helix curve
  Matrix44 M44;                //Transformation matrix
  const int N = 4;             //number of vertices in base

  //two STL vectors to hold base and cap
  vector<Cdouble3>vp0(N), vp1(N);
  Matrix41 p_1;                //transformed point

  //4 vertices of a quad
  //homogeneous coordinates of the four vertices of a quad
  Matrix41 points[4];          //define four points
  points[0] = Matrix41 ( 0, -0.1, -0.1, 1 );  //x, y, z, w
  points[1] = Matrix41 ( 0, -0.1,  0.1, 1 );  //x, y, z, w
  points[2] = Matrix41 ( 0,  0.1,  0.1, 1 );  //x, y, z, w
  points[3] = Matrix41 ( 0,  0.1, -0.1, 1 );  //x, y, z, w

  float p3[3];                 //3-D point, (x, y, z)
  //starting
  setM ( M44, 0, b );          //u = 0
  for ( int i = 0; i < 4; ++i ) {
    p_1 = M44 * points[i];     //transform the point
    p_1.get3( vp0[i].p3 );     //put (x, y, z) in vp0[i].p3[]
  }
  glBegin( GL_QUADS );         //a side has four points
  for ( float u = 0.2; u <=  26; u += 0.2 ) {
    setM ( M44, u, b );
    for ( int i = 0; i < N; ++i ) {
      p_1 = M44 * points[i]; //transform to Frenet Frame system
      p_1.get3( vp1[i].p3 ); //put (x, y, z) in vp1[i].p3[]
    }
    //draw the N sides of tube between 'base' and 'cap'
    for ( int i = 0; i < N; ++i ) {
      int j = (i+1) % N;
      glVertex3dv( vp0[i].p3 );
      glVertex3dv( vp0[j].p3 );
      glVertex3dv( vp1[j].p3 );
      glVertex3dv( vp1[i].p3 );
    }
    copy ( vp1.begin(), vp1.end(), vp0.begin() ); //copy vp1 to vp0
  } //for u
  glEnd();
}
```

In Listing 14-2, we have made use of the C++ Standard Template Library (STL) to simplify our implementation. In the program, we have included two STL headers:

```
#include <vector>
```

```
#include <algorithm>
```

These allow us to use the C++ *vector* class and the function **copy**(). As we can see from the Listing, the function **setM**() sets up the Frenet frame transformation matrix M at a certain value of u of a helix curve. The class *Cdouble3* only has one data member, *p3*, which is an array of 3 doubles. We define this class because we cannot copy an array directly using the C/C++ assignment operator '=' with one simple statement. However, we can perform this copy operation for class objects. The statement

```
vector<Cdouble3>vp0(N), vp1(N);
```

declares two vectors, *vp0*, and *vp1* each with capacity N and of data type *Cdouble3*. They save the vertices of the base and the cap of a segment respectively. When we sweep the cross section, the cap of the previous segment becomes the current base. So we copy the previous cap vector to the current base vector. This is done by the statement

```
copy ( vp1.begin(), vp1.end(), vp0.begin() ); //copy vp1 to vp0
```

The new cap is obtained from transformation. Note that the x-axis **i** maps to the unit tangent **T** of the Frenet frame and we sweep the cross section, which is a square here, along the curve. To construct the tube, we want the square to be perpendicular to the curve with its center on the curve. In other words, the square is centered around the **T** axis. Therefore, we define our cross section (the square) to lie on the y-z plane and centered around the x-axis like the following:

$$\text{vertex } 0 : (0, \quad -0.1, \quad -0.1)$$
$$\text{vertex } 1 : (0, \quad -0.1, \quad 0.1)$$
$$\text{vertex } 2 : (0, \quad 0.1, \quad 0.1)$$
$$\text{vertex } 3 : (0, \quad 0.1, \quad -0.1)$$

In the above code, the vertices coordinates are stored in the array *points*; each *points* object is a 4×1 matrix.

The variable *p_1* defines a point (a 4×1 matrix in homogeneous coordinates). This variable is used to calculate the new position of a point transformed by the transformation matrix such as

```
for ( int i = 0; i < N; ++i ) {
   p_1 = M44 * points[i]; //transform to Frenet Frame system
   p_1.get3( vp1[i].p3 ); //put (x, y, z) in vp1[i].p3[]
}
```

where the member function **get3**(double a[]) of *p_1* extracts the x, y, z values of *p_1* and puts them in the array a[], which is a function argument.

Figure 14-7 (b) above shows an output of this program and Figure 14-9 below shows an output with lighting effect and tube segments drawn as solid polygons.

Figure 14-9 Solid Tube Created using Frenet Frame

In some cases, the curve $C(u)$ may have a complicated form and it is difficult to find the derivatives of it. In these situations, we can approximate the derivatives using numerical techniques like the following:

$$\mathbf{T}(u) \sim \frac{dC(u)}{du} = \frac{C(u+\epsilon) - C(u-\epsilon)}{2\epsilon} \qquad (14.19a)$$

$$\mathbf{N}(u) \sim \frac{d^2C(u)}{du^2} = \frac{C(u+\epsilon) - 2C(u) + C(u-\epsilon)}{\epsilon^2} \qquad (14.19b)$$

The numerical differentiations usually produce good approximations for the Frenet frame basis vectors. However, the method may sometimes give unstable solutions.

14.3.3   Toroidal Spirals and Other Examples

We may use toroidal spirals to create interesting tubes. Toroidal spiral curves can be described by the equations,

$$C(u) = \begin{pmatrix} x(u) \\ y(u) \\ z(u) \\ 1 \end{pmatrix} = \begin{pmatrix} (R + r\cos(qu))\cos(pu) \\ (R + r\cos(qu))\sin(pu) \\ r\sin(qu) \\ 1 \end{pmatrix}, \qquad 0 \leq u \leq 2\pi \qquad (14.20)$$

where $R, r, p,$ and q are some constants. Such a curve wraps around the surface of a torus centered at the origin (see Figure 13-2); the constants R and r are the large and small radii of the torus as shown in Figure 13-2 of Chapter 13. The parameter q determines the number of times the curve wraps around the torus, and the parameter p defines the number of times the curve winds around the origin.

In this case the tangent at u is $\mathbf{T}(u) \sim \frac{dC(u)}{du}$ with

$$\begin{aligned} \frac{dx(u)}{du} &= -p(R + r\cos(qu))\sin(pu) - rq\sin(qu)\cos(pu) \\ &= -py(u) - rq\sin(qu)\cos(pu) \end{aligned} \qquad (14.21a)$$

and

$$\begin{aligned} \frac{dy(u)}{du} &= p(R + r\cos(qu))\cos(pu) - rq\sin(qu)\sin(pu) \\ &= -px(u) - rq\sin(qu)\sin(pu) \end{aligned} \qquad (14.21b)$$

$$\frac{dz(u)}{du} = rq\cos(qu)$$

The normal vector $\mathbf{N}(u)$ is obtained from the second derivatives of $C(u)$:

$$\begin{aligned} \frac{d^2x(u)}{du} &= -p\frac{dy}{du} + rq(p\sin(qu)\sin(pu) - q\cos(qu)\cos(pu)) \\ \frac{d^2y(u)}{du} &= p\frac{dx}{du} - rq(p\sin(qu)\cos(pu) + q\cos(qu)\sin(pu)) \\ \frac{d^2z(u)}{du} &= -rq^2\sin(qu) \end{aligned} \qquad (14.22)$$

The binomial vector $\mathbf{B}(u)$ is obtained by $\mathbf{B} = \mathbf{T} \times \mathbf{N}$.

The following code segment shows an implementation of calculating the transformation matrix M for a toroidal spiral:

```
//toroidal-spiral
void get_C ( double C[4], double u, double R, double r,
                                      double p, double q ) {
  double t1 = q * u, t2 = p * u;
  C[0] = (  R + r * cos ( t1 )) * cos ( t2 );
  C[1] = ( R + r * cos ( t1 ) ) * sin ( t2 );
  C[2] = r * sin( t1 );
  C[3] = 1;
}
//Tangent
void get_T ( double T[4], double C[4], double  u, double r,
                                      double p, double q ) {
  double  t1, t2;
  t1 = q * u;  t2 = p * u;
  T[0] = -p * C[1] - r * q * sin ( t1 ) * cos ( t2 );
  T[1] = p * C[0] - r * q * sin ( t1 ) * sin ( t2 );
  T[2] = r * q * cos ( t1 );
  T[3] = 0;
}
//Normal
void get_N ( double N[4],  double C[4], double T[4], double u,
                          double r, double p, double q ){
  float t1, t2;
  t1 = q * u;  t2 = p * u;
  N[0] = -p*T[1] + r*q*(p * sin(t1) * sin(t2) - q * cos(t1) * cos(t2));
  N[1] = p * T[0] - r * q*(p * sin(t1) * cos(t2) + q* cos(t1)*sin(t2));
  N[2] = -q * q * r * sin ( t1 );
  N[3] = 0;
}
//Matrix for transforming to Frenet frame
void setM( Matrix44 &M, double u, double R, double r, double p, double q ) {
  double C[4], T[4],  N[4], B[4];
  get_C ( C, u, R, r, p, q );
  get_T ( T, C, u, r, p, q );
  get_N ( N, T, C, u, r, p, q );
  vector_normalize ( T );   //normalize the vector
  vector_normalize ( N );   //normalize the vector
  vector_cross ( B, T, N ); //B = T X N

  M.setCol( 0, T );     //Tangent   T
  M.setCol( 1, N );     //Normal    N
  M.setCol( 2, B );     //Binormal  B
  M.setCol( 3, C );     //The curve C
}
```

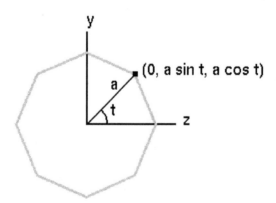

Figure 14-23 Approximating a Circle with an N-sided Polygon

If we want a tube with circular cross section, we can approximate the base with an n-sided regular polygon as shown in Figure 14-23 above. The following code segment shows an implementation of approximating a circular base with a 16-sided polygon:

```
const int N = 16;                //number of vertices in base
Matrix41 points[N];              //define N points
double a = 0.15;
double x, y, z;
double dtheta = 2 * 3.1415926/ N;
double theta = 0;
for ( int i = 0; i < N; i++ ) {
  z = a *   cos ( theta );
  y = a *   sin ( theta );
  x = 0;
  points[i] = Matrix41( x, y, z, 1 );
  theta += dtheta;
}
```

Figure 14-24 below shows a couple of outputs of the implementations.

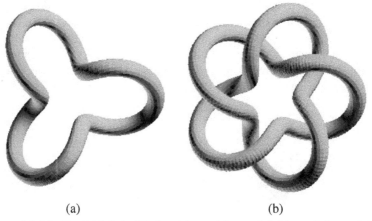

(a)   (b)

Figure 14-24 Toroidal Spiral Tubes (a) p = 1.0, q = 3.0 (b) p = 2.0, q = 5.0

There are a lot of variations of using Frenet frames to construct tubes. We can multiply the Frenet frame transformation matrix by another matrix to obtain tubes with special shapes. For example, we can construct a seashell by wrapping a growing radius about a helix. This can be achieved by multiplying the matrix M of Equation (14.18) by a scaling matrix, where the scaling factors may depend on the parameter u:

$$M' = M \times \begin{pmatrix} g_1(u) & 0 & 0 & 0 \\ 0 & g_2(u) & 0 & 0 \\ 0 & 0 & g_3(u) & 0 \\ 0 & 0 & 0 & 1 \end{pmatrix} \qquad (14.23)$$

Figure 14-25 below shows an example of a seashell, where we have set $g_1(u) = 1, g_2(u) = g_3(u) = u/10$.

Figure 14-25 Seashell Produced by Matrix of (14.23)

14.4   Surface of Revolution

14.4.1   Revolving a Profile

Another simple and popular way to create the surface of a 3D object is to rotate a two-dimensional curve around an axis. A surface thus obtained is referred to as a **surface of revolution**, and the 2D curve is also called a **profile**. The surface always has azimuthal symmetry. For example, the walls of a cone, a conical, a cylinder, a hyperboloid, a lemon, a sphere and a spheroid can all be created by revolving a line or a curve around a vertical axis. Figure 14-26(a) below shows the surface of a pawn obtained by revolving a profile around the vertical axis; the profile is a spline curve defined by the control points shown in the figure. Figure 14-26(b) shows the corresponding wireframe of the surface.

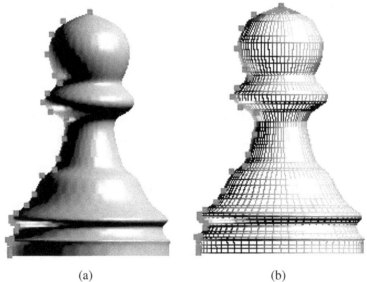

(a)   (b)

Figure 14-26   Pawn Created by Revolving a Spline Curve

14.4.2   Area of a Surface of Revolution

In many situations, we are interested to find the area of a surface of revolution. Understanding how we calculate the area would also give us insight on how to use OpenGL to construct the surface.

Suppose we rotate the curve $y = f(x) > 0$ from $x = a$ to $x = b$ and we assume that the second derivatives of $f(x)$ exist for $a \leq x \leq b$. Figure 14-27 (a) shows an area element of the surface of revolution thus obtained, and Figure 14-27 (b) shows the cross-section of revolution when viewed along the negative x-axis. Note that the value of y considered here is evaluated at a point on the surface at $z = 0$. For points not at $z = 0$, the y value is given by $r cos\theta$ and $z = r sin\theta$ as shown in Figure 14-27 (b), where r is the y value at $z = 0$.

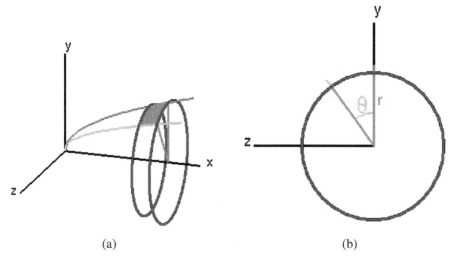

(a)   (b)

Figure 14-27   Area Element and Cross Section of Surface of Revolution

Suppose Δs is the segment length of the area element along the curve. Then the area ΔA_x of the element (shaded region of Figure 14-27(a)) is given by

$$\Delta A_x = 2\pi y \Delta s$$

but

$$(\Delta s) = \sqrt{(\Delta x)^2 + (\Delta y)^2} = \Delta x \sqrt{1 + \frac{(\Delta y)^2}{(\Delta x)^2}}$$

When $\Delta x \to 0$, we have $\Delta A_x \to dA_x$, and

$$ds = dx \sqrt{1 + \left(\frac{dy}{dx}\right)^2}$$

Therefore,

$$dA_x = 2\pi y \sqrt{1 + \left(\frac{dy}{dx}\right)^2} dx$$

So the surface area is

$$A_x = 2\pi \int_a^b y \sqrt{1 + \left(\frac{dy}{dx}\right)^2} dx \qquad (14.24)$$

Similarly, if we rotate the curve $x = g(y) > 0$ from $y = c$ to $y = d$ about the y-axis, the area of the surface of revolution is given by

$$A_y = 2\pi \int_c^d x \sqrt{1 + \left(\frac{dx}{dy}\right)^2} dy \qquad (14.25)$$

If we instead specify the curve parametrically by $(x(u), y(u))$, and we rotate the curve about the x-axis for $u \in [a, b]$ with $x(u) > 0$ in the interval, then the surface area obtained is given by

$$A_x = 2\pi \int_a^b y(u) \sqrt{\left(\frac{dx}{du}\right)^2 + \left(\frac{dy}{du}\right)^2} \, du \qquad (14.26)$$

The corresponding equation for y-axis rotation is

$$A_y = 2\pi \int_c^d x(u) \sqrt{\left(\frac{dx}{du}\right)^2 + \left(\frac{dy}{du}\right)^2} \, du \qquad (14.27)$$

Example 14-2:
Suppose $y = f(x) = \sqrt{x}$, what is A_x for $1 \le x \le 4$?

Solution:
Here, $y = \sqrt{x}$. So

$$\left(\frac{dy}{dx}\right)^2 = \left(\frac{1}{2\sqrt{x}}\right)^2 = \frac{1}{4x}$$

Substituting this into Equation (14.24), we have

$$\begin{aligned}
A_x &= 2\pi \int_1^4 \sqrt{x} \sqrt{1 + \frac{1}{4x}} \, dx \\
&= \pi \int_1^4 \sqrt{4x + 1} \, dx \\
&= \frac{\pi}{6} (4x + 1)^{3/2} \big|_1^4 \\
&= \frac{\pi}{6}(17\sqrt{17} - 5\sqrt{5}) \\
&= 30.85
\end{aligned}$$

14.4.3   Volume of a Surface of Revolution

The volume enclosed by a surface of revolution can be found by first dividing the volume into thin discs; the total volume is the sum (integration) of the volumes of all the discs. If we rotate the curve around the x-axis like the one shown in Figure 14-27, the volume of each disc is

$$dV_x = \pi y^2 dx$$

Therefore, the total volume for $a \le x \le b$ is

$$V_x = \int_a^b dV_x = \pi \int_a^b y^2 dx \qquad (14.28)$$

Similarly, the volume enclosed by the surface of revolution by rotating a curve $x = g(y) > 0$ for $c \le y \le d$ is given by

$$V_y = \pi \int_c^d x^2 dy \qquad (14.29)$$

Example 14-3:
Find the enclosed volume V_x for surface shown in Figure 14-28 below, which is obtained by revolving $y = f(x) = 2 + sin(x), 0 \le x \le 2\pi$ about the x-axis.

Solution:

From Equation (14.28), we have

$$V_y = \pi \int_0^{2\pi} (2 + sin(x))^2 dx$$

$$= \pi \int_0^{2\pi} (4 + 4sin(x) + sin^2 x) dx$$

$$= \pi \left[4x - 4cos(x) + \frac{x}{2} - \frac{sin(2x)}{4} \right]_0^{2\pi}$$

$$= \pi [8\pi - 4 + \pi - 0 - 0 + 4 - 0 + 0]$$

$$= 9\pi^2$$

Figure 14-28   Revolving about x-axis for $f(x) = 2 + sin(x)$, $0 \le x \le 2\pi$

14.4.4 Computing a Surface of Revolution

The procedure of computing a surface of revolution is like finding its area by integration. We decompose the surface into thin disks and compute an area element, which is a quad on the disk like that shown in Figure 14-27. The following steps show the details of constructing a surface of revolution:

1. Define a curve $y = f(x)$ in the xy plane and determine a set of discrete points, say $(x_i, y_i, 0)$ for $i = 0$ to $N - 1$, on the curve.
2. For each pair of two adjacent points, rotate them about the x-axis by a small angle $\Delta\theta$.
3. The rotation generates a polygon (quad) consisting of four points, the original two points and the points after they have been rotated.
4. Calculate the normal to the quad by finding the cross product of two vectors formed by the differences among three points of the polygon.
5. Draw the quad.
6. Rotate the two new points about the x-axis by another $\Delta\theta$ to create two newer points.
7. Form the quad between the new points and the newer points; calculate its normal and draw it.
8. Continue the process until a rotation of 360° has been made.
9. Move to the next two points in the 2D curve (corresponding to a new disc) and repeat the steps above until all of the points have been used.

Program Listing 14-3 below shows the implementation of these steps, which are used to generate the vase image shown in Figure 14-28 above.

Program Listing 14-3   Computing Surface of Revolution

```
-------------------------------------------------------------------------
//function defining profile of revolution
double f1 ( double x )
{
  double y = 2 + sin ( x );

  return y;
}

void vase(int nx, int ntheta, float startx, float endx )
{
   const float dx = (endx - startx)/nx; //x step size
   const float dtheta = 2*PI / ntheta;  //angular step size
   float theta = PI/2.0;                //from pi/2 to3pi/2

   int i, j;
   float x, y, z, r;                    //current coordinates
   float x1, y1, z1, r1;                //next coordinates
   float t, v[3];
   float va[3], vb[3], vc[3], normal[3];
   int nturn = 0;
   x = startx;
   r = f1 ( x );
   bool first_point = true;
   for ( int si = 1; si <= nx; si++ ) {
      theta = 0;
      int start=0, nn=60, end=nn;
      x1 = x + dx;
      r1 = f1 ( x1 );
      //draw the surface composed of quadrilaterals by sweeping theta
      glBegin( GL_QUAD_STRIP );
      for ( j = 0; j <= ntheta; ++j ) {
        theta += dtheta;
        double cosa = cos( theta );
        double sina = sin ( theta );
        y = r * cosa;   y1 = r1 * cosa;  //current and next y
        z = r * sina;    z1 = r1 * sina;        //current and next z
        if ( nturn == 0 ) {
          va[0] = x;   va[1] = y;     va[2] = z;
          vb[0] = x1;  vb[1] = y1;    vb[2] = z1;
          nturn++;
        } else {
          nturn = 0;
          vc[0] = x;    vc[1] = y;     vc[2] = z;
          //calculates normal of surface
          plane_normal ( normal, va, vb, vc );
          glNormal3f ( normal[0], normal[1], normal[2] );
        }
        //edge from point at x to point at next x
        glVertex3f (x, y, z);
```

```
        glVertex3f (x1, y1, z1);
        //forms quad with next pair of points with incremented theta value
    }
    glEnd();
    x = x1;
    r = r1;
  } //for k
}
```

We can call the function **vase**() directly to render the graphics object. For example, the function

   vase(64, 128, 0, 2 * 3.1415926); //x: 0 to 2pi

generates the vase image of Figure 14-28. Alternatively, one can make use of the OpenGL command **glCallList**() to make the rendering process more convenient and sometimes more efficient. This command takes the integer handle of a display list as the input parameter and executes the display list, which is a group of OpenGL commands that have been saved in memory for later execution. When we invoke a display list, the OpenGL functions in the list are executed in the order in which they were issued. In other words, the commands saved in the list are executed as if they were called without using a display list. In an OpenGL program, we can mix the rendering in the usual immediate mode and the display list mode. In our example here, we create the display list as follows:

```
GLuint theVase;
theVase = glGenLists (1);
glNewList(theVase, GL_COMPILE);
vase(64, 128, 0, 2 * 3.1415926 );   //x: 0 -> 2pi
glEndList();
```

The variable *theVase* in the above code is an integer handle, which is used to refer to the display list. To execute the commands saved in the list, we simply issue the command in the program:

   glCallList (theVase);

14.5   Anaglyphs by Extrusion and Revolution

14.5.1   Stereo Images with Black Background

We have discussed the general process of creating anaglyphs in Chapter 10. The main idea of the method as shown in Program Listing 10-2, is to 'render' the image with the camera at the left-eye position with a red-filter and then 'render' the image again with the camera at the right-eye position with a blue-filter; the accumulation buffer is used to superimpose the left and right images and render the composite image. The process of creating an image and the process of rendering it as a red-blue composite image is independent of each other. Therefore, the code for generating anaglyphs with images created by extrusion or surface of revolution is the same as that presented in Program Listing 10-2. All we need to do is to call the functions that create the extrusion or revolution images in the function **drawScene**(). Of course, we can always make changes in the **init**() function to have different graphical environments. For example, we can include lighting in the scene by declaring white light sources and enabling lighting in OpenGL. Figure 14-29 shows an anaglyph version of the seashell of Figure 14-25, which is created using the technique of time-variant extrusion. Figure 14-30 shows an anaglyph of three pawns, each of which can be created independently like the one shown in Figure 14-26, which is constructed using the technique of surface-of-revolution with use of a cubic spline.

Figure 14-29 Stereoscopic Seashell

Figure 14-30 Stereoscopic Pawns

14.5.2 Stencil Buffer

We have discussed in Chapter 10 that an anaglyph should have a black background. Any background that is not totally black will somewhat compromise the 3D effect. If in some cases, we do need a background, we can create the composite image with the help of the stencil buffer, which has been discussed briefly in Chapter 6. The main purpose of using the stencil buffer is to create a mask so that certain regions of an image can be masked off and not rendered. That is, we can use the stencil buffer to restrict drawing to a certain portion of the screen.

The stencil buffer can be turned on or off. If it is on, a pixel value is rendered only if it passes the stencil test. The stencil test at each rendering pixel position is performed in the following way:

1. It takes place only if the there is a stencil buffer and stencil test has been enabled.

2. It compares a reference value with the stencil buffer value at the pixel position.
3. The value of the stencil buffer at the pixel position may be modified, depending on the result of the test.

OpenGl provides the functions **glStencilFunc**() and **glStencilOp**() to specify the details of a stencil test. The following are their prototypes:

void **glStencilFunc** (GLenum *func*, GLint *ref*, GLuint *mask*);
This function sets the comparison function (*func*), the reference value (*ref*), and a mask (*mask*) which are used in the stencil test. The reference value is compared with the value in the stencil buffer at each rendering pixel position in a way specified by the comparison function. However, only bits with corresponding bits of *mask* having values of 1 are compared. The following table lists the possible values of the comparison function *func*, where the symbol & denotes the bitwise-and operation:

func	comparison between (*ref* & *mask*) and stencil value
GL_NEVER	always fails
GL_ALWAYS	always passes
GL_LESS	passes if *ref* $<$ stencil value
GL_LEQUAL	passes if *ref* $\leq$ stencil value
GL_EQUAL	passes if *ref* $=$ stencil value
GL_GEQUAL	passes if *ref* $\geq$ stencil value
GL_GREATER	passes if *ref* $>$ stencil value
GL_NOTEQUAL	passes if *ref* $\neq$ stencil value

void **glStencilOp** (GLenum *fail*, GLenum *zfail*, GLenum *zpass*);
This function specifies how the value in the stencil buffer at each rendering pixel is modified when the pixel passes or fails a stencil test:

fail specifies what to do to the stencil value at the pixel location when the stencil test fails,
zfail specifies what to do when the stencil test passes, but the depth test fails, and
zpass specifies what to do when both the stencil test and the depth test pass, or when the stencil test passes and either there is no depth buffer or depth testing is not enabled.

The following table lists the possible stencil operations and the resulted action of each operation on the stencil value:

Stencil operation	Resulted action on stencil value
GL_KEEP	stencil value unchanged
GL_ZERO	stencil value set to 0
GL_REPLACE	stencil value replaced by reference value
GL_INCR	stencil value incremented
GL_DECR	stencil value decremented
GL_INVERT	stencil value bitwise-inverted

Program Listing 14-4 below shows an example of using the stencil buffer to restrict drawing of certain portions of the screen. In the callback function **display**(), the statement "$glClear(GL\_STENCIL\_BUF$

clears the stencil buffer (in this case, it fills the whole buffer with zeros). The call to the function **drawTriangle**() fills the the triangle region of the stencil buffer with ones. Before calling the first **drawSquare**() function, it executes the statement "*glStencilFunc (GL_NOTEQUAL, 0x1, 0x1);*" to ensure that only regions outside the triangle will be rendered because the reference value is 0x1 and inside the triangle, the stencil values are also 1, which fail the stencil test of "GL_NOTEQUAL". Therefore, a red square region minus a triangle is rendered. Before calling the second **drawSquare**() function, it executes *glStencilFunc (GL_EQUAL, 0x1, 0x1);*, which has the opposite effect. Because now the comparison function is "GL_EQUAL" and the reference value is 0x1, only pixels inside the triangle will pass the stencil test. Therefore, a green triangle is rendered even though we draw a square. Figure 14-31 shows the output of this example.

Program Listing 14-4   Use of Stencil Buffer to Mask Regions

```
------------------------------------------------------------------------
/*
 *   stencil-demo.cpp
 *   This program demonstrates the use of the stencil buffer to
 *   mask  pixels for rendering.
 *   Whenever the window is redrawn, a value of 1 is drawn
 *   into a triangular-region in the stencil buffer and  0 elsewhere.
 */
void init (void)
{
   glEnable ( GL_DEPTH_TEST );
   glEnable ( GL_STENCIL_TEST );
   glClearColor (1.0f, 1.0f, 1.0f, 0.0f);
   glClearStencil ( 0x0 );
}

void drawSquare( float z )
{
  glBegin ( GL_POLYGON );
      glVertex3f (-1.0, 1.0, z);
      glVertex3f (1.0, 1.0, z);
      glVertex3f (1.0, -1.0, z);
      glVertex3f (-1.0, -1.0, z);
   glEnd();
}

void drawTriangle( float z )
{
  glBegin ( GL_POLYGON );
      glVertex3f ( 0.0,  0.0, z );
      glVertex3f (-1.0, -1.0, z );
      glVertex3f ( 1.0, -1.0, z );
   glEnd();
}

//green triangle inside red square
void display(void)
{
   glClear(GL_COLOR_BUFFER_BIT | GL_DEPTH_BUFFER_BIT );
   glClear(GL_STENCIL_BUFFER_BIT);  //fill stencil buffer with 0s
   glStencilFunc (GL_ALWAYS, 0x1, 0x1);
   glStencilOp (GL_REPLACE, GL_REPLACE, GL_REPLACE);
```

```
    drawTriangle( -0.5 ); //stencil buffer: triangle region filled with 1s
                          //  but outside triangle, stencil values  are 0

    //fail inside triangle, pass outside; so triangle region not rendered
    glStencilFunc ( GL_NOTEQUAL, 0x1, 0x1 );
    glStencilOp(GL_KEEP,GL_KEEP,GL_KEEP); //no change in stencil values

    glColor3f ( 1, 0, 0 );                   //red
    drawSquare( -0.5 );                      //z = -0.5,
    glStencilFunc ( GL_EQUAL, 0x1, 0x1 ); //pass in triangle region,fail outside
    glStencilOp ( GL_KEEP, GL_KEEP, GL_KEEP );//no change in stencil buffer values
    glColor3f ( 0, 1, 0 );                   //green
    drawSquare ( 0 );                        //z = 0, so in front of red region
    glFlush();
}
void reshape ( int w, int h )
{
    glViewport(0, 0, (GLsizei) w, (GLsizei) h);

    glMatrixMode(GL_PROJECTION);
    glLoadIdentity();
    if (w <= h)
       gluOrtho2D(-3.0, 3.0, -3.0*(GLfloat)h/(GLfloat)w,
                  3.0*(GLfloat)h/(GLfloat)w);
    else
       gluOrtho2D(-3.0*(GLfloat)w/(GLfloat)h,
                  3.0*(GLfloat)w/(GLfloat)h, -3.0, 3.0);

    glMatrixMode(GL_MODELVIEW);
    glLoadIdentity();
}
```

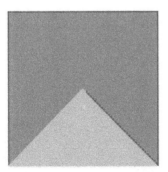

Figure 14-31   Triangular Mask with Stencil Buffer

14.5.3   Stereo Images with Background

After we have learned the usage of the stencil buffer, we can use it to add a background to a stereo composite image. The background could be a texture or simply a grey area. The background should be defined by a rectangular region that covers the entire screen minus the regions taken up by the composite image. In the two-center method of rendering an anaglyph, the top and bottom values of the rectangular region are the same for the left and right eyes. The left and right boundary values can be obtained by the left and right boundary values of the viewing frustum. Suppose we use the right eye frustum parameters to set the left and right boundary values for the rectangular background. Then the left boundary is the same as that of the frustum. The right boundary value is that of the frustum plus half of the eye separation. The background should be at the near plane. Thus its z value is equal to the difference between the focal length and the near distance that defines the frustum (i.e. $z = f - N$). In summary, using the notations of Equation (10.11) of Chapter 10, the rectangular region is defined by the parameters,

$$
\begin{aligned}
top &= T_r \\
bottom &= B_r \\
left &= L_r \\
right &= R_r + \frac{e}{2} \\
z &= f - N
\end{aligned}
\tag{14.30}
$$

Program Listing 14-5 below shows a sample code segment that renders an anaglyph with a background using the stencil buffer. Figure 14-32 shows the image of the seashell of Figure 14-29 with a grey background produced by this code segment.

Program Listing 14-5   Rendering Anaglyphs With a Background

```
---------------------------------------------------------------------------
//rectangular region
void background ( double L, double R, double B, double T, double N )
{
  glDisable ( GL_DEPTH_TEST );
  glDisable( GL_CULL_FACE );
  glDisable ( GL_LIGHTING );
  glColor3f (0.2, 0.2, 0.2 );   //grey background
  glBegin( GL_POLYGON );
    glVertex3f ( L, B, N );
    glVertex3f ( R, B, N );
    glVertex3f ( R, T, N );
    glVertex3f ( L, T, N );
  glEnd();
  glEnable ( GL_LIGHTING );
  glEnable( GL_CULL_FACE );
  glEnable ( GL_DEPTH_TEST );
}

void display (void)
{
  glClearAccum ( 0, 0, 0, 0 );      // The default
  glClear( GL_DEPTH_BUFFER_BIT );
  glClear(GL_STENCIL_BUFFER_BIT);   //fill stencil buffer with 0s

  double theta2, near,far;
  double L, R, T, B, N, F, f, e, a, b, c, ratio;
  glClearColor(0, 0, 0, 0.0);       //black background
  glClear ( GL_COLOR_BUFFER_BIT );

  near = camera.f / 5;
  far = 1000.0;
  f = camera.f;
```

```
glDrawBuffer ( GL_BACK );
glReadBuffer ( GL_BACK );
glClear(GL_ACCUM_BUFFER_BIT);

// Left eye filter (red)
glColorMask ( GL_TRUE, GL_FALSE, GL_FALSE, GL_TRUE );

// Create the projection
glMatrixMode(GL_PROJECTION);
glLoadIdentity();
theta2 = ( 3.1415926 / 180 ) * camera.fov / 2; //theta/2 in radians
ratio  = camera.w / (double)camera.h;
a = f * ratio * tan ( theta2 );
b = a - camera.es / 2.0;
c = a + camera.es / 2.0;
N = near;
F = far;
T = N * tan ( theta2 );
B = -T;
L = -b * N / f;
R =  c * N / f;
glFrustum( L, R, B, T, N, F );
// Create the model for left eye
glMatrixMode(GL_MODELVIEW);
glLoadIdentity();
camera.p = Point3( -camera.es/2, 0, f );        //change camera viewpoint
camera.focus = Point3 ( -camera.es/2, 0, 0 );
camera.lookAt();

glDrawBuffer ( GL_BACK );
glReadBuffer ( GL_BACK );
glClearColor(0, 0, 0, 0.0);       //black background
glClear ( GL_COLOR_BUFFER_BIT );
glEnable( GL_STENCIL_TEST );     //enable stencil test

//Fill scene region of stencil buffer with 1s
glStencilFunc ( GL_ALWAYS, 0x1, 0x1);
glStencilOp (GL_REPLACE, GL_REPLACE, GL_REPLACE);

drawScene();
glFlush();
// Write over the accumulation buffer
glAccum ( GL_LOAD, 1.0 );

glClear ( GL_COLOR_BUFFER_BIT | GL_DEPTH_BUFFER_BIT );

//now handle the right eye
glMatrixMode(GL_PROJECTION);
glLoadIdentity();

// Obtain right-eye parameters from left-eye, no change in T and B
double temp;
temp = R;
R = -L;
L = -temp;
```

```
    glFrustum( L, R, B, T, N, F );

    // Right eye filter   (blue)
    glColorMask ( GL_FALSE, GL_FALSE, GL_TRUE, GL_TRUE );
    glMatrixMode(GL_MODELVIEW);
    glLoadIdentity();
    camera.p = Point3( camera.es/2, 0, f );   //change camera viewpoint
    camera.focus = Point3 ( camera.es/2, 0, 0 );
    camera.lookAt();

    glClear ( GL_COLOR_BUFFER_BIT | GL_DEPTH_BUFFER_BIT );
    drawScene();    //scene region of stencil buffer filled with 1s
    glFlush();
    // Add  the new image
    glAccum ( GL_ACCUM, 1.0 );

    //disable stencil test to render composite scene
    glDisable ( GL_STENCIL_TEST);

    // Allow all color components
    glColorMask ( GL_TRUE, GL_TRUE, GL_TRUE,GL_TRUE );
    glAccum ( GL_RETURN, 1.0 );

    //enable stencil test to add background minus scene
    glEnable ( GL_STENCIL_TEST );
    //only pixels not occupied by scene will be rendered
    glStencilFunc (GL_NOTEQUAL, 0x1, 0x1);
    glStencilOp (GL_KEEP, GL_KEEP, GL_KEEP);   //no change in stencil values
    background ( L, R + camera.es/2 , B, T, f-N );
    glFlush();
    glutSwapBuffers();
}
```

Figure 14-32 Anaglyph with Grey Background

Chapter 15   Stereoscopic Displays

In chapters 8 through 10, we have discussed the principles and programming of stereoscopic graphics. We have concentrated on discussing the creation of anaglyphs and the use of color-coded glasses to view anaglyphs. Nowadays, there are a lot of new 3D display systems that can provide new advantages to end users. Some new systems are able to support an auto-stereoscopic, no-glasses, 3D display that provides enhanced image quality over older generation systems. In recent years, auto-stereoscopic displays have seeked their way into desktop computing as the cost of micro-optics, LCD displays, image processing and 3D graphics technologies have been dropping rapidly. Low cost high-resolution stereoscopic displays and associated equipment are readily available, which help drive the development of applications, ranging from science and engineering to entertainment and education, using stereoscopic imaging and graphics technologies to create higher quality products or provide better services. For example, stereoscopic commercial 3D DVDs and PC games are popular and widely available to the public; NASA mounted four stereoscopic cameras on the 2004 Mars rovers (Spirit and Opportunity) as shown in Figure 15-1 below.

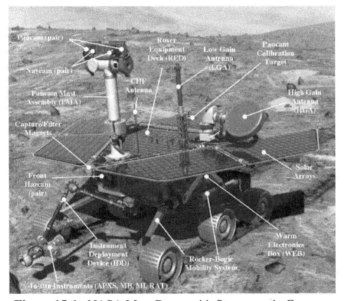

Figure 15-1   NASA Mars Rover with Stereoscopic Cameras
(Image from *http://marsrover.nasa.gov/mission/spacecraft_surface_rover.html*)

The wider availability of stereoscopic applications in turn brings down the cost of stereoscopic displays. Today, there are many vendors of 3D display systems, including Barco, Christie Digital, Dimension Technologies Inc. (DTI), Opticality, Sharp, StereoGraphics, SeeReal, and VREX. The traditional display device, Cathode Ray Tube (CRT) has given way to a new generation of displays such as Liquid Crystal Displays (LCD), Plasma Displays, and Digital Light Processing (DLP) Displays.

Whatever method a stereoscopic display device uses, it always relies on some undelying method to present to each of our eyes a different perspective image. In the following sections, we discuss some commonly used display technologies.

15.1 Anaglyph

We have discussed anaglyphs in detail in Chapters 9 and 10. In short, this method uses different colors to render left and right eye images. In general we display the left perspective image with red color and the right perspective image with blue and/or green colors. A viewer wears a pair of glasses which has a red left lens and a cyan right lens. It is possible to use other combinations of color primaries such as a combination of red and green. Anaglyphs are easy to produce and the glasses are cheap, which have made this method cost-effective. Moreover, the color composite of an anaglyph is compatible with all full color displays. In other words, we do not need to purchase any special display device to display an anaglyph. All we need is a pair of color-coded glasses. However, compared to other stereoscopic methods, the anaglyph technique produces relatively poor quality of images and cannot create truly full-color stereoscopic images. Research has revealed that anaglyph image quality depends on the spectral color purity of the display and the glasses. A study on anaglyph ranks display devices for anaglyph images in following order, from best to worst: 3-chip LCD projector, 1-chip DLP projector, CRT display, LCD display.

15.2 Time-Sequential

Time-sequential is also referred to as field-sequential or frame-sequential because the stereo display presents a sequence of fields or frames alternately to the left and right eyes of the viewer. The viewer wears a pair of shutter glasses whose left and right shutter 'opens' and 'closes' in synchronization with the left and right perspective images shown on the display device so that the left eye sees only the 'left' perspective images and the right eye sees only the 'right' perspective images. The shutter glasses and corresponding projectors could be mechanical or based on liquid crystal (LC). A mechanical shutter projector uses a spinning disc, half transparent and half opaque to present two sequences of images alternately. Liquid crystal shutters are widely used for shutter glasses. (See Figure 9-1 of Chapter 9 for an LCD shutter glasses.)

The image quality of time-sequential stereoscopic stereo display depends on the persistence and refresh rate of the display device and the quality of the particular LC shutter glasses used. In general, shorter persistence pixels and faster refresh rates produce better stereoscopic image quality.

15.3 Spatially Multiplexed Polarized

The VREX company has introduced a series of stereoscopic display designs that are based on polarizing micro-optics. Left and right image elements are spatially-multiplexed as shown in Figure 15-2 below. A single display is divided into two differently polarized views. A viewer wears a pair of polarized 3D glasses to view the image composed of the polarized views. The two different resolution views may be achieved using a checkerboard pattern of image multiplexing and polarization. In Figure 15-2, left (L) and right (R) image pixels are spatially-multiplexed together and the resulted image is placed behind a patterned micro-polarizer element. When viewed with polarized glasses, our left eye sees only the P_1 polarized pixels, and our right eye only sees the P_2 polarized pixels.

When the micro-polarizer is mounted over the LCD, a gap (g in Figure 15-2) forms between the substrates. This gap could induce undesired parallax, which is particularly pronounced for direct view LCD based displays. If the head is not at the right position, the adjacent normally invisible pixels may become visible as a result of crosstalk. A simple way to reduce the effect is to interlace the images in alternate rows so that the lateral head movement is not affected by parallax. This problem may be fully solved if the LCD manufacturers make the micro-polarizer element within the LCD pixel cells, which can reduce the parallax between polarizer and pixel.

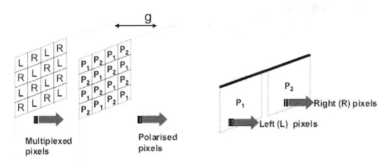

Figure 15-2   VREX Spatially Multiplexed Image (SMI)

15.4   Polarized Projection

In this method, we optically overlay two images for display and use polarization to code images. Two images are projected onto the same screen or display through different filters. A viewer wears polarized 3D glasses that contains a pair of different polarizing filters to view the overlayed images. As each filter passes only the light that is similarly polarized and blocks the light polarized in the opposite direction, each eye sees a different image. Figure 15-3 shows a pair of glasses containing polarized filters.

Figure 15-3   A Pair of Polarized Glasses

15.4   Lenticular, Parallax Barrier and Parallax Illumination

These methods are some of the **autostereoscopic** display techniques, in which a viewer can view stereo pairs without wearing a pair of glasses. The methods are similar in the way that they need to work with a fixed-pixel display; the display device consists of spatially-grouped pixels that are aligned with an optical element. The views of the two eyes of a viewer fall into two zones, each of which is only visible to one eye. As a consequence, this creates a 3D sensation without the use of 3D glasses. Figure 15-4 below illustrates this principle. In the figure, the white light lines are the optical element. The LCD pixels are illuminated by the light lines and form viewing zones where particular groups of pixels are only visible from a particular direction as shown in (b).

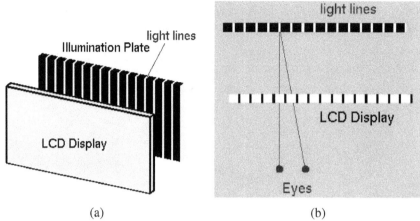

(a)   (b)

Figure 15-4 Illumination Zones

In lenticular display, the optical element consists of a series of vertical lenslets (lenticules) fitted over the display surface. Lenticules are tiny lenses on a special film. The lenses direct the light from the stereoscopic images to our eyes with each image visible to only one eye. To sense the 3D effect, our eyes must be in a sweet spot so that each eye sees light from one zone. (See also the discussion on integral method below.) If we were to move to the left or right from one of the sweet spots, the image on the screen would appear blur. Future televisions may include a camera that tracks our position. The television may be able to adjust the image so that our eyes are always in a sweet spot.

In parallax barrier display, the optical element consists of a series of opaque vertical strips placed over the display surface, similar to the black strips of Figure 15-4(b) of the LCD display.

In parallax illumination display, vertical strips of light are fitted behind the display similar to the one shown in Figure 15-4. As illustrated in the figure, such a system displays left and right images of stereo pairs on alternate columns of pixels on the LCD. The left image may appear on the odd numbered columns and the right image may appear on the even numbered columns. If the LCD has 1024 columns and 768 rows of pixels, then each complete stereoscopic image has 512 columns and 768 rows. Both halves of a stereo pair are displayed simultaneously; a special illumination plate located behind the LCD directs them to corresponding eyes. The illumination plate, consisting of compact intense light sources, generates a lattice of very thin and bright, and uniformly spaced vertical light lines, in this case 512 of them, which are precisely spaced with respect to the pixel columns of the LCD so that the left eye sees all of the lines through the odd columns of the LCD, while the right eye sees the even column pixels as shown in Figure 15-4(b). This technology may allow several people to view the stereo on the same screen at the same time.

15.5 Dual-View Twin-LCD Systems

Using two LCD elements has been a successful approach to building high quality autostereoscopic displays. In this method, one LCD directs an image of a stereo pair to the left eye while the other LCD directs the other image to the right eye. Figure 15-5 below shows one of the Sharp designs of dual-view system, which produces high quality 3D stereoscopic video over a wide horizontal range. The display has two viewing windows with a single illuminator.

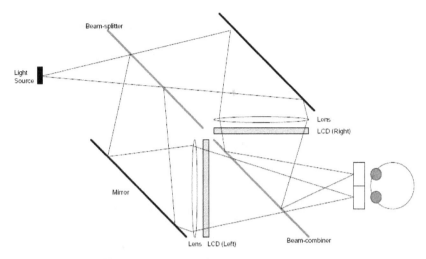

Figure 15-5   The Sharp Twin-LCD Display

As shown in the figure, horizontally offset images are generated from the optical elements. An eye can only see one image passing through the viewing window. Therefore, if we place a stereo pair images on the left LCD and the right LCD, we will see a stereoscopic 3D image. This optical arrangement can be used in a low cost desktop PC system.

The viewing windows play an important role in determining the quality of autostereoscopic displays. Undesirable visual effects such as image flickering, reduced viewing freedom and increased inter-channel cross-talk could result from degradation of the windows due to unresolved issues in the optical design. When designing the windows, designers have to carefully take into consideration the windows' shape and size, and the lateral and longitudinal viewing freedom.

15.6   Other Methods

There are many other methods of displaying stereoscopic 3D images. We breifly discuss a few here.

Autostereogram

Autostereogram refers to the single-image form of stereograms that can give a visual illusion of a 3D scene from a 2D image without using any special visual aid. For us to perceive 3D in an autostereogram, we have to overcome the coordination between vergence and focusing that normally occurs automatically in our brain.

To create an autostereogram, we modulate a repeated horizontal pattern to create an image that can be viewed with an abnormal convergence (or divergence) angle; the image would give an illusion of 3D within the space of the pattern. Figure 15-6 shows such an image, which is a structured pattern autostereogram of a heart on a ground of roses; the image is downloaded from Magic Eye (*http://www.magiceye.com/*). If we view the image with normal convergence, we will see it as a flat repeating pattern. However, a hidden 3D scene would appear if we view it with the correct vergence. Recall that we perceive depth via binocular disparity, in which our left eye and right eye see the same object from slightly different angles, leading to two slightly different perspective images. With autostereogram, when we look at the repeated pattern at a distance that our eyes either diverge or converge, our brain is not able to match the images from the eyes correctly and the small differences between adjacent pattern cycles could provide binocular disparity. Consequently, we see a 3D scene.

In creating an autostereogram, we may construct the disparity structure to correspond to the depth map of the desired 3D scene. We will obtain the 3D sensation when our eyes are at the appropriate convergence angle while looking at the image. However, to perceive the 3D scene, the viewer must overcome the nominal tendency of the eyes that focus at the convergence distance; the viewer has to refocus at the plane of the image. (For Figure 15-6, it is easier to see the 3D scene if you print the image on a piece of paper, not necessarily colorful. You first hold the paper near your eyes and focus on the whole image which appears blur. Then you move the image slowly away; at a certain distance, you will see a heart structure pops out.)

We can also create 3D animation by showing a series of autostereograms one after another, in the same way we normally render animated graphics.

Figure 15-6   Magic Eye Image (from *http://www.magiceye.com/*)

Volumetric Display

Volumetric displays are true 3D display systems, meaning that each spatial position (x, y, z) is displayed physically in a real 3D space volume. The displays use a voxel, the 3D analog to a pixel in 2D image, to describe a displayed position. Traditional volumetric displays have multiplanar displays, giving rise to multiple display planes; they also have rotating panel displays to sweep out a volume. Newer technologies may use projection of light dots in the air above a device; by focusing an infrared laser beam at a point in space, we can generate a small bubble of plasma that emits visible light.

Figure 15-7 shows a volumetric device from Sony.

Figure 15-7   A Sony Volumetric 3D Display

Holographic Display

Holographic displays are another kind of true 3D display systems. They can provide a viewer various depth cues, including motion parallax, binocular disparity, accommodation and convergence and the images they display are scalable; the images can be created with one light wavelength and viewed with another. Again a viewer does not need any special glasses to view 3D objects and the viewing will not cause any visual fatigue.

The principles of the displays are based on holography, which is a technique that makes use of the coherent properties of laser beams to record the 3D structure of an object. The recorded image is referred to as a hologram, which is **not** recorded as a conventional image on a film, but as an interference pattern of light on the film. Holograms must be recorded with coherent light. Coherent light consists of light waves that are "in phase" with one another, which is typically produced by lasers. Light from the sun or light bulbs are incoherent light.

Scattering, reflection and refraction of light waves by a surface can change the phase of the waves. Different surface shapes will change the phase in different ways, leaving a distinct footprint of the surface in the light waves. When two waves interact, they interface with each other to generate an interference pattern, which may be a standing wave. If the two interacting light waves do not change, the resulted standing wave will remain unchanged. The standing wave is what is recorded onto a hologram.

In the process of creating a hologram, a coherent light beam from a laser is split into two beams, an illumination beam and a reference beam, as shown in Figure 15-8. The illumination beam shines the object and is reflected or scattered by the object. The reflected beam, referred to as object beam in the Figure, is combined with the reference light beam at the film. The recorded interference pattern allows one to reconstruct the 3D scene; a viewer sees a different appearance of the object when viewing the hologram at a different angle.

When a hologram is viewed with a coherent light source as shown in Figure 15-9, the original light waves are reconstructed, creating a 3D virtual object in space. We can view the virtual object (image) from different angles, as if it were actually there. When viewing from the front, we see the front of the object, and when viewing from the side, we see the side of the object. Even if we cut the hologram into two halves, we still can see the whole virtual object from each piece. This is because each point of a hologram contains information about light reflected from every point of the real object. This is in analogy of seeing a mountain through a window. We still can see the whole mountain through a smaller window with half the size; all we need to do is to tilt our head to change our viewing angle. This makes holograms good data storage media as they inherently have the fault tolerant property.

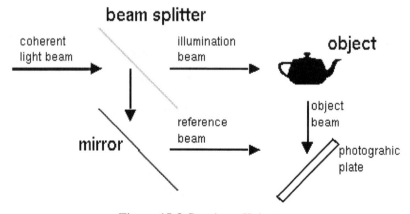

Figure 15-8 Creating a Hologram

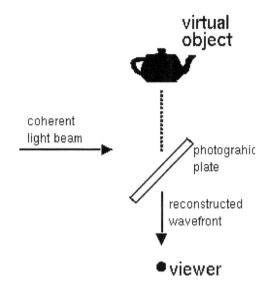

Figure 15-9 Reconstructing Scene From a Hologram

Integral Imaging

Integral imaging is also an autostereoscopic method, similar to the lenticular method. It makes use of an array of spherical convex lenses, each containing a micro-image, to create 3D viewing. The lens array is known as a fly's eye or integral lens array. Parallel incident light rays are focused on a flat surface, known as focal plane, which is on the opposing side of the array as shown in Figure 15-10. (Note that a light path is reversible meaning that it is always bidirectional.) Different sets of parallel light rays will focus onto different points. This implies that our eyes will see different focal points of a lens as our eyes look at the lens at different angles. On the focal plane, one micro-image is placed at the focal point of one lens. Consequently our left and right eyes will never see the same spot of a micro-image; the eyes always see different spots as parallel light rays along the paths from the eyes always focus on different spots. For example, if a micro-image consists of only a white dot and a black dot which are carefully placed by pre-calculations, then it is possible that the left eye can see only the black dot and the right eye can see only the white dot. Therefore, by carefully decomposing a composite image into micro-images, we can have our left eye sees one image and the right eye sees another one.

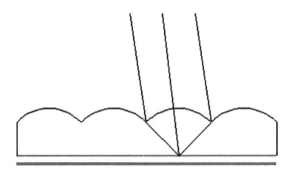

Figure 15-10 Light Rays Focus on Flat Panel of Lens Array

15.7 Stereoscopic Compatibility

When we develop a stereoscopic application, we need a display device to show the image pairs. The display must be compatible with the stereoscopic display method we intend to use otherwise a stereo pair cannot be properly displayed. Unfortunately, current display products are not always compatible with existing stereoscopic display methods. Therefore, stereo image developers need to have a knowledge about the compatibility of current display products with commonly used stereoscopic display methods.

Besides some special cases such as autostereogram and volumetric display, the compatibility between a display and a stereoscopic display method is determined by a few factors, including native polarization, image persistence (also called refresh rate or response time), color purity, and the spatial configuration of the pixels. There has been quite a lot of study on this subject in recent years.

LCD

Conventional Liquid Crystal Displays (LCD) are not well-suited to time-sequential 3D because of the scanning image update method and the hold-type operation of LCDs, and in some cases slow pixel response time. The maximum speed at which a display can render a sequence of images is determined by the display's maximum refresh rate. If the refresh rate is not high enough, the rendered images cannot be synchronized with the shutter glasses. Also, it takes a finite amount of time for to a display to switch the state of an individual pixel. It takes a long time for the brightness of a pixel of an LCD display to stabilize. The refresh rate of an LCD is effectively halved when displaying time-sequential stereo images. For time-sequential 3D viewing, the Liquid Crystal Shutter (LCS) should be closed until the changed state of the pixel has stabilized sufficiently. If the pixel response time is not fast enough, the rendered image could not be stabilized before the next image is displayed, and hence give poor visual effect for time-sequential 3D viewing. LCD's image update method also hinders its usage for time-sequential 3D because a new image is written to an LCD one line at a time from top to bottom. This is similar to the way that an image is scanned on a CRT, except that an LCD is a hold-type display whereas a CRT is an impulse-type display. This means that there is no single image shown exclusively on the whole LCD panel at a time. This implies that we cannot see exclusively a single perspective image when the shutters in the LCS glasses open. However, the improvement in the pixel response time and refresh rate could mitigate this effect, and LCD will become more compatible with time-sequential 3D in the future.

On the other hand, LCDs are compatible with anaglyphs, polarized projections and other fixed-pixel methods. The color purity of an LCD affects the quality of a rendered 3D image; this quantity varies considerably from display to display.

CRT

For many years in the last century, the Cathode Ray Tube (CRT) was the dominant display technology. However, in the past couple of decades, CRT has given way to better emerging new display technologies such as LCD, Plasma, and DLP. Pixel brightness of CRT or plasma phosphorus changes a lot faster than that of LCD. Therefore, CRT is naturally well-suited for time-sequential 3D viewing. The technology is also compatible with anaglyph, and polarized projection methods. However, a CRT is a device with a photosensor that detects a scanning electron beam; it is not compatible with fixed-pixel methods.

Plasma

Plasma is a collection of charged particles (positive and negative ions) in the form of gas-like clouds or ion-beams that respond strongly and collectively to electromagnetic fields and is often described as an *ionized gas*. Plasma display panels (PDP) consist of small plasma cells that change color with the strength of an electromagnetic field like what a fluorescent lamp does.

Plasma displays are usually bright and have a wide color gamut, and have fairly large sizes (up to 3.8 meters diagonally). They are now commonly used for both commercial information display and consumer television applications. Studies show that plasma displays are not ideal for use with time-sequential stereo. While many plasma displays do support time-sequential, they usually have a maximum display frequency of 60Hz and most have long phosphor persistence which produces a lot of stereoscopic crosstalk. The compatibility of plasma display and 3D stereos is expected to be similar to that of CRT.

DLP

Digital Light Processing (DLP) is a rear-projection technology that competes against LCD and plasma flat panel displays in the high-definition TV (HDTV) market. The image formed by a DLP projector is created by a Digital Micromirror Device (DMD) which is a semiconductor chip consisting of microscopically small mirrors laid out in a matrix form. Each of the micromirrors represents one or more pixels of the projected image. This technology is compatible with polarized and time-sequential methods. It is not usually considered for fixed-pixel methods as the technology is currently only used in projection displays. The anaglyph compatibility ranges from poor to good as the color purity of different DLP displays varies significantly.

Others

There are also many other emerging display products available or becoming available in the market. These include Light Emitting Diode (LED), Organic Light Emitting Diode (OLED), Ferro-Electric Liquid Crystal Display (FELCD), and Liquid Crystal on Silicon (LCoS). Currently, there have not been many studies on the compatibility of the emerging display technologies and stereoscopic display methods.

Chapter 16   Ray Tracing

16.1   Local vs. Global Illumination

The Phong lighting model that we discussed in the previous chapters is called a **local illumination** model. In the model, the shaded color or the illumination at a point of a surface depends purely on the local surface configuration such as the surface normal, the viewing direction, and the light direction. A light ray from a source only causes a point of the surface to glow; the reflected light ray has no effect on any other surface. Even if a surface is emissive (e.g. *glMaterialfv(GL_FRONT, GL_EMISSION, ..);*), it only glows itself but does not illuminate any other surface. Also, an object does not block the light source from illuminating another object and thus it won't cast any shadows. Figure 16-1 shows an example of illuminating two sphere by the same distant light source on the right. In reality, the sphere on the left should not be illuminated as the light is blocked by the right sphere. However, using the Phong model, the light source illuminates both spheres identically. Therefore, in situations like this, local illumination is a poor approximation to reality.

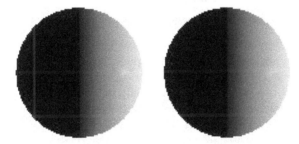

Figure 16-1   Two Spheres Illuminated by Same Source using Phong Model

Global illumination would make a lit scene look a lot more realistic. In a global illumination model, objects can block light to create shadows. A light ray reflected off a surface may illuminate other objects. Therefore, the image of an object may appear on a reflective surface. Also, emissive surfaces and refracted light rays may illuminate other objects. **Ray tracing** is one of the global illumination techniques; it eliminates the use of a depth buffer to determine hidden surfaces and allows for many special effects.

In summary, ray tracing unifies in one framework hidden surface removal, shadow computation, reflection of light, refraction of light, and global specular interaction. With all these advantages, ray tracing is a wonderful tool for creating sophisticated images. However, ray tracing is very computing intensive; a single image generated by ray tracing may take minutes, hours or even days to render. Despite the high computational costs, ray tracing has been widely used to create high quality and photorealistic images especially in animated movies. It is fortunate that each frame of an animated movie can be rendered independently by a different computer using ray tracing; it is common that hundreds of computers are used in parallel to produce a movie.

Another popular global illumination technique is **radiosity**. Ray tracing follows the paths of light rays around a 3-D scene to compute the illumination and shading on various surfaces. It assumes light sources to be point sources. On the other hand, radiosity simulates the diffuse propagation of light starting at the light sources, which may be broad surfaces.

16.2 Ray Tracing Concepts

To follow the paths of light rays, ray tracing makes use of the characteristics of light:

1. Light rays travel in straight lines.
2. Light rays do not interfere with each other even if they cross over.
3. Light paths are reversible. If a light ray can travel from point A to point B, then it is able to travel from B to A.

A straightforward way to do ray tracing is to follow light rays bounced off surfaces that will reach the viewplane as shown in Figure 16-2. However, as one can see from the figure, many of the rays originated from the light source may not hit the viewplane and thus cannot be seen by the viewer. Therefore, a lot of the computing work of following light paths is wasted.

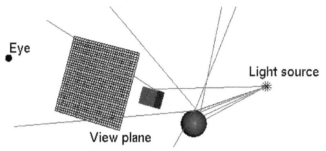

Figure 16-2 Tracing Rays From a Light Source

In practice, we only want to track those rays that can finally reach the eye. Since light paths are reversible, we can start tracing rays from the viewpoint, passing through viewplane pixels to the light source. You may ask: *Won't many of the rays miss the light source and thus the method is just as inefficient as the one before?* You are certainly right! Ray tracing actually does not work by tracing light paths only. It must work with a local lighting model, in which a light 'source' illuminates a surface like the Phong model. The task of ray tracing is to find out whether a surface that is visible to the viewer is illuminated by various light 'sources'. Visibility of surfaces can be found by throwing (or casting) light rays from the viewpoint, passing through pixels of the viewplane, into the scene as shown in Figure 16-3. This simple process is usually referred to as **ray casting**. If a ray hits an object, the eye will see the object at the intersection point, which is illuminated by the light source and the intensity value at the point is calculated according to the local lighting model. Furthermore, this point will be mapped to the pixel of the viewplane that the ray passes through.

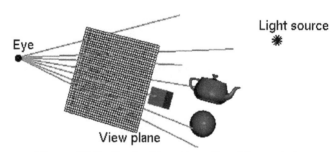

Figure 16-3 Casting Rays From Eye (Viewpoint)

Ray casting, which throws rays from the viewpoint to the scene to determine the visibility of surfaces, can be considered as a special case (the simplest case) of ray tracing. Conversely, we can consider ray tracing as an extension of ray casting. In ray casting, a light source is a point source that gives out light. In ray tracing, a light 'source' can be a point reflecting or transmitting a light ray incident on it. Therefore, ray tracing is a recursive process. It recursively casts from the points of intersections between light rays and object surfaces as shown in Figure 16-4 below.

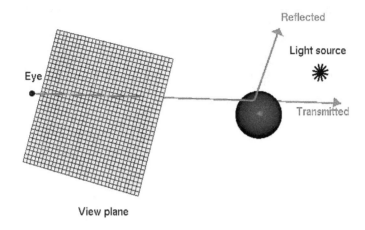

Figure 16-4   Recursive Ray Tracing

16.3   Basic Ray Tracing

16.3.1   Ray Casting (Nonrecursive Ray Tracing)

In this method, we determine the color of a pixel P on a viewplane by sending a ray from the eye through the pixel center to find out the first point where the ray hits an object in the scene. This first point of intersection is colored (shaded) according to a local lighting model such as the Phong model. This point is mapped to the pixel of the viewplane and is what the eye sees at that pixel. The following is the basic algorithm for ray casting:

```
for each pixel
{
   Shoot a ray from the eye through a pixel of viewplane.
   Find the first primitive intersection point by ray.
   Determine color at intersection point using local model.
   Draw color at the intersection point.
}
```

For example, Figure 16-5 below shows a ray that would intersect both the sphere and the lower cube. However, the ray hits the sphere first. So we will only see this point on the pixel. Note that using this simple ray casting model, we have not achieved any new visual effects as compared to the local lighting model. We have simply replaced the method of discarding hidden surfaces using a depth buffer by a ray tracing method to determine visible surfaces. To obtain more interesting visual effects, we must trace the paths recursively to include reflection rays, transmission rays and shadow feelers.

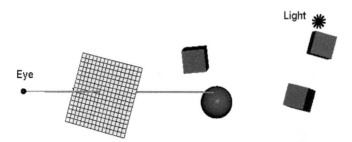

Figure 16-5 Determining First Intersection Point of Ray

16.3.2 Recursive Ray Tracing

In recursive ray tracing, the path tracing for a pixel deos not stop after the ray has hit a surface. We have to reflect the ray off the surface specularly (mirror-like) and continue the tracing along the reflected path. If the surface is that of a translucent media such as water, in addition to the reflected ray, we also have to shoot a ray through the surface along the refraction direction. The reflected and refracted ray are referred to as *secondary rays*. We carry on this process recursively until the secondary rays could 'see' the light source.

In ray tracing, there are several kinds of rays we need to consider, depending on the material properties of the scene.

Shadow Rays

A *shadow ray*, also called *shadow feeler*, is a ray sent from an intersection point to the light source to determine whether the intersection point is in shadow (the point is not visible from the light source) or not. As we discussed above, local light models like Phong model assume that every light source is always visible and no objects block light rays. Therefore, a local light model alone does not create shadows (see Figure 16-1). However, by casting rays into a scene and emitting shadow rays from the intersection points, we can create shadows in a scene from a simple local light model.

Figure 16-6 below shows an example of four shadow feelers shown as four broken lines. Four primary rays are sent from the eye through four pixels of the viewplane to determine four intersection points. From each of the intersection points, a shadow ray (shown as broken line) is sent to the light source. If the shadow ray hits an object before reaching the light source, then the intersection point is occluded and is in a shadow, not illuminated by the light. In the figure, two intersection points labeled "I" are illuminated and the other two intersecion points labeled "S" are shadowed.

Reflection Rays

When a light ray is bounced off a surface, the reflected ray may hit another surface and illuminates it. The reflected ray may be reflected again and illuminates other objects. To account for this effect, we add *reflection rays* in a ray tracing algorithm. When a ray intersects a surface and reflected, we treat the intersection point as the view point (eye) and follow the path of the reflected ray to continue the ray tracing. When this reflected ray hits a surface, we use a shadow ray discussed above to determine whether the hit point is shadowed or illuminated by a light source.

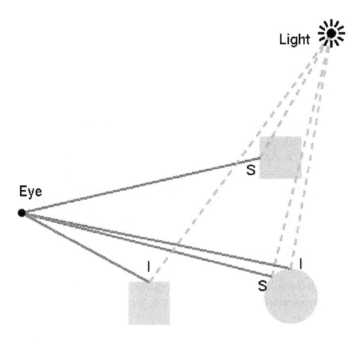

Figure 16-6   Shadow Feelers (S = shadowed, I = illuminated)

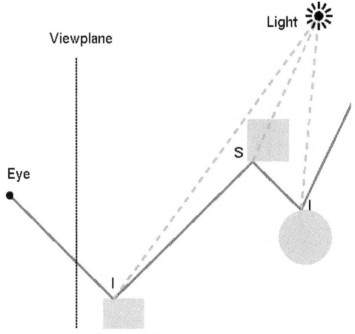

Figure 16-7   Reflection Rays

This process is carried on recursively as shown in Figure 16-7. Therefore, the illumination at a point is the sum of direct local illumination (if the point is not shadowed) from the local light model plus illumination due to reflection. This can be computed by a formula of the form

$$\mathbf{I} = \mathbf{I}_{local} + \rho_{rg}\mathbf{I}_r \tag{16.1}$$

where **I** denotes a color vector consisting of the red, green, and blue color components:

$$\mathbf{I} = \begin{pmatrix} R \\ G \\ B \end{pmatrix} \tag{16.2}$$

The subscript g denotes "global" and r denotes reflection. The brightness (color vector) $\mathbf{I}_{local}$ is the illumination at the reflection point computed using a local lighting model such as Phong lighting. The brightness I_r is the illumination due to reflection from the reflected direction. It is computed recursively by Equation (16.1); at the very end (the reflection point on the sphere of Figure 16-7), there is no more reflection, and $I = I_{local}$. The reflection coefficient ρ_{rg}, depending on the material property of the surface, is the fraction of incident light from the reflection direction that will be reflected.

Transmission (Refracted) Rays

When a light ray passes through the boundary between two different media (such as air and glass), it is partially reflected and partially refracted. Part of the light is blent and transmitted through the media. By adding **transmission rays** in ray tracing, we can simulate transparency effects in a scene.

When a ray hits a translucent object, besides the reflection ray, a transmission ray is generated as shown in Figure 16-8.

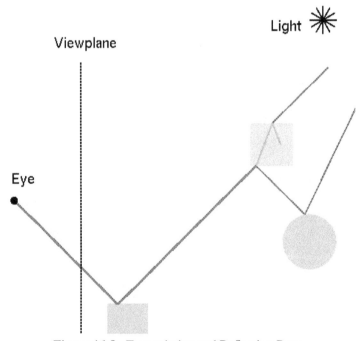

Figure 16-8 Transmission and Reflection Rays

The direction of the transmission ray is different from that of the original ray due to refraction. The degree of refraction is calculated using the the refraction indices of the media as discussed in the next section. When the transmission ray hits the other boundary of the object like that shown in Figure 16-8, it will be refracted and reflected again. Therefore, transmission rays also need to be traced recursively like the reflection rays.

When both transmission rays and reflected rays have been traced, the intensity (color vector) I

at a point is calculated according to the formula

$$\mathbf{I} = \mathbf{I}_{local} + \rho_{rg}\mathbf{I}_r + \rho_{tg}\mathbf{I}_t \tag{16.3}$$

where the subscript t denotes transmission. The intensity $\mathbf{I}_t$ is the transmission illumination due to refraction in the transmission direction and is calculated recursively. The transmission coefficient ρ_{tg} is the fraction of light transmitted through the surface.

16.4   Global Intensity Calculation

16.4.1   Basic Ray Tracing Vectors

Figure 16-9 below shows the basic ray tracing vectors at an intersection point Q. In the figure we hava a surface between two media with different refractive indices η_v and η_t. The refractive index of a medium is the ratio of the speed of light in vacuum to the light speed in the medium. The two media could be air ($\eta \approx 1$), water ($\eta \approx 1.33$), glass ($\eta \approx 1.5$) or any other materials. It does not matter which refractive index, η_v or η_t, is greater. All that matters is that η_v is the refractive index of the medium the ray comes from (incident ray), and η_t is that of the medium it transmits (refractive ray).

We trace the path of a ray originated from the viewpoint, which intersects a surface at point Q. In the figure, this direction is $-\mathbf{v}$; we assume that this vector and others in the figure are normalized (i.e. magnitude=1). Besides v, vectors of reflection, transmission, and other related rays are shown in Figure 16-9:

$$
\begin{aligned}
\mathbf{v} \quad &= \text{ viewing vector from } Q \text{ to the viewpoint} \\
\mathbf{r_v} \quad &= \text{direction of perfect reflection of tracing ray} \\
\mathbf{t} \quad &= \text{perfect transmission direction of tracing ray} \\
\mathbf{L} \quad &= \text{direction from } Q \text{ to the light source at same side as viewpoint} \\
\mathbf{L_t} \quad &= \text{direction from } Q \text{ to the light source at opposite side of viewpoint} \\
\mathbf{r} \quad &= \text{perfect reflection direction of light source vector } \mathbf{L} \\
\mathbf{n} \quad &= \text{normal to the surface at } Q \\
|\mathbf{n}| \quad &= |\mathbf{v}| = |\mathbf{r_v}| = |\mathbf{t}| = |\mathbf{L}| = |\mathbf{r}| = 1
\end{aligned}
\tag{16.4}
$$

We can split the direction vector in components orthogonal (perpendicular) and parallel to the surface at Q. We call these the normal component $\mathbf{b}_\perp$ and the tangential component $\mathbf{v}_\parallel$ of a vector $\mathbf{v}$.

The normal component of $\mathbf{v}$ can be found by orthogonal projection of $\mathbf{v}$ on $\mathbf{n}$:

$$\mathbf{v}_\perp = (\mathbf{v} \cdot \mathbf{n})\mathbf{n} = \cos\theta_v \mathbf{n} \tag{16.5}$$

The sum of the normal component $\mathbf{v}_\perp$ and tangential component $\mathbf{v}_\parallel$ is equal to $\mathbf{v}$. Therefore, the difference between $\mathbf{v}$ and $\mathbf{v}_\perp$ gives the tangent componet:

$$\mathbf{v}_\parallel = \mathbf{v} - \mathbf{v}_\perp = \mathbf{v} - (\mathbf{v} \cdot \mathbf{n})\mathbf{n} \tag{16.6}$$

The dot product of $\mathbf{v}_\perp$ and $\mathbf{v}_\parallel$ is zero:

$$
\begin{aligned}
\mathbf{v}_\perp \cdot \mathbf{v}_\parallel \quad &= \mathbf{v}_\perp \cdot \mathbf{v} - \mathbf{v}_\perp \cdot \mathbf{v}_\perp \\
&= (\mathbf{v} \cdot \mathbf{n})\mathbf{n} \cdot \mathbf{v} - (\mathbf{v} \cdot \mathbf{n})^2 \mathbf{n} \cdot \mathbf{n} \\
&= ((\mathbf{v} \cdot \mathbf{n})^2 - (\mathbf{v} \cdot \mathbf{n})^2 \\
&= 0
\end{aligned}
\tag{16.7}
$$

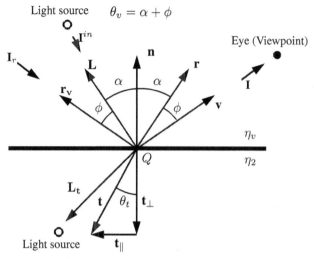

Figure 16-9   Basic Vectors for Ray Tracing

Note that all the normal components and **n** are parallel to each other and all the tangent components are parallel as well. Also,

$$\cos \theta_v = |\mathbf{v}_\perp|$$
$$\sin \theta_v = |\mathbf{v}_\parallel|$$

$$(16.8)$$

16.4.2 Reflection

The direction of perfect reflection is $\mathbf{r_v}$ of Figure 16-9. It can be calculated from the normal and viewing vector:

$$
\begin{aligned}
\mathbf{r_v} &= \mathbf{r_{v\perp}} + \mathbf{r_{v\parallel}} \\
&= \mathbf{v}_\perp - \mathbf{v}_\parallel \\
&= 2\mathbf{v}_\perp - \mathbf{v} \\
&= 2(\mathbf{v} \cdot \mathbf{n})\mathbf{n} - \mathbf{v}
\end{aligned}
$$

$$(16.9)$$

Note that $|\mathbf{r_v}|^2 = |\mathbf{v}|^2 = 1$.

Suppose we have used a Phong lighting model as our local lighting model. From Figure 16-9, we see that $\mathbf{r_v} \cdot \mathbf{L} = \mathbf{r} \cdot \mathbf{v}$, and from Equation (7.15) of Chapter 7, the direct illumination at Q due to the light source is given by

$$
\begin{aligned}
\mathbf{I}_{local} &= \mathbf{I}_a + \mathbf{I}_d + \mathbf{I}_s + \mathbf{I}_e \\
&= \mathbf{c}_a \odot \mathbf{I}_a^{in} + \mathbf{c}_d \odot \mathbf{I}_d^{in}(\mathbf{L} \cdot \mathbf{n}) + \mathbf{c}_s \odot \mathbf{I}_s^{in}(\mathbf{r_v} \cdot \mathbf{L})^f + \mathbf{I}_e
\end{aligned}
$$

$$(16.10)$$

There could be more than one light source in the scene. Suppose there are N lights and we use subscript i to associate a vector with light i. So $\mathbf{L_i}$ is the unit vector in the direction of light i. We introduce the variable δ_i to denote whether the intersection point Q is illuminated by light i ($\delta_i = 1$) or it is shadowed ($\delta_i = 0$) from that light source. To determine the value of δ_i, we first check whether $\mathbf{L_i} \cdot \mathbf{n} > 0$. If so, the light is above the surface and we need to use a shadow ray to determine its visibility.

The total local lighting due to all the light sources above the surface is the sum of the illumination of all the visible lights:

$$
\mathbf{I}_{local} = \mathbf{c}_a \odot \mathbf{I}_a^{in} + \mathbf{c}_d \odot \sum_{i=1}^{N} \delta_i \mathbf{I}_d^{in,i}(\mathbf{L_i} \cdot \mathbf{n}) + \mathbf{c}_s \odot \sum_{i=1}^{N} \delta_i \mathbf{I}_s^{in,i}(\mathbf{r_v} \cdot \mathbf{L_i})^f + \mathbf{I}_e \qquad (16.11)
$$

As mentioned in Chapter 7, the coefficient vectors $\mathbf{c}_*$ are tuples of coefficients of red, green, and blue intensities. The symbol $\odot$ denotes a component-wise multiplication.

In addition to the local illumination, the intensity$\mathbf{I}$ at Q as seen from the ray direction $\mathbf{v}$ consists of intensity from reflection:

$$\mathbf{I} = \mathbf{I}_{local} + \rho_{\mathbf{rg}} \odot \mathbf{I}_r \tag{16.12}$$

where ρ_{rg} is the reflection coefficient of the surface. This coefficient can be a scalar independent of the light wavelength for simple applications or it can be a 3-tuple consisting of three differents values for the red, green and blue colors if we need more accurate calculation of the reflected light.

16.4.3   Transmission

The transmission ray can be calculated using Snell's law, which states that the ratio of the refractive indices is equal to the inverse of the ratio of the sines of the angles:

$$\frac{\eta_v}{\eta_t} = \frac{\sin \theta_t}{\sin \theta_v} \tag{16.13}$$

The transmission angle θ_t can be calculated by:

$$\sin \theta_t = \frac{\eta_v}{\eta_t} \sin \theta_v \tag{16.14}$$

Equation (16.14) implies a special situation when $\eta_v \sin \theta_v > \eta_t$, leading to $\sin \theta_t > 1$ which is impossible. Physically, this means that total internal reflection has occurred. Therefore, we have to put the constraint, $\eta_v \sin \theta_v \leq \eta_t$ in (16.14).

Our goal is to calculate the transmission vector $\mathbf{t}$ from the normal $\mathbf{n}$ and viewing vector $\mathbf{v}$ in Figure 16-9. Recall that all the vectors in the the figure are normalized (magnitude=1) and a vector can be decomposed into a normal component and a parallel component. So

$$\mathbf{t} = \mathbf{t}_\perp + \mathbf{t}_\| \tag{16.15}$$

The parallel component $\mathbf{t}_\|$ is in the opposite direction of $\mathbf{v}_\|$ which is given by (16.6). Thus

$$|\mathbf{t}_\|| = \sin \theta_t = \frac{\eta_v}{\eta_t} \sin \theta_v = \frac{\eta_v}{\eta_t} |\mathbf{v}_\|| \tag{16.16}$$

and

$$\mathbf{t}_\| = -\frac{\eta_v}{\eta_t} \mathbf{v}_\| = \frac{\eta_v}{\eta_t} ((\mathbf{v} \cdot \mathbf{n})\mathbf{n} - \mathbf{v}) \tag{16.17}$$

Also, $\mathbf{t}_\perp$ is in the negative direction of the normal $\mathbf{n}$ and $|\mathbf{t}_\perp|^2 + |\mathbf{t}_\||^2 = 1$. So

$$\mathbf{t}_\perp = -\sqrt{1 - |\mathbf{t}_\||^2}\, \mathbf{n} \tag{16.18}$$

The transmission vector is obtained by summing the two components, that is $\mathbf{t} = \mathbf{t}_\perp + \mathbf{t}_\|$.

In the situation that $\sin^2 \theta_t = |\mathbf{t}_\||^2 \geq 1$, total internal reflection occurs and there will be no transmission light. The incoming angle at which total internal reflection occurs is called the *critical angle* θ_c. The calculation of the transmission vector $\mathbf{t}$ can be easily implemented as follows, makng use of *Vector3* class discussed in previous chapters:

```
//calculating transmission director; vector returned in t
bool transmitDir(double eta_v, double eta_t, const Vector3 &v,
                                const Vector3 &n, Vector3 &t)
{
   Vector3 t_parallel = (eta_v / eta_t ) * ((v * n) * n - v );
   double tp_square = t_parallel * t_parallel;
   if ( tp_square >= 1.0 )     //total internal reflection
      return false;
   Vector3 t_perp = -sqrt ( 1 - tp_square ) * n;
   t = t_parallel + t_perp;    //transmission vector

   return true;
}
```

16.4.4 Phong Lighting for Transmission

When we consider the illumination due to reflection, we have to apply a local lighting model to calculate the lighting due to different material surfaces as we did in (16.11) where a Phong lighting model has been used. We can extend Phong lighting to calculate the transmission illumination in a similar way. For transmission illumination, the light may come from the opposite side of the surface from the viewer or incoming ray. Just like reflection illumination, transmission illumination is modeled as consisting of two types of lighting, specular and diffuse lighting as shown in Figure 16-10.

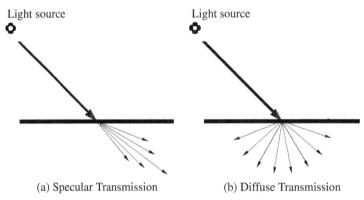

(a) Specular Transmission   (b) Diffuse Transmission

Figure 16-10 Phong Lighting for Transmission

Specular transmission transmits primarily along the direction of perfect transmission, the direction t found using Snell's law. Diffuse transmission transmits equally in all directions. In this model, we define $\mathbf{L_t}$ as the direction from the intersection point Q to a light source (see Figure 16-9). Similar to the illumination of the Phong reflection lighting model, the local transmission illumination due to light source i is given by

$$\mathbf{I}_{local}^i = \mathbf{c}_a \odot \mathbf{I}_a^{in,i} + \delta_i^t (\mathbf{c}_{td} \odot \mathbf{I}_d^{in,i} (\mathbf{L_{ti}} \cdot (-\mathbf{n})) + \mathbf{c}_{ts} \odot \mathbf{I}_s^{in,i} (\mathbf{t} \cdot \mathbf{L_{ti}})^f \qquad (16.19)$$

where $\mathbf{c}_{td}$ and $\mathbf{c}_{ts}$ are transmission coefficients for diffuse and specular materials respectively. The variable δ_{ti} is 1 if the light and the viewpoint are on opposite side of the surface (i.e. $\mathbf{L_{ti}} \cdot \mathbf{n} < 0$), otherwise it is equal to 0; this can be determined by a shadow feeler. The total local transmission lighting at the point is the sum of all illumination due to light sources that are on the opposite side of the surface.

The total lighting, including both reflection and transmission illumination, is given by

$$
\begin{aligned}
\mathbf{I}_{local} = \quad &\mathbf{c}_a \odot \mathbf{I}_a^{in} + \mathbf{c}_d \odot \sum_{i=1}^{N} \delta_i \mathbf{I}_d^{in}(\mathbf{L_i} \cdot \mathbf{n}) + \mathbf{c}_s \odot \sum_{i=1}^{N} \delta_i \mathbf{I}_s^{in}(\mathbf{r_v} \cdot \mathbf{L_i})^f + \mathbf{I}_e \\
&+ \mathbf{c}_{td} \odot \sum_{i=1}^{N} \delta_{ti} \mathbf{I}_d^{in,i}(\mathbf{L_{ti}} \cdot (-\mathbf{n})) + \mathbf{c}_{ts} \odot \sum_{i=1}^{N} \delta_{ti} \mathbf{I}_s^{in,i}(\mathbf{t} \cdot \mathbf{L_{ti}})^f
\end{aligned}
\tag{16.20}
$$

Note that for each light i, both δ_i and δ_{ti} may be 0, but only one of them can be 1 as the light source cannot be above and below the surface at the same time.

Appendix C discusses an open-source ray-tracing package.

Chapter 17 Intersection Testing

This chapter discusses the methods of determining the intersection between a ray and a surface or an object. The technique also applies to finding collisions between objects in game development.

17.1 Rays, Lines, and Planes

17.1.1 Representing Lines and Planes

For clarity of presentation, we first distinguish between a line, a ray, and a line segment. Figure 17-1 shows their characteristic, which can be described as follows:

1. A **line** is defined by two points. It is infinite in length and passes through the points, extending forever in both directions.
2. A **line segment** (**segment** for short) is defined by two end points and its length is finite.
3. A **ray** is defined by a point and a direction. It is semi-infinite, extending to infinity in one direction.

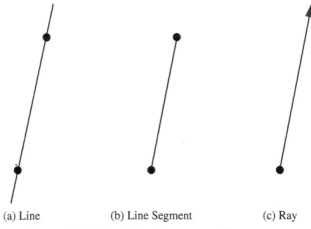

(a) Line   (b) Line Segment   (c) Ray

Figure 17-1 Line, Line Segment, and Ray

So we can regard a line, a segment, or a ray as a set of points. Recall that the difference between two points is a vector. We can simply define them by two points, P_1 and P_2. We let $\mathbf{D} = P_2 - P_1$ be the vector pointing from P_1 to P_2. Then all of them can be represented by a single parametric function $L(t)$,

$$L(t) = P_1 + \mathbf{D}t \tag{17.1}$$

with different restrictions on the parameter t:

$$
\begin{aligned}
\text{Segment:} &\quad 0 \le t \le 1 \\
\text{Ray:} &\quad 0 \le t < \infty \\
\text{Line:} &\quad -\infty < t < \infty
\end{aligned}
\tag{17.2}
$$

The point P_1 is often called the starting point or the origin of the ray. Using the classes *Vector3*, and *Point3* discussed in previous chapters, we can easily implement a ray as a class like the following:

```
class Ray {
public:
  Point3  O;       //starting point (origin)
  Vector3 D;       //direction vector
  Ray()            //default constructor
  {
     O = Point3( 0.0, 0.0, 0.0 );
     D = Vector3( 1.0, 1.0, 1.0 );     D.normalize();
  }
  //constructor
  Ray ( const Point3 &origin, const Vector3 &dir ){
     O = origin;
     D = dir;     D.normalize();
  }

  //return point L(t) at t
  Point3 getPoint ( const double t )
  {
     return O +  t * D;
  }
};
```

17.1.2 Ray-Plane Intersection

As discussed above, we can specify a ray by its starting position O and a unit vector $\mathbf{D}$. We can consider a ray as a set of points given by

$$L(t) = O + t\mathbf{D} \qquad 0 \le t < \infty \qquad (17.3)$$

as shown in the figure on the right. One can see that a ray is actually part of a line. The line that contains the ray is referred to as a **ray-line**.

A **plane** is specified by a point $P' = (x', y', z')$ on the plane and a normal $\mathbf{n} = (n_x, n_y, n_z)$ perpendicular to it. It can be described by an equation in the form,

$$(P - P') \cdot \mathbf{n} = 0$$

impling that

$$(x - x')n_x + (y - y')n_y + (z - z')n_z = 0$$

or in the form

$$ax + by + cz + d = 0 \qquad\qquad (17.4)$$

with

$$(a, b, c) = (n_x, n_y, n_z),$$
$$d = -(x'n_x + y'n_y + z'n_z)$$

Conversely, if a plane is described by an equation of (17.4), its normal is given by $\mathbf{n} = (a, b, c)$.

Suppose P is the intersection point of the ray $L(t)$ and the plane $(P - P') \cdot \mathbf{n} = 0$ as shown below. As P is on both the ray and the plane, we have

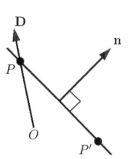

$$0 = (P - P') \cdot \mathbf{n} = (O + t\mathbf{D} - P') \cdot \mathbf{n}$$

Soving for t, we get

$$t = \frac{(P' - O) \cdot \mathbf{n}}{\mathbf{D} \cdot \mathbf{n}} \qquad (17.5)$$

There are three cases that imply the ray and plane do not intersect:

1. If $\mathbf{D} \cdot \mathbf{n} = 0$, the ray L that contains P is parallel to the plane (perpendicular to $\mathbf{n}$). So they don't intersect.
2. If $\mathbf{D} \cdot \mathbf{n} < 0$, the ray is downward relative to the plane. So they don't intersect.
3. if $t < 0$, the ray L does not intersect the plane.

Example 17.1:

A plane passes through the points $P_1 = (3, 4, 0)$, $P_2 = (4, 4, 0)$, and $P_3 = (5, 3, -1)$. Determine whether the ray that originates from $O = (2, 1, 0)$ and passes through the point $P_0 = (1, 3, 0)$ will intersect with the plane. If yes, what is the intersection point?

Solution:

Here
$$\mathbf{D} = (P_0 - O) = (1, 3, 0) - (2, 1, 0) = (-1, 2, 0)$$
Let
$$\mathbf{A} = P_2 - P_1 = (4, 4, 0) - (3, 4, 0) = (1, 0, 0)$$
$$\mathbf{B} = P_3 - P_1 = (5, 3, -1) - (3, 4, 0) = (2, -1, -1)$$
Then
$$\mathbf{n} = \mathbf{A} \times \mathbf{B} = (0, 1, -1)$$
$$\mathbf{D} \cdot \mathbf{n} = (1, 2, 0) \cdot (0, 1, -1) = 2$$
So
$$t = \frac{(P_1 - O) \cdot \mathbf{n}}{\mathbf{D} \cdot \mathbf{n}}$$
$$= \frac{((3, 4, 0) - (2, 1, 0)) \cdot (0, 1, -1)}{2}$$
$$= \frac{(1, 3, 0) \cdot (0, 1, -1)}{2}$$
$$= 3/2$$

Thus, the ray intersect the plane at the point
$$P(t) = P(3/2) = (2, 1, 0) + (3/2)(-1, 2, 0) = \boxed{(1/2, 4, 0)}$$

The implementation of a plane is simple. We implement it as a class by specifying a point on it along with its normalized normal like the following:

```
class Plane {
public:
  Point3 p0;           //one point and a normal define a plane
  Vector3  n;
  Plane (){            //default is xy plane
    p0 = Point3( 0.0, 0.0, 0.0 );
    n = Vector3 ( 0, 0, 1 ) ;
  }
  Plane ( const Point3 &aPoint,  const Vector3 & aNormal )
  {
    p0 = aPoint;
    n = aNormal;
    if ( n.magnitude() == 0 )    //special case
      n = Vector3 ( 0, 0, 1 );
    else
      n.normalize();             //make it a unit vector
  }
};
```

We implement the testing of the intersection of a ray and a plane as the function **intersect_ray_plan**() presented below. The function returns **true** and the value of t if they intersect and *false* if they do not. The calculation of the parameter t is a straightforward implementation of Equation (17.5).

```
bool intersect_ray_plane(const Ray &ray, const Plane &plane,
                                                     double &t)
{
  t = 0;
  if ( ray.O == plane.p0 )
    return true;

  //vector from origin to p0
  Vector3 origin_to_p0 = plane.p0 - ray.O;
  double op_dot_n = origin_to_p0 * plane.n;//dot product
  double d_dot_n = ray.D * plane.n;        //dot product

  if (fabs(d_dot_n) < 0.0000001)    //ray parallel to plane
    return false;

  t = op_dot_n / d_dot_n;
  if ( t < 0.0 )
    return false;

  return true;
}
```

17.1.3 Ray-Slab Intersection

A slab consists of two parallel planes as shown in the figure on the right below. Therefore, it is specified by two points and a normal. If intersection occurs, the ray intersects the slab at two points which are specified by two values of the parameter values, t_1 and t_2.

$$L(t) = O + t\mathbf{D}$$

At intersection points, we have

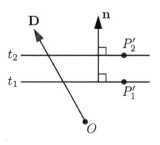

$$t_1 = \frac{(P_1' - O) \cdot \mathbf{n}}{\mathbf{D} \cdot \mathbf{n}} \qquad (17.6a)$$

$$t_2 = \frac{(P_2' - O) \cdot \mathbf{n}}{\mathbf{D} \cdot \mathbf{n}} \qquad (17.6b)$$

17.1.4 Ray-Box Intersection

A box is bounded by six planes, which can be used both as an object and a bounding volume. We only consider the special case of boxes that have parallel faces with normals parallel to the coordinate axes; the box faces are contained in a set of slabs. In this case, the intersection of the slabs defines the box. We specify the box by two points, the minimum extent at $p_l = (x_l, y_l, z_l)$, and the maximum extent at $p_h = (x_h, y_h, z_h)$. This is shown in Figure 17-2 below.

Ray : $L(t) = O + t\mathbf{D}$
Box :   minimum extent $p_l = (x_l, y_l, z_l)$
        maximum extent $p_h = (x_h, y_h, z_h)$

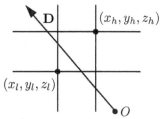

Figure 17-2   Ray-Box Intersection

To determine whether a ray intersects a box, we examine the intersection of each pair of slabs by the ray, calculating t_{far}, the intersection value of t at the far-side slab, and t_{near}, value at the near-side. If the largest overall t_{near} value is larger than the smallest t_{far} value then the ray misses the box, otherwise it hits the box as shown in Figure 17-3 below.

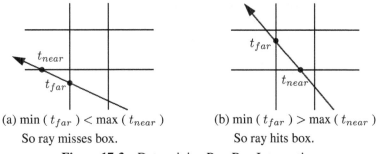

(a) min (t_{far}) < max (t_{near})   (b) min (t_{far}) > max (t_{near})
So ray misses box.   So ray hits box.

Figure 17-3   Determining Ray-Box Intersection

Also, if the ray is parallel to an axis, we can simplify the process by first checking whether the origin of the ray lies between the corresponding parallel planes. If not, the ray will not hit the box.

Suppose we call planes parallel to yz-plane the X-planes (normal along x-axis), planes parallel to zx-plane the Y-planes (normal along y-axis), planes parallel to xy-plane the Z-planes (normal along z-axis). Using Equations (17.6), we present a commonly used algorithm for determining whether the ray $L(t) = O + t\mathbf{D}$ intersects with the box discussed above:

1. Set $t_{near} = -\infty$, $t_{far} = +\infty$

2. For the pair of X-planes, do the following

    2.1 if ($\mathbf{D}_x = 0$), the ray is parallel to the X-planes (normal $\mathbf{n} = \mathbf{x}$), so

        if ($O_x < x_l$ or $O_x > x_h$) return **false** (origin not between planes)

    2.2 else the ray is not parallel to the planes, so calculate the ray parameter t values at the intersections:

- $t_1 = \dfrac{x_l - O_x}{\mathbf{D}_x}$ (point at which ray intersects minimum X-plane)
- $t_2 = \dfrac{x_h - O_x}{\mathbf{D}_x}$ (point at which ray intersects maximum X-plane)
- if ($t_1 > t_2$) swap t_1 and t_2, so that t_1 is always at the near-plane and t_2 is at the far-plane
- if ($t_1 > t_{near}$) set $t_{near} = t_1$ (find largest t_{near})
- if ($t_2 < t_{far}$) set $t_{far} = t_2$ (find smallest t_{far})
- if ($t_{near} > t_{far}$) ray misses box so return **false**
- if ($t_{far} < 0$) box is behind ray so return **false**

3. Repeat step 2 for Y-planes and Z-planes.
4. If all tests were survived, return **true** with t_{near} as parameter value at intersection point and t_{far} at exit point.

We implement such a box as a class by specifying the minimum and maximum extents:

```
class Box {
public:
  Point3 pl;                //minimum extent
  Point3 ph;                //maximum extent
  Box (){ //default box center at origin
    pl = Point3( -1, -1, -1 );
    ph = Point3( 1, 1, 1 );
  }
  Box ( const Point3 &p1,  const Point3 &p2 )
  {
    assert(p1.x < p2.x && p1.y < p2.y && p1.z < p2.z);
    pl = p1;
    ph = p2;
  }
};
```

We could implement the intersection testing of a box and a ray with use of the **intersect_ray_plane**() function discussed above. However, it is a lot more efficient to implement directly using the ray-box intersection algorithm presented above. We present this implementation below, where the function **intersect_ray_box**() determines whether a ray intersects a box; if yes it returns true and ray parameters $t1$ and $t2$ at the intersection and exit points respectively:

```
bool intersect_ray_box(Ray &ray,Box &box,double &t1,double &t2)
{
  double t_near = -1.0e+10, t_far = 1.0e+10;
  double D[3];  //ray direction
  double O[3];  //ray origin
  double pl[3]; //minimum extent
  double ph[3]; //maximum extent
  ray.D.getXYZ ( D );   //put ray direction (x,y,z) in D[]
  ray.O.getXYZ ( O );   //put ray origin (x,y,z) in O[]
  box.pl.getXYZ ( pl ); //put (x,y,z) of minimum point in pl[]
  box.ph.getXYZ ( ph ); //put (x,y,z) of maximum point in ph[]

  for ( int i = 0; i < 3; i++ ) {  //test 3 planes (X, Y, Z)
    if ( D[i] == 0 ) {  //ray parallel to axis plane
      if ( O[i] < pl[i] || O[i] > ph[i] )
        return false;    //origin not between points
    } else {
        t1 = ( pl[i] - O[i] ) / D[i];
        t2 = ( ph[i] - O[i] ) / D[i];
        if ( t1 > t2 ) {  //swap t1, t2
          double temp = t1;
          t1 = t2;
          t2 = temp;
        }
        if ( t1 > t_near ) t_near = t1;   //find max (t_near)
        if ( t2 < t_far  ) t_far  = t2;   //find min (t_far)
        if (t_near > t_far) return false;
        if (t_far < 0 ) return false;
    }
  } //for
  t1 = t_near;   //returns maximum t_near (intersection)
  t2 = t_far;    //returns minimum t_far  (exit)

  return true;   //ray hits box
}
```

17.2   Ray-Triangle Intersection

17.2.1 Ray-Triangle Intersection Test

Since any surface can be approximated by triangles, ray-triangle intersection algorithms are very important in ray-tracing or game development.

A triangle is a subset of a plane; it is the region of the plane bounded by the three edges of the triangle which is defined by three vertices. Therefore, we can break up the ray-triangle intersection testing into two stages:

1. Test whether the ray intersects the plane that contains the triangle.
2. If ray-plane intersection occurs, check whether the intersection point is inside the triangle.

Recall that a plane is specified by a point p' lying on the plane and a normal $\mathbf{n}$ of the plane. That is,

$$\text{Plane} = (p', \mathbf{n}) \tag{17.7}$$

Suppose a triangle is defined by three vertices, (p_0, p_1, p_2) and is contained in a plane as shown in Figure 17-4 below. We refer to this plane as triangle-plane.

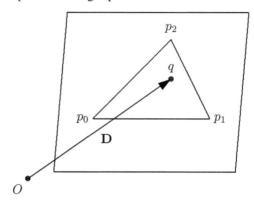

Figure 17-4 Ray-Triangle Intersection

As the difference between two points is a vector, we can compute a unit normal $\mathbf{n}$ to the plane by the cross product of two vectors along two triangle edges originated from the same vertex:

$$\mathbf{N} = (p_1 - p_0) \times (p_2 - p_0)$$
$$\mathbf{n} = \frac{\mathbf{N}}{|\mathbf{N}|} \tag{17.8}$$

Since P_0 is a point of the triangle, it is also a point of the plane containing the triangle. Therefore, the triangle-plane is specified by

$$\text{Tri-plane} = (p_0, \mathbf{n}) \tag{17.9}$$

We can always substitute p_0 by p_1 or p_2 in (17.9) as all three points are on the plane. The intersection point q is determined by the ray-plane intersection test, which calculates the ray parameter $t(q)$ at q if they intersect:

$$t(q) = \frac{(P_0 - O) \cdot \mathbf{n}}{\mathbf{D} \cdot \mathbf{n}} \tag{17.10}$$

Once we have found q, we have to check whether it lies inside the triangle. (Of course, if the ray does not hit the plane, it does not hit the triangle either, and we do not need to make further tests.) This test is easier to be done using Barycentric coordinates.

We have learned that a point can be expressed as an affine combination of other points. Therefore, a point p on a triangle-plane can be expressed as

$$p = A_0 p_0 + A_1 p_1 + A_2 p_2 \quad (17.11)$$

where A_0, A_1, A_2 are proportional to the areas of the corresponding subtriangles as shown in the figure above and

$$A_0 + A_1 + A_2 = 1 \tag{17.12}$$

The values (A_0, A_1, A_2) are referred to as **Barycentric coordinates** of p. If the area of the triangle is normalized to 1, then A_i $(i = 0, 1, 2)$ becomes the area of the actual subtriangle, and the coordinates are called **homogeneous Barycentric coordinates**. The criterion for p to be inside the triangle is:

$$0 \leq A_i \leq 1 \quad i = 0, 1, 2 \tag{17.13}$$

Therefore, if we know the Barycentric coordinates of the hit point q, we can accept or reject the ray with very simple tests: Point q is outside the triangle if one of the Barycentric coordinates A_i is smaller than zero. So our task is to find the Barycentric coordinates of q.

Suppose vertices v_0, v_1, and v_2 form a triangle and (α, β, γ) are Barycentric coordinates of a point q on the triangle-plane. Then

$$q = \alpha v_0 + \beta v_1 + \gamma v_2 \tag{17.14}$$

Substituting with $\alpha = 1 - \beta - \gamma$, we can rewrite (17.14) as

$$\beta(v_1 - v_0) + \gamma(v_2 - v_0) = q - v_0 \tag{17.15}$$

It is easier to solve for the Barycentric coordinates of (17.15) if we project the triangle in a 2D plane. Projecting both the triangle and the hit-point q onto another plane does not change the Barycentric coordinates of q because the projection does not change the ratios of the subtriangle areas. After projection, all computations can be performed more efficiently in 2D. For example, we can project them into the xy-plane (Z-plane). We first define three vectors:

$$\begin{aligned} \mathbf{c} &= & (v_1 - v_0) \\ \mathbf{b} &= & (v_2 - v_0) \\ \mathbf{h} &= & (q - v_0) \end{aligned} \tag{17.16}$$

We can then express (17.15) as

$$\beta \mathbf{c} + \gamma \mathbf{b} = \mathbf{h} \tag{17.17}$$

When projected into the Z-plane, we obtain the following equations:

$$\begin{aligned} \beta \mathbf{c}_x + \gamma \mathbf{b}_x &= \mathbf{h}_x \\ \beta \mathbf{c}_y + \gamma \mathbf{b}_y &= \mathbf{h}_y \end{aligned} \tag{17.18}$$

So we have two equations and two unknowns (β, γ), which can be easily solved. Upon solving (17.18), we obtain

$$\boxed{\beta = \frac{\mathbf{b}_x \mathbf{h}_y - \mathbf{b}_y \mathbf{h}_x}{\mathbf{b}_x \mathbf{c}_y - \mathbf{b}_y \mathbf{c}_x}} \qquad \boxed{\gamma = \frac{\mathbf{h}_x \mathbf{c}_y - \mathbf{h}_y \mathbf{c}_x}{\mathbf{b}_x \mathbf{c}_y - \mathbf{b}_y \mathbf{c}_x}} \tag{17.19}$$

If either $\beta < 0$, or $\gamma < 0$, or $\alpha = 1 - \beta - \gamma < 0$, then the intersection point q is outside the triangle. Otherwise it is inside.

If the triangle-plane is almost parallel to the Z-plane (i.e. $\mathbf{n}_z \approx 0$), then the denominator in (17.18) is close to zero and could cause significant rounding errors in the calculation. In this case, we should project it into the X-plane or Y-plane. In other words, we should first calculate the normal components $(\mathbf{n}_x, \mathbf{n}_y, \mathbf{n}_z)$ and project into the axis plane associated with the largest normal component. For example if $|\mathbf{n}_y|$ is largest, we should project the triangle into the Y-plane.

17.2.2 Triangle Implementation

As a triangle can be specified by three points, we implement it as the class *Triangle* that has three *Point3* members. The following code segment shows the implementation.

```
class Triangle {
public:
  Point3 p0;       //three points determine a triangle
  Point3 p1;
  Point3 p2;

  Triangle ()    //default Triangle
  {
    p0 = Point3( 0.0, 0.0, 0.0 );
    p1 = Point3( 1.0, 0.0, 0.0 );
    p2 = Point3( 0.0, 1.0, 0.0 );
  }
  Triangle(const Point3 &v0, const Point3 &v1,
                                const Point3 &v2)
  {
    p0 = v0;   p1 = v0;   p2 = v2;
  }
};
```

17.2.3 Ray-Triangle Intersection Test Implementation

Implementation of the ray-triangle intersection test consists of a few steps:

1. Construct a plane containing the triangle.
2. Perform the ray-plane intersection test. If the ray misses the plane, return **false**. Otherwise test whether the ray-plane intersection point is inside the triangle according to steps 3-6.
3. Construct the three vectors of **b**, **c**, **h** of (17.16).
4. Find the axis that the normal to the triangle has the largest absolute component and choose this axis-plane to be the plane of projection.
5. Project the three vectors into the axis-plane and calculate the Barycentric coordinates of the ray-plane intersection using formulas (17.18) and (17.19).
6. If any of the Barycentric coordinates is smaller than 0, return **false**. Otherwise return **true**.

The function **intersect_ray_triangle**() of Listing 17-1 below shows the actual implementation:

Program Listing 17-1   Ray-Triangle Intersection Test

```
-------------------------------------------------------------------
//assume that x, y, z are positive
char max_axis ( float x, float y, float z )
{
  char a;
  if ( x  > y )
    if ( x > z )
       a = 'x';
    else
       a = 'z';
  else
    if ( y > z )
       a = 'y';
    else
       a = 'z';

  return a;
}
```

```
bool intersect_ray_triangle(Ray &ray, const Triangle &triangle,
                                                  double &t )
{
  Vector3 v01 = triangle.p1 - triangle.p0;
  Vector3 v02 = triangle.p2 - triangle.p0;
  Vector3 normal = v01 ^ v02;         //normal to triangle
  Plane plane(triangle.p0, normal); //plane containing triangle
  bool hit_plane = intersect_ray_plane ( ray, plane, t );
  if ( !hit_plane ) return false;

  Point3 q = ray.getPoint( t );       //ray-plane intersection

  //check whether q is inside triangle
  double bx, by, cx, cy, hx, hy;
  double beta, gamma;
  Vector3 b, c, h;

  c = v01;
  b = v02;
  h = q - triangle.p0;

  //find the dominant axis
  char axis = max_axis ( fabs ( normal.x), fabs ( normal.y), fabs(normal.z) );

  switch ( axis ) {
    case 'x': //project on X-plane (yz)
      bx = b.y; by = b.z;
      cx = c.y; cy = c.z;
      hx = h.y; hy = h.z;
      break;
    case 'y': //project on Y-plane (zx)
      bx = b.z; by = b.x;
      cx = c.z; cy = c.x;
      hx = h.z; hy = h.x;
      break;
    case 'z': //project on Z-plane (xy)
      bx = b.x; by = b.y;
      cx = c.x; cy = c.y;
      hx = h.x; hy = h.y;
      break;
  }

  double denominator =  bx * cy - by * cx;
  beta = ( bx * hy - by * hx ) / denominator;
  gamma = ( hx * cy - hy * cx ) / denominator;

  if ( beta < 0 ) return false;
  if ( gamma < 0 ) return false;
  if ( 1 - (beta + gamma) < 0 ) return false;

  return true;
}
```

17.3 Ray-Sphere Intersection

17.3.1 Ray-Sphere Intersection Test

A sphere is specified by the location of its center C and its radius R. If P is a point on the sphere, we can express the sphere as

$$(P - C)^2 - R^2 = 0 \qquad\qquad (17.20)$$

A ray is described by (17.3) (i.e., $P(t) = O + t\mathbf{D}$). If P is an intersection point of the ray and the sphere as shown in Figure 17-5 below, it satisfies both (17.20) and (17.3). Then

$$(O + t\mathbf{D} - C)^2 - R^2 = 0 \tag{17.21}$$

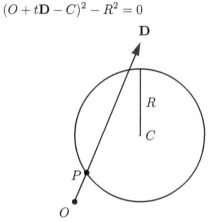

Figure 17-5 Ray-Sphere Intersection

Equation (17.21) can be expanded and expressed in the form,

$$at^2 + bt + c = 0 \tag{17.22}$$

where

$$a = \mathbf{D}^2$$
$$b = 2(O - C) \cdot \mathbf{D}$$
$$c = (O - C)^2 - R^2$$

Equation (17.22) is a quadratic equation in t, and we can easily solve for t. Its solution is given by

$$t = \frac{-b \pm \sqrt{b^2 - 4ac}}{2a} \tag{17.23}$$

There are three different cases for the solutions of (17.23) depending on the discriminant $b^2 - 4ac$:

(a) $b^2 - 4ac < 0$ no solution, ray misses sphere
(b) $b^2 - 4ac = 0$ one solution, ray may touch sphere at one intersection point
(c) $b^2 - 4ac > 0$ two solutions, ray may intersect sphere at two points

These three cases are shown in Figure 17-6 below. If the ray 'intersects' the sphere at two points, then the point with smaller t value is nearer and is the real intersection point. However, if the larger t value is negative, the ray points away from the sphere implying that the ray misses the sphere. Another situation is that the ray origin is inside the sphere. In this case, one root is positive and the other is negative; the positive root (larger t value) gives the real intersection point.

For the case of (b), if the t value is positive, the ray touches the sphere. If it is negative, it points away from the sphere and thus misses it (if we extend the ray backward, it then touches the sphere).

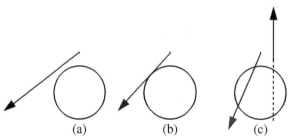

(a)   (b)   (c)

Figure 17-6 Three Cases of Ray-Sphere Intersection

17.3.2 Ray-Sphere Intersection Implementation

We can represent a sphere using a class with a *Point3* data member to denote the sphere center, and a double data member to denote the radius as shown below:

```
class Sphere {
public:
  Point3 C;    //sphere center
  double R;    //sphere radius
  Sphere (){  //default
    c = Point3( 0.0, 0.0, 0.0 );
    R = 1.0;
  }
  Sphere ( double r0 ) {
    C = Point3( 0.0, 0.0, 0.0 );
    R = r0;
  }
  Sphere ( const Point3 &c0, double r0 ){
    C = c0;
    R = r0;
  }
};
```

The following function, **intersect_ray_sphere**() of Listing 17-2, implements the ray-sphere intersection test.

Program Listing 17-2   Ray-Sphere Intersection Test

```
--------------------------------------------------------------------------
bool intersect_ray_sphere(const Ray& ray,   const Sphere &sphere, double &t)
{
    double r = sphere.R;

    //Compute a, b and c coefficients
    double a =  ray.D * ray.D;     //dot product

    Vector3 oc = ray.O - sphere.C;
    double b = 2 * oc * ray.D;
    double c = oc * oc - r * r;

    //Find discriminant
    double disc = b * b - 4 * a * c;

    // if discriminant is negative there are no real roots, so return
    // false as ray misses sphere
    if (disc < 0)
        return false;

    // compute the roots
    double distSqrt = sqrtf(disc);
    double t0 = (-b - distSqrt ) / ( 2 * a );
    double t1 = (-b + distSqrt ) / ( 2 * a );
    // make sure t0 is smaller than t1
    if (t0 > t1) {
        // if t0 is bigger than t1, swap them around
        double temp = t0;
```

```
        t0 = t1;
        t1 = temp;
    }

    // if t1 < 0, object is in the ray's negative direction
    // as a  consequence the ray misses the sphere
    if (t1 < 0)
        return false;

    // if t0 is less than zero, the intersection point is at t1
    if (t0 < 0)  {
        t = t1;
        return true;
    } else {  // else the intersection point is at t0
        t = t0;
        return true;
    }
}
```

17.4   Ray-Tapered Cylinder Intersection

A tapered cylinder is a frustum cone with unequal base and cap as shown in Figure 17-4 (b). For simplicity, we consider the side of the tapered cylinder as a wall along the z-direction, with radius of 1 at $z = 0$ and a smaller radius s at $z = 1$. Then the equation of the wall is given by:

$$x^2 + y^2 - (1 + (s - 1)z)^2 = 0 \quad \text{for } 0 \le z \le 1 \tag{17.24}$$

When $s = 1$, it is reduced to a generic cylinder and when $s = 0$, it is a generic cone.

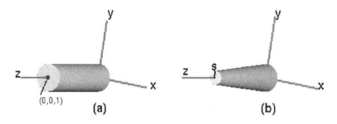

Figure 17-7   (a) A generic cylinder   (b) A tapered cylinder

There are four situations that a ray can intersect with a tapered cylinder:

1. The ray hits the wall twice.
2. The ray enters through the cap and hits the wall once.
3. The ray hits the wall and exits through the the base.
4. The ray enters the base and exits through the cap.

Ray-Wall Intersection

We again assume that a ray is given by (17.3) $(L(t) = O + t\mathbf{D})$. To determine whether the ray hits the wall, we substitute this into (17.24) for the intersection point, and obtain a quadratic equation of the form:

$$at^2 + 2bt + c = 0 \tag{17.25}$$

where

$$\begin{aligned} a &= \mathbf{D}_x^2 + \mathbf{D}_y^2 - d^2 \\ b &= O_x \mathbf{D}_x + O_y \mathbf{D}_y - Fd \\ c &= O_x^2 + O_y^2 - F^2 \\ d &= (s-1)\mathbf{D}_x \\ F &= 1 + (s-1)O_z \end{aligned}$$

Whether the ray hits the wall or not is determined by the discriminant Det of the quadratic equation (17.25), which is

$$Det = (2b)^2 - 4ac = 4(b^2 - ac) \qquad (17.26)$$

We have the following situations:

1. If $Det < 0$, no intersection occurs (the ray passes by the cylinder).
2. If $Det \geq 0$, the ray hits the infinite wall and the parameter t_{hit} can be found. To determine whether the ray hits the cylinder wall, we can check whether $0 \leq z \leq 1$ at t_{hit}. If yes, the ray hits the cylinder wall.

Ray-Base Intersection

To determine whether the ray hits the base, we apply the ray-plane intersection check with the plane (plane containing base) described by $z = 0$. If the ray hits the plane at point $(x, y, 0)$, then the hit spot lies within the base if $x^2 + y^2 < 1$.

Ray-Cap Intersection

In this case we apply the ray-plane intersection check with plane $z = 1$ (plane containing cap). If the ray hits the plane at point $(x, y, 1)$, then the hit spot lies within the cap if $x^2 + y^2 < s^2$.

17.5 Ray-Quadric Intersection

A *quadric* is a surface in Euclidean space consisting of points that satisfy a polynomial of degree 2, which is of the form,

$$f(x, y, z) = Ax^2 + By^2 + Cz^2 + Dxy + Exz + Fyz + Gx + Hy + Jz + K = 0 \qquad (17.27)$$

where $A, B, C, D, E, F, G, H, J, K$ are some constants. Examples of quadrics include spheres, cylinders, ellipsoids, paraboloids, hyperboloids, and cones.

To determine whether the ray hits the quadric, we can again substitute the ray equation,

$$(x(t), y(t), z(t)) = L(t) = O + t\mathbf{D} \qquad (17.28)$$

into the quadric equation (17.26). We will again obtain a quadratic equation of t,

$$at^2 + 2bt + c = 0 \qquad (17.29)$$

and the discriminant in the form of (17.26) determines whether the ray hits the object:

1. If $Det > 0$, the ray may hit the quadric surface twice (two t_{hit} solutions).
2. If $Det = 0$, the ray may hit the quadric surface once (one t_{hit} solution).
3. If $Det < 0$, the ray misses the quadric (no solution).

Chapter 18   Vertex Array

18.1   Function Calls

We have discussed that we can specify the shapes of a graphics object by calling a sequence of **glVertex*** commands, which are enclosed within a pair of **glBegin/glEnd** functions. Actually, each **glVertex*** command is also a function. This is not an efficient method because function calls are expensive as they involve pushing and popping parameters onto a stack, and this method involves a lot of redundant function calls; the shared vertices have to be specified again and again. For example, consider rendering a cube, which is shown in Figure 18-1 below. A cube has 6 faces and 8 vertices. We need 4 vertices to specify a face. To render a cube using **glBegin/glEnd**, we will process a total of $6 \times 4 = 24$ vertices though only 8 different vertices exist.

   To avoid redundant function calls, OpenGL provides vertex array routines to process arrays of vertices with fewer function calls. Vertex arrays make graphics programming more efficient and effective.

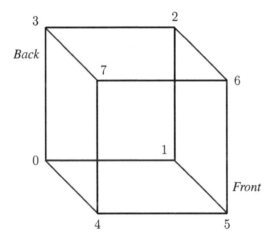

Figure 18-1   A Cube With Indexed Vertices

18.2   Vertex Array Process

There are three steps in the process of using vertex array routines:

1. **Enabling Arrays**.
   We enable the usage of vertex arrays with the command **glEnableClientState**, which has protocol:

void glEnableClientState(GLenum array)
Specifies the array to enable.
Acceptable Symbolic constants:
GL_VERTEX_ARRAY, GL_COLOR_ARRAY, GL_INDEX_ARRAY,
GL_NORMAL_ARRAY, GL_TEXTURE_COORD_ARRAY, and
GL_EDGE_FLAG_ARRAY

For example, if we use lighting, we need to define a surface normal for each vertex. In this situation, we have to activate both the surface normal and vertex coordinate arrays with:

315

```
glEnableClientState ( GL_NORMAL_ARRAY );
glEnableClientState ( GL_VERTEX_ARRAY );
```

The lighting effect can be turned off by:

```
glDisableClientState(GL_NORMAL_ARRAY);
```

2. **Specifying Data for the Arrays**.
We specify the data for a vertex array with the function **glVertexPointer**:

void glVertexPointer(GLint size, GLenum type, GLsizei stride, const GLvoid *pointer);
Specifies where spatial coordinate data can be accessed; *pointer* is the memory address of the first coordinate of the first vertex in the array; *type* specifies the data type (GL_SHORT, GL_INT, GL_FLOAT, or GL_DOUBLE) of each coordinate in the array; *size* is the number of coordinates per vertex, which must be 2, 3, or 4; *stride* is the byte offset between consecutive vertexes; if *stride* is 0, the vertices are tightly packed in the array.

Commands for specifying other array data include:

```
void glColorPointer(GLint size,GLenum type,GLsizei stride,
                                      const GLvoid *pointer);
void glIndexPointer(GLenum type,GLsizei stride,
                                      const GLvoid *pointer);
void glNormalPointer(GLenum type,GLsizei stride,
                                      const GLvoid *pointer);
void glTexCoordPointer(GLint size,GLenum type,GLsizei stride,
                                      const GLvoid *pointer);
void glEdgeFlagPointer(GLsizei stride, const GLvoid *pointer);
```

The following table shows various vertex array sizes (Values per Vertex) and data types:

Command	**Sizes**	**Values for type Argument**
glVertexPointer	2, 3, 4	GL_SHORT, GL_INT, GL_FLOAT, GL_DOUBLE
glNormalPointer	3	GL_BYTE, GL_SHORT, GL_INT, GL_FLOAT, GL_DOUBLE
glColorPointer	3, 4	GL_BYTE, GL_UNSIGNED_BYTE, GL_SHORT, GL_UNSIGNED_SHORT, GL_INT, GL_UNSIGNED_INT, GL_FLOAT, GL_DOUBLE
glIndexPointer	1	GL_UNSIGNED_BYTE, GL_SHORT, GL_INT, GL_FLOAT, GL_DOUBLE
glTexCoordPointer	1, 2, 3, 4	GL_SHORT, GL_INT, GL_FLOAT, GL_DOUBLE
glEdgeFlagPointer	1	no type argument (type of data must be GLboolean)

The following is an example of enabling and loading vertex arrays, which specify 6 vertices, each with 2 coordinates and 6 different colors, each with 3 values for the RGB components:

```
int vertices[] = { 20,  20,           100, 300,
                  180,  20,           180, 300,
                  245,  20,           300, 300};
float colors[] = {0.8, 0.2, 0.2,     0.2, 0.8, 1.0,
                  0.6, 1.0, 0.2,     0.8, 0.8, 0.6,
                  0.3, 0.3, 0.3,     0.6, 0.6, 0.6};

glEnableClientState (GL_COLOR_ARRAY);
glEnableClientState (GL_VERTEX_ARRAY);

glColorPointer (3, GL_FLOAT, 0, colors);
glVertexPointer (2, GL_INT, 0, vertices);
```

In the above example, the *stride* values are 0, meaning that the data are closely packed. To show the usage of the parameter *stride*, which tells OpenGL how to access the data we provide, we consider another example where the vertex coordinates and color values are stored in the same array:

```
float mixed_data[] = { 20.0,  20.0,0.0,     0.8,0.2,0.2,
                      100.0,300.0,0.0,     0.2,0.8,1.0,
                      180.0, 20.0,0.0,     0.6,1.0,0.2,
                      180.0,300.0,0.0,     0.8,0.8,0.6,
                      245.0, 20.0,0.0,     0.3,0.3,0.3,
                      300.0,300.0,0.0,     0.6,0.6,0.6};
```

In this *mixed_data* array, the left column contains the vertex coordinates and the right column contains the corresponding color values. The *stride* parameter allows a vertex array to access its desired data at regular intervals in the array, and its value should be the number of bytes between the starts of two successive pointer elements, or zero, which is the special case when the data are tightly packed. So in this example, we provide access to the vertex coordinates with the command:

```
glVertexPointer(3,GL_FLOAT,6*sizeof(float),mixed_data);
```

For the color values, we start from the fourth element of the array *mixed_data*. This can can be accomplished by the command:

```
glColorPointer(3,GL_FLOAT,6*sizeof(float),mixed_data+3);
```

3. **Dereferencing and Rendering**.
   We dereference **a single array element** with **glArrayElement**:

void glArrayElement(GLint ith)
Obtains the data of one (the *ith*) vertex for all currently enabled arrays. For the vertex coordinate array, the corresponding command would be **glVertex**[*size*][*type*]v(), where *size* is one of [2,3,4], and *type* is one of [s,i,f,d] for GLshort, GLint, GLfloat, and GLdouble respectively. Both *size* and *type* were defined by **glVertexPointer**(). For other enabled arrays, **glArrayElement**() calls **glEdgeFlagv**(), **glTexCoord**[*size*][*type*]v(), **glColor**[*size*][*type*]v(), **glIndex**[*type*]v(), and **glNormal**[*type*]v(). If the vertex coordinate array is enabled, the **glVertex*v**() routine is executed last, after the execution (if enabled) of up to five corresponding array values.

The following is an example of drawing a triangle using this command:

```
glEnableClientState (GL_COLOR_ARRAY);
glEnableClientState (GL_VERTEX_ARRAY);
glColorPointer (3, GL_FLOAT, 0, colors);
glVertexPointer (2, GL_INT, 0, vertices);

glBegin(GL_TRIANGLES);
  glArrayElement (2);
  glArrayElement (3);
  glArrayElement (4);
glEnd();
```

When we execute the above code, the last five statements has the same effect as the following code:

```
glBegin(GL_TRIANGLES);
  glColor3fv(colors+(2*3));
  glVertex2iv(vertices+(2*2));
  glColor3fv(colors+(3*3));
  glVertex2iv(vertices+(3*2));
  glColor3fv(colors+(4*3));
  glVertex2iv(vertices+(4*2));
glEnd();
```

We dereference **a list of array elements** with **glDrawElements**:

void glDrawElements(GLenum mode, GLsizei count, GLenum type, void *indices)
Specifies multiple geometric primitives with very few subroutine calls. Instead of calling a GL function to pass each vertex attribute, we can use **glVertexAttribPointer** to prespecify separate arrays of vertex attributes and use them to construct a sequence of primitives with a single call to **glDrawElements**.
When **glDrawElements** is called, it uses count sequential elements from an enabled array, starting at *indices* to construct a sequence of geometric primitives; *type* specifies the type of *indices* values, which must be GL_UNSIGNED_BYTE or GL_UNSIGNED_SHORT. *mode* specifies what kind of primitives are constructed and how the array elements construct these primitives (GL_POLYGON, GL_POINTS,...). If more than one array is enabled, each is used. We can call **glEnableVertexAttribArray** and **glDisableVertexAttribArray** to enable and disable a generic vertex attribute array.

This command almost has the same effect as:

```
int i;
glBegin (mode);
  for (i = 0; i < count; i++)
    glArrayElement(indices[i]);
glEnd();
```

18.3   Drawing a Cube

As an example of illustrating the usage of the vertex array commands discussed above, we discuss drawing a colored cube here. Suppose the vertices of the cube is numbered as shown in Figure 18-1 above, and the vertex and color data are defined by:

```
GLint vertices[] = {-1, -1, -1,    //vertex 0
                     1, -1, -1,    //vertex 1
                     1,  1, -1,    // 2
                    -1,  1, -1,    // 3
                    -1, -1,  1,    // 4
                     1, -1,  1,    // 5
                     1,  1,  1,    // 6
                    -1,  1,  1};   // 7

GLfloat colors[] = {1.0, 0.2, 0.2,    //color at vertex 0
                    0.2, 0.2, 1.0,    //color at vertex 1
                    0.8, 1.0, 0.2,
                    0.7, 0.7, 0.7,
                    0.3, 0.3, 0.3,
                    0.5, 0.5, 0.5,
                    1.0, 0.0, 0.0,
                    0.0, 1.0, 0.0};   //color at vertex 7

glVertexPointer (3, GL_INT, 0, vertices);
glColorPointer (3, GL_FLOAT, 0, colors);
```

Suppose we have made the appropriate setup of viewing and have enabled the usage of vertex array. We can render the cube with the commands:

```
glBegin( GL_QUADS );
  glArrayElement ( 4 );      // front face (see notes)
  glArrayElement ( 5 );
  glArrayElement ( 6 );
  glArrayElement ( 7 );

  glArrayElement ( 0 );      // back face
  glArrayElement ( 3 );
  glArrayElement ( 2 );
  glArrayElement ( 1 );

  glArrayElement ( 1 );      // right face
  glArrayElement ( 2 );
  glArrayElement ( 6 );
  glArrayElement ( 5 );
  .....
glEnd();
```

In this method, we have to call **glArrayElement** 24 times. A better method is to define the indices of each face and draw it with the **glDrawElements** command:

```
GLubyte frontIndices[] = {4, 5, 6, 7};
GLubyte backIndices[]  = {0, 3, 2, 1};
GLubyte rightIndices[] = {1, 2, 6, 5};
GLubyte leftIndices[]  = {0, 4, 7, 3};
GLubyte topIndices[]   = {2, 3, 7, 6};
```

```
GLubyte bottomIndices[]= {0, 1, 5, 4};

glDrawElements(GL_QUADS, 4, GL_UNSIGNED_BYTE, frontIndices);
glDrawElements(GL_QUADS, 4, GL_UNSIGNED_BYTE, rightIndices);
glDrawElements(GL_QUADS, 4, GL_UNSIGNED_BYTE, bottomIndices);
glDrawElements(GL_QUADS, 4, GL_UNSIGNED_BYTE, backIndices);
glDrawElements(GL_QUADS, 4, GL_UNSIGNED_BYTE, leftIndices);
glDrawElements(GL_QUADS, 4, GL_UNSIGNED_BYTE, topIndices);
```

Using **glDrawElements**, we only need to call the function 6 times. Also note that we do not need to enclose the functions with the **glBegin/End** pair. Better still, we can put all indices in one array and draw the cube with only one command:

```
GLubyte allIndices[] = {4, 5, 6, 7, 0, 3, 2, 1, 1, 2, 6, 5,
                        0, 4, 7, 3, 2, 3, 7, 6, 0, 1, 5, 4};
glDrawElements(GL_QUADS, 24, GL_UNSIGNED_BYTE, allIndices);
```

Figure 18-2 shows two cubes that are rendered with these methods.

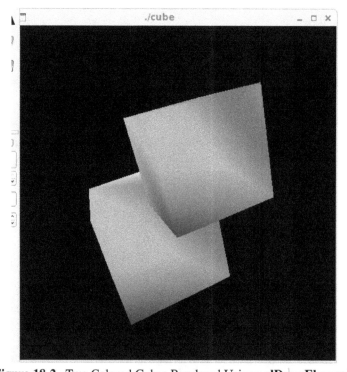

Figure 18-2 Two Colored Cubes Rendered Usinge **glDrawElements**

Chapter 19 OpenGL Shading Language (GLSL)

19.1 Extending OpenGL

The OpenGL architecture we have presented in previous chapters is called fixed-pipeline architecture, in which the functionality of each processing stage is fixed. The user can control the parameters to the functions but the underlying processing of the functions are fixed. All OpenGL versions up to 1.5 are based on this fixed-function pipeline. Figure 19-1 below shows this traditional fixed function pipeline architecture:

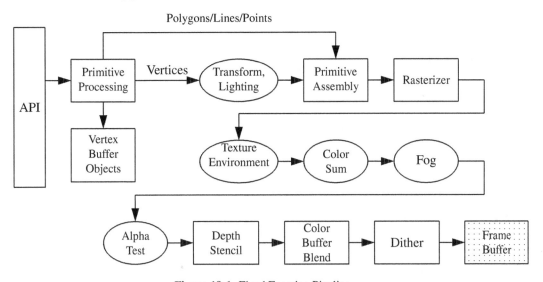

Figure 19-1. Fixed Function Pipeline

Before version 2.0, to modify OpenGL we must define the new features through extensions. Consequently, a lot of OpenGL functionality is available in the form of extensions that expose new hardware functionality. OpenGL has well-defined extensions for hardware vendors to define and implement special graphics features. For complex applications, there is a trend in graphics hardware to replace fixed functionality with programmability, including vertex processing and fragment processing.

Since version 2.0, besides supporting the fixed pipeline architecture, OpenGL also supports the programmable pipeline, which replaces the fixed function transformations and fragment pipeline by programmable shaders as shown in Figure 19-2 below.

The OpenGL Shading Language (glsl) is designed to address the programmable issue and is part of the OpenGL distribution. It allows programmers to write shaders to alter the processing of the graphics attributes along the pipeline. GLSL is an extension of the original OpenGL with the following properties:

1. GLSL is included in OpenGL 2.0, which was released in 2004.
2. Other competing shading languages include Cg (C for Graphics), which is cross platform and HLSL (High Level Shading Language) by Microsoft, which is used in DirectX.
3. GLSL is part of OpenGL. Therefore, it is naturally easily integrated with OpenGL programs.
4. It is a C-like language with some C++ features,
5. It is mainly used for processing numerics, but not for strings or characters.
6. OpenGL 1.5 has fixed function pipeline.
7. OpenGL 2.0 allows processors to be programmed, introducing GLSL, which is approved by OpenGL Architectural Review Board (ARB).

8. With programmed shaders, data flow from the application to the vertex processor, on to the fragment processor and ultimately to the frame buffer. This allows vendors to produce faster graphics hardware with more parallel features.

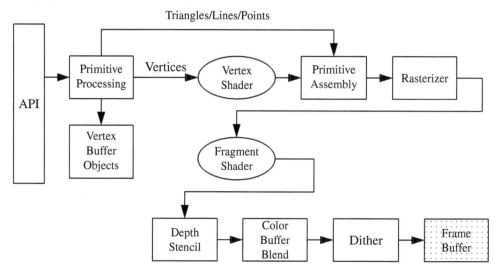

Figure 19-2. Programmable Pipeline

19.2   OpenGL Shaders Execution Model

We can consider a driver as a piece of software that manages the access of a hardware. In this sense, we can view OpenGL libraries as drivers because they manage shared access to the underlying graphics hardware; applications communicate with graphics hardware by calling OpenGL functions. An OpenGL shader is embedded in an OpenGL application and may be viewed as an object in the driver to access the hardware. We use the command **glCreateShader**() to allocate within the OpenGL driver the data structures needed to store an OpenGL shader. The source code of a shader is provided by an application by calling **glShaderSource**() and we have to provide the source code as a null-terminated string to this function.. Figure 19-3 below shows the steps to create a shader program for execution.

There are two kinds of shaders, the vertex shaders and the fragment shaders. A **vertex shader** (program) is a shader running on a **vertex processor**, which is a programmable unit that operates on incoming vertex values. This processor usually performs traditional graphics operations including the following:

1. vertex transformation
2. normal transformation and normalization
3. texture coordinate generation
4. texture coordinate transformation
5. lighting
6. color material application

The following is an example of a simple "pass-through" vertex shader, which does not do anything:

```
//A simple pass-through vertex shader
void main()
{
   gl_Position = gl_ProjectionMatrix * gl_ModelViewMatrix * gl_Vertex;
}
```

A **fragment shader** is a shader running on a **fragment processor,** which is a programmable unit that operates on fragment values. A fragment is a pixel plus its attributes such as color and depth. A fragment shader is executed after the rasterization. Therefore a fragment processor operates on each fragment rather than on each vertex. It usually performs traditional graphics operations including:

1. operations on interpolated values
2. texture access, and application
3. fog effects
4. color sum
5. pixel zoom
6. scaling
7. color table lookup
8. convolution
9. color matrix operations

The following is an example of a simple fragment shader which sets the color of each fragment for rendering.

```
//A simple fragment shader
void main()   {
  gl_FragColor = gl_FrontColor;
}
```

19.3   OpenGL Shading Language API

Figure 19-3 below shows the development steps of a glsl shader program.

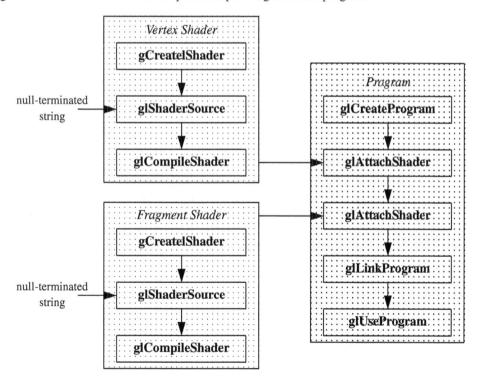

Figure 19-3 Shader Program Development

Table 19-1 below lists the OpenGL functions involved in the process.

Table 19-1 OpenGL Commands for Embedding Shaders

glCreateShader()	Creates one or more shader objects.
glShaderSource()	Provides source codes of shaders.
glCompileShader()	Compiles each of the shaders.
glCreateProgram()	Creates a program object.
glAttachShader()	Attach all shader objects to the program.
glLinkProgram()	Link the program object.
glUseProgram()	Install the shaders as part of the OpenGL program.

The following are the normal steps to develop an OpenGL shader program.

1. **Creating a Shader Object**

   We first create an empty shader object using the function **glCreateShader**, which has the following prototype:

   Gluint **glCreateShader** (GLenum *shaderType*)

   Creates an empty shader.

   shaderType specifies the type of shader to be created. It can be either GL_VERTEX_SHADER or GL_FRAGMENT_SHADER.

   Return: A non-zero integer handle for future reference.

   ---

2. **Providing Source Code for the Shader**

   We pass the source code to the shader as a null-terminated string using the function **glShaderSource** which has the prototype:

   ---

   void **glShaderSource** (GLuint *shader*, GLsizei *count*, const GLchar ****string*, const GLint **lengthp*)

   Defines a shader's source code.

   shader is the shader object created by glCreateShader().

   string is the array of strings specifying the source code of the shader.

   count is the number of strings in the array.

   lengthp points to an array specifying the lengths of the strings. If NULL, the strings are NULL-terminated.

   The source code can be hard-coded as a string in the OpenGL program or it can be saved in a separate file and read into an array as a null-terminated string. The following example shows how this is done.

   ```
   struct stat statBuf;
   FILE* fp = fopen ( fileName, "r" );
   char* buf;

   stat ( fileName, &statBuf );
   buf = (char*) malloc ( statBuf.st_size + 1 * sizeof(char) );
   fread ( buf, 1, statBuf.st_size, fp );
   buf[statBuf.st_size] = '\0';
   fclose ( fp );
   return buf;
   ```

   In the example, the **stat**() function gives detailed information about a file; from it we obtain the size of the file containing the shader source code and allocate the buffer *buf* to hold the string. At the end of the string we save the null character '\0' to indicate its end.

3. **Compiling Shader Object**

We use the function **glCompileShader** to compile the shader source code to object code. This function has the following prototype.

---

void **glCompileShader** (GLuint *shader*)

Compiles the source code strings stored in the shader object *shader*.

The function **glShaderInfoLog** gives the compilation log.

---

4. Linking and Using Shaders

Each shader object is compiled independently. To create a shader program, we need to link all the shader objects to the OpenGL application. These are done within the C/C++ application using the functions **glCreateProgram, glAttachShader, glLinkProgram**, and **glUseProgram**, which have the prototypes listed below. These are done while we are running the C/C++ application. Performing the steps of compiling and linking shader objects are simply making C function calls.

GLuint **glCreateProgram** (void)

Creates an empty program object and returns a non-zero integer handle for future reference.

void **glAttachShader** (GLuint *program*, GLuint *shader*)

Attaches the shader object specified by *shader* to the program object specified by *program*.

void **glLinkProgram** (GLuint *program*)

Links the program objects specified by *program*.

void **glUseProgram** (GLuint *program*)

Installs the program object specified by *program* as part of current rendering state.

If *program* is 0, the programmable processors are disabled, and fixed functionality is used for both vertex and fragment processing.

---

5. **Cleaning Up**

At the end, we need to release all the resources taken up by the shaders. The clean up is done by the commands,

void **glDeleteShader** (GLuint *shader*),

void **glDeleteProgram** (GLuint *program*),

void **glDetachShader** (GLuint *program*, GLuint *shader*).

Listing 19-1 (a)-(c) below is a complete example of a shader program; the OpenGL application is the C/C++ program **tests.cpp**, which does the shader creation, reading shader source code, shader compilation and shader linking. The shader source code for the vertex shader is saved in the text file **tests.vert**, and the code for the fragment shader is saved in **tests.frag**. In compiling **tests.cpp**, we need to link the GL extension library by "-lGLEW". If we compile "tests.cpp" to the executable "tests", we can run the shader program by typing "./tests" and press 'Enter'. Note that when we change the code of a shader ("tests.vert" or "tests.frag"), we do not need to recompile the C/C++ program "tests.cpp". We just need to execute "./tests" and the changed features will take place. Figure 19-4 below shows the output of executing "tests".

Program Listing 19-1   Complete Example of a Shader Program

(a) tests.cpp

```
/*
  tests.cpp
  Sample program showing how to write GL shader programs.
  Shader sources are in files "tests.vert" and "tests.frag".
*/
#include <stdlib.h>
#include <stdio.h>
#include <string.h>
#include <fcntl.h>
#include <sys/stat.h>
#include <GL/glew.h>
#include <GL/glut.h>

using namespace std;

// Global handles for the current program object, with its two shader objects
GLuint programObject = 0;
GLuint vertexShaderObject = 0;
GLuint fragmentShaderObject = 0;
static GLint win = 0;

int readShaderSource(char *fileName, GLchar **shader )
{
    // Allocate memory to hold the source of our shaders.
    FILE *fp;
    int count, pos, shaderSize;

    fp = fopen( fileName, "r");
    if ( !fp )
        return 0;
    struct stat statBuf;
    stat ( fileName, &statBuf );
    shaderSize = statBuf.st_size;
    if ( shaderSize <= 0 ){
        printf("Shader %s empty\n", fileName);
        return 0;
    }

    *shader = (GLchar *) malloc( shaderSize + 1);

    // Read the source code
    count = (int) fread(*shader, 1, shaderSize, fp);
    (*shader)[count] = '\0';

    if (ferror(fp))
        count = 0;

    fclose(fp);

    return 1;
}
```

```
int installShaders ( const GLchar *vs, const GLchar *fs )
{
    GLint  vertCompiled, fragCompiled;  // status values
    GLint  linked;

    // Create a vertex shader object and a fragment shader object
    vertexShaderObject = glCreateShader ( GL_VERTEX_SHADER );
    fragmentShaderObject = glCreateShader ( GL_FRAGMENT_SHADER );

    // Load source code strings into shaders, compile and link
    glShaderSource ( vertexShaderObject, 1, &vs, NULL );
    glShaderSource ( fragmentShaderObject, 1, &fs, NULL );

    glCompileShader ( vertexShaderObject );
    glGetShaderiv ( vertexShaderObject, GL_COMPILE_STATUS, &vertCompiled );

    glCompileShader ( fragmentShaderObject );
    glGetShaderiv( fragmentShaderObject, GL_COMPILE_STATUS, &fragCompiled);

    if (!vertCompiled || !fragCompiled)
        return 0;

    // Create a program object and attach the two compiled shaders
    programObject = glCreateProgram();
    glAttachShader( programObject, vertexShaderObject);
    glAttachShader( programObject, fragmentShaderObject);

    // Link the program object
    glLinkProgram(programObject);
    glGetProgramiv(programObject, GL_LINK_STATUS, &linked);

    if (!linked)
        return 0;

    // Install program object as part of current state
    glUseProgram ( programObject );

    return 1;
}

int init(void)
{
    GLchar *VertexShaderSource, *FragmentShaderSource;
    int loadstatus = 0;

    const char *version  = (const char *) glGetString ( GL_VERSION );
    if (version[0] < '2' || version[1] != '.') {
       printf("This program requires OpenGL >= 2.x, found %s\n", version);
       return 0;
    }
    readShaderSource("tests.vert", &VertexShaderSource );
    readShaderSource("tests.frag", &FragmentShaderSource );
    loadstatus = installShaders(VertexShaderSource, FragmentShaderSource);
    if ( !loadstatus ) {
      printf("\nCompilation of shaders not successful!\n");
    }

    return loadstatus;
}

static void reshape(int width, int height)
{
    glMatrixMode(GL_PROJECTION);
```

```
   glLoadIdentity();
   glFrustum(-1.0, 1.0, -1.0, 1.0, 5.0, 25.0);
   glMatrixMode(GL_MODELVIEW);
   glLoadIdentity();
   glTranslatef(0.0f, 0.0f, -15.0f);
}
void CleanUp(void)
{
   glDeleteShader(vertexShaderObject);
   glDeleteShader(fragmentShaderObject);
   glDeleteProgram(programObject);
   glutDestroyWindow(win);
}

void display(void)
{
   glClearColor ( 1.0, 1.0, 1.0, 0.0 ); //get white background color
   glClear ( GL_COLOR_BUFFER_BIT | GL_DEPTH_BUFFER_BIT );
   glColor3f ( 0, 1, 0 );          //green, no effect if shader is loaded
   glLineWidth ( 4 );
   glutWireSphere ( 2.0, 16, 8 );
   glutSwapBuffers();
   glFlush();
}

int main(int argc, char *argv[])
{
   glutInit(&argc, argv);
   glutInitWindowPosition( 0, 0 );
   glutInitWindowSize ( 300, 300 );
   glutInitDisplayMode ( GLUT_RGB | GLUT_DOUBLE | GLUT_DEPTH );
   win = glutCreateWindow(argv[0]);
   glutReshapeFunc ( reshape );
   glutDisplayFunc ( display );
   // Initialize the "OpenGL Extension Wrangler" library
   glewInit();

   int successful = init();
   if ( successful )
     glutMainLoop();

   return 0;
}
```

(b) tests.vert
_____

```
// tests.vert : a minimal vertex shader
void main(void)
{
   gl_Position = gl_ModelViewProjectionMatrix * gl_Vertex;
}
```

(c) tests.frag
_____

```
// tests.frag : a minimal fragment shader
void main(void)
{
   gl_FragColor = vec4( 1, 0, 0, 1);   //red color
}
```

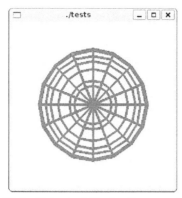

Figure 19-4   Output of Shader Program **tests.cpp**

19.4   Data Types in GLSL

There are four main data types in GLSL: **float, int, bool**, and **sampler**. Vector types are available for the first three types:

vec2, vec3, vec4	2D, 3D and 4D floating point vector
ivec2, ivec3, ivec4	2D, 3D and 4D integer vector
bvec2, bvec3, bvec4	2D, 3D and 4D boolean vectors

For floats there are also matrix types:

mat2, mat3, mat4	$2 \times 2, 3 \times 3, 4 \times 4$ floating point matrix

Samplers are types used for representing textures:

sampler1D, sampler2D, sampler3D	1D, 2D and 3D texture
samplerCube	Cube Map texture
sampler1Dshadow, sampler2Dshadow	1D and 2D depth-component texture

Attributes, Uniforms and Varyings

GLSL shaders have three different input-output data types for passing data between vertex and fragment shaders, and the OpenGL application. The data types are **uniform, attribute** and **varying**. They must be declared as global (visible to the whole shader object). The variables have the following properties:

1. **Uniforms** : These are read-only variables (i.e. A shader object can only read the variables but cannot change them.). Their values do not change during a rendering. Therefore, Uniform variable values are assigned outside the scope of **glBegin/glEnd**. Uniform variables are used for sharing data among an application program, vertex shaders, and fragment shaders.

2. **Attributes**: These are also read-only variables. They are only available in vertex shaders. They are used for variables that change at most once per vertex in a vertex shader. There are two types of attribute variables, user-defined and built-in. The following are examples of user-defined attributes:

    attribute float x;

attribute vec3 velocity, acceleration;

Built-in variables include OpenGL state variables such as color, position, and normal; the following are some examples:

gl_Vertex
gl_Color

3. **Varyings**: These are read/write variables, which are used for passing data from a vertex shader to a fragment shader. They are defined on a per-vertex basis but are interpolated over the primitive by the rasterizer. They can be user-defined or built-in.

Built-in Types

The following tables list some more of the GLSL built-in types.

Table 19-2   Built-in Attributes (for Vertex Shaders)

gl_Vertex	4D vector representing the vertex position
gl_Normal	3D vector representing the vertex normal
gl_Color	4D vector representing the vertex color
gl_MultiTexCoord$n$	4D vector representing the texture coordinate of texture n

Table 19-3   Built-in Uniforms (for Vertex and Fragment Shaders)

gl_ModelViewMatrix	4×4 Matrix representing the model-view matrix
gl_ModelViewProjectionMatrix	4×4 Model-view-projection matrix
gl_NormalMatrix	3×3 Matrix used for normal transformation

Table 19-4   Built-in Varyings (for Data Sharing between Shaders)

gl_FrontColor	4D vector representing the primitives front color
gl_BackColor	4D vector representing the primitives back color
gl_TexCoord[n]	4D vector representing the n-th texture coordinate
gl_Position	4D vector representing the final processed vertex position (vertex shader only)
gl_FragColor	4D vector representing the final color written in the frame buffer (fragment shader only)
gl_FragDepth	float representing the depth written in the depth buffer (fragment shader only)

GLSL has many built in functions, including

1. trigonometric functions: **sin, cos, tan**
2. inverse trigonometric functions: **asin, acos, atan**
3. mathematical functions: **pow, log2, sqrt, abs, max, min**
4. geometrical functions: **length, distance, normalize, reflect**

Built-in types provide users an effective way to access OpenGL variables as they are mapped to the OpenGL states. For example, if we call **glLightfv**(GL_LIGHT0, GL_POSITION, *myLight-Position*), its value is available as a **uniform** using gl_LightSource[0].position in a vertex and/or fragment shader.

The following is an example of using various data types; it consists of a vertex shader and a fragment shader for defining a modified Phong lighting model.

Program Listing 19-2   Shaders for Modified Phong Lighting

(a) Vertex Shader: phong.vert

```
//phong.vert
varying vec3 N;   //normal direction
varying vec3 L;   //light source direction
varying vec3 E;   //eye position

void main(void)
{
  gl_Position =gl_ModelViewMatrix*gl_Vertex;
  vec4 eyePosition = gl_ModelViewProjectionMatrix*gl_Vertex;
  vec4 eyeLightPosition = gl_LightSource[0].position;

  N = normalize( gl_NormalMatrix*gl_Normal );
  L = eyeLightPosition.xyz - eyePosition.xyz;
  E = -eyePosition.xyz;
}
```

(b) Fragment Shader: phong.frag

```
//phong.frag
varying vec3 N;
varying vec3 L;
varying vec3 E;
void main()
{
  vec3 norm = normalize(N);
  vec3 lightv = normalize(L);
  vec3 viewv = normalize(E);
  vec3 halfv = normalize(lightv + viewv);
  float f;
  if(dot(lightv, norm)>= 0.0) f =1.0;
  else f = 0.0;

  float Kd = max(0.0, dot(lightv, norm));
  float Ks = pow(max(0.0, dot(norm, halfv)), gl_FrontMaterial.shininess);
  vec4 diffuse = Kd * gl_FrontMaterial.diffuse*gl_LightSource[0].diffuse;
  vec4 ambient = gl_FrontMaterial.ambient*gl_LightSource[0].ambient;
  vec4 specular = f*Ks*gl_FrontMaterial.specular*gl_LightSource[0].specular;
  gl_FragColor = ambient + diffuse + specular;
}
```

19.5   The OpenGL Extension Wrangler Library

To develop applications with glsl, we also need the *OpenGL Extension Wrangler Library* (GLEW), which is a cross-platform open-source C/C++ extension loading library. It is a simple tool providing efficient run-time mechanisms to determine the OpenGL extensions that are supported on the target platform. An application uses the OpenGL core and extension functionality in a single header file. The library has been tested on a various operating systems, including Windows, Linux, Mac OS X, FreeBSD, Irix, and Solaris. Currently, the library supports OpenGL 4.4 and the following extensions:

1. OpenGL extensions
2. WGL extensions
3. GLX extensions

We can download the package from the site:

```
http://sourceforge.net/projects/glew/
```

The compilation and installation process is simple and is described in the *README.txt* file of the package. The version that we have used to test the programs described here is *glew-1.11.0*.

19.6   Drawing Polygons

To make our code easier to be ported to OpenGL ES platforms, the graphics objects of many of our examples are drawn using triangles. OpenGL ES, where ES stands for *embedded systems*, is a streamlined version of OpenGL for rendering sophisticated 3D graphics on handheld and embedded devices.

19.6.1   Creating a *Shader* Class

We have seen in Section 19.3 that we always need to call the same few functions to create shaders that render graphics objects. It will be more convenient if we create a base class called *Shader* to call these functions and do the miscellaneous initializations such as compiling and linking. When we draw an actual shape such as a triangle or a rectangle, we can always create a corresponding class that extends this base class to draw the actual shape. This concept is shown in Figure 19-5 below.

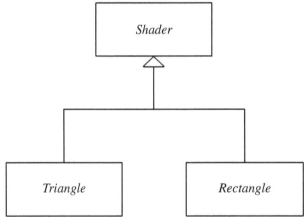

Figure 19-5 *Shader* Class and Typical Subclasses

Subclasses or applications should provide the shader source codes to the functions of the *Shader* class, which does the routine work of creating shader programs and objects, compiling the shader source code, linking the shaders, attaching the shaders, using the shader programs and cleaning up as shown in Figure 19-3 above. The following shows the members of this class:

```
------------------------------------------------------------------
//Shader.h
class Shader
{
  public:
    int program;
```

```
      int vertexShader;
      int fragmentShader;
      char *infoLog;
      Shader();
      ~Shader();
      int loadShader (int shaderType, const string *shaderCode );
      bool createShader( const string *vs, const string *fs );
      void cleanUp();
   };
```

Typically, an application (or a subclass) calls the function **createShader** of this class to create a vertex shader and a fragment shader. The application provides pointers as input string parameters, pointing to the source code of the vertex shader (*vs* and that of the fragment shader (*fs*). If the application only needs to create one shader, it can set the other pointer pointing to **NULL**. The following is its implementation:

```
bool  Shader::createShader( const string *vs, const string *fs )
{
  // create empty OpenGL Program, load, attach, and link shaders
  program = glCreateProgram();
  if ( vs != NULL ) {
    vertexShader = loadShader( GL_VERTEX_SHADER, vs);
    // add the vertex shader to program
    glAttachShader(program,vertexShader);
  }
  if ( vs != NULL ) {
    fragmentShader = loadShader( GL_FRAGMENT_SHADER, fs);
    // add the fragment shader to program
    glAttachShader(program,fragmentShader);
  }
  glLinkProgram(program); // creates program executables
  int linked;
  glGetProgramiv(program, GL_LINK_STATUS, &linked);

  if (!linked) {
    printf( "Shader not linked!\n" );
    return false;        // mission failed
  }

  glUseProgram( program); // use shader program

  return true;           // mission successful
}
```

This function actually calls the other member function, **loadShader** to create a shader object and compile it. The function **loadShader** also saves the log information in memory, and the data member pointer *infoLog* points at the memory. If necessary, the application can examine the log for debugging or other purposes. The following is its implementation:

```
int Shader::loadShader (int shaderType, const string *shaderCode)
{
  // create a vertex shader type ( GL_VERTEX_SHADER)
```

```
  // or a fragment shader type ( GL_FRAGMENT_SHADER)
  int shader =  glCreateShader( shaderType);

  // pass source code to the shader and compile it
  char *strPointer = (char *) shaderCode->c_str();
  glShaderSource(shader, 1, &strPointer, NULL);
  glCompileShader(shader);
  int compiled;
  glGetShaderiv( shader, GL_COMPILE_STATUS, &compiled);
  if ( !compiled )
    printf("Compiling %d failed!\n", shaderType );

  int maxLength;
  glGetShaderiv( shaderType, GL_INFO_LOG_LENGTH, &maxLength);

  // maxLength includes NULL character
  infoLog = (char *) malloc ( sizeof( char ) * maxLength );
  glGetShaderInfoLog(vertexShader,maxLength,&maxLength,infoLog);

  return shader;
}
```

19.6.2 Drawing a Triangle

As a very simple example, we write a class called *Triangle*, which extends the classs *Shader* to create shaders to draw a triangle with a specified color. For simplicity, the shader source codes are hard-coded in the *Triangle* class:

```
class Triangle : public Shader
{
 private:
  static const string vsCode;   // Source code of vertex shader
  static const string fsCode ;  // Source code of fragment shader
  static const int vertexCount = 3;
  static const int COORDS_PER_VERTEX = 3;
  static const float triangleCoords[];
  static const float color[];
 public:
  Triangle( int &success );
  void draw();
};

const string Triangle::vsCode =
   "attribute vec4 vPosition;   \
      void main() {             \
      gl_Position = vPosition;  \
    }";


const string Triangle::fsCode =
    "uniform vec4 vColor;        \
     void main() {               \
```

```
      gl_FragColor = vColor;    \
    }";

const float Triangle::triangleCoords[] =
{   // in counterclockwise order:
   0.0f,  0.9f, 0.0f, // top vertex
  -0.5f, -0.3f, 0.0f, // bottom left
   0.5f, -0.2f, 0.0f  // bottom right
};


// Set color of displaying object
// with red, green, blue and alpha (opacity) values
const float Triangle::color[] = {0.89f, 0.6f, 0.4f, 1.0f};
```

This class makes use of the functions of its parent and provides the source codes to do the initilization of the shaders in the constructor:

```
// Create a Triangle object
Triangle::Triangle ( int   &success )
{
  string *vs, *fs;
  vs = (string *) &vsCode;
  fs = (string *) &fsCode;
  success = createShader ( vs, fs );
  if ( !success )
    printf("infoLog: %s\n", infoLog );
}
```

The **draw** function of *Triangle* shown below draws the triangle using the OpenGL command **glDrawArrays**. Before calling this command, it must pass the values of the triangle vertices to the vertex shader and the color values to the fragment shader. We pass the vertex data via the **attribute** variable *vPosition* and use the command **glVertexAttribPointer** to point to where the vertex data are located. The color value is passed to the fragment shader via the **uniform** variable *vColor*. The command **glUniform4fv** points to the location of the color data. The function **glUniform** has 1 to 4 dimensional forms and a vector (v) version, and we can use it to set scalar or vector values.

```
void Triangle::draw()
{
  // get handle to vertex shader's attribute variable vPosition
  int positionHandle= glGetAttribLocation(program, "vPosition");

  // Enable a handle to the triangle vertices
  glEnableVertexAttribArray( positionHandle );

  // Prepare the triangle coordinate data
  glVertexAttribPointer(positionHandle, COORDS_PER_VERTEX,
                        GL_FLOAT, false, 0, triangleCoords);

  // get handle to fragment shader's uniform variable vColor
  int colorHandle =  glGetUniformLocation(program, "vColor");
  if ( colorHandle == -1 )
    printf("No such uniform named vColor\n");
```

```
// Set color for drawing the triangle
glUniform4fv ( colorHandle, 1, color );

// Draw the triangle
glDrawArrays( GL_TRIANGLES , 0, vertexCount);

// Disable vertex array
glDisableVertexAttribArray(positionHandle);
}
```

We can now render the triangle with a code similar to the following:

```
.....
int  loadStatus = 0;
Triangle *triangle = new Triangle( loadStatus );
triangle->draw();
triangle->cleanUp();
glutSwapBuffers();
glFlush();
```

The *Triangle* constructor calls the functions of its parent *Shader* to do all the initialization of the shaders and returns the status of loading the shaders via the reference variable *loadStatus*, with a value of 1 meaning successful loading and 0 meaning failure. The shader source codes are hard-coded in the *Triangle* class. The **draw** method passes the necessary information to the shaders to render a triangle. The example here has not setup any world window or viewing volume; default values are used. In the vertex shader, we have not applied any transformation operation to the vertex values. Figure 19-6 below shows the output of this code.

Figure 19-6 Output of Triangle Shader

19.6.2 Temperature Shader

Our next example is a temperature shader where we use colors to represent temperatures with red meaning hot and blue meaning cold. We draw a square with temperature gradient where a warm temperature is a mixture of red and blue. We can imagine that the square is a metallic sheet with each corner connected to a heat or a cooling source. We can express smoothly the surface temperature as a mixture of red and blue. In the example, we assume that the lowest temperature is 0 and the highest is 50.

To accomplish this we pass the temperature value at each square vertex via an **attribute** array variable called *vertexTemp* to the vertex shader. The shader normalizes it to a value between 0 and 1 before passing the value to the fragment shader via the **varying** variable *temperature*. We create a class called *Square*, which is similar to the *Triangle* class above, to load the shaders and pass values to them:

```
------------------------------------------------------------------------
 class Square : public Shader
 {
   private:
    static const string vsCode;    //Source code of vertex shader
    static const string fsCode ;   //Source code of fragment shader
    static const int vertexCount = 4;
    static const int COORDS_PER_VERTEX = 3;
    static const float squareCoords[];
    static const float vertexTemp[];
   public:
    Square( int &success );
    void draw();
 };
------------------------------------------------------------------------
```

In this example, instead of hard-coding the shader source codes in the class, we read them from external files. So we add a function called **readShaderFile**() to the parent class *Shader*; it loads a shader source code from a file to a character array:

```
------------------------------------------------------------------------
 int Shader::readShaderFile(char *fileName, char **shader)
 {
    // Allocate memory to hold the source of our shaders.
    FILE *fp;
    int count, pos, shaderSize;

    fp = fopen( fileName, "r");
    if ( !fp )
        return 0;

    pos = (int) ftell ( fp );
    fseek ( fp, 0, SEEK_END );                    //move to end
    shaderSize = ( int ) ftell ( fp ) - pos;      //calculates file size
    fseek ( fp, 0, SEEK_SET );                    //rewind to beginning

    if ( shaderSize <= 0 ){
        printf("Shader %s empty\n", fileName);
        return 0;
    }
    // allocate memory
    *shader = (char *) malloc( shaderSize + 1);

    if ( *shader == NULL )
      printf("memory allocation error\n");
    // Read the source code
    count = (int) fread(*shader, 1, shaderSize, fp);
    (*shader)[count] = '\0';

    if (ferror(fp))
        count = 0;
    fclose(fp);
```

```
      return 1;
  }
```

In this function, *fileName* is the input parameter holding the file name of the shader source and *shader* is the output parameter pointing to the address of a character array that stores the shader source. The function simply opens the file, calculating its length, allocating memory for the shader, and reading the source code into the allocated character array. The function returns 1 for success and 0 for failure.

We can load the shaders and peform the initialization in the constructor of *Square*, assuming that the source codes of the vertex shader and the fragment shader are saved in the files *temp.vert* and *temp.frag* respectively:

```
// Create a Square object
Square::Square ( int   &success )
{
  string *vs, *fs;
  char *vsSource, *fsSource;

  // Read shader source code.
  readShaderFile( (char *) "temp.vert",  &vsSource);
  readShaderFile( (char *)"temp.frag",  &fsSource);
  vs = new string ( vsSource );
  fs = new string ( fsSource );
  success = createShader ( vs, fs );
  if ( !success ) {
    printf("infoLog: %s\n", infoLog );
    return;
  }
  delete vs;       delete fs;
  delete vsSource; delete fsSource;
}
```

On the other hand, we hard-code the coordinates of the square vertices and their associated temperatures in the class *Square*. These data are passed to the vertex shader in the **draw**() function, where the command **glVertexAttribPointer** is used to point to the data array:

```
//  Coordinates of a square
const float Square::squareCoords[] =
{ // in counterclockwise order:
  -0.8f,  0.8f, 0.0f,  // top left vertex
  -0.8f, -0.8f, 0.0f,  // bottom left
   0.8f, -0.8f, 0.0f,  // bottom right
   0.8f,  0.8f, 0.0f   // upper right
};

// Temperature at each vertex
const float Square::vertexTemp[] = {
    5.0f,              // v0 cold (top left)
   12.0f,              // v1 cool
   22.0f,              // v2 warm
   40.0f               // v3 hot (upper right)
};
```

```
void Square::draw()
{
 // get handle to vertex shader's attribute variable vPosition
 int positionHandle= glGetAttribLocation(program,"vPosition");
 int vertexTempHandle= glGetAttribLocation(program,"vertexTemp");

 // Enable a handle to the square vertices
 glEnableVertexAttribArray( positionHandle );

 // Prepare the square coordinate data
 glVertexAttribPointer(positionHandle, COORDS_PER_VERTEX,
                       GL_FLOAT, false, 0, squareCoords);
 glEnableVertexAttribArray( positionHandle );

 // Enable a handle to the temperatures at vertices
 glEnableVertexAttribArray( vertexTempHandle );
 // Pointing to the vertex temperatures
 glVertexAttribPointer (vertexTempHandle, 1,
                        GL_FLOAT, false, 0, vertexTemp);

 GLchar names[][20] = { "coldColor", "hotColor", "tempRange" };
 GLint handles[10];
 for ( int i = 0; i < 3; ++i ) {
   handles[i] = glGetUniformLocation(program, names[i]);
   if (handles[i] == -1)
     printf("No such uniform named %s\n", names[i]);
 }

 // set uniform values
 glUniform3f(handles[0], 0.0, 0.0, 1);    //cold color
 glUniform3f(handles[1], 1.0, 0.0, 0.0);  //hot color
 glUniform1f(handles[2], 50.0);           //temperature range

 // Draw the square
 glDrawArrays( GL_QUADS, 0, vertexCount);

 // Disable vertex array
 glDisableVertexAttribArray(positionHandle);
 glDisableVertexAttribArray(vertexTempHandle);
}
```

In the **draw** function the integer handles *positionHandle* and *vertexTempHandle* point to the attribute variables, *vPosition*, a **vec4**, and *vertexTemp*, a **float**, defined in the vertex shader. Through these handles, the application assigns data to *vPosition* that specifies the vertex coordinates and to *vertexTemp* that specifies the temperature at each vertex. The command **glVertexAttribPointer**() tells the handle where the actual data are located, and in our case, the vertex data and the temperature data are hard-coded in the arrays *squareCoords* and *vertexTemp* respectively. The command **glDrawArrays** sends these data to the shader on a per-vertex basis. The **draw** function declares another 3 integer handles to pass the color data representing hot and cold temperatures to the fragment shader and the temperature range to the vertex shader. The commands **glUniform*()** send the data.

The vertex and fragment shaders, which are saved in the files *temp.vert* and *temp.frag* respectively, are relatively simple:

```
----------------------------------------------------------------------
// temp.vert   (temperature vertex shader)
attribute vec4   vPosition;
attribute float  vertexTemp;
uniform    float tempRange;
varying    float temperature;

void main(void)
{
  temperature = ( vertexTemp - 0.0 ) / tempRange;
  gl_Position = vPosition;
}

// temp.frag  (temperature fragment shader)
uniform vec3 coldColor;
uniform vec3 hotColor;
varying float temperature;

void main()
{
  vec3 color = mix ( coldColor, hotColor, temperature );
  gl_FragColor = vec4 ( color, 1 );
}
----------------------------------------------------------------------
```

The vertex shader and the fragment shader communicate via the **varying** varialbe *temperature*, which is a **float**. The vertex shader calculates *temperature* from **uniform** variables *vertexTemp* and *tempRange*, whose values are obtained from the application or from interpolation. The *temperature* value, which has a value ranges from 0.0 to 1.0 is passed to the fragment shader to evaluate a color using the glsl **mix** function that interpolates a new color from two provided colors, *color*1 and *color*2, and a fraction f:

$$mix(color1, color2, f) = color1 \times (1 - f) + color2 \times f$$

When we execute this program, we will see a color square like the one shown in Figure 19-7 below. Again, in this example no world window and viewing volume has been setup and no transformation matrix operation has been applied to the vertex values.

Figure 19-7 Output of Temperature Shader

19.6.3 Drawing a Wireframe Tetrahedron

A tetrahedron is composed of four triangular faces, three of which meet at each vertex and thus it has four vertices. It may be the simplest kind of 3D objects.

A tetrahedron can be considered as a pyramid, which is a polyhedron with a flat polygon base and triangular faces connecting the base to a common point. A tetrahedron simply has a triangular base, so it is also known as a **triangular pyramid**.

A **regular tetrahedron** is one in which all four faces are equilateral triangles. The vertices coordinates of a regular tetrahedron with edge length 2 centered at the origin are

$$(1,0,\frac{-1}{\sqrt{2}}),\ (-1,0,\frac{-1}{\sqrt{2}}),\ (0,1,\frac{1}{\sqrt{2}}),\ (0,-1,\frac{1}{\sqrt{2}}) \tag{19.1}$$

The following example illustrates the basic techniques of drawing 3D objects with glsl. We will setup the viewing and projection paramters in the application and the vertex shader will multiply the model-view projection matrix to the vertex coordinates.

In the application, the class *Tetrahedron*, which is similar to classes *Triangle* and *Square* above, defines the coordinates of the four tetrahedron vertices and the indices of the four faces:

```
const float Tetrahedron::tetraCoords[] =
{
  1, 0, -0.707f,  -1, 0, -0.707f,
  0, 1,  0.707f,   0, -1, 0.707f
};

const int nIndices = 8;  // number of indices
// Order of indices of drawing the tetrahedron
const short indices[nIndices] = {0, 1, 2, 0, 3, 1, 2, 3};
```

It passes the drawing color to the fragment shader through a **uniform** variable named *vColor*. We set the drawing color to cyan and use line stripes to draw the 3D tetrahedron as a wireframe. So the *draw* function can be implemented as:

```
-------------------------------------------------------------------
void Tetrahedron::draw()
{
  // get handle to vertex shader's attribute variable vPosition
  int positionHandle= glGetAttribLocation(program,"vPosition");

  // Enable a handle to the tetrahedron vertices
  glEnableVertexAttribArray( positionHandle );
  // Prepare the tetrahedron coordinate data
  glVertexAttribPointer(positionHandle, COORDS_PER_VERTEX,
                   GL_FLOAT, false, 0, tetraCoords);

  int colorHandle  = glGetUniformLocation(program, "vColor");
  if (colorHandle == -1)
      printf("No such uniform named %s\n", "vColor" );
  // set drawing color
  glUniform4f ( colorHandle, 0.0, 1.0, 1.0, 1.0 );
  glLineWidth(5);
  // Draw the tetrahedron
  glDrawElements( GL_LINE_STRIP, nIndices,
                   GL_UNSIGNED_SHORT, indices);
```

```
  // Disable vertex array
  glDisableVertexAttribArray(positionHandle);
}
```

In this example, the application defines the projection and model-view transformations; we can implement the **reshape** function of the *renderer* as:

```
static void reshape(int width, int height)
{
    glViewport(0, 0, width, height);
    glMatrixMode(GL_PROJECTION);
    glLoadIdentity();
    glFrustum(-1.0, 1.0, -1.0, 1.0, 5.0, 50.0);
    glMatrixMode(GL_MODELVIEW);
    glLoadIdentity();
    gluLookAt (0.0, 0.0, 6.0, 0.0, 0.0, 0.0, 0.0, 1.0, 0.0);
}
```

The vertex shader (*tetra.vert*) and the fragment shader (*tetra.frag*) are very simple:

```
// tetra.vert : tetrahedron vertex shader
attribute vec4  vPosition;
void main(void)
{
    gl_Position = gl_ModelViewProjectionMatrix * vPosition;
}

// tetra.frag :  tetrahedron fragment shader
uniform vec4 vColor;
void main()
{
    gl_FragColor = vColor;
}
```

The built-in glsl variable **gl_ModelViewProjectionMatrix** is the product of the projection matrix and the model-view matrix, and is multiplied to the vertex coordindates for every vertex. The shader statement is equivalent to

```
gl_Position=gl_ProjectionMatrix*gl_ModelViewMatrix*vPosition;
```

In principle we should get the same transformation as the fixed-pipeline architecture. However, in practice the order of transforming the vertices in our shader may differ from that of the fixed functionality due to the optimization in a graphic card, that special built-in functions may take advantage of the optimization to speed up calculations. Also, rounding errors may generate different results for different methods of calculations. Therefore, **glsl** provides a function that guarantees the result to be the same as when using the fixed functionality:

vec4 **ftransform** (void);

This function does the matrix calculations in the order as that of the fixed functionality and produces the same results.

Alternatively, we can pass in the transformation matrices from the application as **mat4 uniform** variables rather than using the built-in variables.

The color of drawing is set by the variable *vColor* in the fragment shader. Note that if we declare a variable in a shader and do not actually use it in the shader program, the variable will be removed in the compilation process for optimiazation purposes. Consequently, the application will not be able to find the variable even though it has been declared in the shader.

Figure 19-8 below shows the output of this program.

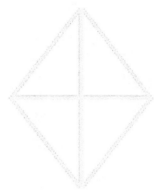

Figure 19-8   Output of Tetrahedron Shader

19.6.4   Drawing a Color Solid Tetrahedron

In this example, we draw a solid 3D tetrahedron, specifying the data inside a class named *Tetrahedrons*. We draw each face independently with a different color. Therefore, we have to specify the vertex indices of each face and the associated colors like the following:

```
//  Coordinates of a tetrahedron
const float Tetrahedrons::tetraCoords[] =
{
    1.0f, 0.0f, -0.707f, // vertex v0
   -1.0f, 0.0f, -0.707f, // v1
    0.0f, 1.0f,  0.707f, // v2
    0.0f, -1.0f, 0.707f  // v3
};

// draw indices for each face
const short Tetrahedrons::drawOrders[][3] = {
   {0, 1, 2},   {0, 2, 3},   {0, 3, 1},   {3, 2, 1}
};

// color for each face
const float Tetrahedrons::colors[][4] = {
   {1.0f, 0.0f, 0.0f, 1.0f},    // 0,1, 2 red
   {0.0f, 1.0f, 0.0f, 1.0f},    // 0, 2, 3 green
   {0.0f, 0.0f, 1.0f, 1.0f},    // 0, 3, 1 blue
   {1.0f, 1.0f, 0.0f, 1.0f}     // 3, 2, 1 yellow
};
```

As a demonstration of the alternative method of transforming vertices, we pass in a 4×4 transformation matrix from the application to the vertex shader instead of using the built-in variable *gl_ModelViewProjectionMatrix* like what we did above.

In this example, we rotate the tetrahedron about an axis by dragging the mouse and perform our own matrix operations. Alternatively, one may use the OpenGL Mathematics (glm), which is a C++ mathematics library for 3D software based on the glsl specification to do matrix operations. The package can be downloaded from:

http://sourceforge.net/projects/ogl-math/

But for simplicity, we have not used this math library in our examples. We calculate the composite transformation matrix in our display call-back function:

```
Tetrahedrons *tetrahedron;
float mvMatrix[4][4];    //model-view matrix
float mvpMatrix[4][4];   //model-view projection matrix
float angle = 0;         //rotation angle
.....
void display(void)
{
  glClear(GL_COLOR_BUFFER_BIT | GL_DEPTH_BUFFER_BIT);
  glClearColor( 1.0, 1.0, 1.0, 1.0 );  //set white background
  glMatrixMode(GL_MODELVIEW);
  glLoadIdentity();
  gluLookAt (0.0, 0.0, 6.3, 0.0, 0.0, 0.0, 0.0, 1.0, 0.0);
  glRotatef ( angle, 1.0f, 0.2f, 0.2f );
  // retrieve model-view matrix
  glGetFloatv(GL_MODELVIEW_MATRIX, &mvMatrix[0][0]);

  glMatrixMode(GL_PROJECTION);
  glLoadIdentity();
  glFrustum(-1.0, 1.0, -1.0, 1.0, 5.0, 50.0);
  // multiply projection matrix by model-view matrix
  glMultMatrixf ( &mvMatrix[0][0] );
  // retrieve model-view projection matrix
  glGetFloatv(GL_PROJECTION_MATRIX, &mvpMatrix[0][0]);
  // pass transformation matrix to vertex shader
  tetrahedron->draw( mvpMatrix );
  tetrahedron->cleanUp();
  glutSwapBuffers();
  glFlush();
}
```

The code uses the command **glGetFloatv**() to obtain the 4×4 model-view matrix *mvMatrix*. It then multiplies it to the projection matrix, and the product is retrieved into the model-view projection matrix *mvpMatrix*, which is an input parameter to the **draw**() function of the class *Tetrahedrons*, where it passes it to the vertex shader. The code also rotates the object by *angle* degrees around the axis $(1.0, 0.2, 0.2)$. The rotation angle is changed by the mouse-movement callback function, **movedMouse**():

```
const int screenWidth = 200;
const int screenHeight = 200;
float previousX=0, previousY=0, dx = 0, dy = 0;
void movedMouse(int mouseX, int mouseY)
{
  dx = mouseX - previousX;
  dy = mouseY - previousY;
  // reverse direction of rotation above the mid-line
  if (mouseY > screenHeight / 2)
```

```
      dx = dx * -1 ;
    // reverse direction of rotation to left of the mid-line
    if (mouseX < screenWidth / 2)
      dy = dy * -1 ;
    angle = angle + (dx + dy) / 2;   //scale factor of 2
    previousX = mouseX;
    previousY = mouseY;
    glutPostRedisplay();
}
```

The following is the **draw**() function with some non-significant code omitted. The main thing new here is that it passes the 4 × 4 model-view projection matrix to the vertex shader via the **uniform** variable *mvpMatrix* declared in the vertex shader.

```
void Tetrahedrons::draw( float mvpMatrix[4][4] )
{
   int positionHandle = glGetAttribLocation(program,"vPosition");
   glEnableVertexAttribArray( positionHandle );
   glVertexAttribPointer(positionHandle, COORDS_PER_VERTEX,
                         GL_FLOAT, false, 0, tetraCoords);
   int mvpMatrixHandle = glGetUniformLocation(program, "mvpMatrix");
   glUniformMatrix4fv(mvpMatrixHandle, 1, GL_FALSE, &mvpMatrix[0][0] );
   int colorHandle  =  glGetUniformLocation(program, "vColor");
   glEnable (GL_CULL_FACE);
   glCullFace(GL_BACK);
   for ( int i = 0; i < N_FACES; i++ ) {
     glUniform4fv(colorHandle, 1, &colors[i][0]);
     glDrawElements( GL_TRIANGLES, 3,
                            GL_UNSIGNED_SHORT, &drawOrders[i][0]);
   }
}
```

The following is the vertex shader, which mulitplies the model-view projection matrix, a **mat4** obtained from the application to the vertex coordinates:

```
// tetra.vert : tetrahedron vertex shader
attribute vec4  vPosition;
uniform    mat4  mvpMatrix;
void main(void) {
  gl_Position = mvpMatrix * vPosition;
}
```

The fragment shader does nothing special. It simply sets the color at a fragment to the corresponding vertex color obtained from the application:

```
// tetra.frag : tetrahedron fragment shader
uniform vec4 vColor;
void main() {
  gl_FragColor = vColor;
}
```

Figure 19-9 below shows a few sample outputs of this program when the mouse is dragged to rotate the tetrahedron.

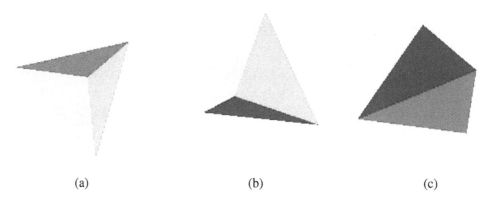

(a)   (b)   (c)

Figure 19-9 Sample Outputs Color Tetrahedron Shader

19.7 Drawing Spheres

19.7.1 Spherical Coordinates

We can use a mesh of triangles to approximate a spherical surface. We have to define the vertices coordinates of each triangle and every vertex is on the surface of the sphere. In practice, it is easier to calculate the position of a point on a sphere using spherical coordinates, where a point is specified by three numbers: the radial distance r of that point from a fixed origin, its polar angle θ (also called inclination) measured from a fixed zenith direction, and the azimuth angle ϕ of its orthogonal projection on a reference plane that passes through the origin as shown in Figure 19-10. So in spherical coordinates, a point is defined by (r, θ, ϕ) with some restrictions:

$$
\begin{aligned}
&r \geq 0 \\
&0^o \leq \theta \leq 180^o \\
&0^o \leq \phi < 360^o
\end{aligned}
\tag{19.2}
$$

Cartesian coordinates of a point (x, y, z) can be calculated from the spherical coordinates, (radius r, inclination θ, azimuth ϕ), where $r \in [0, \infty)$, $\theta \in [0, \pi]$, $\phi \in [0, 2\pi)$, by:

$$
\begin{aligned}
x &= r \sin \theta \cos \phi \\
y &= r \sin \theta \sin \phi \\
z &= r \cos \theta
\end{aligned}
\tag{19.3}
$$

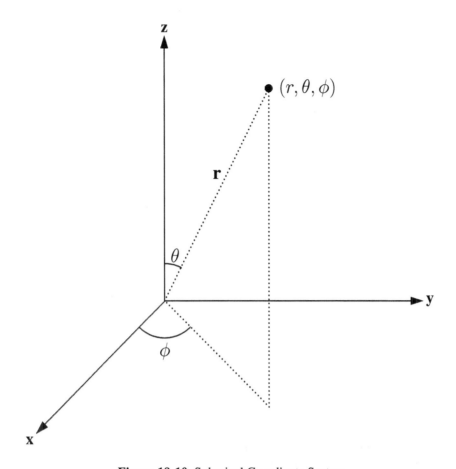

Figure 19-10 Spherical Coordinate System

Conversely, the spherical coordinates can be obtained from Cartesean coordinates by:

$$r = \sqrt{x^2 + y^2 + z^2}$$
$$\theta = \cos^{-1}\left(\frac{z}{r}\right)$$
$$\phi = \tan^{-1}\left(\frac{y}{x}\right)$$

(19.4)

19.7.2 Rendering a Wireframe Sphere

To render a sphere centered at the origin, we can divide the sphere into slices around the z-axis (similar to lines of longitude), and stacks along the z-axis (similar to lines of latitude). We simply draw the slices and stacks independently, which will form a sphere. Each slice or stack is formed by line segments joining points together. Conversely, each point is an intersection of a slice and a stack.

Suppose we want to divide the sphere into m stacks and n slices. Since $0 \le \theta \le \pi$, the angle between two stacks is $\pi/(m-1)$. On the other hand, $0 \le \phi < 2\pi$, the angle between two slices is $2\pi/n$ as the angle 2π is not included. That is,

$$\delta\theta = \frac{\pi}{m-1}$$
$$\delta\phi = \frac{2\pi}{n}$$

(19.5)

Figure 9-11 below shows a portion of two slices and two stacks, and their intersection points.

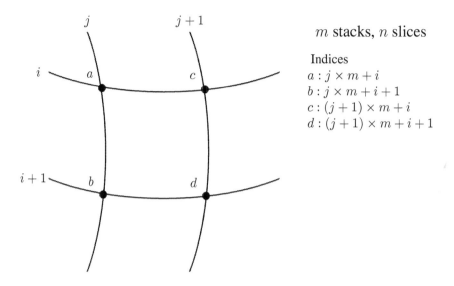

Quad $abdc = \triangle abc + \triangle cbd$

Figure 9 - 11. Spherical Surface Formed by Stacks and Slices

Our task is to calculate the intersection points. Suppose we calculate the points along a slice starting from $\phi = 0$, spanning θ from 0 to π, and then incrementing ϕ to calculate the next slice. We apply equation (19.3) to calculate the x, y, and z coordinates of each point. For convenience, we define a class called *XYZ* that contains the x, y, z coordinates of a point, and save the points in a C++ Standard Template Library (STL) class *vector* called *vertices*. Suppose we have declared a class called *Sphere*, which is similar to the *Tetrahedron* class discussed above. The following code, where **createSphere** can be a member function of the class *Sphere*, shows an implementation of such a task, assuming that r is the radius of the sphere:

```
class XYZ{
public:
  float x, y, z;
};

void Sphere::createSphere ( float r, int nSlices, int nStacks )
{
    double phi,  theta;
    XYZ *p = new XYZ();
    const double PI = 3.1415926;
    const double TWOPI = 2 * PI;

    for ( int j = 0; j < nSlices; j++ ) {
      phi = j * TWOPI / nSlices;
      for ( int i = 0; i < nStacks; i++ ) {
        theta = i * PI / (nStacks-1);  //0 to pi
        p->x = r * (float) ( sin ( theta ) *  cos ( phi ));
        p->y = r * (float) ( sin ( theta ) *  sin ( phi ));
        p->z = r * (float)  cos ( theta );
        vertices.push_back ( *p  );
      }
    }
}
```

In the code, the **push_back**() function of *vector* simply inserts an item into the *vector* object at its back. So the *vector vertices* contains the coordinates of all the points on the sphere.

Now we have obtained all the intersection points. The remaining task is to define a draw order list that tells us how to connect the points. We use a **short** array, named *drawOrderw* to hold the indices of the vertices in the order we want to connect them. Suppose we first draw the slices. The following code shows how to calculate the indices for the points of the slices:

```
int k = 0;
for ( int j = 0; j < n; j++ ) {
  for ( int i = 0; i < m-1; i++ ) {
    drawOrderw[k++] = (short) (j * m + i);
    drawOrderw[k++] = (short)( j* m + i + 1 );
  }
}
```

The two indices $(j * m + i)$ and $(j * m + i + 1)$ define two points of a line segment of a slice. Each slice is composed of $m - 1$ line segments. The following code shows the calculations for the stacks:

```
for ( int i = 1; i < m - 1; i++) {
  for ( int j = 0; j < n; j++){
    drawOrderw[k++] = (short) (j * m + i);
    if ( j == n - 1)   //wrap around: j + 1 --> 0
      drawOrderw[k++] = (short) ( i);
    else
      drawOrderw[k++] = (short) ((j+1)*m + i);
  }
}
```

Each pair of indices defines two end points of a line segment of a stack. When j equals $n - 1$, the next point wraps around so that the last point of the stack joins its first point to form a full circle. So each stack is composed of n segments. Also we do not need to draw the poles, and there are only $m - 2$ stacks. Therefore, the total number of indices in *drawOrderw* is

$$2 \times n \times (m - 1) + 2 \times (m - 2) \times n = 4 \times m \times n - 6 \times n$$

So we can calculate the *drawOrderw* array size and allocate the approximate memory for the array before using it:

```
short *drawOrderw;
int drawOrderwSize = 4 * m * n - 6 * n;
drawOrderw = new short[drawOrderwSize];
```

In order to use the OpenGL command **glDrawElements**, we put all the vertex coordinates in a float array called *sphereCoords*:

```
int nVertices = vertices.size();
float *sphereCoords = new float[3*nVertices];
int k = 0;
for ( int i = 0; i < nVertices; i++ ) {
  XYZ v = vertices[i];
  sphereCoords[k++] = v.x;
  sphereCoords[k++] = v.y;
  sphereCoords[k++] = v.z;
}
```

(The tasks of calculating the *drawOrderw* and *sphereCoords* arrays can be done in the constructor of *Sphere*, after calling the member function **createSphere**.)

To draw the sphere, we simply join these points together. When we draw all the slices and stacks, we get a wireframe sphere:

```
void Sphere::draw( float mvpMatrix[4][4] )
{
    int positionHandle= glGetAttribLocation(program,"vPosition");
    glEnableVertexAttribArray( positionHandle );
    glVertexAttribPointer(positionHandle, COORDS_PER_VERTEX,
                          GL_FLOAT, false, 0, sphereCoords);
    int mvpMatrixHandle = glGetUniformLocation(program, "mvpMatrix");
    glUniformMatrix4fv(mvpMatrixHandle, 1, GL_FALSE, &mvpMatrix[0][0] );
    ......
    glDrawElements(GL_LINES,drawOrderwSize,GL_UNSIGNED_SHORT,drawOrderw);
    ......
}
```

Since the first index in *drawOrderw* references the point that is the north pole of the sphere, we can draw the pole using the statement:

```
glDrawElements(GL_POINTS,1,GL_UNSIGNED_SHORT, drawOrderw);
```

The shaders are very simple and similar to those described in previous examples:

```
// sphere.vert: Source code of vertex shader
attribute vec4  vPosition;
uniform    mat4  mvpMatrix;
void main(void)
{
  gl_Position = mvpMatrix * vPosition;
}

// sphere.frag: Source code of fragment shader
uniform vec4 vColor;
void main()
{
  gl_FragColor = vColor;
}
```

Suppose we set the number of slices to 24 and the number of stacks to 16. When we run the program, we will see a wireframe sphere like the one shown in Figure 9-12 below. The point near the top of the sphere is its north pole. It has been rotated by the mouse dragging movement.

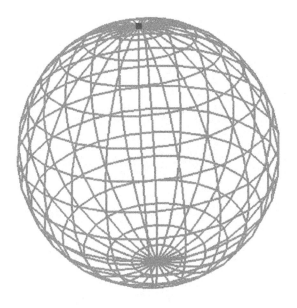

Figure 9-12   A Rendered Wireframe Sphere

19.7.3   Rendering a Color Solid Sphere

Rendering a color solid sphere is similar to rendering a color solid tetrahedron except that we have to calculate the vertices of the triangle mesh. We have already learned how to decompose a sphere into slices and stacks in the previous section. Suppose we have saved all the vertices in the *vector* variable *vertices* as we did in the previous example. The shaders are the same as those in the previous example, which are very simple.

As shown in Figure 9-11, the intersection points of two latitudes and two longitudes form a quadrilateral, which can be decomposed into two triangles. Since all the vertices coordinates have been calculated, we just need to find out the order of drawing them in the form of triangles.

As shown in the figure, to draw the quad abcd, we first draw the triangle abc and then draw the other triangle cbd, both in a counter-clockwise direction. That means the drawing order of the vertices is a, b, c, c, b, d. The following code shows the implementation of this procedure:

```
// 2n(m-1) slices + 2(m-2)n stacks
int nTriangles = 2 * n * (m - 1);      //number of triangles
short *drawOrders = new short[3*nTriangles];
for ( int j = 0; j < n; j++ )
{
   for ( int i = 0; i < m-1; i++ ) {
      short j1 = (short)(j + 1);
      if ( j == n - 1 ) j1 = 0;    //wrap around
      short ia = (short)( j * m + i ) ;
      short ib = (short)( j * m + i + 1);
      short ic = (short) (j1 * m + i );
      short id = (short)( j1 * m + i + 1 );
      drawOrders[k++] = ia;
      drawOrders[k++] = ib;
      drawOrders[k++] = ic;
```

```
      drawOrders[k++] = ic;
      drawOrders[k++] = ib;
      drawOrders[k++] = id;
    }
 }
```

Suppose we just use the four colors, red, green, blue, and yellow to draw the whole sphere, alternating the colors between adjacent triangles. We can define a **float** array to hold the four colors:

```
const float Spheres::colors[][nColors] = {
   {1.0f, 0.0f, 0.0f, 1.0f},    // red
   {0.0f, 1.0f, 0.0f, 1.0f},    // green
   {0.0f, 0.0f, 1.0f, 1.0f},    // blue
   {1.0f, 1.0f, 0.0f, 1.0f}     // yellow
};
```

To draw the sphere, we simply draw all the triangles, each of which is defined by three vertices and a color. In this example, only four colors, red, green, blue, and yellow have been used for coloring the triangles. The following is the **draw** function of the class *Sphere* that draws a color solid sphere composed of triangles; the user can rotate the sphere by dragging the mouse:

```
void Spheres::draw( float mvpMatrix[4][4] )
{
   int positionHandle= glGetAttribLocation(program,"vPosition");
   glEnableVertexAttribArray( positionHandle );
   glVertexAttribPointer(positionHandle, COORDS_PER_VERTEX,
                         GL_FLOAT, false, 0, sphereCoords);

   int mvpMatrixHandle = glGetUniformLocation(program,"mvpMatrix");
   glUniformMatrix4fv(mvpMatrixHandle,1,GL_FALSE,&mvpMatrix[0][0]);

   int colorHandle =  glGetUniformLocation(program, "vColor");
   for ( int i = 0; i < nTriangles; i++ ) {
     int j = i % 4;
     glUniform4fv(colorHandle, 1, colors[j]);

     glDrawElements( GL_TRIANGLES, 3,
                         GL_UNSIGNED_SHORT, (drawOrders + i*3 ));
   }
   glDisableVertexAttribArray(positionHandle);
}
```

In the code, the array pointer argument of the OpenGL function **glDrawElements** is
        *drawOrders + i * 3*
which points to the three indices of the vertices of the *i-th* triangle to be drawn. For instance, if the first index value is *j* (i.e. *j = *(drawOrders+i*3)*), then the coordinates of the triangle vertices are given by
        sphereCoords[j], sphereCoords[j+1], sphereCoords[j+2]
These values are passed to the vertex shader via the attribute variable *vPosition*.

The vertex and fragment shaders are the same as those presented in the previous section, *Rendering a Wireframe Sphere*. When we run the program, we will see an output similar to the one shown in Figure 19-13 below, where the sphere has been rotated by the mouse.

Figure 19-13   A Rendered Color Solid Sphere

19.7.4   Lighting a Sphere

Lighting is an important feature in graphics for making a scene appear more realistic and more understandable. It provides crucial visual cues about the curvature and orientation of surfaces, and helps viewers perceive a graphics scene having three-dimensionality. Using the sphere we have constructed in previous sections, we discuss briefly here how to add lighting effect to it.

To create lighting effect that looks realistic, we need to first design a lighting model. In graphics, however, such a lighting model does not need to follow physical laws though the laws can be used as guidelines. The model is usually designed empirically. In our discussion, we more or less follow the simple and popular Phong lighting model that we discussed in Chapter 7 to create lighting effect. In the model we only consider the effects of a light source shining directly on a surface and then being reflected directly to the viewpoint; second bounces are ignored. Such a model is referred to as a local lighting model, which only considers the light property and direction, the viewer's position, and the object material properties. It considers only the first bounce of the light ray but ignores any secondary reflections, which are light rays that are reflected for more than once by surfaces before reaching the viewpoint. Nor does a basic local model consider shadows created by light. In the model, we consider the following features:

1. All light sources are modeled as point light sources.
2. Light is composed of red (R), green (G), and blue (B) colors.
3. Light reflection intensities can be calculated independently using the principle of superposition for each light source and for each of the 3 color components (R, G, B). Therefore, we describe a source through a three-component intensity or illumination vector

$$\mathbf{I} = \begin{pmatrix} R \\ G \\ B \end{pmatrix} \qquad (19.6)$$

Each of the components of **I** in (19.6) is the intensity of the independent red, green, and blue components.

4. There are three distinct kinds of light or illumination that contribute to the computation of the final illumination of an object:

  - **Ambient Light**: light that arrives equally from all directions. We use this to model the kind of light that has been scattered so much by its environment that we cannot tell its original source direction. Therefore, ambient light shines uniformly on a surface regardless of its orientation. The position of an ambient light source is meaningless.
  - **Diffuse Light**: light from a point source that will be reflected diffusely. We use this to model the kind of light that is reflected evenly in all directions away from the surface. (Of course, in reality this depends on the surface, not the light itself. As we mentioned earlier, this model is not based on real physics but on graphical experience.)
  - **Specular Light**: light from a point source that will be reflected specularly. We use this to model the kind of light that is reflected in a mirror-like fashion, the way that a light ray reflected from a shinny surface.

5. The model also assigns each surface material properties, which can be one of the four kinds:

  - Materials with **ambient reflection properties** reflect ambient light.
  - Materials with **diffuse reflection properties** reflect diffuse light.
  - Materials with **specular reflection properties** reflect specular light.

In the model, ambient light only interacts with materials that possess ambient property; specular and diffuse light only interact with specular and diffuse materials respectively.

Figure 19-14 below shows the vectors that are needed to calculate the illumination at a point. In the figure, the labels *vPosition*, *lightPosition*, and *eyePosition* denote points at the vertex, the light source, and the viewing position respectively. The labels **L, N, R**, and **V** are vectors derived from these points (recall that the difference between two points is a vector), representing the light vector, the normal, the reflection vector, and the viewing vector respectively. The reflection vector **R** is the direction along which a light from **L** will be reflected if the the surface at the point is mirror-like. Assuming that the center of the sphere is at the origin $O = (0, 0, 0)$, some of them can be expressed as

$$
\begin{aligned}
\text{light vector } \mathbf{L} &= lightPosition - vPosition \\
\text{normal } \mathbf{N} &= vPosition - O \\
\text{view vector } \mathbf{V} &= eyePosition - vPosition
\end{aligned} \tag{19.7}
$$

We can normalize a vector by dividing it by its magnitude:

$$
\mathbf{l} = \frac{\mathbf{L}}{|\mathbf{L}|}, \quad \mathbf{n} = \frac{\mathbf{N}}{|\mathbf{N}|}, \quad \mathbf{v} = \frac{\mathbf{V}}{|\mathbf{V}|}, \quad \mathbf{r} = \frac{\mathbf{R}}{|\mathbf{R}|} \tag{19.8}
$$

One can easily show that the normalized reflection vector **r** can be calculated from **l** and **n** by the formula,

$$
\mathbf{r} = 2(\mathbf{n} \cdot \mathbf{l})\mathbf{n} - \mathbf{l} \tag{19.9}
$$

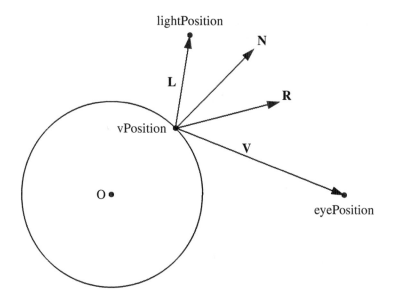

Figure 19-14 Lighting Vectors

Suppose I^{in} denotes the incident illumination from the light source in the direction l. The ambient, diffuse, and specular illumination on the point *vPosition* can be calculated according to the following formulas.

The ambient illumination is given by

$$I_a = c_a I_a^{in} \tag{19.10}$$

where I_a^{in} is the incident ambient light intensity and c_a is a constant called the *ambient reflectivity coefficient*.

The diffuse illumination is

$$I_d = c_d I_d^{in} \mathbf{l} \cdot \mathbf{n} \tag{19.11}$$

where $\mathbf{l} \cdot \mathbf{n} = \mathbf{r} \cdot \mathbf{n}$, I_d^{in} is the incident diffuse light intensity and c_d is a constant called the *diffuse reflectivity coefficient*.

The specular illumination can be calculated by

$$I_s = c_s I_s^{in} (\mathbf{r} \cdot \mathbf{v})^f \tag{19.12}$$

where c_s is a constant called the *specular reflectivity coefficient* and the exponent f is a value that can be adjusted empirically on an ad hoc basis to achieve desired lighting effect. The exponent f is ≥ 0, and values in the range 50 to 100 are typically used for shinny surfaces. The larger the exponent factor f, the narrower the beam of specularly reflected light becomes.

The total illumination is the sum of all the above components:

$$\begin{aligned} I &= I_a + I_d + I_s \\ &= c_a I_a^{in} + c_d I_d^{in} (\mathbf{l} \cdot \mathbf{n}) + c_s I_s^{in} (\mathbf{r} \cdot \mathbf{v})^f \end{aligned} \tag{19.13}$$

This model can be easily implemented in the glsl shader language. In our example, where the illuminated object is a sphere, the shader code is further simplified. The positions of the light source, the vertex, and the eye position (viewing point) are passed from the the application to the vertex shader as **uniform** variables. The vertex shader calculates the vectors **L**, **N**, and **V** from the positions and pass them to the fragment shader as **varying** variables:

```
// Source code of vertex shader
uniform mat4 mvpMatrix;
attribute vec4 vPosition;
uniform vec4 eyePosition;
uniform vec4 lightPosition;
varying vec3 N; //normal direction
varying vec3 L; //light source direction
varying vec3 V; //view vector
void main() {
   gl_Position = mvpMatrix * vPosition;
   N = vPosition.xyz;   //normal of  a point on sphere
   L = lightPosition.xyz - vPosition.xyz;
   V = eyePosition.xyz - vPosition.xyz;
}
```

In the code, we have used the **swizzling** operator to access the x, y, and z components of the **vec4** and **vec3** variables. In glsl, a swizzling operator is a variant of the C selection operator (.). It allows us to read and write multiple components of the matrix and vector variables. For example,

N = vPosition.xyz;

is to assign the x, y, and z components of *vPosition* to the corresponding components of *N*. (We may even use it to swap elements like *a.xy = a.yx*.)

The fragment shader obtains the vectors **L**, **N**, and **V** from the vertex shader, normalizes them, and calculates the reflection vector **r**. It then uses formulas (19.10) to (19.12) to calculate the illumination at the vertex. The following is the fragment shader code that calculates the illumination at each pixel:

```
// Source code of fragment shader
varying vec3 N;
varying vec3 L;
varying vec3 V;
uniform vec4 lightAmbient;
uniform vec4 lightDiffuse;
uniform vec4 lightSpecular;
//in this example, material color same for ambient, diffuse, specular
uniform vec4 materialColor;
uniform float shininess;

void main() {
  vec3 norm = normalize(N);
  vec3 lightv = normalize(L);
  vec3 viewv = normalize(V);
  // diffuse coefficient
  float Kd = max(0.0, dot(lightv, norm));

  // calculating specular coefficient
  // consider only specular light in same direction as normal
  float cs;
  if(dot(lightv, norm)>= 0.0) cs =1.0;
  else cs = 0.0;
  //reflection vector
  vec3 r = 2.0 *  dot (norm, lightv) * norm  - lightv;
  float Ks = pow(max(0.0, dot(r, viewv)), shininess);
  vec4 ambient = materialColor * lightAmbient;
  vec4 specular = cs * Ks * materialColor *lightSpecular;
  vec4 diffuse = Kd * materialColor *  lightDiffuse;
```

```
   gl_FragColor = ambient + diffuse + specular;
 }
```

One can modify the code or juggle with it to obtain various lighting effects empirically.

Similar to previous examples, the OpenGL application has to provide the actual values of the **uniform** and **attribute** parameters. The sphere is constructed in the same way that we did in the previous example. However, we do not need to pass in the colors for each triangle as the appearance of the sphere is now determined by its material color and the light colors, and the color at each pixel is calculated by the fragment shader using the lighting model. Suppose we call the class of the drawn sphere *Sphere1*. We define the light and material properties as follows:

```
const float Sphere1::eyePos[] = {0, 0, 6.3, 1};
const float Sphere1::lightPos[] = {5, 10, 5, 1};
const float Sphere1::lightAmbi[] = {0.1, 0.1, 0.1, 1};
const float Sphere1::lightDiff[] = {1, 0.8, 0.6, 1};
const float Sphere1::lightSpec[] = {0.3, 0.2, 0.1, 1};
//material same for ambient, diffuse, and specular
const float Sphere1::materialColor[] = {1, 1, 1, 1};
```

The **draw** function of the class passes the variable values to the shaders and draws the lit sphere:

```
-----------------------------------------------------------------------
void Sphere1::draw( float mvpMatrix[4][4] )
{
  int positionHandle= glGetAttribLocation(program,"vPosition");
  glEnableVertexAttribArray( positionHandle );
  glVertexAttribPointer(positionHandle, COORDS_PER_VERTEX,
                        GL_FLOAT, false, 0, sphereCoords);
  int mvpMatrixHandle = glGetUniformLocation(program, "mvpMatrix");
  glUniformMatrix4fv(mvpMatrixHandle,1,GL_FALSE,&mvpMatrix[0][0]);
  glUniformMatrix4fv(mvpMatrixHandle,1,GL_FALSE,&mvpMatrix[0][0]);
  int eyePosHandle = glGetUniformLocation(program, "eyePosition");
  int lightPosHandle=glGetUniformLocation(program,"lightPosition");
  int lightAmbiHandle=glGetUniformLocation(program,"lightAmbient");
  int lightDiffHandle=glGetUniformLocation(program,"lightDiffuse");
  int lightSpecHandle=glGetUniformLocation(program,"lightSpecular");
  int materialColorHandle=glGetUniformLocation(program,"materialColor");
  int shininessHandle =  glGetUniformLocation(program, "shininess");
  glUniform4fv(eyePosHandle, 1, eyePos);
  glUniform4fv(lightPosHandle, 1, lightPos);
  glUniform4fv(lightAmbiHandle, 1, lightAmbi);
  glUniform4fv(lightDiffHandle, 1, lightDiff);
  glUniform4fv(lightSpecHandle, 1, lightSpec);
  glUniform1f(shininessHandle, shininess);
  glUniform4fv(materialColorHandle, 1, materialColor);

  // Draw all triangles
  for ( int i = 0; i < nTriangles; i++ ) {
    glDrawElements( GL_TRIANGLES, 3,
                    GL_UNSIGNED_SHORT, (drawOrders + i*3 ));
  }
  glDisableVertexAttribArray(positionHandle);
}
-----------------------------------------------------------------------
```

Figure 19-15 below shows an output of this application, where the same sphere of Figure 19-13 has been used. Note that in this example, the light source is rotated together with the sphere. That is, the light source position relative to the sphere is fixed.

Figure 19-15   Example of Rendered Lit Sphere

We can obtain similar outputs if we draw the sphere using the functions **glutSolidSphere** or **glu-Sphere** instead of drawing the triangles (i.e. replacing the for-loop of **glDrawElements** by **glut-SolidSphere** or **gluSphere**) in the above code. In our example, we calculate the normal of the object at a vertex in the vertex shader. This could be inconvenient if we need to render several different kinds of objects using the same shader program. In general we calculate the normal in the application and specify it using the command **glNormal*()**; the normal is passed to a shader via the the built-in variable *gl_Normal*, which has been transformed by the model-view matrix. To recover the normal value in the original world coordinates, we need to perform an inverse transformation on *gl_Normal* by multiplying it by the ineverse of the model-view matrix, which is gl_NormalMatrix:

$$gl\_NormalMatrix * gl\_Normal ;$$

19.8   Animation

We can animate objects using glsl by changing their vertex positions at specified time intervals, which means that we need a variable to keep track of time. However, a vertex shader does not have built-in features to keep track of elapsed time. Therefore, we have to define a time variable in the OpenGL application, and pass its value to the shader via a uniform variable. We can calculate the lapsed time of running the program in the **idle** callback function of the application. We first consider an example of animating the color sphere presented above.

19.8.1   Animating a Color Sphere

In this example, we animate the color solid sphere discussed in Section 19.7.3. We need to first include in the **main** function of the application the idle function callback command
         glutIdleFunc (idle);
which sets the global idle callback to be the function **idle** so that a GLUT program can perform background processing tasks or continuous animation when window system events are not being received. The idle callback is continuously called when there are no events. So we make use of this function to find the elapsed time for animation. We define in the renderer the idle function as follows (with some minor details omitted):

```
void idle(void) {
  float t = glutGet ( GLUT_ELAPSED_TIME );
  sphere->setTime ( t );
  glutPostRedisplay();
}
```

In this function, the command **glutGet (GLUT_ELAPSED_TIME)** returns the number of milliseconds since **glutInit** was called (or first call to **glutGet(GLUT_ELAPSED_TIME)**). The function **setTime** is a new function that we add to the class *Spheres* discussed above. It passes the elapsed time to the vertex shader using the function **glUniform1f**:

```
void Spheres::setTime ( float t ) {
  glUniform1f ( timeHandle, t );    // send the lapsed time to vertex shader
}
```

The variable *timeHandle* is a data member of the class *Spheres* and its value is set in the **draw** function:

```
void Spheres::draw( float mvpMatrix[4][4] ) {
  .....
  timeHandle = glGetUniformLocation(program, "timeLapsed");
  .....
}
```

The variable *timeLapsed* is defined in the vertex shader for animating the sphere:

```
// sphere.vert
attribute vec4  vPosition;
uniform    mat4  mvpMatrix;
uniform    float  timeLapsed;    // time in milliseconds
void main(void)
{
  float t = timeLapsed / 1000.0;  // time t in seconds
  float s = sin ( t );     // s varies between -1 and 1
  mat4 m = mat4( 1.0 );    // 4 x 4 identity matrix
  m = s * m;               // try to create scale matrix
  m[3][3] = 1.0;           // set last matrix element to 1
                           //  to form a proper scale matrix
  gl_Position = m * mvpMatrix * vPosition;
}
```

The vertex shader simply receives the time parameter *timeLapsed* value from the application and divides it by 1000 to convert it to seconds. It then makes use of the **sin** function to obtain the value *s*, which varies between -1 and 1. The *s* value is multiplied to an identity matrix to obtain the scaling matrix *m*, which is multiplied to the model-view projection matrix. Therefore, the vertex values will change sign and vary. This gives us an animated sphere, which shrinks and expands repetitively, and the poles may flip over depending on the orientation of the sphere. The fragment shader is the same as before. Figure 19-16 below shows a few frames of the output of the program.

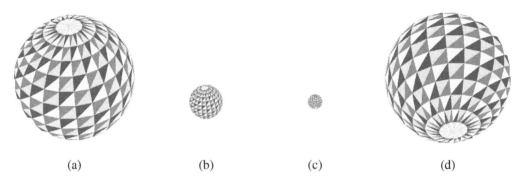

(a)   (b)   (c)   (d)

Figure 19-16 Four Frames of Animated Sphere

Note that the constructor **mat4** (*c*) constructs a 4×4 array, setting the diagonal elements to the parameter *c* and other elements to 0. Thus **mat4** (1.0) creates an identity matrix.

In the above discussion, we have used a default frame rate, which depends on how the OpenGL library calls the **idle** function. If we need to animate the sphere at a specified frame rate, we can declare a **float** variable called *previousTime* that records the time at which the most recent frame was rendered. We render a new frame only if the time lapsed has exceeded the specified period between two consecutive frames. For example, if we want the frame rate to be 5 frames per second, the period is 100 ms and we can modify the code of the **idle** function to:

```
void idle(void)
{
  float t = glutGet ( GLUT_ELAPSED_TIME );
  if ( t - previousTime  > 100.0 ){
    sphere->setTime ( t );
    previousTime = t;
    glutPostRedisplay();
  }
}
```

In the above example, the center of the sphere is fixed. If we need to move the sphere in space as a solid object, we can set the translational matrix according to the desired object movements. Recall that the transformation matrix of translation is given by:

$$T = \begin{pmatrix} 1 & 0 & 0 & \mathbf{d}_x \\ 0 & 1 & 0 & \mathbf{d}_y \\ 0 & 0 & 1 & \mathbf{d}_z \\ 0 & 0 & 0 & 1 \end{pmatrix} \tag{19.14}$$

This matrix translates an object by the values d_x, d_y, and d_z in the x, y, and z directions respectively. Therefore, to translate an object, we just need to set the appropriate entries of the transformation matrix m[][] in the vertex shader to the translation values. Since in OpenGL, a matrix is column-major, where m[i][j] is the element of the i-th column and the j-th row. That is, m[3] represents column 3 of the matrix. So we set the entries in the following way:

$$m[3][0] = d_x, \quad m[3][1] = d_y, \quad m[3][2] = d_z$$

Suppose we want the sphere to move under gravity in the y direction and assume that the sphere's initial velocity in the z direction is 0. Then the translation values are given by:

$$d_x = v_x t$$
$$d_y = v_y t + \tfrac{1}{2} g t^2$$

(19.15)

where v_x, and v_y are initial velocities in the x and y directions respectively and are constants, and g is the gravitational constant. If we set all the constants to 1 (i.e. $v_x = v_y = g = 1$), we can modify our above vertex shader to simulate the motion:

```
// spheres.vert
attribute vec4  vPosition;
uniform   mat4  mvpMatrix;
uniform   float timeLapsed;    // time in milliseconds
void main(void)
{
   float t1 = timeLapsed / 1000.0;   // time t1 in seconds
   vec3 d;

   float t = sin ( t1 );        // t varies between -1 and 1
   mat4 m = mat4( 1.0 );        // 4 x 4 identity matrix
   m = 0.2 * m;                 // shrink sphere by a factor of 5
   d.x = t;                     // translation in x-direction
   d.y = t + 0.5*1.0*t*t;       // translation in y-direction
   m[3][0] = d.x;
   m[3][1] = d.y;
   m[3][3] = 1.0;               // reset last matrix element to 1
   gl_Position =   mvpMatrix * m *  vPosition;
}
```

In the code, the time t is sinusoidal, varying between -1 and 1. This makes the sphere oscillates along a parabolic curve. Figure 19-17 below shows a few frames of this shader output.

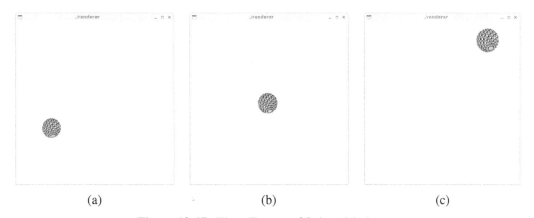

| (a) | (b) | (c) |

Figure 19-17   Three Frames of Sphere Motion

19.8.2   Animated Particle Systems

We have mentioned in Chapter 11 about the creation and applications of a particle system, which uses a large number of very small sprites or graphic objects to simulate certain kinds of *fuzzy* phenomena or objects such as clouds, dust, explosions, falling leaves,fire, flowing water, fog smoke, snow, sparks, meteor tails, stars and galaxies, or abstract visual effects like glowing trails, and magic spells.

The basic idea in a particle system is that we model the motion of points in space using physical laws or empirical experience. For each time step, we calculate the new position of each particle for rendering. This works well with a vertex shader where it receives a time parameter from the application. As a simple example, we use the technique in animating a sphere discussed above to animate a cloud of randomly formed color particles, each of which is a point. We declare a class called *Particles*, which is similar to the *Spheres* class discussed above except that now we do not need to create any sphere. In addition, we also declare a class called *ColorPoint* that holds the position and color of a "particle":

```
class ColorPoint{
public:
  float position[4];
  float color[4];
  ColorPoint (float position0[], float color0[]){ //constructor
    for ( int i = 0; i < 4; i++ ) {
      position[i] = position0[i];
      color[i] = color0[i];
    }
  }
};
```

In the constructor of the class *Particles*, we create *Npoints ColorPoint* objects with random positions and colors, and save them in an array (a *vector* object) named *pointArray* (both *Npoints* and *pointArray* are data members of *Particles*):

```
//create Npoints particles
float position[4];
float color[4];
for ( int i = 0; i < Npoints; ++i ){
  for ( int j = 0; j < 3; j++ ) {
    position[j] = (float)(rand()%32000)/16000.0-1.0; //-1 --> 1
    color[j] = (float) ( rand() %32000 ) / 32000.0;  // 0 --> 1
  }
  color[3] = position[3] = 1;             //not used
  ColorPoint cp = ColorPoint ( position, color );
  pointArray.push_back ( cp );            //save in vector
}
```

The **draw** function of *Particles* send the position and the color of each particle to the vertex shader:

```
void Particles::draw( float mvpMatrix[4][4] )
{
  int positionHandle= glGetAttribLocation(program,"vPosition");
  int mvpMatrixHandle=glGetUniformLocation(program,"mvpMatrix");
  // pass model-view projection matrix to vertex shader
  glUniformMatrix4fv(mvpMatrixHandle,1,GL_FALSE,&mvpMatrix[0][0]);

  int colorHandle =  glGetUniformLocation(program, "vColor");
  timeHandle =  glGetUniformLocation(program, "timeLapsed");

  ColorPoint *cp;
  for ( int i = 0; i < Npoints; i++ ) {
    cp = &pointArray[i];
    glUniform4fv(colorHandle, 1, cp->color);
```

```
      glBegin ( GL_POINTS );
        glVertex4fv ( cp->position );
      glEnd();
   }
}
```

The vertex shader and the fragment shader are the same as those of the *animated color sphere* presented in the previous section:

```
// particles.vert : vertex shader
attribute vec4   vPosition;
uniform    mat4  mvpMatrix;
uniform  float  timeLapsed;    // time in milliseconds
void main(void)
{
   float t = timeLapsed / 5000.0;  // adjust time
   float s = sin ( t );        // s varies between -1 and 1
   mat4 m = mat4( 1.0 );       // 4 x 4 identity matrix
   m = s * m;                  // try to create scale matrix
   m[3][3] = 1.0;              // set last matrix element to 1
                               //   to form a proper scale matrix
   gl_Position = m * mvpMatrix * vPosition;
}

// particles.frag : fragment shader
uniform vec4 vColor;

void main()
{
   gl_FragColor = vColor;
}
```

Figure 19-18 below shows three frames of the output of this shader; two thousand particles are randomly palced on the screen.

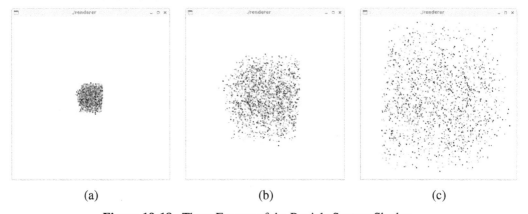

| (a) | (b) | (c) |

Figure 19-18 Three Frames of the Particle System Shader

19.8.3 Morphing

Morphing (shortened term of *metamorphosing*) is a technique that changes an object smoothly from one object to another, a generalization of the tweening technique we discussed in Chapter

11. The points of an intermediate shapes are calculated using interpolation techniques from the initial and final objects. We assume that the two objects have the same number of vertices, which can be saved in arrays. Suppose we use linear interpolation, and we want to morph objects A to B. Suppose A_i and B_i are the corresponding vertices of the objects. A corresponding point C_i of an intermediate shape is given by the affine combination of A_i and B_i:

$$C_i = (1-t)A_i + tB_i \quad 0 \le t \le 1 \tag{19.16}$$

Initially, when $t = 0$, $C_i = A_i$. As t increases to 1, C_i changes to B_i. Equation (19.16) can be easily evaluated using the glsl function **mix**. For instance, suppose $vPostion$ and $vPosition1$ are two **vec4** that have the coordinate values of vertices A_i and B_i. Then the interpolated vertex can be calculated by

vec4 inPosition = mix(vPosition, vPosition1, t);

where, for example, the first component of *inPostion* is calculated according to:

inPosition.x = (1 - t) * vPosition.x + t * vPosition1.x

The implementation of this technique is straight forward. As an example, we declare a class called *Morph*, which is similar to the classes discussed above such as *Spheres* and *Particles*. In the class, we declare two static **float** constant arrays, *figureA* and *figureB*, to store the vertex values of the initial and final objects respectively:

```
const float Morph::figureA[][3] =
    {{0,0,0}, {3,3,0}, {6,0,0}, {6,-6,0}, {4,-6,0},
     {4,-4,0}, {2,-4,0}, {2,-6,0}, {0,-6,0}};
const float Morph::figureB[][3] =
    {{0,0,0}, {3,0,0}, {6,0,0}, {6,-2,0}, {4,-2,0},
     {4,-6,0}, {2,-6,0}, {2,-2,0}, {0,-2,0}};
```

In the example, *figureA* defines a wedge-like shape and *figureB* defines a T-shape. Both of them have 9 vertices.

We pass the blending parameter t, which we call *timeStep* from the *Morph* class to the vertex shader. This parameter, varying between 0 and 1, is incremented or decremented in the **idle** callback function of the renderer:

```
static void idle(void)
{
  static float timeStep = 0;
  static bool  increase = true;
  float t = glutGet ( GLUT_ELAPSED_TIME );
  if ( t - previousTime  > 500.0 ){
    if ( timeStep > 0.91 )
       increase = false;
    else if ( timeStep < 0.09 )
       increase = true;
    if ( increase )
     timeStep += 0.1;
    else
     timeStep -= 0.1;
    morph->setTime ( timeStep );
    previousTime = t;
    glutPostRedisplay();
  }
}
```

In the code, we have used a frame rate of 2 fps (frames per second). That is, the period between two frames is 500 ms. The variable *timeStep* increases from 0 to 1 with step 0.1 and then decreases from 1 to 0 and so on. So the animation morphs *A* to *B* and reverses direction, morphing the figure from *B* to *A* and so on.

Like before, the **draw** member function passes the vertex data and other parameters to the shaders:

```
void Morph::draw( float mvpMatrix[4][4] )
{
   int posHandle = glGetAttribLocation(program,"vPosition");
   int posHandle1 = glGetAttribLocation(program,"vPosition1");
   glEnableVertexAttribArray( posHandle );
   glEnableVertexAttribArray( posHandle1 );
   glVertexAttribPointer(posHandle,3,GL_FLOAT,false,0,figureA);
   glVertexAttribPointer(posHandle1,3,GL_FLOAT,false,0,figureB);
   //timeHandle and Npoints are data members of class
   timeHandle =  glGetUniformLocation(program, "timeStep");
   .....
   glDrawArrays( GL_LINE_LOOP, 0, Npoints );
}
void Morph::setTime ( float t )
{
   glUniform1f(timeHandle, t); //send timeStep to vertex shader
}
```

The following is the corresponding vertex shader, which is similar to those discussed above for animation:

```
// morph.vert
attribute vec4  vPosition;    //vertex of figureA
attribute vec4  vPosition1;   //vertex of figureB
uniform   mat4  mvpMatrix;
uniform   float timeStep;     //interpolation time parameter
void main(void)
{
   vec3 d;                    //displacement
   float t = timeStep;
   mat4 m = mat4( 1.0 );      // 4 x 4 identity matrix
   //interpolated figure move along diagonal of screen
   d.x = 8.0 * t;             // translation in x-direction
   d.y = 8.0 * t;             // translation in y-direction
   m[3][0] = d.x;
   m[3][1] = d.y;
   m[3][3] = 1.0;             // reset last matrix element to 1
   gl_Position = mvpMatrix * m * mix(vPosition, vPosition1, t);
   }
}
```

Figure 19-19 below shows four frames of this shader's output.

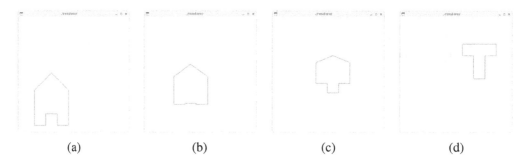

Figure 19-19   Four Frames of the Morphing Shader

19.9   Texture Shaders

One method to perform texture operations in glsl is to access the texture coordinates for each vertex through built in attribute variables, one for each texture unit. The following are the available built in variables that a shader can use:

```
attribute vec4 gl_MultiTexCoord0;
attribute vec4 gl_MultiTexCoord1;
attribute vec4 gl_MultiTexCoord2;
attribute vec4 gl_MultiTexCoord3;
attribute vec4 gl_MultiTexCoord4;
attribute vec4 gl_MultiTexCoord5;
attribute vec4 gl_MultiTexCoord6;
attribute vec4 gl_MultiTexCoord7;
```

The texture matrix of each texture unit can be accessed through a uniform array:

```
uniform mat4 gl_TextureMatrix[gl_MaxTextureCoords];
```

The vertex shader has to compute the texture coordinates for the vertex and store the values in the pre-defined varying variable *gl_TexCoord*[*i*]. For example, we need to declare in the fragment shader a special type of variable called **sampler**. Each sampler variable in a program represents a single texture of a particular texture type. It provides access to a particular texture object, including all its parameters. OpenGL supports a variety of sampler types for accessing one-dimensional (**sampler1D**, two-dimensional (**sampler2D**), three-dimensional (**sampler3D**), and cube-map (**samplerCube**) textures. The following table lists the sampler types that OpenGL supports; the prefix *t* preceding *sampler* in a sampler name represents any of the 3 possible prefixes (nothing for **float**, i for **signed int**, and u for **unsigned int**). The rest of the sampler's name refers to the texture type of the sampler:

Table 19-3   Names Map of GLSL Samplers

GLSL Sampler	OpenGL Texture enum	Texture Type
*t*sampler1D	GL_TEXTURE_1D	1D texture
*t*sampler2D	GL_TEXTURE_2D	2D texture
*t*sampler3D	GL_TEXTURE_3D	3D texture
*t*samplerCube	GL_TEXTURE_CUBE_MAP	Cubemap Texture
*t*sampler2DRect	GL_TEXTURE_RECTANGLE	Rectangle Texture
*t*sampler1DArray	GL_TEXTURE_1D_ARRAY	1D Array Texture
*t*sampler2DArray	GL_TEXTURE_2D_ARRAY	2D Array Texture
*t*samplerCubeArray	GL_TEXTURE_CUBE_MAP_ARRAY	Cubemap Array Texture (requires GL 4.0 or ARB _texture_cube_map_array)
*t*samplerBuffer	GL_TEXTURE_BUFFER	Buffer Texture
*t*sampler2DMS	GL_TEXTURE_2D_MULTISAMPLE	Multisample Texture
*t*sampler2DMSArray	GL_TEXTURE_2D _MULTISAMPLE_ARRAY	Multisample Array Texture

For example,

```
uniform sampler2D texHandle;
```

declares a two-dimensional sampler with **float** data type.

The function **texture2D**() gives us a texel (texture element). It takes a sampler2D and texture coordinates as inputs and returns the texel value:

```
vec4  texture2D(sampler2D texHandle, vec2 gl_TexCoord[0].st );
```

We can pass the texture coordinates to the fragment shader using gl_TexCoord[*i*], for example,

```
gl_TexCoord[0]  = gl_MultiTexCoord0;
```

The simple example presented in the next section shows how to use these features to render an object with texture.

19.9.1   A Simple Texture Example

In this example, we apply a two-dimensional texture, which is a black-and-white checkerboard pattern to a graphics object created by the **glu** utilities. The vertex shader is simple enough, receiving the texture coordinates with the built-in variable *gl_MultiTexCoord0* and passing them to the fragment shader using the built-in array variable *gl_TexCoord*:

```
//simpletex.vert
attribute vec4  vPosition;
uniform   mat4  mvpMatrix;

void main(void)
{
  gl_TexCoord[0]  = gl_MultiTexCoord0;
  gl_Position = mvpMatrix * vPosition;
}
```

The fragment shader is also very simple. It obtains the texture color from a sampler and blends it with another color specified by the application using the **mix** function:

```
// simpletex.frag
uniform sampler2D texHandle;
uniform vec4 vColor;

void main (void)
{
  vec3 texColor = vec3 (texture2D(texHandle, gl_TexCoord[0].st));
  vec4 color = mix ( vColor, vec4 (texColor, 1.0), 0.6 );
  gl_FragColor = color;
}
```

In the application, we make use of the **glu** utilites to create some quadric objects and a teapot that support texturing. We do the usual initialization for texture as we discussed in Chapter 7. Suppose we declare a class called *Simpletex*, which is similar to classes such as *Morph* or *Spheres* discussed above, and suppose the texture image data is stored in a two-dimensional array named *checkimage*. The following code shows the specification of texture features:

```
void Simpletex::init2DTexture()
{
 glGenTextures(1, &texName);
 glBindTexture(GL_TEXTURE_2D,texName); //now we work on texName
 glTexParameteri(GL_TEXTURE_2D,GL_TEXTURE_WRAP_S, GL_REPEAT);
 glTexParameteri(GL_TEXTURE_2D,GL_TEXTURE_WRAP_T, GL_REPEAT);
 glTexParameteri(GL_TEXTURE_2D,GL_TEXTURE_MAG_FILTER,GL_LINEAR);
 glTexParameteri(GL_TEXTURE_2D,GL_TEXTURE_MIN_FILTER,GL_LINEAR);
 glTexImage2D(GL_TEXTURE_2D, 0, GL_RGB, iWidth,
                iHeight,0,GL_RGB,GL_UNSIGNED_BYTE,checkImage);
 glActiveTexture(GL_TEXTURE0);
 glBindTexture(GL_TEXTURE_2D, texName);
}
```

In the code, *iwidth* and *iwidth* are the image width and height of the checkerboard texture image; they are set to 64 in the example.

The texture data and other parameters are passed to the shaders in the **draw** routine for rendering:

```
void Simpletex::draw( float mvpMatrix[4][4] )
{
  int posHandle = glGetAttribLocation(program,"vPosition");
  glEnableVertexAttribArray( posHandle );

  int mvpMatrixHandle=glGetUniformLocation(program,"mvpMatrix");
  glUniformMatrix4fv(mvpMatrixHandle,1,GL_FALSE,&mvpMatrix[0][0]);

  int colorHandle =  glGetUniformLocation(program, "vColor");
  glUniform4f(colorHandle,  0, 1, 1, 1);      //set color of object
  GLUquadric *qobj=gluNewQuadric(); //create quadric objects
  gluQuadricTexture(qobj,GL_TRUE);  //requires texture coordinates
  if ( objType == 0 )
    gluSphere(qobj,0.8,32,32);
  else if ( objType == 1 )
    gluCylinder(qobj, 0.8, 0.8, 1.2, 32, 32);//top, base height
  else
     glutSolidTeapot(0.6f);              //has texture coordinates
  gluDeleteQuadric(qobj);
}
```

The code allows us to choose an object to be rendered, which can be a sphere, a cylinder or a teapot, depending on the value of the **int** variable *objType*, which represents object types. The function **gluNewQuadric** creates and returns a pointer to a new quadric object. A quadric surface is described by a polynomial with each term in the form $x^m y^n z^k$, with $m + n + k \leq 2$. Any quadric can be expressed in the form

$$q(x, y, z) = Ax^2 + By^2 + Cz^2 + Dxy + Exz + Fyz + Gx + Hy + Iz + J = 0 \quad (19.17)$$

wehre $A, ..., J$ are constants. The function **gluQuadricTexture** specifies whether texture coordinates should be generated for the quadric for rendering with the quadric object. A value of GL_TRUE indicates that texture coordinates should be generated. The *renderer*, which is not shown here, allows a user to press the key 't' to toggle the object types, and to press other keys to rotate, translate or magnify the object. Figure 19-20 below shows a sample output of each textured object in the example.

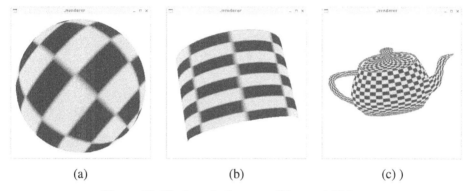

| (a) | (b) | (c)) |

Figure 19-20   Sample Outputs of Textured Objects

Actually in this example, we make use of the command **gluQuadricTexture** to map the texture coordinates and have not shown you how the texture coordinates are set. We have already discussed the texture coordinate mapping principles in Chapter 7. Here, again we use the *Spherel* shader example discussed in Section 19.7 above to review how this is done.

We have presented in Equation (7.29) of Chapter 7 that the texture coordinates of a spherical surface is given by:

$$s = \frac{\phi}{2\pi}$$
$$t = \frac{\theta}{\pi} \quad\quad\quad (19.18)$$

To implement the texture mapping for our *Spherel*, we declare another *XYZ* **vector** named *texPoints*, which saves the texture coordinates at all the vertices. The **createSphere** function becomes (we call our new class *Spherelt*):

```
void Spherelt::createSphere ( float r, int nSlices, int nStacks )
{
    double phi,  theta;
    XYZ *p = new XYZ();
    XYZ *t = new XYZ();    //for texture coordinates
    const double PI = 3.1415926;
    const double TWOPI = 2 * PI;

    for ( int j = 0; j < nSlices; j++ ) {
      //phi: 0 to 2pi  (modified for texture coordinates)
      phi = j * TWOPI / (nSlices-1);
```

```
      for ( int i = 0; i < nStacks; i++ ) {
        theta = i * PI / (nStacks-1);   //0 to pi
        p->x = r * (float) ( sin ( theta ) * cos ( phi ));
        p->y = r * (float) ( sin ( theta ) * sin ( phi ));
        p->z = r * (float)  cos ( theta );
        t->x = phi / TWOPI;       // s (column)
        t->y = 1 - theta / PI;    // t (row)
        vertices.push_back ( *p );
        texPoints.push_back ( *t );
      }
    }
  }
```

The texture coordinates are then saved in an array named *texCoords* along with the saving of the spherical coordinates in the *SphereIt* class constructor:

```
  sphereCoords = new float[3*nVertices];
  texCoords = new float[2*nVertices];
  int k = 0;
  int kk = 0;
  for ( int i = 0; i < nVertices; i++ ) {
    XYZ v = vertices[i];
    sphereCoords[k++] = v.x;
    sphereCoords[k++] = v.y;
    sphereCoords[k++] = v.z;
    v = texPoints[i];
    texCoords[kk++] = v.x;
    texCoords[kk++] = v.y;
  }
```

After we have also incorporated the texture features of *Simpletex* in *SphereIt*, we only need to add two statements in the **draw** function to access the texture coordinates:

```
void SphereIt::draw( float mvpMatrix[4][4] )
{
  ..... //Same as draw() of SphereI
  glEnableClientState (GL_TEXTURE_COORD_ARRAY);
  glTexCoordPointer ( 2, GL_FLOAT, 0, texCoords );
  // Draw all triangles
  for ( int i = 0; i < nTriangles; i++ ) {
    glDrawElements( GL_TRIANGLES, 3,
                    GL_UNSIGNED_SHORT, (drawOrders + i*3 ));
  }
}
```

For the vertex shader, we just need to add the statement in **main**():

$$gl\_TexCoord[0] = gl\_MultiTexCoord0;$$

which passes the texture coordinates to the fragment shader, where we mix the light intensity obtained from the Phong model to the texture color:

```
//fragment shader
void main()
{
  ..... //same as fragment shader of SphereI
  vec4 intensity =  ambient + diffuse + specular;
  vec4 color = mix ( intensity, vec4 (texColor, 1.0), 0.2 );
  gl_FragColor = color;
}
```

Figure 19-21 below shows an output of this shader program.

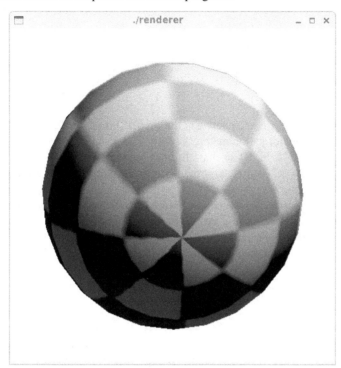

Figure 19-21   Sample Output of Textured Lit Sphere

19.9.2   Bump Mapping with Shaders

Bump mapping is a texture mapping technique that can make a smooth surface appear rough, looking more realistic without increasing the geometry complexity. For example, we can apply bump mapping to the surface of a sphere to make it look like an orange, which has bumpy skin.

The idea of the technique is to perturb the normal for each fragment. The perturbations can be generated from an algorithm or saved as textures (called normal-map or bump-map) in memory.

The normal vector contained in a texel of a normal-map represents the vector perpendicular to the surface of an object at the considered texel. Without deformation, the proper normal vector is $(0, 0, 1)$ as its XYZ components. We can modulate the vector to make it differ slightly from the proper one. For example, a modulated normal with components $(0.1, 0.2, 0.975)$ indicates a modification of the surface. A normal vector considered here is always normalized, having unit length, i.e. $(X^2 + Y^2 + Z^2) = 1$.

In the technique, we form an orthonormal frame of reference using vectors normal, tangent and binormal (tangent space) at each vertex of the surface:

X-axis = (1, 0, 0) (tangent vector **t**)
Y-axis = (0, 1, 0) (binormal vector **b**)
Z-axis = (0, 0, 1) (normal vector **n**)

This is similar to the Frenet frame we discussed in Chapter 14. To work in this orthonormal frame whose origin is at a vertex of the surface, we need a transformation to project a vector **a** = (x, y, z) expressed in our world coordinate system (**i, j, k**) to a' in the new coordinate system with basis (**t, n, b**). This can be done by first translating the origin of our coordinate system to the surface vertex and make an appropriate rotation. If all vectors and points are represented in homogeneous coordinates as 4×1 matrices, the 4×4 transformation matrix that brings the basis $(\mathbf{i}, \mathbf{j}, \mathbf{k})$ to the orthonormal frame at a vertex $p = (p_x, p_y, p_z)$ and performs a rotation is given by:

$$M = \begin{pmatrix} t_x & t_y & t_z & 0 \\ b_x & b_y & b_z & 0 \\ n_x & n_y & n_z & 0 \\ 0 & 0 & 0 & 1 \end{pmatrix} \begin{pmatrix} 0 & 0 & 0 & p_x \\ 0 & 0 & 0 & p_y \\ 0 & 0 & 0 & p_z \\ 0 & 0 & 0 & 1 \end{pmatrix} = \begin{pmatrix} t_x & t_y & t_z & p_x \\ b_x & b_y & b_z & p_y \\ n_x & n_y & n_z & p_z \\ 0 & 0 & 0 & 1 \end{pmatrix} \quad (19.19)$$

Note that there is a subtle difference between the Frenet frame transformation matrix of (14.11) in Chapter 14 and the transformation matrix M here. The former transformation rotates the basis $(\mathbf{i}, \mathbf{j}, \mathbf{k})$ to the new basis $(\mathbf{T}, \mathbf{N}, \mathbf{B})$ so that all cross-sections will be rotated accordingly. Here, the transformation matrix M lets us express the components of a vector (or a point) in the new coordinate system $(\mathbf{t}, \mathbf{n}, \mathbf{b})$.

For some parametric surfaces, a tangent at a point can be calculated conveniently by differentiating each coordinate with respect to a surface parameter. For example, a unit sphere centered at the origin O is described by the parametric equations of (19.3) with $r = 1$. At a point $P = (x, y, z)$ on the sphere, we can calculate the unit normal $\mathbf{n}$ and a unit tangent $\mathbf{t}$ easily:

$$\mathbf{n} = P - O = \begin{pmatrix} x \\ y \\ z \end{pmatrix}, \quad \mathbf{t} = \frac{\partial \mathbf{n}}{\partial \phi} = \begin{pmatrix} -sin\theta sin\phi \\ sin\theta cos\phi \\ 0 \end{pmatrix} = \begin{pmatrix} -y \\ x \\ 0 \end{pmatrix}, \quad (19.20)$$

However, the tangent vector of (19.20) is undefined at the poles when $\theta = 0$, or $180°$, which makes all three components of $\mathbf{t}$ in (19.20) become 0. For these special situations, we can set the vector to point along the y-axis, i.e.,

$$\mathbf{t} = \begin{pmatrix} 0 \\ 1 \\ 0 \end{pmatrix} \quad \text{when } z = 1, -1 \quad (19.21)$$

A binormal vector $\mathbf{b}$ is given by the cross product of $\mathbf{t}$ and $\mathbf{n}$ (i.e. $\mathbf{b} = \mathbf{t} \times \mathbf{n}$). So the transformation matrix $\mathbf{M}$ $(z \neq \pm 1)$ is

$$M = \begin{pmatrix} -y & x & 0 & x \\ b_x & b_y & b_z & y \\ x & y & z & z \\ 0 & 0 & 0 & 1 \end{pmatrix} \quad (19.22)$$

In glsl, the transformation matrix can be easily implemented like the following:

```
attribute vec4 vPosition;
.....
vec3 t, b, n;
.....
mat4 M = mat4(vec4 (t, vPosition.x), vec4(b, vPosition.y),
              vec4( n, vPosition.z), vec4(0.0, 0.0, 0.0, 1.0));

}
```

Any vector or vertex can be transformed to this surface-local coordinate system by multiplying it by M. (Note that OpenGL matrices are column-major; their columns are our rows.)

In the following, we use the textured sphere (i.e. *Spherelt*) we discussed above as an example to illustrate the principle of a bump mapping shader. We call our new class *Bump*, which is a slight modification of *Spherelt*. For simplicity and clarity of presentation, some parameters are hard-coded in the shaders and we discard many fancy lightling features such as diffuse and ambient lights and material properties. The light intensity is 'made up' inside the fragment shader. We only pass to the shaders the light postion and eye position (viewing point). However, we do need the texture features for reasons explained later. The following is the vertex shader for the example:

```
// bump.vert: Source code of vertex shader
uniform mat4 mvpMatrix;
attribute vec4 vPosition;
uniform vec4 eyePosition;
uniform vec4 lightPosition;

varying vec4 lightVec;   //light direction vector
varying vec4 eyeVec;     //eye direction vector
void main()
{
  vec4 O = vec4 ( 0.0, 0.0, 0.0, 1 );   //origin

  // Normalized normal in object coordinates
  // Normal can be also obtained by:
  //   vec3 n = normalize ( gl_NormalMatrix * gl_Normal );
  vec3 n = normalize(vPosition.xyz - O.xyz);
  vec3 t;                  //tangent
  //tangent for sphere (usually from application)
  if ( n.z < 1.0 && n.z > -1.0  ) {
     t.x = -n.y;           //t perpendicular to n;
     t.y = n.x;
  } else {
     t.x = 0.0;            //special treatment at poles
     t.y = 1.0;
  }
  t.z = 0.0;
  vec3 b = cross(n, t); //binormal
  //Since n is normalized, so b and t are also normalized

  //Transformation matrix, which transforms objects
  //   to surface-local system (t, b, n)
  mat4 M = mat4(vec4(t,vPosition.x), vec4(b,vPosition.y),
               vec4(n,vPosition.z), vec4(0.0,0.0,0.0,1.0));

  //vectors in surface-local system
  lightVec = normalize ( M * (lightPosition - vPosition) );
  eyeVec = normalize( M * ( eyePosition - vPosition ) );

  //texture coordinates for fragment shader
  gl_TexCoord[0] = gl_MultiTexCoord0;

  gl_Position = mvpMatrix * vPosition;
}
```

In the code, the **varying** variables *lightVec* and *eyeVec* are the light direction vector and the eye direction vector, corresponding to **L** and **V** at the surface point *vPosition*, of Figure 19-14 respectively. They are calculated, transformed to the surface-local system and normalized and are passed to the fragment shader.

On the spherical surface we need to select some bump centers, where the normals of the regions around them will be perturbed. However, our application has only passed in the coordinates and attributes of a limited number of points, the vertices of the triangles that form the sphere. The attributes of all other pixels are obtained by interpolation. How do we know the coordinates of a point on the surface? The trick is to make use of the texture coordinates, which can specify any point on the surface as the whole spherical surface has been mapped to the 1×1 st domain with $0 \le s \le 1$ and $0 \le t \le 1$. That's why we need the statement

$$\text{gl\_TexCoord[0]} = \text{gl\_MultiTexCoord0};$$

in the vertex shader.

The following is a corresponding fragment shader, a simplied version of one used by many authors. We explain this code below.

```
// bump.frag: Source code of fragment shader

varying vec4 lightVec;//light dir vector in surface-local system
varying vec4 eyeVec;  //eye direction vector in surface-local system
void main()
{
  float bumpDensity = 10.0;
  float bumpSize = 0.1;
  vec3 litColor;
  vec2 c = bumpDensity * gl_TexCoord[0].st;
  vec2 b = fract( c ) - vec2(0.5, 0.5 );   //a texsel on surface
  vec3 n1;                 //modulated normal

  float r2;                //square of radius of bump
  r2 = b.x * b.x + b.y * b.y;

  if ( r2 <= bumpSize ) { //modulate normal
    n1 = vec3 ( b, 1.0 ); //n1.z = 1
    n1 = normalize ( n1 );
  } else                  //do not perturb normal
    n1 = vec3 ( 0, 0, 1 );

  vec3 surfaceColor = vec3 ( 1.0, 0.6, 0.2 );
  litColor = surfaceColor * max(dot(n1, lightVec.xyz), 0.0 );
  vec3 reflectVec = reflect ( lightVec.xyz, n1 );
  float specularLight = max( dot(eyeVec.xyz, reflectVec), 0.0);
  float specularFactor = 0.5;
  specularLight = pow ( specularLight, 6.0 ) * specularFactor;
  litColor = min ( litColor + specularLight, vec3(1.0) );

  gl_FragColor = vec4 ( litColor, 1.0 )
}
```

This fragment shader defines the bump locations implicitly through the variable *bumpDensity*, which is the one-dimensional density of bumps, and the fucntion **fract**. The **fract** (x) function returns the fractional part of x, i.e. x minus **floor** (x). The input parameter can be a **float** or a **float** vector. In the latter case, the operation is done component-wise. After the multiplication of *bumpDensity*, the 1×1 st domain is magnified as shown in Figure 19-22 below, where *bump-Density* is 5. The total number of bumps on the surface is the square of *bumpDensity* and is equal to $5^2 = 25$ in the example of Figure 19-22. This is because the new domain can be divided into equally spaced grid lines in the s and the t directions. Each intersection point of the grid lines is described by two integer coordinates like point b in Figure 19-22(b) that has coordinates $(1, 1)$. In Figure 19-22(b), the integer values of the components of any point in the shaded region are always

$(1,1)$. Therefore, the unit shaded square represent the group of points where the integer parts of their coordinates is $(1,1)$. Their fractional parts represents how far the point is from $(1,1)$, an intersection point. If we shift the fraction components by $(0.5, 0.5)$, then the center of the grid square can be regarded as a bump center. This is done by the statement:

$$\text{vec2 b = fract(c) - vec2(0.5, 0.5); //a texsel on surface}$$

We 'bump' a point (modulate the unit normal $n1$ at the point) only if it lies within the radius of a circle as shown in the figure, otherwise the normal is left unchanged (i.e. $n1 = (0,0,1)$). In the code the **float** variable $r2$ is the square of the radius of the circle, which is inside the square.

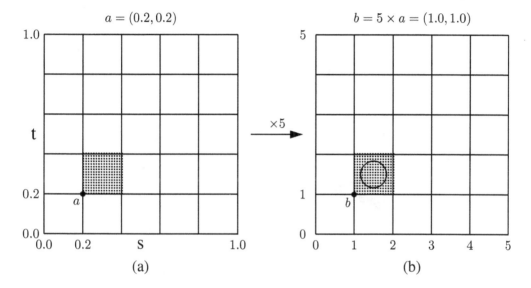

Figure 19-22 Texture Coordinates Multiplied by *bumpDensity* (=5)

The **vec3** variable *reflectVec* is the ray reflection direction vector, which is the vector **R** of Figure 19-14. Its value is calculated using the function **reflect**.

We hard-code the surface-color and compute the diffuse and specular reflection intensity values in the usual way except that vector values are in surface-local systems. Figure 19-23(a) below shows an output of this shader.

In the above example, we modulate normals using an algorithm. Alternatively, we can store the normal perturbations as a texture, which is referred to as a **bump map** or a **normal map**. Using our textured sphere as an example, we can create a bump map with minor modifications to our checkerboard texture data:

```
void Bump::makeCheckImage(void)
{
  int i, j, r, g;
  for (i = 0; i < iWidth; i++) {
    for (j = 0; j < iHeight; j++) {
      r = rand() % 32;
      g = rand() % 32;
      checkImage[i][j][0] = (GLubyte) r;
      checkImage[i][j][1] = (GLubyte) g;
      checkImage[i][j][2] = (GLubyte) 255;
    }
  }
}
```

The red and green components of the texture are randomly assigned an integer value betwenn 0 and 32, and the blue component is assigned a value of 255. When the RGB components are normalized to $[0, 1]$, the red and green values are in $[0, 0.125]$ and the blue value is always 1. The RGB components are mapped to the XYZ values of a normal at the surface. This means that we only perturb the X and Y components with small values and always keep the Z component, which is perpendicular to the surface, to be 1. (Of course, after we have normalized the normal vector, the Z value also changes.) The following is the code for the fragment shader that uses this normal map. An output of it is shown in Figure 19-23(b).

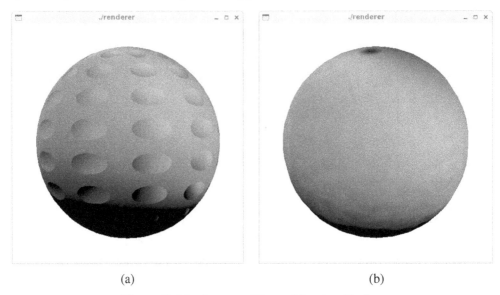

(a)   (b)

Figure 19-23 Outputs of Bump Mapping Shaders

```
// bump.frag: Source code of fragment shader

varying vec4 lightVec;   //light dir vector in surface-local system
varying vec4 eyeVec;     //eye direction vector in surface-local system
uniform sampler2D texHandle;
void main()
{
  vec3 litColor;
  vec3 n1;                   //modulated normal
  n1 = texture2D(texHandle, gl_TexCoord[0].st).rgb;
  n1 = normalize ( n1 );
  vec3 surfaceColor = vec3 ( 1.0, 0.6, 0.2 );
  litColor = surfaceColor * max(dot(n1, lightVec.xyz), 0.0 );
  vec3 reflectVec = reflect ( lightVec.xyz, n1 );
  float specularLight = max ( dot(eyeVec.xyz, reflectVec), 0.0 );
  float specularFactor = 0.5;
  specularLight = pow ( specularLight, 6.0 ) * specularFactor;
  litColor = min ( litColor + specularLight, vec3(1.0) );

  gl_FragColor = vec4 ( litColor, 1.0 );
}
```

Complete related programs of this chapter can be downloaded from the web site of this book.

Chapter 20   Shaders of Lighting

20.1   Lighting Models

We have discussed that the Phong lighting model is a **local illumination** model, in which the shaded color or the illumination at a point of a surface depends purely on the local surface configuration such as the surface normal, the viewing direction, and the light direction. The model only considers light rays originated from point sources and ignores illumination due to second bounces of rays. Also, the model does not consider occlusion of light rays and thus it won't create any shadows in a scene. The main advantage of the model is its simplicity and efficiency in computation.

The ray tracing technique discussed in Chapter 16 is a **global illumination** model. It is a sophisticated technique that considers multiple bounces of light rays, casting shadows and producing lighting effects resembling real scenes. However, it is computing intensive and many real-time games may not be able to use the method.

In this chapter, we consider some simple and popular lighting models that approximate global lighting effects. We implement the models using the OpenGL Shading Language (glsl).

20.2   Hemisphere Lighting

Hemisphere lighting can give additional approximation of ambient or diffuse lighting in scenes that have two distinct lighting colors. For example, a scene consisting of a blue sky and green mountains can be illuminated by blue color light from above and and green color light from below. The Phong model only uses fixed colors and is not able to produce such effect.

Figure 20-1 below shows the hemisphere lighting model. The surface of an object receives light from an upper hemisphere and a lower hemisphere as shown in Figure 20-1(a).

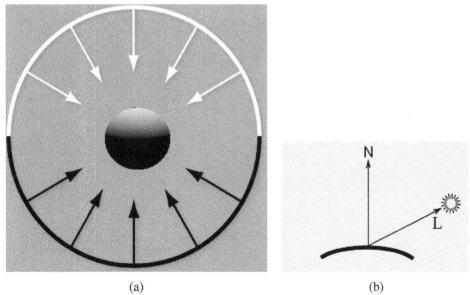

(a)   (b)

Figure 20-1 Hemishpere Lighting Model

In the model, we assume that each point of a hemisphere around a surface acts as a light source in the direction of **L** (a unit vector) as shown in Figure 20-1(b) (see also Figure 19-14). The unit normal at the illuminated point is **N**. The illumination at an area from each point source is proportional to

$$F(\mathbf{N}, \mathbf{L}) = max(0, \mathbf{N} \cdot \mathbf{L}) \tag{20.1}$$

Therefore, an area with its normal pointing straight up receives all its illumination from the upper hemisphere as $\mathbf{N} \cdot \mathbf{L}$ is negative for all light sources on the lower hemisphere. Similarly, an area with its normal pointing straight down receives all the illumination from the lower hemisphere. For areas with other surface normals, the illumination on the area is a mixture of illuminations from the upper and lower hemispheres.

Suppose **U** is the unit vector that points in the straight up direction (Figure 20-2b), and f is the fraction of illumination on a surface area due to the upper hemisphere. The fraction f is proportional to the integration of the contribution of each point source over the the hemisphere. In spherical coordinates (see Figure 19-10 of Chapter 19), an infinitesimal area is given by $dA = (rsin\theta d\phi)(rd\theta)$ (Figure 20-2a). For the upper hemisphere, we need to integrate over θ from 0 to π, and ϕ from 0 to π. So

$$f \propto \int_0^\pi \int_0^\pi F(\mathbf{N}, \mathbf{L})(rsin\theta d\phi)(rd\theta) \tag{20.2}$$

That is,

$$f = c \times r^2 \int_0^\pi \int_0^\pi F(\mathbf{N}, \mathbf{L})sin\theta d\phi d\theta \tag{20.3}$$

where c is a constant. When **N** is pointing straight up, in the same direction as **U**, f is 1 as there is only contribution from the upper hemisphere, and $F = \mathbf{N} \cdot \mathbf{L} = sin\theta sin\phi$. Therefore,

$$\begin{aligned} 1 \quad &= c \times r^2 \int_0^\pi \int_0^\pi sin^2\theta sin\phi d\phi d\theta \\ &= c \times r^2 \pi \end{aligned} \tag{20.4}$$

Thus $c = 1/(\pi r^2)$. Substituting this back to (20.3), we have

$$f = \frac{1}{\pi} \int_0^\pi \int_0^\pi F(\mathbf{N}, \mathbf{L})sin\theta d\phi d\theta \tag{20.5}$$

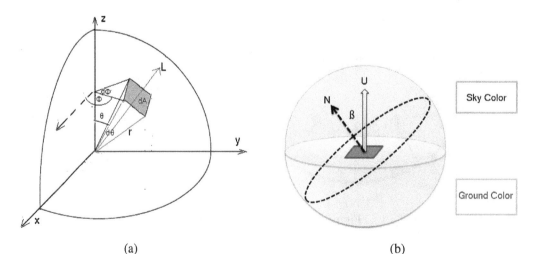

(a)   (b)

Figure 20-2 Integration Over Upper Hemisphere (y-axis is up)

If **N** is not in the same direction as **U**, and the angle between them is β like that shown in Figure 20-2b, then illumination of the upper hemisphere is only from a spherical wedge with ϕ ranging from β to π. The faction f is calculated by integrating over ϕ from β to π:

$$
\begin{aligned}
f &= \tfrac{1}{\pi} \int_0^\pi \int_\beta^\pi (\mathbf{N} \cdot \mathbf{L}) sin\theta d\phi d\theta \\
&= \tfrac{1}{\pi} \int_0^\pi \int_\beta^\pi sin^2\theta sin\phi d\phi d\theta \\
&= \tfrac{1}{2}(1 + cos\beta) \\
&= \tfrac{1}{2}(1 + \mathbf{N} \cdot \mathbf{U})
\end{aligned}
\tag{20.6}
$$

The value of f represents the contribution of the upper hemisphere, so the contribution from the lower hemisphere is $1 - f$. If C_{sky} and C_{ground} are the illumination from the the upper and lower hemispheres respectively, the total illumination C at a surface point is

$$
\begin{aligned}
C &= fC_{sky} + (1 - f)C_{ground} \\
&= \tfrac{1}{2}(1 + cos\beta)C_{sky} + \tfrac{1}{2}(1 - cos\beta)C_{ground}
\end{aligned}
\tag{20.7}
$$

Implementation of the shader of this model is straightforward. Suppose our illuminated object is the *Sphere* object we have discussed in Chapter 19; the normal at each point is easy to calculate. The following is the code for the vertex shader and the fragment shader:

Program Listing 20-1   Shaders for Hemisphere Lighting

(a) Vertex Shader: sphereh.vert

```
// sphereh.vert: Source code of vertex shader
uniform mat4 mvpMatrix;
attribute vec4 vPosition;

varying vec3 N; //normal direction

uniform int objType;

void main()
{
   if ( objType == 0 )
     N = vPosition.xyz;    //normal of  a point on sphere
   else
     N = gl_NormalMatrix * gl_Normal;

   gl_Position = mvpMatrix * vPosition;
}
```

(b) Fragment Shader: sphereh.frag

```
// spherel.frag Source code of fragment shader

varying vec3 N;

uniform vec4 skyColor;
uniform vec4 groundColor;
uniform vec3 skyDirection;
```

```
void main()
{
    vec3 norm = normalize(N);
    float cosbeta = dot ( norm, skyDirection );
    float f = 0.5 + 0.5 * cosbeta;
    vec4 color = mix (groundColor, skyColor, f);
    gl_FragColor = color;
}
```

The glsl built-in function **mix** has been used to combine the color contributions from the lower and upper hemispheres using equation (20.7). In the fragment shader, the **uniform** variables *sky-Color, groundColor*, and *skyDirection* are passed from the application. The code is simple and efficient, appropriate to be used in applications for model preview, or in conjunction with traditional graphics lighting models. Hemisphere lighting can also be superimposed with directional or spot lights to provide more detailed illumination to certain parts of the scene. Figure 20-3 shows a sample output of the code, where *skyColor, groundColor*, and *skyDirection* are set to $\{0.5, 0.5, 1, 1\}$, $\{0.2, 1, 0.2, 1\}$, and $\{0, 1, 0\}$ respectively and the y-axis is the up direction.

Figure 20-3 Lit Sphere Using Hemisphere Lighting

20.3 Image-Based Lighting (IBL)

Image-based lighting (IBL) is the process of lighting graphical scenes and objects using images of light from the real world. It evolves from the reflection-mapping technique in which panoramic images are used as texture maps to simulate shiny objects reflection of real and synthetic environments.

IBL utilizes an image to simulate lighting in a scene. The image represents omni-directional real world lights and is often captured by a special camera and projected onto a dome or a sphere. The image may contain detailed real-world lighting information saved as an enironment map. The technique has been popularized by research professor Paul Debevec of USC (http://www.pauldebevec.com/), who gives a tutorial on the subject at the site

   http://ict.usc.edu/pubs/Image-Based%20Lighting.pdf

20.3.1   High-Dynamic Range Image

The method often uses a **light probe** to capture the lighting of a real-world scene and saves it as a **high-dynamic range** (HDR) image, usually referred to as a light probe image, which is used to create an environment map, such as a cubemap, where a light probe sphere is projected onto six unwrapped cube faces. One may obtain light probe images from Debevec's web site mentioned above.

A scene's dynamic range is the contrast ratio of its brightest region to its darkest region. An 8-bit image can have a range of 256 to 1. A high-dynamic range (HDR) image is an image with a greater dynamic range than one that can be shown on a standard display device or captured by a standard camera that uses only one exposure. Its value at a pixel value is proportional to the amount of light in the world region mapped to that pixel, unlike a normal image in which pixel values are nonlinearly encoded. The higher range can be achieved by capturing several different narrower range exposures of the same subject and then combining them to form a single HDR image. Non-HDR cameras take photographs with a limited exposure range, which may result in a loss of highlight or shadow details. To represent a larger range, HDR pixel values are represented by floating-point numbers. On the other hand, traditional low-dynamic range image pixels are usually represented by eight bits per channel, with each pixel value ranging as integers from 0 to 255.

Figure 2-4 compares some images, which are downloaded from the site *http://www.hdrshop.com/*, that are originated from an HDR image and a normal 8-bit image. As shown in (a) and (b), the two images look the same when they are displayed on a computer screen as each screen pixel channel is of 8 bits. However, as shown in (c) and (d), when the image brigtnesses are reduced by 64, the two images appear significantly different. A tool called *HDRshop* is available at the site for manipulating HDR images.

Normal 8-bit Image	HDR Image
(a) Not processed	(b) Not Processed

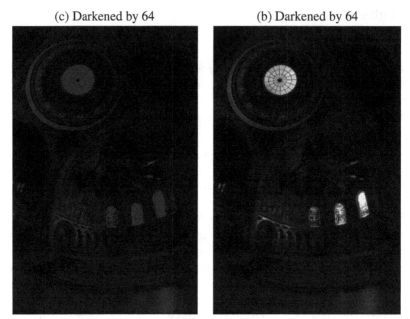

(c) Darkened by 64   (b) Darkened by 64

Figure 20-4 Comparing HDR Image with Normal 8-bit Image
(Images downloaded from *http://www.hdrshop.com/*)

More detailly, image-based lighting using HDR images involves a few steps:

1. Capture real-world illumination as an omnidirectional HDR image.
2. Create from the HDR image a representation of the environment such as an environment map.
3. Put the 3D graphical object inside the environment.
4. Simulate lighting from the environment representation of step 2.

However, if we do not have HDR images at hand, we still can apply the technique of image-based lighting to illuminate objects using images as light sources as we do here.

20.3.2 Cubemaps

Cube mapping can be used for environment mapping, where the reflection color at a point of a surface area is looked up from the the *environment* along the area's reflection vector, and the *environment color* is stored in a texture map (see also Figure 20-6 below). In cube mapping, we typically map six images as textures to the six faces of a large cube surrounding a scene. The color that we see along a direction in the environment is represented by a texture pixel on the cube. The GLSL data type **samplerCube** is specifically provided for cube mapping; when shading a point of a scene, we can treat the surface area at the point as a perfect reflecting surface and get the environment data by calculating the reflection direction of the viewing direction. Another popular application of cube mapping is for creating sky boxes, which provide the illusion of 3-dimensional backgrounds looked like a sky; in the process a big box is created to encase the camera as it moves around.

In OpenGL, we can create a *cubemap*, which is a texture, the way we create any other textures. We generate a texture and bind it to the target GL_TEXTURE_CUBE_MAP:

```
int texName;
glGenTextures(1, &texName);
glBindTexture(GL_TEXTURE_CUBE_MAP, texName);
```

As a cube has 6 faces, we need to provide 6 images, one for each face, to be used as textures. To simplify the task, OpenGL provides 6 special texture targets for mapping an image to a face of the cube:

Texture target	Orientation
GL_TEXTURE_CUBE_MAP_POSITIVE_X	Right
GL_TEXTURE_CUBE_MAP_NEGATIVE_X	Left
GL_TEXTURE_CUBE_MAP_POSITIVE_Y	Top
GL_TEXTURE_CUBE_MAP_NEGATIVE_Y	Bottom
GL_TEXTURE_CUBE_MAP_POSITIVE_Z	Front
GL_TEXTURE_CUBE_MAP_NEGATIVE_Z	Back

The texture targets are of **enum** data type and their values are linearly incremented by 1. So we could loop through all texture targets by starting from GL_TEXTURE_CUBE_MAP_POSITIVE_X and incrementing the **enum** texture target by 1 in each iteration, like the following:

```
char *cubeMapImages[6] =
     {"right.png", "left.png", "top.png", "bottom.png",
                                  "front.png", "back.png"};
for ( int i = 0; i < 6; i++ ) {
   GLubyte *texImage = makeTexImage ( (char *) cubeMapImages[i] );
   glTexImage2D(GL_TEXTURE_CUBE_MAP_POSITIVE_X + i, 0, GL_RGBA,
     texImageWidth,texImageHeight,0,GL_RGBA,GL_UNSIGNED_BYTE,texImage);
   delete texImage;
}
```

Or better if we specify the targets explicitly:

```
GLuint targets[] = {
     GL_TEXTURE_CUBE_MAP_POSITIVE_X, GL_TEXTURE_CUBE_MAP_NEGATIVE_X,
     GL_TEXTURE_CUBE_MAP_POSITIVE_Y, GL_TEXTURE_CUBE_MAP_NEGATIVE_Y,
     GL_TEXTURE_CUBE_MAP_POSITIVE_Z, GL_TEXTURE_CUBE_MAP_NEGATIVE_Z
};
.....
for ( int i = 0; i < 6; i++ ) {
   GLubyte *texImage = makeTexImage ( (char *) cubeMapImages[i] );
   glTexImage2D(targets[i], 0, GL_RGBA, texImageWidth,
              texImageHeight, 0, GL_RGBA, GL_UNSIGNED_BYTE, texImage);
   delete texImage;
}
```

As a cubemap is a texture, we could also specify its filtering and wrapping methods like what we do to other textures:

```
glTexParameteri(GL_TEXTURE_CUBE_MAP,GL_TEXTURE_MAG_FILTER,GL_LINEAR);
glTexParameteri(GL_TEXTURE_CUBE_MAP,GL_TEXTURE_MIN_FILTER, GL_LINEAR);
glTexParameteri(GL_TEXTURE_CUBE_MAP,GL_TEXTURE_WRAP_S,GL_CLAMP_TO_EDGE);
glTexParameteri(GL_TEXTURE_CUBE_MAP,GL_TEXTURE_WRAP_T,GL_CLAMP_TO_EDGE);
glTexParameteri(GL_TEXTURE_CUBE_MAP,GL_TEXTURE_WRAP_R,GL_CLAMP_TO_EDGE);
```

In the code, (S, T, R) represents a texel's 3-dimensional coordinates. (Because the images are mapped to a cube, the texture is 3-dimensional.) So GL_TEXTURE_WRAP_R simply sets the wrapping method for a texel's R coordinate. The wrapping method is set to GL_CLAMP_TO_EDGE so that a texture coordinate is clamped within the range of edges; that is, it is clamped to $[\frac{1}{2N}, 1 - \frac{1}{2N}]$ where N is the size of the texture in the direction of clamping.

GLSL provides the sampler type **samplerCube** to handle cubemaps. A fragment shader that calculates the color at a point due to a cubemap texel would look like the following:

```
uniform samplerCube cubeEnvMap;
varying vec3 envReflectDir;    //texel direction

void main()
{
  vec3 envColor = vec3 (textureCube(cubeEnvMap, envReflectDir));
}
```

Let us consider a very simple example that utilizes cube mapping to shade a sphere. In the application, we use the same *Sphere* class that we have developed in the previous chapter. Instead of using the Phong model, for simplicity, we use a simplified lighting model, in which the illumination at a point on a surface due to a point light source is given by

$$I = I^{in} \times F(\mathbf{N}, \mathbf{L}) \tag{20.8}$$

where $F(\mathbf{N}, \mathbf{L})$ is given by (20.1) and the vectors $\mathbf{N}$ and $\mathbf{L}$ are shown in Figure 20-1 (b). The total illumination is a mixture of this illumination and that due to the environment. The sphere is inside the cube so that the environment the sphere sees is the texture images of the cube.

Figure 20-5 shows the 6 images that we will use for the cubemap:

Right (+X)	Left (-X)	Top (+Y)
Bottom (-Y)	Front (+Z)	Back (-Z)

Figure 20-5   Images for Cubemap

Our vertex shader and fragment shader are simple. The vertex shader calculates the perfect reflection direction of the viewing vector using the formula

$$\mathbf{r_v} = 2(\mathbf{v} \cdot \mathbf{n})\mathbf{n} - \mathbf{v} \tag{20.9}$$

which is also shown in Equation (16.9) of Chapter 16. Figure 20-6 again shows this relation.

A Face of Cubemap

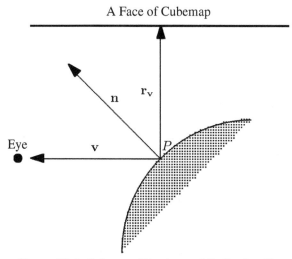

Figure 20-6 Cubemap Viewing and Reflection Vectors

```
// sphereibl.vert: Source code of vertex shader
uniform mat4 mvpMatrix;
attribute vec4 vPosition;
uniform vec4 eyePosition;
uniform vec4 lightPosition;
uniform vec4 lightDiffuse;
uniform vec4 materialColor;
varying vec4 lightReflection;
varying vec3 envReflectDir;   //environment reflection direction

void main() {
   vec3 N = vPosition.xyz;   //normal of  a point on sphere
                             // (= vPosition.xyz - origin.xyz)
   vec3 L = lightPosition.xyz - vPosition.xyz;
   vec3 V = eyePosition.xyz - vPosition.xyz;

   N = normalize(N);   //unit normal direction
   L = normalize(L);   //unit light source direction
   V = normalize(V);   //unit view vector

   // using a simplified lighting model
   float F = max(0.0, dot(N, L));
   lightReflection =  F * materialColor *  lightDiffuse;
   //environment reflection direction
   envReflectDir = 2.0 *  dot ( N, V) * N - V;
   gl_Position = mvpMatrix * vPosition;
}
-------------------------------------------------------------------
// sphereibl.frag: Source code of fragment shader
uniform samplerCube cubeEnvMap;
varying vec4 lightReflection;
varying vec3 envReflectDir;   //environment reflection direction

void main()    {
  vec4 envColor = vec4(vec3(textureCube(cubeEnvMap,envReflectDir)),1);
```

```
    float envPercent = 0.7;
    vec4 color = mix ( lightReflection, envColor, envPercent );
    gl_FragColor = color;
}
```

The vertex shader passes the reflection vector to the fragment shader, which utilizes it in the glsl function **textureCube** to fetch the environment color (texel color) along that reflected direction, saving its value in the **vec4** variable *envColor*. We use the formula (20.9) to calculate the reflection vector. (Alternatively, one may use the glsl function **reflect** to calculate it with **-v** and **n** as input parameters.) The function **textureCube** performs a cube mapping operation, in which the (s, t, r) texture coordinates are treated as a direction vector (r_x, r_y, r_z) emanating from the center of the cube, and the texture color at that position is returned. Therefore, when we pass $\mathbf{r_v}$ to **textureCube**, the cube center is at the point P on the sphere (Figure 20-6), which is only an approximation to the real scene.

The **varying vec4** variable *lightReflection* calculates the illumination by the point light source in the vertex shader according to the formula (20.8) and passes its value to the fragment shader. The overall illumination is a combination of this illumination and the environment illumination *envColor*, which are combined by the glsl function **mix** with the weight of *envColor* specified by the variable *envPercent*, which is equal to 0.7 in the example.

Note that as discussed in Chapter 3, a point is not the same as a vector and the difference between two points (positions) is a vector. So the statement

vec3 N = vPosition.xyz;

actually means

vec3 N = vPosition.xyz - origin.xyz;

and the origin is at $(0, 0, 0)$. (Also note that a translation transformation changes a point but has no effect on a vector.)

A sample output of this application is shown in Figure 20-7(a) with the following parameters:

```
    materialColor[] = {1, 1, 1, 1};
    lightDiffuse[] = {1, 0.8, 0.6, 1};
    lightPosition[] = {5, 10, 5, 1};
    eyePosition[] = {0, 0, 6.3, 1};
```

(a)   (b)

Figure 20-7 Outputs of Cubemap Shader

One can see that the mapped images are "upside-down". This is due to the way that **textureCube** maps the textures, which is explained in the official GLSL specifications. A simple way to 'fix' this problem is to rotate all the texture images by 180°; Figure 20-6(b) shows the output of the shader when the images of Figure 20-5 have been rotated by 180°.

20.3.3 Cubemaps for Image-based Rendering

Each texel in a cubemap can be regarded as a light source. We can describe static lighting environments by a cubemap, which can be considered as an environment map. In an image-based lighting model, we compute the lighting by an arbitrary number of light sources with a single texture lookup in a cubemap.

Referring to Figure 20-1(b), the diffuse illumination at an area due to a light source is given by

$$I_d = I_d^{in} c_d \times max(0, \mathbf{N} \cdot \mathbf{L}) \tag{20.10}$$

where I_d^{in} is the incoming diffuse illumination, c_d is the diffuse reflection coefficient, and I_d is the resulted diffuse illumination. (This is also the point source light model we have used in the previous section with c_d set to 1.) Suppose the environment is mapped to the six faces of a cube as textures (i.e. cubemap). Then the light sources are the texels of the cube surfaces and the light direction $\mathbf{L}$ is the direction from the cube center to the texel in the cube map.

For a static cube map, we can speed up the process by precomputing the diffuse lighting for all possible surface normals $\mathbf{N}$ and storing them in a lookup table. The lighting from a source at a point on a surface with a normal $\mathbf{N}$ can be found by looking up the diffuse illumination for the specific normal from the lookup table, and the total illumination at the point is the sum of the diffuse illumination of all texels of the cube map. This summed diffuse illumination for a specific normal can be stored in a second cube map, which is usually referred to as the *diffuse irradiance environment map* or *diffuse environment map*.   This second cube map is simply a lookup table, where each normal $\mathbf{N}$ is mapped to a color. The diffuse environment can be created using the graphics tool HDRshop. (Irradiance is the flux of light incident on a unit area, measured in $watts/meter^2$. Our color intensity at a pixel represents the corresponding irradiance.)

The illumination due to specular lights can be similarly treated. The specular illumination due to one point source is:

$$I_s = I_d^{in} c_s \times max(0, \mathbf{r_v} \cdot \mathbf{L})^f \tag{20.11}$$

where c_s is the reflection coefficient, r_v is the reflection direction, and f is the surface shininess. Using this equation, we can compute a cubemap (used as lookup table) that contains the sum of specular illumination from many source for any r_v.

If the cubemaps are given and we use our *Sphere* object as the scene to be illuminated, the shader codes are quite simple. The vertex shader just needs to compute the normal and the reflected view direction at each vertex and sends their values to the fragment shader via varying variables. The values are interpreted across each polygon and the fragment shader utilizes the interpreted values to lookup the illuminations from two cubemaps and combine them using the **mix** function to obtain the resulted illumination:

```
// sphereibl.vert: Source code of vertex shader
uniform mat4 mvpMatrix;
attribute vec4 vPosition;
uniform vec4 eyePosition;
varying vec3 reflectDir;    //environment reflection direction
varying vec3 N;             //normal at a point

void main()
```

```
{
   N = vPosition.xyz;   //normal of  a point on sphere
                        // (= vPosition.xyz - origin.xyz)
   vec3 V = eyePosition.xyz - vPosition.xyz;

   N = normalize(N);    //unit normal direction
   V = normalize(V);    //unit view vector

   //environment reflection direction
   reflectDir = 2.0 *  dot ( N, V) * N - V;

   gl_Position = mvpMatrix * vPosition;
}
------------------------------------------------------------------
// sphereibl.frag: Source code of fragment shader
uniform samplerCube diffuseMap;
uniform samplerCube specularMap;
varying vec3 reflectDir;   //environment reflection direction
varying vec3 N;

void main()
{
  float c_d = 0.8, c_s = 0.7;

  vec4 diffuseColor=c_d*vec4(vec3(textureCube(diffuseMap, N)), 1);
  vec4 specularColor = c_s * vec4(vec3(textureCube(specularMap,
                                                 reflectDir)), 1 );

  vec4 color = mix ( diffuseColor, specularColor, 0.5 );

  gl_FragColor = color;
}
```

20.4 Spherical Harmonic Lighting

20.4.1 Irradiance Environement Map

Spherical Harmonic lighting (SH lighting) computes the diffuse illumination on 3D scenes from broad light sources by expressing light intensities using spherical harmonics. It is based on the observation that the reflected intensity from a diffuse surface varies slowly as a function of surface orientation. Consequently, one can decompose a light source image into spherical harmonic terms so that it can be represented by an analytic expression to reproduce the lighting effects of image-based or environment mapping models without using the actual image source at the runtime.

   Ravi Ramamoorthi and Pat Hanrahan of Stanford University showed in 2001 that the irradiance at an area is not sensitive to the high frequency components of the light source and one only needs to compute 9 coefficients of an analytic formula, which correspond to the lowest-frequency modes of the light, to achieve average errors of only 1%. They showed that the irradiance can be procedurally represented explicitly as a quadratic polynomial of the surface normal. Ravi and Pat refer to a diffuse reflection map indexed by the surface normal, as an *irradiance environment map* because the map at each pixel location essentially stores the irradiance for a particular orientation of the surface.

   Suppose $L(\theta, \phi) = |\mathbf{L}(\theta, \phi)|$ denotes the remote light intensity distribution from the unit direction $1(\theta, \phi) = \frac{L}{L}$ as shown in Figure 20-2(a). Neglecting the effects of cast shadows and near-field illumination, the irradiance E is then a function of the unit surface normal $\mathbf{n}$ only and is calculated by integrating L over the upper hemisphere $\Omega(\mathbf{n})$:

$$E(\mathbf{n}) = c \times \int_{\Omega(\mathbf{n})} \mathbf{n} \cdot \mathbf{L}(\theta, \phi) \, d\phi d\theta \qquad (20.12)$$

where c is a proportional constant. Then the radiosity of a surface, the rate at which energy leaves that surface (energy per unit time per unit area), can be found by multiplying E by ρ, the fraction of incident light that is reflected by the surface, and may depend on position p and be described by a texture:

$$B(p, \mathbf{n}) = \rho(p)E(\mathbf{n}) \qquad (20.13)$$

The radiosity B corresponds directly to the brightness at a position of the scene. We want to find an analytic expression, which can be computed efficiently in real time, to approximate E. It turns out that spherical harmonics are good basis functions for this purpose.

20.4.2 Spherical Harmonics

Spherical harmonics, analogous to Fourier series which are a series of functions on a line or a circle, are a series of functions defined on the surface of a sphere, in terms of spherical coordinates. Denoted by $Y_l^m(\theta, \phi)$, spherical harmonics are the angular portion of the solution to *Laplace's equation* with the absence of azimuthal symmetry. In our notation, θ is the polar (colatitudinal) coordinate with $\theta \in [0, \pi]$, and ϕ the azimuthal (longitudinal) coordinate with $\phi \in [0, 2\pi)$. (See Figure 19-9 or Figure 20-2.) Spherical harmonics can be defined as

$$Y_l^m(\theta, \phi) = \left(\frac{2l+1}{4\pi} \frac{(l-m)!}{(l+m)!} \right)^{\frac{1}{2}} P_l^m(cos\theta) e^{im\phi} \qquad (20.14)$$

where $P_l^m(x)$ is an *associated Legendre polynomial*, which are orthonormal:

$$P_l^{-m} = (-1)^m \frac{(l-m)!}{(l+m)!} P_l^m \qquad (20.15)$$

and

$$\int_{\theta=0}^{\pi} \int_{\phi=0}^{2\pi} Y_l^m \overline{Y}_{l'}^{m'} (sin\theta) d\phi d\theta = \delta_{ll'} \delta_{mm'} \qquad (20.16)$$

where $\overline{z}$ denotes the complex conjugate of z, and δ_{ij} is the Kronecker delta. (It equals 1 when $i = j$, and equals 0 when $i \neq j$.) One can also show that normalized spherical harmonic functions satisfy the relation:

$$\overline{Y}_l^m(\theta, \phi) = (-1)^m Y_l^{-m}(\theta, \phi) \qquad (20.17)$$

The following list the first few analytic expressions of $Y_l^m(\theta, \phi)$:

$$Y_0^0 = \frac{1}{2} \left(\frac{1}{\pi} \right)^{\frac{1}{2}}, \qquad\qquad Y_1^{-1} = \frac{1}{2} \left(\frac{3}{2\pi} \right)^{\frac{1}{2}} sin\,\theta\, e^{-i\phi}$$

$$Y_1^0 = \frac{1}{2} \left(\frac{3}{\pi} \right)^{\frac{1}{2}} cos\,\theta, \qquad Y_1^1 = -\frac{1}{2} \left(\frac{3}{2\pi} \right)^{\frac{1}{2}} sin\,\theta\, e^{i\phi}$$

$$Y_2^{-2} = \frac{1}{4} \left(\frac{15}{2\pi} \right)^{\frac{1}{2}} sin^2\,\theta\, e^{-i2\phi}, \qquad Y_2^{-1} = \frac{1}{2} \left(\frac{15}{2\pi} \right)^{\frac{1}{2}} sin\,\theta\, cos\,\theta\, e^{-i\phi} \qquad (20.18)$$

$$Y_2^0 = \frac{1}{4} \left(\frac{5}{\pi} \right)^{\frac{1}{2}} (3cos^2\,\theta - 1), \qquad Y_2^1 = -\frac{1}{2} \left(\frac{15}{2\pi} \right)^{\frac{1}{2}} sin\,\theta\, cos\,\theta\, e^{i\phi}$$

$$Y_2^2 = \frac{1}{4} \left(\frac{15}{2\pi} \right)^{\frac{1}{2}} sin^2\,\theta\, e^{i2\phi}, \qquad Y_3^{-3} = \frac{1}{8} \left(\frac{35}{\pi} \right)^{\frac{1}{2}} sin^3\,\theta\, e^{-i3\phi}$$

Note that in (20.14), when $m = 0$, the harmonics does not depend on the azimuthal coordinate ϕ. In SH lighting, we use a real basis of spherical harmonics denoted by Y_{lm}, which can be defined in terms of the complex basis denoted by Y_l^m:

$$Y_{lm} = \begin{cases} \sqrt{2}(-1)^m Im[Y_l^{|m|}] & \text{if } m < 0 \\ Y_l^0 & \text{if } m = 0 \\ \sqrt{2}(-1)^m Re[Y_l^m] & \text{if } m > 0 \end{cases} \tag{20.19}$$

The spherical coordinates and Cartesian coordinates are related by:

$$(x, y, z) = (\sin\theta\cos\phi, \ \sin\theta\cos\phi, \ \cos\theta) \tag{20.20}$$

Applying the formulas

$$\begin{aligned} e^{i\phi} &= \cos\phi + i\sin\phi \\ \sin 2\phi &= 2\sin\phi\cos\phi \\ \cos 2\phi &= \cos^2\phi - \sin^2\phi \end{aligned}$$

to (20.19) and evaluating the numeric constants, one can obtain the first 9 spherical harmonics in cartesian coordinates:

$$\begin{aligned} Y_{00} &= 0.282095 & \text{constant} \\ (Y_{1-1}; Y_{10}; Y_{11}) &= 0.488603(y; z; x) & \text{linear} \\ (Y_{2-2}; Y_{2-1}; Y_{21}) &= 1.092548(xy; yz; xz) & \text{quadratic} \\ Y_{20} &= 0.315392(3z^2 - 1) & \text{quadratic} \\ Y_{22} &= 0.546274(x^2 - y^2) & \text{quadratic} \end{aligned} \tag{20.21}$$

These 9 spherical harmonics are simply constant ($l = 0$), linear ($l = 1$), and quadratic ($l = 2$) polynomials of the cartesian components (x, y, z).

The spherical harmonics will be used as basis functions, which can be scaled and summed to produce an approximation to a specified function. The process of calculating how much of each basis function contributes to the approximation is referred to as *projection*.

We can decompose the light intensity distribution $L(\theta, \phi)$ and the irradiance $E(\theta, \phi)$ in terms of spherical harmonics with coefficients, L_{lm} and E_{lm}:

$$\begin{aligned} L(\theta, \phi) &= \sum_{l,m} L_{lm} Y_{lm}(\theta, \phi) \\ E(\theta, \phi) &= \sum_{l,m} E_{lm} Y_{lm}(\theta, \phi) \end{aligned} \tag{20.22}$$

We can also expand the dot product $a(\theta) = (\mathbf{n} \cdot \mathbf{l})$ with coefficients a_l. Since a does not depend on ϕ, $m = 0$, so we only use the index l:

$$a(\theta) = max(\cos\theta, 0) = \sum_l a_l Y_{l0}(\theta) \tag{20.23}$$

One can show that

$$E(\theta, \phi) = \sum_{l,m} A_l L_{lm} Y_{lm}(\theta, \phi) \tag{20.24}$$

where

$$A_l = \left(\frac{4\pi}{2l+1}\right)^{\frac{1}{2}} a_l$$

In fact, $A_l = 0$ for odd values of $l > 1$, and for even values, it falls off rapidly as $l^{-5/2}$. With these, one can derive an analytic formula for A_l:

$$A_l = \begin{cases} \dfrac{2\pi}{3} & \text{if } l = 1 \\[2mm] 0 & \text{if } l > 1, odd \\[2mm] 2\pi\dfrac{(-1)^{\frac{l}{2}-1}}{(l+2)(l-1)}\dfrac{l!}{2^l\left(\dfrac{l}{2}!\right)^2} & \text{if } l \ even \end{cases} \tag{20.25}$$

The following are numerical values of the first few terms:

$$\begin{aligned} A_0 &= 3.141593 \quad A_1 = 2.094395 \quad A_2 = 0.785398 \quad A_3 = 0 \\ A_4 &= -0.130900 \quad A_5 = A_7 = 0 \quad A_6 = 0.049087 \quad A_8 = -0.024543 \end{aligned} \tag{20.26}$$

As one can see from these numerical values, A_l decays exponentially with l, and we just need to consider low-frequency lighting coefficients, of order $l \leq 2$. Practically, approximating the irradiance with only 9 coefficients (1 for $l = 0$, 3 for $l = 1, -1 \leq m \leq 1$, and 5 for $l = 2, -2 \leq m \leq 2$) gives very good results.

The lighting coefficients can be found by integration:

$$L_{lm} = \int_{\theta=0}^{\pi} \int_{\phi=0}^{2\pi} L(\theta, \phi) Y_{lm}(\theta, \phi)(\sin\theta)d\phi d\theta \tag{20.27}$$

The expressions for Y_{lm} are given in (20.21). In the case of environment mapping, the integrals are basically sums of the pixel values in the environment map L, weighted by the values of Y_{lm}, and this can be preprocessed.

20.4.3   Analytical Light Source

Some simple light sources such as directional, disc, and spherical sources can be represented by analytical expressions. For a directional light source, light comes from a single direction. Under this situation, integration against basis functions is reduced to evaluating basis functions in the light direction.

For a disc source, light is originated from a disc object. For instance, consider that the light is from a disc centered around the z-axis as shown in Figure 20-8 on the right. This could be a good approximation to illumination from the sun or the moon. The light intensity distribution $L(\theta, \phi)$ can be described by the equation:

$$L(\theta, \phi) = d_\alpha(\theta, \phi) = \begin{cases} 1 & \text{if } \theta \leq \alpha \\ 0 & \text{if } \theta > \alpha \end{cases} \tag{20.28}$$

This light distribution has rotational symmetry around the z-axis (i.e. $L(\theta, \phi)$ is independent of ϕ). Therefore, it only has non-zero coefficients for modes $m = 0$. We can evaluate numerically the first few non-zero terms using (20.21) and (20.27). For example, using $z = cos\ \theta$, and consider only $l = 1, m = 0$, we have,

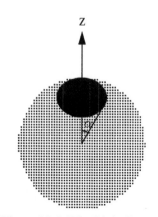

Figure 20-8 Disc Light Source

$$L_{10} = \int_{\theta=0}^{\alpha} \int_{\phi=0}^{2\pi} Y_{10}(\theta,\phi)(\sin\theta)d\phi d\theta$$

$$= \int_{\theta=0}^{\alpha} \int_{\phi=0}^{2\pi} 0.488603 \times \cos\theta(\sin\theta)d\phi d\theta$$

$$= 0.488603 \times 2\pi \int_0^{\alpha} \cos\theta \sin\theta \, d\theta$$

$$= 1.53499 \sin^2\alpha$$

We can similarly obtain other terms. The first three non-zero terms are:

$$\begin{aligned} L_{00} &= 1.77245(1-\cos\alpha) \\ L_{10} &= 1.53499\sin^2\alpha \\ L_{20} &= 1.98166\,(\cos\alpha - \cos^3\alpha) \end{aligned} \tag{20.29}$$

The irradiance $E(\theta,\phi)$ of (20.24) can be approximated by,

$$E(\theta,\phi) = A_0 L_{00} Y_{00} + A_1 L_{10} Y_{10} + A_2 L_{20} Y_{20}$$

$$= 1.57079(1-cos\alpha) + 1.57080(sin^2\alpha)z + 0.490874(cos\alpha - cos^3\alpha)(3z^2-1) \tag{20.30}$$

If α is 20°, this is reduced to

$$E(\theta,\phi) = 0.0947305 + 0.183748z + 0.0539584(3z^2-1) \tag{20.31}$$

The following shaders code shows an implementation of (20.30) using our *Sphere* class.

```
// Vertex shader for spherical harmonics lighting with disc source

uniform mat4 mvpMatrix;
attribute vec4 vPosition;
varying vec3  diffuseColor;

const float C0 = 1.57079;
const float C1 = 1.57080;
const float C2 = 0.490874;

void main(void)
{
   vec3 baseColor = vec3 ( 1.0, 1.0, 1.0 );
   vec3 N = vPosition.xyz;   //normal for sphere
   N = normalize ( N );
   float z = N.z;

   float alpha = radians ( 20 );   // angle is 20 degrees
   float cs = cos ( alpha );
   float sn = sin ( alpha );
   float intensity = C0*(1.0 - cs) + C1*sn*sn*z +
                  C2 * cs * (1.0 - cs*cs) * (3.0*z*z - 1.0);
   diffuseColor = baseColor * intensity;

   gl_Position = mvpMatrix * vPosition;
}
-----------------------------------------------------------------
// Fragment shader for spherical harmonics lighting with disc source
```

```
varying vec3  diffuseColor;

void main(void)
{
    gl_FragColor = vec4(diffuseColor, 1.0);
}
```

Figure 20-9(a) shows an output of this shader.

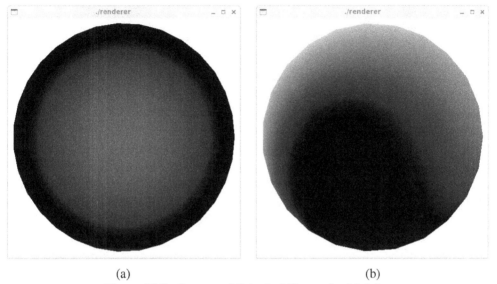

(a)   (b)

Figure 20-9 Outputs of Spherical Harmonics Lighting

As we have mentioned, any function constructed using spherical harmonics has rotational symmetry around z-axis only has non-zero coefficients for modes $m = 0$. For the first 5 bands, only 5 out of the 25 coefficients are non-zero. This also makes the operation of rotating the light source more efficient.

For spherical light sources, we may approximate them as disc sources. Suppose the distance of a spherical light center to the origin is d and the sphere radius is r, then the size of the approximated disc can be determined by:

$$\sin \alpha = \frac{r}{d} \tag{20.32}$$

20.4.4 Environment Map Light Source

The lighting due to an environment map is approximated by 9 lighting coefficients, L_{lm} for $l \leq 2$, which can be found by integrating against the spherical harmonic basis functions according to (20.27). Each color channel is treated independently. So we have to do the integration 3 times, one for each of the RGB color values. The integrals are simply sums of the pixel values of the environment map $L(\theta, \phi)$, weighted by the basis functions Y_{lm}. The integrals can be computed using Monte-Carlo integration, a popular statistical numerical technique for evaluating integrals. The computation of the coefficients are preprocessed.

If the size (total number of pixels) of the environment map is S, the preprocessing computation takes $9S$ steps, one for each pixel, as 9 sets of coefficients are computed for each pixel color. This is significantly more efficient that traditional method of computing an irradiance environment map texture that requires $T \times S$, where T is the number of texels in the irradiance environment map. Table 20-1 below shows the computed RGB values of the coefficients for a few environments, taken from the paper *An Efficient Representation for Irradiance Environment Maps* by Ravi Ramamoorthi and Pat Hanrahan of Stanford University.

Table 20-1 RGB Lighting Coefficients For a Few Environments

	Grace Cathedral			Eucalyptus Grove			St. Peters Basilica		
L_{00}	.79	.44	.54	.38	.43	.45	.36	.26	.23
$L_{1,-1}$	.39	.35	.60	.29	.36	.41	.18	.14	.13
L_{10}	-.34	-.18	-.27	.04	.03	.01	-.02	-.01	-.00
L_{11}	-.29	-.06	.01	-.10	-.10	-.09	.03	.02	.01
$L_{2,-2}$	-.11	-.05	-.12	-.06	-.06	-.04	.02	.01	.00
$L_{2,-1}$	-.26	-.22	-.47	.01	-.01	-.05	-.05	-.03	-.01
L_{20}	-.16	-.09	-.15	-.09	-.13	-.15	-.09	-.08	-.07
L_{21}	.56	.21	.14	-.06	-.05	-.04	.01	.00	.00
L_{22}	.21	-.05	-.30	.02	-.00	-.05	-.08	-.06	.00

We can calculate the irradiance due to an environment map using equation (20.24). We will combine the constants A_l of (20.26) and the numeric coefficients of Y_{lm} given by (20.21) and call the product constant c_i, where i is labeled in a convenient way to organize the terms. For example, c_4 is the product of A_0 and Y_{00}:

$$c_4 = A_0 \times Y_{00} = 3.141593 \times 0.282095 = 0.886227$$

With (20.21) and (20.26), we can express (20.24) as

$$E(\mathbf{n}) = c_1 L_{22}(x^2 - y^2) + c_3 L_{20}z^2 + c_4 L_{00} - c_5 L_{20} + 2c_1(L_{2,-2}xy + L_{21}xz + L_{2,-1}yz) + 2c_2(L_{11}x + L_{1,-1}y + L_{10}z) \quad (20.33)$$

where

$$c_1 = 0.429043 \quad c_2 = 0.511664 \quad c_3 = 0.743125$$

$$c_4 = 0.886227 \quad c_5 = 0.247708$$

The following shaders code shows an implementation of the the lighting from the coefficients of *Grace Cathedral* shown in Table 20-1. Our *Sphere* is the illuminated object. Figure 20-9(b) shows an output of the shader.

```
// Vertex shader for SH lighting of Grace Cathedral

uniform mat4 mvpMatrix;
attribute vec4 vPosition;

varying vec3  diffuseColor;

const float c1 = 0.429043;
const float c2 = 0.511664;
const float c3 = 0.743125;
const float c4 = 0.886227;
const float c5 = 0.247708;
```

```
// Constants for Grace Cathedral lighting
const vec3 L00  = vec3( 0.79,  0.44,  0.54);
const vec3 L1_1 = vec3( 0.39,  0.35,  0.60);
const vec3 L10  = vec3(-0.34, -0.18, -0.27);
const vec3 L11  = vec3(-0.29, -0.06,  0.01);
const vec3 L2_2 = vec3(-0.11, -0.05, -0.12);
const vec3 L2_1 = vec3(-0.26, -0.22, -0.47);
const vec3 L20  = vec3(-0.16, -0.09, -0.15);
const vec3 L21  = vec3( 0.56,  0.21,  0.14);
const vec3 L22  = vec3( 0.21, -0.05, -0.30);


void main(void)
{
   vec3 N;
   N = vPosition.xyz;  //normal of  a point on sphere
   N = normalize( N ); //normalize

   float x = N.x, y = N.y, z = N.z;

   diffuseColor = c1 * L22 * (x*x - y*y) +
                  c3 * L20 * z*z +
                  c4 * L00 - c5 * L20 +
                  2.0 * c1 * (L2_2 * x*y + L21 * x*z + L2_1 * y*z) +
                  2.0 * c2 * (L11  * x + L1_1 * y + L10  * z);

    gl_Position = mvpMatrix * vPosition;

}
---------------------------------------------------------------------
// Fragment shader for SH lighting of Grace Cathedral

varying vec3  diffuseColor;

void main(void)
{
    gl_FragColor = vec4(diffuseColor, 1.0);
}
```

The calculations are done in the vertex shader, which passes the color at each vertex via the **varying** variable *diffuseColor* to the fragment shader. The fragment shader simply takes the colors at vertices calculated by the vertex shader and renders it. For pixels not at any vertice of any ploygon, interpolation is used to obtain the color during rasterization. This is justified for diffuse reflection, which typically varies slowly across the scene.

20.5 Lighting of Cinematography

20.5.1 Introduction

Lighting on cinematography can contribute to the storytelling, mood, image composition, and special effects. For cinematography, physical light sources, such as desk or ceiling lamps, are rarely major contributors to the illumination. Instead, illumination effects are often created by placing various types of lamps and spotlights off-camera, and the lighting does not need to be restricted by physical laws. To achieve special effects, a lighting designer often employs whatever necessary tricks and cheats such as suspending a cloth in front of a light to soften shadows, positioning opaque cards or graded filters to shape a light, or focusing a narrow *tickler* light to get extra high-light.

Ronen Barzel of Pixar Animation Studios published a paper in *Journal of Graphics Tools* in 1997, presenting a lighting model, which was developed over several years in response to the needs of computer graphics film production, in particular for making the movie *Toy Story*. The model gives lighting designers control over the shape, placement, and texture of lights, so that their real-world cinematographic talent can be applied to computer images. The model does not empha-size on real physically simulating tools but on taking advantage of various sorts of imaginary art work available. The model became known as *überlight* model and its *RenderMan* implementation known as *überlight* shader.

20.5.2 Superellipse

The *ü*berlight model uses a pair of superellipses to define the shape of light and to model a gradual dropoff of light at the edge of the shape from full to zero intensity.

A superellipse, first discussed by *Lamė* in 1818, is a curve described by the Cartesian equation:

$$\left(\frac{x}{a}\right)^{\frac{2}{d}} + \left(\frac{y}{b}\right)^{\frac{2}{d}} = 1 \qquad (20.34)$$

where d, a, and b are positive numbers. This formula describes a closed curve contained in the rectangle $-a \leq x \leq a$ and $-b \leq y \leq b$. The variable d can be regarded as a "roundness" parameter varying the shape from pure ellipse when $d = 1$ to a pure rectangle as $d \rightarrow 0$. Figure 20-10 shows superellipses for various d values.

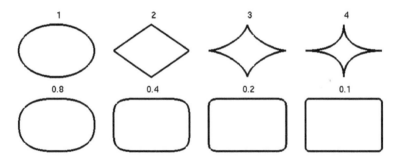

Figure 20-10 Superellipses with Various d values

A superellipse may be described parametrically by:

$$\left.\begin{array}{l} x(\theta) = \pm a \, \cos^d \theta \\ y(\theta) = \pm b \, \sin^d \theta \end{array}\right\} \quad 0 \leq \theta < \frac{\pi}{2} \qquad (20.35)$$

We can use two nested superellipses with radii a, b and A, B as shown in Figuure 20-11 to specify a shape, at which light intensity transitions smoothly. Given a point P, we compute a clip factor, which has a value of 1 if P lies within the inner superellipse, and 0 if lies outside the outer superellipse, and varies smoothly from 0 to 1 for points between the superellipses.

20.5.3 Step Transitions

To achieve soft-cliping, we need a step function to provide control values between 0 and 1 for a variable s. The function varies slowly from 0 to 1 when s changes from c to d. It returns 0 if $s < c$ and 1 if $s > d$. Then 1 minus the function gives us the desired clipping factor.

A linear step function gives these effects and is described by:

$$\text{linearstep}(c,d,s) = \begin{cases} 0 & s \leq c \\ \frac{s-c}{c-d} & c \leq s \leq d \\ 1 & s \geq d \end{cases} \qquad (20.36)$$

The function **linearstep** given in (20.36) and shown on the left of Figure 20-12, is simple and fast to compute. However, it is not C^1-continuous as it changes abruptly at the boundaries. It can causing Mach banding, a physical illusion named after the physicist Ernest Mach. It exaggerates contrast between edges of slightly different shades of gray.

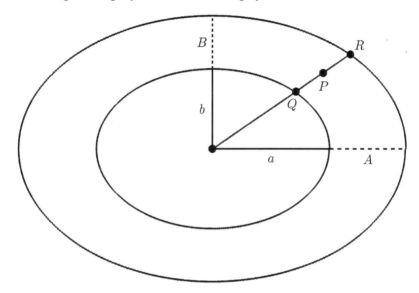

Figure 20-11 Nested Superellipses

A better function to use is a smooth step function, where the interpreting function is defined by a cubic curve so that the tangent is horizontal at the start and the end, and the curve is C^1-continuous. (i.e. Its first derivative at every point exists and is continuous.) A commonly used curved is a special Hermite Spline, a cubic spline defined by two interpolating points and two tangents. Such a step function is shown on the right of Figure 20-12 and can be described by:

$$\text{smoothstep}(c,d,s) = \begin{cases} 0 & s \leq c \\ 3t^2 - 2t^3 & c \leq s \leq d \\ 1 & s \geq d \end{cases} \qquad (20.37)$$

where

$$t = \frac{s-c}{c-d} \qquad (20.38)$$

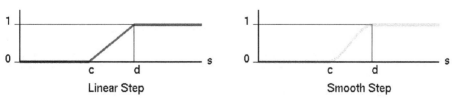

Figure 20-12   Linear and Smooth Step Functions

The **smoothstep** function is supported by the OpenGL shading language and is also in the *RenderMan* liabrary. The glsl function **smoothstep**() works exactly as described in (20.37).

To evaluate the step function, we need to first compute the parameters c, d, and s of (20.37). Referring to Figure 20-11, given a point P, we express the ray through P, and originating from the origin $O = (0,0)$ as $L(s) = O + s(P - O) = sP$. Suppose the ray intersects the inner superellipse at Q, and the outer at R. To find Q, and R, we can express the points as:

$$P = pP, \quad Q = qP, \quad R = rR \tag{20.39}$$

Trivially, $p = 1$. Assuming $P = (x, y)$, we can compute q by:

$$
\begin{aligned}
1 &= \left(\frac{qx}{a}\right)^{\frac{2}{d}} + \left(\frac{qy}{b}\right)^{\frac{2}{d}} \\
&= q^{\frac{2}{d}} \left(\left(\frac{x}{a}\right)^{\frac{2}{d}} + \left(\frac{y}{b}\right)^{\frac{2}{d}} \right)
\end{aligned}
\tag{20.40}
$$

from which, we can solve for q as:

$$q = ab \left((bx)^{\frac{2}{d}} + (ay)^{\frac{2}{d}} \right)^{\frac{-d}{2}} \tag{20.41}$$

We can similarly obtain an expression for r by replacing a and b in (20.41) by A and B respectively:

$$r = AB \left((Bx)^{\frac{2}{d}} + (Ay)^{\frac{2}{d}} \right)^{\frac{-d}{2}} \tag{20.42}$$

So the final clip factor is given by $1 - smoothstep(q, r, 1)$.

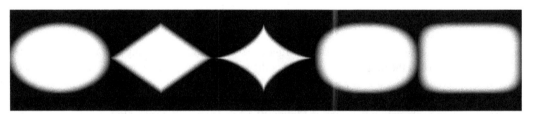

Figure 20-13 Nested Superellipses Shading with Smooth Step (left to right: $d = 1, 2, 3, 0.8, 0.4$)

If the center of the light beam is on the z-axis and the beam is aimimg along the z-axis, the illumination across a cross section of the beam can be implemented using (20.41) and (20.42) as follows in a fragment shader:

```
uniform float a;            //inner superellipse width
uniform float b;            //inner superellipse height
uniform float A;            //outer superellipse width
uniform float B;            //outer superellipse hight
uniform float d;            //roundness of shape

float superEllipseShape(vec3 pos)
{
   // Project point onto z = 1.0 plane; consider absolute values
   float x = abs(pos.x/pos.z);
   float y = abs(pos.y/pos.z);
   float e1 = 2.0 / d, e2 = -d / 2.0;
```

```
float q = a * b * pow(pow(b * x, e1) + pow(a * y, e1), e2);
float r = A * B * pow(pow(B * x, e1) + pow(A * y, e1), e2);

return 1.0 - smoothstep(q, r, 1.0);
}
```

To do such an implementation, we need to consider the relative position and orientation of the light source with respect to the vertex to be shone.

Suppose $P = (x, y, z)$ is the vertex and the light source center is at the point $Q = (x_l, y_l, z_l)$ as shown in Figure 20-14 below. We want to move the origin O of the world coordinate system to the point Q; this is simply a translation by the vector $\mathbf{L} = Q - O = (x_l, y_l, z_l)$. To simplify the calculations, we align the light vector $\mathbf{L} = Q - O$ with the z-axis, so that the shape formed on the object at P is simply the projection of the light source on the rotated $x - y$ plane. To rotate L onto the z-axis, we need to

1. rotate $\mathbf{L}$ about the x-axis to put $\mathbf{L}$ on the xz-plane,
2. rotate $\mathbf{L}$ about the y-axis to align it with the z-axis.

Suppose $\mathbf{L} = (L_x, L_y, L_z)$ is normalized (i.e. $|L| = 1$). The components L_x, L_y, and L_z are the direction cosines of x, y, and z axes respectively. That is, if the angles between $\mathbf{L}$ and the x, y, and z axes are A, B, and C respectively, then $L_x = \cos A$, $L_y = \cos B$, and $L_z = \cos C$.

For the rotation about the x-axis, we need to find $\cos \alpha$ and $\sin \alpha$, where α is the angle between the projection of $\mathbf{L}$ (in the yz-plane) and the z-axis. Let $d = (L_y^2 + L_z^2)^{\frac{1}{2}} = (1 - L_x^2)^{\frac{1}{2}} = (1 - \cos^2 A)^{\frac{1}{2}} = \sin A$, which is the length of the projection. Then

$$\cos \alpha = \frac{L_z}{d}, \quad \sin \alpha = \frac{L_y}{d} \qquad (20.43)$$

(See Figure 20-15 the projection of $\mathbf{L}$ on y-z plane.)

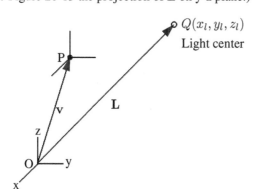
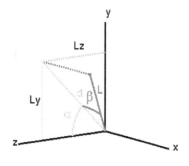

Figure 20-14   Lighting Coordinates   Figure 20-15   Aligning $\mathbf{L}$ with z-axis

Using (3.32) of Chapter 3, the rotation matrix about x-axis is:

$$R_x(\alpha) = \begin{pmatrix} 1 & 0 & 0 & 0 \\ 0 & \cos \alpha & -\sin \alpha & 0 \\ 0 & \sin \alpha & \cos \alpha & 0 \\ 0 & 0 & 0 & 1 \end{pmatrix} = \begin{pmatrix} 1 & 0 & 0 & 0 \\ 0 & L_z/d & -L_y/d & 0 \\ 0 & L_y/d & L_z/d & 0 \\ 0 & 0 & 0 & 1 \end{pmatrix} \qquad (20.44)$$

For the rotation about the y-axis, we need to rotate the vector for an angle $\beta = -(90^\circ - A)$. So $\sin \beta = -\cos A = -L_x$. Also, $\cos \beta = \sin A = d$. Using (3.30) of Chapter 3, we obtain the rotation matrix:

$$
R_y(\beta) = \begin{pmatrix} \cos\beta & 0 & \sin\beta & 0 \\ 0 & 1 & 0 & 0 \\ -\sin\beta & 0 & \cos\beta & 0 \\ 0 & 0 & 0 & 1 \end{pmatrix} = \begin{pmatrix} d & 0 & -L_x & 0 \\ 0 & 1 & 0 & 0 \\ L_x & 0 & d & 0 \\ 0 & 0 & 0 & 1 \end{pmatrix} \tag{20.45}
$$

The composite matrix $R = R_y R_x$ will bring the unit vector **L** to coincide with the z axis.

Using our *Sphere* class as an example, the following is the complete code of a vertex shader that implements these features with some parameters hard-coded. The rotation matrix can be easily calculated evenly if the light source position is changing with time.

```
// Vertex Shader of uberlight-like model
uniform mat4 mvpMatrix;
attribute vec4 vPosition;
uniform vec4 lightPos;      // light position in world coordinates
uniform vec4 eyePos;        // view position in world space

varying vec3 vPosLC;        // vertex position in light coordinates
varying vec3 normLC;        // normal in light coordinates
varying vec3 eyeLC;         // view point in light coordinates

void main()
{
    vec3 L = normalize ( lightPos.xyz );
    float d = sqrt (L.y*L.y + L.z*L.z);
    mat3 Rx, Ry, R;    // rotation matrices

    Rx = mat3 ( 1, 0,      0,          //1st column
                0, L.z/d, L.y/d,       //2nd column
                0, -L.y/d, L.z/d );    //3rd column
    Ry = mat3 ( d,   0, L.x,           //1st column
                0,   1, 0,             //2nd column
                -L.x, 0, d );          //3rd column

    R = Ry * Rx;                       //the composite matrix
    vPosLC = R * (vPosition.xyz - lightPos.xyz);
    eyeLC  = R * (eyePos.xyz - lightPos.xyz);
    normLC = R * vPosition.xyz;

    gl_Position = mvpMatrix * vPosition;
}
```

20.5.3 Distance Falloff

Besides the intensity falloff across a beam, which is modeled by nested superellipses, the light intensity also drops off with distance from the light source. To simplify the controls, people often employ near and far distances, also known as cuton and cutoff values to define regions illuminated by the beam as shown in Figure 20-16. Smooth transitions between zones are desired and they can be implemented using the glsl **smoothstep**() function.

This kind of lighting control does not follow any physical laws. It is introduced for lighting designers to create special imaginary effects in cinematograhy.

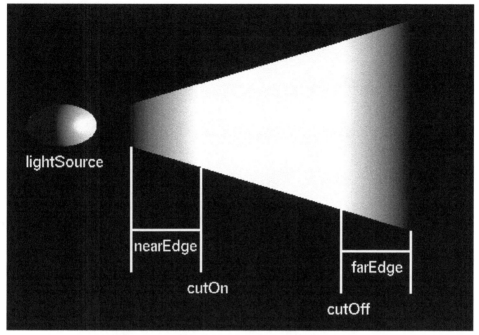

Figure 20-16   Distance Effects of Illumination

Besides zone transitions, the light intensity falls off with distance and is often expressed using the inverse power formula:

$$I(d) = K \left(\frac{d_0}{d} \right)^{\alpha}$$

(20.46)

where d is the distance from the light source, α is an attenuation exponent, and K is the desired intensity at the canonical distance d_0. In the expression, I goes to infinity as d approaches 0. A simple solution is to clamp the intensity to a maximum value, but this creates discontinuities, which may cause Mach banding. A better method is use a Guassian-like curve for a distance smaller than the canonical distance:

$$I(d) = \begin{cases} M e^{s\left(\frac{d_0}{d}\right)^{\beta}} & d < d_0 \\[2mm] K \left(\frac{d_0}{d}\right)^{\alpha} & d > d_0 \end{cases}$$

(20.47)

where $s = ln\left(\frac{K}{M}\right)$ and $\beta = -\alpha/s$ are chosen so that the two expressions for $d < d_0$ and $d > d_0$ give the same value, $I(d_0) = K$ at $d = d_0$ and give the same slope $I'(d) = -K\alpha/d_0$. If $K = 1$, and $\alpha = 1$, then $s = ln(1/M)$ and $\beta = -1/s$.

The following is the fragment shader code that works with the vertex shader presented above; it implements these lighting features. For simplicity and clarity of presentation, we hard-code a number of parameters.

```
------------------------------------------------------------------

// Fragment Shader of uberlight-like model

// Super ellipse shaping parameters
uniform float a;              //inner superellipse width
```

```
uniform float b;              //inner superellipse height
uniform float A;              //outer superellipse width
uniform float B;              //outer superellipse hight
uniform float d;              //roundness of shape

// Distance attenuation parameters
uniform float zNear;
uniform float zFar;
uniform float nearEdge;
uniform float farEdge;

varying vec3 vPosLC;          // vertex position in light coordinates
varying vec3 normLC;          // normal in light coordinates
varying vec3 eyeLC;           // view position in light coordinates

float superEllipseShape(vec3 pos)
{
   // Project point onto z = 1.0 plane, and consider absolute values
   float x = abs(pos.x/pos.z);
   float y = abs(pos.y/pos.z);

   float e1 = 2.0 / d, e2 = -d / 2.0;

   float q = a * b * pow(pow(b * x, e1) + pow(a * y, e1), e2);
   float r = A * B * pow(pow(B * x, e1) + pow(A * y, e1), e2);

   return 1.0 - smoothstep(q, r, 1.0);
}

float distanceAttenuation(vec3 pos,float maxIntensity,float d0,float alpha)
{
   float z = abs(pos.z);

   // attenuation in various light zones (Figure 20-16)
   float a =  smoothstep(zNear - nearEdge, zNear, z) *
              (1.0 - smoothstep(zFar, zFar + farEdge, z));

   // attenuation due to distance
   if ( z > d0 )
     a *= pow ( d0/z, alpha );
   else {
     float s = log ( 1.0 / maxIntensity );
     float beta = -alpha / s;
     a *=  maxIntensity * exp ( s * pow(z/d0, beta) );
   }

   return a;
}

void main()
{
   float attenuation;
   attenuation = superEllipseShape(vPosLC) *
                 distanceAttenuation(vPosLC, 2.0, 1.0, 1.0 );
```

```
    vec3 N = normalize(normLC);
    vec3 L = -normalize(vPosLC);
    vec3 V = normalize(eyeLC-vPosLC);
    vec3 H = normalize(L + V);    // half-vector

    vec3 baseColor = vec3(1.0, 1.0, 1.0);
    float shinness = 4.0;
    float NdotL = dot(N, L);
    float NdotH = dot(N, H);

    float diff = max(NdotL, 0.0);
    float spec =  max(NdotH, 0.0);

    vec3 ambient = vec3 (0.5, 0.2, 0.2);
    vec3 diffuse = attenuation * baseColor  * diff;
    vec3 specular = attenuation * baseColor * pow(spec, shinness);

    gl_FragColor = vec4(diffuse + specular + ambient, 1.0);
}
```

Figure 20-17 shows an output of this shader with the following parameters provided by the main OpenGL application:

lightPos[]:	{1, 1, 2, 1}	eyePos[]:	0, 0, 6.3, 1
a, b, A, B, d:	0.2, 0.3, 0.3, 0.4, 0.8	zNear, zFar:	1.0, 2.0
nearEdge:	0.4	farEdge:	0.8

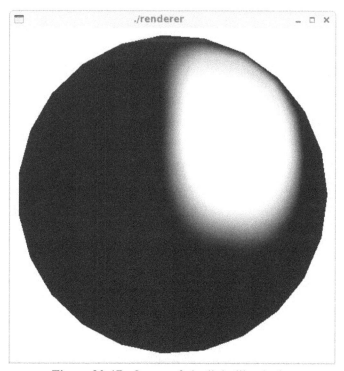

Figure 20-17 Output of uberlight-like shader

Appendix A FFmpeg Libraries

A.1 Introduction

FFmpeg has been a popular open-source video library for processing videos. One can also make use of this library to make interesting graphics as discussed below. It can be downloaded from its official site at *http://ffmpeg.org/* . FFmpeg is a complete, cross-platform solution to record, convert and stream audio and video. The code is written in C. It provides executable programs for users to process and play videos. We do not intend to present the details of using their executables as they are well documented in their web site. We are more interested to learn to use their libraries so that we can incorporate their features and functions into our own applications such as graphics or video games. In this appendix, we make use of what we have learned about graphics and the libraries to embed a simple video player in a graphical application. The materials presented here are mostly obtained from the official FFmpeg web site (http://ffmpeg.org). Interested readers may obtain further information about FFmpeg directly from the site.

A.2 Getting and Compiling FFmpeg

You may download the source code from their web site directly (http://ffmpeg.org/download.html). At the time of this writing, their version is 0.5 and you will obtain from the site the zipped file "ffmpeg-0.5.tar.bz2". You may unzip it into a directory using the command:

```
$bunzip2 -c ffmpeg-0.5.tar.bz2 | tar xvf -
```

It creates the directory "ffmpeg-0.5". You may go into the directory to configure your installation. As an example, suppose you want to install the package in the directory "/apps/mpeg". You may do the configuration using the command:

```
$./configure --prefix=/apps/mpeg --enable-cross-compile
```

After the configuration, you are ready to compile and make the executables and libraries. However, you need the GNU Make utility version 3.81 or later. (You may check your system's make version by the command "make –version".) If your system's **make** is earlier than 3.81, you need to download version 3.81 or later from the GNU web site (*http://www.gnu.org/*). If the version is correct, simply type "make" to build FFmpeg. Then type "make install" to install all binaries and libraries built into "/apps/mpeg". After "make install", you should find the three directories:

```
$/apps/mpeg/bin
$/apps/mpeg/lib
$/apps/mpeg/share
$/apps/mpeg/include
```

Directory "bin" contains the executable programs, "ffmpeg", "ffplay", and "ffserver". The program "ffmpeg" is a very fast video and audio converter, allowing you to grab from a live audio/video with command-line interface. The program "ffserver" is a streaming server for both audio and video, supporting several live feeds, streaming from files and time shifting. If you want to play a video, you need to use "ffplay", which is a very simple and portable media player built using the FFmpeg libraries and the SDL library, and is mostly used as a testbed for various FFmpeg APIs. SDL here stands for Simple DirectMedia Layer, which is a cross-platform multimedia library designed to provide low level access to 3D hardware via OpenGL. For details, please refer to its official web site at *http://www.libsdl.org/*.

The libraries "libavcodec.a", "libavdevice.a", "libavformat.a", and "libavutil.a" are in the directory "lib" and the corresponding include header-files are in the directory "include". Therefore, in building your applications, your include-path should contain "/apps/mpeg/include" and your library-path should contain "/apps/mpeg/lib". Actually, we also need another header file, "libswscale" for building some ffmpeg applications. This header directory is not built by default in the installation process because it requires a different distribution license from other ffmpeg libraries. To create this directory in the installation process, you need to choose a special option in the configuration stage. To simplify the process, we just simply copy these files manually to the appropriate directories:

```
$mkdir /apps/mpeg/include/libswscale
$cp /apps/ffmpeg-0.5/libswscale/*.h /apps/mpeg/include/libswscale/.
```

Note that the library "libswscale.a" does **not** exist. Its functions can be found in the library "libavcodec.a". Their usages are to replace the "imgconvert" functions of earlier ffmpeg versions. If you do not like the"libswscale" functions, simply use "imgconvert".

For the convenience of explanation, let us make the directories "/apps/mpeg/work" and "/apps/mpeg/data" where we shall save our project programs and sample video files respectively.

A.3 Using FFmpeg Libraries

Opening the File

To use FFmpeg libraries, we have to include their header files. Since FFmeg is written in pure C and our programs are written in C/C++ with extension ".cpp", we have to use the keyword "extern" in specifying the include:

```
extern "C" {
  #include <libavcodec/avcodec.h>
  #include <libavformat/avformat.h>
  #include <libswscale/swscale.h>
}
```

If we do not use "extern", the compiler will generate errors. Before opening any video file, we need to use **av_register_all**() to register all available file formats and codecs so that they will be used automatically when a file with the corresponding format/codec is opened:

```
av_register_all();
```

We only have to call this function once in our application. We now can actually open the video file:

```
AVFormatContext *pFormatCtx;
char filename[100];
.....

// Open video file
if(av_open_input_file(&pFormatCtx, filename, NULL, 0, NULL)!=0)
  return -1; // Couldn't open file
```

We provide the filename as input parameter to this function, which reads the file header, saving information about the file format in the **AVFormatContext** structure. The last three arguments are used to specify the file format, buffer size, and format options, but by setting them to NULL or 0, **libavformat** will auto-detect the correct parameter values. The information is returned via *pFormatCtx* which is a pointer pointing to the AVFormatContext structure the function has created; the structure contains the miscellaneous video and audio information such as author, timestamp, packet size and bit rate of the date in the file.

Next, we may retrieve the information from the stream and may dump the information to the screen:

```
// Retrieve stream information
if(av_find_stream_info(pFormatCtx)<0)
   return -1; // Couldn't find stream information

// Dump information about file onto standard error
dump_format(pFormatCtx, 0, filename, 0);
```

The field *pFormatCtx->streams* is an array of pointers, of size *pFormatCtx->nb_streams*, each pointing to an **AVStream** structure. We can search through it to find a video stream:

```
//Find the first video stream
videoStream=-1;
for(int i=0; i<pFormatCtx->nb_streams; i++) {
  if(pFormatCtx->streams[i]->codec->codec_type==CODEC_TYPE_VIDEO){
     videoStream=i;
     break;
  }
}

if(videoStream==-1)
   return -1; // Didn't find a video stream

// Get a pointer to the codec context for the video stream
pCodecCtx=pFormatCtx->streams[videoStream]->codec;
```

The information of the codec used to enclose the video stream is referred to as "codec context", which contains all the information about the codec that the stream is using. Now we have a pointer to the "codec context", and we need to find the actual codec to open it:

```
AVCodec *pCodec;
// Find the decoder for the video stream
pCodec=avcodec_find_decoder(pCodecCtx->codec_id);
if(pCodec==NULL) {
  fprintf(stderr, "Unsupported codec!\n");
  return -1; // Codec not found
```

```
}
//open codec
if(avcodec_open(pCodecCtx, pCodec)<0)
  return -1; // Could not open codec
```

Decoding the Stream

We have found the video stream and know about its codec context. We need to allocate some memory to buffer the data of one or more frames so that we can further process them. We shall use the same producer-consumer concept, where a producer thread produces data and a consumer thread consumes data, to process the decoded data. For instance, we can allocate memory to buffer 4 frames:

```
int width = pCodecCtx->width;
int height = pCodecCtx->height;

char *buf[4];
for ( int i = 0; i <  4; ++i ) {
  buf[i] = ( char * ) malloc ( width * height * 3 );
  if ( buf[i] == NULL )
    return -2;
}
```

In this case the decoder is our producer and the player is our consumer. The decoder thread just needs to decode data and put them in the buffer. The player thread reads the data from the buffer and displays them on the screen. We can write a class **Video** to store the relevant decoding information of the file:

```
class Video {
private:
  SDL_Thread *producer, *consumer;

public:
  SDL_Surface *screen;
  unsigned long head;
  unsigned long tail;
  int width;
  int height;
  int x0;          //play position
  int y0;
  bool quit;
  AVCodecContext *pCodecCtx;
  AVFormatContext *pFormatCtx;
  int videoStream;

  ........
};
```

We use FFmpeg function **avcodec_alloc_frame**() to allocate a frame structure to hold one frame. Also, we need the data to be stored in RGB (or BGR) format so that we can use an SDL function to blit the data on the screen:

```
AVFrame *pFrame, *pFrameRGB;
if(pFrame==NULL)
  return -1;

// Allocate video frame buffer for holding one frame of data
pFrame=avcodec_alloc_frame();

// Allocate an AVFrame structure for holding one frame of RGB data
pFrameRGB=avcodec_alloc_frame();
if(pFrameRGB==NULL)
  return -1;
```

We have to convert our frame from its native format to RGB. Our decoder makes use of the FFmpeg function **avcodec_decode_video**() to decode the video stream and it uses **sws_getContext**() and **sws_scale**() to convert the image from its native format to RGB. In older FFmpeg versions, the function **img_convert**() is supplied to make the conversion, but now this function has been deprecated. We shall also use FFmpeg function **av_malloc**() to temporarily allocate memory to buffer one frame of data and use **avpicture_fill**() to associate the frame with the newly allocated buffer. The following shows the decoder thread:

Program Listing A-1

```
//Producer Thread
int decoder ( void *data )
{
  Video *vi = ( Video * ) data;
  SDL_Surface *screen = ( SDL_Surface * ) vi->screen;
  AVCodecContext *pCodecCtx =  vi->pCodecCtx;
  .......
  int frameFinished;
  AVPacket packet;
  AVFrame *pFrame;
  // Allocate video frame
  pFrame=avcodec_alloc_frame();
  // Allocate an AVFrame structure
  AVFrame *pFrameRGB;
  pFrameRGB=avcodec_alloc_frame();
  if(pFrameRGB==NULL)
    return -1;
  uint8_t *buffer;
  int numBytes;
  // Determine required buffer size and allocate buffer
  numBytes=avpicture_get_size(PIX_FMT_RGB24, pCodecCtx->width,
                         pCodecCtx->height);
  while ( !vi->quit ) {
    if ( vi->tail >= vi->head + 4 ) {  //buffer full
      SDL_Delay ( 30 );
      continue;
    }
    //produce data
    if (av_read_frame(pFormatCtx, &packet)>=0) {
      // Is this a packet from the video stream?
      if(packet.stream_index==videoStream) {
        // Decode video frame
        avcodec_decode_video(pCodecCtx, pFrame, &frameFinished,
                      packet.data, packet.size);
        // Did we get a video frame?
        if(frameFinished) {
          // Convert the image from its native format to RGB
          SwsContext * encoderSwsContext = sws_getContext(
```

```
      pCodecCtx->width, pCodecCtx->height, pCodecCtx->pix_fmt,
      pCodecCtx->width, pCodecCtx->height, PIX_FMT_RGB24,
      SWS_BICUBIC, NULL,NULL,NULL);

      sws_scale( encoderSwsContext, pFrame->data,
      pFrame->linesize, 0, pCodecCtx->height, pFrameRGB->data,
      pFrameRGB->linesize);

      char *pb = vi->buf[vi->tail%4]; //points to buffer slot
      int size = vi->width * 3;

      //copy decoded data to our buffer
      for ( int y = 0; y < height; y++ ){
          char *pc =(char *)
              (pFrameRGB->data[0]+y*pFrameRGB->linesize[0]);
          int k = 0;
          char *p = pb + y * size;
          for ( int i = 0; i < vi->width; ++i ) {
            p[k] = pc[k+2];
            p[k+1] = pc[k+1];
            p[k+2] = pc[k];
            k += 3;
          }
      }
      vi->tail++;
    }
  }
  // Free the packet that was allocated by av_read_frame
  av_free_packet(&packet);
} else
    vi->quit = true;
} //while
//free resources here
.......
return 0;
}
```

After we exited the while loop near the end of the decoder, we need to free the resources allocated by FFmpeg functions. We again call the FFmpeg functions to free them:

```
// Free the RGB image
av_free(buffer);
av_free(pFrameRGB);

// Free the YUV frame
av_free(pFrame);

// Close the codec
avcodec_close(pCodecCtx);
// Close the video file
av_close_input_file(pFormatCtx);
```

When we initialize the SDL, its better to use the double buffering feature so that we can carry out the decoding and put the decoded data at the background. We later swap the background and foreground buffers to avoid any flickering effect:

```
    //initialize video system
    if ( SDL_Init( SDL_INIT_VIDEO ) < 0 ) {
        fprintf(stderr, "Unable to init SDL:%s\n",SDL_GetError());
        exit(1);
    }

    //set video mode of  with 24-bit pixels
    screen = SDL_SetVideoMode(640, 480, 24, SDL_DOUBLEBUF);
    if ( screen == NULL ) {
        fprintf(stderr, "Unable to set video:%s\n",SDL_GetError());
        exit(1);
    }
```

Playing the Video Data

The player thread which sends the decoded data to the screen is our consumer. It 'consumes' the data generated by the decoder. It puts a frame on the screen at the position (x0, y0) specified by the user. A background buffer is created to hold a frame of RGB data. The data are sent to the screen by **SDL_BlitSurface**() and **SDL_UpdateRect**():

Program Listing A-2

```
//Consumer Thread
int player ( void *data )
{
  Video *vi = ( Video * ) data;
  SDL_Surface *screen = ( SDL_Surface * ) vi->screen;
  Uint32 prev_time, current_time;
  current_time = SDL_GetTicks();//ms since library starts
  prev_time = SDL_GetTicks();   //ms since library starts

  SDL_Surface *background;
  background = SDL_CreateRGBSurface(SDL_SWSURFACE,
                        vi->width, vi->height, 24, 0, 0, 0, 0);
  if ( background == NULL ) {
    fprintf(stderr, "Unable to set  video: %s\n",SDL_GetError());
    return -1;
  }
  while ( !vi->quit ) {
    if ( vi->head == vi->tail ){//buffer empty (data not available)
      SDL_Delay ( 30 );         //sleep for 30 ms
      continue;
    }
    //consumes the data
    background->pixels = vi->buf[vi->head%4];
    current_time = SDL_GetTicks();   //ms since library starts
    if (current_time - prev_time < 50)//20 fps ~ 50 ms / frame
      SDL_Delay ( 50 - (current_time - prev_time) );
    prev_time = current_time;

    SDL_Rect source_rect, dest_rect;
    source_rect.x = 0;                source_rect.y = 0;
    source_rect.w = vi->width;
    source_rect.h = vi->height;
    dest_rect.x = vi->x0;            dest_rect.y = vi->y0;
    dest_rect.w = vi->width;
    dest_rect.h = vi->height;

    SDL_BlitSurface(background, &source_rect, screen, &dest_rect);
```

```
      SDL_UpdateRect ( screen, 0, 0, 0, 0 );   //update whole screen
      vi->head++;
   } //while

   return 0;
}
```

Sample Makefile

The following is a typical **Makefile** for compiling and linking programs that use ffmpeg libraries:

```
#Sample Makefile for using ffmpeg libraries.
#"video.cpp" and "vplayer.cpp" are the application files

#users may need to modify the SDL path
LIBSDL =  -L/usr/local/lib -L/usr/local/lib -lSDL  -lpthread

PROG=vplayer
CC=g++
BASE=/apps/mpeg
FI = $(BASE)/include
FLIBS = -L$(BASE)/lib -lavcodec -lavdevice -lavformat -lavutil \
        -L/usr/lib
INCLS = -I/usr/include  -I$(FI)/libavcodec  -I$(FI)/libavdevice \
        -I$(FI)/libavformat -I$(FI)/libavutil -I$(FI)
#source codes
SRCS = $(PROG).cpp
#substitute .cpp by .o to obtain object filenames
OBJS = $(SRCS:.cpp=.o) video.o
FLAGS= -D_ISOC99_SOURCE -D_POSIX_C_SOURCE=200112  -g
FLAGS2=-rdynamic -export-dynamic -Wl,--warn-common -Wl,\
        --as-needed -Wl,
PATHS=-rpath-link,-Wl,-Bsymbolic
fflibs=-lavdevice -lavformat -lavcodec -lavutil
otherlibs=-lz -lbz2 -lm  -lasound -ldl

#$< evaluates to the target's dependencies,
#$@ evaluates to the target
$(PROG): $(OBJS)
    $(CC) -o $@ $(OBJS) $(FLAGS) $(FLIBS) $(FLAGS2)$(PATHS)\
            $(fflibs) $(otherlibs) $(LIBSDL)

$(OBJS):
    $(CC) -c  $*.cpp $(INCLS)

clean:
    rm $(OBJS)
```

A.4   Using FFmpeg Functions in Graphics

In the above sections, we discuss the usage of FFmpeg libraries. In the example, the decoded data are in RGB form and saved in a buffer. We can regard each frame as an image and make further processing on it. A typical application is to incorporate a video in a graphics application. This is commonly used in video game software. As an example, we discuss how we can use the techniques we have discussed to play videos in an OpenGL (Open Graphics Library) application.

First, we have to set the SDL video mode with the "SDL_OPENGL" option:

```
SDL_Surface *screen;
screen = SDL_SetVideoMode(640, 480, 24, SDL_SWSURFACE|SDL_OPENGL);
```

We may then initialize our graphics as usual. The following is a typical initialization of a graphics application that has a yellow light source at (20, 40, 20) and the camera (view point) is located at (0, 0, 10), viewing at the origin (0, 0, 0) with the up direction along the y-axis (0, 1, 0):

```
void init_gl ( SDL_Surface *screen ) {
  glutInitDisplayMode (GLUT_DOUBLE | GLUT_RGB);
  glViewport( 0, 0, screen->w, screen->h );
  glMatrixMode( GL_PROJECTION );
  glOrtho( -2.0, 2.0, -2.0, 2.0, -20.0, 20.0 );  //world window
  //camera at (0, 0, 10), looking at (0, 0, 0) with up-axis (0, 1, 0)
  gluLookAt ( 0, 0, 10, 0, 0, 0, 0, 1, 0 );

  glMatrixMode( GL_MODELVIEW );
  glEnable(GL_DEPTH_TEST);
  glDepthFunc(GL_LESS);
  glShadeModel(GL_SMOOTH);
  glClearColor( 1.0, 1.0, 1.0, 1.0 );              //white background
  glClear(GL_COLOR_BUFFER_BIT | GL_DEPTH_BUFFER_BIT);
  GLfloat light[] = { 1.0, 1.0, 0 };               //yellow light
  //light source at (20,40,20)
  GLfloat light_position[]={20.0,40.0,20.0,1.0};
  glEnable(GL_LIGHTING);
  glEnable(GL_LIGHT0);
  glLightfv(GL_LIGHT0, GL_DIFFUSE, light );
  glLightfv(GL_LIGHT0, GL_SPECULAR, light );
  glLightfv(GL_LIGHT0, GL_POSITION, light_position);
}
```

With the OpenGL functions available, we no longer need to use the SDL functions like **SDL_UpdateRect**() to send the image data to the screen. Instead, we can use the OpenGL functions **glDrawPixels**() to write the image data to the graphics frame buffer at a location specified by **glRasterPos**(). The data in the frame buffer are rendered to the screen. Using this method, we can play the video at more than one position of the screen simultaneously. The following is an example of simultaneous display of a video at two positions with a lit sphere revolving around:

```
//vi points to an object of the video class
//width = image width, height = image height
while ( !vi->quit ) {
  if ( vi->head == vi->tail ) {        //buffer empty
    SDL_Delay ( 30 );                  //sleep for 30 ms
    continue;
  }
  //consumes the data
```

```
      current_time = SDL_GetTicks();        //ms since library starts
      if ( current_time - prev_time < 50) //20 fps ~ 50 ms / frame
        SDL_Delay ( 50 - (current_time - prev_time) );
      prev_time = current_time;
      glClear( GL_COLOR_BUFFER_BIT | GL_DEPTH_BUFFER_BIT);
      glPushMatrix();
      glRotatef ( vi->az,0, 0, 1 );
      glTranslatef ( 1.5, 0, 0 );
      glutSolidSphere ( 0.25, 22, 16 );    //creates a solid sphere
      glPopMatrix();
      vi->az += 1.0;
      glRasterPos2i ( -2, -2 );
      //may use GL_BGR depending on how data are organized in buf[]
      glDrawPixels(width, height, GL_RGB, GL_UNSIGNED_BYTE,
                                               vi->buf[vi->head%4]);
      glRasterPos2i ( 0, 0 );
      glDrawPixels (width, height, GL_RGB, GL_UNSIGNED_BYTE,
                                               vi->buf[vi->head%4]);

      glFlush();
      SDL_GL_SwapBuffers();
      vi->head++;
   } //while
```

As another example of graphics application we may use each video frame as a texture image and paste it on any object we want. In other words, we can play the video on any object surface. The following code listing shows how we can play the video on the 6 faces of a rotating cube. In the code, the array *texImages[]* points to the video images saved in the buffer array *buf[]* that we have discussed before.

```
if ( !tex_initialized ) {
   glShadeModel ( GL_FLAT );
   glEnable(GL_DEPTH_TEST);

   glPixelStorei(GL_UNPACK_ALIGNMENT, 1);
   glGenTextures(6, texName);
   for ( int i = 0; i < 6; ++i ) {
     //now we work on texName
     glBindTexture(GL_TEXTURE_2D, texName[i]);
     glTexParameteri(GL_TEXTURE_2D, GL_TEXTURE_WRAP_S, GL_REPEAT);
     glTexParameteri(GL_TEXTURE_2D, GL_TEXTURE_WRAP_T, GL_REPEAT);
     glTexParameteri(GL_TEXTURE_2D, GL_TEXTURE_MAG_FILTER, GL_NEAREST);
     glTexParameteri(GL_TEXTURE_2D, GL_TEXTURE_MIN_FILTER, GL_NEAREST);
   }
   tex_initialized = true;
}

glEnable(GL_TEXTURE_2D);
glTexEnvf(GL_TEXTURE_ENV, GL_TEXTURE_ENV_MODE, GL_DECAL);
float x0 = -1.0, y0 = -1, x1 = 1, y1 = 1, z0 = 1;
//defining the 6 faces of a cube
float face[6][4][3] =
  {{{x0, y0, z0},{x1, y0, z0}, {x1, y1, z0},{x0, y1, z0}},//front
   {{x0, y1, -z0},{x1, y1, -z0},{x1, y0, -z0},{x0,y0,-z0}},//back
   {{x1, y0, z0},{x1, y0, -z0},{x1,y1,-z0}, {x1, y1, z0}},//right
   {{x0, y0, z0},{x0, y1, z0},{x0, y1, -z0}, {x0, y0, -z0}},//left
```

```
{{x0, y1, z0},{x1, y1, z0},{x1, y1, -z0}, {x0, y1, -z0}},//top
{{x0, y0, z0},{x0, y0, -z0},{x1, y0, -z0},{x1, y0, z0}}//bottom
};
glEnable( GL_CULL_FACE );
glCullFace ( GL_BACK );
glPushMatrix();
glRotatef( ax, 1.0, 0.0, 0.0);//rotate the cube along x-axis
for ( int i = 0; i < 6; ++i ){//draw cube with texture images
    glTexImage2D(GL_TEXTURE_2D, 0, GL_RGB, width,
             height, 0, GL_RGB, GL_UNSIGNED_BYTE, texImages[i]);
    glBindTexture(GL_TEXTURE_2D, texName[i]);
    glBegin(GL_QUADS);
      glTexCoord2f(0.0, 0.0); glVertex3fv ( face[i][0] );
      glTexCoord2f(1.0, 0.0); glVertex3fv ( face[i][1] );
      glTexCoord2f(1.0, 1.0); glVertex3fv ( face[i][2] );
      glTexCoord2f(0.0, 1.0); glVertex3fv ( face[i][3] );
    glEnd();
}
glPopMatrix();
glFlush();
glDisable(GL_TEXTURE_2D);
```

Figure A-1 is an image captured from the output of the program that plays two instances of a video with a revolving sphere and Figure A-2 shows that the video is played on a cube with a lit sphere revolving around it.

The blending of image processing and computer graphics is a new field of study. Many objects can be synthesized by computer graphics techniques. Therefore, the scene of a video may be specified by a few parameters and a computer model can reconstruct the scene based on the parameters. It can result in very high compression and pleasant presentation of the video. The international standard MPEG-4 has introduced the concept of hybrid synthetic and natural video objects for visual communication. In this method, we code the 'natural' or 'real world' objects using the traditional coding techniques we have discussed, but we employ some tools from the 2D/3D animation community to render synthetic or computer-generated visual scenes.

Figure A-1 Graphics Playing Two Video Instances

Figure A-2 Graphics Playing Video on Rotating Cube

Using computer graphics techniques, one can generate any 3D visual objects using polygon meshes. A polygon mesh models a 3D object as a collection of polygons, which may be simply triangles. One can rotate, translate, or scale the mesh to simulate the motion of any rigid body. Moreover, by deforming a couple polygons in a mesh, we can use the mesh to synthesize non-rigid objects like human bodies. For example, MPEG-4 specifies support for animated face and body models by defining the geometric shape of a body or face model and sending animation parameters to animate the body/face model. Developers use Facial Definition Parameters (FDPs) to describe a face model and Facial Animation Parameters (FAPs) to describe its animation. One can use the default FDPs to render a generic face at the decoder, and obtain a custom set of FDPs sent by the encoder to create a specific face. The FAPs sent by the encoder are used to animate the face model. A typical application of this is to 'compress' the scene of a TV news announcement where the scene is fairly static with the main motion in the picture due to lips movement of the announcer; also in such an application, the exact motion of other parts of the body of the news announcer is not very crucial. In a similar way, MPEG-4 specifies the use of Body Definition Parameters (FDPs) and Body Animation Parameters (BAPs) to render a human body. Using these parameters, one can render generic body models as well as a customized synthetic body to represent a 'real world' human. In general, an application for face and body animation consists of the generation of virtual scenes containing face and/or body meshes, as well as model-based coding of natural (real world) face or body scenes, where face and/or body movement is analyzed, coded and transmitted by the encoder as a set of BAPs and FAPs; upon receiving the BAPs and FAPs, the decoder utilize them to synthesize the face and body.

Appendix B   Video Compression using Graphics Models

B.1   Introduction

In the past two decades, a new development in video compression is to utilize synthesized images to represent some natural scenes that do not change much for a substantial period of time. For example, in a TV news announcement like the one shown in Figure B-1, the major scene change is the lip movement of the announcer. The background of the scene is fixed and in many cases may not be very important. This is also true for the situation of a video conference.

Figure B-1 News Announcer

To compress this kind of frames, one can use a graphics model to synthesize the announcer; the encoder just has to send the parameters of the lip movements of the announcer. Upon receiving the parameters, the decoder reconstructs the scene using the parameters and the graphics model. Of course, the parameters can be compressed before sending. One can easily see that this can give a very high compression ratio of the video as the encoder does not need to send the details of the images. It only has to send some parameters that will be used by the graphics model of the decoder to reconstruct the scene. The advance in computer graphics software and hardware technologies will make the use of graphics techniques play a more important role in video compression. The recent success of real 3D movies such as "Avatar" and "Alice and Wonderland" will further accelerate this trend.

In the 1990s, MPEG began to integrate synthetic audio and video data into audio and visual samples acquired from the natural world. The MPEG Synthetic-Natural Hybrid Coding was based on technologies developed by the Virtual Reality Modeling Language (VRML) Consortium (now Web3D). In later versions of MPEG-4 International Standard, efficient coding of shape and animation of human faces and bodies is specified. The specifications include standardizing Facial Animation (FA) and Face and Body Animation (FBA). MPEG-4 Visual specifies support for animated face and body models within the Simple Face Animation and simple FBA. A face model described by Facial Definition Parameters (FDPs) and animated using Facial Animation Parameters (FAPs) is specified. The body is described by body animation parameters (BAP). The basic idea of these technologies is to use graphics models to create synthesized human bodies or faces which are modified or deformed by parameters extracted from the real scene.

The next question is: *how do we generate synthesized human bodies or in general graphics objects?* It turns out that most 3D objects can be described using polygon meshes. Polygon meshes (or simply meshes) are collections of polygons that fit together to form the skin of the object. They have become a typical way of representing a broad class of solid graphical shapes. The simplest polygon is the triangle, which is one of the most useful geometric figures. The triangle is commonly used in the construction of buildings and bridges as it is the strongest geometric figure. Moreover, the vertices of a triangle always lie on the same plane. Therefore, it is the most popular polygon used to construct 3D graphical objects. The two images of Figure B-2 show the use of triangles to represent a rabbit; by deforming a triangle, one can change the shape of the object.

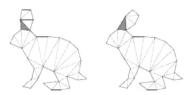

Figure B-2 Changing a Rabbit's Shape by Deforming a Polygon

There exist a lot of geometric modeling software packages that construct a model from some object, which can be a surface or a solid; it tries to capture the true shape of the object in a polygonal mesh. By using a sufficient number of polygons, a mesh can approximate the underlying surface to any desired degree of accuracy. For example, 3D Max is one of such 3D modeling software packages that run on Windows. Blender (*http://www.blender.org/*) is a popular free open-source 3D creation suite that lets users create sophisticated 3D graphical objects and do animation, and is available in all major operating systems, including Linux, Windows, and Mac OS/X. Typically, an artist creates an object using one of those packages and save it as a mesh in a file. A programmer writes programs in a computer language such as C/C++ or java to parse the polygons and manipulate the object. Artists may even post their graphical objects on some 3D graphics sites such as 3D Cafe (*http://www.3dcafe.com/*) for sale or for sharing. Specifically, **MakeHuman** (*http://www.makehuman.org/*) is an open-source tool for making 3D characters. Using MakeHuman, a photorealistic character can be modeled in less than 2 minutes and the character can be saved as a polygon mesh. MakeHuman is released under an Open Source Licence (GPL3.0) , and is available for Windows, Mac OS X and Linux. Xface is an MPEG4-based open-source toolkit for 3D facial animation. .

Figure B-3 shows two more synthetic images for video compression taken from the web site *http://coven.lancs.ac.uk/mpeg4* that does Synthetic-Natural Hybrid Coding (SNHC) conformed to the MPEG-4 standard.

Figure B-3a Animating Sign Language   **Figure B-3b** Animating Business Meeting

B.2   MPEG-4 Facial Animation

To accomplish the representation of synthetic visual objects, MPEG-4 had to choose a scene description language to describe the scene structure. MPEG-4 selected Virtual Reality Modeling

Language (VRML) standard as the basis with some additional new nodes to form the scene description language. Rather than constructing an object using purely triangles, the standard composes human face or body and other generic objects using a variety of geometric primitives such as cones, rectangles, triangles, and spheres. This makes the task of creating an object easier, and the object may look more realistic with the same number of polygons. To make the processing of the geometric primitives more efficient, the standard uses an indexed face set to define vertices and surface patches. It also uses nodes such as Transform to define rotation, scale, or translation and uses IndexedFaceSet nodes to describe the 3-D shape of an object. There are three problems that one has to address in animating human faces: a head needs to be specified; facial expressions have to be animated in real-time; animation and speech need to be synchronized.

MPEG-4 Facial Animation (FA) specifies the procedures to create a talking agent by standardizing various necessary parameters. The procedures of creating a talking agent consist of two phases. Phase one specifies the feature points on a static 3D model that defines the regions of deformation on the face. Phase two involves generation and interpolation of parameters that are used to modify the feature points to produce the actual animation. The two phases are cleanly separated from each other so that application developers can focus on their field of interest.

Face Definition Parameters (FDPs) and Face Animation Parameters (FAPs) are used to define head models and primitive facial expressions respectively. FDPs define the shape and texture of the model and FAPs are used to animate the face. FAPs are based on the study of minimal perceptible actions (MPA) and are closely related to muscle actions, including movements of lips, jaw, cheek and eyebrows. They make up a complete set of basic facial actions that represent the most natural facial expressions. Exaggerated parameter values may be used for Cartoon-like characters. Figure B-4 shows some common facial expressions.

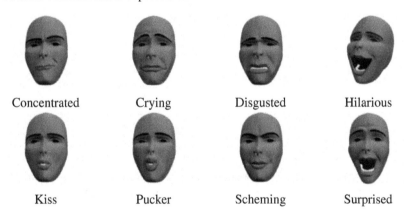

Concentrated   Crying   Disgusted   Hilarious

Kiss   Pucker   Scheming   Surprised

Figure B-4 Common Facial Expressions

The FAP values are usually defined and normalized in face animation parameter units (FAPUs) so that interpolations of the FAPs on any facial model are made in a consistent way. FAPUs measure spatial distances of facial expressions from its neutral state and are defined in terms of the fractions of distances between the marked key features. MPEG-4 defines a generic face model in its neutral state along with some feature points as shown in Figure B-5. The neutral state of a face model may be defined by the following features:

1. gaze is along the Z-axis,
2. all face muscles are relaxed,
3. eyelids are tangent to the iris,
4. the pupil is one third of the diameter of the iris,
5. lips are in contact,
6. the mouth is closed and the upper teeth touch the lower ones,

7. the tongue is flat, horizontal with the tip of tongue touching the boundary between upper and lower teeth,
8. FAPUs (Face Animation Parameter Units) are defined as fractions of distances between key facial features in the neutral state as shown in the following table:

Iris diameter	IRISD = IRISD0 / 1024
Eye Separation	ES = ES0 / 1024
Eye-nose Separation	ENS = ENS0 / 1024
Mouth-nose Separation	MNS = MNS0 / 1024
Mouth width	MW = MW0 / 1024
Angle unit (AU)	10^{-5} rad

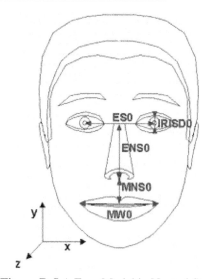

Figure B-5 A Face Model in Neutral State

For creating a standard conforming face, MPEG-4 specifies 84 feature points (FPs) on the neutral face. Feature points are arranged in groups such as cheeks, eyes and mouth. Applications need to define the locations of these feature points in order to conform to the standard. The feature points provide spatial references for defining FAPs as well as calibration between models when switched from one player to another. Figure B-6 shows the set of FPs which are used to provide spatial reference for defining FAPs. The 68 FAPs are classified into 10 groups as shown in the following table:

Table B-1 FAP Groups

Group	Number of FAPs
1. visemes and expressions	2
2: jaw, chin, inner lowerlip, cornerlips, midlip	16
3. eyeballs, pupils, eyelids	12
4. eyebrow	8
5. cheeks	4
6. tongue	5
7. head rotation	3
8. outer lip positions	10
9. nose	4
10. ears	4
Total	68

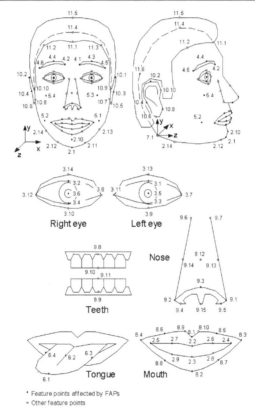

Figure B-6 MPEG-4 Feature Points

B.3   Computing Face Mesh Vertices

We use FAP values to animate a facial model, creating desired facial expressions. MPEG-4 further divides the FAPs into two subgroups. The first subgroup consists of FAPs that control simple motion of human face such as rotation, translation and scaling. The second subgroup FAPs are used for animating more complex motions that do not have any regular order such as frowning, blinking, and mouth-opening.

The first subgroup FAP values are fairly easy to process. For example, FAP23 is used to animate horizontal orientation of left eyeball. Suppose we have the following parameters,

$$
\begin{aligned}
\text{AU (Angle Unit)} &= 10^{-5} \text{ rad} \\
\text{Rotation Axis} &= (0, -1, 0) \\
\text{Rotation factor } \theta &= 1 \\
\text{Value of FAP23} &= 10000
\end{aligned}
$$

then the left eyeball needs to be rotated by an angle α given by,

$$\alpha = 10^{-5} \times 10000 \times 1 = 0.1 \ radian$$

The mesh vertex oordinates are more difficult to obtain from the second subgroup of FAPs. We have to perform a piecewise linear interpolation to obtain the new vertex coordinates of the mesh in the affected region. Figure B-7 shows two phases of a left eye blink along with the neutral phase. The eyelid motion is controlled by FAP19. In the blinking animation, the eyelid movement is along an acred trajectory but we can using 2D coordinates to specify the trajectory as shown in the figure.

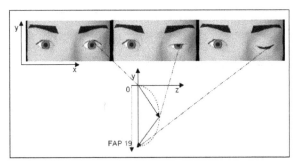

Figure B-7 Two Phases of Movement of Upper Left Eyelid

In general, we can compute the displacements of mesh vertices using piecewise linear interpolation. We approximate the motion trajectory of each mesh vertex as a piecewise linear one as shown in the figure below:

Suppose P_m is the position of vertex m when the face is in neutral state (FAP = 0) and $D_{m,k}$ is the 3D displacement that defines the piecewise linear function in the kth interval as shown in Figure B-8. If P'_m is the new position of the same vertex after animation with the given FAP value, we can compute

P'_m according to the following algorithm which is slightly different from that of MPEG-4, which requires 0 to be on an interval boundary all the time.

1. Assume that the range of FAP is divided into max intervals:

$$[I_0, I_1], [I_1, I_2], [I_2, I_3], ..., [I_{max-1}, I_{max}]$$

where

$$I_0 = -\infty, \ I_{max} = +\infty$$

2. Assume that the received FAP is in the jth interval, $[I_j, I_{j+1}]$, and 0 is in the kth interval, $[I_k, I_{k+1}]$, with $0 \le j, k < max$. (See Figure B-8.)

3. If $j > k$, we compute the new position P'_m of the mth vertex by:

$$P'_m = \begin{aligned} &P_m + FAPU \times [(I_{k+1} - 0) \times D_{m,k} + (I_{k+2} - I_{k+1}) \times D_{m,k+1} \\ &+ ... + (I_j - I_{j-1}) \times D_{m.j-1} + (FAP - I_j) \times D_{m,j}] \end{aligned} \qquad (B.1)$$

4. If $j < k$, we compute P'_m by:

$$P'_m = \begin{aligned} &P_m + FAPU \times [(I_{j+1} - FAP) \times D_{m,j} + (I_{j+2} - I_{j+1}) \times D_{m,j+1} \\ &+ ... + (I_k - I_{k-1}) \times D_{m.k-1} + (0 - I_k) \times D_{m,k}] \end{aligned} \qquad (B.2)$$

5. If $j = k$, we compute P'_m by:

$$P'_m = P_m + FAPU \times FAP \times D_{m,k} \qquad (B.3)$$

6. If the range of FAP contains only one interval, the motion is strictly linear, and we compute P'_m by:

$$P'_m = P_m + FAPU \times FAP \times D_{m,0} \qquad (B.4)$$

For example, suppose the FAP range is divided into three intervals:

$$[-\infty, 0], [0, 500], [500, +\infty].$$

The coordinates (x, y, z) of the displacements of vertex m controlled by the FAPs in these intervals are:

$$\begin{pmatrix} 1 \\ 0 \\ 2 \end{pmatrix}, \quad \begin{pmatrix} 0.8 \\ 0 \\ 0 \end{pmatrix}, \quad \begin{pmatrix} 1.5 \\ 0 \\ 4 \end{pmatrix}$$

respectively. The coordinates of vertex m in neutral expression is P_m. Suppose the received FAP value is 600 and the corresponding FAPU is Mouth Width, MW = 0.1. Since this FAP value is in the third interval $[500, +\infty]$ and 0 is in the second interval $[0, 500]$, we have the situation $j > k$. Thus we apply (B.1) to calculate the new position P'_m of vertex m:

$$P'_m = P_m + 0.1 \times [(500 - 0) \times \begin{pmatrix} 0.8 \\ 0 \\ 0 \end{pmatrix} + (600 - 500) \times \begin{pmatrix} 1.5 \\ 0 \\ 4 \end{pmatrix}] = P_m + \begin{pmatrix} 55 \\ 0 \\ 40 \end{pmatrix}$$

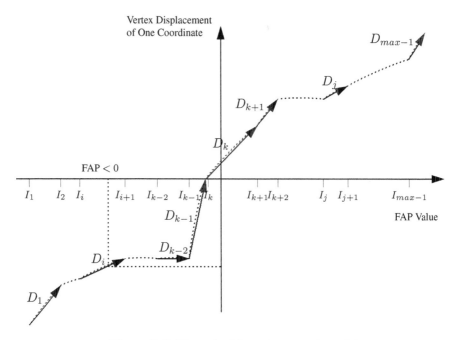

Figure B-8. Piecewise Linear Interpolation of FAP Values

To speed up the animation process, we may save the relation between FAP intervals and 3D displacements in the so called *FaceDefTables*. When we get the value of an FAP, we need to look up the *FaceDefTables* to get information about the control region of the FAP and the three dimensional displacements of vertices within the control region to convert the FAP into facial animation as shown in the figure below:

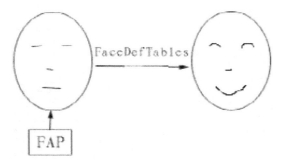

B.4 Keyframing

To animate realistic facial expressions, one can first calculate the animation parameters for key frames from photographs. A key frame in animation and film making is an image that defines the starting and ending points of any smooth transition. **Keyframing** is the process of creating animated motion by specifying objects at key frames and then interpolating the motion in intermediate frames. For traditional animation of movies, the key frames, also known as keys, are drawn by a senior artist. Other artists, *inbetweeners* and *inkers*, draw the intermediate frames and fill in the complete detailed drawings. The key frames are drawn for critical poses or when there is a sharp change in motion. At the beginning, the key frames could be very brief without fine details. The inbetweener would draw the intermediate poses to ensure that the motion appear fluid and natural.

Keyframing is particularly important in the animation of a full-length movie, which plays 24 frames per second. A 90-minute movie consists of 129,600 frames, which are way too many for a single artist to handle. On the other hand, if many artists draw different portions of the movie, the style or even appearance could be inconsistent. The movie has much better look if the production company employs a few senior animators to draw the key frames and a larger number of inbetweeners and linkers to draw the frames in between. A single senior animator can draw all the key frames of a particular character in a movie, producing more consistency of style.

In a similar spirit, computer animation uses interpolation to do keyframing. We specify the crucial parameters such as positions, orientations, and shapes of objects in the scene at key frames. Then, we obtain the parameters as smooth functions of time by using interpolating curves. This often can be done fully automatically but manual editing may be needed at some stages.

B.5   Extracting FAPs From Video

We have discussed how to use FAPs to animate facial expressions. This actually is a relatively easy part. When the animation parameters are given, one can basically use any appropriate model to perform animation. The more difficult problem is how to extract the FAPs from a given video. The extraction of facial parameters from video is not a completely solved problem. The process involves face detection, identification, recognition and tracking which are still active research topics in the academic and the industry. Automatic and accurate location of facial features is always difficult. The variety of human faces, expressions, facial hair, glasses, poses, and lighting contribute to the complexity of the problem.

A quick and simple way to find a human face in an image is to search for some common characteristics of human faces, such as color and shape. Some people use Delaunay triangulation and Voronoi diagrams to locate facial features of humans. However, this method is usually not very robust.

More sophisticated methods in general involve some statistical techniques and deformable models. A human is a deformable object and the tracking and recognition of it is usually tackled by making simplified assumptions concerning the motion or imposing constraints on it. Very often, the first step towards human tracking is to segment human figures from the background. A popular and relatively simple method to extract and track a deformable object in an image is the Active Contour Model (also called "snake"), which finds the contour of an object by balancing the effects of several energy terms. Variations of the Active Contour Model also exist. The gradient vector flow (GVF) snake is an improved model that includes the gradient vector flow, a new non-irrotational external force field. Another approach for tracking a deformable object is to employ deformable templates to automatically detect the objects. In general, retrieval by shape requires object detection and segmentation. Some researchers had used model-based region-grouping techniques to detect and retrieve deformable objects and found that using this method along with perceptually-motivated splitting strategy yields good image segmentation results of deformable shapes. In this section, we present a practical and popular technique for extracting FAPs from a video, the active appearance model (AAM).

B.5.1   Active Appearance Model (AAM)

An active appearance model (AAM) considers a face as a pattern in an image and makes use of a statistical model to match its appearance and shape with a pattern in the image. The approach is widely used for matching and tracking faces and for medical image interpolation.

AAM is an extension of the active shape model (ASM), which is a statistical model of the shape of objects that iteratively deform to fit to an example of the object in a new image. The shapes are constrained by the PDM (point distribution model) Statistical Shape Model to vary only in ways seen in a training set of labeled examples.

The shape of an object can be represented by a mesh of polygons or represented by a set of points (controlled by the shape model). Typically, it works by alternating the following steps:

1. Look in the image around each point for a better position for that point.
2. Update the model parameters to best match these new found positions.

To locate a better position for each point one may need to look for strong edges, or a match to a statistical model of what is expected at the point.

Usually the points that represent a shape are referred to as *landmarks*. In general, a *landmark* is a distinguishable point present in most of the images under consideration and people use landmarks to locate features of an image. In our case, we locate facial features by locating landmarks. Figure B-9 shows an image with correctly positioned landmarks.

Figure B-9 A face with correctly positioned landmarks

A set of landmarks forms a shape. Therefore, a shape s consists of a set of points. We can express s as an n-tuple:

$$s = \begin{pmatrix} p_1 \\ p_2 \\ \cdot \\ \cdot \\ \cdot \\ p_n \end{pmatrix} \tag{B.5}$$

where

$$p_i = \begin{pmatrix} x_i \\ y_i \\ z_i \end{pmatrix} \tag{B.6}$$

is a point with three coordinates if we consider 3D space. The z_i component of (B.6) will be dropped if we consider 2D space. In general, the points of a shape are vertices of a mesh composed of triangles.

One can align one shape to another with an affine transformation (translation, scaling, or rotation) that minimizes the average Euclidean distance between shape points. The mean shape is the mean of the aligned training shapes, which are manually landmarked faces. (Note that the average of points is a linear affine combination of points and thus the average is also a valid point.) In general, a shape s is typically controlled by adding a linear combination of shape/deformation modes to the average shape $\bar{s}$:

$$s = \bar{s} + \Phi b \tag{B.7}$$

where b is a set of vectors consisting of deformation parameters and Φ is a matrix whose columns contain the deformation modes. A deformation is a displacement of a point and can be regarded as a vector. The operation Φb gives us another set of vectors. Therefore, in (B.7) we add a set of points to a set of vectors and the operation is legitimate; the result is another set of points as the sum of a point and a vector yields another point.

We can generate various shapes with Equation (B.7) by varying the deformation parameters in b. By keeping the elements of b within limits (determined during model building) we ensure that the generated face shapes are lifelike. Conversely, given a suggested shape s, we can calculate the parameter b that allows Equation (B.7) to best approximate s with a model shape s'. One can use an iterative algorithm to find b and T that minimize a 'distance' D described by

$$D = ||s, T(\overline{s} + \Phi b)|| \tag{B.8}$$

where T is an affine transformation that maps the model space into the image space.

ASM is relatively fast but it is too simplistic, not robust when new images are introduced. It may not converge to a good solution. Another disadvantage of ASM is that it only uses shape constraints and does not take advantage of all the available information like the texture of the target object.

It turns out that an equation similar to (B.7) can be also used to describe the texture of objects based on statistical models. A texture t of an object is also a set of points at various locations of the objects:

$$t = \overline{t} + \sigma w \tag{B.9}$$

where $\overline{t}$ is the average texture, σ describes texture modes and w is a set of texture parameters.

Active appearance models (AAMs), also known as "smart snakes" as they conform to some explicit shape constraints like what an active contour model (snake) does, combine shape and texture into a single statistical model. We can express an AAM as

$$\begin{aligned}
s &= \overline{s} + \phi \mathbf{v} = \overline{s} + \sum_{j=1}^{n} \phi_{ij} v_j \\
t &= \overline{t} + \sigma \mathbf{v} = \overline{t} + \sum_{j=1}^{n} \sigma_{ij} v_j
\end{aligned} \tag{B.10}$$

That is, we use the same displacement vectors to control both shape and texture. In (B.10), each v_i is a vector and the coefficients ϕ_i and σ_i are shape and texture parameters respectively. Note that

$$v_i = \begin{pmatrix} v_{ix} \\ v_{iy} \\ v_{iz} \end{pmatrix}$$

AAMs are normally computed from training data. The standard approach is to apply Principal Component Analysis (PCA) to the training meshes. The mean shape $\overline{s}$ is usually referred to as the base shape. Figure B-10 shows an example of AAM, where $\overline{s}$ is the average shape and v_i's are shape vectors.

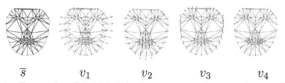

$$\overline{s} \qquad v_1 \qquad v_2 \qquad v_3 \qquad v_4$$

Figure B-10 An Example of AAM. $\overline{s}$ is the average shape. v_i's are shape vectors.

B.5.2   An AAM Search Algorithm

Face modeling has been the most frequent application of AAMs. Typically an AAM is first fit to an image of a face. That is, we search for model parameters that maximize the "match" between the model instance and the input image. The model parameters are then used in whatever the application is. Fitting an AAM to an image is a non-linear optimization problem. The usual approach is to iteratively solve for incremental additive updates to the parameters (the shape and appearance coefficients.) We briefly describe an AAM search algorithm here that is based on such an iterative update.

For an input image I and a model parameter vector $\mathbf{v}$, we can map the image onto the model and reshape the model to the standard shape to create a normalized image J:

$$J = J(I, s(\mathbf{v})) \tag{B.11}$$

For simplicity, we assume that the input image I is fixed. Therefore, the normalized image J is a function of $\mathbf{v}$ only. The residual image R is given by

$$R(\mathbf{v}) = J(\mathbf{v}) - s(\mathbf{v}) \tag{B.12}$$

We want to find $\mathbf{v}$ so that the error measure

$$E(\mathbf{v}) = ||R(\mathbf{v})||^2 \tag{B.13}$$

is minimized. Suppose we roughly know that the optimal $\mathbf{v}$ is near $\mathbf{v_0}$. Then the optimization process can be approximated by finding $\delta \mathbf{v}$ so that $E(\mathbf{v_0} + \delta \mathbf{v})$ is optimized. We can make a Taylor expansion of $R(\mathbf{v_0} + \delta \mathbf{v})$ and simplify the expression by retaining only the first two terms:

$$R(\mathbf{v_0} + \delta \mathbf{v}) \approx R(\mathbf{v_0}) + D\delta \mathbf{v} \tag{B.14}$$

where

$$D = \frac{\partial R(\mathbf{v})}{\partial \mathbf{v}}$$

is evaluated at $\mathbf{v} = \mathbf{v_0}$. Thus, our optimization is reduced to minimizing

$$E(\mathbf{v_0} + \delta \mathbf{v}) \approx ||R(\mathbf{v_0}) + D\delta \mathbf{v}||^2 \tag{B.15}$$

The least square solution to Equation (B.15) is

$$\delta \mathbf{v} = -(D^T D)^{-1} D^T R(\mathbf{v_0}) \tag{B.16}$$

We can use Equation (B.16) to update $\mathbf{v}$ in the search space; we use the $\delta \mathbf{v}$ to compute a new vector $\mathbf{v}$ and a new error measure:

$$\begin{aligned} \mathbf{v}' &= \mathbf{v_0} + \delta \mathbf{v} \\ E' &= E(\mathbf{v}') \end{aligned} \tag{B.17}$$

If $E' < E$, we update $\mathbf{v}$ accordingly ($\mathbf{v}' \to \mathbf{v_0}$) and repeat the steps until convergence occurs. If $E' > E$, we do not perform the update but try smaller update steps. If the smaller steps still do not improve the error measure, we assume that convergence has reached.

We can estimate the gradient matrix D from a set of training data. For example, the ith row of D can be estimated as:

$$D_i = \sum_k [R(\mathbf{v} + \delta \mathbf{v}_{ik}) - R(\mathbf{v})] \tag{4.18}$$

where $\delta \mathbf{v}_{ik}$ is a vector that perturbs $\mathbf{v}$ in the ith component to the amount of $k \times c$ for some suitable constant c. We can then compute the update matrix U as the negative pseudoinverse of D:

$$U = -D^* = -(D^T D)^{-1} D^T \tag{B.19}$$

We can apply a similar procedure to the texture of Equation (B.10).

Some tools for studying AAM can be downloaded from the web site of Professor Tim Cootes (*http://personalpages.manchester.ac.uk/staff/timothy.f.cootes/*).

B.6   Conclusions

The application of graphics techniques to video compression has become an interested research topics in recent years. If your interest is mainly on utilizing existing video compression libraries, you may use open-source video codecs for your applications. One can make use of the libraries to easily integrate videos in a graphics or video game application. The use of these open-source video compression libraries will tremendously shorten your software development cycle. Because of the huge advancement and demand of Internet and multi-media applications, video technologies and computer graphics are blending together more each year. The technologies will be even more important in the coming decades. Their applications are only limited by your imagination.

Appendix C An Open-Source Ray Tracing Package

C.1 Radiance

RADIANCE, an open-source package, is a a suite of programs that generates highly accurate ray-tracing scenes, and is readily to be run in UNIX platforms. It was developed with primary support from the U.S. Department Of Energy and additional support from the Swiss Federal Government, and its copyright owner is the Regents of the University of California. Detailed information of the package can be found at its official web site:

http://radsite.lbl.gov/radiance/framew.html

where one can download the complete package of it. It is easy and straight forward to install and use.

Radiance yields better results over simpler lighting calculation and rendering tools as it has no limitations on the geometry or materials for simulations. Architects and engineers use Radiance to predict illumination, visual quality and appearance of innovative design spaces, and researchers use it to evaluate new lighting and daylighting technologies.

The following are some features of Radiance:

1. Input parameters such as the scene geometry, materials, luminaires, time, date and sky conditions (for daylight calculations) can be specified in files.
2. Typical ray tracing outputs such as spectral radiance (ie. luminance + color), irradiance (illuminance + color) and glare indices are calculated.
3. Simulation results may be displayed as color images, numerical values or contour plots.
4. Generator programs are provided for the creation of more complex shapes from the basic surface primitives, such as boxes, prisms and surfaces of revolution.
5. A transformation utility permits the simple duplication of objects and hierarchical construction of a scene.

Tutorials and usage of the package can be found at the sites:

1. *http://radsite.lbl.gov/radiance/refer/tutorial.html*, or
2. *http://netghost.narod.ru/gff/vendspec/radnce/tutorial.txt*

Examples of using this package presented in the next section are based on these tutorials.

C.2 Using Radiance

In this section, we present a brief tour of using Radiance. To get an image, we need a minimum input of a source of illumination and an object to reflect light to the *camera*. One can think of a Radiance renderer as an invisible camera observing a simulated world. As presented in the first example below, we begin with two spheres, one emissive and one reflective. We first define the materials, then the spheres themselves.

I. First Example

This example shows the basic formats. A scene description file represents a three-dimensional physical environment in Cartesian world coordinates, stored as ASCII text, with the following basic format:

```
# comment
```

```
modifier type identifier
n S1 S2 "S 3" .. Sn
0
m R1 R2 R3 .. Rm

modifier alias identifier reference

! command
...
```

The following are the steps to create a red plastic sphere shone by bright light. The keyword **light** defines the basic material for self-luminous; in the example, its (R, G, B) values are $(100, 100, 100)$. The **plastic** material requires 5 parameters: (red, green, blue, specularity, roughness). A **sphere** is defined by its center and radius; so $(7\ 1.125\ .625\ .125)$ means its center is at $(7, 1.125, .625)$ and its radius is .125.

1. Use a text editor (e.g. vi) to create a file named *room0.rad* with the following code:

```
# My first scene.

# The basic primitive format is:
#
# modifier TYPE identifier
# number_of_arguments [arguments...]
# arguments are of the same type, and
# could be strings, integers or reals
#
#The special modifier "void" means no modifier.

# Material for my light source:
void light bright
0
0
3 100 100 100

  # Material for my test ball:
  void plastic red_plastic
  0
  0
  5 .7 .05 .05 .05 .05

  # Here is the light source:
  bright sphere fixture
  0
  0
  4 2 1 1.5 .125

  # Here is the ball:
  red_plastic sphere ball
  0
  0
  4 .7 1.125 .625 .125
```

Figure C-1 First Example

2 Create Octree. As now we have a simple scene description, we can examine it using the interactive viewing program, *rview*. However, we need to first create an **octree** file, which will be used to speed up the rendering process. This is done by the command:

```
$ oconv room0.rad > test0.oct
```

Note that the file extensions *.rad* and *.oct* are not enforced, but merely a convenience for recognizing the files.

3 Get information about the Octree. The command **getinfo** can be used to retrieve information from the unviewable binary *.oct* file. Try entering the command:

```
$ getinfo test0.oct
```

4 Use the command **rview** to render the scene:

```
$ rview -vp 2.25 .375 1 -vd -.25 .125 -.125 -av .5 .5 .5 test0.oct
```

The output is shown in Figure C-1. Note that within the *rview* display menu, we can save the viewing configuration to the file *default.vp* (or a file with other file names), by entering the following command near the bottom of the display screen:
  : view default.vp
We can retrieve a view file with the command:
  : last *filename*
Details of the command *rview* can be found at the site:
http://www.siggraph.org/education/materials/HyperGraph/raytrace/radiance/man_html/rview.1.html

II.   Second Example:

1. Modify *room0.rad* to *room1.rad* by adding the following code:

```
# the wall material:
void plastic gray_paint
0
0
5 .5 .5 .5 0 0

# a box shaped room:
!genbox gray_paint room 3 2 1.75 -i
```

The command **genbox** generates a box (6 rectangles) with lower left corner at $(0, 0, 0)$, and upper right corner at $(3, 2, 1.75)$.

2. Convert to octtree:
    $ oconv room1.rad > test1.oct

3. Render the scene with configuration file *default.vp*:
    $ rview -vf default.vp -av .5 .5 .5 test1.oct
    An output is shown in Figure C-2(a).

4. Rotate scene with command **rotate** or **r** at the render prompt. Example:
    :r 5 -20
    A sample output is shown in Figure C-2(b).

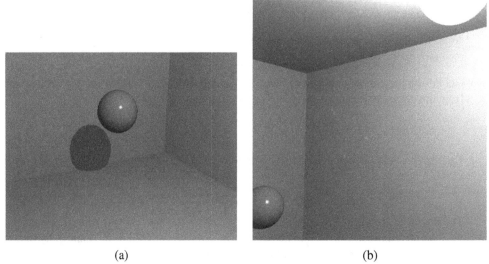

(a)   (b)

Figure C-2 Example 2

III.   Third Example:

1. Modify *room1.rad* to *room2.rad* by adding more features:

```
# a shiny blue box:
void plastic blue_plastic
0
0
5 .1 .1 .6 .05 .1

!genbox blue_plastic box .5 .5 .5 |xform -rz 15 -t .5 .75 0

# a chrome rod to suspend the light
# from the ceiling:
void metal chrome
0
0
5 .8 .8 .8 .9 0

chrome cylinder fixture_support
0
0
7
    2    1    1.5
    2    1    1.75
    .05
#Note: cylinder has 7 parameters: x0 y0 z0
#                                  x1 y1 z1  radius
# denoting the top and bottom disc centers, and radius
```

2. Convert and render:

```
$ oconv room2.rad > test2.oct
$ rview -vf default.vp \
      -av .5 .5 .5 test2.oct
```

A sample output is shown in Figure C-3.

Figure C-3   Third Example

IV.   Example 4:

1. Try different materials, modifying *room2.rad* to room3.rad with the following changes:

```
#
# room3.rad
#

# this is the material for my light source:

void light bright
0
0
3 100 100 100

# this is the material for my test ball:

# solid crystal:

void dielectric crystal
0
0
5 .5 .5 .5 1.5 0

# dark brown:

void plastic brown
0
0
5 .2 .1 .1 0 0

# light gray:

void plastic white
0
0
5 .7 .7 .7 0 0

# here is the light source:
```

```
bright sphere fixture
0
0
4 2 1 1.5 .125

# here is the ball:

crystal sphere ball
0
0
4 .7 1.125 .625 .125
```

```
# the wall material:

void plastic gray_paint
0
0
5 .5 .5 .5 0 0
```

```
# a box shaped room:

!genbox gray_paint room 3 2 1.75 -i

# a shiny blue box:

void plastic blue_plastic
0
0
5 .1 .1 .6 .05 .1
```

Figure C-4 Example 4

```
!genbox blue_plastic box .5 .5 .5 |xform -rz 15 -t .5 .75 0

# a chrome rod to suspend the light from the ceiling:

void metal chrome
0
0
5 .8 .8 .8 .9 0

chrome cylinder fixture_support
0
0
7
    2    1    1.5
    2    1    1.75
    .05
```

2. Convert and render:

```
$ oconv room3.rad > test3.oct
$ rview -vf default.vp -av .5 .5 .5 test3.oct
```

Note "—" means piping. The statement
  xform -rz 15 -t .5 .75 0
means to transform the object by rotating the scene by 15° about the z-axis, and translating the scene by $(.5, .75, 0)$.

3. One can create an image from the scene using the command *rpict* like:

```
$ rpict -vf default.vp -av .5 .5 .5 test3.oct > test3.pic
```

You may convert the *.pic* file to a *.png* file using the Unix utility *convert* like:

```
$ convert test3.pic test3.png
```

An output is shown in Figure C-4.

V.   Example 5:

This example shows how to change the color of ceiling and floor.

1. Generate room externally:

```
$ genbox gray_paint room 3 2 1.75 -i >> room4.rad
```

2. Edit the file *room4.rad* to make floor (all z values = 0) with brown color:

```
genbox gray_paint room 3 2 1.75 -i >> room4.rad
```

3. and make ceiling (all z values = 1.75) white:

```
white polygon room.6457
```

4. An output of the scene is shown in Figure C-5.

Figure C-5   Example 5

VI.   Example 6:

This example shows how to add a window to the previous example. This is a two-steps process.

1. Copy *room4.rad* to *room5.rad*.
2. Step 1:
   (a) Cut a hole in the wall and put in a piece of glass. (Use coincident edges to make a seam to give the appearance of a hole.) Edit *room5.rad*, changing *room.5137* to:
```
gray_paint polygon room.5137
0
0
30

3      2       1.75
3      2       0
3      0       0
3      0       1.75
3      .625    1.75
3      .625    .625
3      1.375   .625
3      1.375   1.375
3      .625    1.375
3      .625    1.75
```
   (b) Create a separate file named *window.rad* for the widnow:
```
# transmittance glass window has a transmission of 96%:
void glass window_glass
0
0
3 .96 .96 .96

window_glass polygon window
0
0
12
3      .625     1.375
3      1.375    1.375
3      1.375    .625
3      .625     .625
```
3. Step 2:
   (a) Create a scene outside the window (sky and sun). Save the scene in a separate file named *sky.rad*:
```
$ gensky 3 20 10 -o 0 -m 0 -a 40 > sky.rad
```
   (b) Create a file named *outside.rad* that contains a generic background of the outside scene:
```
#Standard sky and ground to follow a gensky sun & sky distribution.
```

```
skyfunc glow sky_glow
0
0
4 .9 .9 1.15 0

sky_glow source sky
0
0
4 0 0 1 180

skyfunc glow ground_glow
0
0
4 1.4 .9 .6 0
ground_glow source ground
0
0
4 0 0-1 180
```

(c) Put everything in one octree:

```
$ oconv sky.rad outside.rad window.rad room5.rad > test5.oct
```

(d) Render with:

```
$ rview -vf default.vp -av .5 .5 .5 test5.oct
```

We may adjust the illumination (exposure) with the render command ":e" (e.g. e 0.8). Figure C-6(a) shows an image of the scene with exposure 0.8 and rendered with:

```
$rview -vtv -vp -2.25 -0.375 1 -vd 0.25 -0.125 -0.125\
        -vu 0 0 1 -vh 45 -vv 45 -vo 0 -va 0 -vs 0 -vl 0
```

Figure C-6(b) is with exposure 0.4 and rendered with:

```
$rview -vtv -vp 1.7823 0.15627 0.99132 -vd 0.23949 0.19006 -0.01653\
        -vu 0 0 1 -vh 45 -vv 45 -vo 0 -va 0 -vs 0 -vl 0
```

We save the configuration file for rendering Figure C-6(b) as *test5b.vp*.

(a)   (b)

Figure C-6   Example 6

VII.   Example 7:

This example adds illumination to the window.

1. Copy *window.rad* to *srcwindow.rad* and add the following:

```
# An emissive window

# visible glass window_glass

void glass window_glass
0
0
3 .96 .96 .96
  # window distribution function, including angular
  # transmittance:
  skyfunc brightfunc window_dist
  2 winxmit winxmit.cal
  0
  0

  # illum for window,using 88%
  # transmittance at normal
  # incidence:
  window_dist illum window_illum
  1 window_glass
  0
  3 .88 .88 .88

  # the source polygon:
  window_illum polygon window
  0
  0
  12
      3        .625    1.375
      3       1.375    1.375
      3       1.375     .625
      3        .625     .625
```

Figure C-7 Example 7

2. Compile with:

```
$oconv sky.rad outside.rad srcwindow.rad room5.rad > test5s.oct
```

3. Render with:

```
$rview -vf test5b.vp -av .5 .5 .5 test5s.oct
```

An ouput is shown in Figure C-7.

Bibliography

1. N. Abramson, *Information Theory and Coding*, McGraw-Hill, 1963.

2. T. Budd, *Data Structures in C++: Using The Standard Template Library*, Addison Wesley, 1997.

3. S. R. Buss, *3-D Computer Graphics: A Mathematical Introduction with OpenGL*, Cambridge, 2003.

4. K. Chen, R. Kambhamettu, and D. Goldgof, *Extraction of MPEG-4 FAP Parameters from 3D Face Data Sequences*, CiteSeer, 1998.

5. T. M. Cover and J.A. Cover, *Elements of Information Theory*, Second Edition, John Wiley, 2006.

6. P. Debevec, *Image-Based Lighting*, IEEE Computer Graphics and Applications, vol 22, no. 2, p. 26-34, 2002.

7. P.F. Drucker, *The Essential Drucker*, Harper Business, 2001.

8. M. Ezhilarasan, and P. Thambidural, *A Hybrid Transform Coding for Video Codec*, 9th International Conference on Information Technology (ICIT06), IEEE Computer Society, 2006.

9. D. Genzel and E. Charniak, *Entropy Rate Constancy in Text*, Proceedings of the 40th Annual Meeting of the Association for Computational Linguistics (ACL), Philadelphia, pp. 199-206, July 2002.

10. A. Gersho and R.M. Gray, *Vector Quantization and Signal Compression*, Kluwer Academic Publishers, 1992.

11. R.G. Gonzalez and R.E. Woods, *Digital Image Processing*, Addison-Wesley, 1992.

12. E. L. Hall, *Computer Image Processing and Recognition*, Academic Press, 1979.

13. B. G. Haskell, A. Puri, and A. N. Netravali, *Digital Video: An introduction to MPEG-2*, Springer, 1996.

14. D. Hearn, and M.P. Baker, *Computer Graphics, C Version*, Second Edition, Prentice Hall, 1996

15. D. Hearn, M.P. Baker, and W.R. Carithers, *Computer Graphics with OpenGL*, Fourth Edition, Prentice Hall, 2011.

16. F.S. Hill, Jr. and S. M. Kelley, Jr., *Computer Graphics Using OpenGL*, Third Edition, Pearson Prentice Hall, 2007.

17. A.K. Jain, *Fundamentals of Digital Image Processing*, Prentice Hall, 1989.

18. Eric Lengyel, *Mathematics for 3D Game Programming & Computer Graphics*, Second Edition, Course Technology, 2004.

19. Loki Software with J. R. Hall, *Programming Linux Games: Building Multimedia Applications with SDL, OpenAL, and Other APIs*, Linux Journal Press, 2001.

20. Bernard Mendiburu, *3D Movie Making: Stereoscopic Digital Cinema from Script to Screen*, Focal Press, 2009.

21. Larry E. Mansfield, *Linear Algebra with Geometric Applications*, Dekker, 1976.

22. John Miano, *Compressed Image File Formats*, Addison-Wesley, 1999.

23. I.S. Pandzic and R. Forchheimer (editors), *MPEG-4 Facial Animation: The Standard, Implementation and Applications*, John Wiley & sons, 2002.

24. W. B. Pennebaker and J. L. Mitchell, *JPEG: Still Image Data Compression Standard*, Van Nostrand Reinhold, 1993.

25. Edited by Matt Pharr, *GPU Gems 2*, Addison-Wesley, 2005.

26. Ravi Ramamoorthi and Pat Hanrahan *An Efficient Representation for Irradiance Environment Maps*, SIGGRAPH 2001 Proceedings, p.497-500, 2001.), p.497-500,

27. Randi J. Post, *OpenGL Shading Language*, Second Edition, Addison-Wesley, 2006.

28. Recommendations ITU-R BT.601-5, *Studio encoding parameters of digital television for standard 4:3 and wide-screen 16:9 aspect ratios*, ITU-T, 1995.

29. Iain E.G. Richardson, *H.264 and MPEG-4 Video Compression: Video Coding for Next-generation Multimedia*, John Wiley & Sons, 2003.

30. David Salomon, *Curves and Surfaces for Computer Graphics*, Springer, 2005.

31. N. Sarris and M. G. Strintzis, *3D Modeling and Animation: Synthesis and Analysis Techniques for the Human Body*, IRM Press, 2005.

32. Linda G. Shapiro and George C. Stockman, *Computer Vision*, Prentice Hall, 2001.

33. Allen Sherrod, *Game Graphics Programming*, Course Technology, 2008.

34. Dave Shreiner, et al., *OpenGL Programming Guide*, Fourth Edition, Addison Wesley, 2004.

35. Richard Szeliski, *Computer Vision: Algorithms and Applications*, Springer, 2010.

36. H. Tao and H. H. Chen et. al., *Compression of MPEG-4 Facial Animation Parameters for Transmission of Talking Heads*, IEEE Transactions on Circuits and Systems for Video Technology, 9(2), pp. 264-276, 1999.

37. T.L. Yu, *A Framework for Very High Performance Compression of Table Tennis Video Clips*, Proceedings of IASTED on Signal and Image Processing, pp. 167-172, Kailua-Kona, Hawaii, August 2008.

38. Gady Agam, *Introduction to programming with OpenCV*, 2007, http://www.cs.iit.edu/ agam/cs512/lect-notes/opencv-intro/opencv-intro.html

39. M. Stokes, et al. *A Standard Default Color Space for the Internet - sRGB*, 1996, http://www.w3.org/Graphics/Color/sRGB.html

40. John Wattie, *Principles of stereoscopic photography using an ordinary camera*, http://nzphoto.tripod.com/sterea/stereotake.htm

41. Andrew J. Woods, *Compatibility of Display Products with Stereoscopic Display Methods*, International Display Manufacturing Conference (IDMC), Taiwan, February 2005.

42. Paul T. Burns, *The History of the Discovery of Cinematography*,
    http://www.precinemahistory.net/

43. Aditi Majumder, *Perceiving Depth and Size*,
    http://www.ics.uci.edu/ majumder/vispercep/depthsize.pdf

44. *Stereo Projections: Background, Mathematics, and Use*,
    http://people.eecs.ku.edu/ miller/Stereo/Section_05/Page_0010.php

45. *Stereoscopic Displays and Applications XXI (2010) Conference Proceedings*,
    http://www.stereoscopic.org/2010/preface.html

46. http://www.3dcafe.com/

47. http://www.android.com

48. http://www.blender.org/

49. http://blenderart.org/

50. https://collada.org/

51. http://coven.lancs.ac.uk/mpeg4

52. http://eclipse.org/

53. http://www.makehuman.org/

54. http://www.opengl.org/

55. http://www.pauldebevec.com/

56. http://personalpages.manchester.ac.uk/staff/timothy.f.cootes/

57. http://radsite.lbl.gov/radiance/

58. http://xface.fbk.eu

59. http://xmlsoft.org/

Index

Books by Fore June:

1. *An Introduction to Video Compression in C/C++*
2. *An Introduction to Digital Video Data Compression in Java*
3. *An Introduction to 3D Computer Graphics, Stereoscopic Image, and Animation in OpenGL and C/C++*
4. *Android Programming and Open Source Tools*

See

http://www.forejune.com/

www.ingramcontent.com/pod-product-compliance
Lightning Source LLC
Chambersburg PA
CBHW080135060326
40689CB00018B/3801